Boeing B-29 Superfortress

Boeing B-29
Superfortress

The Ultimate Look:
From Drawing Board to VJ-Day

William Wolf

Schiffer Military History
Atglen, PA

Acknowledgments

My lifelong hobby has been WW-II aerial combat, and over the past 35 years I have collected over 15,000 books and magazines, along with hundreds of reels of microfilm on the subject. I probably have nearly every book written on WW-II aviation, and a complete collection of every aviation magazine published since 1939. Also included in my collection are many hundreds of aviation unit and pilots' histories, crew manuals, and aircraft technical, structural, and maintenance manuals. My microfilm collection includes vintage intelligence reports, USAF, USN, and USMC group and squadron histories, complete Japanese Monograph series, and U.S. Strategic Bombing Surveys, as well as USAF Historical Studies. Over the years I have been fortunate to meet many fighter aces, other pilots, and fellow aviation buffs who have shared stories, material, and photographs with me (I have over 5,000 photos of fighter aces alone). I have made many multi-day expeditions to various military libraries, museums, and photo depositories with my copy machine and camera, accumulating literally reams of information and 1,000s of photographs. I also had a photo darkroom where I developed 1,000s of rare photos from microfilm negatives.

I have always intended to write a book on the B-29, and for many years I have collected material and photographs for this project. The author wishes that every person who contributed over the past quarter century could be specifically mentioned. Over the years the origin of many of the 1,000s of photos I have been lent to copy or have copied and collected myself have become obscured. Most are from military and government sources, but many are from private individuals, and I apologize in advance if some of the photos are miscredited. Also, some of the photos are not of the best quality because of their age and sources, especially those copied from microfilm, but were used because of their importance to the book.

A particular thank you goes to Scott Marchand, curator of the Pima Air & Space Museum, and Kate DeMeester, archivist of that museum, who were of invaluable help in aiding in photographing *Sentimental Journey* and gathering and copying the B-29 aircraft and crew manuals. Through them I was able to make this book into the detailed, ultimate book on the B-29. A belated thank you goes to Judy Endicott of the Albert F. Simpson Historical Research Center, Maxwell AFB, Alabama. Ms. Endicott was of great help during my 10 day expedition to that facility in the mid-1980s to collect material on fighter aces and the B-29 and B-32 (which is the subject of my next book). Thanks also go to the personnel at the Air Force Museum Archives at Wright-Patterson, Dayton, Ohio, and those at the Ferndale Photographic facility, Washington, D.C., who aided me during my visits there. Thanks also to Pima ASM docent Louis Prawitz for the loan of *Sentimental Journey* photos.

Again, thanks go to my persevering wife, Nancy, who allows me to spend many hours researching and writing, and patiently (mostly) waits while I browse bookstores and visit air museums in search of new material and photos. Also, I thank her because her car sits out in the hot Arizona sun as my WW-II library luxuriates in the remodeled, air-conditioned three-car garage.

Book Design by Ian Robertson.

Printed in China.
ISBN: 0-7643-2257-5

We are interested in hearing from authors with book ideas on related topics.

Published by Schiffer Publishing Ltd.
4880 Lower Valley Road
Atglen, PA 19310
Phone: (610) 593-1777
FAX: (610) 593-2002
E-mail: Info@schifferbooks.com.
Visit our web site at: www.schifferbooks.com
Please write for a free catalog.
This book may be purchased from the publisher.
Please include $3.95 postage.
Try your bookstore first.

In Europe, Schiffer books are distributed by:
Bushwood Books
6 Marksbury Avenue
Kew Gardens
Surrey TW9 4JF
England
Phone: 44 (0) 20 8392-8585
FAX: 44 (0) 20 8392-9876
E-mail: Info@bushwoodbooks.co.uk.
Free postage in the UK. Europe: air mail at cost.
Try your bookstore first.

Contents

Foreword:
General Dwight Montieth

After serving as the commander of the B-24 equipped 491st Bombardment Group during its formation in 1943, I was assigned to the B-29 equipped 20th Bomber Command by Gen. Blondie Saunders as its Deputy A-3 in December 1943. Previous to this time I had never heard of the B-29 and its developmental problems. When I first encountered the B-29 the bomber was continuing to have troubles and flight testing was ongoing, but it was imperative that training begin, and to get the bomber into combat as soon as possible. After flying the bomber several times I had no doubt about its potential, and was convinced that its engine cooling problems and other lesser problems would soon be solved. The so-called Battle of Kansas began in earnest in February 1944; the bomber's major problems were solved and the minor ones ignored, and the B-29 was considered "good enough" for combat when we departed for India in April 1944. I was Operations Staff Advisor and flew the first heavy bombardment mission over Japan, bombing the Yawata steelworks on 15 June 1944. In the CBI our B-29s not only served as bombers, but also carried gasoline and bombs to their forward bases in China, and were relentlessly flown by their overtaxed crews. Slowly but surely the mechanical and operational bugs were worked out as I became commander of the Forward Echelons in China, bombing targets on Japan and Okinawa. The major tactical turning point for the bomber in the CBI was the appointment of Gen. Curtis LeMay—an experienced combat commander—as commander of the 20th at the end of August 1944. By the time the 20th was ordered to withdraw and regroup from the CBI in January 1945 the B-29 was ready to assume its role as a "Superfortress." I was assigned as Chief of Staff of the 58th Bombardment Wing and led the Wing's advance echelons to Tinian for the initial operations from the Marianas. The early capture of the Marianas was to be decisive for the B-29 to carry out operations against Japan. Fuel and ordnance were abundantly available and the bomber could be flown at low, fuel-saving altitudes until the Japanese mainland was approached. The new bombers sent to us off the production lines were considerably improved and reliable. With each mission over Japan the B-29 and its crews became an increasingly efficient and devastating weapon, totally destroying Japanese cities and the Japanese will, especially after LeMay's switch to the devastating low altitude night incendiary raids. However, it was the dropping of the atomic bombs that convinced the stubborn Japanese military and leaders that it would be futile to continue to resist. The B-29 was largely responsible for winning the Pacific War. It did the job it was designed for and was one hell of a bomber!

Gen. Dwight Montieth

Author and Gen. Kelly Montieth (left) at the General's home in Scottsdale, AZ.

Foreword:
Scott Marchand

As the world plunged into conflict at the close of the 1930s a whole host of aircraft had been designed to perform specialist roles in aerial combat. One of the predominate beliefs in the war colleges and Air commands of the day was that the *bomber would always get through*. In many instances this was wishful thinking, and was rapidly proved wrong in the European theatre, forcing the British to adopt night bombing, and nearly crippling the 8th Air Force's B-17s and B-24s until long range fighter escort was available. One of the only aircraft to which this adage could arguably be said to be true is the Boeing B-29 Superfortress.

Although beset by developmental difficulties and a relative latecomer in the world war, the impact of the B-29 on the outcome and duration of the war was truly monumental. The B-29 was also the zenith of bomber design, with innovative features that would not be unfamiliar to the modern crews on B-52s and B-1Bs two generations later, a phenomenal legacy. This book is not only about the airplane, it is about all the people who shared in the saga of the Superfortress; people with a difficult, dangerous, and unpleasant task to execute. From the skills of the Boeing design and production teams, to the youthful crews who took her to war, this book covers the entire story, from each cameo of personal experience to the meticulous exposition of technical knowledge.

This book is a fitting tribute to a magnificent airplane, as well as the crews, designers, and workers who labored to make vision a reality. The B-29's contribution to the final victory over the Axis powers and peace has too often been unsung, often denigrated and misunderstood. A book such as this has been long awaited. Its meticulously researched text, outstanding photo collection—many published here for the first time—pay fitting tribute to all associated with the Superfortress. However, the author has taken a very daunting scope, and through a well-written and well-organized text has, for the first time, presented anyone with an interest in the B-29 a concise and definitive reference, while also paying homage to all the sacrifices that produced such an enduring legend and legacy.

The author has performed a very necessary and worthwhile task in having presented the history of the B-29 so thoroughly and effectively before living memory was lost.

Scott Marchand, M.Phil.
Director of Collections & Aircraft Restoration
Pima Air & Space Museum

Preface

Of all the aircraft of World War II, the B-29 probably had the most profound influence on the outcome of the war. Strategic aerial planning in the Pacific war hinged on the troubled development and deployment of this superbomber. From the time of its first test flight on 21 September 1941 until its first combat mission over Bangkok on 5 June 1944, the bomber had one of the shortest gestation periods of any combat aircraft, fighter, or bomber, despite chronic problems with its Wright R-3350 engines. Although the B-29 forever will be linked to the atomic bombings of Hiroshima and Nagasaki as the "A-Bomber" and be given credit for ending the Pacific war, the bomber's missions from the Marianas had previously devastated the Japanese homeland to the brink of submission. There were 3,970 B-29s built before the last B-29A-BN rolled off the Boeing-Renton line on 28 May 1946. The bomber was truly an innovative air weapon—a true Superfortress—as it was the first heavy bomber produced to include a tricycle landing gear, autopilot, tandem bomb bays, pressurized crew compartments, and remote central fire control. It was the forerunner of today's "systems" aircraft.

Although many books have been published about the B-29, none has been an in-depth look, with most being either superficial pictorials or focusing on the bombing campaigns, particularly the incendiary attacks and atomic bombings. Generally, descriptions of the bomber and crew have been cursory, and tend to be similar from book to book. This book, using rare, previously unexplored sources, intends to be the definitive look at the bomber and crew, detailing every facet for the air enthusiast, historian, and modeler. The author was granted access to the Pima Air & Space Museum's restored B-29 *Sentimental Journey* for inspection and photography, resulting in the most extensive photographic documentation of the B-29 ever published. The Pima Museum's archives, filled with B-29 technical and crew manuals, gave the author access to extensive information that also had not been previously used. The utilization of these sources and the author's personal library has produced the first detailed look at the bomber and its crew in the context of the bomber's development and operational use.

Author, Dr. Bill Wolf, and the Pima Air & Space Museum's B-29 *Sentimental Journey.* (Author/Pima)

Part One

Design, Development, Testing, and Production

During the two-decade period between the World Wars aircraft technology—particularly aircraft engines, propellers, and airframes—became comparatively more developed than any other military weapons systems. The other two major weapons developed in World War I, the tank and submarine, made no similar giant strides in technology during that period. Aircraft engines increased in horsepower from the Spad's 220hp to the Spitfire's 1,030hp in 1936. Propellers developed from fixed pitch that were adjusted on the ground to variable pitch, which could be altered in flight by the pilot to increase performance at different altitudes and for different circumstances. Also, a propeller on a multi-engine aircraft could be feathered if the engine became inoperative. Previously the prop of a disabled engine continued to windmill, even further decreasing the aircraft's performance. Airframe development was the most apparent of the new technology. Monoplanes appeared with all metal flush riveted construction, enclosed crew compartments, engine cowlings, and retractable landing gear. Another innovation was the wing flap, which increased wing area, thus increasing lift and drag and allowing heavier aircraft to take off and land at slower airspeeds and in shorter distances.

By the mid-1930s the global situation had begun to change, with the rise of Hitler and Mussolini in Europe and the Japanese militarism in the Far East. In 1933 the disciples of Billy Mitchell's strategic air power theories had been promoted to levels of some importance in the Army Air Corps, particularly its research and development branch, the Air Materiel Command at Wright Field, Dayton, OH. Out of this branch came "Project A," a thoroughly crafted feasibility study for a four-engined bomber that could fly 5,000mi carrying a ton of bombs. At the time the top echelon of the Army General Staff were former cavalry officers, and on 14 April 1934 they grudgingly approved Project A, but not as an "offensive" weapon, but one for "hemispheric defense." Gen. Conger Pratt, head of the Air Materiel Command, mailed out four requests for proposals for a bomber design. The Glenn Martin Company of Baltimore and the Boeing Company of Seattle were chosen.

1

The Boeing Company Heads Towards the Long-Range Bomber

Bill Boeing and Boeing Aircraft 1917 to 1933

Today the Boeing Aircraft Company is one of the world's foremost manufacturers of military and commercial multiengine aircraft, but its history is one of struggle and near bankruptcy, and finally preeminence in producing World War II heavy bombers. In 1903 William E. "Bill" Boeing, the son of a wealthy northwest lumber magnate, left Yale's Sheffield Scientific School to join his father in the lumber business. The young Boeing soon became successful, and along the way became preoccupied with aviation. On Independence Day, 1914, he took his first flight with a barnstormer named Terah Maroney, who flew 100hp flying boats off of Lake Washington, and left the lumber business behind. It is interesting to note that northwest lumber investor Reuben Fleet, the future president of Consolidated Aircraft, also took his first flight with Maroney that same year and became an aviation enthusiast. By the end of 1915 Boeing had built an aircraft hangar,

In 1903, William E. "Bill" Boeing left Yale's Sheffield Scientific School to join his father in the lumber business and soon became successful and along the way became preoccupied with aviation. On Independence Day, 1914, he took his first and left the lumber business behind. (USAF)

called "Bill Boeing's Lake Union Hanger," on the west shore of that lake in Seattle. Two years after his first flight he established the Pacific Aero Products Co. with partner Lt. Conrad Westervelt, a naval officer and aeronautical engineer. Westervelt designed the Model 1 B&W (Boeing & Westervelt) that became a two seat utility seaplane powered by a 125hp Hall-Scott A-5 engine. Only two Model 1s were built, and with America's increasing involvement in World War I Westervelt, a naval career officer, left the company, as he was transferred to the East Coast. The Navy awarded the company a subcontract for 50 Curtiss HS-2L flying boats, and to build them Boeing founded the Boeing Airplane Co. on 26 April 1917 (today the original factory building is part of the Museum of Flight at Boeing Field, Seattle). After the war ended the unfinished half of the Curtiss flying boat order was canceled, and the Boeing Company struggled to remain viable by building boats, canoes, and even furniture. In 1920 contracts to build 200 Thomas Morse MB-3A single seat fighters and to modernize 111 de Havilland DH-4s revived company finances. Ironically, it was contracting officer Maj. Reuben Fleet who signed the purchase order to keep his future competitor in business. In 1922 Boeing received its first sizable order with a contract to build its own design, the Model B-15 fighter, which became the Army PW-9 and the Navy FB-1. Boeing continued to develop and manufacture U.S. Army and Navy fighters during the 1920s and into the 1930s, culminating with 586 P-12/F-4Bs built from 1929 to March 1933.

The Civilian and Transport Market: Late 1920s and Early 1930s

Boeing entered the potentially more profitable civilian and transport market in the late 1920s and early '30s. When the Post Office Department opened its transcontinental airmail routes to private operators in 1927, Boeing won the San Francisco-Chicago route with a low bid and then created a new airline subsidiary named Boeing Air Transport to do the job. Boeing redesigned its 1925 Model 40 as the Model 40A by adding a radial, air-cooled Wasp engine that enabled it to carry 1,200lbs of airmail and two passengers in a small cabin located forward of the open cockpit. Boeing built 82 Model 40As, and its success motivated the company to expand by purchasing the Pacific Air Transport (PAT) in 1928, adding a Seattle-San Francisco route to the new Boeing System. The company's first successful civilian type was the Model 200 Monomail that first flew in May 1930. The Monomail team consisted of project manager Monty Montieth, designer Robert Minshall, project engineer John Kylstra, and structural de-

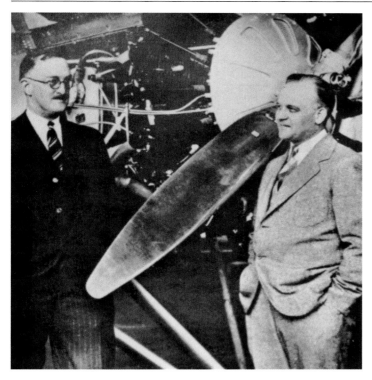

Bill Boeing (left) was only 51 years old but wished to retire, and in August 1933 he relinquished the Boeing Airplane Company chairmanship to Philip Johnson (right), and Clairmont Egtvedt became the Boeing president. (USAF)

signer Lysle Wood. The single engine, all metal Monomail was a revolutionary design, being a cantilever monoplane with retractable wheels and a modified, drag reducing streamlined cowling for its Hornet engine. However, the Monomail design was too advanced for contemporary engines and would not reach its full potential until a variable pitch propeller was fitted, by which time it was superseded by the multi-engine designs it influenced. Boeing followed the Monomail with its renowned Model 80 series of monoplane, tri-motor passenger aircraft that were able to compete with the contemporary Ford 5-A and Fokker F.VII tri-motor airliners.

Boeing Bomber Development: Early 1930s
Over the years Boeing had not developed a successful bomber, but Boeing executive Clairmont Egtvedt had visited European aircraft companies and

was particularly impressed by the monoplane bombers coming off English drawing boards. Egtvedt had joined the company as a draftsman in 1917 and quickly rose to chief experimental engineer, and in 1926 became General Manager and was a rising star in the company. Without Army requirements or funding, but with Egtveldt's urging, Boeing utilized the successful design features of its Monomail and Model 80s to develop the Model B-214 and B-215 bombers under project manager John Sanders. Except for the engines the two models were to be virtually identical. The B-215 was to be powered by two 575hp air-cooled Pratt & Whitney R-1860-13 Hornet B radial engines, while two 600hp liquid-cooled inline Curtiss V-1570 Conqueror inline engines would power the second bomber. The Model B-214 was first flown on 29 April 1931 by test pilot Les Tower and surpassed the performance and speed (163mph) of its contemporaries. In June pilots Slim Lewis and Erik Nelson, with Sanders as a passenger, flew the bomber from Seattle to Wright Field, OH. The flight to Dayton, with stops at Cheyenne and Chicago, averaged 158mph, and subsequent testing so impressed the Army that it ordered both models on 14 August 1931, even though the B-214 was not completed! The B-215 was initially designated the XB-901 (X=experimental and 901= the 901st AAC test aircraft), and then was redesignated as the YB-9. The B-214 was given the military designation Y1B-9 and was first flown on 5 November 1931. The 175mph speed of the B-9s made them faster than most contemporary fighters, and they had a ceiling of just over 19,000ft that was also higher than most fighters. The Model B-246 (the military designation of the Y1B-9A) was a development of the B-214/215 bombers, and had been ordered at the same time as the 214/215s. Design improvements of the B-246 were an enclosed cockpit (which was never built into the finished aircraft), more powerful engines, and a modified vertical tail. It weighed 8,941lbs and had a gross weight of almost 14,000lbs. Its wingspan was 76ft, 10in (wing area of 954square feet), and measured 52ft in length and was 12ft high. It was powered by two 630hp Pratt & Whitney R-1860-11 radial engines that gave the bomber a top speed of 186mph, a range of 540mi, and a ceiling of over 20,000ft; all of which made the performance of the B-246 higher and faster than most contemporary pursuit aircraft. The bomber had a four-man crew and was armed with a .30 caliber machine gun in a nose and dorsal turret, and carried a 2,200lb bomb load. The Army contracted for five service test bombers, but by the time the prototype first flew on 14 July 1932, and then by the time it was ready for quantity production in October, it had been superseded by the performance of the new generation of Martin built bombers, the B-10 (121 built) and B-12s (32 built). The

In 1922 Boeing received its first sizable order with a contract to build its own design, the Model B-15 fighter, which became the Army PW-9 and the Navy FB-1. (USAF)

When the Post Office Department opened its transcontinental airmail routes to private operators in 1927 Boeing won the San Francisco-Chicago route with a low bid and created a new airline subsidiary named Boeing Air Transport to do the job. Boeing redesigned the 1925 Model 40 by adding a radial, air-cooled Wasp that was able to carry 1,200lbs of airmail and two passengers in a small cabin located ahead of the open cockpit. (USAF)

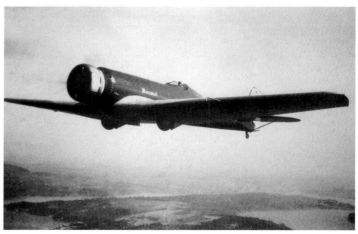

The company's first successful civilian aircraft type was the Model 200 Monomail that first flew in May 1930. The single engine, all metal Monomail was a revolutionary design being a cantilever monoplane with retractable wheels and modified, drag-reducing streamlined cowling for its Hornet engine. However, the Monomail design was too advanced for contemporary engines and would not reach its full potential until a variable pitch propeller was fitted by which time it was superseded by multi-engine designs it influenced. (USAF)

Martin bombers had a higher speed (193mph cruising), longer range (1,240mi), and could carry a heavier bomb load (2,260lbs), and Boeing's lead in the bomber race was short-lived.

Boeing and Civilian Transport: 1930s

Meanwhile, Boeing continued its exploration of the civilian transport field, utilizing the experience it had gained with the development of the Model 80 airliners and B-9 bombers. In mid-1932 the United Aircraft & Transport group decided to consolidate Boeing Air Transport, Pacific Air Transport, National Air Transport, and Varney Air Lines into the 120 plane United Air Lines and Transport Company, with Philip G. Johnson as president. Johnson would retain his position as the Boeing Airplane Company President, but would delegate much of his duties to the young 40 year old Claire Egtvedt as his vice president. At this time there was the tri-motor bi-plane versus monoplane controversy in progress in airliner design. Johnson wanted to equip his newly formed United Airlines Company with the best aircraft available, and he and Egtvedt felt their successful experience with the Monomail and B-9 made the monoplane design the wave of the future. They assigned Robert Minshall to lead the program, with Frank Canney as his project manager. The result was the development of the world's first true airliner, the superlative all-metal, low-wing monoplane Model 247, which flew its maiden flight on 8 February 1933. The aircraft could carry 10 passengers at 180mph (more than 60mph faster than the tri-motors of the day) over 500mi, at altitudes of up to 20,000ft. The Model 247s were powered by either the 525hp Pratt & Whitney Wasp or Twin Wasp Junior. Johnson's enthusiasm for the airliner sold United Airlines president Frederick Rentschler into placing a $3 million, 60 aircraft order to be delivered at the end of 1932. Despite 24-hour shifts to meet Johnson's target delivery date the Model 247 did not make its first flight until 8 February 1933. The 247 revolutionized the airline industry, and William Boeing was awarded the Guggenheim Medal for "successful pioneering and achievement in aircraft manufacture and air transportation." Bill Boeing was only 51 years old but wished to retire, and in August 1933 he relinquished the Boeing Airplane Company chairmanship to Johnson, and Egtvedt became the Boeing president. Once the initial 60 Model 247s had been delivered, the Boeing Company committed a critical business error by refusing to sell the Model 247 to other airlines, particularly Transcontinental and Western Airlines (later TWA). But Boeing actually had no choice, as it first needed to give its in-house United Airlines its allocation of the airliner. In response TWA issued a request to other manufacturers to design an alternative. Douglas Aircraft countered by developed its outstanding DC-1, DC-2, and DC-3 series that surpassed and ultimately ended the short-lived supremacy of the Boeing airliner.

Without Army requirements or funding the Boeing Company utilized the successful design features of the Monomail and Model 80s to develop the Model B-214 and B-215 bombers. Except for the engines the two models were virtually identical. It was first flown on 29 April 1931 by test pilot Les Tower. (USAF)

The Model 247 was the result of the superlative all-metal, low-wing monoplane designs of the Monomail and B-9 that were the wave of the future. It flew its maiden flight on 8 February 1933 and was the world's first true airliner. The aircraft could carry ten passengers at 180mph (more than 60mph faster than the tri-motors of the day), over 500 miles, at altitudes of up to 20,000ft. (USAF)

The Model 266 made its first flight as the P-26A Peashooter on 10 January 1934. The ultimate design, the P-26C fighter was a small, open cockpit low-wing monoplane that had a top speed of 235mph. The aircraft was moderately successful with 136 of all types sold to Army and as export versions to Spain and China. (USAF)

Boeing Returns to Fighter Development

Johnson and Egtvedt turned next to the development of a fighter and designed the Model 248 at its own expense to an Army Air Corps specification. The fighter was redesignated the Model 266 P-26A/B/C and made its first flight as the P-26A "Peashooter" on 10 January 1934. The ultimate design, the P-26C fighter, was a small, open cockpit low-wing monoplane that had a top speed of 235mph. The aircraft was moderately successful, with 136 of all types sold to the Army, and as export versions to Spain and China. But it was not long until the design was succeeded by more advanced designs from Seversky (P-35 and P-36), Bell (P-39), Curtiss-Wright (P-40), and Lockheed (P-38). To make matters worse, United Air Lines and Transport was in deep financial trouble and had to be split into three new companies: United Air Lines; Pratt & Whitney; and Boeing Airplane Company (Seattle and Stearman Aircraft, Wichita). With the division of United Aircraft & Transport Boeing Aircraft received $582,000 in cash, but had obligations and a payroll of $743,000 for the year.

In 1932, America was in the midst of the "Great Depression," and the voters had elected Franklin Roosevelt as president. In 1931 the Congressional five-year plans (approved and funded in 1926) for Army Air Corps and U.S. Navy aviation were completed. By 1933 Congressional appropriations for the armed services had fallen to half of projected requirements. The aircraft industry was in dire straits, as labor was demanding more pay and shorter hours, and Congress was threatening an investigation, and even possible nationalization of the industry. At the beginning of 1935 the AAC had only 1,500 operational aircraft in its inventory, a number

ber that was 300 less than the 1,800 authorized by Congress years earlier. It was only the enormous expansion of commercial aviation that kept the American aircraft industry solvent during the period.

Boeing and the B-307 Stratoliner

Boeing was again left behind, as it had no other fighter aircraft in development, and once more turned to the design, development, and manufacture of bombers for the AAC and airliners, and transport aircraft for the fledgling transport and airline industry. Boeing engineers had begun the development of the Model B-307 Stratoliner in late 1935 and continued on through 1936. They borrowed heavily from the Model 299, which was the B-17 precursor being developed concurrently. They used many of its components and assemblies: the wings and nacelles; horizontal and vertical stabilizers; and engines in the B-307 design. The aircraft weighed 42,000lbs, had a 107ft, 3in wingspan, stood 20ft, 9in high, and was 74ft, 4in long. What distinguished the Stratoliner was its fully pressurized cylindrical fuselage that could carry 33 passengers and a five-person crew, making it the benchmark airliner until the Douglas DC-4 came on line. The Stratoliner was powered by four Wright GR-1820 Cyclone radial engines that developed 900hp, giving it a top speed of 246mph. The airliner first flew over Seattle on the last day of 1938. Pan American Airways (PAA) ordered the Stratoliner first, and was followed by Trans World Airlines (TWA). Because the Douglas DC-4 Skymaster (AAC C-54) and the Lockheed L-49 Constellation (AAC C-69) soon superseded the Stratoliner only 10 were built. These aircraft were later commandeered in 1942 by the Air Transport Service Command (ATSC) and were designated the C-75.

Boeing engineers had begun the development of the Model B-307 Stratoliner in late 1935, and borrowed heavily from the B-17C Flying Fortress, using many of its components and assemblies: the wings and nacelles, horizontal and vertical stabilizers, and engines. What distinguished the Stratoliner was its fully pressurized cylindrical fuselage, which could carry 33 passengers and a five-person crew, making it the benchmark airliner until the Douglas DC-4 came on line. (USAF)

2

The Long-Range Bomber

Pre-War Aircraft Procurement Policy

The Air Corps Act of 1926 was to establish a statutory means to procure new aircraft. It provided for a design competition that would lead to the purchase of one or more prototypes, the issue of contracts for "experimental" aircraft by the Secretary of War at "his discretion without competition," and competition where aircraft could be procured on grounds other than the first two provisions, with the Secretary able to "exercise discretion in determining the lowest responsible bidder." Another procurement possibility was for the negotiated purchase contract without competition of a design "of sufficient interest to justify immediate procurement." The Act required the use of a design competition, with the designs to be submitted to and evaluated at Wright Field, and a winner was to be selected and awarded a contract to build one prototype for service testing. If the service tests were successful a production order was then to be issued. However, in effect design competition was impractical, as when bids went out Wright Field received a large number of design proposals that the designers claimed met or exceeded the specifications. Until a prototype was built it could not be determined from the submitted design if specifications had been met and, if not, time passed and money was spent without result. Also, bidders were given inadequate time (several months) to design and submit their proposals, and once the winner was chosen its design had to be detailed; then it was often found that the original dollar bid was inadequate, and the manufacturer would lose money on the building of the prototype and production models. This ineffective design competition gave way to the negotiated purchase contract, but the manufacturer with the winning bid lost money, as they intentionally low-balled the bid, expecting to recoup this loss on the quantity production order. But the Act made no provision for a quantity order, and a new bid for a quantity order needed to be issued, and another manufacturer could be contracted to build the winning design of another manufacturer. In June 1929 the Navy announced that, despite the fact that Reuben Fleet's Consolidated Aircraft had invested an additional $500,000 more for the development of the Admiral Flying Boat than the original $150,000 Navy contract awarded, it would accept bids from "qualified companies" (later Glenn Martin) to manufacture nine flying boats to Consolidated's design. Manufacturers were reluctant to submit designs and bids, and Army Regulation 5-240 was resurrected from the mass of regulations to accommodate procurement. The Regulation stipulated that "competition might be avoided in certain special circumstances in which competition was impractical." By interpreting AR 5-240 to classify the manufacturer of an experimental aircraft purchased under the Air Corps Act of 1926 as the only source the manufacturer could be awarded the production contract. Between 1926 and 1934 awards were issued of $16 million for contracts under the "experimental" provision of the Act and $22 million under the non-competitive, and entirely legal under the terms of AR 5-240. There had been a public record, and an annual aircraft procurement report to Congress every year from 1926, of every procurement, all of which were completely legal. Nonetheless, in January 1934 the *Washington Post* reported that the House of Representatives was about to investigate seven years of wrongful aircraft procurement by the War Department in violation of the Air Corps Act of 1926.

In late 1933 the ambitious Alabama Senator, H.D. Black, was aggressively investigating the federal subsidies to private airmail contractors that were U.S. airlines to such an extent that the newspapers soon led the public to believe that most of the nation's airlines were guilty of flagrant wrongdoing and excessive profits. Since many of America's aircraft manufacturers were associated with airlines (e.g. Boeing/United Airlines), they were also incriminated by the newspapers. When the Navy and Army came to Congress to present their appropriations bill in January and February 1934, respectively, both were attacked with accusations of profiteering and excess profits by the aircraft manufacturers at the expense of the taxpayers. The Chairman of the House Naval Affairs Committee, Georgia Representative Carl Vinson, appointed a subcommittee headed by New York Representative, J.J. Delaney, to investigate the supposed widespread procurement corruption. After two months and hearing 800 pages of testimony the Delaney Committee's final report found that the charges against the Navy's procurement policies were unfounded, and that said policies were "prudent and practicable" and fostered competition. The Committee found that the major airframe manufacturers made only 0.2% on cost profit on their sales to the military and commercial interests. The average profit earned by airframe and engine manufacturers between 1926 and 1934 was a not-so-excessive 9% on cost. Further figures showed that aircraft manufacturers lost an average of 50% on cost on "experimental" aircraft, and when combining these losses with production profits (if the aircraft went into production) the return was 11.5%, which was not considered excessive for the high risk involved. However, while the *New York Times* had headlined the Committee's appointment and printed titillating accusation stories during the Committee's investigation, it only spent one day reporting the story exonerating the Navy, and that was carried on page 15! To exacerbate the situation, one member of the Committee charged publicly that the majority had "whitewashed" the Navy, and then wrote a minority report that reached the *Congressional Record*, while the majority report languished in obscurity. Of course, the newspapers cited this minority report and mentioned the "indication of new evidence of illegal procurement." Strangely, the majority members did not refute this report and the misleading indication of new evidence that would never surface. In the turmoil the Air Corps also soon came under fire from South Carolina Representative John McSwain, Chairman of the Military Affairs Committee, who put New Hampshire Representative, W.N. Rogers, in charge of the eight man committee that took his name. In closed hearings the Rogers Committee found the Chief of the Air Corps guilty of "gross misconduct" and "deliberate and willful and intentional violation of the law," and the Air Corps both "inefficient" and "expensive," using "various subterfuges" for "pernicious" and "unlawful" procurement. It made the recommendation that there be a return to "aggressive design competition for experimental aircraft" and "competition on all contracts for procurement in quantity." Perhaps due to the closed nature of the hearings to the insistent Press, Congress did nothing about the Air Corps Act of 1926, but passed a law limiting profits and provided for the recapture of all earnings in excess of 10% (but provided nothing to put a floor under losses). This excess profits law raised questions and a mandate for further revisions to it.

A new administrative procurement policy was devised by Assistant Secretary of War, H.H. Woodring, that essentially supported competitive bids, and thus circumvented the Congress from amending the Air Corps Act by statute. During fiscal 1933 the Congress appropriated $10 million for the AAC, but the new Roosevelt Administration, under the economic pressure of the Depression, impounded $7 million as an economic emergency measure. The AAC urgently needed more than 700 new aircraft to equip active units, and many more were needed to replace aircraft that were, or were going to be, obsolete. At the end of the year the administration transferred $7.5 million to the AAC from the Public Works Administration (PWA). To expedite the purchase of the best aircraft available the AAC negotiated production contracts with the manufacturers of these top-quality aircraft using Army Regulation 5-240, maintaining that the manufacturer was the "sole source" of the required aircraft. Two companies complained about not getting the AR 5-240 negotiated contract awards. The Depression put the War Department under pressure to award contracts to a number of aircraft companies to keep them viable, and the Assistant Secretary of War, Woodring, was forced to reconsider the contract awards. In order to award contracts equally throughout the aircraft industry and also obtain aircraft of maximum performance at a minimum cost, Woodring was in a Catch-22 situation. Aircraft contracted on the basis of price competition would save the government money but not insure purchasing aircraft with the best performance. On the other hand, aircraft contracted on the basis of having the best performance would cost more. Either way, the intention of spreading the wealth was not met, as whether contracts were awarded on cost or performance, most of the contracts tended to be awarded to a few efficient companies who had the best designs and production capacity. Woodring asked the Air Corps to devise a policy before Congress reconvened in January 1934. The AAC responded with the 1934 War Department Aircraft Procurement Policy, which had "competition" as its foundation. The AAC's solution was to allow each manufacturer to bid on his

own specification, but required a minimum high speed, thus allowing competition as to performance; however, it disqualified all companies but those that fell within a narrow margin of specified performance. The competition was also limited to companies that had previously submitted similar aircraft for approval to Wright Field for evaluation, so that there was some assurance that the submitted aircraft proposal had some design and safety substance behind it. The 1934 Procurement Policy went on to state that if the aircraft with the highest performance was not the lowest bidder then the Secretary could award the contract "at his discretion to the best advantage of the Government." Each submitting company was required to supply a prototype for flight testing, eliminating "paper promises," and would provide a basis for an assessment of the aircraft for production contracts. The Secretary's timely submission of the 1934 Procurement Policy undercut a Congressional Committee that was infuriated over the alleged profiteering by the aircraft industry and bent on amending the Air Corps Act.

Now the competition procedure was to mail a circular containing "type specifications in terms of the minimum acceptable performance." The aircraft's maximum performance was then left to the talents of the manufacturer's design team, whose design performance was to be verified by flight tests of the prototype aircraft. The AAC needed to require a necessary "degree of uniformity and standardization" on the aircraft industry to prevent the "collection of heterogeneous aircraft and equipment" and "insure a high degree of uniformity and interchangeability." The aircraft manufacturers were asked to submit designs based on the performance specifications issued by the AAC. With their invitations to the aircraft industry for designs and bids the AAC issued the

Handbook for Aircraft Designers and an "index of all pertinent Army, Navy, and federal specifications for materials and subassemblies." In addition, the industry was required to use Government Furnished Equipment (GFE), which included instruments, armament, communications, oxygen equipment, etc., and use mandatory engine and propeller installations. The *Handbook* and use of GFE decreased the number of variables to be incorporated in the prototype design, thus limiting the range of the competing designs, and made the competition more evenhanded among the qualified competitors. In June 1936 the Secretary of War reported to Congress that the new policy was a success, as it had increased the number of bidders, and the designs submitted were far advanced compared to contemporary aircraft. But the question remained as to equating price to performance. To which bidder should a contract be awarded when one manufacturer submitted a superior design at a higher cost, while another submitted a much lower bid on an inferior design? If performance was the main prerequisite then the manufacturer with the superior design could ask an unreasonable price for his design. During the design competition for an AAC transport the larger, twin engine Douglas DC-2, already in successful service as a commercial airliner, was clearly the far superior design over the single engine transport designs submitted by Curtiss Wright (Condor) and Fairchild (C-8). But the Douglas bid was $49,500 per aircraft, compared to the $29,500 for Curtiss Wright and $29,150 for Fairchild. The transport design proposal stipulated that the primary consideration would be performance, not price, and the Douglas DC-2 was given the production contract. But Fairchild protested, and the Comptroller General deferred payment to Douglas, pointing out that the performance of the Fairchild transport "was far in excess of the *minimum* performance required." The Comptroller General did not realize that in combat, having the minimum acceptable performance would not be sufficient against the superior aircraft being designed in Europe. The CG believed that the AAC's competition was illegal, as it did not provide any method of establishing a precise relationship between cost and performance and left the choice only on performance. The Secretary of War held that no formula could evaluate price vs. performance, and that the Air Corps Act of 1926 gave him legal discretion to make decisions regarding the weight of price versus performance when evaluating bids "in order to serve the best interests of the air arm." Meanwhile, Douglas delivered aircraft on the contract but was not paid, as the disagreement between the CG and Secretary of War continued. The Attorney General was asked to intervene, and after four months ruled significantly in favor of the Secretary of War, and Douglas was finally paid. Even though the Attorney General had ruled in favor of the Secretary of War, AAC procurement officers realized that price would remain a problem with the Comptroller General and General Accounting Office. In order to expedite their procurement programs, and for their aircraft contractors to receive timely payments, the AAC agreed to include price as a factor for evaluation in all future competition. The AAC's evaluation proposal was to determine a "figure of merit" on the basis of performance that was to be divided by the dollar cost bid by the manufacturer. This "price facto" would favor the bidder with the lowest price and the highest performance. However, the War Department continued to be adamant that final selection would be the decision of the Secretary of War, and the figure of merit and price factor would serve as a guideline for the final selection.

With this procedure in place the manufacturers found drawbacks lingered. The circulars (design proposals) had to be composed so that the manufacturers had enough design autonomy to incorporate innovations, but it also had to be specific as to the design requirements so that the manufacturer knew what the circular required. To make the competition as fair as possible the manufacturers could not consult Wright Field engineers, which, in turn, prevented Wright from offering suggestions that could enhance the design. The manufacturers were also not allowed to submit mock up aircraft to Wright for evaluation that could discover design defects that could be more easily corrected in this mock up stage than in the prototype phase. Changes in the prototype phase, once it reached Wright Field, could only be made by change orders to amend the contract, which was time and money intensive. The overriding factor in issuing a circular was getting a design into quantity production as soon as possible, and the AAC assumed that the manufacturers would submit a wholly developed prototype that would be ready to go into production. But to win the competition the manufacturers had to design aircraft with innovations that were not yet combat proven, and thus the prototypes tended to be more experimental in nature and would later require numerous contract change orders. Prototypes were very expensive to build, especially four engine bombers, whose airframe costs rose 300 to 400%, and the time for their fabrication increased from months to as much as two years during the 1930s. Also, the manufacturers always faced the possibility of not having their design and prototype accepted and having to absorb the entire cost of the project, as there was a very slight chance that the design could be sold to foreign air forces or used commercially. The manufacturers were between the proverbial rock and hard place, as they were forced into bidding simply because they needed the business in the poor economic environment of the Depression, and failure to enter the competition would result in leaving the manufacturer behind its contemporaries in developing combat technology. But then not

entering competition would save them the costs of developing a design and building a prototype without assurance of a contract. In the late 1930s the result was a declining number of bidders for government contracts, as the economic conditions improved and the large manufacturers were receiving contracts from commercial airlines and air transport. In 1938 manufacturers led by Consolidated Aircraft Corporation's Reuben Fleet suggested remedies to increase bidding. Fleet had once been a procurement officer for the Army in the early 1920s and had been committed to the problems of aircraft procurement and legislation. Over the years Fleet had made several proposals that culminated in his suggesting that legislation be passed to authorize the War Department to procure aircraft in production quantities by negotiated contracts, rather than bids involving prototypes. Of course, the War Department could not endorse this idea without rankling Congress and their desire for competition. When in a dilemma the government's solution was to convene another board to study yet again another revised procurement recommendation. The AAC and various aircraft manufacturers testified, and the board recommended a solution that was a compromise between competition with prototypes and a simple design competition. Before issuing circular proposals for production aircraft the AAC would invite aircraft manufacturers to submit designs for evaluation. One or more designs would be selected and be granted experimental contracts for the construction of one or more prototypes. There was also the proviso that a quality data from losing designs could be purchased. Detailed type specifications would not be prepared until the winning design(s) passed the final mock up phase, allowing the AAC and manufacturers to discuss changes. Once the design was finalized the AAC was to issue its circular proposal for a prototype aircraft to be built by manufacturers interested in procuring a contract for the production aircraft. The War Department would subsidize the building of the prototype of the winning manufacturer(s). Usually the winner could expect to be awarded a production contract with his prototype, but other manufacturers who could afford to build a prototype to specifications could also enter the competition and preclude any accusations that free competition was being thwarted. An impartial evaluation of the design was now based on the performance of the prototype, and was to reduce the number of design changes and get the aircraft into production sooner. Finally a workable procurement proposal seemed to have been realized. The Chief of Staff approved the board's proposal in October 1938, but the threat of an impending European war soon made the proposal mute.

In February 1939 the chairman of the House Military Affairs Committee introduced a bill authorizing 6,000 aircraft for the fiscal year 1940 that was passed in April, authorizing $57 million for new equipment. The next day the AAC issued contracts worth $19 million to build 571 aircraft. In July, in response to an appeal by President Roosevelt, a supplementary $89 million was authorized for immediate disbursement and authorized an additional $44 million. On 10 August 1939 the AAC issued $86 million in aircraft contracts. By 1941 the same Congress that was so adamant about financial prudence and competitive bidding in 1934 were now voting billions of dollars for defense, and endorsing negotiated contracts to expedite the placement of contracts to meet the President's call for 50,000 aircraft. All the legislation from the Air Corps Act of 1926 onward, and all the boards and committees and their investigations and recommendations were to be invalidated by the Japanese attack on Pearl Harbor, which would open the procurement flood gates.

Air Materiel Command and the Long-Range Bomber Requirements

In the early 1930s the Army Air Corps realized they needed a bomber with both speed and range. However, range was contingent on aircraft size; the more fuel carried for longer range meant a bigger aircraft and larger wing to carry the increased fuel supply. Large aircraft were dependent on the availability of a sufficient power plant. In 1933 the requirements of a Long-Range bomber were discussed at Wright Field by chief engineer James Howard, his assistant Al Lyons, aircraft branch chief James Taylor, Hugh Kneer of the field service section, and Leonard "Jake" Harman, the Air Materiel Command representative. The group decided to categorize the future bomber types that would be required:

1) Wingspan, 75ft; gross weight 15,000lbs (already contemporary in the B-9 and B-10)
2) 100ft span; 40,000lbs gross weight
3) 150ft span; 60,000lbs gross weight
4) 200ft span; 150,000lbs gross weight
5) 250ft span; 200,000lbs gross weight
6) Etc.

In the fall of 1933 it was decided to disregard the #2 category, and category #3 was considered as a feasible choice; it was identified as "Project A." Jake Harman drew up the requirement, and Gen. Conger Pratt of the Air Materiel Command authorized the money for engineering designs and sent the request to Washington for approval. At the time strategic air power had few advocates, but Long-Range defensive patrol aircraft did have their proponents in Air Chief Benjamin Foulois and the General Staff. In 1933 Foulois commanded his assistant, Brig.Gen. Oscar Westover, to fly missions testing the defense of the West Coast. Westover's report to the General Staff found the observation and patrol aircraft that flew these missions to be "woefully obsolete." But he suggested that modern bombers flying in formation with increased speed and range could frustrate any "known agency." Pratt was able to sell the idea of the 5,000-mile bomber, as it could protect Alaska and Hawaii, and was a step in establishing a mobile GHQ Air Force.

In the early 1930s there was a dichotomy in the War Department. The conflict engaged the traditionalists, led by Army Chief of Staff Gen. John J. Pershing, who believed that the infantry ruled the battlefield, while the Army Air Arm, led by the defrocked Gen. Billy Mitchell, espoused the future role of air power in warfare. The government organized a number of boards and committees to study air doctrine and its role in future warfare. The most influential of these groups was the Baker Board Report of July 1934, which recommended America's national defense policy was not based on aggression, and its purpose was to defend the homeland and overseas possessions, with the Army fending off any invader until civilian forces could be mobilized. The Report stated:

"The idea that aviation can replace any of the other elements of our armed forces is found on analysis, to be erroneous. Since ground forces alone are capable of occupying territory, the Army with its own air forces remains the ultimate decisive factor in war."

Baker Board member Jimmy Doolittle voiced the minority dissent, supporting the separation of the Army and its air forces, and advocating the development of air doctrine for its employment.

Although the Baker Board rejected an independent strategic air force, it did support the creation in March 1935 of a General Headquarters Air Force that would be under the control of the Army commander in the field. However, there were conflicting opinions of the role of the GHQ Air Force. One was that it would be apportioned and attached to field armies and utilized under their direct control. Another view had the GHQ AF engaged as an integrated force acting to further the mission of the Army. The view held by most airmen was to have it act as a unified force not to support the Army, but also act beyond the realm of the Army with missions of its own. Maj.Gen. Frank Andrews was the CO of the GHQ AF and forcefully advocated the airmen's point of view. As the possibility of a war in Europe approached the War Department was in a state of flux, and the GHQ AF and its concepts were replaced by ideas formulated by the Joint Army-Navy Board that culminated in the First Strategic Air Plan (AWPD-1), which will be discussed later.

On 14 April 1934 Pratt released a secret requirement for a bomber that could fly 5,000mi (five times the B-9 or B-10) at 200mph carrying a one-ton bomb load designated as top secret "Project A." No production was to be actualized, as Project A was more of a proof-of-concept than a production military bomber. On 12 May 1934 Pratt was authorized to begin negotiations for the initial designs. On the 14th he met with Boeing President, Clairmont Egtvedt, and Martin President, C.A. Van Dusen, at Wright Field. Pratt's aide, Jake Harman, explained the importance of Project A. He presented the ambitious proposal, outlined design and cost estimate procedures, and told the two company representatives that he would like to have them by 15 June—only a month away! Sikorsky later entered the Long-Range bomber project with the XBLR-3, but it did not progress beyond the initial stages of development and was not given the "B" (Bomber) designation. Back in Seattle Boeing began a flurry of activity by drawing up the preliminary design for its Model 294, and AAC designated it XBLR-1 (eXperimental Bomber, Long-Range, Number-1). But an obstacle was met in the proposed use of the four 850hp Pratt & Whitney R-1830-11 Twin Wasp, 14 cylinder, 2-row radial engines, which would only provide the minimum power required for the projected weight of the aircraft. Another possible engine choice was four 1,600hp 24-cylinder Allison XV-3420 liquid-cooled inline engines. The Allison V-3420 engine consisted of two of its capable V-1710 engines (e.g. 2x1710=3420) tied together by a single crankshaft to yield a V-24 (two V-12s). This engine had critical developmental problems and was not available (until 1940). On 28 June Boeing was awarded a $600,000 contract to build its Project A design, which was then designated the XB-15, and Martin was given another $600,000 contract for its Model 145 to be called the XB-16.

Martin XB-16

The Martin XB-16 was never given a XBLR designation, as it only reached the design stage. It was to utilize four bulky 1,000hp Allison V-1710 air-cooled radial engines embedded entirely in its wings, with extended drive shafts to drive the 12ft, 3in propellers. The inboard nacelles were enlarged to house the large five-foot tires of the retracted landing gear. Its supercharged top speed was estimated to be 237mph, with a cruising speed of 120mph over a range of 5,040mi carrying 2,500lbs of bombs. Innovations included the addition of 360square feet of Fowler flaps that would lower the landing speed to 60mph. The XB-16 was to have retractable dorsal, fuselage, and belly turrets, in addition to its Plexiglas nose and tail gun positions. Further design development led to an odd-looking giant bomber

The gigantic and remarkable Boeing XB-15 was the first four-engined bomber ordered by the AAC, and at the time was the largest aircraft ever built. The XB-15 project was an all-metal 70,700lb giant with a 149ft wingspan, an 87ft, 7in length and 19ft, 5in height that was very similar in appearance to the B-17 except for the severe taper of its wing. The XB-15 was underpowered that made its performance mediocre to the Model 299, the future B-17 design that had made its first flight two years before the XB-15. (USAF)

with a huge wing with twin tail booms attached. The fuselage was a bulky nacelle-like cabin suspended under the wing, and carried the 10-man crew and payload. The curious feature of the new design was the six embedded Allison V-1710-3 engines that were arranged in a unique four tractor, two pusher arrangement, whose propellers were driven via extension shafts. The first appearance of a tricycle landing gear was proposed in the model. No models of either XB-16 were ever built, but the engineering designs were purchased by the AAC.

Boeing XB-15

Engineering work began on the Boeing design in January 1934, and the result would be a single remarkable research model that was the largest aircraft ever built. On 29 June 1935 the Boeing proposal was officially designated the XB-15, with the AAC serial number 35-277, but would not

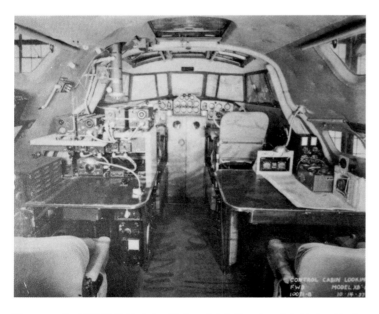

The pressurized XB-15 flight deck with the pilot (left) and copilot side-by-side, the bombardier forward of them, and the navigator's position (right) and for the first time a flight engineer's position (left) (USAF)

be ready until mid-1937. The XB-15 was an all-metal 70,700lb giant with a 149ft wingspan, an 87ft, 7in length, and 19ft, 5in height that was very similar in appearance to the B-17, except for the severe taper of its wing. It made its first flight on 15 August 1937, and the four 1,000hp (rated) Pratt & Whitney R-1830-11 engines were found to be insufficient; thus the XB-15 was underpowered and its performance was mediocre. Its 197mph speed, rate of climb, and operational ceiling were each inferior to the Model 299 that had made its first flight on 28 July 1935, two years before the XB-15. In the meantime, the Model 299 had been officially designated the Y1B-17 and 13 had already been completed. Nonetheless, the design work on the XB-15 had provided Boeing engineers with beneficial experience toward the future development of the B-29, as the design was unique in many ways. It was the most heavily armed bomber ever built, as it was defended by three .30 caliber and three .50cal machine guns supplied with 7,200 rounds located in six turrets. It had the first 110-volt A.C. electrical system, with generators driven by two auxiliary power plants. It had a "comfort conditioned" living and sleeping quarter, including a kitchenette and lavatory for its crew of 10 including, for the first time, a flight engineer. There was a passageway leading through the thick wing for inflight servicing of the engines. The XB-15 project was continued as Model-294-2, the service test type that was designated the Y1B-20. In late 1937 the AAC ordered two more aircraft to be powered by the 1,400hp Pratt & Whitney R-2180-5 engines. The proposed 80,000lb model was similar in appearance to the XB-15 with a 152ft wingspan and 90ft length, but was canceled in the mockup stage. Later the original XB-15 had a large door cut into its fuselage and continued its days as the XC-105 transport, based in Panama with the 6th Air Force. It would set several payload and load-to-altitude records, and flew relief supplies to earthquake victims in Chile before it was scrapped in 1945.

Boeing Model 299

In a memorandum of 14 July 1934 the Air Materiel Command had changed its thinking, and decided that a second bomber that was not as grand as the Project A bomber could more easily be realized and put into production. The new AAC bomber was to have the same 2,000lb bomb load as the proposed XB-15 in development, but its speed was to be 200mph, and its range was to be at least 1,020mi, but 2,200mi was much preferred. The AAC proposal was for "multi-engines," which to the AAC meant two, but to Boeing it meant four. On 26 September 1934 the board of directors of the newly independent Boeing Airplane Company met for the first time after United Aircraft & Transport was finally dissolved. The board bravely voted $275,000 to design and build a bomber to meet the new AAC specification. Egtvedt assigned his project engineer, E.G. "Giff" Emery, with Ed Wells as his assistant, and Frederick Laudan as the construction supervisor to work on the Model 299. The bomber was to be a low-wing monoplane that would have four engines to power it, and was essentially a scaled up version of Boeing's streamlined Model 247 twin-engine airliner that was first flown in February 1934. Concurrently, Egtvedt ordered Emery to develop a four-engine airliner based on Model 299 that was to become the Model 307 Stratoliner. With Emery running the Model 307 project, Egtvedt placed 24 year old Edward Wells as project manager of the Model 299, which had been unofficially designated the "XB-17" by Boeing before it had been approved by the AAC. After four months the Boeing Company had lost $226,000 and needed another $150,000 to continue running. The Model 299 made its first flight on 28 July 1935, and the media was im-

The Model 299, unofficially designated as the "XB-17" by Boeing, made its first flight on 28 July 1935 and so impressed the media by it size that it was dubbed the "Flying Fortress." Boeing put the Model 299 into production as the Y1B-17 and the first rolled off the Seattle line on 2 December 1936 (USAF)

pressed by it size and dubbed it the "Flying Fortress." On 20 August project test pilot, Leslie "Les" Tower, flew it cross-country 2,100mi to Wright Field for evaluation at an average speed of 232mph.

During testing at Wright Field the four-engine Boeing Model 299 was to challenge Douglas Aircraft's twin-engine DB-1 bomber, the XB-18 that had been developed from the company's successful DC-3 airliner design. From August and into October the AAC examined both bombers, and the Boeing's better range and reliability earned it the lead in gaining a contract. On 30 October 1935 Boeing test pilot Les Tower, and AAC pilot, Maj. P.P. "Pete" Hill, and the test crew took off in the Model 299. But once it became airborne the bomber became uncontrollable, and as it passed over the end of the runway it crashed in a nearby pasture. Hill was killed on impact, but Tower survived with horrible burns, though he died 20 days later. Lt. Donald Putt was pulled from the burning wreckage and given little chance of survival, but Putt did survive, and four years later was to become the project manager of the B-29 program. Investigation showed that the ground crew had not unlocked the tail control surfaces, thus causing the crash that would put the Boeing program in jeopardy. The Douglas XB-18 had also done well in tests, and two of the twin-engine Douglas bombers could be manufactured for the cost of one Model 299. On 17 January 1936 the Army General Staff decided to order 133 production B-18s and only 13 of the Model 299s, now designated the YB-17 (the "Y" meant that the aircraft was not experimental, but a "service test" model that could, or not, precede production aircraft). Boeing put the now Y1B-17 (the 1 because they were purchased out of F-1 fiscal year supplementary funds) into production. The first Y1B-17 rolled off the Seattle line on 2 December 1936, and the last of the 13 was finished on 5 August 1937, 10 days before the XB-15 was finally completed and slated to make its first flight on 15 August. One X1B-17 was sent to Wright for testing, and the other 12 were assigned to the Second Bombardment Group at Langley Field, VA, under Lt.Col. Robert Olds.

Douglas B-18

The Douglas B-18 "Bolo," developed from the Douglas DC-2 airliner/transport design, was the winner of the 1936 bomber competition, but the bomber was nothing more than a transport with a bomb bay! The prototype was known as the Douglas Model DB-1 and was distinguished by its short pug nose and large belly, which transported its six-man crew in a spacious cabin. The Bolo, powered by two 930hp Wright R-1820-45 Cyclones, had a top speed of 217mph and a cruising speed of 167mph, and with its full bomb load of 4,400lbs had a range of 1,200mi. The AAC ordered a total of 217 B-18As, but the Bolos proved to be inadequate and were later converted to 122 radar-equipped anti-submarine B-18Bs. The AAC finally came to its senses and pressed Boeing, a company that had lost $334,000 in 1936, for the production of the B-17. From this point America would lead the world in the development of four-engine, Long-Range bombers. Despite the success of the B-17 design and its potential in strategic bombing there were many opponents to the concept. Military appropriations were limited, and airpower opponents felt that military dollars would be better spent on more conventional naval and ground weapons. Conservative military strategists were of the time-honored opinion that wars could only be won by troops on the battlefield. They felt military aircraft should be developed and utilized to aid ground and naval forces, and not fly off on independent missions behind enemy lines. Traditionalists in the Army and Navy also realized that if airpower were successful it could lead to a new aerial branch of the military that would vie not only for status, but for Congressional tax dollars. Opponents doubted the enthusiastic claims of airpower advocates that heavy bombers could bring about the defeat of the enemy by destroying his major military and industrial installations via so-called "pin-point" bombing missions. Their doubts would ultimately prove to be correct, but at the time airpower proponents had two trump cards in their hand: the B-17, and the menacing global situation with the ascendancy of Germany and Japan.

The Douglas B-18 "Bolo," developed from the Douglas DC-2 airliner/transport design, was the winner of the 1936 bomber competition, although the bomber was nothing more than a transport with a bomb bay! The prototype was known as the Douglas Model DB-1 and was distinguished by its short pug nose and large belly. (USAF)

The superbomber concept went off on tangent with the Douglas XB-19. The design was initiated in 1935 but by mid-1938 it had fallen behind schedule and changes had substantially increased the bomber's weight and thus decreased its anticipated performance. It required seven years of development before the bomber took flight for the first time on 27 June 1941 and by then the design was obsolete in view of contemporary advances in aircraft design. (USAF)

Douglas XB-19

In the meantime, the superbomber concept went off on a tangent with the Douglas XB-19. The design was initiated in 1935 as the XBLR-2, and one plane was ordered on 29 September 1936 to be powered by four new 2,000hp Wright 3350-5 engines. It was designated the XB-19 by the AAC in mid-November 1937 and given the serial number 38-471. By mid-1938 work on the XB-19 had fallen behind schedule, and design changes had substantially increased its weight and decreased anticipated performance; realistically the design was obsolete in view of contemporary advances in aircraft design. Douglas had spent a substantial amount of company funds on the project, and on 30 August 1938 requested it be released from the program, as it needed its design team to concentrate on more promising aircraft that could reach production. The Air Materiel Division persisted and ordered Douglas to complete the XB-19, which was to be as a test aircraft. It required seven years of development before the bomber took flight for the first time over Clover Field, Santa Monica, CA, on 27 June 1941. Maj. Stanley Umstead and a crew of seven flew the bomber to March Field for testing and evaluation, first by Douglas, and then by the Army. Since the bomber was considered obsolete, its "impressive" numbers (mostly its size and anticipated performance) were released to the press. Great public hoopla ensued:

"America's millions, given (its) breath-taking statistics, have probably been nursing a secret desire to hear that it bombed Tokyo" (Edward Churchill, *Flying Magazine*, August 1942).

Since it did not bomb Tokyo, or anywhere else, its "bigger job" as a flying laboratory was emphasized. President Roosevelt personally telegraphed congratulations to Donald Douglas on his company's accomplishment. The XB-19, which was tentatively accepted in October 1941 by the Air Corps, was a gigantic all-metal stressed skin monoplane that measured 132ft, 4in; its rudder towered 42ft above the tarmac, and it weighed 84,431lbs (162,000lbs maximum gross weight). The bomber had the largest wing ever built at 212ft and, like the XB-15, had 45ft ailerons, and its eight-foot main tire retracted almost flush into the lower wing surface. A prototype tricycle landing gear was tested on a Douglas OA-4B Dolphin amphibian on loan from the Army, and then fitted to the XB-19. Initially it was to be powered by four 1,600hp Allison XV-3420-1 24 cylinder in-line engines that were to power Boeing's model 247. The XV-3420-1 was two coupled V-1710 12-cylinder "V" engines driving a single propeller, but the engine ran into teething problems, and on 2 November 1936 Douglas decided on four 2,000hp Wright R-3350-5 18 cylinder Cyclones. The XB-15 had a top speed of 224mph and a cruising speed of 135mph, could carry 16,000lbs of bombs internally, and exterior bomb racks were able to carry 20,000 additional pounds. The aircraft had a crew of 16 that included an aircraft commander, pilot, co-pilot, flight engineer, navigator, radio operator, bombardier, and nine gunners. An additional crew of two flight mechanics and six relief crewmen could be accommodated in a special cabin with eight seats and six bunks built in the fuselage above the bomb bay. There were passageways built into the lower wing to give flight mechanics access to service the engines in flight. There was also a complete galley to prepare hot meals in flight. Defensive armament was an impressive total of 12 guns with 4,770 rounds of ammunition. The nose and top forward power turrets each contained one 37mm cannon and a .30 caliber machine gun. Single .50cal machine guns were positioned in the powered rear dome, the two waist positions, a belly fairing, and in the tail. Two more .30s were at each side of the bombardier and in the sides of the empennage. Self-sealing fuel tanks and protective armor for the crew were not included in the test model, but would have been placed in a production version—and would have further denigrated the bomber's performance. After Pearl Harbor, as a precaution against a possible Japanese attack, the bomber was flown to Wright Field, Dayton, OH, where it was painted in camouflage and flew with loaded guns for its final test flights. In June 1942 the XB-19 was officially accepted, and the Air Force paid Douglas $1.4 million; however, Douglas had invested $4 million. Further testing was uneventful and mostly trouble free, except for the typical Wright 3350 engine cooling difficulties that were solved by opening the engine cowl flaps during extended flights and lowering the maximum speed under 16,000ft. In 1943 the XB-19 was redesignated as the XB-19A when it was finally fitted with four Allison V-3420-11 engines that increased its top speed to 265mph. The XB-19A was tested at length, and was eventually converted to a transport; it remained the largest American aircraft ever built until the construction of the Convair B-36 in August 1946. Its ultimate fate was to be scrapped at Davis-Monthan, Tucson, AZ, in June 1949.

The 1937-1938 "Superbomber" Requisites

In October 1937 the AAC Chief of Staff, Oscar Westover, decided to initiate informal design requisites for a "super bomber" that would succeed the B-17. The super bomber was to be much larger and heavier than the B-17, and also to be able to fly farther and faster with a heavier bomb load. Previously, scant attention had been paid to improving bomber operational efficiency by totally redesigning and cleaning up its airframe configuration and making the fuselage larger to accommodate the interchangeability of fuel and bomb loads. The tricycle landing gear concept was in vogue with designers, and while it did ease ground handling, take offs and landings, it added weight to the design (a ton in the case of the B-29). A super bomber that was to fly faster and farther would require designing new and more powerful engines. Designers understood the means to increase range and speed was to fly at altitudes above 25,000ft, but this presented problems of extreme cold and lack of oxygen, not only for the crew, but also for the engines. The engines would have to be "supercharged" which compressed and heated their intake of air. The crew compartments were to be "pressurized" to avoid having the crew wear warm heavy clothing and to use oxygen gear for long periods at high altitudes.

Aircraft companies were reluctant to take on new designs as, unlike today's cost-plus contracts, the AAC was by law only permitted to let fixed-price contracts, with no money paid in advance. Compensation was only made when the contracted aircraft was built and had flown. Aircraft companies had to use their own money to buy materials and tools, and also pay the salaries of their engineers and employees, and the time from contract signing to prototype flight could range from months to years. Contracts had no "cost overruns clauses," and there was no guarantee that the prototype would be accepted for production.

Only four companies responded to Westover's request: Boeing in Seattle; Consolidated in San Diego; Douglas in Los Angeles; and the United Aircraft Sikorsky Division in Hartford. The design submissions were mediocre, and the Douglas design was considered the best of the lot. Even though Douglas was the only profitable company of the four, its design was merely a lackluster upgrade of its new DC-4 airliner. Despite having four-engine bomber expertise, Boeing's submission was nothing more than a reworked XB-15 design whose mid-1930s technology was obsolete. Despite having been awarded the B-17 contract Boeing had received no funds, and was having problems on the early production phase; the AAC also refused to purchase more of the bombers. In fact, it would take a Federal loan in 1940 to keep the company from going bankrupt.

On 21 September 1938 Gen. Oscar Westover died in an aircraft accident. He was succeeded by Col. Henry Harley "Hap" Arnold, who had risen through the ranks, starting as a fledgling Lieutenant in the new Aeronautical Division of the Signal Corps in 1911. By the mid-1930s Arnold and other disciples of Billy Mitchell's theory of airpower had gradually gained prominent positions in the Army Air Corps, and were able to exert an "air" influence in the "horse soldier" dominated Army. When Arnold took over the AAC his bomber force consisted of 14 B-17s. In January 1939 President Roosevelt, after a review of American air power at Bolling Field, requested the production of "500 bombers a month." On 30 March 1939 the AAC approved Consolidated's Model 32 design that would lead

In late 1938, Maj.Gen. Arnold called a secret meeting of AAC officers and aviation experts to discuss the future of the AAC and the heavy bomber predicament. Brig.Gen. Walter Kilner (pictured) headed the so-called Kilner Board and was aided by Col. Carl Spaatz, Col. Earl Naiden, Maj. Alfred Lyon and the renowned Charles Lindbergh. The Board issued its report in June 1939 concluding that in a European war Germany would not only overrun the Continent but also conquer Great Britain and then Africa and perhaps establish bases in South America. (USAF)

to the B-24. The Liberator would make its first flight on 29 December 1939 and join the B-17 as America's primary heavy bombers in the upcoming war.

The super bomber concept languished until late 1938, when Maj.Gen. Arnold called a secret meeting of AAC officers and aviation experts to discuss the future of the AAC and the heavy bomber predicament. Charles Lindbergh had visited Hitler's Germany and was impressed and alarmed over the emphasis that the Luftwaffe had put on bombardment aircraft. Arnold asked Lindbergh to serve on a board headed by Brig.Gen. Walter Kilner and aided by Col. Carl Spaatz, Col. Earl Naiden, and Maj. Alfred Lyon. The Kilner Board issued its report in June 1939, and members of the group thought that in a European war Germany would not only overrun the Continent, but also conquer Great Britain and then Africa, and perhaps establish bases in South America. If the Japanese began a war in the Pacific, it would have to be fought over long expanses of ocean, extending from Alaska to Hawaii to the Philippines, and as far as Australia. In this scenario the B-17 would surely be inadequate, and the super bomber notion was revived. The role of the super bomber was no longer thought to be as a strategic bomber, but was to be a defensive bomber, able to fly long distances to strike an enemy advancing on the American Continents. The Board proposed a five-year research and development program for new aircraft and engines. Engine development was to be liquid-cooled and range in horsepower from 1,500 to 2,400, and eventually to 3,000hp. The Board recommended that two-engine light and medium bombers and a 2,000 mile four-engine heavy bomber be developed, along with another heavy bomber with a large fuselage that could carry bombs and/or enough fuel to give it a range of 5,000mi. From the latter specification the B-29 would eventually be developed for hemispheric defense. Although the Kilner recommendation was accepted by the AAC, at the time there was an isolationist sentiment in America, and the AAC could do nothing until Congress appropriated funds.

In September 1938, Chief of the Army Air Corps, Gen. Oscar Westover, died in an aircraft accident. He was succeeded by Col. Henry Harley "Hap" Arnold who had risen through the ranks starting as a fledgling Lieutenant in the new Aeronautical Division of the Signal Corps in 1911. By the mid-1930s, Arnold and other disciples of Billy Mitchell's theory of airpower had gradually gained elevated positions in the Army Air Corps and were able to exert an "air" influence in the "horse soldier" dominated Army. (USAF)

3

Boeing Long-Range Bomber Entries

The Boeing design teams continued work on two analogous studies of the basic super bomber design prerequisite; developing a large airframe that would be able to carry the most bombs and as much fuel as feasible. One design team reworked the Boeing XB-15 design into the Model 316, and the other reconfigured the B-17 into the Model 322.

Model 316

The Boeing design team under Lysle Wood reworked the XB-15 (Model 294) into a high wing monoplane with four 1,600hp Wright GR-2600 Cyclone 14 cylinder engines that gave 60% more power than the XB-15's four 1,000hp Pratt & Whitney R-1830-11 engines. A tricycle landing gear—the first on a Boeing aircraft—was adopted, and along with the non-stepped, all glass nose of the Stratoliner, the two would become a hallmark of the B-29 design. The Model 316 was to have a wingspan of 157ft (2,020square feet), a length of 109ft, 2in, was to be 23ft, 4in high, and to weigh 50,680lbs

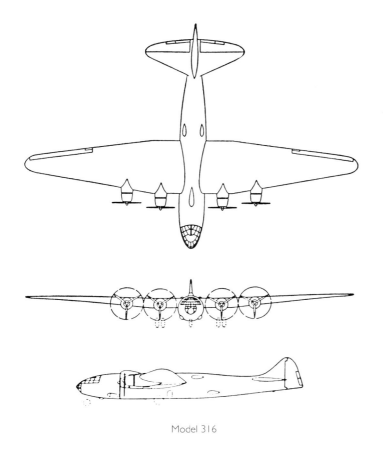

Model 316

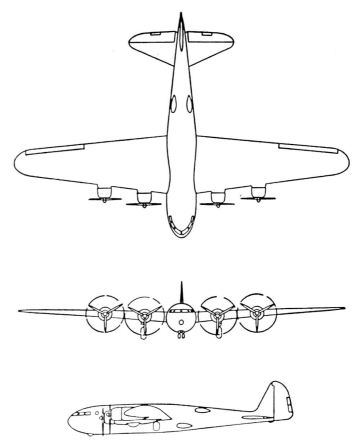

Model 322 (Pima)

empty and 87,600lbs gross. Its bomb load ranged from 16 1,000lb or 42 100lb bombs. It was to be armed with four .50cal and three .30 caliber machine guns mounted in teardrop-shaped turrets. It was given a pressurized cabin to carry a crew of nine. The four Wright 1,600hp engines were to carry a ton of bombs (maximum bomb load was to be 9.7 tons) over 4,000mi at 248mph at 15,000ft. To support the massive bomber, the main wheels would have to have been very large, and could not have been fully retracted into the engine nacelles. To rectify the problem Boeing engineers designed each main undercarriage leg with two proportionally smaller wheels that would fit into the nacelles. The Model 316 design was ready in March 1938, and the AAC showed enough interest in it to assign it a provisional Y1B-20 in June 1938, but then canceled the program.

Model 322

In March 1938 Boeing was contracted to pressurize the cabin of the B-17 as a continuation of the work it had done on its Stratoliner. The Model 322 was to be smaller than the Model 316, and was a mid-wing monoplane (as opposed to the B-17 low-wing), having a wingspan of 108ft, 7in, a length of 75ft, 5in, and was to carry a crew of six and was to be armed with four .50cal machine guns. Only four machine gun positions were provided because of the difficulty in pressurizing them. The Model 322 employed the standard B-17 wings, four engines, and tail assembles, but incorporated a large cylindrical fuselage to facilitate pressurization. The fuselage layout for pressurization moved the center of gravity forward, and a tricycle undercarriage was used. Two nose wheels were to be used in combination with the existing B-17 main undercarriages. Four 1,400hp Pratt & Whitney R-2180 engines were to power the Model 322, providing for a maximum bomb load of 9,928lb at a top speed of 307mph at 25,000ft. Further diffi-

culties arose in pressurization, and finally Boeing engineers were forced to admit that they were on the wrong track in trying to pressurize their B-17 hybrid.

Model 333

On 26 January 1939, before AAC requirements were posted, Boeing had already designed the Model 333, which suspended their previous design notions and incorporated the most recent aerodynamic concepts of a cleaner design for maximum efficiency, but maintained the pressurized cabins. Allison had just introduced their liquid-cooled 1,150hp V-1710 in-line engine that presented a much thinner profile than bulky air-cooled radial engines. Choosing the Allisons, Boeing designers then concentrated on cleaning up the bomber configuration and set the engines in tandem; pusher/puller in a single nacelle, but this engine layout presented problems in cooling the rear engines. The single wheeled tricycle undercarriage would have to be heavily built, and would have to have very high clearance for the pusher propellers on take off and landing. The design had a wingspan of 109ft, a length of 80ft, 8in, and a gross weight of 48,600lbs (design gross weight was 41,000lbs). The Model 333 was to fly at 307mph at 15,000ft with a ton of bombs (maximum bomb load was 2.9 tons) over a range of 3,400mi with a crew of six. For the first time a tail .30cal machine gun position was introduced (to go with the five fuselage .50cal machine guns). The fuselage was fitted with tandem bomb bays, and significantly, a small diameter tunnel—a feature that would be standard on all B-29s—connected the two pressurized crew compartments across the bomb bays. After wind tunnel testing Boeing engineers found that the Model 333 would have to be redesigned, as there was a distribution of dead weight in the wing that caused vibration and torque.

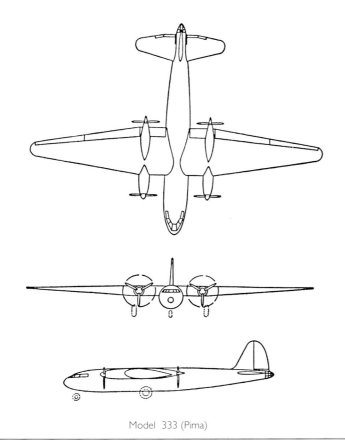

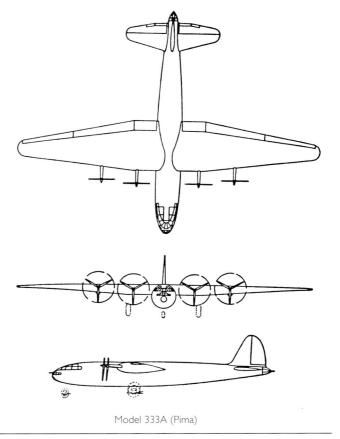

Model 333 (Pima)

Model 333A (Pima)

Model 333A

The advantages of the Allison V-1710 tandem pusher/puller engine arrangement on the Model 333 were impracticable. The Model 333A was initiated on 27 January 1939, and was identical to the Model 333, except that the Allisons were completely enclosed separately in the wings, and the propellers were extended to the leading edge of the wing via long shafts. The sumps of the outer engines projected below the surface of the wing and were enclosed in streamlined fairings. The Model 333A was 21mph faster than the Model 333, but its range with a ton of bombs was 420mi less. The engine/wing arrangement and higher wing loading, along with the tricycle undercarriage, tail gun position, pressurized compartments, and tunnel made the 333A the precursor of the B-29. However, the Allisons were soon found to be underpowered at altitude, and a different engine was required.

Model 333B

In the first three months of 1939 Boeing designers concentrated on a pressurized bomber with a clean, high wing, tricycle landing gear, and engine installations completely "submerged" in the wing. At the time both Pratt & Whitney and Wright were planning to develop flat profile, liquid-cooled engines that would make these wing installations viable, and the 333B and 334 were developed using the Pratt & Whitney engines.

The Model 333B of 21 February 1939 utilized four 1,850hp Wright 1800 flat engines, and the airframe was identical to the Model 333A, except that the wingspan was slightly longer at 111ft. The larger engines increased the gross loaded weight to 52,180lbs (design weight 46,000lbs)

and produced a top speed of 364mph at 20,000ft. However, with the engines submerged in the wing there was less space available for fuel and, consequently, the range with one ton of bombs was only 2,500mi—insufficient for future Pacific heavy bomber operations.

Model 334

The Model 334 of 4 March 1939 used the Pratt & Whitney 1800 flat engine, and was basically similar to the Model 333B, except in wing and tail configurations. The wing was redesigned to completely enclose the engines, and to increase fuel capacity. This design had an estimated range of 4,500mi carrying a ton of bombs. By the late 1930s the Germans and British had developed monoplane fighters with heavy machine gun and cannon armament, and the AAC redesigned the tail assembly on the Model 334 with twin tail fins and rudders so as to increase the field of fire of its eight turret machine guns. But soon the twin tail was discarded, as the small gains in fields of fire were not compensated by the decrease in structural integrity. The new engine/wing installation and tail assembly, along with the already clean lines of the 333B increased the top speed to 390mph (at 20,000ft), and the bomb load from 2,000lbs to 7,800lbs. Tests showed that the drag from the thick, high wing had increased wing loading almost 18%, from 34lbs per square foot to 40lbs. The new concept of a completely submerged engine placement caused cooling problems, and did not improve aerodynamics enough to justify the increased fuel storage and complicated wing structure, and this model was the last to have a completely submerged engine.

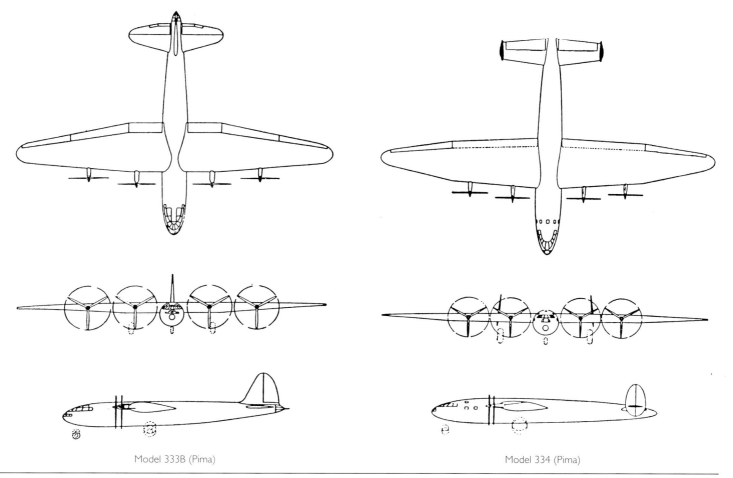

Model 333B (Pima) Model 334 (Pima)

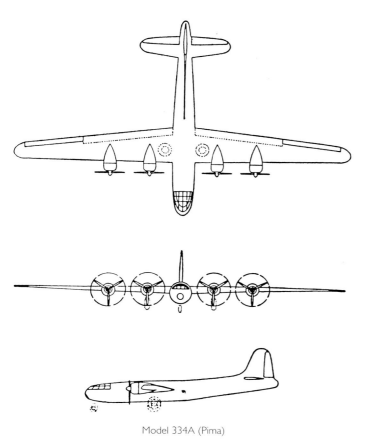

Model 334A (Pima)

the wooden mockup stage, but Boeing engineers were on the right track, and set out to develop a wing flap to negate the drawbacks of highly loaded wings.

During the first half of 1939 Boeing representatives began exploratory dialogue with the AAC at Wright Field on the design direction a new super bomber would take. The Boeing representatives included Boeing President Claire Egtvedt, the force behind the development of the B-17; Boeing chief engineer Wellwood Beall, the designer of the Clipper and Boeing chief assistant engineer; and Edward Wells, the primary designer of the B-17. During the meetings the AAC was variously represented by its Chief, Gen. H.H. Arnold; Brig.Gen. Frank Andrews, commander of Gen-

Model 334A

Once Boeing engineers recognized that the submerged engine was not the answer to developing the new super bomber they were seeking they returned to the drawing boards. Their new design was a complete break from the Model 334 but was, nonetheless, designated as the Model 334A. At the time a major premise of aircraft design was to keep wing loading (the weight carried by each square foot of wing area) to a minimum. Designers thought that a high wing loading was dangerous, as it meant take off problems and very high landing speeds. However, high wing loading after take off was advantageous in its lower drag and greater range, and Boeing designers believed they could design a wing flap to abet takeoffs and reduce landing speeds and distances. At the time the prototype Consolidated XB-24 Liberator was being developed with the high aspect ratio Davis Wing, and Boeing followed that developmental direction. The Model 334A (July 1939) came off the drawing boards with a wing very similar to the XB-24. The long, narrow wing planform spanned 120ft, and the main wheels of the tricycle undercarriage folded sideways into the wings like the XB-24, instead of into the engine nacelles. The bomber's length increased to 83ft, 4in, and the maximum gross weight increased to 66,000lbs (49,750lbs design gross weight). The tail assembly reverted to a high single dorsal fin and rudder that was to be another trademark of the B-29. The 2,200hp Wright 3350 engine was coming online, and promised to yield a speed of 390mph at 16,000ft over a range of 5,333mi carrying a ton of bombs and a crew of nine. The bomber was to be armed with five .30 caliber and three .50cal machine guns. The Model 334A was never built and only reached

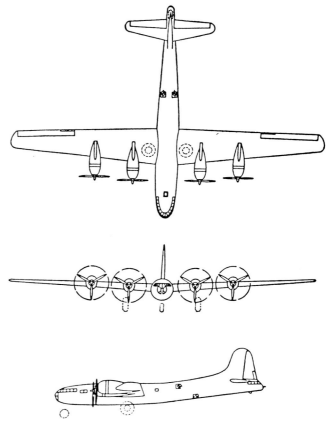

Model 341 (Pima)

eral Headquarters Air Forces (Langley Field, VA); Col. Oliver Echols, commander of the Materiel Command; and Col. Frank O'Carroll, commander of the engineering division of the Materiel Command, along with Col. Frank Craigie, Maj. William Irvine, and Maj. Turner Simms, all technical assistants to Arnold. Also included were two officers who would later play a large part in the B-29 program: Lt.Col. Donald Putt of Materiel Command's experimental engineering division, who was later the AAF project engineer for the XB-29; and Lt.Col. Frank Cook, who would later head B-29 production engineering. The obvious conclusion of these discussions was that the new super bomber was primarily to possess great range and bomb-carrying ability. In August 1939 Boeing engineers decided to begin its design on the Model 341, which would give the company a head start on any future AAC bomber request (which would be in six months time).

Model 341

The experimentation and lessons learned with the Model 333 and 334 designs contributed to the preliminary designs for the Model 341, begun in August 1939 at Boeing Plant #1. To increase speed and range Boeing designers, the Flight Test Department, and Aerodynamic Department worked closely on producing a bomber with clean aerodynamics. The fuselage joints were smooth, and all external rivets flush. They enclosed the turbosuperchargers and eliminated or streamlined fuselage vents, drains, and scoops. In December 1939, confident in the design, Boeing built a full-scale wooden mockup at its own expense. Its wingspan was 124ft, 7in—10 feet less than the 334A—and its length of 85ft, 6in, was five feet more. But with its shorter wingspan its wing area was 70 square feet less, which raised the wing loading from 47lbs/square foot to 64lbs/square foot. The maximum gross weight (85,672lbs) was about 20,000lbs more than the 334A, but it could carry twice the payload. The aerodynamically clean 341 design was the zenith of Boeing's expertise in designing and building bombers. When the AAF's Request for Data R-40-B was let on 29 January 1940, Boeing was ready to redesign the Model 341 to meet its specifications.

The superbomber developmental project was an immense undertaking; fortunately, Boeing President Philip G. Johnson and Executive Vice President H. Oliver West were the men to tackle it. Johnson joined Boeing as a draftsman after his graduation from the University of Washington in 1917. In five years he rose to vice president and general manager, and in 1926 he was named president. By 1929, at 39, he not only headed Boeing, but also was president of United Aircraft & Transportation Corporation, which manufactured Pratt & Whitney engines and controlled United Air Lines. In 1934 he resigned from these corporations, as the Black Airmail Committee canceled airmail contracts and ravaged Boeing finances and

plans. The disillusioned Johnson left the aviation industry and entered the truck manufacturing business, but three years later formed Trans-Canada Air Lines on the request of the Canadian government. At the time Roosevelt's rearmament program was forthcoming, and Boeing faced the possibility that the B-17 would not be ordered in large numbers because of its production problems. Boeing Chief Consul William Allen suggested to Claire Egtvedt that he ask Johnson to return to Boeing as president, as production had been Johnson's forte during his previous tenure as Boeing president. On 9 September 1939 Johnson became president and Egtvedt chairman. On his return Johnson took over a company with a nine-month loss of $2.6 million dollars, no credit line, a backlog of $28 million in orders, and the need to borrow money ASAP to buy materials for the planes on order. Johnson began a refinancing program and called a stockholders' meeting to authorize 450,000 shares of new stock which, in part, would be used to retire the almost $3.5 million in debt. He also was able to secure a $5.5 million RFC loan for new working capital. As his first astute personnel move, Johnson named H. Oliver West as his executive vice president. West started at Boeing in 1921 as an inspector of raw materials, moving quickly on to production chief, then to superintendent of Boeing Air Transport Maintenance, and then moved to the same position at United Air Lines. West joined Johnson at Air Canada and went with him back to Boeing in 1939. Johnson delegated West to expand Boeing's factory and machine tool capacity to meet the demands of the upcoming B-17 production. The antiquated Boeing Plant #1 was to be replaced by a vast expansion of Plant #2, a small portion of which had been previously constructed. West's chief contribution to Boeing was Multi-line Production, which entailed the prefabrication of the B-17 in large sections or components that were then placed on production lines that converged, and these sections or components were united into a completed aircraft and rolled out the door. Under West Boeing would produce more pounds of airplane per square foot of factory space than any other aircraft company.

Chief of Staff Malin Craig established an Air Board to conduct a study of hemisphere defense, and ordered it to make its report before his term expired on 1 September 1939, the day George C. Marshall would start his six-year reign as Chief of Staff. The Air Board report was issued on that day, and found that U.S. naval forces and coastal defenses were insufficient to protect America. The report pointed out that contemporary bombers made America vulnerable to aerial attack, and the only answer was a flexible, long-range air fleet. When Edward Wells visited Dayton in late 1939 Col. Oliver Echols, head of the Air Materiel Command, encouraged Boeing to continue work on the superbomber by telling Wells that there would be a new bomber requirement soon.

4

R-40-B Contracts

The Role of the Air Materiel Command

The Air Materiel Command, headquartered at Wright Field, Dayton, OH, was an important factor in the B-29 saga. For mostly good, and sometimes bad, it acted as a liaison between the taxpayer, government, Army Air Corps, and the aircraft industry in formulating military aircraft designs, developing these designs, purchasing the completed design, and placing it into production as soon as possible. The Air Materiel Command did not design aircraft, but after receiving a list of requirements from the Air Staff it formulated performance—but not dimensional—specifications for the requisite aircraft. The Command's Procurement Division then sent out requests to aircraft manufacturers to draw up and tender designs for the specified aircraft. Air Materiel Command engineers considered the submitted designs and consulted with the designers to determine if the design met specifications, was workable, and if the manufacturer was capable of producing the specified aircraft. If these criteria were met then the manufacturer was contracted to build mockups and conduct wind tunnel tests, followed by contracts to build one or more experimental models. Finally, if the experimental model met specifications better than other contracted designs, the manufacturer was issued a contract to build combat aircraft and service test them.

The Air Materiel Command merged with the Air Service Command in 1944 to become the Air Technical Service Command (ATSC). The ATSC was made up of six divisions: Engineering, Procurement, Supply, Maintenance, Personnel, and Base Services. Of the six ATSC Divisions, the Engineering and Procurement Divisions had a direct affect on aircraft development and manufacture.

The function of the Engineering Division's 10 extensively equipped laboratories was to research, develop, test, and evaluate every aspect of aircraft design, including those of the enemy. It had separate sections, such as Armament, Power Plant and Propeller, Aero-Medical, Radio and Electronics, etc. to study, test, develop, and approve equipment and systems in these sections. The Procurement Division evaluated design proposals, let contracts, and then followed up on the terms of the contract. At one time this division had 40,000 contracts with over 26,000 individual contractors comprising 400,000 plus items. The Production Section of the Procurement Division was responsible for the correct and timely supply of raw materials to over 15,000 manufacturers. It guaranteed the steady supply of combat-worthy aircraft into battle by providing for the expansion or con-

struction of manufacturing facilities, dispersing government-furnished equipment (GFE) and parts, and obtaining and supervising subcontractors. Another responsibility of this division that was to greatly affect the B-29 program was its function to prescribe changes to aircraft and equipment as determined by fight testing and combat experience, and then incorporate them into the production line. Another Procurement section was the Quality Control Section, which employed thousands of officers and civilians to inspect and accept all aircraft, aircraft accessories, and equipment for the AAF. The inspection ran the gamut from raw materials to the finished article. Larger manufacturing plants often had a resident representative who supervised inspection personnel who had been trained by the Division. There was a chronic shortage of ATSC Quality Control personnel to staff the thousands of factories doing defense work, and the factories also provided quality control that could range from meticulous to negligent.

RB-40-B Contracts

Due to Maj.Gen. Henry Arnold's energetic campaign in November 1939 Congress approved funding, and Arnold was authorized by Gen. George Marshall to let R-40-B study contracts (R-40-B translates to Requirement number 40, Bomber) for the very Long-Range heavy bomber. Capt. Donald Putt of the Air Materiel Command at Wright Field established a statement of the military characteristics of the new bomber. The bomber was to have a range of 5,333mi and be able to carry a bomb load of a ton over half that distance and have a speed of 400mph. In early 1940, after the experience of five months of war in Europe, the AAF saw that there were limitations in its earlier requirements, and issued another specification to succeed its R-40-B specs. The AAF then restructured its heavy bomber requirements, requesting self-sealing fuel tanks, increased armor protection, and multiple turrets with heavier caliber machine guns and cannons. On 29 January 1940 the AAC sent the Request for Data R-40-B and Spec XC-218 to a number of aircraft companies that designed heavy bombers. The request was sent via mail marked as "Urgent" from Washington D.C. The companies were given 30 days to submit design proposals, and then were expected to finish a full-scale engineering mockup by 5 August 1940; the first completed aircraft was to be ready by 1 July 1941, and subsequent aircraft one month later. Four West Coast companies would submit designs: Lockheed and Consolidated of San Diego; Douglas of Los Angeles; and Boeing of Seattle. Again, none of the companies was motivated to submit far-reaching designs. Whatever resources they had available were being invested in expanding their factories and work force to build established, but mediocre contemporary aircraft for the three American military services and foreign air forces that were at war, and in dire need of anything that would fly.

It was not until 5 February 1940 that Boeing President Philip Johnson received the blizzard-delayed Data R-40B and Spec XC-218 specs from across the continent. Boeing had previous experience in heavy bomber design, and since 1938 had engaged a few of their best young designers—led by Claire Egtvedt, Wellwood Beall, George Schairer, and Edward Wells—on working on the super bomber concept. Johnson placed his Chief Engineer, Wellwood Beall, to head the project. The 33-year-old Canon City, CO, native was a good choice. After he had graduated from the University of Colorado and New York University, he joined Boeing and taught at their School of Aeronautics at Oakland, CA, and then became Boeing's Far Eastern Manager, marketing the company's P-26 pursuit planes to the Chinese. In 1935 he returned to Seattle and was assigned to the engineering division, where he became Vice President in Charge of Engineering, and was instrumental in the design of the Model 314 Clipper that was being built in conjunction with the XB-15 project. The Clipper was a massive commercial flying boat that Pan American Airway's Juan Trippe put on his trans-Atlantic and trans-Pacific routes. Beall appointed Lyle Pierce as the B-29 project engineer, and Donald Euler was put in charge of preliminary design. Edward Wells, assisted by N.D. Showalter, was to head the detail design groups. Wells was a 29 year old Stanford cum laude graduate who had immediately joined Boeing's design team and designed large portions of the B-17; he would be Assistant Chief Engineer on the XB-29 project design. The redoubtable Edmund Allen was to supervise wing, tail, and performance data, and John Ball and his assistant, George Martin, were to head structures. George Schairer, 27, a Swarthmore and MIT graduate, was Boeing's Chief of Aerodynamics after a stint at Consolidated Aircraft.

His first task at Boeing was to improve the Model 307 Stratoliner after its crash in mid-March 1939. Schairer designed the Boeing Company's trademark dorsal tail fin that was used on all B-17s from the D Model onward, and then was used in a larger version on the B-29. Shairer was then assigned to work on reducing drag on the B-29 design, and would devise the revolutionary "117" airfoil wing and its large, high lift wing flaps.

The Boeing design team consisted of:

1) The Preliminary Design Engineers designed the bomber according to R-40B and Spec XC-218 parameters to produce the mock-ups that led to the experimental versions.
2) The Project Engineer was in charge of seeing that the experimental XB-29 met the original design requirements, and approved all designs before they went to manufacturing for fabrication and assembly.
3) The Staff Engineers directed research and development in relation to aerodynamics, armament, acoustics and electrical, flight test, master layout, photo template, mechanical equipment, metallurgical laboratory, power plant, structural test, vibration, and weight control.
4) The Project Group Engineers designed the components for manufacture: the fuselage and nacelles; wing and control surfaces; power plant installations; electrical and hydraulic systems; landing gear and controls; and all internal equipment.
5) The Group Engineers created the detail design for the components.

Boeing also began a program to recruit engineers from colleges and universities throughout America, and collected over 400 qualified men and women in 26 engineering fields. Under a War Manpower Commission training program, Boeing hired several hundred more employees, mostly women, to act as "tracers" for the thousands of engineering drawings of the B-29 project.

Boeing's engineering "Dream Team" (left to right): George Schairer (Chief of Aerodynamics), Edward Wells (Chief Engineer), Wellwood Beall (Engineering VP), N. D. Showalter (Chief of Flight Test), and Lysle Wood (Assistant Chief Engineer). (USAF)

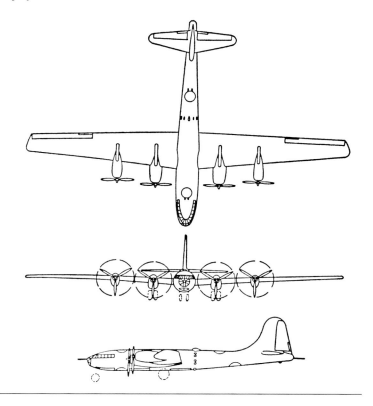

Model 345 (Pima)

Model 345

Boeing continued to evaluate its Model 341 proposal, and made numerous improvements that led to the Model 345. Compared to the Model 341, the Model 345 was to reflect the exigencies of the European air war in its design. After working day and night for two months, Boeing responded by sending the preliminary design for the Model 345 to Wright Field on 11 May 1940. The Model 345 was essentially a reworked Model 341, with a crew of 12 contained in a pressurized cabin. The Boeing design team worked in close association with the Flight Test and Aerodynamics Division to produce the most aerodynamic design possible. The fuselage skin joints were to be smooth, and all external rivets were to be flush. All "normal" protuberances—lights, thermometers, antennas, de-icers, drains, vents, and air scoops—were to be streamlined, enclosed, or flush. The new design requirements increased the gross weight of the Model 345 to 112,300lbs, which was 27,000lbs more than the Model 341. The weight increase decreased its speed by 23mph (to 382mph) compared to the Model 341's 405mph (at 25,000ft). The weight of the new remote armament system was 4,153lbs, as compared to the Model 341's armament of 1,646lbs. This ton and a quarter increase in weight required 1,680lbs of additional fuel to carry the bomber over a constant range, while the self-sealing fuel tanks weighed 3,000lbs more and required 2,000lbs more fuel. Generally, for each pound added to the Model 345 there was two-thirds pounds of fuel needed to carry it over the required 5,333mi. To accommodate these increases the Model 345 had 17ft more wingspan (141ft, 3in), and was almost 16ft longer than the Model 341. Edward Wells and Wellwood Beall of Boeing's Aerodynamics Department had continued their work on high lift wings from the Model 334A in August 1939 and developed the Boeing 115 Aerofoil. On the drawing board the Model 334A had a promising 124ft, 7in, very high aspect wing that was to be fitted with four 2,000hp Pratt &

Whitney R-2800 engines. The 115 Aerofoil had a wing area 70square feet less than the 334A, and a wing loading of 64lbs per square foot, as compared to the 334A's 47lbs. The Boeing 115 Aerofoil had the potential of increased range due to its lower drag. The AAF was unconvinced about the wing, as it was concerned that, because of its high wing loading, its operational ceiling would be reduced and affect its take off and landing characteristics. After comprehensive wind tunnel tests a wing flap that would offset the high wing loading was developed that precluded the Air Force's worries. The wing had an unusually high aspect ratio of 11.5, but was of a laminar flow type, which gave it a good lift/drag ratio. Compared to conventional wings the 115 was deep between the main spars, giving it greater strength, increasing the space for fuel tanks, and had more gradual stalling characteristics. The 115 was later developed into the 117 airfoil by George Schairer, and would characterize the B-29. A Fairchild PT-19A, a small two seat primary trainer, was fitted with a scaled down wing and tail, and Schairer used it as a flying test bed for aerodynamic evaluations. The bomber was supported by a tricycle landing gear with double wheels, with the main wheels retracting into the inboard engine nacelles instead of into the wing, as in previous models. It was powered by four new Wright air-cooled R-3350 twin-row radial engines, and more than met the one-ton bomb load over 5,333mi requirement, as it was capable of an eight ton maximum bomb load over 6,950mi. While the Model 341 mounted only six flexible manual .50cal machine guns, the Model 345 bristled with 10 .50cal machine guns and one 20mm cannon. The machine guns were mounted in pairs in four Sperry retractable turrets, and one pair plus a 20mm cannon were mounted in the power operated tail turret. The previous problem of pressurizing the gun positions was solved in a new innovative way. Instead of having the gunners positioned inside each turret, they controlled the guns remotely via sighting periscopes from stations within pressurized compartments inside the fuselage.

Boeing B-29 Precursors

Model	Design Complete	Engine	HP	Wing Span	Wing Area	Wing Load	Length	Gross Wt	Range	Max. Speed
316	3/38	Wright R-3350	2000	157" 0'	2920	31	109' 2"	89900	4000	248@ 15000'
322	6/38	P&W R-2100	1400	108' 7"	1530	35	75' 5"	53100	4000	307@ 25000'
333	1/26/39	Allison V-1710	1150	109' 0"	1420	34	80' 8"	48600	4220	307@ 15000'
333A	1/27/39	Allison V-1710	1150	108' 6"	1420	34	80' 8"	48600	3000	328@ 15000'
333B	2/21/39	Wright X-1800	1850	111' 0"	1522	34	80' 8"	52180	2500	364@ 20000'
334	3/4/39	P&W X-1800	1850	120' 0"	1644	40	83' 4"	66000	4500	390@ 20000'
334A	7/39	Wright R-3350	2200	135' 0"	1400	47	80' 0"	66000	5333	390@ 16000'
341	8/39-3/41	P&W R-2800	2000	124' 7"	1332	64	85' 6"	85672	7000	405@ 25000'
345	3-4/40	Wright R-3350	2200	141'3"	1736	65	93' 0"	112300	6950	382@ 25000'
XB-29	3/40-2/42	Wright R-3350	2200	141' 3"	1736	66	98' 2"	114500	5333	382@ 25000'

5

Other Long-Range Bomber Contracts

Besides Boeing, Lockheed and Douglas Consolidated (and later Martin) also tendered their R-40-B proposals to the Air Materiel Command. All had met the requirements, and on 14 June all were awarded contracts to construct full-sized wooden scale models for wind tunnel testing and evaluation, and also were to furnish comprehensive engineering drawings and data, along with cost estimates. The Air Materiel Command initiated negotiations for price and delivery dates for a pair of prototypes, with an option to purchase 200 production bombers. The Boeing proposal was designated the XB-29, the Lockheed XB-30, the Douglas XB-31, and the Consolidated XB-32. The contracts were valued at only $85,652, which was a pittance compared to the $3 billion dollar military aircraft allotment Congress had approved for 1940.

Lockheed XB-30
Lockheed based its proposal, the Model 51-81-01 XB-30, on its triple-tailed Model 49 C-69 Constellation cargo/transport design that was, in turn, based on its Model 49 Airliner. The design was similar in dimension to the airliner, except for the lengthening of the nose, which was covered by Plexiglas for the bombardier, and the tail, which contained the two .50cal machine guns and a 20mm cannon. The design had a wingspan of 123ft, a length of 104ft, 8in, a height of 23ft, 10in (at the vertical stabilizer), and an empty weight of 51,725lbs (gross 86,000lbs). It was powered by four 2,200hp Wright R-3350-13 radial engines that were predicted to have a top speed of 450mph (cruise at 240mph), a service ceiling of 40,000ft, and a range of 3,380mi. It was to have an eight-man crew, with the pilot and co-pilot seated side-by-side under separate bubble canopies. However, on 6 September the Lockheed Board of Directors made a policy decision and withdrew its proposal from the super bomber competition.

Douglas XB-31
Douglas continued to rework its basic DC-4 transport design into the proposed XB-31, but their project never progressed beyond the drawing board. There was no XB-31 as such, but the designation denoted a series of engineering studies that created a range of shapes and sizes. The Model 423 was typical of the designs spawned from the bomber development of the commercial DC-4 airliner. The design was the largest and heaviest of all the proposals, and was submitted in the fall of 1941. It was to have a wingspan of 207ft (five feet less than the XB-19), a length of 117ft, 3in (only

3in less than the XB-19), and a height of 40ft, 5in (vertical stabilizer). It weighed 109,000lbs empty and grossed at 176,000lbs, and could drop 25,000lbs of bombs through its double bomb bays. It was to be powered by four 28-cylinder 3,000hp Pratt & Whitney R-4360 X-Wasps (later named the Wasp Major) radial engines to turn the huge 25ft three-bladed propellers. The fuel load was 13,000gals, and its 450-gallon oil tank capacity exceeded the fuel load of many of the bombers of the 1930s! The eight-man crew was lodged in a beautifully streamlined, pressurized fuselage, with the pilot and co-pilot stations located in two small Plexiglas bubble canopies protruding from the top of the fuselage behind the nose. The potentially remarkable XB-31 never progressed beyond the design study phase, but some innovations shaped other later Douglas aircraft. The Douglas C-74 transport utilized the twin bubble canopies, and on a smaller scale the B-26 Invader tail assembly resembled the Model 423 tail.

Consolidated XB-32 Cinderella's Sister
In December 1940 the Vultee Aircraft Company (Nashville) acquired 34% of the stock of the Consolidated Aircraft Corporation (San Diego), and although the final merger did not consummate until March 1943, by January 1942 the two firms were closely linked in management and engineering. This led to some confusion over nomenclature, as after the 1943 merger most sources referred to the bomber as the Consolidated-Vultee B-32, but the AAF referred to it as the Consolidated B-32 throughout the war.

On 6 October 1940, contract #15549 ordered two XB-32 prototypes (contract #15429 ordered the two XB-29 prototypes). The first prototype (#41-141) was to be delivered in 18 months (March 1942), and the second (#41-142) three months later (June 1942). A third prototype (#41-18336) was added to the contract in late 1940, and it was to be delivered in March 1943.

The prototype schedule proved to be too optimistic, as the first prototype was not ready for flight testing until September 1942, six months late. The XB-32 had some likeness to its older B-24 Consolidated sister. It had the same high-aspect ratio, slim Davis Wing, and the same two vertical tails mounted at the ends of the horizontal stabilizer. Although this twin-tail configuration appeared to be identical to the B-24, a closer inspection showed that each half of the "horizontal" stabilizer was tilted, instead of at an upward angle (dihedral), which was Consolidated's PB2Y-2 Coronado's twin-tail configuration. In contrast to the B-24's squat, slab-sided profile, the XB-32 had flowing cylindrical lines and a more conventional stepped windshield that replaced the Liberator's rounded nose before the first prototype flew. The XB-32 had twice the gross weight of the B-24, weighing in at 100,000lbs. An interesting footnote to the use of the Davis Wing was that Consolidated paid the Davis-Brookins Aircraft Company a $5 royalty for each wing used—$43,000 for all the B-24s, and $650 for the 130 B-32s!

The XB-32 mockups, designated the Model 33 by the company, were built in late December 1940, and were modified to incorporate changes prompted by the wind tunnel tests at Wright Field. The revised mockups were approved on 6 January 1941, and 13 test YB-32s were ordered in June 1941 to be developed in parallel with the construction of the three XB-32s. Compared to the XB-29, the XB-32 was physically slightly smaller, but weighed ten tons less. It had the same defensive armament (although the XB-32's turrets were retractable), and the same 10 ton bomb load, crew number, and power plants (four Wright R-3350s). Given these statistics alone, the XB-32 should have had better performance than the XB-29, but actually had a top speed of only 10mph more, and a range of 100mi less at similar loads and altitude. The XB-32 was powered by two R-3350-13 inboard engines and two R-3350-21 outboard engines with three-bladed Hamilton Standard propellers.

The problem-plagued Sperry remote gun system and turrets were not installed so as not to interfere with flight testing. The first taxi tests were conducted on 3 September 1942 at Lindbergh Field, Consolidated's San Diego home base. Four days later, test pilots Russ Rogers and Richard McMakin took the first XB-32 (41-141) on its maiden flight. Rogers was compelled to make an emergency landing at the nearby North Island Navy airfield after only 20 minutes when forces on one of the vertical tail surfaces fractured a rudder trim tab that set up a flutter. Along with seemingly endless other problems, the tail flutter continued to remain a major problem despite modifications. In February 1943 the YB-32 contract was canceled, but in March a contract for 300 B-32s and several TB-32 transition trainers was placed, and they were to be built at Consolidated's Fort Worth Plant (although the XB-32s were built in San Diego). At this time the popular nickname "Terminator" was chosen.

On 10 May 1943, after 30 test flights, test pilot Richard McMakin took off on a routine test flight, but the aircraft did not gain sufficient speed at the moment of lift off and crashed, without burning, over the end of Lindbergh Field's runway. McMakin was killed, and the other six crewmen were injured, but three Marine recruits were killed and 57 injured while watching a training film in a temporary mess hall located at the crash site. The definite cause of the crash was not determined, but was thought to be flap malfunction. At the time of the crash the second XB-32 (41-142) would not be ready for almost two months, and this delay caused serious problems in the test program, as most of the test records were destroyed in the crash and would need to be repeated. The second prototype was outwardly similar to the first, but many internal modifications were made. On 2 July flight testing began again, but the rudder trim tabs continued to cause serious directional stability problems, along with a profusion of niggling technical problems of all kinds. The third prototype (#41-18336) was finally ready on 9 November—eight months late—and it too experienced rudder trim tab problems, and while many minor problems were solved, others cropped up during 25 test flights. The B-32 program was threatened, and an AAF engineering survey team was called in to inspect the two prototypes. Their report of 3 December found the B-32 to be "obsolete when compared with 1943 combat airplane requirements," and recommended a number of major changes. Among these changes was a complete redesign of the engine nacelles, removal of any fuselage pressurization, replacement of the remote turrets with manned turrets, and installation of four blade propellers. The most significant change was the replacement of the twin tail with a single large vertical stabilizer, which was to finally resolve the trim tab flutter. Ironically, in 1942 Consolidated engineers had concluded that the B-24 twin tail design would also have better stability with a single fin and rudder, and tests using a tail-modified B-24D proved this conjecture. In April 1944 Consolidated decided all future B-24s, starting with the B-24N, would have a single tail, but only seven were built before all B-24 production was halted. However, 740 of the independently developed, single-finned PB4Y-2 Privateer B-24 spin-offs were built for the Navy. Soon, the third XB-32 had a 16ft, 8in B-29 tail grafted to it, but subsequent tests showed this tail to be inadequate, and the problem was

The Consolidated-Vultee B-32 was built as a back up to the troubled B-29 project, but ultimately ran into many developmental problems of its own. As the B-29's problems were solved the B-32 was relegated to a secondary role, and flew only 18 combat missions during the war. (USAF)

later corrected by increasing the tail height to 19ft, 6in. The revised prototype had all pressurization deleted, manned gun stations installed, and most of the other recommended changes. So, when the third prototype was ready in November 1943 the AAF had already taken delivery of its first production B-29s. The AAF had placed its initial order for 300 production B-32s in March 1943, and this order was amended to include the subsequent revisions. Despite the continued XB-32 prototype problems, orders for an additional 1,713 Model 34 B-32s was made in mid-1943, as the AAF continued to have lingering doubts about the production B-29s, which continued to have problems of their own. In case the B-29 ultimately failed, the B-32 was the only backup available.

The first production B-32 models were built at the Consolidated-Vultee factory at Fort Worth, which had the world's longest straight assembly lines, requiring 27,000 tools for manufacture. Numerous internal and external modifications on the bombers were made on the production line. The new extended single tail much improved directional control on the XB-32 #3 prototype, but the first two B-32-1-CF production aircraft (#42-108471 and 42-108472) were given the modified grafted B-29 tails. The production line was stopped so the eight bombers on the line could be given the new extended 19.5ft tail. Ironically, the other major B-32 production model changes were caused by the B-29, which was on its way to truly becoming a superfortress. The B-29 left little doubt that it would fulfill its high altitude, VHB specifications, and soon the B-32 would not even be needed as a backup. To get production B-32s into combat, to satisfy the AAF orders, and to keep the Fort Worth factory occupied, Consolidated eliminated the pressurized cabins and substituted oxygen masks, eliminated the balky Sperry remote gunnery system, and substituted five manned turrets. These two major alterations changed the character of the B-32 from a high altitude VHB to the status of an ordinary heavy bomber, like the B-17 or B-24. Perhaps, the change in its name from "Terminator" to the less authoritative "Dominator" in August 1944 reflected this downgrading. The Fort Worth plant built only 114 B-32-CFs (one B-32-CO was built by the San Diego plant at the end of the canceled production order).

The bomber flew only 18 combat missions in World War II, all with the Far Eastern Air Force's (FEAF) 386th Bomb Squadron of the 312BG, "The Roarin' 20's" out of Clark Field and Floridablanca Field, Luzon, and Yonton, Okinawa. Fourteen of these missions were flown against targets first in the Philippines, and then over the Formosa area, and the last four were flown against targets in the Tokyo area. The final B-32 mission was a disaster, as two aircraft were lost, though not by enemy action. One bomber skidded off the runway on take off and all 13 crewmen were killed. On the return from the target another bomber lost two engines and the pilot ordered a bailout, and two crewmen were lost. The B-32 was never a contender.

Martin XB-33 and XB-33A

In late 1940, when the AAC was continuing to solicit high altitude twin-engine medium bomber designs, the Martin Company presented the Model 190, to be designated the XB-33, as a possible twin-engined replacement for its B-26 Marauder. The design featured a pressurized fuselage, and resembled Martin's recently developed PBM Mariner Navy Patrol bomber. It was slated to use two 1,800hp Wright P-3350 engines, and was to measure 71ft long, 22ft, 6in high, and have a 100ft wingspan. The continued evolution of the design caused a great increase in weight that precluded Martin from achieving the performance specifications required by the AAC. Martin set aside the XB-33 program and expanded it to a four-engined program, the XB-33A.

At the time Martin was in competition with Boeing and Consolidated for a Long-Range heavy bomber design, and felt its Model 190 showed promise. Martin was awarded a contract (AC-18645) to begin construction of two prototype XB-33A airframes. On paper the "Super Marauder" was to have a 79ft, 10in fuselage, 24ft height, and 134ft wingspan (1,500square feet). It was to be powered by four 1,800hp Wright R-2600-15 Cyclones with two-stage GE CMC-3 turbosuperchargers that were to give the bomber a top speed of 345mph at 39,000ft (cruise at 242mph) over a range of 2,000mi. The empty weight was 65,000lbs (gross 98,000lbs), with a bomb capacity of 10,130lbs. The fuselage was to house a remote firing system that operated power turrets of twin .50cal machine guns in the nose, forward belly, and upper rear and tail. Three thousand rounds of ammunition fed the eight .50cal machine guns. The proposed performance specs were so promising, the AAC ordered 400 more XB-33As before the prototypes were built! But by this time the course of the war pointed toward a Japanese defeat, and the need for a third Long-Range heavy bomber was redundant, as the B-29 was proving itself over Japan and the B-32 had been relegated to a non-player. The XB-33A order was canceled, and the two unfinished prototypes were dismantled.

6

Boeing and the XB-29

AAC Contracts for the First Two XB-29s

By the late 1930s Boeing finances were finally recovering, as Clairmont Egtvedt sold 240 Douglas A-20 attack bombers built under license to the French for $23 million with a down payment of $3.5 million. At the time the Boeing engineering department was stretched thin, as the Boeing B-17 venture was ready for mass production, and the AAC was about to place an order for 250 B-17Es. Over the previous two years the preliminary design engineers and aerodynamic engineers had developed the Model 345 into the XB-29 design from performance specifications set by the AAC Air Materiel Command, and issued by its Procurement Division into a detailed plan with dimensional specifications. The project engineers were to take these plans and create an aircraft that would function as specified. Engineers were assigned as individuals or in groups for research and development, and to systems and parts design for the mockup. The war in Europe was escalating, and Gen. Oliver Echols summoned Boeing President Philip Johnson and Earl Schaefer, vice president of the existing Boeing-Wichita factory, to Dayton. Because of a threatened strike, Oliver West went in Johnson's place. Schaefer was a West Point graduate, and served as a flight instructor in World War I. In 1927 he prompted 10 Wichita businessmen to

invest $60,000 to move Lloyd Stearman's factory from Venice, CA, to begin building mail planes. Schaefer was the plant manager, and when the Depression threatened to close the plant, he persuaded parent United Aircraft & Transport to start building training aircraft there. At the meeting Echols told the two Boeing representatives that the AAC was going to contract for 512 B-17s and two XB-29s. The Seattle plant would need to be doubled to accommodate the new B-17 production, and when B-29 orders came in, Plant #2 would have to be built in Wichita, as the B-29 would not be built on the West Coast. In order to get part of the Wichita plant built, B-17 tails were to be fabricated there until B-29 production began.

On 24 August 1940, before the mockup was even completed, the AAC was so impressed by wind tunnel data that it let a contract for two flyable Model 345 prototypes at a cost of $3,615,095. The first prototype was scheduled to be delivered in April 1942, and the second in June. The AAC redesignated the Model 345 as the XB-29 experimental bomber 29, as it was the twenty-ninth Army bomber since the Martin B-1 of 1918. Soon the mockup was approved, and wind tunnel tests of a detailed scale model were begun. The XB-29 was to be the largest and fastest bomber ever built, at 116,000lbs and a cruising speed of 380mph (at 25,000ft). The bomber

The AAC redesignated the Model 345 as the XB-29 (experimental bomber 29), as it was the twenty-ninth Army bomber since the Martin B-1 of 1918. On 24 August 1940, before the mockup was even completed, the AAC was so impressed by wind tunnel data that it let a contract for two flyable prototypes at a cost of $3,615,095. The first prototype was to be delivered in April 1942, and the second in June. Pictured is the first prototype. (USAF)

would have a wingspan of 141ft and a fuselage length of 99ft. It would carry a crew of 10 (five in the nose compartment: airplane commander, copilot, engineer, navigator, and bombardier, and four in the rear pressurized compartment: Central Fire Control gunner, two more gunners and radio operator, and a lone gunner in the tail). The pressurized forward and rear compartments were to be connected by crawl tunnel across the top of the bomb bay. The XB-29 was truly to be a super bomber, at twice the weight and horsepower of the B-17, and half again as large dimensionally. With the government contract in hand, Boeing was able to obtain loans and buy material from suppliers, and begin in earnest its long quest to develop the XB-29 into the finest bomber in World War II.

Boeing was to build the XB-29 not on a fixed cost basis, but on a cost plus a fixed 6% management fee basis. Once the contracted aircraft were finished the cost basis was the expense of salaries, materials, and depreciation, less any advances and progress payments. Boeing would receive a 6% fee of the total cost for managing the project. To give the company an incentive to keep costs down, it was to be awarded a percentage of the savings under the expected cost. The 6% essentially was the company's profit. Unlike cost plus aircraft manufacturing contracts of today, when a wrench can be billed at hundreds of dollars, there was little abuse of the system, as Boeing's books were audited and found to have fair profits. In a program of the magnitude of the XB-29 program the government and Army more or less had a laissez-faire policy that was to pay dividends in the successful completion of the program.

The XB-29 Languishes in Development
In October 1940 Gen. Arnold wanted 12 more XB-29s to be ordered, but had to wait until after the 1940 elections the following month. At the time the majority of Americans opposed the war, and even though the government was spending millions of dollars on the military, President Roosevelt assured voters that the spending was for the defense of America. The wooden XB-29 mockup was completed in November, and in December Arnold did not get his wish for more XB-29s, as only a third prototype was ordered to be built, and a fourth airframe was approved for static tests. The XB-29 languished as a wooden mockup and on thousands of blueprints into late spring 1941. By May 1941, Roosevelt decided that Long-Range bombers

were to be the focal point of American military strategy, and ordered 500 per month to be a target B-29 production rate.

On 4 May 1941 the XB-29 engineering plans were completed, and the first bomber was ready to be started in Boeing Seattle Plant #1, six months before aerodynamic tests were completed, and a year before detailed drawings were completed. The Boeing "production line" consisted of 50 mechanics who built the first fuselage by hand in one piece on wooden jigs. As new drawings arrived that particular component was fabricated and added to the bomber.

On 17 May 1941 Col. W.F. Volandt, AAC contracting officer at Wright Field, informed Boeing President Johnson that the Air Force had $10 million presently available toward the manufacture of 250 B-29s and 335 B-17s. This order was "conditioned on the expansion of facilities at Boeing-Wichita to permit the monthly productive capacity of 65 B-17 and 25 B-29 airplanes by 1 July 1942 and 1 February 1943, respectively." In October 1940 groundbreaking for a new $13 million Boeing B-17 factory in Wichita had been initiated around the Stearman Aircraft Company factory, which Boeing had acquired in 1939. The Secretary of War, wanting to expedite production, authorized Boeing to:

"...purchase such jigs, dies, and fixtures (except machine tools and production machines), and such critical material and equipment as are necessary to the production of such aircraft, and spare parts in anticipating of the placing of such order or orders."

On 6 September 1941 this contract for 250 B-29s, plus $19.5 million in spare parts (the equivalent of 25 B-29s in spare parts), was formalized.

Meanwhile North American Aviation, which was operating the government's new B-25 Mitchell medium bomber factory in Kansas City, MO, advised the AAC that it could produce 200 B-29s if and when the Boeing design was ready. In December 1941 the AAC granted a contract worth $187 million for B-29 airframes, with a 6% management fee to North American, and with Boeing to receive a $1.3 million licensing fee to use their design. The government issued North American large advances, and they began to purchase equipment, machinery, and supplies to begin to manufacture B-29s in September 1943.

In the manufacture of the components of the B-29, the world's largest aircraft, jigs to hold them were to be necessarily larger than normal aircraft jigs. Boeing engineers adopted techniques used in shipbuilding, but needed to keep the jigs simple but rigid enough to hold the component being built to the highest tolerances ever. (USAF)

The order finally pushed Boeing onto the fast track of what would be a gargantuan endeavor that it had worked toward since October 1937. Oliver West was assigned the job of planning and contracting a fully integrated factory at Wichita. Wellwood Beall was to quickly expand the Wichita engineering staff to 1,000 men, who were to work on executing 10,000 drawings requiring 1.5 million man-hours and costing nearly $3 million. Drawings came slowly, as did the materials required to build the first XB-29. Thousands of man-hours were spent on development of production procedures that led nowhere. West's original plans called for the fuselage, inboard center section, and main wing to be built at Seattle, and the outer wings and tail surfaces to be built at Wichita, with Seattle's components shipped to Wichita for assembly.

To West, tooling was the key to success in mass-producing the B-29. His credo was:

"Put your planning in the tools, then the job must come out accurately and well done."

Since work had just started on the first XB-29 and engineering would not be completed for a year, tooling had to anticipate manufacture. To do this West and his staff broke down the aircraft into component parts, and from there tried to simplify construction and assembly to the lowest common denominator, so that the inexperienced, hurriedly trained work force—many women—could turn out the best product in the least amount of time.

Seattle would design the main jigs for the wing and body sections, design the dies for the draw presses, and design the main handling equipment. Seattle would also layout the design and manufacture of all Wichita's tools for intermediate parts, such as ribs, spars, bulkheads, and frames, and the myriad of subassemblies that made up the main components of the B-29.

The jigs were to be simple, but rigid enough to hold the component being built to the highest tolerances ever demanded in aircraft manufacture. Single piece jigs, rather than lighter jigs requiring elaborate bracing, were used whenever possible, as bracing reduced speed and efficiency of the personnel working around them. Since the jigs were to hold components for the world's largest aircraft, they necessarily were larger than normal aircraft jigs, and Boeing engineers adopted techniques used in shipbuilding. To reduce the stress natural to large welded structures the jigs were heated ("normalized") in large outdoor kilns. At the height of B-29 tooling the Seattle design department had 60 design engineers and about 1,500 men in the tooling shops transforming these designs into tools. The master gauges used in setting up the jigs were designed and built in Seattle. These gauges supposedly guaranteed the maintenance and interchangeability of 40,450 B-29 parts anywhere they were built—Wichita, Marietta, Renton, or Omaha. There were 72 master gauges used in the B-29, and the control master gauges were kept at Seattle and used for correcting the master gauges.

On 7 May 1941 Gen. Arnold called Boeing President P.G. Johnson in Dayton, OH, and asked him to submit the cost for 14 so-called YB-29s, service test B-29s, and many additional B-17s. Arnold gave Johnson only until the next morning to make a submission! After a long night, Johnson called Arnold the next morning with an outline for the most audacious and ambitious aircraft production programs ever attempted. Johnson made four recommendations that he had jotted down. They were:

1) Establish the principle of one or two proven production models of heavy bombardment aircraft.
2) Arrange for the models selected to be built in factories now used for other purposes.
3) Give first priorities to such factories for materials and machine tools.
4) Continue the development of replacement types for the models selected so that in time they can become the production model.

The B-17 BDV program arose from this recommendation. Boeing's Plant #2 in Seattle, the massive new Douglas-operated factory in Long Beach, CA, and the Vega (Lockheed) final assembly plant in Los Angeles—known collectively as the BDV consortium—were to produce 100s of B-17s. Planners had originally anticipated that the B-17 production lines could be shut down and converted to B-29 production in late 1942. As part of this plan the War Department approved a $20 million contract for 14 YB-29s. The plan was when the YB-29s were ready they would not be experimental, and could be used for testing and to train crews as service test aircraft. The contract included Boeing's 6% management fee, but not the cost of government supplied engines, instruments, and other equipment. New factories and equipment were also needed, and the government's Defense Plant Corporation and the Army Corps of Engineers were to pay for these. In exchange Boeing assured a January or February 1943 delivery date for the YB-29s.

On 20 June 1941 President Roosevelt signed the War Powers Act of 1941 that authorized the creation of the U.S. Army Air Forces (USAAF), which in effect merged the Army Air Corps and the General Headquarters, Air Force into a solitary, self-governed entity with its own Air Staff, and that was no longer answerable to the Army General Staff. Although the USAAF was not entirely independent of the Army or War Department, it could operate autonomously and was able to administer its own training, procurement, and operations. By the end of the year Arnold, the head of the new USAAF, would also be to all intents and purposes a member of the Joint Chiefs of Staff.

Both the contracts for the B-29 and B-32 were too optimistic, and both fell far behind scheduled delivery. The first XB-32 model was not ready for flight until September 1942; six months late, but two weeks before the XB-29. Because of the delay the AAC requested that the XB-32 testing be started:

"...as soon as possible, even if the aircraft must be flown in a 'stripped condition.'"

At the time, both the unproven B-29 and B-32 had a major role in the AAC's long range bombing plans for the war over Europe. The urgency of rearmament increased on 22 June 1941 when the German armies invaded Russia. On 9 July 1941 President Roosevelt sent a letter to the Secretaries of War and Navy asking them to prepare "an estimate of overall production requirements required to defeat our potential enemies." To forestall the War Plans Division from preparing a plan that would relegate the Army Air Force into a supporting role to the Army, Arnold's Air Chief of Staff, Brig.Gen. Carl "Toohey" Spaatz, and member of the 1939 Kilner Board, formed the Air War Plans Division (AWPD). The AWPD was to be headed by Lt.Col. Harold George, CO of the Second Bombardment Group, and newly appointed Chief of the War Plans Division Lt. Colonels; Kenneth

Walker, Chief of the War Plans Group; Maj. Haywood Hansell, Chief of the European section of the War Plans Group; Lawrence Kuter, G-3 from the General Staff; and Orvil Anderson and Howard Craig. The responsibility of the AWPD was to formulate a general plan for the employment of air power to defeat the Axis that would utilize air power to its fullest capability. The AWPD was to determine the size of the air forces required to defeat Germany first, and then defeat Japan. Their plan, called AWPD-1, was submitted in nine days to the Army General Staff War Plans Division on 12 August 1941. Generally, it called for 24,500 combat aircraft, of which approximately 10,000 were to be four and six engine bombers. On 11 September 1941 Gen. Marshall accepted AWPD-1, and the B-29 and B-32 were an important element in the plan. In the 1939 Kilner Board recommendation the future B-29 and B-32 were to be hemispheric bombers to operate from American bases, but by early 1941 Britain appeared to be safe from German invasion. If the United States entered the war, English and American planners envisioned the Very Long-Range (VLR) Bomber to operate from bases in England and the Mediterranean to bomb Germany. In those dark days AWPD-1 projected that by summer 1944 24 B-29 and 24 B-32 groups would be sent to bomb Germany from England and Egypt as part of the "48 Very Heavy Group Program." As part of this plan, several B-24 groups in the MTO would initially transition to B-32s and B-29s as soon as the bomber's service tests were completed. Then the remaining Eighth and Fifteenth Air Force B-17 and B-24 groups in the MTO and ETO would transition to the two new longer range bombers. Gen. Spaatz also saw the bomber as a weapon against Japan in a future war in the Pacific that seemed to be inevitable, so also embodied in AWPD-1 was the provision for two B-29 and B-32 groups to be available to bomb Japan from Luzon if the Japanese entered the war. This was the beginning of the "Europe first" strategy, in which the Anglo-American forces concentrated their efforts against Germany. Until Germany was defeated Japan would be contained in a defensive battle in which naval forces would predominate. Even after the great post-Pearl Harbor Japanese successes, American long-term air strategy focused on Europe. AWPD-41 (15 December 1941) and AWPD-42 (9 September 1942) both deployed the B-29 and B-32 to Europe, after which they would be transferred to Pacific bases that were captured in the island battles to bomb Japan. The *Casablanca Conference* in January 1943 continued the Europe first strategy and approved a Combined Bomber Offensive against Germany; it also projected that the B-29 and B-32 would take part in the offensive. The plan was to deploy Very Long Range bombers in shuttles between North Africa and England. Maj.Gen. Ira Eaker of the 8AF was to develop a Combined Bomber Offensive, and in March 1943 requested a tentative deployment schedule for the B-29 and B-32 groups. By early 1944 both the B-29 and B-32 were experiencing developmental problems, and it was apparent that the 48 Group Plan could not be implemented on schedule, so Arnold advised Eaker that the VLR groups would be sent to the Pacific.

Meanwhile, progress on the XB-29 proceeded slowly through fall 1941 and continued on into 1942. By May the prototype was only one-third completed, as work was slowed by a myriad of tests to confirm the structural integrity of the various components. George Schairer and his aerodynamics team tested the new 117 wing model at the University of Washington, and then at MIT. Along with its aerodynamics they tested the structural strength. During their testing they found that when the wind flowing over the wing approached the speed of sound it began to act more like a solid than a fluid. It would tumble around the wing, and a new type of stall

was created, not due to low speed, but to high speed. This finding had no effect on the XB-29, but would become an important factor later in testing high-speed fighters. Schairer rechecked the wing for a third time in the Cal Tech wind tunnel, and these wind tunnel tests seemed to confirm the soundness of the wing's aerodynamics and design. Ed Wells tackled the problem of controlling the large aircraft, as previous attempts at powered controls had been unsuccessful. What was needed was to design small tabs and hinges on the control surfaces that used the wind's force to help move them. After hours of wind tunnel testing that included trial and error and mathematical calculations Wells came upon a solution.

XB-29: Engineering and Testing
Engine Considerations Affect Aerodynamic Development

The basic engineering problem facing Boeing engineers was to solve the problem of how to build a bomber that was twice the weight of the B-17, and to give it 30% more speed with only 83% more horsepower. The laws of aerodynamics state with all other factors equal, that doubling an aircraft's speed requires eight times the horsepower (horsepower requirements rise as a cube of the velocity). This calculation does not take into account the doubled weight and the increased drag of a larger aircraft. At the time the four 1,200hp Wright R-1820 engines powering the B-17 developed a total 4,800hp. The 18-cylinder R-3350 Wright Cyclone, originally fitted to the XB-19, developing 8,800hp, and was the largest power plant available. Calculations, however, determined that this horsepower was inadequate to power the bomber. The answer was to improve the aerodynamics of the airframe, and Boeing engineers designated 13 areas to be evaluated through engineering analysis, wind tunnel tests, and flight-testing:

1) Airspeed Indicator: required negligible errors due to pitch, yaw, power, flaps, mach number, etc. were required (20 B-29 tests and 7 XB-29 tests).

2) Propellers: intensive studies were made on the basis of their effect on aircraft efficiency. A change from three to four blades was made after flight B-17 tests of wide blade propellers.

3) Nacelles: shapes were governed by consideration of low drag, compressibility effects, clean wing flow and good stalling characteristics (7 nacelles were tested on the Model 307, 5 on the Model 341 and 27 tests on the B-29).

4) Cowlings: proportions were governed by considerations of engine cooling, low drag and compressibility effects (40 nacelle-cowl changes were tested on 1/8-scale nacelle models of the XB-29-1 and XB-29).

5) Wing Planform and Dihedral: determined range, stalling, lateral stability and longitudinal balance (predicted values were confirmed on a complete model).

6) Wing Ailerons: required to give larger rolling moments than on previous aircraft in order to give adequate control with asymmetrical power or fuel (4 ailerons were tested on Model 307, 3 on the Model 341, 2 on the B-29 and 1 tested on a 1/4 scale model at high speed).

7) Wing Flap Tabs: required to reduce wing bending moments and to cut down drag at cruising speed. Fillets were required to reduce drag (10 flap tabs were tested on B-29 and 8 fillets were tested on the B-29).

8) Elevators: design was dictated by the necessity for obtaining adequate control. Favorable elevator motion in hands-off flight and one hand-on landings were required (5 elevators were tested on the Model 307, 2 on the Model 341, 6 on the B-29, 15 on the B-17 in flight and 2 on

the B-29 in flight).

9) Rudder: design was dictated by problems of control under asymmetrical power at low speed, and by the necessity of eliminating rudder boost without incurring serious overbalance (1 rudder tested on Model 307, 20 on the B-17E, 22 on the XB-29-1, 30 on the B-29, 1 rudder flight tested on the B-17E and minor adjustments were required on the B-29).

10) Tail Size and Setting: determined considerations of stability, trim and control without tail stall under all conditions of power, both symmetrical and asymmetrical, with flaps up and down (horizontal tails were tested on 3 Model 307s, 2 B-17Es, 1 Model 341, 3 B-29s and 2 B-17Gs in flight).

11) Armament: all turrets contemplated were tested at low and high speeds on a B-29 model and armament drag and other effects were evaluated in determining the final aircraft armament.

12) Flaps: a high lift, low drag flap was required because of the high wing loading and high altitude characteristics of the aircraft (7 flaps were tested on the Model 307, 4 on the Model 341, 15 on the B-29 flap model and 1 on the B-29). Flap deflection was found to be desirable at high weights and altitudes.

13) Airfoil Section: required low drag at cruising speed, small moments and stall, as well as good compressibility characteristics (eight three-dimensional wing models with different airfoil sections were tested to determine the basic airfoil, 20 two-dimensional tests, and 10 complete model tests were made in search of airfoil improvements).

Weight Control

Many large aircraft of the 1930s failed because their designers disregarded weight control factors. The German Dornier DOX Flying Boat and the Russian Maxim Gorky are examples of this. The weight control engineer used the weights of previous aircraft to make estimates of the weights of new designs. But these past precedents were only partially useful in the case of the B-29 with its many new innovations and requirements: its unequaled size and extreme operating altitude that required new heating and insulating prerequisites; pressurized cabins; its avant-garde remote fire control system; tricycle landing gear; and untested new Wright engines. The engineers broke the bomber down into the fuselage, wing and its components, landing gear, engines, and equipment. Cost estimates for aircraft were based on design weight estimates, and Boeing weight engineers provided Boeing cost analysts with a component weight itemization of the empty B-29. The weight engineers, along with stress engineers, then conducted an exhaustive analysis of the structural components, and a preliminary design was established.

After the preliminary design stage the Project and Weight Group leader, known as the "Weight Controller," assumed the responsibility of maintaining the weight of the B-29 to plus or minus 0.5% of the originally estimated weight of the aircraft, as stipulated in the company's contract with the AAC. With the aircraft's weight divided into components a "weight budget" was set for each component. The engineers responsible for designing each part of a component were limited to a specified weight allowance for that part, and could not exceed that allowance without jeopardizing the component. The design engineer could "borrow" weight from another part that came in under its weight requirement, but this rarely happened.

Weight engineers were concerned with maintaining the balance of the bomber, as the center of gravity had to remain in an established correlation to the center of lift of the wings. If there was a sizable overweight in any part or group of parts it would have disrupted the estimated balance to such an extent that redesign or repositioning of equipment to compensate would have been necessary. However, at this time the detailed design of the B-29 was relatively flexible, and minor changes were made daily. The Air Materiel Command Mockup Board had examined the mockup, and approved the final layout with "recommended" changes and additions of equipment. The Weight Controller then had to estimate how these changes would affect the overall weight of the B-29. The AAC recognized that their recommendations would add weight and granted a "weight allowance," which meant they would accept a reduction in performance in exchange for weight additions.

Weight engineers then provided the Structures Unit with a "panel point breakdown" of the B-29, showing the distribution of weight of the wing and fuselage based on preliminary estimates. From this data the Structures Unit was able to establish the flight and landing loads to be required, and so determined the structure sizes. The Structure Unit then sent their figures to the Weight Unit, which determined and checked the weight distribution that had already been allowed on the panel points.

Structural Testing

The B-29 was said to be the most tested aircraft ever built. This was the result of experimental B-29s being built before detailed plans were completed, and because the Air Force ordered the bomber into large-scale production before the first XB-29 was completed. The Air Force ordered three flying XB-29s, and a fourth without engines for "testing to destruction." As the first XB-29 was being built, all key load-bearing components of the airframe were built in full scale and tested to destruction by Boeing's Structural Test Group to determine the accuracy of design strength calculations. Boeing conducted their tests in a building they called the "Cathedral" because of its shape and size. The testing to destruction was in three stages:

1) Testing of component parts while the parts were held in special jigs.
2) Testing of component parts in relation to others after they had been installed on the bomber.
3) Testing of the completed bomber (without engines and other special equipment)

Because the tail surfaces, elevators, stabilizers, rudders, and fins of the XB-29 were the first components to be completed, they were also the first to be tested. In fall 1940 some B-29 control surfaces were scaled down to the size of the B-17 and flight tested on a B-17C. In spring 1941 B-29 ailerons were scaled down and tested on the B-17, with the objective being to develop an aileron that was lighter and at least 50% more effective than a B-17 aileron. A scaled down B-29 tail surface was also tested on a B-17. In testing to destruction these components were held in jigs in the same position they would have in the aircraft, and all tested to at least 110% of design load.

For years the standard structural test was to distribute 65lb bags of lead shots on the part to be tested, conforming to actual in flight loads until the weight broke the part. To test the wing of the XB-29 it was estimated that 300,000lbs of lead, or over 4,600 bags of shot would be required. The

XB-29 wing was designed to flex to 100in, and that presented the problem of keeping the bags from sliding off during the loading for the test. Another testing method was needed, and Boeing engineers suggested the use of hydraulic jacks. However, there were no jacks available of that size, and it took Boeing a year to find a jack manufacturer that was interested in developing them. The jacks were 115in long—the maximum length of the manufacturer's lathes—but that was just over the expected 100in flex of the XB-29 wing.

The wings were attached to the test fuselage, and a complicated system of hydraulic jacks was applied with accurate pressures of more than 300,000lbs. Special extra large test jigs were constructed to hold the wing, and if a jig failed its loss would delay the B-29 program and cost hundreds of thousands of dollars and thousands of man-hours labor. To anticipate failure, and to preserve the wing for further testing, strain gauges were used with sensor wires attaching to over 300 points on the wing. When the recording apparatus warned that the applied forces were about to cause structural failure the test was stopped, and the structure was reinforced and retested. The first wing test to destruction failed at 97% of the design load, and proved the B-29 wing could withstand four times the loads it would ever carry.

Testing the innovative Fowler Flap tested the testers. No previous flap had been designed to endure such high loads, and available bearings to move the flaps could not tolerate these large loads. The bearings needed to be small, as they were rolling in small spaces, and in testing they spiraled and bound in their steel tracks. These tracks also were not strong enough, and distorted when the bearings rolled in them. As a solution the tracks were specially heat-treated, and the bearings manufactured of the strongest steel.

When the control systems were tested it was discovered that their electric motors did not meet the test standards. The motor manufacturers only tested their product for electrical output, but when Boeing engineers put them on the brake stands for low (-75F) to high (120F) temperature performance the motors failed at low temperatures. The grease in the motors was unable to tolerate very low temperatures, and the motor parts stuck and broke. It was not until the third XB-29 was ready for testing that the motors passed testing.

Another major test of the completed airframe was the drop test, to determine if it could withstand the AAF stipulated 27in free drop. The airframe was loaded with weights to simulate full load of equipment, bombs and ammunition, fuel, and crew. Two drop tests were conducted, with the bomber being lifted 27in off the floor in a horizontal, and then in an inclined position. In another test 20mm cannon and .50cal machine gun bullets were fired at sections of the airframe to determine the bomber's ability to withstand gunfire. Fuselage pressurization was to be tested to 13.5lbs/sqin. When the nose section was tested it blew out at 13.1lbs, which was twice the actual pressure it would ever be subjected to in flight, but to meet specifications the nose section was reinforced and passed later tests.

7

B-29 Contracted and Production Planned

During January 1942, the AAC began to contract numerous companies to supply parts and components for the B-29 project. General Electric, Schenectady, NY, was contracted to supply fire-control units, General Motors A.C. Spark Plug division was to supply autopilots, and GM's Dayton, OH, Frigidaire plant was given a huge $40 million contract to produce 6,600 propellers under license. After Pearl Harbor the AAC increased Boeing's Wichita contract to an unheard of $408 million to produce 750 B-29s at 50 per month by June 1943. Another $20 million was added to expand the Wichita plant to produce these additional bombers.

On 10 February 1942 Under Secretary of War Robert Lovett had directed Maj.Gen. Oliver Echols, head of the Air Material Command, to convene a subcommittee of America's leaders in the automotive and aircraft industries at the General Motors Building in Detroit; they were to discuss the plans for a bomber with Long-Range striking power, principally the B-29. O.E. Hunt, General Motor's Vice President, presided over the meeting, and representing the Air Force was Brig.Gen. George Kenney, Col. Kenneth Wolfe, and Col. A.M. Drake, while Col. E.M. Powers represented the War Department. Company president Lawrence Bell, along with Ray Whitman and O.L. Woodson represented Bell Aircraft. Fred Collins, sales manager, and Edward Wells, assistant engineer, represented Boeing. Representing Fisher Body (a division of GM) was general manager Edward Fisher, and Don Berlin, director of aircraft development. North American Aviation sent its President, J.H. Kindelberger, and CEO Ernest Breech. T.B. Wright of the Aircraft Branch and E.C. Watson and Merrill Meigs represented the War Production Board. February 1942 was a dire time for American industry, as aluminum and steel were in such short supply that there were drives in American neighborhoods to collect scrap. There was a severe shortage of machine tools, as all were in use, and machine tool manufacturers could not keep up with demand.

Hunt addressed the meeting as the representative of America's industrial leader General Motors, and explained that GM was already overburdened, and that the aircraft industry would have to take on the B-29 project without it. The subcommittee agreed, especially those from the aircraft industry, who feared that GM would make inroads in their bailiwick. When Gen. Echols addressed the meeting he took GM's Hunt to task, and demanded that GM become part of the B-29 program. From this meeting a joint B-29 production plan patterned after the 1941 B-17 BDV production plan was formulated.

Boeing-Wichita would produce and assemble B-29s; North American Aviation—then a GM division—would produce B-29s in its Kansas City plant, and Bell Aircraft of Buffalo, NY, and GM's Fisher Body Division of Cleveland, OH, would build B-29s in plants to be built in Marietta, GA, and Cleveland, respectively. To expedite and coordinate the joint project the B-29 Liaison Committee was formed, with headquarters in Seattle, to coordinate design and maintain a schedule for production. Boeing was represented by Frederick Collins, the company sales manager who had established the BDV Liaison Committee under the direction of Boeing President Philip Johnson. B.A. Winter represented Bell Aircraft, and A.P. Ripley represented Fisher (GM). The Committee also included major B-29 subcontractors, such as Republic and McDonnell Aviation, Wright (engines), Chrysler (fuselage sections), Hudson Motors (outer wings and three major body sections), Briggs (outboard wing and empennage), Murray (wing tips), and Goodyear (stabilizers, vertical fins, and center sections). Although Army Gen. Kenneth Wolfe headed the Committee, any decisions needed the unanimous consent of the four companies. The B-29 Committee was to take on the biggest and most complex large-scale manufacturing endeavor ever undertaken. To make their undertaking more difficult was that they were working with a concept that would not fly until September 1942. Fortunately, President Roosevelt and his advisor, Harry Hopkins, personally favored the B-29 program, and it was given free financial reign. Boeing agreed

On 10 February 1942, Under Secretary of War Robert Lovett had directed Maj.Gen. Oliver Echols (pictured), head of the Air Material Command, to convene a subcommittee of America's leaders in the automotive and aircraft industries at General Motors to discuss the plans for a bomber with long range striking power, namely the B-29. (USAF)

to furnish the three other companies with the blueprints and thousands of tool designs so that production could begin ASAP, and to insure that B-29 production in the four factories was identical. The Committee subcontracted numerous companies to supply parts, materiel, and machinery to the four plants, with Boeing alone having over 140 subcontractors. In April Wright Aeronautical Corporation received an order to triple the original order for the R-3350 engine. In addition to building B-29s, Fisher was to supply North American and Bell with outer wing panels, tail surfaces, ailerons, flaps, control columns, wing tips, and completed engine nacelles.

The XB-29 was on the drawing board, and instead of waiting for flight trials of the prototype to be completed, the AAF and Boeing were so convinced of the XB-29's potential that, to facilitate future B-29 production, as early as 1941 plans were made to build factories and to supply equipment, tools, and personnel for these factories. Boeing was confident that its XB-29 would be successful, as had previously been verified in its Clipper and Stratoliner designs, and that the actual XB-29 problems would be with the new Wright engines and the remote control defensive armament system, and not the Boeing airframe and components. Boeing anticipated that the B-17 production lines could be shut down and converted to B-29 production in late 1942. The B-17 BDV consortium was producing 100s of B-17s, aided by subcontractors that supplied parts and components to their production lines. But the heavy demand for the B-17 and B-24 not only precluded the conversion of B-17 production lines to the B-29, but also utilized so many of the nation's engineers and workers that Boeing did not have enough of these personnel to design and build the B-29 on schedule.

In January 1941 the AAC investigated sites for a new B-29 factory in the Atlanta, GA, area, and decided on Marietta, a small town northwest of Atlanta. The government was building the new Government-owned Aircraft Assembly Plant #6, Atlanta, Georgia, and obtained a commitment from the Bell Aircraft Co. of Buffalo, NY, to build 400 B-29s. General Motor's Fisher Body Plant agreed to build 200 B-29s at the yet-to-be-built government plant at Cleveland, OH.

Once the B-29s were ready for production it was estimated that each bomber was to cost $700,000 in salaries, materials, and operating costs, plus about $200,000 for government furnished equipment (GFE), such as engines, armament, electronic equipment, etc. Contracts were awarded on the $700,000 per bomber basis. North American was given $250 million for 300 B-29s in April 1942. Bell agreed to a $342 million contract for 400 B-29s to be produced in the Marietta plant starting in September 1943.

Fisher-GM also agreed to a contract to build 200 B-29s for $195 million at the Cleveland factory, which would assemble components from GM plants in Detroit, Memphis, and Muncie. Letters of Intent made up 30% of these contracts, and were sent out months before the contracts were finalized.

By June 1942 the demands of the B-29 production plan began to cause rifts among the Committee. Boeing was late in furnishing blueprints, and its executives were concerned about losing their control over the program to rival aircraft companies. Boeing regarded American industrial kingpin General Motors as a potential competitor in the aircraft industry, as GM owned Fisher Body and had a large stake in North American Aviation. The great American victory over the Japanese Navy at the Battle of Midway in June had changed the tide of battle in the Pacific, and with it strategic plans changed. In August the AAF and Navy were ordered to change aircraft production requirements. To fulfill its need for a medium bomber the Navy took over the North American plant at Kansas City that was building the B-25. In exchange the AAF took over the Boeing plant at Renton, WA, where the Navy Sea Ranger flying boat prototype project was underway, but then abandoned it to free up the factory for B-29 production. This eliminated North American from the B-29 plan, and the AAF transferred that B-29 production to the Renton plant. Canceling the North American contract led to a tangle of involved legal and accounting problems with North American and its subcontractors. In July 1942 Boeing was committed to building 800 B-29s at its plants at Renton and Wichita. Its contracts were valued at $750 million, and furthermore, the government was required to build and expand the factories and provide the tools and equipment.

After engineers from the three other B-29 licensees studied the B-29 data supplied by Boeing they questioned the figures. They felt the bomber would have 40mph less speed, 5,000ft less ceiling, and 1,000mi less range than estimated. These doubts led a very worried Hap Arnold to appoint Oliver Echols, who had pushed for the B-29, and a legation led by Donald Putt to go to Seattle to meet with Wellwood Beall. At the meeting, attended by Boeing representative Ed Wells, N.D. Showalter, George Schairer, and Eddie Allen, Echols said that studies and data showed the aircraft to need a bigger wing. When questioned Schairer, backed by Allen, told the committee that much of the data explored new frontiers of flight, and that changes would be disastrous to performance. Beall used his figures from three wind tunnel tests as substantiation. Donald Putt, who worked with Boeing in the B-17 program, was familiar with Schairer's reputation, and recommended Echols accept the Boeing wing data.

8

First Flight, 21 September 1942

Boeing Flight Testing

In its development of the Stratoliner, Boeing had initiated a comprehensive and extensive testing program that had produced a magnificent four-engined airliner with a pressurized cabin. Later Boeing used these testing procedures on the new B-17s, and the Boeing Flight Test and Aerodynamic Research Unit placed comprehensive scientific instruments and recording apparatus on board the XB-29 test aircraft to be monitored during the flight. The XB-29 Flight Test and Aerodynamic Research Unit would conduct the most exhaustive and comprehensive test programs in aviation history. Their primary objective was to establish "airworthiness," and to substantiate that the B-29 met contractual requirements set by the Air Force: maximum speed; range; take off and landing distance over an obstacle and military load; and to prove "detailed performance characteristics to comply with requisites of engine cooling and control." The Boeing test crews were comprised of fight test engineers trained to operate these instruments, and to monitor and interpret the data. Before a flight test, the flight engineers were briefed on the objective of the flight and their responsibilities in the test. After the test flight the flight engineers were debriefed and the data collected and analyzed. By the next day an extensive transcript was ready, denoting the results and conclusions of the test flight.

Since the production program had been initiated before the first prototype had been completed, there were literally hundreds of items that were not flight-tested, but were to be part of the production aircraft, and could require some degree of change once they were flight-tested. The factories relied on Flight and Aerodynamics Unit test information on the new engines and new electric and control systems. The Flight and Aerodynamics Unit put the XB-29 to rigorous tests, first for general function, and then for the "measure and range of their efficiency." The aircraft was tested as an entirety, and each element was tested under every condition, at all altitudes.

Edmund T. "Eddie" Allen, 46, was the Boeing Chief of the Test Flight and Aerodynamics staff. After graduating from high school Allen worked for three years to support his family when his father died. The Chicago native then attended the University of Illinois for a year, and while there became a flying cadet at Scott Field, IL. During World War I he enlisted in the Army and served in the Aviation Section of the Signal Corps. While in England he was assigned to the British flight-testing center, and when he returned to America he became a test pilot at the Army flight test center at

McCook Field. After the Armistice he became the first test pilot for the newly formed National Advisory Committee for Aeronautics (NACA). In 1919 he reentered the University of Illinois for a year and transferred to MIT for two years to study aeronautical engineering. While at MIT he designed and built gliders and entered competitions in Europe. From 1923 to 1925 he went on to a varied career in aviation doing freelance flight-testing, and was the civilian test pilot at McCook Field. From mid-1925 to mid-1927 Allen was a pioneer airmail pilot for the Post Office Department, flying rebuilt DeHavilands for the Mountain Division across the Rocky Mountains. After the Post Office relinquished its airmail business Allen flew airmail for Boeing Air Transport, flying their Boeing 40As on the new San Diego route. Over the next five years he did more and more test flying and consulting, and served in those capacities for a host of air transport companies. He became the authority on flying heavy aircraft, particularly for the Boeing Airplane Company, an affiliate of Boeing Air Transport that was to become United Air Lines. By 1932 Allen became a respected aeronautical authority, and had established a scientific approach to flight-testing, collaborating with both the designers and engineers while the aircraft was in the design stages. Along with Boeing, he worked for the principal aircraft manufacturers and for Pan American Airways and Eastern Airlines. During his career Allen was to make the first test flight on more than 30 new aircraft models, mostly for Boeing (F83, XB-15, Model 307 Stratoliner, Model 314 Clipper, B-17B through F, and the XB-29), but

Edmund T. "Eddie" Allen, 46, was the Chief of Boeing's Test Flight and Aerodynamics staff. During his career Allen was to make the first test flight on more than 30 new aircraft models, mostly for Boeing (F83, XB-15, Model 307 Stratoliner, Model 314 Clipper, B-17B through F, and the XB-29), but also for Douglas (DC-2), Lockheed (Constellation), and Sikorsky (S43). (USAF)

also for Douglas (DC-2), Lockheed (Constellation), and Sikorsky (S43). Insurance companies often lowered the premiums on new aircraft tested and approved by Allen.

Allen was an aeronautical engineer first and a test pilot second. Allen stressed patience and thoroughness in the program, stating:

"Patience is one of the prime requisites of a good flight test pilot or engineer. Some of the less experienced persons engaged in flight test work find it difficult to understand why such pains are required. They feel it should be quite possible to go out and get data with much less bother."

After the crash of the Model 307 Stratoliner on 18 March 1939, Allen believed that the future of aircraft development was through comprehensive design research, followed by laboratory and wind tunnel tests, and only then were flight tests to be conducted by specialized test teams consisting of engineers using sophisticated instruments. Allen presented his ideas to Boeing, and on 26 April 1939 he was named Boeing's first Director of Aerodynamics and Flight Research. During the next four years he helped to lift the fortunes of Boeing, a company that was on the brink of bankruptcy. His flight research facility consisted of three independent test Departments. The first was the Research Flight Test Department, which directed research, experimental, and engineering flight testing. The Production Flight Test Department was charged with flying all new production aircraft to inspect the aircraft for manufacturing and quality control problems, and to make any corrections before the aircraft was released to the buyer. The third group was the Flight Acceptance Department, which in the case of military aircraft was the Army Air Corps officers who flew and accepted the aircraft.

The Flight Research Department director was Al Reed, the Chief of Flight Test and Chief Test Pilot. Allen divided the Department into functional groups:

1)   Pilots and co-pilots;
2)   Specialized flight crewmen (mostly flight test engineers);
3)   Instrumentation group (that was responsible for all the standard and specialized instruments and photographic equipment);
4)   Analysis group (that collected, analyzed and prepared test data);
5)   Liaison group (coordinated the aircraft configuration and instrumentation requirements established by the Project Flight Test Engineer with the mechanics and shops);
6)   Flight Equipment group (serviced, stored and maintained equipment e.g. parachutes, oxygen apparatus, etc.) and;
7)   Administration group.

Before each flight test the aircraft test crew was prepared to adhere to explicit written test and configuration stipulations, called the Plan of Test, which was formulated implementing precise test conditions and procedures. The flight test crew considered the Plan in detail during a pre-flight meeting. During the flight the crew carried out their normal duties, however, the Project Flight Engineer would position himself between and slightly behind the test pilot and co-pilot (the flight engineer's position in the B-29) for better communication. The Project Test Engineer coordinated the action of the entire crew, maintained a master log of the test, and set the applicable recording frequency of all cameras from his master control. On the B-17 and B-29 there were usually 10 men, linked by interphones, responsible for flying and the special testing equipment and instruments. The instrumentation commonly included two or three manometer panels to record 40 to 50 pressures; two photo-recorders with a camera in each and 40 to 50 instruments; one or two potentiometers to record 50 to 100 temperatures; a Brown Recorder set to continuously record vital selected temperatures; and oscilloscopes to record strain, flutter, or vibration. Each instrument was wired to transmitters on the component under examination, and a data recording was made to the specifications of the Plan of Test. At all recording stations there was a coordination light and coordination counter that moved once a second to provide accurate coordination of all manual and photographic data from before take off and after landing. The test pilot would focus on flying the aircraft to precisely stabilize and maintain the specified flight test plan. The co-pilot was to set engine power, wing flap, or cowl flap positions, and to monitor everything occurring inside and outside the aircraft. On the XB-29 the co-pilot was aided by the flight engineer to operate the engines. After the flight test an informal, but very structured meeting was held and recorded by a stenographer. It was headed by the Project Flight Test Engineer, or sometimes by the Project Test pilot. The flight crew and the following important ground personnel attended:

1)   Design project and staff engineers who had stipulated specific tests;
2)   Technical and management representatives of outside suppliers whose components were being tested;
3)   Data analysis supervisor;
4)   Quality control supervisor;
5)   Flight test instrumentation engineers;
6)   Customer representatives (USAAC in the case of military aircraft)

The agenda was based on the Plan of Test, but to expedite matters, short items were discussed first, so as to allow personnel to return to work. The various tests were discussed and preliminarily analyzed, and questions were asked and answered. Tentative plans were made, and suggestions were entertained for the next flight test before the meeting was adjourned. The stenographer prepared the transcript of the meeting so that it was available the next morning. The Project Flight Test Engineer would prepare his "The Report of Test," which was a written summary of the flight test conditions and his log sheet.

In early 1942 Eddie Allen had his engineering flight testing organization functioning and had expanded it, adding seven new pilots to supplement him and four other pilots. Most of their early work involved flying engineering flight tests of the B-17. Allen prepared a preliminary report that stated that to prove the XB-29 for production, 200 hours of flight testing would be required, "compressed into a four or five month period." The AAC requested that the Boeing Flight and Aerodynamics Unit conduct their tests at their air bases at either Spokane or Yakima, WA. But Boeing already had a large and comprehensive testing ground and a large staff of engineers at its Seattle facility, and the Air Force agreed to conduct tests at Boeing Field. After 1.4 million man-hours had been invested in engineering and 764 B-29 production bombers had been ordered, the first XB-29 (41-002) was scheduled to arrive at Boeing Field on 30 August. A troubling result of ground tests was that no engine could run longer than 57 hours without having some type of problem. An immediate problem was that factory tests showed that the landing gear electric motors were faulty, and the electric cowl flap motors could not delivered on time. So it was not until 9 September that the XB-29 was ready for engine run up and taxi tests on the short 5,200ft Boeing Field in Seattle. In the meantime, the flight test crews practiced emergency and bail out procedures.

Constant carburetor and other engine problems further slowed progress, and new engines or engine accessories were installed. On 15 September the XB-29 was finally able to undergo fast taxiing tests, and it became airborne briefly, as it bounded 15 feet into the air three times. But during the test a torque meter (an instrument put on the propeller to measure power output) to an oil hose coupling malfunctioned, and mechanics had to work through the night to replace all hoses so the aircraft could ready for the first flight tests.

First Flight, 21 September 1942
Initial flight tests were made with stripped aircraft, without turrets/armament or other equipment unnecessary to its performance. The four R-3350-13 engines featured 16ft, 7in Hamilton-Standard three-bladed hydromatic propellers. A prominent commander's dome was placed just aft of the cockpit. The rudder extended down to the base of the horizontal stabilizer, into the space that would later be occupied by the tail gunner's position. There was a large fixed tail bumper located below the horizontal stabilizer. Dual pitot probes were placed on top of the horizontal stabilizer.

At 3:40 PM, Test Pilot Eddie Allen taxied and took off with his six man crew:

Co-pilot:	A.C. Reed
Flight Test Engineer:	W.F. Milliken
Asst. Flight Test Engineer:	E.I. Wersebe
Flight Engineer:	M. Hanson
Radio Operator:	A. Peterson
Observer:	K.J. Laplow

Allen took the aircraft to 6,000ft and tested the longitudinal, directional, and lateral stability and control. He checked the effectiveness, re-

sponse, and forces of the controls, and then the controllability and performance with the #1 engine throttled, followed by power off stalls. An hour and a quarter later the plane landed, and Allen was swarmed by anxious Boeing executives and engineers, who had devoted two years of time, hundreds of thousands of man-hours, and millions of dollars in the results of this test. The laconic Allen smiled and declared, "She flies!" His postflight report stated that the aircraft had:

"Exceptionally good aerodynamic characteristics; aileron and rudder turns were satisfactory, illustrating effect of dihedral angle of the wings; yaw stability satisfactory; stalling characteristics excellent; spiral stability and controls generally satisfactory; window arrangement affords good vision in attitudes of flight, particularly good in landing."

That night after the test, Boeing Engineering VP Wellwood Beall sent Washington this brief but ardent telegram: "Eddie Allen reports that we have an excellent airplane." The next day AAF pilot Donald Putt flew the prototype, and reported that it was "unbelievable for such a large aircraft to be so easy on the controls."

Tests and Changes Continue
But everything was not well with the XB-29, as on 30 September, after only seven hours of flight, the new, unproven Wright engines delayed the test program for 10 days, awaiting modification. Carburetors were adjusted to reduce the forces needed to open and close the throttles, and new carburetors were installed for testing on engine #4, and another type of carburetor was placed on #2 engine for evaluation. Propeller governors were adjusted, and the four blade props were installed (it was to become standard). Other significant changes were made during this down time: elevator trim tab anti-creep brakes were added; turrets were installed without guns; the flight engineer's station was changed; the oxygen system was installed; bomb bay racks were added, and auxiliary fuel tank racks were fitted to them; and the braking system for ground control was improved. Inspec-

Eddie Allen made the first flight on 21 September 1942 with this XB-29 (41-002), which was a stripped aircraft without turrets/armament or other equipment unnecessary to its performance. The R-3350-13 engine featured 16ft, 7in Hamilton-Standard three-bladed hydromatic propeller. 41-002 continued to be flown in Boeing flight testing, and eventually was sent to the B-29 School to give students experience in repair. (USAF)

tions were made of the hydraulic system operating the brakes, and the fuel tank doors were removed so inspections could be made of the fuel cells. Instruments were added to measure and record engine vibration and pressure and temperature.

It was not until the end of October that the XB-29 flew again, and once more there was an engine failure, causing the engine to be replaced. While the XB-29 was grounded engineers performed ground checks on the throttle, carburetion, landing gear retraction, the electrical system, propeller function, and the fuel tanks. In November flight tests were again plagued by engine failure. The XB-29 was put into power off stalls to evaluate controllability and the aircraft passed the test, stalling slowly and coming easily back under control. At the end of November engine operation was primarily tested; carburetion and fuel flow was examined, and supercharger and engine cooling was assessed in power climbs and level flight.

It would not be until 2 December that XB-29 #1 would be taken to 25,000ft. In the 18 hours of test flying the XB-29 had shown excellent aerodynamics at the altitudes it had flown, and continued to do so at high altitude. However, engine problems continued unabated. In mid-December Eddie Allen flew tests to determine minimum distances for take offs and landings at specified gross weights, and the bomber met all specifications. During the last week of December weather was bad, and canceled test flights to 35,000ft and take off tests were hampered by cross winds and poor visibility. Other tests assessed fuel flow and supercharger regulation, nose gear controllability and stability (there was a shimmy), propeller feathering checks, aileron forces, and effectiveness, and air speed calibration. On the 28th a test flight was aborted after 26 minutes at 6,800ft, as the #1 engine failed, and ground inspection showed that the #2 engine had metal fragments in the sump, and both were replaced. The situation was so bad that XB-29 #1 would not fly for another seven months.

On 30 December the second XB-29 prototype (41-003) made its first flight to check the aircraft, and its instrumentation in general. Soon after take off, at 3,000ft the #4 engine governor became erratic, and the engine could not be feathered. The engine raced to 3,500rpm, and at six minutes into the flight, smoke and sparks came out of the exhausts, and then caught on fire. The weather that had been marginal at the start of the flight was quickly deteriorating as Allen turned back toward Boeing Field. Allen shut off the fuel and activated the Lux fire extinguisher, but the fire reignited and continued to become worse. In another two minutes it was burning intensely in the accessory compartment, and flames and smoke were streaming from the nacelle access door and intercooler exit area. Soon flames and heavy smoke were flowing off the wing and from the bomb bay into the

cabin. Choking and partially blinded, Eddie Allen calmly returned to the small field after 32 minutes, where the fire crew was waiting and extinguished the fire. Allen was later to receive the Air Medal for his cool skill and courage in saving his crew and aircraft.

Frank Crosby, who was a Flight Test Instrument Technician at the Flight Test Hanger at Boeing Field on the XB-29 project in Seattle, describes his experience after the fire:

"We called the new Wright R-3350 the 'corn cob' engine," as the cooling baffles on the air cooled engine were staggered to direct enough air over the four banks of cylinders, and this made it look like a twisted corn cob. The two front and two rear banks of cylinders each had a supercharger, and the hot exhaust gases were conducted through the inside of the nacelle from the engine to drive the superchargers. These hot gases passed through an elbow directly adjacent to the magnesium encased accessories behind the firewall, and a stainless steel shroud casing that protected the engine accessory compartment in the monocoque nacelle. In this compartment four autosync engine instrument transmitters and other accessories were attached on shockproof mountings in a very tight space. The CO_2 fire extinguishing equipment was also located there. Eddie Allen did a wonderful job bringing the down the burning plane. He used all the CO_2 for that engine, and then the fire truck also used all its CO_2 supply, and finally extinguished the fire with water. The fire was difficult to put out because the magnesium—used to save weight—burns well, and is very difficult to extinguish, although it works well on oil, gas, and electrical fires.

While the damaged nacelle was being replaced I was instructed to remove the instruments from the other three nacelles and test them so that they would be ready for the next test flight. The instruments in the nacelle were very difficult to get to because of the cramped space, and I noticed that the magnesium casing had been distorted from the exhaust heat, and reported it to the test engineers who, at the time, did not place much importance on it."

Inspection on the ground showed that the #1 engine also had a small fire, and the #3 engine was about to fail. The intense fire in the #4 engine so severely damaged the #4 nacelle that it had to be replaced with #1 XB-29's #4 nacelle. These three engines had been rated for 35 hours of use, but all three combined had only a total of less than three hours of ground and flight time on them! Because there was a shortage of engines, two of the three engines were to be replaced by engines from #1 XB-29 that were

On 30 December the second XB-29 prototype (41-003) made its first flight to check the aircraft, and its instrumentation in general. Soon after take off, at 3,000ft, the #4 engine governor became erratic, and the engine could not be feathered and caught on fire. Choking and partially blinded, Eddie Allen calmly returned to the small field after 32 minutes, where the fire crew was waiting and extinguished the fire. Allen was later to receive the Air Medal for his cool skill and courage in saving his aircraft and crew. (USAF)

rated as "unlimited." The only positive factor now was that #2 XB-29 had four "unlimited" engines installed. The type of fire in engine #4 continued to plague the B-29 program, and would cause 19 severe accidents between February 1943 and September 1944. Although Boeing and Wright tried to correct the problem, they naturally pointed the finger at each other. It was not until late March 1944 that it was established that the Wright R-3350 was vulnerable to induction system fires that quickly became intense, uncontrollable magnesium fires that eradicated all evidence of the fire's cause.

So, by the end of December Allen had only made 23 flights totaling 27 hours of air time. The longest was 2 hours 19 minutes, and the average was 1:10, but much of that time was spent trying to get back safely on the ground after problems arose. The short flights meant that significant quantitative data was not collected. In these three months there had been 16 engine changes, 22 carburetor changes, and 19 exhaust modifications, and the propellers had chronic governing and feathering problems. On the plus side of the ledger the aerodynamics, performance, and handling of the aircraft were excellent.

During January 1943 the XB-29s were grounded for major changes, as the engines were overhauled, and major structural changes were performed, such as reinforcing the wing at the wheel wells, landing gear, and wing flaps, and reinforcing the fuselage at the turrets and the nose windows. Other changes were made to the nacelles, engine controls, generators, instrumentation, and the electrical system. The Washington winter weather was particularly harsh and made work difficult, and completely stopped it several days, as the hanger was not large enough to enclose the XB-29. Then, as a low point an icicle fell and punctured the right aileron! Problems continued on 31 January when the #2 engine of the XB-29 packed up at 20,000ft. Then, on 17 February, #2 was on a test flight to check the trailing antenna, air speed indicator, and brake reaction when climbing past 5,000ft; gasoline leakage was seen to come from the #4 tank filler cap behind the #4 (right) engine. The leakage increased as the aircraft leveled off, and then further increased as the right wing banked to return safely to the field. XB-29 #2 had flown eight test flights totaling only 7:27 hours—an average of 56 minutes in preparation for high altitude tests at the end of the month. The aircraft was unproved and dangerous. But it could not be grounded, as by this time over 1,600 production B-29s had been ordered, testing was far behind schedule, and the bomber was a priority in the Pacific. Further, more intensive testing was urgently needed to gather the data to make the major improvements required to get the aircraft into production with minimal delays, and to develop training and operational procedures and manuals.

Eddie Allen Accident, 18 February 1943

The Accident

A flight test was scheduled to take off at 1040 on a cold and overcast morning, with Allen to evaluate climb and level flight performance, and to measure engine-cooling figures with two and four engines operating. The flight test was to be restricted to 25,000ft, as the Wright R-3350 Cyclone engines had problems with gasoline leakage and low nose oil pressures the previous day. The XB-29 took off at design gross of 105,000lbs and with maximum fuel (5,410gals). The 11 crewmen included:

<cap>1-09-01 Eddie Allen

Test Pilot:	Eddie Allen
Co-pilot:	Robert Dansfield
Flight Test Engineers:	
	Edward Wersebe
	Thomas Lankford
	Charles Blaine
	Raymond Basel
Flight Engineer:	Fritz Mohn
Instrument Monitoring:	Robert Maxfield
Photo-Recorder Observer:	Barclay Henshaw
Aerodynamicist:	Vincent North
Radioman:	Harry Ralston

Edward Wersebe was the major scientific member on board, as his reputation as an Aerodynamics Engineer and his time at high altitudes (30,000ft+) was among the best in the world.

The XB-29 took off to the south at 1209, and five minutes after takeoff, climbing at rated power through 5,000ft, a fire was reported in the #1 engine nacelle. Allen cut the mixture and fuel to the engine and feathered the prop, while Mohn, the flight engineer, closed the cowl flaps and discharged the Lux CO_2 fire extinguisher, and the fire appeared to have been extinguished. Allen turned the bomber back toward Boeing Field and descended for a routine landing from the north over Sumner on Runway 13 to the SSE into a 5mph wind, rather than a downwind landing on the longer, 5,200ft runway. After five minutes Allen radioed that he was at 2,400ft descending and asked for immediate clearance, as his #1 engine had been on fire and the prop had been feathered. He said that the trouble was not

serious, but crash equipment should stand by. Two minutes later Allen radioed that he was over the Lake Washington Bridge, four miles NE of the field on the downwind leg. Turning left into the base leg at 2,500ft he corrected his altitude to 1,500ft, passing over the heavily populated west shore of Lake Washington. The XB-29 continued a normal descent over Seattle at 1,200ft, but heavy smoke and pieces began to come from the #2 engine, and the stricken bomber was headed for Seattle's industrial and commercial area south of downtown. The bomber continued to head south, losing altitude as the fire spread across the wing into the bomb bay. Two minutes later an explosion occurred that could be heard on the ground. The radio operator peered into the forward bomb bay and saw that the center wing section forward wing spar was on fire. The control tower overheard the radio operator on his open microphone tell Allen:

"Allen, better get this thing down in a hurry. The wing spar is burning badly."

Allen's last message to Boeing Field was to order that the fire equipment be ready, as he was coming in with a wing on fire. Allen turned the XB-29 south on an oblique final approach at 250ft, anxiously trying to

Eddie Allen and 10 crew took off in the late morning of 18 February 1943 in XB-29 (41-003), and five minutes after takeoff an engine fire began. Allen valiantly tried to bring the bomber back to base. (USAF)

reach the field, which was still three to four miles away. Witnesses later reported seeing the leading edge of the wing missing between the #1 and #2 engines (parts were later found on the ground). Two crewmen in the forward compartment tried to bail out, but their parachutes failed to open at the low altitude. The radioman, Harry Ralston, hit a high-tension wire, and his parachute snagged and he was strung over the wire. Flight Test Engineer Edward Wersebe jumped, but his chute never opened. At 1226, three miles from the runway, Allen tried to pull back on the controls into a left turn, but the XB-29 crashed into the Frye Meat Packing Plant, killing him and pilot Bob Dansfield, as well as the remaining seven crew on board. The crash and the ensuing fire killed another 20 people, including workers in the factory and several firemen, and destroyed much of the plant. Frank Crosby describes his experience and reaction to the crash:

"I heard the whole thing over the air to ground radio in the flight test hangar. It was terrible, as these flight test crews, engineers, and ground crews all lived and worked together, and were like family. We all stood around stunned, and many of us were crying. We couldn't believe it could happen to Eddie, not only because he was so capable, but because we all loved him. He wasn't a big man, but was very debonair, with his clipped mustache and the tweed suit he always wore. Always a gentleman, he'd come in and say to me, 'Would you test such and such, I'm a little concerned about the readings we're getting; I want to be sure they were accurate.' He was a stickler for doing everything by the book, but was always cordial and never put down a mechanic, even if he was wrong."

Post-crash investigation showed that the fire and heavy smoke had moved through the bomb bay into the cockpit, as the three crew who had attempted to bail out had burns on their bodies and clothing. Since the XB-29 was a top-secret project, the news releases described the crashed aircraft as a "four-engine bomber." Since the second XB-29 was unpainted, unlike the first XB-29, the many witnesses either thought it was an airliner, or assumed it to be a B-17. However, the *Seattle City Transit Weekly*, a newspaper for transit company employees, nearly exposed the secret

bomber. A bus driver who had been near the crash site had taken photos of the crashed aircraft before it completely burned, and submitted them to the *Transit Weekly*, which published them with its story of the crash. The FBI quickly investigated and confiscated all but a few of the 500 copies printed.

There has been some controversy over which XB-29 crashed. On 6 September 1940 the AAC let contract AC-15429 for two flyable XB-29s and a non-flying, static test aircraft. On 14 December 1941 the contract was revised to add a third flyable XB-29. The first two XB-29s were assigned AAC serial numbers 41-002 and 41-003, but Boeing serial numbers (c/n, for contractor numbers) for the aircraft were c/n 2482 for 41-002 and c/n 2481 for 41-003—the numbers were not mutually sequential. This has lead to confusion as to which XB-29 was involved in the Allen crash. Some news accounts said it was the "first" XB-29 (41-002) that crashed, but Boeing records show that 41-003 crashed. 41-002 continued to be flown in Boeing flight testing, and eventually was sent to the B-29 School to give students experience in repair. It remained with the company until it was scrapped in 1948. The third XB-29 was given the AAC serial number 41-18335 and the Boeing c/n 2484. The other Boeing c/n (2483) was assigned to the last Douglas DB-7 that Boeing built for the RAF (c/n 2485 was the first Douglas A-20C built for the AAC). As a footnote, on 23 April 1946 Allen's widow, Florence, was presented the Air Medal by the direction of President Harry S. Truman. Maj.Gen. Benjamin Chidlaw pinned the medal on Allen's six-year-old daughter, Turney.

Post Allen Crash Investigation and Remedies

The Allen crash devastated the Boeing XB-29 test program, as in eight years the company had lost three chief test pilots, three large experimental aircraft, and the 10 highly qualified men on Allen's valuable XB-29, which was thoroughly equipped with test instruments. In 1935 the experimental Model 299 prototype of the B-17 crashed after Boeing had invested both great amounts of money and time in the project, and they also lost chief test pilot Les Tower (who was not at the controls, but a passenger). Three years later, the first Stratoliner crashed and all aboard perished. In both instances Boeing persevered and corrected the problems. But with the Allen

The doomed XB-29 crashed into the Frye Meat Packing Plant and killed all 11 crew. Another 20 people were killed, including workers in the factory and several firemen, and much of the plant was destroyed. (USAF)

tragedy company morale was at a nadir, and the reasons for the crash had to be found before the B-29 program could proceed. To make matters worse, Al Reed, the only pilot alive who had flown the B-29, decided to leave the testing program.

The crash was investigated from every angle; witnesses were questioned, and the remnants of the aircraft were collected not only at the crash site, but also along the flight path, and were intensively examined. The post crash investigation and previous tests had shown that the B-29 was aerodynamically and structurally reliable. Thousands of hours of ground tests and engineering analyses were conducted in lieu of flight-testing. There were 54 major and literally hundreds of other minor changes that were recommended and assigned precedence to be evaluated. The major problems centered on the engines, nacelles, and surrounding structures that needed to be redesign to isolate and minimize the fire potential. There were problems with the nacelle design, and incorporating the changes in the Fisher nacelle plants in Cleveland and Detroit were done without interrupting production. Reducing cowl flap length and the internal airflow decreased nacelle drag, and modifications were made to ventilation and nacelle drainage. The engine was scheduled to be fitted with a computer directed fire control and extinguishing system that was nowhere near ready. The carburetor had to be replaced by fuel injection carburetors, and Minneapolis-Honeywell electric turbo regulators were added. The propellers needed a better feathering system so they would not continue to turn out of control and cause fires. The changes necessary for the wing were the relocation of the filler heads and isolation of the fuel cells, additional bulkheads, and ventilation of the wing leading edge, the seals in the firewalls, and front spars were to be tightened, exhaust shroud cooling improved, and electrical equipment better fireproofed and ventilated. A cockpit ventilation shut off valve and cockpit to nose wheel well pressure release valve were installed. It was found that de-icing boots needed to be installed on the leading edges of the wings. The bomb bay doors opened too slowly, and caused excessive drag and instability when the bomber was most vulnerable to enemy AA fire and interceptors over the target. A mechanism to snap open the doors was developed and installed. At high altitudes windows frosted over, and new glass and a defrosting system needed to be designed and installed. Frank Crosby describes his role in the post crash investigation:

"Then (after the crash) they remembered what I told them about my findings after the December 30th fire, about the magnesium casing around the autosyn engine instruments on the other outboard engine being distorted by heat from being too close to the exhaust shroud elbow. The post crash investigation disclosed that the fire burned through the fire wall, into the engine accessory compartment, and into the fuel cell, and came down the dihedral of the wing and into the fuselage. There were many changes, major and minor, to the nacelle and cooling system, among them the relocation of the magnesium encased accessories to reduce their proximity to the intense heat of the exhaust shrouds. I like to think my findings were instrumental in these changes."

Wright Engine Committee
After the crash Maj.Gen. Oliver Echols, Chief of the Air Materiel Command, instructed Wright engineer W.D. Kennedy and his assistant, Robert

Johnson, to report to the Air Force delegate at the Boeing Seattle plant. They were directed to analyze the installation of Wright engines in the XB-29, and to collect crash data to guide the Wright Engine Committee in its determination of the cause of the accident. The two-man team arrived on 24 February and submitted their conclusions to Echols on 5 March.

Their report stated that there was no conclusive evidence that any of the four engines had a fire during the flight, and that the fire occurred in the leading edge of the wing. They hypothesized the cause of the fire to be in the instrument tubing that was routed from the test instrument manometers in the cockpit, through the leading edge of the wing, to the outboard engine. In a test it was demonstrated that this tubing could ignite by touching the hot exhaust, and then the fire could slowly burn along the tubing until it ignited the fuel leakage that had accumulated in the leading wing edge. The fuel tanks were placed behind the main spar, and their filler necks came through the spar to the filler cap on the top surface of the wing. There was a scupper drain from the filler cap cavity to an outlet on the lower surface of the wing. The investigation showed that when the tanks were full and the aircraft climbing, the gasoline was sucked into the filler cap cavity, and the scupper did not drain because of the upward pressure of the air on the outlet point. Fuel accumulated in the leading edge of the wing and was ignited by the burning tubing, and pieces flew off during the fatal descent, as parts of the leading edge were found for miles along the ground. Design changes on the production aircraft placed the filler behind the spar.

The Engine Committee had been instituted by the Air Force in order to accelerate decisions and production to develop the so-called "combat engine." Col. Clarence "Bill" Irvin directed the Committee, which also sat the vice presidents of engineering of Wright and Pratt & Whitney, members of the power plant and production sections at Wright Field, and a nonpartisan consultant. The Committee's basic responsibility was to reduce the standard five-year engine production period to two years. The principal decision the Committee had to make was to establish the "Bill of Material"—the "how" and "when" for the "combat engine."

Harry Truman—an obscure Senator from Missouri—headed a Senate investigative panel to examine the problems with the new and complex Wright R-3350 engine. The Senate panel concluded that Wright had inadequate quality control procedures, and that the Air Force had exerted too much pressure on Wright to step up production. The R-3350 had a propensity to overheat, throw valves, and catch fire in flight. The crankcase was manufactured from magnesium that, while being very light and strong, was also very flammable. The magnesium crankcase expanded more than the aluminum engine structure around it at operating temperatures, which put the crankcase under heavy compressive stresses. After a while the crankcase would crack and leak oil, and the engine temperature would rise further increasing the stress and the fractures would enlarge. If the engine was not shut down the pistons would freeze, and finally the fuel lines would catch fire, and the magnesium would begin to burn intensely and destroy the wing. The fuel induction system was also inclined to catch fire, and burned long and hot enough to set the magnesium on fire. After months the addition of air baffles to direct more air to the rear row of cylinders, and propeller cuffs to force more air through the engine to reduce heat, were added. But to convert the magnesium crankcase to aluminum would cause a significant design change and extensive production delays. Instead, the SOP was to assign the waist gunners to watch for engine oil leaks and shut down the offending engine at the first sign of an oil leak.

10

Gen. K.B. Wolfe Takes Over the B-29 Program

Contracts

In September 1942—the month the first XB-29 finally left the ground—the government had committed $1.5 billion for B-29 airframes, and had ordered 1,665 B-29s and their spare parts. Boeing had contracts for 1,065 (765 from Wichita and 300 from Renton), Bell for 400, and GM-Fisher for 200. With this huge investment there was pressure on the government, the AAF, and the aircraft companies to produce a super bomber. In April 1943 Generals Arnold and Marshall introduced the "*Plan for the Employment of the B-29 Airplane Against Japan Proper*," and a plan to accelerate the entire B-29 lagging program by restricting further design changes. They wanted at least 100 B-29s on forward bases by the end of 1943, but this was not to come about, as more problems arose. It was not only difficult to build factories and set up assembly lines, but also to procure materials, subcontractors, and personnel in an American economy and industry that was operating at maximum wartime capacity. In July 1943 Fisher-GM was ordered to relinquish B-29 production to concentrate on developing and then building 2,500 XP-75 "Eagle" fighters at the Cleveland plant. However, Fisher was to continue to supply B-29 nacelles. The Glenn Martin Company of Baltimore, which was building B-26 Marauders at its immense Omaha, NE, plant, was now contracted to build B-29s there. A contract was let to Martin-Omaha to produce 20 B-29s a month by July 1944. By October 1943 the AAF had consigned $90 million to Martin-Omaha, in addition to the previous $25 million that the government invested in building the Omaha factory. B-29 production now was to take place at four locations: Boeing-Wichita (BW); Bell-Marietta (BA); Martin-Omaha (MO); and Boeing-Renton (BN).

The B-29 is "Good enough"

As the XB-29 was tested, there were a multitude of changes required to make the aircraft safer and more effective. The list of changes was passed from the AAF to the prime contractors to the subcontractor, and then to the suppliers. The complexity of the bomber design meant that any small change would cause a domino effect of changes throughout the entire aircraft. The exasperated Arnold needed to take strong action; he took the B-29 program out of the "system" and used his considerable influence in Washington to make it a priority program. Gen. Wolfe of the B-29 Committee was allowed to "deal directly" with Boeing, Bell, and Martin without military and governmental bureaucracy and red tape. Arnold ordered that "any change, future or pending, be reviewed or eliminated unless it is necessary for the safety of the crew," and that "the aircraft is good enough now and is to be left alone." He added:

"It is my desire that the airplane be produced in quantity so that it can be used in this war, not the next."

Since Boeing-Wichita was the only plant producing the B-29, Arnold ordered that engineering and production be centralized there, and that essential supplies, materials, tools, and equipment be sent there before the other three factories.

The third XB-29 (AAC serial number 41-18335) had the layout that would be chosen for production, as it was the only XB-29 available after the Allen accident. It had improved engines installed, along with other mandated changes after the Allen accident and Army pilots flew it for the first time at Seattle on 29 May 1943. At the end of June Col. Leonard Harman and Lt.Col. Abram Olson flew the aircraft from Seattle to Wichita in record time. (USAF)

At the time the B-29 project was secret, but Arnold lifted the secrecy to speed the project through bureaucratic channels. To introduce the bomber to the public there was a disagreement between Boeing and Air Force public relations offices over the name of the bomber. Boeing wanted "Superfortress," while the AAF chose "Annihilator," as it felt that the Boeing name was too similar to its "Flying Fortress," and would identify the aircraft as Boeing. Arnold made the decision, and the B-29 was officially the "Superfortress."

KB Wolfe Takes Over the "Special Project"

The Eddie Allen accident was the culmination of the numerous problems that demanded wide-ranging changes and improvements in the XB-29 design. At the end of February 1943 Gen. Kenneth Bonner "KB" Wolfe, head of the Production Division, Air Materiel Command, was appointed by Gen. Henry Arnold to assume all phases of the B-29 program as a Special Project, and to report to Arnold personally. Wolfe was a good choice, as he rose through the ranks as a private in the Signal Corps Aviation Section in World War I, and had a reputation for being tough but fair. Wolfe took control immediately, and directed that in the future the Air Force would take over B-29 flight tests. In June, Wolfe became the Commanding General of the 58th Bombardment Wing, which was to prepare the B-29 for combat and train its officers and personnel. Wolfe was known to surround himself with capable aides, and he brought in Brig.Gen. Laverne "Whitey" Saunders, who had been the CO of the 11th Bombardment Group in the Solomons; Col. Richard Carmichael, CO of the 19th Bombardment Group in the Southwest Pacific; and Col. Leonard "Jake" Harman, Wright Field B-29 flight test officer. On 21 June, Wolfe set up his headquarters near the Bell plant at Marietta, GA, to hasten B-29 modifications at Bell and Wichita, and to direct flight tests.

Further XB-29 #3 Flight Testing

For flight testing Wolfe commandeered the Accelerated Service Test Branch from Wright Field, which was a small group of pilots and engineers that had been running the experimental test flight program at Wright. Col. Harman was named pilot, and Lt. Col. Abram Olson co-pilot for the AAC B-29 test program, which was limited to the remaining (third) XB-29 (41-18335). It was the only B-29 equipped with the extensive instrumentation to carry on testing to gather comprehensive data quickly. After the Allen accident it had improved engines installed, along with the numerous other changes mandated by the post crash investigation. The Army pilots flew it

At the end of February 1943, Gen. Kenneth Bonner, "KB" Wolfe, head of the Production Division, Air Materiel Command was appointed by Gen. Henry Arnold to assume all phases of the B-29 program. (USAF)

for the first time out of Seattle on 29 May, and tests confirmed that the all important engine improvements were successful. While in Washington, the test flight personnel had decided on the name "*The Flying Guinea Pig*," and searched for an artist—which were in short supply—to paint the name on their airplane. Finally a riveter who had been a civilian sign painter was located, and he drew a preliminary sketch of a flying guinea pig using a picture of a guinea pig from a dictionary. A watch showing 4 o'clock was added, because the aircraft had a reputation for not becoming airworthy until after that time. The dictionary drawing was enlarged and painted on each side of the cockpit. The name *Moses Lake Belle* was placed on the nose wheel hubcap to denote the eastern Washington test field of the aircraft.

Three weeks later the XB-29 was ready for its first cross-country flight to Wichita, which Wolfe had chosen for his flight-testing center. Wichita had longer and wider runways, unobstructed approaches, and better and closer alternate fields, and the Kansas spring and summer weather was generally better than the persistently cloudy Seattle weather. Harman and Olson flew the aircraft from Seattle to Wichita in record time. Harman became so enthusiastic over the flight in the revamped XB-29 that, upon his arrival at Wichita, he buzzed the field, and later telegraphed Wolfe extolling the bomber as the best aircraft he had ever flown. By the end of the year the test XB-29 #3 had flown a total of 121 hours and tested 208 components. This, compared to Allen's engine-plagued 27 hours of testing on XB-29 #1, during which time there were 16 engine changes and slightly less than eight flying hours on the XB-29 #2, which had two engine changes. XB-29 #3 was used as Boeing's B-29 flight test ship throughout the war, and it continued flying until 1947.

YB-29 Flight Testing

At the end of March N.D. Showalter, Boeing Chief Military Projects Engineer, was named Chief of Flight Test. Showalter had participated in both the B-17 and B-29 programs, and had flown with Allen on the #2 Stratoliner tests after the death of test pilot Julius Barr in 1939. Showalter remained at Wichita during the post Allen crash testing, and was a Boeing plant manager before becoming Chief of Flight Test. Showalter was energetic and competent; he helped to improve morale, and would be largely responsible for the success of the YB-29 testing. At the same time it ordered 250 production B-29s, the AAC had ordered 14 YB-29 (41-36954 through 41-36967) service test aircraft to be manufactured at the newly constructed Wichita Plant #2. The YB-29s outwardly resembled the XB-29s, but were built almost to production standards, and had most of the military equipment installed, including five gun turrets and three sighting blisters. The engines were the improved R-3350-21, but continued to mount the three blade propellers of the XB-29s. The first YB-29 (41-36954) had been completed on 15 April 1943, but was grounded until 26 June because of the Allen crash investigation. On that day, with thousands of enthusiastic Boeing-Wichita employees watching, Col. Abram Olson taxied and took off on the first YB-29 flight, but soon black smoke spilled from an engine, and the disappointed Olson turned the bomber around for a safe landing. Post-flight inspection showed the cause to be a small loose gasket, which was considered a minor problem, and would not jeopardize the program.

The flight test program was to be a Boeing Wichita-Army partnership to appraise the YB-29's speed, range, and engines (particularly cooling). During the YB-29 Kansas testing, Army Air Force officers (Col. Harman, airplane commander, and Lt.Col. Abram Olson, co-pilot) would fly the

The AAC ordered 14 YB-29 service test aircraft (41-36954 to 41-36967) at the same time it ordered 250 production B-29s. The YB-29s were manufactured at the newly constructed Wichita Plant #2. The YB-29s outwardly resembled the XB-29s but were built almost to production standards and had most of the military equipment installed, including five gun turrets and three sighting blisters. The engines were the improved R-3350-21, but continued to mount the three blade propellers of the XB-29s. (USAF)

bomber in accordance to Boeing Company test flight procedures. The Wichita Boeing plant was to provide the ground crew personnel to maintain the aircraft, as they were experienced and familiar with the complex aircraft. The AAF pilots were to train Boeing flight personnel so that they could fly the big bombers when they rolled off the production line. Boeing test pilot Robert Robbins was to act as a non-flying middleman between the Army test pilots and the Boeing test crews. Robbins was given flying time as a co-pilot, and by the end of the first week of October was checked out as an airplane commander, with Edward Martin as his co-pilot. During the next two weeks the two Boeing pilots flew the majority of the tests, and by 21 October the test program was again totally a Boeing project. From the end of August the initial testing was continued for six weeks, completing 24 flights totaling 72 hours of flying time. There had been no engine failures or other serious problems. Vital aircraft and engine performance data had been collected, particularly engine cooling data. Takeoffs with a 130,000-pound loading were made. An important test flight was a 3,000mi, 14 hour simulated bombing mission with five ton simulated bomb load.

Boeing's Flight Test Engineer N.D. Showalter, and Col. H.S. Estes and Lt. Louis Sibilsky of the Wright Field Test Section worked together in August and September to gather and evaluate flight test data that was sorely

needed, both by the manufacturers, and the AAF B-29 combat groups that were being organized. After the success of the test program Gen. Wolfe had transferred most of the flight-testing to Boeing. Col. Abram Olson replaced Col. Harman as CO of the Accelerated Service Test Branch, and Harman was transferred to Wright Field to work as B-29 liaison officer to Gen. Wolfe. In this capacity Harman was to prove his reputation as an expediter, and cleared many bottlenecks in the upcoming production, testing, modification, and training phases.

The Boeing factory runways at Wichita were not long enough to accommodate the takeoffs for the high gross weight tests. Olson and his staff flew four production bombers (the 10th, 12th, 15th, and 16th) off the Wichita line, and a YB-29 (136963, the ninth YB-29) to the AAF base at Salina, KS. The Accelerated Service Test Branch flew high altitude tests at high gross weights of 130,000lbs to establish the range of the bomber. The bombers took off from Salina, KS, with a bomb load, and flew over the Gulf of Mexico and back across Texas to make a run over a bombing range, then returned to Salina. The Branch conducted a rated power climb with 127,000lbs that revealed that the engines still needed improvements of their exhaust collector rings and rocker arm lubrication. On one of the high altitude tests a sighting blister blew out, and the cabin suddenly depressurized, sucking out loose papers. The crew quickly put on their local emergency oxygen equipment and suffered no bends or other ill effects. On another flight test at 25,000ft one of the side gunners leaned against a blister and it blew out, taking the gunner along with it. Fortunately he was wearing a parachute, and after landing near a Texas town he telephoned the base that he was OK. After concluding testing the Test Branch returned to Marietta, GA, leaving three of its three aircraft behind at Salina.

Showalter and his engineers were under pressure to complete their work at Wichita so they could return to Seattle. At the home factory they would be close to company engineering facilities and staff, where they could flight test suggested modifications that could then be integrated into the bomber more promptly. H.T. "Slim" Pickens and Ernest "Allie" Allison, old hand Boeing test pilots on the B-17 project, were checked out on the B-29, and trained their own check test units to continue the Wichita testing.

Col. Leonard Harman (left) was transferred to Wright Field to work as B-29 liaison officer to Gen. K. B. Wolfe (right). In this capacity Harman was to prove his reputation as an expediter, and cleared many bottlenecks in the upcoming production, testing, modification, and training phases. (USAF)

11

Battle of Kansas

The B-29 Project's Future is Questioned

In early 1944 a faction arose that contended that, despite the time and dollars expended to date on the hapless B-29 project, it should be abandoned to cut losses. Another faction used combat data from Europe to predict that two-thirds of the B-29s would be lost in combat, and that their crews could not expect to survive past 30 missions to back their contention. This second faction also pointed out that precision bombing in Europe was unsuccessful, and that area bombing of city centers would have to be used, resulting in heavy civilian casualties.

Hap Arnold, backed by Secretary of War Robert Lovett, went to the White House and the War Department to bolster the B-29 program, promising increased effort and top echelon changes. A major change was the appointment of Gen. William Knudsen, a past president of General Motors, to coordinate the B-29 project. Under Knudsen, and with Arnold's influence, there would be tangible progress in the B-29 program.

The Battle of Kansas Begins

The "Battle of Kansas" or "Kansas Blitz" was officially named the "PQ Project," and was initially directed by Col. Pearl Robey of the XX Bomber Command. The Battle of Kansas began on 15 February 1944 when Col. Eric Nelson, Lt.Col. Hubbard, Maj. Midel, Capt. Borden, and 1Lt. J.E. Brown flew from Washington, D.C., with personal orders from Gen. Arnold to expedite the completion of command aircraft for overseas deployment. Soon it became obvious the overseas deployment deadlines could not be realized unless sweeping emergency measures were taken.

To expedite getting the B-29 to the CBI, combat units were organized to take part in a combination of testing and training over Kansas. Col. Lewis Parkes was checked out by Col. Abram Olson, and was assigned to organize the 40th Bombardment Group at Pratt, KS. Col. Alva Harvey organized the 444th Bombardment Group when he delivered three production line B-29s at Great Bend, KS. Col. Howard Engler delivered three B-29s to form the 468th Bombardment Group at Salina, KS. Col. Richard Carmichael took over the 462nd Bombardment Group when he flew three B-29s to Walker, KS. In September, Gen. Wolfe moved his command to Smoky Hill Army Air Field at Salina to be closer to his four tactical training units in Kansas: Salina, Walker, Pratt, and Great Bend. Pilots with four-engine experience, flight engineers, navigators, bombardiers, and ground

crews were transferred into the Kansas bases, but there were not enough B-29s available for each crew for testing/training.

With the shortage of Superfortresses, the future B-29 crews trained in B-26 Marauders and B-17 Flying Fortresses, Link Trainers, high altitude pressure chambers, and other artificial training devices. In late December 1943 the average B-29 crew had put in only 18 hours in a B-29, and only a few flights were flown in formation above 20,000ft. Only 67 pilots had checked out as airplane commanders. To further exacerbate the aircraft shortage problem, six B-29s were involved in accidents during the flight training program. Two pilots retracted the landing gear while the aircraft were on the ground! There was one fatal accident on take off, two B-29s made belly landings because their landing gears malfunctioned, and the sixth bomber was lost when the crew abandoned the bomber at high altitude for undisclosed reasons.

For quantity B-29 production to succeed the master production plan had to be adhered to, the tools, jigs, and machinery built, and workers

Gen. H. H. Arnold, backed by Secretary of War Robert Lovett, went to the White House and War Department to bolster the B-29 program, promising increased effort and top echelon changes. A major change was the appointment of Gen. William Knudsen, a past president of General Motors, to coordinate the B-29 project. Shown are (left to right) A. W. Schupp, Boeing-Wichita Assistant Manager, Knudsen, Oliver West, Boeing Executive VP, and J. E. Schaefer Boeing-Wichita VP and General Manager. (USAF)

In September 1943, Gen. Wolfe moved his command to Smokey Hill Army Air Field at Salina (right) to be closer to his four tactical training units in Kansas: Smokey Hill/Salina, Walker, Pratt (left) and Great Bend. (USAF)

trained in their jobs, all without interference. Due to the acceleration of the B-29 program many bombers were delivered before all the recommended changes discovered in testing and later training had been completed, and others were delivered because of the lack of the necessary parts, tools, etc. to make these changes. To make these changes at the factory would have significantly slowed the production lines. The solution was to fly the bombers from the production line to modification centers, where the changes could be made at the beginning of a process, and not in the middle of the production line.

When a B-29 came off the assembly line factory, Flight Check Crews subjected it to three or four flight checks before it was assigned to the four Kansas bases. While the B-29s in operational units were flown by newly trained young men, the Flight Check Crews were veteran professionals

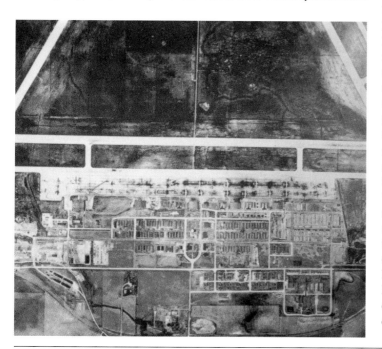

who were air transport and airmail pilots, barnstormers, and instructors. Many of the Flight Test Crews had initially flight checked the B-17, and then moved on to the B-29 program. The Superintendent of Flight Check at Renton and Seattle was veteran pilot H.T. "Slim" Lewis, who was the head pilot for Boeing Air Transport and its successor, United Air Lines. Ernest "Allie" Allison headed the B-29 flight check program at Wichita. Allison was another seasoned pilot, winning his wings in the Signal Corps in 1917, flying Boeing's new airmail routes, and then spending 10 years in the Far East. There he organized China National Airways, went on to expand Chiang Kai-shek's air force and, before returning to Boeing, he aided Gen. Claire Chennault in setting up the American Volunteer Group, the Flying Tigers.

Once the B-29s left the factory they were to be the Army's responsibility, and in November, the AAF set up two modification centers; one at Marietta, GA, managed by Bell Aircraft, and the other smaller center at Birmingham, AL, managed by Bechtol, McCone & Parsons. At the modification centers groups of 10 to 20 workers were trained to perform assigned modification tasks on each B-29. By the end of 1943 it was estimated that each B-29 required 25,000 man-hours for modifications. Col. Carl Cover of the Air Materiel Command was appointed by Wolfe to supervise all engineering issues, and to supervise the modification centers. Cover had been a well-known test pilot, and then a vice president at Douglas Aircraft. By February, Marietta was receiving more aircraft than it could process, so Col. Cover dispersed some B-29s to Martin-Omaha and to Continental Airlines, at Denver's Stapleton Field. A group of the Boeing-Wichita staff, mostly engineers, was assigned to the Omaha Center, and another group from Seattle was sent to the Continental Center. Members of these groups formed what was called the "DEBAC" staff, whose function was to decide how changes were to be made, and directed these procedures to the modification centers. John Saunders was the chief of the DEBAC engineering section, and C.M. "Buck" Weaver was the head of Boeing's modification section. The so-called "war engines," engines with drilled rocker arms and oil sump changes, were to be installed at AAF centers in Oklahoma City and San Antonio under ATSC direction. Despite these changes the B-29 backlog grew. By February 1944 the 20AF at Smokey Hill Air Field, Salina, KS, had not received one combat-ready B-29 for training, and by the first of March it appeared that there would not be enough B-29s available to meet the CBI, 10 March 1944 schedule.

The solution seemed to be to send B-29s from the production line directly to the four Kansas bases and modify them there, so that they could be put into training ASAP. Cover sent civilian and AAF personnel from the civilian modification centers, along with selected modification crews to Kansas. Cover also appointed specialists to sort out the problems associated with modifying B-29s at these Kansas centers. These personnel were responsible for completing the modifications in the field of all B-29s assigned to them by the Air Materiel Command.

While the plan to concentrate the modifications at the four Kansas bases seemed to be practicable, there was an intrinsic flaw. Most of the experienced AAF mechanics schooled to work on the B-29 had already been sent to the CBI, with the forward ground echelon to prepare the new bases in India. This move left the civilians transferred from the modification centers, and inadequately trained Army personnel, who were basically unskilled, and their assigned modifications ranged from inadequate to pathetic. The aircrews did not participate in the modification of their own aircraft to any extent, as they were billeted in nearby small towns, often with their wives, girlfriends, and family. During the day they were attending briefings and being processed for overseas assignment. The Kansas modifications were hastily done at widely separated, generally unorganized centers with material shortages, and sometimes without complete inspections, and B-29s with decidedly "non-standard" equipment were leaving the Kansas modification centers.

On 9 March Gen. Arnold personally flew to Salina, KS, and discovered that no B-29s were ready to leave for India. He found that about 100 B-29s were waiting for modifications, and the completion time for some was two months. The situation angered Arnold, who stated, "The situation as I found it was a disgrace to the Army Air Forces...." The disgruntled Arnold ordered a 15-day deadline for combat-ready B-29s to be prepared to leave for the CBI.

Troubleshooters Arrive and Most Problems Are Solved
Arnold assigned troubleshooters Maj.Gen. Bennett Meyers, Deputy Assistant of the Chief of Air Staff, Col. C.S. "Bill" Irvine, and a staff of statistical officers to take charge of contracting firms and AAF agencies, and to coordinate the responsibilities of AAF officers and civilians. On 10 March Meyers took over a wing of the base hospital at Salina to use as the Kansas modification headquarters. Meyers spent 10 productive days, and then turned over the coordination of the PQ Project to Irvine. Meanwhile, Brig.Gen. Orville Cook, Chief of Production Control at the Air Materiel Command, was called in for a week to assess and step up Col. Cover's work with the Modification Centers, and to minimize difficulties with the aircraft, supplies, and personnel. The AAF was forced to refuse acceptance of these supposedly modified bombers, and Cook ordered all Modification Center contractors to immediately send all their modification personnel and materials to the four Kansas bases—Great Bend, Pratt, Salina, and Walker—to complete modifications there. Maj.Gen. B.M. "Barney" Giles and Maj.Gen. C.E. Branshaw headed the Kansas modification program, and Maj. Thomas Gerrity was in charge of expediting these modifications on the aircraft. In the field the modifications were to be carried out with Maj.Gen. Meyers in charge, and aided by Col. William Irvine, Col. Pearl Robey (head of the technical staff), Colonels Harman and Olson (20BC), and Col. H.A. Shepard. Arnold set another deadline (15 April) by which time sufficient bombers were to be completely modified and combat ready (and ready to carry their own spare engines and spare parts).

On 20 March Brig.Gen. Orval Cook flew to Wichita to meet J. Earl Schaefer, Boeing vice president in charge of the Wichita plant. Schaefer and his Wichita plant manager, H. Fletcher Brown, accompanied Cook on a tour of the four Kansas modification centers/bases to see first hand inadequate personnel performing modifications under appalling conditions. Schaefer and Brown needed only to inspect the Platt facility to determine that something drastic had to be done, and done at once. Schaefer took 600 of his most skilled men off the Wichita production line, even though Boeing's responsibility had ended once the B-29 rolled off its assembly lines, and their transfer would hurt Boeing production (another 170 men

Through intensive post production modifications in the severe winter Kansas weather the first B-29-1 BWs were ready to be deployed to India by late March 1943 when Jake Harmon took off from Smokey Hill with the first of 150 modified B-29s. (USAF)

were transferred from the Marietta lines). The abducted Boeing men had expertise, and were instructed to complete the modifications, and while doing so were to teach the Kansas modification workforce. The situation was so dire that H. Oliver West, Boeing manufacturing mastermind, and Wellwood Beall, head of Boeing engineering, flew in from Seattle to study the situation and make recommendations. Lt.Col. I.W. Stephenson, head of the Domestic Supply Section, Air Service Command, took control of four Kansas supply sub-depots. He was ordered to step up the shipment and issue of supplies to the Kansas centers, and was to establish ways in which supplies and parts could be obtained directly from Boeing-Wichita and sent daily by truck and air shuttles between the sub-depots, and to wherever they were needed. The Battle of Kansas was intensifying, but skirmishes were being won.

The modifications were classified as vital, necessary, and desirable. The vital and necessary modifications were to be completed, and desirable modifications were to be made only if time permitted. Although there were hundreds of modifications, the major modifications were: carburetor-air duct vane reinforcement revisions; emergency relief tank revisions; fabric attachment revisions; flap switch link revisions; flat glass installation in the cockpit for navigation; flux gate compass transmitter installation revisions; fuel gauge revisions; rudder rib and tail rib revisions; side sighting dome revisions; tailskid actuator revisions; tail turret stop revisions; turbo superchargers; radiation shield reinforcement revisions; and the change from circuit breakers to fuses.

Kansas in March certainly is not Miami Beach, and the modification work had to be done under the most demanding conditions. The four Kansas B-29 bases had prefabricated hangars and buildings that were inadequate for the snowbound, sub-freezing weather conditions. A base had just four hangars, and only six bombers could be housed in each. When the modification hangars were full, the remaining bombers waited outside. Only specified procedures were authorized to be completed indoors, and everything else was done outdoors; an estimated 90% of the work was done on outdoor ramps and taxi stands. A "doghouse" was two wooden structures that came together from opposite sides of the bomber to join and totally enclose a section of the fuselage so a modification could be done in cold or wet weather. Hot air gasoline heaters were needed to warm the inside of the aircraft, and for those men working outside on the fuselage and en-

gines. Air Transport Command (ATC) aircraft transported heaters rounded up from all over America. The bases received trainload after trainload of material, parts, equipment, and ammunition, while the ATC flew in personnel, critical equipment, and parts, and operated a shuttle service between the bases. The ATC also performed the essential service of transporting war engines from San Antonio and Oklahoma City, and returning with engines that needed modification. Electricity was vital to complete outdoor work, especially system testing. The bomber's auxiliary power units (APUs/"putt putts") were running continually to power the electric generators. To keep the APUs operating their small three-gallon gasoline tanks had to be constantly filled, and in the beginning 20,000gal tanker trucks used to fuel aircraft were driven up to the APU and three gallons were squirted into the tank. Later, jeeps with trailers with 50gal gasoline drums with spigots filled the putt putts, or delivered a number of Jerry cans to each. Despite the winter conditions, modifications were steadily completed. The 40BG installed or modified 116 engines, 24 superchargers, 124 cowl flaps, 100 propellers, 100 collector rings, 22 rudders, 144 tires, and 36 APQ-13 radar sets. The last of the B-29s left Kansas for the CBI by mid-April, and the Battle of Kansas was won.

B-29s Arrive in India

In mid-March 1944, the combat squadrons were given a "packing list" for each bomber to get ready in order to leave. The list included the spare parts, tools, and test equipment that were to be carried on cargo platforms in the front bomb bay. A spare engine was lowered into a pit; a B-29 was rolled back over the pit, and the engine was hoisted into the rear bomb bay. On 26 March Jake Harmon took off from Smokey Hill, accompanied by the first of 150 modified B-29s, and flew the initial 2,500mi leg toward India; he landed at Gander, Newfoundland, 11 hours later. Harmon was able to leave Gander, but most of the other bombers were caught in a blizzard, and were forced to remain behind for two days. With clear weather they were able to follow him for the next 3,000mi leg to Marrakech, French Morocco. The B-29s had flown across the Atlantic for 10 hours at 300mph at 17,000 to 19,000ft without trouble. As the B-29s took off from Marrakech the first problems appeared, as the flight engineers noticed that the engine temperatures began to rise as the bombers climbed to 16,000ft to clear the Atlas Mountains. One bomber struggled down the runway and failed to lift

Col. Jake Harman (third from right) being greeted by Gen. Claire Chennault (fifth from right) on his arrival at Chakulia, northeastern India. Harman had made the trip from the US in seven days and was followed by the others individually or in pairs. Each B-29 flew 11,500 miles and consumed 21,000gals of fuel in the 50 hours they were in the air. (USAF)

off, crashing in flames into the adjoining farmland. Quick action by the nearby ground staff saved the lives of the 11 crewmen. The bombers labored across the North African deserts and landed at John Payne Field, Cairo. The aircraft's poor performance was checked by the flight engineers, crew chiefs, and recently arrived civilian ground consultants, who found that engine changes and general aircraft overhauling was required. Harman took off from Cairo on the 2,400mi trip to Karachi, India, and over the next few days was followed by the remainder of his refurbished bombers. At Karachi they landed in temperatures that ranged from 110 to 120°F, and the inside temperatures of the B-29s quickly reached 190°F. The engine temperatures reached within 20-degrees of overheating while just standing on their hardstands! Two more B-29s were lost at Karachi as they were taking off for the final 1,500mi to their new base at Chakulia, northeastern India. Harman had made the trip in seven days, and was followed by the others individually or in pairs. By 15 April less than a quarter (32 bombers) had arrived at Chakulia, and as many others were undergoing repairs and engine changes along the way. On 20 April all B-29s enroute were grounded, as the fifth serious accident occurred. Investigation showed that most of these accidents were the result of engine overheating that was mostly caused by poor crew training. Flights were resumed, and by the end of the month 92 bombers had arrived, and by 8 May, there were 130 B-29s in India. Each B-29 had flown 11,500mi and consumed 21,000gals of fuel in the 50 hours they were in the air.

B-29 Factories Continue to Encounter Problems

After the B-29s left for the CBI the modification personnel were returned to their factories and civilian modification centers. By mid-1944 more changes were ordered to be incorporated into the factory production lines. The Bell-Marietta plant received 42 change orders per week, and Bell estimated that they lost one half million production line man-hours making these changes. In April 1944 B-29 production was finally beginning to increase: Boeing-Wichita built 36 B-29s for a total of 267; Boeing-Renton built three to total 11; and Bell-Marietta built 12 to total 31. But increased production, despite more modifications made on the production line, did not result in a better quality bomber, and the civilian modification center were as busy as ever. A B-29 sent to a modification center now required 61,000 man-hours, which equated to a workforce of 1,525 men working a 40hr week. It took half as long to modify a B-29 as it took to build one! The new factories at Renton and Marietta were poor at introducing changes in their assembly lines, with Bell-Marietta having 39 B-29s—most of its production—in modification in May. The situation became so bad at Bell that B-29 coordinators ordered Bell to build only stripped B-29s and forget about modifications, and all Bell B-29s were sent directly to Birmingham for modification. Modification time increased to 10 or more weeks, but even with modifications to the modification lines, the average modification time was only reduced to nine weeks. As the B-29s entered combat it was found that they were too heavy from the modifications; take offs had become hazardous, and range and speed had decreased as the wing loading had increased to 77lbs. To decrease the weight by 20,000lbs all non-essential equipment was deleted, including the proposed camouflage paint, which would also save many man-hours of painting. If it were not for the Boeing-Wichita plant's ability to quickly and efficiently incorporate changes in their assembly lines and increase productivity to turn out quality bombers, the B-29 program could have become the failure predicted by a few.

12

Plans for the Overseas Deployment of the B-29

In early 1941 the War Department, the Joint Chiefs of Staff, and the Air Force had realized that the service test YB-29 would not be ready until June 1943. It would then be a year to test and make the inevitable changes to the bomber, train the crews, build overseas bases, and transfer enough of the production bombers due in mid-June 1944 to combat.

Casablanca Conference: January 1943

The *Casablanca Conference* in January 1943 had approved a Combined Bomber Offensive against Germany, and projected the B-29/B-32 to take part in the offensive. The plan was to deploy Very Heavy Bombers in shuttles between North Africa and England. Maj.Gen. Ira Eaker of the 8AF was to develop a Combined Bomber Offensive, and in March requested a tentative deployment schedule for the B-29 groups. Eaker made several other deployment requests, but the bomber had continual developmental problems, and by December Arnold advised him that the VHB groups would be sent to the Pacific. The mid-June 1944 starting date determined that the Pacific would be the combat theater for the B-29. Gen. Arnold stated:

"We did not consider Germany as a possible target for the B-29s, because we figured that by the time they were ready, the intensive bombing campaign that we were planning with our B-17s and B-24s would have already destroyed most of the industrial facilities, communications systems, and other military objectives within Germany and German-controlled Europe. On the other hand, we figured Japan would be free of aerial bombardment until we could get the B-29s into the picture."

Trident Conference: May 1943

On 11 May 1943 the *Trident Conference* was held in Washington, D.C., with President Roosevelt, Prime Minister Churchill, and the Anglo-American Joint Chiefs of Staff. Although the defeat of Germany was the main consideration of the meeting, another topic was the projected role of the B-29 against Japan and where the bomber would be based. Parts of China were under Allied control, and a plan called *Setting Sun* was formulated in which B-29s would be based along a 400mi line north and south of Changsha, China. B-29s loaded with 10 tons of bombs could operate from these bases and bomb most of the industrial regions of southern Japan that were located 1,500mi away. Ten groups were scheduled to be deployed by October 1944, and 20 by March 1945. Planners estimated that the groups

would fly five missions per month at 50% strength, and that 168 group months would be needed to destroy the designated Japanese targets within the 12 months. All supplies would be transported from Calcutta to Kunming to Changsha. The supplies would be flown by B-24s that had been released from service by the anticipated victory in Europe and converted to C-87 transports. Each of the initial 10 groups was to have 200 C-87s by October 1944 and 4,000 by May 1945. However, the British offensive in Burma had stalled, and had jeopardized the Allied situation in China, where the Japanese were on the offensive. When asked for his position on *Setting Sun* Gen. Joseph Stillwell felt that the plan was too ambitious and not logistically feasible within the time limits, when considering the inadequacy of Calcutta's port facilities. *Setting Sun* was seen as unrealistic and scrapped, and Stillwell offered another plan, *Twilight*. Stillwell's plan would permanently base the B-29s around Calcutta, out of Japanese bombing range, and they would stage through advanced bases in China on their way to Japan. Since the Japanese controlled the land and sea routes to the area around the proposed Chinese bases, the only way to build and maintain a major base in China was to fly all supplies and materials across the Himalayas. Stillwell's plan called for much of the fuel to be carried by the B-29s, and the extra fuel, bombs, and supplies by 45 converted B-24s and 367 C-54s and C-87s. *Twilight* was to provide 10 B-29 groups flying 500 sorties per month. Stillwell realized once the bombing of Japan began the Japanese would react to the Chinese airbases, and asked for 50 American-trained Chinese divisions, plus a reinforced 14AF and five extra fighter groups to protect the Changsha airfields.

Quadrant (Quebec) Conference: August 1943

During the *Quadrant Conference* held in Quebec in August 1943, the Joint Chiefs of Staff rejected the *Twilight Plan* and formulated a new plan that situated B-29 bases in the then Japanese-held Marianas Islands in the mid-Pacific. The invasion of the Marianas was scheduled for early 1946, after Truk and Yap were taken and converted into advanced naval bases. But that date was moved forward to mid-1944 to correspond with B-29s coming off the production lines. Gen. Arnold instructed Haywood Hansell to meet with the influential Adm. Ernest King, commander of the U.S. Fleet, chief of Naval Operations, and a member of the Joint Chiefs of Staff, to discuss preparations for basing the B-29s in the Marianas. Attending the *Quadrant Conference* was China's foreign minister T.V. Soong, who was demanding increased military aid and the basing of B-29s in China. This concession would not only appease China, but would allow the B-29s to bomb Japan at the earliest date, if the Marianas were taken or not. Arnold appointed a special board to analyze this recommendation.

At the end of February 1943, Arnold had directed that Brig.Gen. "K.B." Wolfe, the head of the Production Division of the Materiel Command at Wright Field, to direct B-29 production as a "Special Project." In April 1943 Arnold asked Wolfe to draw up plans to organize, equip, and train B-29 units for combat, and also to draw up a plan for operating B-29s from China. In June Wolfe became the Commanding General of the 58th Bombardment Wing, which was to ready B-29s for combat and train its officers and personnel. Arnold's special board already had a B-29 China plan available, and on 24 September 1943 the "*Wolfe Plan*" was presented as an adaptation of *Twilight*. The plan was established as a self-sufficient undertaking, in which 150 B-29s were to be based in the Calcutta area to function as transports for a strike force of 100 B-29s based in the Kweilin, China, area. The date for the first mission was postponed to 1 June 1944, but this date was too late to comply with Roosevelt's wish for an earlier show of strength in China. Wolfe revised his plan and presented it to Arnold on 11 October 1943, before the *Sextant Conference*.

Sextant (*Cairo*) Conference: November 1943
Roosevelt, Churchill, Stalin, and Chiang Kai-shek attended the *Sextant Conference*, held in Cairo in late November 1943. Roosevelt, backed by Churchill, maintained it was vital that China stay in the war, and so *Sextant* committed the B-29s into combat in China by June 1944 if Chiang Kai-shek promised to have advanced bases built by 15 April 1944. The Joint Chiefs of Staff, as well as the Joint Logistics and Joint Plans Committees, continued to oppose this politically motivated China plan, as the Marianas plan was more viable.

The *Wolfe Plan* and *Matterhorn*
In his plan Wolfe expected to have 150 bombers and 300 crews in the CBI by 1 March 1944, and 300 bombers and 450 crews by 1 September. From this nucleus he would form a bomber command with two wings of four combat groups each. Stillwell and the Chinese were expected to furnish the bases in China and provide armies for protection. All B-29s were to base at Calcutta and stage through advanced bases in the Kweilin area. Operations were to begin on or about 1 April 1944, when the first wing arrived. The plan called for three immediate 100-bomber missions, with the attack to be maintained at 200 sorties per month until September, when the second wing was scheduled to arrive to provide a schedule of 300 sorties per month. The B-29s were expected to supply themselves, aided by 20 C-47s. Three B-29s were to act as transports for every two combat bombers, but none of the combat bombers were to be modified for transport duties. After Col. Claude Duncan drew up the tables of organization and equipment for the B-29s in China, it was obvious that every phase from production line to battlefront would have to be integrated to assure that the program would run efficiently. But Wolfe realized that his plan had flaws, as its supply system was inefficient and vulnerable to Japanese ground attack. Stillwell had maintained that he would need at least 50 divisions to protect the Kweilin air bases, and no new Chinese troops had been allocated for base defense. With no troop reinforcements the B-29 bases were to be relocated at Chengtu, where the B-29s could be better protected from enemy ground and air attack. While safe from Japanese ground attack, Chengtu would have to be protected from enemy air attack, and Chennault activated the 312th Fighter Wing of the 14AF under Brig.Gen. A.H. Gilkeson. This new wing was to be composed of pilots from the 33rd and 81st Fighter Groups, which were flying P-40s over Anzio in the Italian Campaign at the time. The groups were scheduled for transport to India in February 1944, and were to be re-equipped with P-47Ds. To accelerate their activation, 100 assembled P-47s were to be shipped on escort carriers, and another 50 were carried in crates on transport ships. The 100 assembled P-47s would not arrive in Karachi until 30 March 1944, and it would not be available until the end of April, when the pilots of the fighter squadrons of the 33FG were to arrive to begin transitional crew training to the P-47s. This schedule was to delay fighter protection in China until May or June. When he learned of this delay Stillwell became so exasperated that he requested that

The *Sextant* (Cairo) *Conference* in late November 1943 attended by Churchill (right), Roosevelt (center), Chiang Kai-shek (left) and Stalin. At Cairo Gen. Haywood Hansell and the Air Staff, realizing the drawbacks of the China-India B-29 plan, convinced the Joint Chiefs of Staff to order the Navy Pacific Area Command to capture the Marianas as soon as possible for B-29 bases. (USAF)

K. B. Wolfe (left) with Lord Louis Mountbatten had to rework several combat plans for operations from the CBI. *Matterhorn*, the strategic bombing of Japan, was the China-India B-29 plan that based the B-29s at Chengtu and would keep China in the war. Because of the divergent opinions on *Matterhorn* by the various nations, services and personnel involved, the Combined Chiefs of Staff did not approve *Matterhorn* until 10 April 1944 months after the first B-29s were · in China. (USAF)

the B-29 attacks be postponed for a month, but Washington considered it imperative to begin B-29 operations. The 59FS of the 33FG, retaining its P-40Ns, were to be rushed to Karachi during the first week in March, and to leave for China immediately. Wolfe further fine tuned his plan, and on 13 October Arnold approved the Wolfe Plan in principle, and wrote to Wolfe:

"I have told the President that this will be started (the bombing of Japan) on 1 March. See that it is done."

The Air Staff continued to develop the Wolfe Plan, and on 9 November—the day before the *Sextant Conference*—they presented it to the Joint Chiefs of Staff under the title "*Early Sustained Bombing of Japan*."

The day of the *Sextant Conference*, after meeting with Churchill and Chiang Kai-shek, Roosevelt approved "*Early Sustained Bombing of Japan*," which was now coded *Matterhorn*. Soon after *Twilight* was recoded to *Drake* (*Twilight* had been Stillwell's plan to use the bases at Kweilin, but had been used generically to denote any plan to base B-29s in China). *Matterhorn* was the China-India B-29 plan that based the B-29s at Chengtu, and would keep China in the war. Finally, with *Matterhorn* there was a firm proposal for the strategic bombing of Japan. Because of the divergent opinions on *Matterhorn* by the various nations, services, and personnel involved, the Combined Chiefs of Staff did not approve *Matterhorn* until 10 April 1944, after the first B-29s were in China. The B-29 was finally in combat, and missions from the Marianas bases would have to wait.

13

The B-29 Factories

The American aviation industry was a true colossus, as during World War II it outstripped its enemies in engine and airframe production. During 1942 it out-produced both Germany and Japan in engine manufacture by almost 2 to 1, and two years later these figures jumped to 3 to 1, and for the entire war America outproduced the Axis by 2.5 to 1. However, in finished aircraft the ratio fell from 2 to 1 in 1942 to 1.4 to 1 in 1944. The explanation for this decline was that America was building a greater proportion (compared to fighters) of four-engined bombers, which took longer to build than the fighters that the Axis was building in greater proportions (compared to bombers) to counter the American four-engined bombers that were devastating their homelands. American productivity in pounds of airframe built per employee was also much higher, as in 1941 German workers produced 81% of their American counterparts when their industry was intact, and only 45% in 1944 when Allied bombing was taking its toll. The figures for the Japanese worker were 44% in 1941 and 18% in 1945, when bombing and the blockade of raw materials was having their effect.

The manufacturing history of the B-29, despite its many problems, could not be equaled during the war. The first B-29 flew in September 1942, the 100th was accepted in January 1944, and production increased greatly that year when the 500th was accepted in July, and the 1,000th in November. In March 1945 the 2,000th B-29 was accepted, the 3,000th in June, and the 300 per month figure was reached in April; the peak monthly production of 375 was reached during the last full month of production. No other aircraft in World War II that first flew after December 1941 was built in larger numbers, or saw as much service as the B-29. The Consolidated B-32 first flew in September 1942 and only 114 were built; the Northrop P-61 Black Widow night fighter first flew in May 1942 and had 682 production models; and the Luftwaffe Me-262 jet fighter that first flew in July 1942 had 1,400 production models. The RAF developed no comparable bomber during the war, relying on its tried and true Lancaster. The He-177 Grief was Germany's ill-fated attempt to produce a Long-Range strategic bomber equivalent to the Lancaster or B-17. The six-man bomber had impressive dimensions, comparing to the B-17 and B-24, but was dwarfed by the B-29. It measured almost 67ft long (B-17 - 75ft, B-24 - 66ft, and B-29 - 99ft), and had a wingspan of 103ft (B-17 - 104ft, B-24 - 110ft, and B-29 - 141ft). It was designed to have a speed of 335mph and a range of 1,000mi, carrying 4,400lbs of bombs (or 1,800mi with 2,200lbs). The prototype first flew on 19 November 1939, but like the B-29, it was plagued by engine overheating problems. However, the B-29's overheating problems paled compared to those of the He-177. The He-177A-1 was a four-engined bomber, but had two Daimler Benz 601 1,000hp coupled together (called the DB 606) in one nacelle to drive a single propeller. This coupled arrangement was designed to reduce drag, but the He-177 was underpowered (the Luftwaffe never built an engine that developed 2,000hp during the war). Problems were so severe that three of the first five prototypes crashed. A coupled 3,100hp DB 610 was developed later for the A-3 and A-5 versions, but it too was plagued by fires and overheating. There were about 600 He-177s manufactured, and the bomber saw limited service in anti-shipping attacks, and during the unsuccessful one time *Operation Steinbock* shallow dive-bombing attack on London on 18 April 1944, in which 125 He-177s took part. The bomber carried out a number of somewhat successful high altitude strategic bombing attacks on the Eastern Front in the summer of 1944 with KG.1. These raids were terminated due to the increasing German fuel shortages and the need for Luftwaffe fighters to be given the rationed fuel to intercept Allied bombers.

Boeing-Wichita

The plains of south central Kansas, in the middle of America, seem an unlikely location for a huge aircraft plant to be built. But there were several basic reasons that made Wichita a choice location. At the time this inland city was chosen, there was an apprehension in both the American people and government of possible enemy air and naval attacks, and even a possible invasion of American borders and seacoasts. The country's major industrial centers—Baltimore, Los Angeles, San Diego, and Seattle—were not only located on the coastline, but also were the centers for major aircraft plants, and were major ship building areas. Because of the concentrated industry the competition for qualified employees in these areas was intense. The American Heartland had never recovered from the Depression, unemployment continued to be high, and any new job opportunities would be welcomed. Since the cost of living in the area was low, the labor pool large, and labor unions nonexistent, there would not be pressure to increase wages, as there would be in the large industrial areas, where labor was scarce and labor unions strong. There was a strong work ethic among the people, and they would make good aircraft workers, as many had mechanical experience with cars, trucks, and farm equipment. Wichita also had a developed aircraft industry, as small firms such as Stearman, Cessna,

In October 1940, ground was broken and when the Boeing-Wichita project was completed it covered 2.8 million sqft totaling 86 million cuft over 185 acres and cost $26 million. The main assembly floor of Plant #2 covered 1.7 million sqft and the two main assembly lines were 750ft long and were covered by a 300ft roof covered with built-in windows to let in daylight. (USAF)

building B-17s. The RFC had been formed by President Herbert Hoover when the banks failed in 1929. Hoover appointed Houston businessman Jesse H. Jones to head the RFC, which was expanded by President Roosevelt during the Great Depression. Jones became one of the most powerful men in the financial world, and is credited with restoring the American economy. In 1939 Roosevelt appointed Jones as his Federal Loan Administrator (FLA), which managed the RFC. In 1940, when Roosevelt decided to expand America's war economy, he named Jones as his Secretary of Commerce, but also retained his position as head of the FLA. In the Act of June 25, 1940, Congress gave Jones and the RFC almost unlimited power in anything to do with the defense of America and its preparation for war. The RFC was authorized to build factories and shipyards, to stockpile essential supplies and materials, and to pay subsidies to control prices. Jones mobilized industry to make America the "arsenal of democracy" by establishing such subsidiaries as the Defense Plant Corporation and Defense Supplies Corporation. The Austin Co. of Cleveland was awarded a cost plus-fixed fee contract for the design and construction of Plant #2, and was handed virtual carte blanche for materials and equipment. In October 1940 ground was broken, and when the Boeing-Wichita project was completed it covered 2.8 million square feet, totaling 86 million cubic foot over 185 acres, and cost $26 million. The main assembly floor of Plant #2 covered 1.7 million square feet, and the two main assembly lines were 750ft long and were covered by a 300ft roof surfaced with built-in windows to let in daylight. By June 1941 the building was almost complete, and 3,000 workers were building B-17 parts that were shipped to Seattle and Los Angeles. Meanwhile $40 million in machinery and tooling for the B-29 project was being installed, and by August there were 14,000 employees in the plant; in September Boeing received a $215 million contract to manufacture 250 of the secret bombers. By the end of 1941 there were 22,000 employees, of which nearly 8,000 were women. Though few women had any previous mechanical experience, they were able to do most aircraft jobs, but tended to hold the less skilled factory and administrative—thus poorer salaried—jobs, and few rose to management, supervisory, or skilled positions. Many

and Beech had produced small personal aircraft and trainers for the Army and Navy. In early 1940 there was a base of 1,500 skilled and experienced aircraft workers in Wichita, most of whom worked for Stearman. The company became a wholly owned Boeing subsidiary in April 1938, and had built the PT-17 Stearman Kaydet trainer and B-17 parts. Even though 26,000 employees would be eventually hired, these core 1,500 would become the administrators, supervisors, and foremen of the Boeing-Wichita B-29 program. But the new Wichita plant would require more thousands of employees, and in cooperation with the U.S. Employment Service, Boeing recruiters scoured Midwestern towns and cities.

In September 1940 the U.S. Defense Plant Corporation (DPC), a subsidiary of the Reconstruction Finance Corporation (RFC), announced that it was going to finance Plant #2, a massive new factory that was to be built south of the Stearman factory, and was to be operated by Boeing, initially

Factory Assembly Line Procedure (Pima)

The aircraft multi-line system was introduced and instead of one long assembly line there were six groups of lines positioned near two or three final assembly lines that were located near the main doors. This is the reason that aircraft assembly plants are square and auto plants are long rectangles. The bomber's major components were prefabricated with all equipment in place. (USAF)

pay scales. However, workers were paid time and a half for every hour over 40 per week, but their wages were much less than in other defense industries. Shopping areas, highways and parking lots, schools, and housing were built for the influx of new workers. The Federal Housing Authority built 4,500 new homes, and private contractors built 1,500 more.

Boeing-Wichita was the first B-29 factory; it was the most efficient, and it rolled the first B-29 off its assembly lines. The Boeing-Wichita assembly line was fashioned after the innovative "multi-line assembly system" developed by Boeing's Chief of Production Engineering, Oliver West, that was used by Boeing, Douglas, and Lockheed-Vega to manufacture the B-17 in great quantity. This system utilized many of the aspects of the automobile assembly line, but adapted them for aircraft production. The long moving automotive assembly line, where parts were added to the moving chassis until the auto was completed, was not feasible for the manufacture of large and complex bombers. The size of the bomber—and the weight and size of its components—precluded workers reaching up and adding parts. More than 50 stations, and a labyrinth of movable ladders, hoists, and pulleys were required. Aluminum was more difficult and unforgiving to work with, as compared to auto steel, and aircraft tolerances were much more exacting than auto tolerances. The aircraft multi-line system was introduced, and instead of one long assembly line there were six groups of lines positioned near two or three final assembly lines that were located near the main doors. This is the reason that aircraft assembly plants are square and auto plants are long rectangles. The bomber's major components were prefabricated with all equipment in place. There were six main production lines: forward fuselage (nose) section; the center fuselage (bomb bays); the tail section (empennage); the center wing section that was built around the main wing spar; the engine and nacelles; and outboard wing and leading edge assemblies. Each assembly line was supplied parts from nearby shops via carts, forklifts, or conveyor belts. The forming and machine shops fabricated raw aluminum into parts with giant presses and

women were married and had children, and before they were hired they were required to supply a certificate stating that they had provided childcare. There was a high turnover rate among women, as after a 10 hour shift it was difficult to go home to their "duties" as wives and mothers. Unlike other aircraft workers around the country, Wichita workers put in grueling 10 hour shifts, seven days a week, with every other weekend off. There were two shifts, with the first beginning at 6AM and ending at 4:45PM, when the second shift began (it ended at 3:30AM). Both shifts had 45 minute lunch breaks. The majority of the workers were conservative Midwesterners who allowed Boeing to subjectively set job classifications and

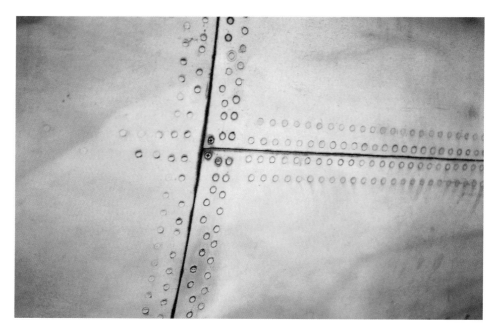

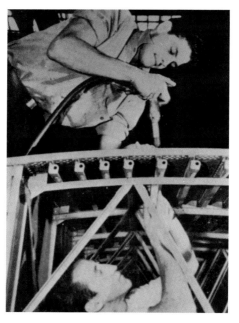

In the assembly and subassembly shops riveters used compressed air guns to hammer the rivets into place. Almost 20% of the workforce were riveters, the majority women. Riveters worked in pairs, a riveter and a bucker. The riveter placed the rivet through the pre-drilled hole in the metal and held a heavy air gun against the rivet head. The bucker placed a heavy steel bar on the other end of the rivet on the other side of the metal and held it there until the air gun squashed that end into a mushroom. The work was an extremely noisy and tedious job that demanded that each rivet was perfectly placed and the surrounding aluminum remain undamaged. (USAF)

cutting machines. Large drill presses cut holes for the thousands of rivets, screws, and bolts. In the assembly and subassembly shops riveters used compressed air guns to hammer the rivets into place. Almost 20% of the workforce was riveters, the majority women. Riveters worked in pairs, a riveter and a bucker. The riveter placed the rivet through the pre-drilled hole in the metal and held a heavy air gun against the rivet head. The bucker placed a heavy steel bar on the other end of the rivet on the other side of the metal and held it there until the air gun squashed that end into a mushroom. Riveting was an extremely noisy and tedious job that demanded that each rivet be perfectly placed and the surrounding aluminum remain undamaged. There was subassembly on equipment, such as instruments, control surfaces, landing gear, etc. When one of the six main sections was completed, large cranes lifted the piece to the final assembly bays. There were four rows of bombers moving through five stations as the six major sections were joined. Here the sections were bolted and riveted together, electrical wiring and control systems were connected, the propellers attached, and the landing gear lowered. At the height of production there were nearly 15,000 workers on the floor, coordinating the 55,000 parts with 600,000 rivets into a completed B-29. The completed bomber was thoroughly inspected and then pulled through the main doors, ready for flight-testing. Since the multi-line system was segmented into sections, it was easier to incorporate the multitude of changes and modifications than on a long, less flexible, auto-type assembly line. Nonetheless, changes could be costly and time consuming, and were often made off the assembly line. At one time during manufacture a change was required on semi-completed wings, and 1,200 assembly line workers were requisitioned to work on the open-air flight apron in the middle of winter to make the change. Another change required the resolder of thousands of plugs connecting the miles of wiring in the wing.

The first 100 B-29s off the production line required 157,000 man-hours to build, 78,000 for the next 100, and 57,000 for the third 100, but even as production efficiency increased, many bombers had to undergo thousands of man-hours of modifications once completed. By late 1944 the production time was down to 30,000 man-hours, but modifications continued, although on fewer aircraft and at much diminished man-hours.

By spring 1945 the B-29s that left the Wichita production line were combat ready without first going to modification centers. On Valentines Day 1945 the 1,000th bomber left Plant #2, and the 1,769 B-29s that Wichita built represented about 44% of the total B-29 production. While the B-29 plants at Omaha, Renton, and Marietta strained and failed to meet production goals in late 1943, the B-29 Committee asked Boeing-Wichita to increase production, and the Committee's confidence was rewarded. In November 1944 the Committee again looked to Boeing-Wichita for increased quality production. A fact that is forgotten is that Boeing-Wichita also built 10,346 PT-17 Trainers (44% of the total), a large number of the CG-4 gliders used in the Normandy D-Day invasion, and most of the B-29 spare parts. Boeing-Wichita was so efficient that it was awarded five Army and Navy E Awards, as compared to only 4% of all American defense plants receiving only one of these awards for production excellence.

Boeing-Seattle and Renton

Since wages were almost half of the cost of building an airplane Boeing was forced to keep wages low, and this gave Boeing a chronic bad reputation in the Seattle area for paying low wages. Until the cost-plus contracts of 1941, Boeing had to bid against its Southern California low wage competitors—Douglas, Lockheed, Consolidated, and North American—for military and commercial aviation fixed price contracts. Finally, in 1940 Boeing workers rebelled, and through a newly elected strong Machinist's Union demanded higher wages. Boeing was losing money on its fixed-price contracts and was nearly bankrupted, and only a government loan guarantee kept the company solvent, so Boeing could only refuse the union's demands. At the time there was a suspicion in America that Communists and other dissidents were behind the labor movement and its strikes in the attempt to keep America from rearming. Powerful factions in Seattle and Washington, D.C., were able to break the union; making Boeing's employees more resentful. "The word" got around, and Boeing had even more difficulties hiring new employees. After America officially entered the war the unions pledged not to strike for the duration.

After Pearl Harbor the government felt that wage increases would lead to national inflation, and throughout the war it kept a lid on aircraft

At the height of production there were nearly 15,000 workers on the B-W floor coordinating the 55,000 parts with 600,000 rivets into a completed B-29. The completed bomber was thoroughly inspected and then pulled through the main doors, ready for flight-testing and most likely modification. (USAF)

On Valentines Day 1945 the 1,000th bomber left B-W Plant #2, and the 1,769 B-29s that Wichita built represented about 44% of the total B-29 production. While the B-29 plants at Omaha, Renton, and Marietta strained and failed to meet production goals in late 1943, the B-29 Committee asked Boeing-Wichita to increase production, and their confidence was rewarded. (USAF)

worker's pay, as they comprised the largest portion of defense workers. The labor turnover rate at Boeing reached 100%, and to make matters worse, many young Boeing workers were drafted into the military. Boeing also had a high absentee rate (as high as 10%) that was fueled by worker bitterness over low wages and a general apathy. But the plain fact was that workers would rather work somewhere else. They trained at Boeing in some basic skill, and then moved on to a better paying job. The Seattle-Tacoma area had large shipyards, and the Navy and Maritime Commission handed out large orders that required a large labor force. Also, the top-secret Manhattan (Atomic Bomb) Project at Hanford, WA, engaged a large workforce. In this labor market, Boeing was paying 25% lower wages than other defense industries. The shipyards were paying $0.95 per hour, Boeing was paying $0.67, and both were outdone by Hanford, which was paying $1.00 per hour, plus travel costs, for day laborers

In March 1942 only 2% of Boeing's Seattle workforce consisted of women. In August 1944, of the 41,564 Boeing Seattle employees 54% were women, who did mainly unskilled and semi-skilled jobs. To relieve the labor demands on the Seattle plants the government built branch plants for B-17 subassemblies in the Puget Sound area: Tacoma (two plants), Everett, Bellingham, Chehalis, and Aberdeen. These plants would later be converted to B-29 subassembly plants. Despite its problems, Boeing-Seattle built 3,600 B-17s and spare parts by November 1943, when manufacture there was to be converted to B-29 production.

The main Boeing facility in Seattle was Plant #2, and was built by the government for $17.5 million for B-17 manufacture. It had been producing a Flying Fortress almost hourly, and needed to continue manufacturing a relatively large number of the bombers at a planned decelerating pace until exclusive B-29 manufacture was ready. In peacetime automobile manufacturers had retooled and converted from one model to another almost yearly, but they closed their factories to do so; Boeing did not have that luxury, as it had to maintain both B-17 and B-29 production schedules. The B-17 lines were to be reduced from three to two, and finally to one. The Seattle operation had the problem of forming two organizations from the existing B-17 lines. Each B-17 production element had to have an equivalent B-29 element. Almost all the usable floor space in the Seattle plant was consigned to B-17 production, as there were 239 B-17 jigs and

239 large new B-29 jigs. The Renton plant, switching from a production plant to an assembly plant, had to maintain its original B-29 contract schedules while giving up much of its fabrication jigs and machinery to Seattle and its satellite plants for subassembly.

The "Big Change," as it was called, was directed by Boeing VP Oliver West and operations manger R.A. Neale. A steering committee headed by Neale and staffed by upper management from Seattle and Renton handled departmental fine points. Factory General Manager J.J. Searle appointed Seattle Production Chief Les Spittler to deal with the problem of shifting B-17 personnel to the B-29 program without affecting the planned B-17 production schedule. Once workers were shifted to the B-29 line they had to be retrained. The changeover took over a year, and began by squeezing a B-29 jig here and there between the B-17 production lines; inch by inch and foot by foot the B-29 tooling took over. Three B-17 lines were reduced to two and then one, as floor space was made for the B-29. Searle directed the tooling engineers in moving the 175 new large jigs (113 for body sections and 62 for wings) and a further 64 large jigs from Renton, along with hundreds of smaller jigs that had to be crammed between the B-17 jigs and assembly lines. In the assembly areas, where there had once been long lines of B-17 jigs, the tails, fuselages, and wings of the B-29 could be seen. B-17 and B-29 parts were moving, side-by-side, out of the fabrication shops. The transport of the completed Seattle subassemblies to Renton met a problem when the existing route had a low overpass, and the alternate route was also inadequate. A new four-lane highway shortcut was built at the cost of $450,000 linking the Pacific Coast Highway out of Seattle to the Sunset Highway to Renton.

Initially the government Defense Plant Corporation built the Renton plant to produce large Navy patrol planes. The Navy traded the Renton plant to the AAF for their North American plant in Kansas City, where the B-25 was being built. The Renton plant was located about eight miles from Boeing's Seattle plant on Lake Washington, and was to be converted into a B-29 facility.

The Boeing-Renton plant measured 1,100ft x 900ft and 1.7 million square feet, and cost $22.5 million, plus $2.5 million more for the adjacent runways. The Navy seaplanes to be built there would have taken off from the adjacent water, and initially plans were considered to move the com-

The Boeing-Renton plant measured 1,100ft x 900ft and 1.7 million sqft and cost $22.5 million plus $2.5 million more for the adjacent runways. The plant was located about eight miles from Boeing's Seattle plant. (USAF)

The Renton plant (BN) was originally built by the government Defense Plant Corporation to produce large Navy patrol planes. The Navy traded the Renton plant to the AAF for their North American plant in Kansas City where the B-25 was being built. The Navy seaplanes to be built there would have taken off from the adjacent water and initially the completed B-29s were moved by barge to the Air Base at Sands Point. (USAF)

The main Boeing facility in Seattle Plant #2, which had been built by the government for $17.5 million, ceased B-17 production, and slowly began tooling up for the B-29. The "Big Change," as it was called, had to find space for the B-29 jigs without interfering with B-17 production. Personnel had to be juggled, as too many workers could not be transferred off the B-17 production line without interfering with its production schedules. (USAF)

pleted B-29s by barge to the Air Base at Sands Point to save on building the expensive concrete runways. To ease congestion the work shifts were staggered, with the first shift's start split between 6:30AM and 7:30AM, and ending when the second shift started between 3:00PM and 4:00PM. A maintenance and cleanup crew started at 11:30PM and 12:30AM. The government financed and developed Boeing Town to be built near the Renton plant. This planned community of 3,000 houses, apartments, and dormitory units, along with transportation, shopping, and health care facilities made Renton more appealing to workers. Boeing VP Fred Laudan, who had supervised the Model 299 (the B-17 precursor), supervised the Renton factory program.

Originally, Renton had been set up to produce complete B-29s, but Boeing production engineers estimated that Renton could turn out twice as many B-29s if it utilized its four production lines as a massive assembly line using subassemblies and parts from outside subcontractors. The bomber subassemblies were to arrive at Renton from Boeing-Seattle and its six (later eight) branch plants. B-29 production planning commenced in July 1942 with the target date set for the first bomber, one year later, in July 1943, with a production rate set at 35 per month. The reality was that Renton B-29s experienced long delays, and the first Renton B-29 came off the production line in January 1944. Renton's problem, along with labor troubles, was that it had to maintain production schedules while giving up much of its fabrication machinery and most of its jigs to Seattle and its branch plants. Ironically, the Boeing-Seattle plant was running at full capacity, turning out B-17s mostly on schedule from 1942 through the "Big Change." However, the death of Boeing President Philip Johnson in November 1944 came at a very bad time, as he had directed the company into becoming the foremost builder of heavy bombers.

The most important reason that the Renton plant never filled its potential was due to a shortage of personnel, ranging from supervisory, engineering, and most significantly, factory workers. In August 1944 Renton employed about 7,500 people working on the B-29: 2,550 women and 2,010 men on the production line; and the remainder (about 2,900) were mostly women in menial administrative jobs. By September 1944 Renton faced a shortage of 4,000 workers that were needed to bring B-29 production to

intended quantities, and to compensate for the continual high absentee and "I quit" rates. Toward the end of 1944 it seemed that the war would soon be over, and since Boeing could not guarantee post-war jobs many aircraft workers quit and looked for jobs that had post-war prospects. Boeing-Renton never was able to fully resolve its labor problems, and B-29 production schedules there were never met; the plant remained months behind schedule. The saving grace of the Renton labor situation was that the changeover from B-17 production to B-29 production was occurring at a time when the women and men at the plant became more efficient.

Employment at all the Boeing Washington state plants crested at 45,000 in February 1945. The Renton plant grew from one 500-man factory to a four-plant 10,000 man (2,500 women) facility, while the other 35,000 worked on all Boeing aircraft projects (e.g. B-29 subassemblies, the C-97 cargo plane, the B-50 bomber, Stratocruiser airliner, and the XB-47 jet medium bomber). Initially, Boeing-Renton was contracted for $700 million to build 1,535 B-29s from October 1944 to September 1945 using mostly in-house manufactured subassemblies. The government cut this figure to 1,065, and it was doubtful that even this quantity could be met; finally, Renton was reduced to manufacturing only a few spare parts and the center wing section, and the plant was used for final assembly of the bomber with outside supplied subassemblies and parts. The B-17 Puget Sound branch plants tooled up to feed B-29 parts to Renton, and later another B-29 branch factory was built at Everett, and two more at Hoquiam. Bomb bay sections were built at a factory in Vancouver, British Columbia, that had produced the PBY Catalina for the Canadian government. The bomb bays were shipped 150mi daily via trucks to Renton. Parts and subassemblies manufactured by these branch factories and other subcontractors were intended to alleviate the demands on Renton B-29 subassembly production, and to facilitate Renton as an assembly plant only. Despite these subcontracted parts, the Renton plant was unable to supply the quantity of on-time B-29s it promised, and the Air Force had to rely on Boeing-Wichita and Martin-Omaha for a reliable supply of new bombers to meet its B-29 training schedule, and consequently its combat timetable. By July 1945 Renton was assembling 160 B-29s per month, more than any other B-29 factory, but because subcontracted components made up these B-29s they needed to spend more time on average at the modification centers. Once at the modification center in Denver the Renton-built (and also Bell-Marietta-built) B-29s took longer to modify than the Wichita-built B-29s, which no longer required modification as they rolled off the assembly lines into combat. During the war Boeing-Renton/Seattle produced a total of 1,119 B-29s, exceeding the 1,065 required by the reduced second contract. On 5 September 1945, despite plans to continue B-29 production after the war, the government canceled all new B-29 production at Renton, and would accept only those already on the assembly lines. Boeing laid off 21,000 of its labor force almost overnight and closed its branch factories, leaving only 8,400 employees.

Martin-Omaha

Except for an existing aircraft industry, Omaha had similar qualifications as Wichita for building a huge new aircraft complex. Nebraska Senior Senator George Norris, supported by Nebraska lobbyists and other delegates, approached President Roosevelt to present their case for building an aircraft factory in Omaha. In December 1940 it was announced that the Glenn L. Martin Company of Baltimore would manage and produce the B-26 Marauder twin-engined medium bomber at a new factory at Fort Crook Army Base, near the town of Bellevue, south of Omaha. The Army Corps of Engineers built aircraft Assembly Plant #1 for an eventual cost of $20 million. Plant D, the final assembly plant, providing floor space of 1.2 million square feet, was the largest building, costing $10 million. It was a duplicate of Martin's Baltimore plant, which had been designed by celebrated industrial architect Albert Kahn.

The 3,500 Army Corps of Engineers construction workers completed the facility's structures in October 1941, but Martin was delayed in starting production by difficulties in setting up machine tools and jigs. The first B-26 was not completed until August 1942, and it was not until the end of that year that the production schedule was met. The B-26, with its high aspect, narrow wing and powerful engines, was difficult for inexperienced pilots to fly, and was given the nickname "Widow Maker" by both its young pilots and the news media. The Air Force, recognizing the pessimistic publicity generated by the bomber, decided to phase out Omaha B-26 production in April 1943 (after 1,536 had been built), and convert the plant and its subcontractors to B-29 production. In October 1943, an initial $90 million was consigned to Martin-Omaha to retool for the B-29 and purchase supplies and materials. The B-29 conversion was to be completed while B-26 manufacture was being phased out. To aid in this conversion, the U.S. Employment Service and National Youth Administration worked with the local high schools and vocational schools and Martin to train thousands of mainly teens and young men and women to acquire the new skills to be

The last of the high quality 536 Martin B-29-MOs came off the assembly line on 19 July 1945 with its undersides painted for night missions. (USAF)

used at the Martin factory. Changes had to made to the factory's structure. Roof trusses were too low to accommodate the B-29 and were raised. The main doors were also too low, but rather than modify them tractors pulled the completed bombers out of the doors with their nose wheels jacked up three feet, which lowered the tail enough to pass through the doors.

Martin was contracted to complete the first B-29 in June 1944, and by August there was to be a production rate of 20 per month. Martin actually produced the first B-29 a month early, despite delays in the fall of 1943 that threatened the program when Martin, its subcontractors, and the Air Force ran into snags. Martin took over the Fisher-Cleveland B-29 contracts and obligations, and Fisher's subcontractors were worried about their exposure in what, at the time, seemed to be a failing B-29 program. They wanted Martin to rewrite the Fisher contracts to protect themselves with assurances from Martin and the government. These demands caused endless legal snarls and slowed the transfer of the Fisher contracts to Martin. The Air Force, already disenchanted with the Martin B-26 program and exasperated with the B-29 delays, alleged that Martin management was playing for time in order to see if the faltering B-29 program was to continue. The AAF thought the Martin management was much too conservative and needed to be more aggressive in getting its program underway again. Finally, Martin and the Fisher subcontractors received reassurances from the government, and by November 1943 employment peaked and leveled at 14,500 workers, with 40% being women. Martin began production after Boeing-Wichita and Bell-Marietta, and was able to learn from them and more easily correct mistakes. Like Boeing-Renton, only the cen-

Plant D, the final Martin assembly plant, provided floor space of 1.2 million sqft and was the largest building at the Omaha facility. Shown is the first Martin B-29, *Satan's Angel* (444BG), rolling off the line in May 1944. (USAF)

ter wing sections were manufactured at Martin-Omaha, and the plant functioned mainly as an assembly point of B-29 components that were subcontracted. Chrysler-Detroit built nose sections, nacelles, center wing flaps, and wing leading edges, and transferred them to Omaha via rail. Hudson Motor-Detroit built the rear pressurized fuselage sections and tail section, while Goodyear-Akron built the bomb bay sections. J.I. Case Tractor and Farm Equipment Company built the outer wing panels, wing tips, and ailerons, as well as the tail assembly, which included the rudder, dorsal, and vertical fin.

Martin-Omaha employees seemed to be more dedicated and motivated to their jobs than in the other B-29 plants because of better working and living conditions. The Martin-Omaha venture was relatively smaller than other B-29 factories, and the demand for housing and services was less. Consequently, the cost of living in the area was lower, and aircraft wages were relatively higher compared to other area wages. Martin-Omaha workers celebrated when their first B-29, named *Satan's Angels*, rolled off the production line a month early. Martin was "rewarded" by the Air Force for its early delivery with a request to increase production. Martin was able to comply despite the familiar B-29 production problems of equipment and material shortages, and the constant design changes and modifications. By early 1945 55 bombers per month were being produced by Martin-Omaha, and these needed far fewer modifications than B-29s from other plants. In 1945 Martin-Omaha employed 13,217 workers: 11,019 in the main production plant, and 2,198 in the modification center. Included in this total were 5,306 women and 765 African Americans. There were 682 inspectors and 127 supervisors and technicians. The plant received the highest recommendations for its quality control from the Air Force, and was awarded the Army-Navy "E" Award four times. Martin Company President J.T. Hartson stated:

"The Martin Company was one of the first to adopt the statistical method of quality control of parts by using visual charts to indicate problem areas. We've taught our employees to make planes, we've trained them, and they have been willing to learn. We have surrounded them with tools and procedures so that they make few mistakes. And those that do occur are caught by inspectors."

Because of their high quality aircraft Martin-Omaha was selected by the AAF for the top-secret *Silver Plate Project* to furnish the modified bombers to carry atomic bomb. The 10,000lb, 10ft, 8in long, 5ft wide atomic bombs were designed specifically to fit into the B-29. The bomb bays were modified, all armament except the tail guns was removed, the gunner's blisters were covered by steel plates, and fuel injection and reversible props were added. Martin produced 36 of these "A-bombers," including the *Enola Gay* and *BOCK's CAR*, the B-29s that bombed Hiroshima (6 August) and Nagasaki (9 August 1945).

Martin-Omaha continued to assemble B-29s from components supplied by subcontractors and modifying B-29s from other plants through the summer of 1945. By the end of the war Martin-Omaha had built 536 quality B-29s, but a month after the war ended 15,000 workers were laid off, and Plant D was mothballed and became a storage center for surplus machine tools. Presently it is part of Offutt AFB, which until 1991 was headquarters of the Strategic Air Command.

Bell-Marietta

The B-29 program was well under way after the Japanese attacked Pearl Harbor, and two weeks after the attack Gen. Arnold contacted Larry Bell, the president of Bell Aircraft Company of Buffalo, NY, to ask him to manage the huge new B-29 plant planned for Atlanta. The dynamic Bell seemed to be a good choice, as he was a respected aircraft designer, manufacturer, and executive whose company was able to meet its commitments while others failed. Bell signed a cost-plus-fixed-fee contract that paid his company to manage and operate the finished government-built plant under an operating lease. Bell and his team moved ahead assuredly and quickly. On New Year's Day 1942 Bell flew to Seattle, accompanied by a team from Fisher to discuss the project with Boeing. The following week Bell sent managers and lawyers to Atlanta to scout plant locations and collect estimates on site, construction, equipment, and labor costs.

In 1940 Atlanta was not a major contender for the new B-29 factories, as it was felt the city was too close to the Atlantic and Gulf Coasts and vulnerable to enemy air attacks. By the time America was at war, Atlanta was one of the few inland locations available with a large enough workforce to accommodate a large plant. Bell executives and the Site Selection Committee of the Army Corps of Engineers agreed that the site for Government Assembly Plant #6 should be a large tract of land near the towns of Marietta and Kennesaw Mountain, about 20mi northwest of Atlanta. This site was chosen because of the low land costs, high unemployment in the area, and the proximity of rail transportation.

After Bell—whose Buffalo plant manufactured the small P-39 fighter—toured the Boeing-Wichita B-29 plant and several B-17 and B-24 facilities, he realized that he had bitten off more than the Bell Aircraft Company could chew. The Marietta production schedule was scaled down to 40 B-29s per month and to a total of 400 bombers, which was still very ambitious. To accomplish this goal the factory would have to be virtually complete in 11 months—by New Years 1943—with trained workers on hand, assembly lines ready, and the tools, jigs, and equipment in place. Standing in the way was the fact that there was little data for engineering and tooling the B-29, and the data that was available was ambiguous and

In late March 1942, the Corps of Engineers was to supervise the construction of the huge Bell-Atlanta (BA) plant for the Defense Plant Corporation, and they did so without sparing costs. They hired Robert & Company to manage plant design and construction. Initially, plans called for a 2.2 million sqft plant, but soon that figure was increased to 3.96 million sqft. By 1944, $47 million taxpayer dollars had been spent on the plant, its equipment, and adjacent runways. (USAF)

incomplete. There also were acute shortages of aluminum, steel, and machine tools.

In late March 1942 the Corps of Engineers supervised the construction of the huge plant for the Defense Plant Corporation, and they did so without sparing costs. They hired Robert & Company to manage plant design and construction. Initially, plans called for a 2.2 million square feet plant, but soon that figure was increased to 3.96 million square feet. By 1944, $47 million government dollars had been spent on the plant, its equipment, and adjacent runways. Since there was the fear of enemy air attacks the plant was to be a "black out" plant with no windows, and thus no natural ventilation, which meant the installation of fluorescent lighting and expensive air conditioning. Robert & Co. promised to have part of the plant ready for the installation of the assembly line by September 1942. The company worked with the B-29 Committee in Seattle to speed the process along. Bell engineers and advisors worked seven-day weeks to plan assembly line layout, and to design the tools and jigs. In May 1942 Bell was officially awarded $342 million to turn out 400 B-29s and spares by January 1945. The first B-29 was optimistically to come off the production lines in less than a year and a half, in September 1943, with an ambitious production target of 65 per month by June 1944. Bell-Marietta was to build the center wing sections, all fuselage pieces and most installations, 69% of its parts and components, and also supply some subassemblies to other B-29 factories. By the end of June 1942 the building was only 3% completed, and Bethlehem Steel could not supply the 32,000 tons of steel frame because of the national shortage. It became obvious that Plant #6 would not be ready until March or April 1943, and the runways not until July. In addition to the plant construction problems, Bell faced the problem of building the aircraft itself. Boeing had promised that by June it would supply manufacturing data, the master gauges and production templates for the tools, presses, and cutting machines that made the myriad of B-29 parts that numbered in the tens of thousands. Boeing, however, did not deliver on much of the promised data, gauges, templates, and machinery. Bell was supposed to manufacture the main wing spar, but had no data on the amounts of material needed, or which parts were to be ordered. Soon animosity developed between Bell, Boeing, and the other companies on the B-29 Committee, and the Air Force blamed Bell for the delays. The Army Corps of Engineers wanted the 700 Bell engineers designing the B-29 tools and jigs to be moved to Marietta, and more be hired to work on the project. Bell requested that the delivery date for the first B-29 be pushed back to December 1943.

Finally, by March 1943, with an army of 5,000 construction workers the plant had been 90% completed. Bell moved many of its executives from Buffalo to expedite the project, and hired consultants from Detroit to advise on production engineering. But Bell was only able to provide 3,000 engineers to work on tooling and production of the first B-29. But also by March 1943 only 40% of the production equipment, machinery, and tools were in place, as Bell was unable to purchase even basic machinery and equipment because of the national demand. Because of the lack of machinery and tooling Bell attempted to fabricate a single B-29 by hand! Because of the delays at the Marietta plant the War Production Board downgraded Bell's demands for the scarce aluminum and steel supplies that were being gobbled up by the American war machine. Bell was now five months behind a schedule that had already been extended, and then Boeing sent engineering changes to further upset the schedule.

It seemed as though the entire B-29 project was on the verge of failure. The B-29 Committee held Boeing primarily responsible for the crisis, as the company had yet to deliver production plans and data and templates. Wright was also cited as a guilty party, in that the R-3350 remained a disappointment. Bell was not immune to criticism, as its engineering department used time-consuming methods called "lofting," in transferring data from Boeing blueprints to metal presses and cutting machines to make parts. Bell draftsmen drew B-29 parts to full size on large sheets of paper, then photographed them and reproduced them on metal templates, a chore that was made worse by the shortage of skilled draftsmen. The B-29 Committee demanded that Boeing supply Bell with the templates from Wichita to get back on schedule and that Bell use them. Bell, nonetheless, insisted that their lofting blueprint transferal method was superior and would produce better templates than Boeing's, and stubbornly continued to use it. To get the Bell B-29s back on schedule, the first few aircraft were to be assembled mainly from parts and components from Wichita. But when the fuselage sections arrived from Wichita they could not be fitted to those built at Marietta due to the incompatibility of Bell's superior templates with Boeing's! To speed production the AAF then permitted Bell to disregard design changes and modifications on its first 25 B-29s, which were to be sent to directly to modification centers.

By July 1943 Plant #6 was essentially completed, and 70% of its tooling was ready, but by this time there were no workers available, as those in the surrounding labor force had found jobs elsewhere, or had been drafted. The South's farms and textile mills prospered, and there was a great building boom that took many workers. Some 40,000 workers would be required at the Bell-Marietta plant, and since surrounding Cobb County only had a population of 35,000, workers would have to be drawn from nearby counties and Atlanta. It would be almost impossible to recruit workers to move to the Marietta area, much less have them commute, as transportation and gasoline were scarce. The government's anti-inflation policy, which did not allow the nation's aircraft companies to raise wages to compete with other industries, did not help matters. The 8,000 workers at the plant in the summer of 1943 complained of the low pay and poor supervision, rumors of which filtered down to the local populace. The government launched a large-scale public relations campaign directed mainly to the unexploited pool of local women. The campaign had as its agenda the appeal to their patriotic duty to make the plant a success to win the war while their men were off fighting the good fight. Transportation facilities were improved, and a four-lane highway was built between Marietta and Atlanta. Incentives included day care services, paid training programs, inexpensive cafeterias, and nightshift bonuses to make working at Bell-Marietta more appealing. In late 1943 the War Manpower Commission and U.S. Employment Service assumed Bell's hiring and labor relations function, and in November 3,379 new workers were hired. By the end of 1944, 17,200 workers were employed at Plant #6, working two nine-hour shifts, seven days a week. The labor force peaked at 27,000 in the spring of 1945.

The large new labor force was finally in place, but it had little to do, and when it did do something, the product suffered from inexperience and poor supervision. Bell continued to have data transferal (template) and tooling problems, and the incessant design changes further delayed the Bell B-29 program. The AAF wanted to reduce Marietta's production program and transfer its supplies and materials that were in short supply to other plants, especially the efficient Wichita plant. Larry Bell spent as much time defending his company's name as he did fighting the threat of production program reductions, and the persuasive Bell managed to garner another $200 million for 300 more B-29s! But Bell was again to bite off more than his company could chew, as his Buffalo plants were tooling up for the P-63 King Cobra and were contracted to develop America's first jet fighter, the XP-59. On 4 November the first "hand-made" Marietta B-29 was completed, and more slowly rolled off the assembly lines. The first 15 were mostly hand-made from components and parts from other factories, and all needed to spend long stretches in modification. Once in full production, most of the Bell B-29s were "stripped-down" versions requiring extensive modifications at other facilities. In July 1944 the Chairman of the Aircraft Production Board, Charles E. Wilson, went on record as being "keenly disappointed with Bell," and the Air Force's Office of Flying Safety found Bell-Marietta's B-29s to be "far below the standards required for aircraft used in combat." It would not be until mid-1945 that Bell was able to incorporate over half of the required modifications into its assembly lines and produce a higher quality aircraft.

In January 1945, after building 357 B-29s, Bell was contracted to exclusively build the B-29B, which was essentially a APQ-7 Eagle radar-carrying bomber, stripped of various radio and electrical equipment, with decreased weight, increased speed, and bomb carrying capacity. Between February and May 1945 Bell sent the stripped "B" bombers to the Oklahoma City Air Depot for installation of electronic equipment; however, by the beginning of May Bell was able to produce a complete aircraft. The B-29B will be discussed later. Finally, by March 1945 Bell-Marietta got its assembly lines to run efficiently, with the workweek reduced to five days and weekends off. It was able to produce a B-29B (albeit still of inferior quality compared to Boeing and Martin B-29s) for $240,000—the cost of a 1940 B-17—and again Bell received a contract on a fixed price basis of $240,000 for 500 more of its troubled B-29s! By June 1945, as the war progressed in the Allies' favor there was a high quitting rate by the Marietta work force, which went to different non-defense related jobs. But remaining worker efficiency kept production high until the late summer of 1945, when Marietta B-29 production and work force was significantly cut, and eventually 358 B-29Bs were produced when production was ceased in September 1945. Despite orders for large numbers of additional B-29s (800 over the original 400) that the persuasive Larry Bell had garnered, only 668 B-29s were built at the large and expensive Marietta facility, and these required extensive modifications during much of the production run.

Plant #6 was closed in 1946, and the AAF used it as a warehouse for machine tools and industrial equipment that were sold to private industry at mere pennies on the dollar. During the Korean War Lockheed reopened the plant. Since then it has become the hub of the aerospace and high tech industry in the South, and a boon to the southern economy. Lockheed has built the B-47 bomber and large military transports, such as the C-130 Hercules, C-141 Starlifter, and C-5 Galaxy. The Lockheed F-22 Raptor fighter is scheduled to be produced in Plant #6.

Fisher-Cleveland

In February 1942 plans for the General Motors Fisher-Cleveland plant were conceived, and within 24 days ground was broken for Fisher's B-29 factory. The Fisher plant was to manufacture 200 bombers, but that order was changed when the new Fisher Cleveland plant was scheduled to build the P-75 fighter. The Bell Marietta plant was scheduled to be ready to turn out

65 B-29s in September 1943, and Fisher was to supply subassemblies to it from its other plants. Fisher's six-story peacetime auto body plant, which employed 9,000 workers, was being converted to manufacture B-29 engine nacelles, and its Michigan plants in Detroit, Grand Rapids, and Lansing were to gear up to build B-29 subassemblies.

Modification Centers

As discussed previously, once a B-29 rolled off the production line it was not ready to be flown directly into combat, as these early production B-29s were virtually test B-29s, and many immediate changes were ordered. Since it was not efficient to make these changes on the assembly lines without upsetting production schedules, the AAF set up modification centers to make them. These changes would later be incorporated into production lines. Four centers were set up: two stand-alone centers located at Birmingham and Denver, and two others associated with the B-29 factories at Omaha and Marietta. Out of 1,000 proposed changes, about two-thirds were incorporated in the B-29, as many proposed changes were rejected because they did not warrant the replacement of a piece of equipment that was "good enough." In mid-October 1944 there were 148 scheduled changes to be made on the B-29s being completed at the four different factories. The new Boeing-Renton plant had the most changes with 75, followed by Boeing-Wichita with 31—19 on the Bell models and 18 on the Martin Omaha versions. In December 1944 the average time to modify a Renton B-29 at Birmingham was a costly 30,000 man-hours, but this figure was reduced to less than 10,000 hours in May 1945, as Renton became more efficient. The Bell models had the low number of ordered changes, because the production line problems there caused them to be pushed out of the factory and sent directly to modification centers.

B-29 Contracts

Designation	Number	Contract #	Date of Approval
XB-29-BO	2	AC 15429	09/06/40
XB-29-BO	1	AC-15429*	12/14/40
		*Amended	
YB-29-BW	14	AC 19673	06/16/41
B-29-1-BW	50	AC19673	09/06/41
B-29-5-BW	50	AC19673	09/06/41
B-29-10-BW	50	AC19673	09/06/41
B-29-15-BW	50	AC19673	09/06/41
B-29-20-BW	50	AC19673	09/06/41
B-29-25-BW	50	AC19673	01/31/42
B-29-30-BW	50	AC19673	01/31/42
B-29-35-BW	50	AC19673	01/31/42
B-29-40-BW	100	AC19673	01/31/42
B-29-45-BW	100	AC19673	01/31/42
B-29-50-BW	100	AC19673	01/31/42
B-29-55-BW	50	AC19673	01/31/42
B-29-1-BA	14	AC27730	07/19/44
B-29-5-BA	16	AC27730	07/19/44
B-29-10-BA	20	AC27730	07/19/44
B-29-15-BA	50	AC27730	07/19/44
B-29-20-BA	50	AC27730	07/19/44
B-29-25-BA	50	AC27730	07/19/44
B-29-30-BA	29	AC27730	07/19/44

B-29B-30-BA	41	AC27730	07/19/44
B-29B-35-BA	70	AC27730	07/19/44
B-29B-40-BA	45	AC27730	07/19/44
B-29-40-BA	4	AC27730	07/19/44
B-29B-40-BA	12	AC27730	07/19/44
B-29-1-MO	1	AC117	06/30/44
B-29-5-MO	7	AC117	06/30/44
B-29-10-MO	8	AC117	06/30/44
B-29-15-MO	16	AC117	06/30/44
B-29-20-MO	28	AC117	06/30/44
B-29-25-MO	50	AC117	06/30/44
B-29-30-MO	69	AC117	06/30/44
B-29-35-MO	18	AC117	06/30/44
B-29A-1-BN	20	AC19673	09/19/42
B-29A-5-BN	30	AC19673	09/19/42
B-29A-10-BN	50	AC19673	09/19/42
B-29A-15-BN	50	AC19673	09/19/42
B-29A-20-BN	50	AC19673	09/19/42
B-29A-25-BN	50	AC19673	09/19/42
B-29A-30-BN	50	AC19673	09/19/42
B-29-35-MO	67	AC117	06/30/44
B-29-40-MO	33	AC117	06/30/44
B-29A-35-BN	100	AC19673	06/30/44
B-29A-40-BN	100	AC19673	06/30/44
B-29A-45-BN	100	AC19673	06/30/44
B-29A-50-BN	100	AC19673	06/30/44
B-29A-55-BN	100	AC19673	06/30/44
B-29A-60-BN	100	AC19673	06/30/44
B-29A-65-BN	100	AC19673	06/30/44
B-29A-70-BN	100	AC19673	06/30/44
B-29A-75-BN	19	AC19673	06/30/44
B-29-55-BW	50	AC19673	06/13/44
B-29-60-BW	100	AC19673	06/13/44
B-29-65-BW	100	AC19673	06/13/44
B-29-70-BW	100	AC19673	06/13/44
B-29-75-BW	100	AC19673	06/13/44
B-29-80-BW	50	AC19673	06/13/44
B-29B-40-BA	5	AC27730	07/19/44
B-29-40-BA	1	AC27730	07/19/44
B-29B-45-BA	42	AC27730	07/19/44
B-29-45-BA	25	AC27730	07/19/44
B-29B-50-BA	23	AC27730	07/19/44
B-29-50-BA	23	AC27730	07/19/44
B-29B-55-BA	24	AC27730	07/19/44
B-29-55-BA	24	AC27730	07/19/44
B-29B-60-BA	24	AC27730	07/19/44
B-29-60-BA	23	AC27730	07/19/44
B-29B-65-BA	25	AC27730	07/19/44
B-29-65-BA	24	AC27730	07/19/44
B-29-40-MO	35	AC117	06/09/44

B-29-45-MO	39	AC117	06/09/44
B-29-50-MO	55	AC117	06/09/44
B-29-55-MO	55	AC117	06/09/44
B-29-60-MO	48	AC117	06/09/44
B-29-80-BW	50	AC19673	06/30/44
B-29-85-BW	50	AC19673	06/30/44
B-29-86-BW	50	AC19673	06/30/44
B-29-90-BW	50	AC19673	06/30/44
B-29-90-BW	50	AC19673	01/13/45
B-29-95-BW	65	AC19673	01/13/45
B-29-96-BW	20	AC19673	01/13/45
B-29-97-BW	15	AC19673	01/13/45
B-29-100-BW	30	AC19673	01/13/45

BO=Boeing Seattle   BW=Boeing-Wichita   BN=Boeing-Renton
MO=Martin Omaha   BA=Bell Atlanta

B-29 Designation and Serial Numbers

The three **XB**s were the prototype models all built by Boeing Seattle (**BO**). The 14 **YB**s were the service test aircraft all built by Boeing-Wichita (**BW**). The B-29 was the production model built by Boeing-Wichita (**BW**), Bell-Atlanta (**BA**), and Martin-Omaha (**MO**). The B-29A was built exclusively by Boeing-Renton (**BN**), while the B-29B was built exclusively by **BA**. Production was in "Block" numbers (e.g. B-29-**45**-BW was a B-29 of Block **45** out of the Boeing-Wichita (BW) plant, while the B-29A-**40**-BN was one of the 100 B-29A models of Block **40** built by the Boeing-Renton (BN) factory). The Block designations indicated variations in the aircraft, starting with Block -1, and then increasing in increments of five. Boeing-Wichita reached Block –100, and Martin and Bell reached –60 and –65 respectively. For example, the Wright R-3350-41 engine replaced the R-3350-23 in the Block –50 Boeing B-29s, while both Bell and Martin installed them on their Block –20 B-29s.

Between the World Wars, when a basic aircraft model was changed the Army assigned it an alphabet letter after the model number (e.g. the P-12E became the P-12F). As World War II began the Army realized that, with the rapid and numerous changes to aircraft models, they would soon run out of letters, and in early 1942 implemented the Block Number System. In this system the series letter was continued, and adding dash numbers to the aircraft designation denoted changes. These were assigned in consecutive blocks grouped in fives after beginning with –1 (e.g. B-29-5-BW, B-29-10-BW, B-29-15-BW, etc.) The reason for the five skipping was to permit for field or factory modifications of the designated dash numbered model. A B-29-1-BW modified significantly in the field or factory would become the B-29-2-BW, while a modified B-29-10-BW would become the B-29-11-BW. Block numbers at Wichita B-29s reached B-29-100-BW (BW=Boeing-Wichita); at Renton they reached B-29-75-BN (BN=Boeing-Renton); at Bell-Marietta they reached B-29-65-BA (BA=Bell-Marietta); and at Martin-Omaha they reached B-29-60-MO (MO=Martin-Omaha). The block numbers of one manufacturer did not reflect the same changes in the same block number of another manufacturer.

Designation	# Built	Serial Numbers
XB-29-BO	2	41-002/-003
XB-29-B0	1	41-18335
YB-29-BW	14	41-36954/-36967
		(41-36954 to XB-39)
B-29-1-BW	17	42-6205/-6221 (1st production B-29s)
B-29-1-BA	1	42-6222 (1st Bell B-29)
B-29-1-BW	1	42-6223
B-29-1-BA	1	42-6224
B-29-1-BW	4	42-6225/-6228
B-29-1-MO	4	42-6229/-6232 (1st Martin B-29s)
B-29-1-BA	1	42-6233
B-29-1-BW	1	42-6234
B-29-1-BA	1	42-6235
B-29-1-BW	1	42-6236
B-29-1-MO	1	42-6237
B-29-1-BW	5	42-6238/-6242
B-29-1-BA	1	42-6243
B-29-1-BW	11	42-6234/-6254
B-29-5-BW	50	42-6255/-6304
B-29-10-BW	50	42-6305/-6354
B-29-15-BW	50	42-6355/-6404
B-29-20-BW	50	42-6405/-6454
B-29-25-BW	50	42-24420/-24469
B-29-30-BW	50	42-24470/-24519
B-29-35-BW	50	42-24520/-24569
B-29-40-BW	100	42-24570/-24669
B-29-45-BW	100	42-24670/-24769
B-29-50-BW	100	42-24770/-24869
B-29-55-BW	50	42-24870/-24919
B-29-1-BA	14	42-63352/-63365
B-29-5-BA	16	42-63366/-63381
B-29-10-BA	20	42-63382/-63401
B-29-15-BA	50	42-63402/-63451
B-29-20-BA	50	42-63452/-63501
B-29-25-BA	50	42-63502/-63551
B-29-30-BA	29	42-63552/-63580
B-29B-30-BA	41	42-63581/-63621 (1st B-29s)
B-29B-35-BA	70	42-63622/-63691
B-29B-40-BA	45	42-63692/-63736
B-29-40-BA	1	42-63737
B-29B-40-BA	6	42-63738/-63743
B-29-40-BA	1	42-63744
B-29B-40-BA	5	42-63745/-63749
B-29-40-BA	1	42-63750
B-29B-40-BA	1	42-63751
B-29-1-MO	3	42-65202/-65204
B-29-5-MO	7	42-65205/-65211
B-29-10-MO	8	42-65212/-65219
B-29-15-MO	16	42-65220/-65235
B-29-20-MO	28	42-65236/-65263
B-29-25-MO	50	42-65264/-65313 (42-65314 canceled)
B-29-30-MO	69	42-65315/-65383
B-29-35-MO	18	42-65384/-65401
B-29A-1-BN	20	42-93824/-93843

Designation	# Built	Serial Numbers
		(1st B-29As & 1st Renton B-29s)
B-29A-5-BN	30	42-93844/-93873
		(42-93845 to XB-44 program)
B-29A-10-BN	50	42-93874/-93923
B-29A-15-BN	50	42-93924/-93973
B-29A-20-BN	50	42-93974/-93023
B-29A-25-BN	50	42-93024/-93073
B-29A-30-BN	50	42-93074/-93123
B-29-35-MO	67	44-27259/-27325
B-29-40-MO	33	44-27326/-27358
B-29-35-BN	100	44-61510/-61609
B-29A-40-BN	100	44-61610/-61709
B-29A-45-BN	100	44-61710/-61809
B-29A-50-BN	100	44-61810/-61909
B-29A-55-BN	100	44-61910/-62009
B-29A-60-BN	100	44-62010/-62109
B-29A-65-BN	100	44-62110/-62209
B-29A-70-BN	100	44-62210/-62309
B-29A-75-BN	19	44-62310/-62328
B-29-55-BW	50	44-69655/-69704
B-29-60-BW	100	44-69705/-69804
B-29-65-BW	100	44-69805/-69904
B-29-70-BW	100	44-69905/-70004
B-29-75-BW	100	44-70005/-70104
B-29-80-BW	50	44-70105/-70154
B-29B-40-BA	4	44-83890/-83893
B-29-40-BA	1	44-83894
B-29B-40-BA	1	44-83895
B-29B-45-BA	4	44-83896/-83899
B-29-45-BA	1	44-83900
B-29B-45-BA	3	44-83901/-83903
B-29-45-BA	1	44-83904
B-29B-45-BA	3	44-83905/-83907
B-29-45-BA	1	44-83908
B-29B-45-BA	2	44-83909/-83910
B-29-45-BA	1	44-83911
B-29B-40-BA	2	44-83912/-83913
B-29-45-BA	1	44-83914
B-29B-45-BA	2	44-8315/-83916
B-29-45-BA	20	44-83917, -83920, -83923, -83926 and even #s through -83940, -83945 and odd #s through -83957, -83960 & -83962
B-29B-45-BA	2	44-83918/-83919
B-29B-45-BA	3	44-83920/-83922
B-29B-45-BA	3	44-83923/-83925
B-29B-45-BA	7	44-83927 and odd #s through -83939
B-29B-45-BA	4	44-83941/-83944
B-29B-45-BA	1	44-83961
B-29-50-BA	23	44-83964 and even #s through -84008
B-29B-50-BA	23	44-83963 and odd #s through -84007
B-29-55-BA	24	44-83010 and even #s through -84056
B-29B-55-BA	24	44-84009 and odd #s through -84055
B-29-60-BA	23	44-84058 and even #s through -84102
B-29B-60-BA	24	44-84057 and odd #s through -84103
B-29-65-BA	24	44-84104 and even #s through -84156

B-29B-65-BA	25	(#s -84140, -84150 & -84154 canceled)
		44-84105 and odd #s through -84155
		(# -84153 canceled)
B-29/-29B-BA	232	44-84157 through 44-84389 canceled
B-29-40-MO	35	44-86242/-86276
B-29-45-MO	39	44-86277/-86315
B-29-50-MO	55	44-86316/-86370
B-29-55-MO	55	44-86371/-86425
B-29-60-MO	48	44-86426/-86473
B-29-MO	217	44-862474/-86691 canceled
B-29-80-BW	50	44-87584/-87633
B-29-85-BW	50	44-87634/-87683
B-29-86-BW	50	44-87684/-87733
B-29-90-BW	50	44-87734/-87783
B-29-90-BW	50	45-21693/-21742
B-29-97-BW	15	45-21743/-21757
B-29-95-BW	35	45-21758/-21792
B-29-96-BW	20	45-21793/-21812
B-29-95-BW	30	45-21813/-21842
B-29-100-BW	30	45-21843/-21842
B-29-BW	919	45-21873/-222792 canceled

B-29 Model Totals

3	XB-29-BO (Boeing-Seattle)
14 YB-29-BW	(Boeing-Wichita)
1,630	B-29-BW (Boeing-Wichita)
	(plus 10 pilot kits to Bell and Martin)
1,119	B-29A-BN (Boeing-Renton)
357	B-29-BA (Bell-Atlanta)
311	B-29B-BA (Bell/Atlanta)
536	B-29-MO (Martin-Omaha)
Totals: 3,970	(Boeing: 2,766/Bell: 668/Martin: 536)

B-29 Monthly Production

1943		1944		1945	
July	7	January	54	January	221
August	4	February	57	February	260
September	15	March	60	March	291
October	13	April	51	April	321
November	18	May	88	May	350
December	35	June	82	June	370
		July	75	July	375
		August	94	August	319
		September	122	Total	3760
		October	125		
		November	163		
		December	190		

Note: The last production B-29 was S/N 44-62328, a B-29A-75-BN that came off the Renton line on 28 May 1946 (the B-29A was built exclusively by Boeing-Renton). Boeing-Wichita produced its last B-29 in October 1945; Martin-Omaha in September 1945; and Bell-Atlanta in January 1945, when it was replaced by the B-29B, which was exclusively built by Bell-Atlanta and ceased production in September 1945.

F-13 and F-13A Photo Recon B-29 Serial Numbers

One B-29-20-BW (serial number 42-6412) served as the prototype of the F-13 (F is the designation for a photographic series), as it had camera installations fitted, along with its standard bombing and defensive armament. The F-13 conversions were done at Boeing's modification center in Denver, CO. Initially, 24 Boeing-Wichita B-29s were converted to the F-13: two Block –35-BWs, five –40-BWs, and 17 –50-BWs. The serial numbers in these F-13s ran from 42-24566 to 42-24881. Denver also converted 42 Boeing-Renton B-29As to the F-13A: 18 –5-BNs; eight –10-BNs; five –15-BNs; five –20-BNs; one –25-BN; and five –30-BNs. This batch of F-13As had serial numbers running from 42-93849 to 42-94114. An additional 55 Boeing-Renton B-29As, with serial numbers running from 44-61528 to 44-62296, were converted. Included in this conversion were: six –35-BNs; one –40 BN; one –45-BN; 16 –50-BNs; 20 –55-BNs; and 11 – 70BNs. Denver finally converted 16 late production Boeing-Wichita B-29s: one –90-BW; nine –95-BWs; one –96-BW; and five –100-BWs to the F-13. These F-13s had serial numbers ranging from 45-21742 to 45-21859.

14
World War II B-29 Models

XB-29

There were three XB-29s built by the Boeing Seattle plant. Externally, the three XB-29s were identical, except for gunsighting blister layout. The first two had four streamlined blisters in the rear pressurized compartment; one low on each side of the fuselage, and two located close together at the top of the fuselage. The third XB-29 had the blister layout that would be chosen for production, one hemispherical blister on each side of the fuselage midway between the top and bottom, and a single blister on top of the centerline. All three XB-29s were the only B-29s to have a commander's astrodome aft of the airplane commander's and co-pilot's seats, which was a B-17 characteristic. Wright R-3350-17 engines equipped with 17ft three-blade propellers powered the three XB-29s. The XB-29 41-002 was later equipped with improved engines and four-blade propellers, and was redesignated as a YB-29 in classified documents.

YB-29 Service Test Models

In June 1941 the AAF let a contract (W535 AC-19673) for the production of 14 YB-29s at a cost of $1,403,623.86 each to be produced at the Boeing-Wichita factory. This contract was later supplemented for the production of the first 250 production B-29s and all subsequent Wichita B-29s. The 14 service test YB-29 models were numbered 41-36954 to 36967 (c/n3325-3338).

They were equipped with the General Electric remote armament system and four R-3350-21 engines mounting three-bladed Hamilton-Standard hydromatic propellers. They were delivered in olive drab (OD) with gray undersides and varied national insignia: blue circle and white star; star and bar with blue surround; and star and bar with red surround. The gunsighting blisters and armament were the same as that developed on the third XB-29. The YB-29s were the first B-29s to be equipped with full military equipment to production standards. All but one YB-29 stayed in the United States, and they were used for training.

The first YB-29 (41-36954) flew on 2 June 1943, and was converted to the only XB-39 by General Motors Fisher (Cleveland) on an Army contract. This program is described later with the XB-39.

The third YB-29 (136957) was sent to Seattle for testing and development. It was fitted with a four-blade propeller and named "*Dauntless Dotty.*"

YB-29 (136958), the fourth YB, was assigned to the 444BG/58BW for crew training, and then went to Boeing's Seattle Trade School.

YB-29 (41-36959) was the fifth production YB built by Boeing-Wichita, and was equipped with electronic equipment and used to train flight leaders and radar operators in Amarillo. It was aptly named "*Amarillo's Flying Solenoid.*"

In April 1944, after it had been decided that the B-29 was to be flown against the Japanese, the ninth YB-29 (136963) flew from Wichita to Mi-

In June 1941 the AAF let a contract for the production of 14 YB-29s at a cost of $1,403,623.86 each to be produced at the Boeing-Wichita factory. The YB-29s were the first B-29s to be equipped with full military equipment to production standards. All but one YB-29 stayed in the United States and were used for training. (USAF)

Dauntless Dotty was the third YB-29 and was sent to Seattle to testing. (Frank Crosby)

ami under secret orders, then headed south over the Atlantic, then north to Gander, Newfoundland, for refueling. It then flew non-stop to Horsham St. Faith, England, and within an hour after its arrival the bomber was discovered and photographed by a Luftwaffe photo-recon aircraft. Part of the point of the mission was to make the Germans believe that the B-29 would be deployed to the ETO. This YB-29 also was to test a new radar bombing system over France as a prelude to "*Project Ruby*"—limited B-29 missions to bomb the *Kriegsmarine* U-boat pens at Farge, Germany, with the RAF 12 ton "Tall Boy" bomb in the summer of 1945. After spending several weeks in England the YB-29 flew directly to the CBI, arriving at Kharagpur on 6 April 1944, the second B-29 to reach the theater. The bomber was assigned to the 462BG and took the name "*Hobo Queen*," and was the only YB-29 to see combat, acting as a tanker to transport gasoline across the Himalayan "Hump."

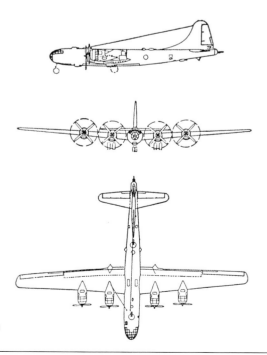

B-29 Production Model (Pima)

B-29 Production Model

The B-29 was the primary production version of the Superfortress, as 2,513 were built (1,620 by Boeing-Wichita, 536 by Martin-Omaha, and 357 by Bell-Marietta). It first came into production at Boeing-Wichita in September 1943, Bell-Marietta in February 1944, and Martin-Omaha in May 1944. The B-29 differed from the service test YB-29s, being fitted with the 16ft, 7in diameter, self-feathering, four-bladed propellers and the Wright R-3350-23 2,200hp engine.

There were many variations within the production blocks, with Boeing-Wichita reaching block number -100 and Bell and Martin reaching -65 and -60, respectively. The R-3350-41 (improved cooling with baffles and oil cross over pipes) was placed in the Boeing Block-50, and Martin and Bell placed that engine in their Block-20s. At the end of the B-29 production run all three manufacturers were using the R-3350-57 engine. The forward top turret armament was increased to four .50cal machine guns on the Boeing Block-40; Bell added it on its Block-10s, and all Martin B-29s had this armament arrangement from the onset. The 20mm tail cannon was deleted from the Boeing Block-55, and the Bell and Martin Block-25s. The first B-29s carried 8,168gals, but later four tanks were added to the center wing section to increase the fuel capacity to 9,438gals. Boeing added the tanks in its Block-50 bombers, and Bell in its Block-5s. All Martin B-29s had these extra tanks from the start of production. Boeing-Wichita produced their last B-29 in October 1945, Martin-Omaha in September 1945, and Bell-Marietta in January 1945.

B-29A

Boeing-Renton exclusively built 1,119 B-29As, with Block numbers reaching –75. There were virtually no external differences between the B-29s built by Boeing-Wichita, Martin-Omaha, Bell-Marietta, and the Boeing-Renton models. However, there was a major difference in the Renton wing installation. The B-29A had a short stub wing center section installed a short distance into the fuselage. The B-29 had a pair of inboard wing panels that passed through the fuselage and were installed as a single unit, and bolted at the centerline of the aircraft. This installation increased B-29A wingspan by a foot, which brought about the "A" designation. The stub mount simplified construction, but had a few undesirable effects on the performance, as the heavier structure increased the weight by 706lbs and reduced the gasoline capacity by 213gals in the center wing tank (1333gals

B-29A (USAF)

B-29B (USAF)

vs. 1083gals). The B-29A was powered by the R-3350-57. The Block –75s had their 20mm tail cannons removed and a pair of .50cal machines guns added to the top forward turret in Block-20.

B-29B

The Bell-Marietta factory exclusively built 311 B-29Bs between January and September 1945 as part of an order that was a follow-up on modifications that were found necessary once the bomber was in combat. The B-29Bs were not built in a single block of consecutive numbered airframes, but in several small blocks, or often individually. As they were based on the Boeing B-29, they all carried the Boeing Model 345-3-0 designation.

Because of Bell's initial production problems their B-29Bs were delivered stripped, and between February and May 1945 Bell sent the stripped bombers to the Oklahoma City Air Depot for installation of electronic equipment. However, by the beginning of May Bell was able to produce a complete aircraft. Various radio and electrical equipment was removed, including the SCR-718 radio altimeter, SCR-274-N command radio, SCR-729 interrogator, AN/ARR-1 homing adapter, the aft Raven station, frequency meter, search antennas and cables, and the AN/ART-13 low frequency radio. The AN/APQ-13 radar was removed and replaced by the AN/APQ-7 Eagle unit, which required the relocation of the radar operator from the aft compartment to the forward compartment, to a position just behind the navigator and opposite the radio operator. There was no AN/APQ-7 repeater for the navigator as there had been for the AN/APQ-13 (*see* AN/APQ-7 and AN/APQ-13).

Decreased aircraft weight, as well as increased speed and bomb carrying capacity, were ordered for the B-29B. Revising the engine baffles and adding louvers to the turbo supercharger well covers increased engine cooling. The airplane commander's throttle override controls were removed. At the time there was little enemy fighter opposition to B-29s operating over Japan, and any attacks were mainly from the rear. All four fuselage turrets, all easily removable turret structure and related turret equipment, all CFC equipment, and all armament were removed. Flush covers overlaid the turrets and sighting blisters. The tail gun and sighting station remained, but the 20mm tail cannon was removed and a third .50cal machine gun was added, along with increased ammunition provisions. The tail guns were aimed by a new AN/APG-15B radar fire control system that was coupled to the GE gun computer and IFF ("Ella") units. The AN/APG-15B detected an incoming enemy aircraft and made the calculations to track and fire on it (*see* AN/APG-15B). Armor was deleted, except the glass forward of the airplane commander's position, and armor and glass in the tail gunner's position. All flak protection was removed except the Dural plate behind the airplane commander's position.

The B-29Bs were crewed by seven or eight crewmen, as the right and left waist gunners were deleted; often the CFC officer stayed behind, but sometimes acted as an observer. The radar operator often replaced the bombardier. The decreased weight and removal of the guns and blisters increased the aircraft's speed to 364mph at 25,000ft, which permitted the bomber to make unescorted "hit-and-run" bombing and photo-reconnaissance missions with increased bomb and/or fuel load. LeMay demanded that there be no delay in the shipment of these bombers to the Pacific, so no waivers in training and equipment were to be made, except for the AN/APG-15 and associated equipment and the third tail machine gun. Most of the B-29Bs were sent to the 315BW, which was scheduled to begin operations on 1 April 1945 for low altitude nighttime pathfinder missions, and what was to become a very successful campaign against the Japanese oil industry.

B-29C

The AAF ordered 5,000 Renton-built B-29Cs with improved R-3350-57 engines, but the order was canceled.

B-29D

The D was an upgrade of the B-29A, built with a 75SST aluminum airframe that was powered by the 3,500hp Pratt & Whitney R-4350 engine housed in the nacelle that P&W developed for its XB-44. The AAF ordered 200 B-29D-BNs in July 1945, but the order was reduced to 50 after the war ended. Even though the changes to the B-29A to make it a B-29D were much greater than those to convert the B-29A-5 to the XB-44, the D remained a B-29. The design was redesignated the B-50 in December 1945 to secure appropriations for continued production when B-29 contacts were under wholesale cancellation. Boeing's ploy was to make the B-50A seem to have so many changes that it was a completely new bomber. The most conspicuous difference was a tail that was five feet taller. The B-50A was placed into production at Boeing–Seattle in 1946 and served in the post war Air Force, along with mothballed B-29s, until the jet-powered B-47s were introduced. They did not see service in Korea, but contributed as tankers in Vietnam.

F-13 and F-13A

In January 1943, the Secretary of War issued requirements for a Long-Range, high altitude photo-reconnaissance aircraft, and in response the twin-engine Hughes XF-11 and four-engine Republic XF-12 Rainbow were contracted for development. The all-wood Hughes XF-11, like the infamous, problem-plagued, all-wood "Spruce Goose" flying boat being developed at the same time by Hughes, also encountered numerous difficulties, as changes were increasing its weight and decreasing performance. It would not be ready before the war ended. The XF-12, which looked much like a more streamlined B-29, languished in mockup and prolonged development and testing, and it would not exceed the performance of stripped B-29s. In April 1944, with the XF-11 and XF-12 nowhere near ready, the B-29 was the only experimental aircraft that was scheduled to go into production that met the January 1943 photo-reconnaissance requirements (except for altitude). On 13 April 1944 the Chairman of the Aerial Mapping Committee proclaimed:

"Due to its size and weight and operational altitude, the B-29 is not considered to be a suitable and economic type for conversion to a photographic airplane."

However, the B-29 was on hand and could be converted into the F-13, and easily included into existing B-29 operational units and their training, and later maintenance and support. However, B-29 operational units felt the conversion of bombing B-29s into photo F-13s interfered with delivery schedules in a program that was already far behind schedule. One B-29-20-BW (s/n 42-6412) was modified as the XF-13 prototype, and was to be followed by 11 more as insurance against eventual XF-11 and XF-12 failure. In any event, the F-13 was considered as a provisional photo-recon aircraft until another purpose-designed aircraft could replace it. In June 1944 a squadron of 12 F-13s was in training and scheduled to be deployed to the XXI Bomber Command, which had only flown its first operational mission from the Marianas four days earlier.

The F-13A was the designation given to photo-reconnaissance versions of the B-29—the F=Foto series started with the Fairchild F-1 in 1930. Batches of 24 and 16 Boeing-Wichita B-29-BWs, and batches of 42 and 55 Boeing-Renton B-29A-BNs were converted to F-13s and F-13As, respectively. In 1945 the F-13 designation was discontinued, and the photo aircraft reclaimed their B-29 identity, but as FB-29s.

The Air Technical Service Command (ATSC) and the Fairchild Photographic Company designed the photo system to equip the B-29 and B-29A aircraft that were diverted from the assembly line to become F-13 and F-13A photo planes. The modification was completed by the Continental Airlines Denver Modification Center at a cost of about $400,000. All defensive armament was maintained, but during 1945 the Japanese fighter

The camera openings were flush doors located in the rear unpressurized compartment. It was the responsibility of the bombardier to have the radar operator open the camera doors when the target was approached. (USAF)

defense, except over important targets, had declined significantly, and only a handful of the Japanese interceptors were able to reach the F-13s at altitude. Additional fuel was carried in both bomb bay tanks to increase flying time up to 25 hours. The front bomb bay could also be used to carry photo flash bombs for night photography, or a cargo platform with special cameras and additional film, with the rear bomb bay fitted with auxiliary fuel tanks. The photo-navigator and cameraman supplemented the normal 10-man crew. The Foto B-29s were designed to carry a bank of six to eight cameras mounted in the rear unpressurized compartment and sighted through small square windows covered with 3/4" glass cut into the fuselage, and included the following cameras: K-17; K-18; K-19 or K-23; K-20; K-24; or F-24. Of the vertical cameras, the K-17 was used for rapid reconnaissance mapping, and the K-18 was used for high altitude mosaic and spotting. They were electric and fully automated, and had a 9 x 18in negative. Two K-17 cameras were located one on the right and one on the left side of the fuselage in an oblique installation. A tri-metrogon camera provided horizon-to-horizon coverage in a single photo, and was composed of three K-17B cameras that were installed for split vertical viewing. These cameras were mounted side-by-side, one pointed straight down, and the other two pointed outward left and right, and could photograph an area 20 to 30mi wide, depending on the altitude. One or two 40in K-22 cameras were located in a vertical mount that was split, so as to cover a two-mile wide area from 20,000ft. The K-22s were used for individual targets, such as factories, rail yards, bridges, etc. One or two K-18s were also used for close range and wide-angle views to obtain pinpoint details. The K-20 handheld camera was manually operated, and held 50 4 x 5in negatives on a roll of film; photographs could be taken through the windows of the aircraft. A bracket was located on the right hand wall forward of the rear entrance door to stow a K-20 portable camera. The cameraman looked through a viewfinder at the upper rear of the camera and tripped the shutter with his right index finger. For night photography the E-17, K-22, and/or K-19B

The cameras used by the 3PRS F-13As ("F" on tail). Shown in this PR photo of the possible F-13 camera arrays is *Suellen J* at Kwajelein during the Bikini Atomic Bomb tests. (USAF)

cameras could be used. Sighting was done through a modified B-3 Driftmeter located in the bombardier's compartment, and operated by the photo-navigator and a cameraman. These cameras used large size film; the K-22 used a 10 x 10in negative film, and the K-17 used a 9 x 18in film. However, much of the camera work of the pioneer radar unit (315BW) was with 35mm film to photograph their radar screens during a bomb run. During July 1945, the 315BW Consolidated Photographic Laboratory operated 24 hours per day to process 1,400,000 negatives and print 55,000.

The 3rd Photo-Reconnaissance Squadron arrived in the Marianas in mid-October 1944 and operated out of Isley Field, on Saipan. Capt. Ralph Streakley, airplane commander of the *Tokyo Rose*—the first F-13A in the Marianas—flew the first photo mission over Japan on 1 November 1944, photographing Tokyo in preparation for the first Marianas-based mission on 24 November. The unit's ground operation, lab, and camera repair department operated from two squadron tents until more permanent build-

The 3rd Photo-Reconnaissance Squadron, arrived in the Marianas in mid-October 1944 and operated out of Isley Field on Saipan. The first F-13A, *Tokyo Rose*, flew the first photo mission over Japan on 1 November 1944 when Capt. Ralph Streakley flew over Tokyo in preparation for the first Marianas-based mission over Japan to follow on 24 November. (USAF)

ings were completed in late March 1945. Often F-13s would take off long after the bombardment mission was under way and catch up with the bombers over the target, then fly back to base for debriefing long before the bombers returned (between 1600 and 2200 hours). The film magazines were picked up immediately and rushed to the photo lab to be processed. The photo intelligence officer scanned the film negatives and selected the negatives to be printed. The prints were then rushed to the photo interpreters of a combined interpretation unit for "flash" information. A "flash" report was prepared for 0800 the next morning, and interim information was forwarded to the CG during the night. Duplicate negatives, complete sets of prints, and mosaics were completed and forwarded to the photo interpreters for damage assessments, surveys, and industrial, airfield, and other special reports. The photos were eventually distributed to 350 different agencies. The 3PRS flew over 440 of the total 755 photo sorties by the end of the war, and claimed it had photographed every square foot of Japan.

SB-29 Super Dumbo

The original Super Dumbos were not a specific model, but makeshift B-29s pressed into Air Sea Rescue (ASR) service. Later Wichita-built B-29-80-BWs were converted to the Super Dumbo, and were referred to as the SB-29. The Super Dumbo carried a crew of 12, with an additional radio operator and navigator, along with radio equipment, a homing transmitter, and survival equipment (they retained all their armament). The Super Dumbos were able to stay on station for 14 hours, and stayed just out of enemy fighter range off the coast of Japan, but could roam into the Inland Sea, if necessary. The first lifeboat rescue was made on 30 May 1945.

The SB-29 could transport a 2,800lb, 27ft Higgins jettisonable lifeboat slung under the bomb bay area by four cables attached to the bomb shackles. The bombardier, using the bomb salvo, released the lifeboat at 1,500ft. After the lifeboat was released a triple cluster of 48-foot parachutes opened by a static line lowered the boat at 25ft per second. The boat entered the water at a 50-degree bow-down attitude to cushion the impact. Pneumatic self-righting chambers were automatically inflated as the boat descended, and as it contacted the water, three rocket-propelled lifelines shot out from the boat for about 300ft. The heavy nylon parachutes acted as sea anchors, holding the boat in place regardless of the wind so the downed crews could swim to the lifeboat. An instruction book was included on the boat to aid the crew who were inexperienced in boat handling. The lifeboat carried survival gear, and was propelled by a 5hp air-cooled engine equipped with a ratchet starter and vertical drives. The engine could maintain a top speed of seven miles per hour, and had a range of 500mi on 50gals of gasoline, which was provided. There were 145square feet of sail area comprised of a jib and mainsail. The interior of the hull was divided into 20 watertight chambers that prevented the boat from being overturned. The chambers and all cockpits were self-bailing, and provided with transparent deck plates to insure the quick detection of leakage. Navigation was by self-reckoning, aided by two types of compasses, an eight-day clock, charts, a parallel rule, and a logbook. There was a supply of rations and water for 12 men to make a 1,500mi voyage. The water supply was provided automatically by two stills operated by the exhaust heat of the engine. Salt water entered through an inlet scoop on the bottom of the boat and traveled through the boilers, and was condensed in the form of drinking water at a rate of one gallon per hour. Thirty Permitit desalting kits supplied additional drinking water, and for immediate use

The original Super Dumbos were not a specific model but makeshift B-29s pressed into ASR service. Later Wichita-built B-29-80-BWs were converted to the Super Dumbo and were referred to as the SB-29. The Super Dumbo carried a crew of 12 with an additional radio operator and navigator along with radio equipment, a homing transmitter and survival equipment (they retained all their armament). (USAF)

there were 30 cans of drinking water. Canned foods were cooked by using the hot water in the condenser stills. Chewing gum, candy, and cigarettes/ matches were also provided. In the main storage locker there was warm clothing and waterproof suits. Air mattresses and wool blankets were stored under the forward and aft self-righting chamber canopies for protection from the weather for eight men at a time. The aft compartment was supplied heat from the engine. A Gibson Girl emergency radio, several types of pyrotechnics, signal mirrors, sea markers, and flashlights were included to aid rescue operations.

XB-39

Allison had developed its V-3420 engine for the Douglas XBLR-2 in the mid-1930s The V-3420 engine was two Allison V-1710 fighter engines totaling 24 cylinders joined to a common shaft to produce 2,600hp takeoff and 2,100hp at 25,000ft. The program was terminated in September 1940 in order to increase conventional V-1710 engine production. Because of the developmental problems of the Wright R-3350 it was decided that a backup engine was needed, and Allison again started priority work on the V-3420 in May 1942. Fisher (GM) was requested to design a nacelle to fit the B-29, and the resulting aircraft was designated the XB-39; to expedite the project Fisher hired Don Berlin, the renowned designer of the P-40 fighter. Because of the unavailability of B-29 airframes the AAF appropriated the XB-19 in September 1942 for V-3420 testing as described previously. Development of this engine fared no better than the R-3350, with only 30 engines being delivered in 1943. The AAF ordered nine V-3420-

11s for the XB-39 and 500 for the first 100 B-39s—the proposed designation for V-3420 powered B-29s. The first V-3420s were to be installed in the fourth YB-29, but this aircraft was unavailable, as it was Wright R-3350 powered due to the urgency of getting enough B-29s ready for combat. The B-29 that became available for testing the Allison engine was the first YB-29, YB-29-BO (41-36954), named the *Spirit of Lincoln*. It arrived at the Fisher factory at the Cleveland Airport in November 1943, where it was fitted with the V-3420-11s that had previously been installed in the XB-19. In the meantime, the General Motors Fisher Division began work on adapting the turbosupercharged V-3420-A for the B-29. During testing various supercharger configurations were tried to increase performance, as the new GM Type CM-2 superchargers were behind contracted delivery dates. The XB-39 project was set aside, as Fisher engineers were to ordered develop the P-75 Long-Range fighter. By October 1944 it became apparent the P-75 would not be ready, and that project was canceled in favor of the new jet fighters. The XB-39 project was resurrected, but the bomber did not make its first flight until 9 December 1944. The XB-39's marginal improvement in performance did not warrant interference with B-29 production for a changeover to B-39 production. Also, the availability of superchargers was critical, and the result was that the XB-39 would not be available before the end of the war. Allison continued to develop the engine and accomplished imposing performance data, including 4,300hp. The company had planned to further develop and sell the engine for the post war market, but Allison's post war business practice was to pursue only programs that would be funded by the client, and did not continue the

The B-29 that became available for testing the Allison engine was the first YB-29, named the *Spirit of Lincoln*. It arrived at the Fisher factory at the Cleveland Airport in November 1943 where it was fitted with the twin Allison V-3420-11 engines that had previously been installed in the XB-19. For the tests it was renamed the XB-39. (USAF)

Quarter scale B-29 wing and tail surfaces in assorted configurations were constructed for flight-testing on a Fairchild PT-19 trainer that had been sent to Boeing by the AAF. (USAF)

Left: When Pratt & Whitney developed its 3,500hp R-4360 Wasp Major engine it needed a B-29A as a test bed to develop an up-powered B-29 that was designated as the XB-44. (USAF)

V-3420. The AAF powered the post war B-29 (the B-50A) with the Pratt & Whitney R-4360-35 engine. This P&W engine had been developed during the war, and the engine would become the premier post war large aero-engine.

XB-44

When Pratt & Whitney developed its 3,500hp four row, 28 cylinder R-4360 Wasp Major engine, it needed a B-29A (42-93845) as a test bed to develop an up-powered B-29 designated as the XB-44. Identification of the XB-44 varies as the Boeing XB-44 or the Pratt & Whitney XB-44. The P&W XB-44 was easily recognized by the engine installation, with the oil cooler intake that was placed further back on the lower part of the engine nacelle. After the new engine was tested and accepted it was scheduled to power 200 B-29Ds, but the end of the war led to their cancellation. An order for 60 of these D models, which were redesignated the B-50A, was placed in December 1945. The production of this improved model was extended to 371 and continued as the TB-50H of 1953.

"Tall Tail Andy Gump" B-29

B-29-35-BW (42-24528) underwent major changes, but was not redesignated or given a new series letter. This B-29 was given the new tall vertical tail that was scheduled for the B-29D/B-50A models, and also the so-called new "Andy Gump" engine nacelles that were to be used on B-29As. The Gump name referred to the nacelle profile, which was reminiscent of the famous Gump cartoon character profile. This B-29 had the Gump name and caricature painted on its nose. The new nacelles were not used on production B-29As, but the six YC-97 cargo planes developed from the B-29 used it.

Fairchild Quarter-Scale B-29

As design and wind tunnel testing of the B-29 advanced, the need for scale model testing arose. Quarter scale B-29 wing and tail surfaces in assorted configurations were constructed for flight testing on a Fairchild PT-19 trainer that had been sent to Boeing by the AAF. Boeing reconfigured the PT-19 forward cockpit to carry test instruments. Boeing tested a number of different wings of various taper and aspect ratios and swept back angles to prove design studies.

15

The Wright R-3350 Cyclone Engine Development and Factories

Introduction

The basic components of an aircraft are its airframe and engines. The success of the B-29 program hinged on the timely development and subsequent dependability and mass-production of the 2,200 hp Wright R-3350 Cyclone engine by the Wright Aeronautical Division of the Curtiss-Wright Company of Paterson, NJ. The first XB-29 used the R-3350-5, which delivered 2,000hp at 2,400rpm, and was later fitted with the –13, rated at 2,200hp at 2,800rpm. A total of 162 R-3350-21s that also delivered 2,200hp at 2,800rpm were ordered for the YB-29s, XB-32s, and the XC-97s (a Boeing cargo spin-off of the B-29). The –21A (2,200hp/2,800rpm) was installed on the YB-29s and the early B-29s. The first R-3350 to be built in quantity was the R-3350-23, of which 1,366 were ordered. Early B-29 production models used the R-3350-23 model built by Dodge-Chrysler, which delivered 2,200hp at 2,600rpm. Once the problems of the –23 engine were remedied it was replaced by the –23A "War Engine." These -23A engines differed from the plain –23s, as they had aluminum cooling fins pressed into the cylinder barrels instead of the machined steel fins. A total of 22,385 R-3350-23As, also built by Dodge, were ultimately ordered. Late production B-29s and B-29As used the improved R-3350-57 engines, which delivered 2,200hp at 2,800rpm. The evolution of the R-3350 engine was slow and arduous, and was the major factor influencing the development of the B-29. The problem with the Wright engine was not with the engine design, as much as the time constraints it was placed under as part of the B-29 project to solve the problems that were inherent in the development of any new engine.

Wright Cyclone R-1820 and R-2600 Engines

At a time when Pratt & Whitney dominated American aircraft engine manufacturing with its Wasp and Hornet engine series, Wright initiated its Cyclone engine series in 1923 with a Navy contract for two of the new radial engines. In 1929 Wright merged with Curtiss, and by 1932 the two engineering departments collaborated to produce the outstanding 9-cylinder 1,000hp Cyclone F (designated the R-1820), that were to power the Douglas airliners and the B-17 bomber. Work on a 14-cylinder engine began in November 1935 and utilized the hard-learned lessons in the development of the R-1820. The 14-cylinder 1,600hp Wright R-2600 Cyclone was the company's first successful two row air-cooled radial engine. It was used to power the Boeing 314 Clippers, and would become a major wartime air-craft engine used in the AAF B-25 and A-20 medium bombers, as well as the Navy's TBM/TBF and SB2C carrier bombers. A larger engine was needed to power the B-29, and the Wright engineering department's developmental objective for the R-3350 was to produce one horsepower for every pound of weight. Wright engineers mounted two 9-cylinder Cyclone engines together at a 90-degree angle from each other to form a "V," with its open ends facing toward the line of flight to yield a displacement of 3,640cuin. Power from each engine was transferred through a common gearbox that combined the power of the two engines and directed it into the propeller main shaft. While single Cyclone R-1820s had flown reliably over millions of airline and military miles, the new combined engine presented Wright engineers with a number of problems. The gearbox added weight, and there was two of every engine accessory: two carburetors, two superchargers, two air scoops, and dual fuel and oil lines. The dual engine had the standard 55in diameter, but its cowl needed to be much wider.

Wright R-3350 Development

Wright engineers soon realized the inherent problems of a combination engine were significant, and went back to the drawing boards to design an entirely new 18-cylinder 3,350hp flat engine that would become the company's financial backbone until well after the end of the war. Wright didn't have enough engineers to devote to the R-3350 project, as they concentrated on the R-1820 and its employment in the pre-war DC-2 and DC-3 commercial market—that would reach 70%—and the military market for the B-17. Also, at the time the potential and marketability of the R-2600 engine was thought to be greater than the R-3350. The company did not assign a large number of engineers to it until 1942, when it was compelled to do so by the awarding of the large B-29 contracts. As Wright and its parent company, Curtiss, rapidly expanded into huge manufacturing entities, Curtiss did not allow Wright management to make high-level decisions. The fact was that Wright executives were not qualified to assume undertaking a project of the magnitude of the R-3350, and consequently failed to support the project as forcefully as they should have. In the late 1930s, under the AAC's prototype/developmental contract system, there was no monetary motivation for airframe builders such as Boeing and engine builders such as Wright to hurry development of their products. Any improvement or innovation in the developmental process was expensive, and Wright had to assume these costs, knowing that there was no guarantee the AAC would purchase the engine once it was ready. Wright could expect no financial help from its parent company, as Curtiss had not been profitable in the 1930s. It was not until 1940, when Congress allowed cost-plus contracts, that engines could be developed and produced without as much financial risk.

Nonetheless work went ahead, and Wright engineers incorporated as many of the established Cyclone engine attributes as possible into the new engine. When it began its development in January 1936 the R-3350 followed the design and construction details of the R-2600. During 1937 and 1938, Wright engineers upgraded and hand-built the new engine in the experimental machine shop. The engine integrated traditional Cyclone steel-barrel cylinders with aluminum heads that increased the cooling area. They kept the Cyclone's strong steel crankcase and strong, light magnesium nose and supercharger sections. There were two banks of nine cylinders each, with one master rod and eight articulated rods directing piston power into a three-piece crankshaft. A 20-pinion reduction gear directed power into the propeller shaft at efficient speeds, and at a weight scarcely over one pound per horsepower. The R-2600 and the R-3350 had the same bore and stroke, with the additional displacement gained by adding four additional cylinders (in two rows' of nine). The R-3350 was an air-cooled, duplex engine that had 18 cylinders, with two radial rings of nine cylinders positioned around the crankshaft. The cylinder heads of the two cylinder rings radiated outward to be cooled by the air stream from the huge propellers. The R-3350 was rated at 2,000hp for cruising and 2,200hp for take off. The engine was twice as powerful as the R-1820 of the Flying Fortress, yet its 55in frontal engine exposure was the same size as the B-17 and provided equivalent cooling!

As mentioned, during the late 1930s the R-3350 was a low priority for Wright, as the company centered its attention on expanding its R-1820 and R-2600 Cyclone engine production. The R-3350 developed slowly from the foundries to the machine shops, to assembly, and finally to the test cells. The testing and development of the Wright engine was very limited, and there was no significant production, as from 1936 to 1939 Wright delivered only seven R-3350-5s to the Air Force. When Wright tested the first R-3350 in 1937 initial problems arose. After running for 135 hours on a test stand the engine's reduction gears failed, and this problem was to continue until 1943. In 1939 two new problems with the exhaust valves and the cooling system occurred that also would never be fully remedied during the war. The R-3350 was scheduled to power the Martin Mars, Lockheed Constellation, and the Boeing Model 341, but it was not until May 1939 that it was first flown in the Douglas XB-19, and tests continued in that aircraft through the summer. In September 1939 the war in Europe began when Hitler invaded Poland, and the French and English demand for Wright Cyclone 9s and 14s increased dramatically. Wright was faced with a glut of orders for its proven R-1820 and R-2600 engines, and in less than two months it built new machine shops to accommodate these orders. These facilities almost equaled the size of the main Wright plant, and were in production by early 1940. The continued high demand prompted Wright to buy vacant silk mills in the Paterson, NJ, area, and these mills were quickly renovated and expanded into six plants and a new foundry to build more R-1820 engines. Wright expanded its main plant in Cincinnati, OH, that would build 50,000 wartime R-2600 engines, and also built its Lockland, OH, plant, which would be the largest single floor factory in America to exclusively manufacture the R-1820. Later Studebaker was

licensed to build the R-1820, and it eventually built 60,000 to power the B-17.

In the R-40-B bomber design invitations of 29 January 1940, all five bidding aircraft companies offered their proposed aircraft to be powered by the Wright R-3350 engine: Boeing XB-29, Lockheed XB-30, Douglas XB-31, Consolidated XB-32, and the Martin XB-33. The engine had been under contract by the AAC since 1936 (XB-19) and by the Navy from 1937 (for the Consolidated Model 31, Boeing XPBB-1, and Martin Mars APB2M-1). All five bidders had experimental aircraft in development using the Wright engine. The reason was that the displacement of the R-3350 was the largest of any contemporary engine, and had the potential for the greatest development. There were no other large contending engines under development at the time except the Pratt & Whitney R-4360, and Allison's large liquid-cooled 1,600hp Allison XV-3420-1 24 cylinder in-line engines. These engines were dropped from consideration, as they were in development, were too large and heavy, and did not provide any increase in power. So by default, on 15 April 1941 the Air Force issued contract No. AC-18971 to Wright for a future production of 30,000 engines—the largest and highest priority production program of the war.

R-3350 Goes into Production
Wright received its first production order for the R-3350 in May 1941 when the AAC ordered 185 for its XB-29s and YB-29s. With all of the fundamental design changes Wright did not have the engine available at that time, and would not have one until December 1941. The R-3350 design was nowhere near ready for the foundries, cutting equipment, and tooling that had been ordered, and thus the government gave Wright a low priority to receive the machine tools and strategic metals that all defense contractors were clamoring after. Fortunately, the War Department continued to support the Wright engine program, and the exigencies caused by the Pearl Harbor attack benefited both the R-3350 and the B-29 programs. To meet the obligations of the R-3350 contract, Wright built a new plant at Woodridge, NJ, exclusively to build the engine, and its entire Cincinnati factory production was also converted to the engine. In January 1942 the Chrysler Corporation and its Dodge Division were awarded a $314 million, 6% cost-plus-fixed-fee contract to build 10,000 R-3350 engines plus spare parts. When Dodge was awarded its contract there was the opportunity for the company to convert the cylinder head design from the forged to the better cast design, but due to delays in the delivery of tooling the existing cast design was continued. In March this contract was increased to 17,653 engines worth $594 million, and Chrysler was to construct a new factory on the west side of Chicago.

In the meantime the B-29 program was in jeopardy, and no one wanted to take responsibility. AAC and engine industry reputations and careers were at risk. Curtiss-Wright, the holding company for the engine, had swelled in size from 10,000 employees in 1939 to 140,000 in 1943, and was still expanding to become the second largest American military contractor after General Motors. But in the expansion Curtiss-Wright continued its archaic, centralized management practices that controlled the 1939 company. The company's many divisions were not allowed any autonomy, and all decisions were to be made through corporate headquarters in New York. Curtiss-Wright Chairman Guy W. Vaughn, and top executives and investors were concerned over losing control of the company during its rapid wartime expansion, as they were looking to the post war, when its military contracts would be canceled, and peacetime endeavors would have to be pursued to stay in business. Consequently, military divisions like Wright Aeronautical found it difficult to draw top-flight executives and managers to fill what would be temporary war industry positions.

R-3350 Test Programs and Problems

In September 1942 three flight test programs commenced using the first 25 Wright R-3350 engines. The Consolidated XB-32 first flew on the 7th, and was followed two weeks later by the XB-29, while Lockheed flew its two engine test aircraft called the "Ventillation" at the end of the month. Very little is known about the Ventillation, except that it was a specially modified two engine Ventura bomber that was the seventh Ventura on the original British contract. It was kept at the Lockheed factory to test nacelle configurations for the Lockheed Constellation airliner, thus the combination of names. The Ventura's nose had to be shortened so it was cleared by the large diameter propellers.

Over the next four months Wright furnished 65 engines for these programs. Due to the small number of test hours of the early lower powered engine's problems, some major, and many minor troubles soon appeared with the cooling system, reduction gear, and piston rings. The Wright service units spent many hours in the field making changes at Consolidated, Boeing, and Lockheed. Among the long list of problems were instances of extremely high oil consumption on the XB-32. All engines shipped before 1 October 1942 had to have all cylinders removed and lapped. During takeoff the propellers developed runaway rpms measuring in the hundreds. Hamilton-Standard, the propeller manufacturer, and Wright discovered the problem was due to low oil pressure, and a stopgap remedy was to set the propeller stop at lower maximum rpms. The final fix was larger internal oil passages and increased oil pressures that would only come with a newly designed, larger engine nose section. Moisture, particularly during rainy periods, was forced into the ignition by outside and inside pressure differentials, and interfered with normal function. To solve this problem Wright used filled harnesses and changed the materials in the ignition components. The original carburetor supplier could not maintain its contract numbers, and other manufacturers were contracted. When the engines were shut down large quantities of fuel were leaked and caused a fire danger (fixed by minor field changes). Also, after engine shutdown oil could leak past the pistons and cause a hydraulic lock at the bottom of the cylinders that could cause damage on the next engine start (special instructions were issued for start up procedures). There was heat buildup from the design of

the nacelles, and from the two external superchargers that could cause exhaust fires. Most of these problems were no more than annoying, and were usually easily corrected. However, a more serious problem soon emerged, as the aircraft were unable to climb to altitude, and high altitude tests had to be suspended until an answer could be found. Investigation determined that as the aircraft climbed the oil pressure decreased to unsafe levels. The solution was to increase the size of the external oil line from the rear of the engine to the nose, reducing oil pressure loss. But this fix would not come for four months, and finally, on 31 December 1942 the Boeing XB-29 finally reached 25,000ft. The engines went through several configurations. Two reduction gear and two supercharger ratios were tested, as were several different compression ratios, and two different master rod locations. By the end of 1942, Wright engineers and designers, as well as their counterparts at component subcontractors, had solved many problems, but in the meantime, solving these problems had reduced the total flight testing times on the 26 engines involved in all three manufacturers' test programs to 365 hours and 10 minutes:

Aircraft	Total Time
Boeing XB-29 #1 *	99:35
Boeing XB-29 #2 *	2:08
Consolidated XB-32*	131:12
Lockheed Ventillation+	132:00
Total	365:10

*=4 engine +=2 engine

The XB-29 #1 required 17 engine changes to reach the 99:35 total hours, and the highest flight time for any of these engines was only 19:35. During the test period the aircraft had encountered three total reduction gear failures and one partial failure, along with a fractured engine nose section on a ground test engine. The XB-32 results were better, because Consolidated utilized Boeing's experience gained earlier in the year. The XB-32s used eight engines to accomplish the 131:12 testing hours and suffered only one reduction gear failure, but the maximum XB-32 engine time was also low at 19:34. The Lockheed tests were much better, as the same two engines were used for the entire 132 hours of testing on both test aircraft, and no major problems were encountered during testing. This significant difference between the two-engine Lockheed and four-engine Boeing/Consolidated test models was due to having each XB-29/XB-32 engine fitted with two external superchargers for each engine nacelle, causing a concomitant increase in heat and mechanical complexity.

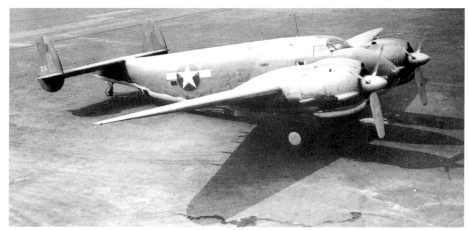

The Ventilation was a specially modified two engine Ventura bomber used to test nacelle configurations for the Lockheed Constellation airliner, thus the combination of names. The Ventura's nose had to be shortened so it was cleared by the large diameter propellers. (USAF)

During the second week of January 1943, Wright did an extensive reexamination of its engine program. The reexamination findings permitted engine production to move forward, as most of the production and operational problems were found, and had been, or were in the process of being remedied. However, time was of the essence. Wright's Woodridge, NJ, plant was still under construction, and then would need to have its machinery and tools installed and staffed by blue-collar laborers and technical personnel. The study determined that the new Woodridge plant, with its new personnel and machinery, and the complexity of R-3350 engine manufacture would require the strict maintenance of quality control.

Just as Wright had received its engine contract and was expanding its facilities, the company was beset by shortages in strategic materials that threatened to jeopardize the program. The East Coast foundries required core sand that was supplied from abroad, and at the time German U-boats threatened the shipment of the supply. A search for alternative local sources was conducted, but none could supply the volume or quality needed, and the foreign sand was scrupulously rationed. Other strategic materials used in engine manufacture were either threatened or in short supply, so Wright was forced to develop substitute materials, and once developed these materials required many hours of engine proof testing.

The B-29 program was hindered by the R-3350's problems, and consequently slowed its development during all of 1943 and into 1944. As described previously, on 18 February 1943 the XB-29 flown by Eddie Allen crashed due to engine fires that killed its crew and 20 people on the ground. A disgruntled Gen. "Hap" Arnold grounded all XB-29s and R-3350s, and formed the special Echol's Board to investigate the engine's problems, conduct tests, and recommend changes. The Air Force Power Plant Laboratory at Wright Field was also assigned to investigate the causes of engine failure, and it compiled an extensive inventory of 82 instances of engine problems occurring between October 1941 and the end of February 1943. Individual engine problems were examined, and Wright suggested a solution, and then considered the urgency of the change and its effect on production.

Engine Failures on Test Aircraft or Test Stands
October 1941 through 28 February 1943

Type of Failure	Total Failures	No. in Flight	No. on Test
High oil consumption	Many	Many	N/A
Reduction gear	23	7*	16
Fires	11+	11	0
Exhaust valves & guides	7	1	6
Cylinders & pistons	7	1	6
Supercharger drive	7	0	7
Oil pressure pumps	6	5	1
Propeller governors	4	4	0
Cam & cam drive	4	0	4
Ignition	4	1	3
Nose section	3	0	3
Master rod & bearing	3	0	3
Intake pipes	2	1	1
Front super housing	1	0	1
Totals	82	31	51

*=Two partial failures were found on ground inspection.
+=No engine fires but due to exhaust system or exhaust shroud failures.

The Wright Lab's findings were that the R-3350 engine design was viable, and that in time, with some basic suggested engineering changes, and given higher priorities would be dependable, and could be put into mass production. Most failures occurred in the reduction gears or nose section of the engine, and these had to be corrected to attain high altitude operation and acceptable propeller rpm control at take off. The nose casting had thicker walls in some areas, requiring larger internal oil conduits, a larger oil pump and sump, and changes to the torque meter. The reduction gear required a new pinion carrier with closer tolerances, which was a very difficult manufacturing process. The machine tools and mass production assembly lines could not be set up until the suggested changes were completed and the engine design frozen. The parts for the first 13 engines shipped from the new Woodridge plant in July 1943 were machined by only one very skilled machinist working long shifts. There were over 2,000 changes made between January and November 1943, of which nearly a quarter caused expensive and time-consuming revisions in tooling that precluded any mass production.

After the installation of the dual turbo-superchargers in each engine, the major potential problem of engine cylinder cooling, especially at high altitudes, emerged, and the lack of time prevented a resolution. The problem was exacerbated when the bombers were made combat ready and their gross weights increased by five to eight tons. Also, each engine had a difference in drag that was caused by opening the cowl flaps to bring down its particular cylinder head temperatures to operating levels. These large differences in the drag of each engine, and concomitantly of each aircraft, made formation flying very difficult. The Wright Engine Committee had anticipated this problem, as it had been remedied in the B-17, powered by R-1800 Cyclones, during its high altitude missions over Europe by replacing cast with forged cylinders. The Committed recommended the same change from cast to forged cylinder manufacture in the Wright R-3350, but there was insufficient forging capacity in the country to meet both B-17 and B-29 requirements, and the B-29 was sent into operational testing with this critical defect.

In the spring of 1943 there were only 32 R-3350s available to Boeing-Wichita, but they could not be used, as Gen. Arnold banned their use after the Allen crash. The first production B-29s rolled out of the plant without engines. The empty nacelles had cement blocks hung below them to balance the aircraft. The Wright Engine Committee decided that these engines could be modified to "flight status,"; the Boeing-Wichita plant made a concerted, round-the-clock effort, and by 29 June 1943 the first production test flight was scheduled. For the test flight work was temporarily halted at the Wichita factory, and the Wichita locals came to watch from a hill near the field. The impressive bomber was towed out, and the engines thunderously run up in preparation for take off. Just after the bomber lifted off smoke billowed out from one engine, and the flight had to be quickly aborted. Inspection on the ground showed the problem to be from a tiny oil leak around a small gasket in the engine nose section that flowed back over the hot exhaust and caused the heavy smoke. By 23 July 1943 143 engines had been shipped, but only 12 were -21 "combat" engines. Fifty of these engines were grounded because their Ceco carburetors needed to be reworked, and another 29 were in the Wright service shops for modification. Once modified only 10 of these engines were declared "combat" ready, and were parceled out for flight (six to the Martin Navy program and four to Bell). Sixteen were only deemed suitable for "school" use and ground testing, and the other three were used for training or flight spares.

On 16 August 1943 a meeting was held at Boeing-Wichita to analyze and discuss the recent R-3350 tests, particularly the engine cooling tests. Comprehensive cooling tests had been conducted using the "combat" type R-3350-21s on the XB-29 #1. During ground testing, problems that would later occur in combat were uncovered: burnt pistons and discolored, charred, burned, or seized parts. Flight tests established that the cowl flaps needed to be wide open for all ground running and partially closed during take offs. A revised take off procedure, considering the bomber's increased heavy gross weights, was tested and instituted, called the "War Emergency Rating." With the increased combat gross weights normal cruise power was not sufficient for climbing, and a much higher power setting was necessary, and with it came the cylinder cooling problem, even with an auto rich mixture. A minimum climb rate of 180mph and a 1,400rpm limit was established to determined to maintain temperature limits.

By October 1943 the engine modifications and problems with the aircraft put everyone concerned with the program under great pressure to meet the original date to get the bomber into combat. Aircraft for flight training were behind schedule, with only 21 B-29s delivered to combat units. The average flight time on these aircraft was about 70 hours (only one plane had 200 flight hours), and only seven had flown with "combat" engines (the highest time on any combat engine was 73 hours). Changes were continuing on a "routine" basis (e.g. the shortest time without interfering with the schedule), and production was rapidly increasing. Major engine and aircraft changes were accompanied by changes in the model "dash" designation, so that it could be easily identified in the field.

Wright-Woodridge Plant
By the summer of 1943 the Wright-Woodridge Plant #7, near New York City (Dodge-Chicago was nowhere near geared up), was built in seven months to exclusively manufacture the R-3350 engine. Despite the supposedly "exposed" east coast location to possible enemy air attack, the large new 1.5 million square feet facility was chosen by Under Secretary of War Robert Patterson, Chief of Staff George C. Marshall, and Assistant Secretary of War Robert Lovett. They chose the site because of the availability of the nearby experienced labor pool and electric power in the area. Seventy million dollars had been invested in the Woodridge plant and machinery by the end of 1944. Plant #7 was scheduled to build 850 engines per month, with the first production engines slated for May 1943 (the first engines were actually shipped in July 1943). The plant was unusual, in that it was built entirely of poured concrete from the floor to the supporting pillars to the roof. The first Woodridge engines were hand-built on a single "pilot line," incorporating changes as they went. Wright engineers reasoned that once the design was frozen the final mass production assembly lines could be easily duplicated from the pilot lines. The first engine was built and tested in July 1943, and it was anticipated that by November all the changes could be incorporated into additional pilot lines/production lines, and relatively large numbers of combat engines could be turned out for the first B-29s coming off the Wichita production lines. But during the summer and into the fall R-3350 production met one delay after another, and there were not enough engines to go around for the B-29s that were now going into an intensive training program over Kansas. The uproar reached Congress, which demanded to know why the R-3350 project fell so far behind schedule. Gen. Arnold was on the hot seat again with the B-29 project, and he made the R-3350 engine the top priority of the Air Force; he ordered a new board to investigate the engine program. Members of the

board included future Supreme Court Justice Col. William Brennan, future mayor of New York William O'Dwyer, and founder of McDonnell Aircraft, James McDonnell. The board found widespread managerial ineptitude and indifference, and shortages in the labor force. Wright-Woodridge Plant #7 was scheduled to have 8,000 workers on the production line, but had only 3,300. Like other companies in the aircraft industry, Wright had problems attracting workers and then holding them after extensive training. Wright's reputation as an employer in the area did not help matters. It had broken a machinist's union strike in 1931, and throughout the 1930s fought the unions and used every means to keep wages low. Wright had planned to attract workers from the New York Boroughs and Newark, but a starting wage of $0.60 per hour, the long commute, and better paying jobs in shipyards closer to New York and Newark left Wright with the dregs of the workforce to manufacture the most complex piece of mass produced machinery built at the time. To cope with this unskilled workforce Wright broke down as much production and assembly as possible into procedures that could be done by machines and watched by workers. Other jobs, such as testing and inspection, were simplified to the lowest common denominator. Wright did little to supervise or train their workers, but there was little work to do until the engine design was finalized. Low pay, an ineffective union, and little or no work led to low morale and excessive wasted time, loitering, absenteeism, and a high quitting rate. By September 1943 the situation at Woodridge became so bad that the War Department sent in advisors to turn things around. An improved training program was established, and workers were made to appreciate the importance of their jobs in the building of the engine of the super bomber that would win the war. Unskilled women and African Americans were also accepted into the workforce, and Wright transferred 300 skilled workers from other plants; the AAF sent men to train new workers. Interchangeable engine parts were to be manufactured by new subcontractors at the Dodge-Chicago plant, and at government-financed Wright plant conversions at East Patterson and Fairlawn, NJ, and Lockland, OH. Gen. Arnold campaigned to have the government raise starting wages to $0.70 per hour, with raises for time on the job and bonuses for work produced. Perks such as child day care, bus transportation to and from New York City, and cafeterias, banks, and stores also attracted new workers. In October the company hired 1,000 new workers to bring its total to 9,700 of the goal of 13,200. In November it seemed that 800 engines per month could be produced starting in January 1944, and the War Department withdrew its advisors and allowed Wright to manage the project at Woodridge. However, with their departure the problems did continue, and production lagged in the spring and early summer, after which the production lines finally churned ahead at the scheduled production rates.

Chrysler-Chicago Plant
The Navy had two important (500 planes each) flying boat projects scheduled requiring their variant of the R-3350 engine. The Consolidated XP4Y-1 was to be built at a new factory at New Orleans, and the Boeing XPBB-1 was scheduled for its new plant at Renton, WA. There were discussions on using the Navy engine, but Boeing and Consolidated were unable to make the necessary engine installation changes to use them. It was determined that the new Chrysler Chicago engine plant could get tooled up to supply these Navy engines without jeopardizing its initial production schedules. However, the Navy production total was finally reduced, and its engine personnel were diverted to the B-29 program.

The first Wright R-3350 factory engine was built and tested in July 1943 and it was anticipated that by November all the changes could be incorporated into additional pilot lines/production lines and relatively large numbers of combat engines could be turned out for the first B-29s coming off the Wichita production lines. But during the summer and into the fall R-3350 production met one delay after another and there weren't enough engines to go around for the B-29s that were now into an intensive training program. (USAF)

Chrysler was contracted to build a new factory complex on 450 acres on the west side of Chicago. The George A. Fuller Co. broke ground in June 1942 for 19 buildings covering 6.3 million square feet. Plant #4, which housed the assembly areas and machine shops, was the largest individual building in existence, as at four million square feet it was larger than the Pentagon. The building was remarkable, containing over 1,000 work bays measuring 30 x 38ft, and located underground were 10 acres of lavatories, nine cafeterias, kitchens, and other services connected by two lengthwise and one cross tunnel. The complex also had the world's largest parking lot, which was a block wide and a mile long, and was capable of parking 8,000 automobiles. The other buildings contained administration, tool and die shops, magnesium and aluminum foundries, light and heavy forge buildings, a heat treating building, two powerhouses, and oil and chip recovery facilities. By 1944 $750 million had been spent on the Chicago-Dodge development, including $175 million on the land, construction, and equipment. Chrysler was to begin engine delivery in March 1943, but there were difficulties in starting up, buying the land, contracting architects, and then construction. Chrysler then had problems obtaining engine blueprints and other data from Wright, which had few to give, as the engine was under development. Crucial metals, such as aluminum, steel, and magnesium, were in high demand and short supply, and Chrysler President K.T. Keller was forced to ask for a July 1943 delivery date extension.

Dodge-Chicago continued to run into problems and delays in the fall of 1943. Dodge was tooling up before the engine had passed its type test, and as a consequence suffered an enormous 48,500 engineering changes that, of course, affected production schedules. The immense plant had been finished in April at a cost of $100 million, but shortages of machine tools, the relentless engineering changes, and problems in the exchange of technical data with Wright prevented Dodge-Chicago from setting up so much as a pilot line. After most of the design problems had been eliminated the first Dodge engine was finally produced in January 1944. The production line was fully equipped and manned, and from that point the engine manufacture moved efficiently, turning out 18,500 R-3350s by the end of the war. The Chicago operation was mammoth, with an average of 33,000

workers: 16,000 on the production line (8,800 on the day shift, 6,600 on the night shift, and 600 maintenance workers in the morning), and 17,000 on the managerial staff. Women comprised 36% of the labor force, and African Americans 20%, mostly in the hot, grueling foundry. The plant commonly surpassed production quotas, building not only engines, but also thousands of vital parts for the Wright Woodridge and Lockland plants. In November 1944 the plant turned out 1,079 engines, and by the end of the year the cost of an engine was down to $15,080. The number of new engines that did not survive hours of testing (called "penalty engines") dropped from 31% in early 1944 to 2% a year later. So good was the tooling set up at the Chicago plant that its parts were interchangeable with those from the Woodridge plant. When the Woodridge plant production faltered in the spring and early summer of 1944, the Chicago plant made up the deficit. Subcontractors supplied the electrical components, such as the generators,

Chrysler was to begin engine delivery in March 1943, but there were start up difficulties in buying the land, contracting the architects, and then construction, which did start until June 1942. Chrysler then had problems obtaining engine blueprints and other data from Wright, and crucial metals, such as aluminum, steel, and magnesium were in high demand and short supply. Chrysler President K.T. Keller (shown with Gen. Henry Arnold) was forced to ask for a July 1943 delivery date extension. (Chrysler)

motors, magnetos, spark plugs, and wiring. Carburetors were also subcontracted.

In the Dodge-Chicago plant, the engine production moved from the forge buildings, die shops, and heat treating building and foundries to the machining and assembly buildings. The forge shop contained 41 hammers that weighed up to 35,000lbs, and were able to strike with a force of 56,000lbs to shape rough steel forgings, such as crankcases, master and articulating rods, and cylinder barrels. From the forge shops the slowly cooling forgings were moved to the heat treating building, where they were subjected to heating, cooling, and an oil bath. The Chicago magnesium and aluminum foundries poured more metal than any other plant in the world at capacity. The aluminum foundry produced intricate castings of finned cylinder heads in sand molds. Originally, Chicago was scheduled to tool up to produce forged cylinder heads that were preferred for greater high altitude cooling, but was unable to do so because of the delays they would cause. (Wright produced their cylinder heads by forging). Each die was half a cylinder head that was placed into molding sand, which was placed into the molding machine that compressed and vibrated the sand

The engine testing facility had 50 test cells (shown) where each engine underwent evaluation. Every month 2.25 million gallons of fuel was used for testing but most of the power generated by the engines was recaptured by means of an unique power recovery system which resupplied one-quarter of the electric current used by the entire Chicago-Dodge facility. (Chrysler)

around the head die. The die was carefully removed, leaving its form in the sand. A binding liquid was sprayed on the delicate sand mold, and then the mold was placed on a slowly moving conveyor that moved it through a furnace for baking to harden it. The hardened mold was inspected and then burned with a blowtorch to keep the poured metal from adhering to the sand. The other half of the cylinder head mold was fitted to its opposite, and the two were clamped together. About a 100 steel pins (1,400 in first production molds) were placed in the mold to keep it from breaking during metal pouring. The clamped mold then had aluminum poured into it, and after it cooled the clamps were removed and the mold was pried open with a bar. The finned casting was removed from the mold and rough machined, inspected, and ready for fine machining and assembly in these automated plants.

The magnesium foundry produced the supercharger housing and the engine nose section. Caution had to be observed in the magnesium foundry due to the metal's inflammability, and the magnesium pouring pots were connected to temperature gauges that were constantly monitored. The molds had to be pumped full of sulfur gas and sprinkled with sulfur to keep oxygen away to prevent flare ups.

The main building contained the automated machining and assembly functions. The raw castings were machined, polished, and fabricated into subassemblies, and moved onward for final assembly. The completed engine was moved off the line on special mounts and run on test cells for several hours. The Chicago engine testing facility had 50 test cells, where each engine underwent evaluation. The engines underwent preliminary "green" tests that gradually ran the engine up from 1,400rpm to full take off throttle at 2,800rpm. Initial green tests lasted seven hours, but by 1945, after the engines became more reliable, this was reduced to 3.75 hours. Any failure of an engine or its auxiliaries during the green test caused the engine to be transferred for repair, and then it was put through the "penalty" tests. After the engine passed the green test it was returned to the factory for disassembly and detailed inspection of every part. It was then reassembled and then retested for another 3.5 hours (later reduced to 2.75 hours) before it was shipped to one of the B-29 factories for installation.

To save weight the cylinder heads were integral aluminum castings with a lacework of W-type cooling fins that were grooves cut on the exterior of the steel barrel as deep as four inches and as little as 1/16-inch thick, spaced five per inch. (Chrysler)

Every month 2.25 million gallons of fuel were used for testing, but most of the power generated by the engines was recaptured by means of a unique power recovery system that resupplied one-quarter of the electric current used by the entire Chicago-Dodge facility.

By the fall of 1944, the Chrysler and Wright plants were exceeding the demand for the R-3350, not only for the B-29, but also for the other aircraft mounting the engine: the Martin Mars Flying Boat; the Douglas BTD Skyraider carrier borne attack plane; and Lockheed's Constellation airliner. There were so many engines produced that it was easier and less expensive to replace a worn engine with a new one than to overhaul it. By August 1944 R-3350 production had to be decreased, as engines had to be stored as the supply outstripped the demand.

Dodge Chicago supplied the majority of the R-3350s manufactured in World War II; 18,413 as compared to Wright's 13,791. The Wright engines averaged more time between overhauls (285 vs. 267 hours). In all, Wright and its licensees produced over 281,000 engines of all types by the end of the war.

Engine Model	Shipped 1937-40	Shipped 1940-45	Shipped Licensee	Total Shipped
975 Whirlwind	1,963	3,288	52,651	57,902
1820 Cyclone	7,770	34,192	63,789	105,751
2600 Cyclone	2,138	83,152	-0-	85,290
3350 Cyclone	17	13,791	18,413	32,221
Total	11,888	134,423	134,843	281,164

B-29 Wright R-3350			
Dash #	Model	HP	RPM
-13+	XB-29	2,200	2,400
-21	YB-29	2,200	2,800
-21A	YB-29	2,200	2,800
-21*	B-29	2,200	2,600
-23	B-29	2,200	2,800
-23	B-29A &B	2,200	2,600
-23	XB-29E	2,200	2,600
-23A*	B-29	2,200	2,800
-23A	B-29A&B	2,200	2,800
-23B*	B-29	2,200	2,800
-37A	B-29	2,200	2,800
-39	B-29	2,200	2,800
-57	B-29	2,200	2,800
-57	B-29A&B	2,200	2,600
-57	XB-29E	2,200	2,600
-57A	B-29	2,200	2,800
-57A	B-29A&B	2,200	2,600
-59	B-29	2,200	2,800
-59	B-29A&B	2,200	2,600
-59	XB-29A	2,200	2,600
-59A*	B-29	2,200	2,800
-59A	B-29A&B	2,200	2,600
-59A	XB-29E	2,200	2,600

+ also used in the XB-32
* also used in the B-32

Part Two

B-29 Described

The B-29 required 23,652 lbs of sheet aluminum held together by 600,000 rivets, 1,000lbs of copper, 1,418 forgings, 618 castings, 11,308 separate extrusions, 140 electric motors, 9.5mi of wiring, and two miles of tubing. It had 40,500 numbered parts and was the first true systems aircraft.

Principal Dimensions

Airplane General

Overall Span	141ft 2.76in
Overall Length	99ft
Overall Height (at rest)	27ft 9in
Overall Height (taxi)	29ft 6.7in
Max. Fuselage Diameter	9ft 6in
Height Centerline Prop Hub	9ft 5.6in
Inboard Engines	9ft 5.6in
Outboard Engines	10ft 8in
Ground Clearance Inboard Prop Tips	14.1in

Wings

Airfoil Section	Boeing 117
Root	22%
Tip	9%
Chord Root	17ft
Chord Tip	7ft 5in
Incidence	4-degrees
Dihedral	4-degrees 29min 23sec
Sweepback	7-degrees 1min 26sec

Stabilizer

Span	43ft
Maximum Chord	11ft 2.4in

Areas

Wing (less ailerons)	1609.7square feet
Wing (flaps extended + ailerons)	2070.9square feet
Ailerons (including tabs)	129.2square feet
Aileron trim tabs (total)	12square feet
Flaps (total)	332square feet
Stabilizer & Elevators (including tabs)	333square feet
Elevators (total including tabs)	115square feet
Elevator Trim Tabs (total)	10.12square feet
Vertical Fin	131.9square feet
Dorsal Fin	40.6square feet
Rudder (including tabs)	65.5square feet
Rudder Trim Tab	5.79square feet

<cap>2-Intro-02 Major Assembly Exploded View folder

<cap>2-Intro-03 Boeing Factory Exploded Major Assembly folder

<cap>2-Intro-04 B-29 Exterior Items folder

<cap>2-Intro-05 B-29 Interior Items folder

<cap>2-Intro-06 Loading and performance folder

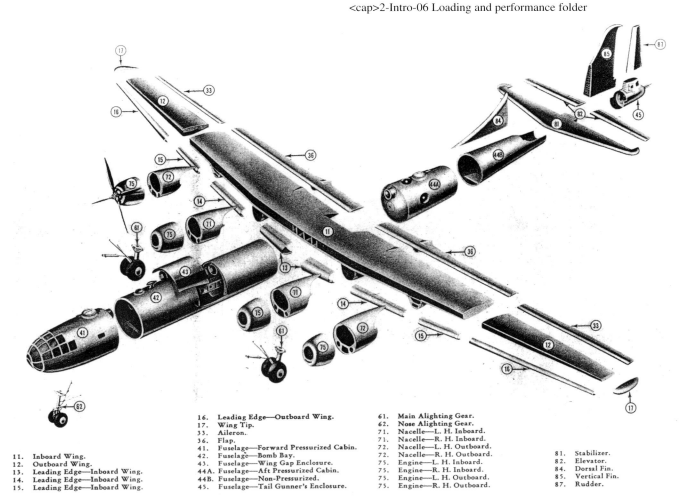

11. Inboard Wing.	16. Leading Edge—Outboard Wing.	61. Main Alighting Gear.	81. Stabilizer.
12. Outboard Wing.	17. Wing Tip.	62. Nose Alighting Gear.	82. Elevator.
13. Leading Edge—Inboard Wing.	33. Aileron.	71. Nacelle—L. H. Inboard.	84. Dorsal Fin.
14. Leading Edge—Inboard Wing.	36. Flap.	71. Nacelle—R. H. Inboard.	85. Vertical Fin.
15. Leading Edge—Inboard Wing.	41. Fuselage—Forward Pressurized Cabin.	72. Nacelle—L. H. Outboard.	87. Rudder.
	42. Fuselage—Bomb Bay.	72. Nacelle—R. H. Outboard.	
	43. Fuselage—Wing Gap Enclosure.	75. Engine—L. H. Inboard.	
	44A. Fuselage—Aft Pressurized Cabin.	75. Engine—R. H. Inboard.	
	44B. Fuselage—Non-Pressurized.	75. Engine—L. H. Outboard.	
	45. Fuselage—Tail Gunner's Enclosure.	75. Engine—R. H. Outboard.	

Major Assembly Exploded View (USAF)

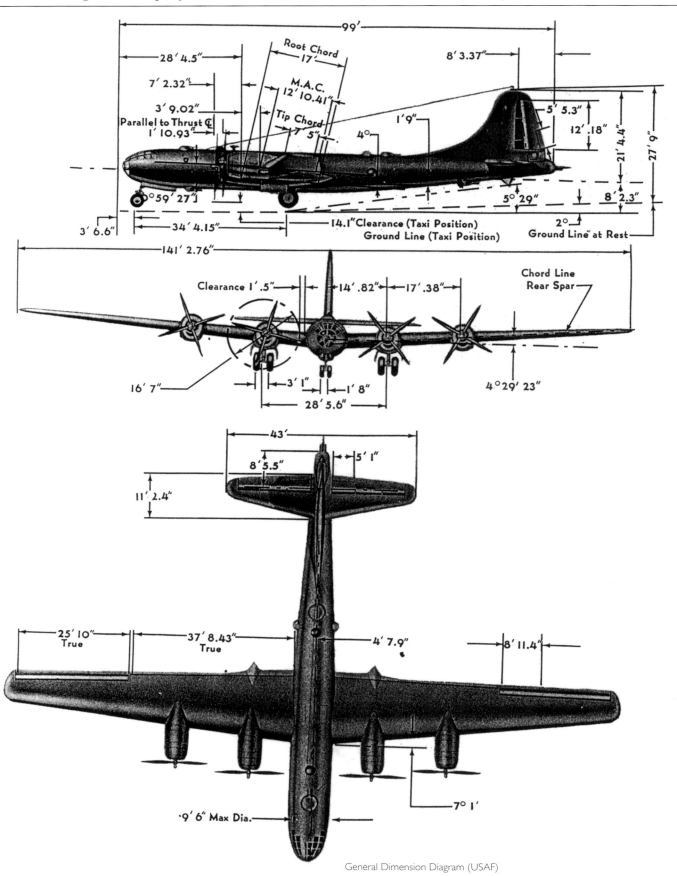

General Dimension Diagram (USAF)

Loading and Performance—Typical Mission

CONDITIONS		BASIC MISSION I	MAX BOMB II	HIGH ALTITUDE III	NORMAL WEIGHT IV	FERRY RANGE V
TAKE-OFF WEIGHT	(lb)	140,000	140,000	140,000	133,500	138,278
Fuel at 6.0 lb/gal (grade 100/130)	(lb)	47,196	39,396	47,196	41,496	56,178
Payload (Bombs)	(lb)	10,000	20,000	10,000	10,000	None
Wing loading	(lb/sq ft)	81.4	81.4	81.4	77.6	80.4
Stall speed (power off)	(kn)	103	103	103	101	102
Take-off ground run at SL ①	(ft)	5230	5230	5230	4575	5050
Take-off to clear 50 ft ①	(ft)	7825	7825	7825	6765	7530
Rate of climb at SL ②	(fpm)	500	500	500	585	520
Rate of climb at SL (one engine out) ②	(fpm)	400	400	400	480	420
Time: SL to 10,000 ft ②	(min)	20	20	20	18	19.5
Time: SL to 20,000 ft ②	(min)	52	52	52	45	49
Service ceiling (100 fpm) ②	(ft)	23,950	23,950	23,950	28,000	25,000
Service ceiling (one engine out) ②	(ft)	19,400	19,400	19,400	23,800	20,650
COMBAT RANGE ③	(n. mi.)					4809
COMBAT RADIUS ③	(n. mi.)	1717	1384	1493	1523	
Average speed	(kn)	220	217	248	221	178
Initial cruising altitude	(ft)	5000	5000	25,000	5000	5000
Target speed	(kn)	312	298	312	314	
Target altitude	(ft)	30,000	25,000	30,000	30,000	
Final cruising altitude	(ft)	25,000	25,000	30,000	25,000	5000
Total mission time	(hr)	15.35	12.77	12.22	13.5	27.03
COMBAT WEIGHT	(lb)	101,082	96,815	98,862	98,550	82,400
Combat altitude	(ft)	30,000	25,000	30,000	30,000	5000
Combat speed	(kn)	347	333	348	348	282
Combat climb (500 fpm) ①	(fpm)	1120	1420	1185	1195	1650
Combat ceiling (500 fpm) ①	(ft)	36,250	37,300	36,650	36,750	40,300
Service ceiling (100 fpm) ②	(ft)	39,650	40,700	40,100	40,150	43,750
Service ceiling (one engine out) ②	(ft)	34,800	36,200	35,400	35,550	39,650
Max rate of climb at SL ①	(fpm)	1630	1770	1690	1700	2250
Max speed at optimum altitude ①	(kn/ft)	347/30,000	348/30,000	348/30,000	348/30,000	353/30,000
Basic speed at 25,000 ft	(kn)	331	333	332	332	339
LANDING WEIGHT	(lb)	84,314	83,250	84,314	83,971	82,400
Ground roll at SL	(ft)	2250	2225	2250	2245	2210
Total from 50 ft	(ft)	2980	2950	2980	2975	2925

NOTES:
① Max power
② Normal power
③ Detailed descriptions of RADIUS and RANGE missions given on page 6.

PERFORMANCE BASIS:
(a) Data source: Flight test
(b) Performance is based on powers shown on page 6.

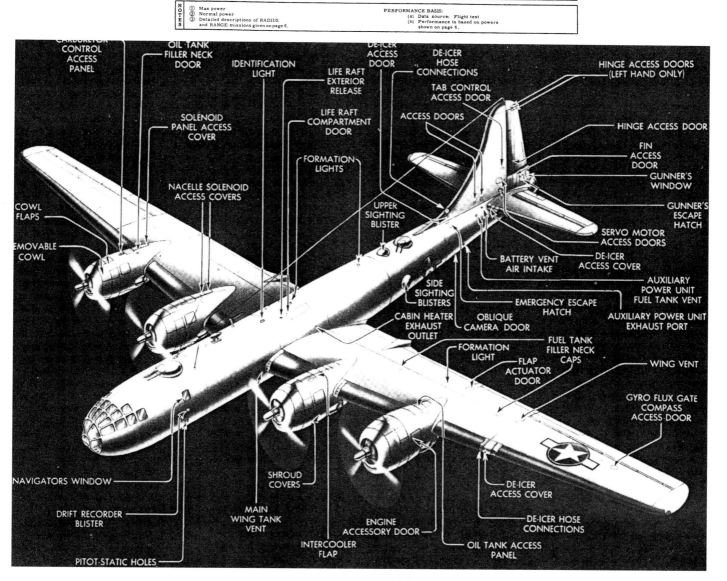

B-29 Exterior Items (USAF)

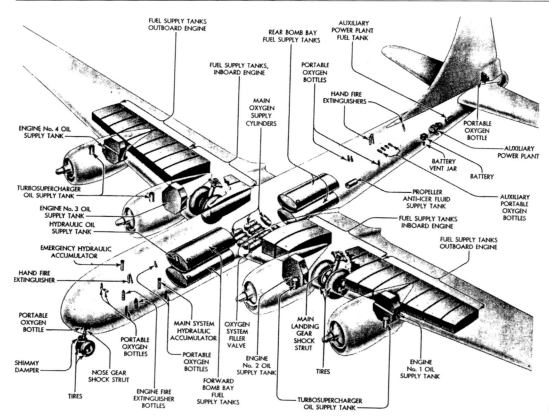

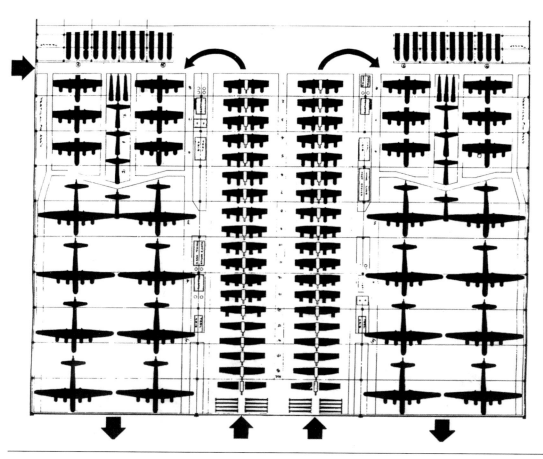

B-29 Interior Items (USAF)

1

From Aluminum Sheet to Aluminum Part

Aluminum

Aluminum is one of the most important metals in aircraft construction because of its light weight, high strength, corrosion resistance, and relative ease of manufacture. Pure aluminum has a tensile strength of 13,000psi, but with rolling and other cold processes its strength could be doubled, and by alloying it with other metals and with heat-treatment its strength could be increased as much as six-fold.

Commercial aluminum is divided into casting alloys and wrought alloys. Casting alloys are those used for casting into sand, permanent mold, and die-casting. While not used too extensively in aircraft manufacture, they are used for engine cylinder heads and pistons. Wrought aluminum alloys are those that can be shaped by rolling, drawing, or forging, and is widely used in aircraft construction for stringers, skin, bulkheads, rivets, and extruded sections.

Wrought alloy articles are fabricated from cast ingots rolled down to plate, sheet, bar, rod, and other shapes. The principal aluminum alloys are copper, silicon, manganese, iron, magnesium, chromium, zinc, and nickel, either used singly, or in combination to yield alloys with desirable properties. Wrought alloys are designated by a number followed by the letter "S," and sometimes the "S" is followed by another letter, such as 75S-T4. The first number (75) denotes the composition of the alloy, the "S" denotes wrought, the last letter (T) denotes it was heat-treated and strain-hardened, and the number (4) denotes the type of treatment. Therefore, 75S-T4 is a wrought aluminum alloy containing 1.6% copper, 0.3% silicon, 2.5% manganese, 5.6% zinc, and 0.7% iron that have been heat-treated and strain-hardened (T), and cold-hardened (4) to give it added strength. Heat-treated wrought alloys are referred to as the duralumin type of alloys. The 24S was the most extensively used type of aluminum alloy, but in 1944 the Aluminum Company of America and Reynolds developed and produced a new type of aluminum alloy called 75S and 310R, respectively. The two alloys were produced in Alclad (Aluminum Co.) and Pureclad (Reynolds) sheets that had very high corrosion-resisting qualities, and in sheet form had high tensile strengths of 88,000psi and 69,000psi, respectively. The sheet consisted of an aluminum alloy core (24ST) coated on each side with commercially pure aluminum to a depth of 5.5% of the core width.

Master Layout Photo Template

One of the most important manufacturing techniques for mass-producing World War II aircraft was the master layout photo template. The evolution from a sheet of aluminum to an aluminum part was an ingenious process. Once the design of a part left the drafting room it needed to be reproduced. The part could range in size from several square feet to several hundred square feet, and patterns resembling a blueprint of the part were drawn to actual size on a paint-coated .038 steel sheet called the "master layout." The exacting (+ or - 1/5000th of an inch) drawing was done on the steel sheet with a plastic pencil holding a silver solder point in a process called "lofting." Once completed, the master layout was ready to be photographed. A large, six ton, specialized camera and easel were wheeled into place, and a photo plate was exposed of the master layout, and the negative was developed. The negative was projected on a blank sheet of metal that became a master photo template. The master photo template was carefully checked for precision and had to be sharp and exact. The master photo template could then be used to cut hundreds of master templates that were then mounted, catalogued, and stored. The negatives were also stored and filed so more prints could be developed for master photo templates, and allowed Boeing to supply Martin and Bell with them when these companies began to build their B-29s.

To fabricate a part a plain, flat aluminum sheet was cut into a predetermined size to fit the master template. The template was then held in place over the aluminum sheet or a number of sheets (the number of sheets depended on the thickness or procedure) to be fabricated into the part(s). The template, still held in place on the sheet(s), could go to a punch press or drill press to create cutouts or holes that were guided exactly by the same cutouts or holes on the master template. After the sheets were cut or holed they were rough and had to be "burred." Since very few parts of an aircraft were flat the part had to be run through a hydraulic press that could form a flat piece of aluminum into almost any shape. The hydraulic press had a very hard-formed rubber component above that put heavy pressure against the aluminum sheet and pressed it into the corresponding hard-formed rubber component below to produce a shaped part. The shaped piece then was placed into a 920°F sodium nitrate bath to harden it, and it was then quenched. The piece was degreased with trichloroethylene and then anodized to add a protective coating against corrosion, then undercoated with a paint primer. These pieces were often one part of a component, and for ease of installation into the aircraft the component parts were put together in groups known as subassemblies.

2

Costs and Quantities

Costs

As the size of the B-29 orders increased the manufacturers were able to lower costs per unit, because their mass production techniques and assembly line workers became more efficient. The B-29-40-BA cost $971,373, while the end-of-production B-29-90-BW was listed at $495,780. These figures compared to the cost of the rival B-32, which was $822,195 initially and $731,040 later because only 145 were produced. The original estimated cost of the World War II production run of 3,943 B-29s (5,092 on order were canceled) was $3.7 billion, resulting in an average cost of $930,000 per bomber. This was 2.7 times more expensive than a 1945 B-17 when the Flying Fortress was nearing the end of its production run. When the airplane commander accepted his B-29 he actually signed a form assuming financial responsibility for $930,000!

The cost of a B-29-55-BW was **$618,045**:

Aircraft	$363,036
Government Furnished Equipment (GFE):	
Engines	$98,930
Engine equipment	$5,796
Propellers	$10,328
Aircraft equipment	$102,415
Radio	$34,328
Ordnance	$3,802

Note: Vega Aircraft Company had fixed price cost for producing its B-17Fs at $337,025 each plus GFE

Man-hours per Airframe

B-29 Wichita		B-24 Willow Run	
Sept/43	5.60	Jan/43	5.03
Nov/43	3.25	Mar/43	1.72
Jan/44	2.60	May/43	1.03
Mar/44	2.36	July/43	1.13
May/44	1.55	Sept/43	0.81
July/44	1.39	Nov/43	0.70
Sept/44	1.13	Jan/44	0.56
Dec/44	0.86	Mar/44	0.52

Although no direct comparisons can be made from these figures, they do show the progressive decrease in time required from initial production runs.

B-29 Weight Control

Coming in overweight was SOP for new aircraft designs, and the B-29 was not immune. As the design processes unfolded more equipment was added and structural changes were required, all adding weight. The four Wright R-3350s weighed slightly over 1,000lbs more than projected; each turret was 588lbs overweight, while the new tailskid and radar added more weight until the basic weight (aircraft plus its fixed equipment) of 71,200lbs increased to 83,100lbs. The range of this heavier bomber decreased, as did its top speed from 378mph to 358mph at 25,000ft. In August 1944 the AAF established the Weight Reduction Committee, which faced the conundrum: reducing the aircraft's weight would increase the performance, but then every piece of additional equipment had been installed for a valid purpose. It was found previously that when equipment had been removed from other aircraft, such as the B-26 and P-40, it had to be reinstalled later. After surveying the bomber the Committee eliminated the crew bunks, sound proofing material, and some of the protective armor. Later the deicing equipment was removed, along with some radio equipment, and when Japanese fighter opposition decreased the turrets, ammunition, and 20mm tail gun were removed, saving about 6,000lbs.

3

Fuselage

Design and Development

The pivotal aerodynamic problem Boeing designers encountered was how to create a bomber that weighed twice as much as the B-17, but would have a much higher top speed. The new Wright Cyclone engine powering the B-29 produced 2,200 horsepower, which gave the bomber a total 8,800hp—nearly twice the power of the 4,800hp of the B-17. But aerodynamically, to attain twice the speed, total horsepower has to be more than just doubled, and generally, the horsepower required to double the speed is the cube of speed (e.g. eight times rather than two times). Doubling the speed increases the drag (wind resistance) four times that, consequently, requires more horsepower to overcome. Engineering vice-president Wellwood Beall realized that instead of "piling horsepower on horsepower," Boeing needed to design an airplane that would have no more drag than the B-17, even though it would be twice as big. The answer was the design of a clean fuselage and a low drag wing.

Boeing had pioneered all-metal aircraft in developing its Monomail, B-9 bomber, 247-D transport, Model 299, B-15 bomber, Stratoliner, Clipper, and B-17. The company had used this experience to fabricate the conventional all metal, semi-monocoque formers and stringers layout for its aluminum alloy B-29 airframe. Unlike the previous Boeing single unit fuselages, the B-29 fuselage was fabricated in five sections that were coupled together on the assembly line. Boeing engineers streamlined the fuselage of the XB-29 so that its total drag was the same as the much smaller, "lumpy" B-17. The fuselage was of a continuous circular cross-section throughout its entire length, varying only at its wing and stabilizer. The nose was configured into a half sphere and fitted to a smooth, straight cylinder that ran 40ft before it began to taper gently into a cone. The pressure bulkheads and frames were spaced at intervals along the length of the body, and were the main structural units. The cylindrical fuselage allowed standardization of parts and eased fabrication, and provided minimum aerodynamic drag and maximum strength for pressurization, as the body was of uniform tensile strength.

Fuselage Construction

A monocoque structure was the basic aircraft structural design. It was a thin-walled, tubular shell that, though relatively light, was able to support and resist the basic structural stresses. This was the ideal design, as there was no internal bracing to interfere with the installation of controls. The monocoque design was ideal for small aircraft, where the shell could support the stresses imposed on it. But for larger aircraft the heavy skin also needed to support the stresses, and the semi-monocoque design was developed. The semi-monocoque design was similar to the monocoque, except that longitudinal stringers were added to help carry the load, and to maintain the shape of the structure.

The major problem of aircraft design was to provide the structure with stiffening against compression. A large diameter covered with thin sheet metal skin would wrinkle, and an initial remedy was to corrugate the outer skin, as in the Ford Tri-motor. However, these corrugations interfered with the aerodynamics of the aircraft, and to retain the smooth exterior skin the corrugations became the stringers that were riveted to the inside of the metal skin. The stringers carried the bending load of the structure and distributed it evenly, so that no concentrated stresses existed at any one area. The body stringers were mainly bulb section angles or channels. These longitudinal members were spaced eight inches apart and ran the length of the fuselage. The circumferential frames—"ribs"—were attached to the longitudinal members by metal clips.

These ribs were inset 1.125in inside the 24ST stressed skin of variable gauge, depending on the local stress requirements. The skin was only riveted to the longitudinal members and not to the ribs, as was usual. This method was used in submarine construction and saved thousands of man-hours in B-29 construction. The B-29 aluminum skin was 0.1875in thick, which was the thickest gage metal ever used on an aircraft skin. This aluminum alloy stressed skin was butt-joined, rather than overlapped, and was attached with hundreds of thousands of countersunk flush head rivets directly to the bulkheads, frames, and stringers. Brazier head rivets were used in the gun blast areas around the turret mounts for strength, and round head rivets were used only in areas out of the slipstream. Twenty miles per hour was added to the bomber's speed by using butt joints and flush rivets. The Boeing engineers were able to make the B-29 39% cleaner than the B-17.

Sections of the B-29 Fuselage
Fuselage Station Numbering

Boeing design engineers sited reference points called fuselage stations on the fuselage of their aircraft from a reference location they called "Point Zero," which was the tip of the nose, and all locations aft were identified in inches from this point. However, when the nose of the B-17F was lengthened the result was a negative measurement to the tip of the nose. On the B-29 and on all later Boeing aircraft the Point Zero was positioned in front of the actual nose. Reference points on the wing and horizontal and vertical stabilizers were taken from a Point Zero that was the centerline of the fuselage in inches. For example, the tailskid was located between fuselage stations 1039-1076 (or 86.6ft to 89.7ft from Point Zero). The reference to station number, such as Bulkhead 646, represented the distance in inches measured from Point Zero to that station reference number.

Fuselage Sections
The all-metal B-29 fuselage was built in five joined sections:
1)   Forward pressurized compartment
2)   Bomb bays
3)   Wing gap closure
4a) Rear pressurized compartment
4b) Rear non-pressurized compartment
5) Tail gunner's compartment

Forward Pressurized Compartment Section
The forward pressurized compartment, sometimes called the nose pressurized compartment, extended aft to the forward (first) pressure bulkhead, station 218. This section was bolted directly to the forward end of the bomb bay section. This compartment contained the operating positions for the airplane commander, co-pilot, bombardier, flight engineer, navigator, and radio operator. Entrance to the compartment was through the nose gear wheel well.

Bomb Bay Section
The wing center section divided the bomb stowage section (station 218 forward pressure bulkhead to station 646 front bulkhead of the rear pressurized compartment) into the forward and aft bomb bays. A catwalk on each side of the bomb bay provided a walkway between the pressure bulkheads and provided longitudinal strength. Two main frames attached to the catwalks provided the terminal attachment for the inboard wing section. A pressurized tunnel extended over the top of the bomb bay and provided pressurized access from the front to rear pressurized sections. The front and rear tunnel sections were riveted to the bomb bay section.

Wing Gap Section
The wing gap section was directly above the wing center section, and was installed after the wing was in place. It was the connecting junction between the two bomb bays, and was bolted to the bomb bay section and riveted through angles to the wing center section. The center tunnel section was riveted to the upper side of the wing gap section. A life raft compartment was located on each side of this section, with release handles on the inside of the wing gap section and on the outside, flush with the fuselage skin.

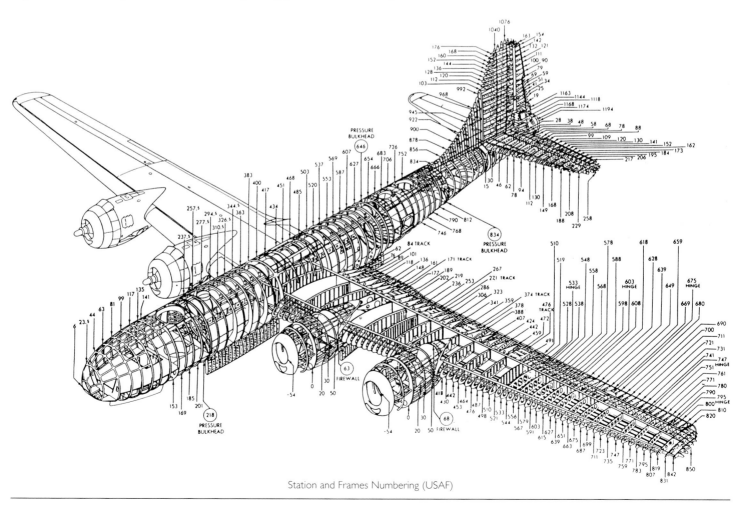

Station and Frames Numbering (USAF)

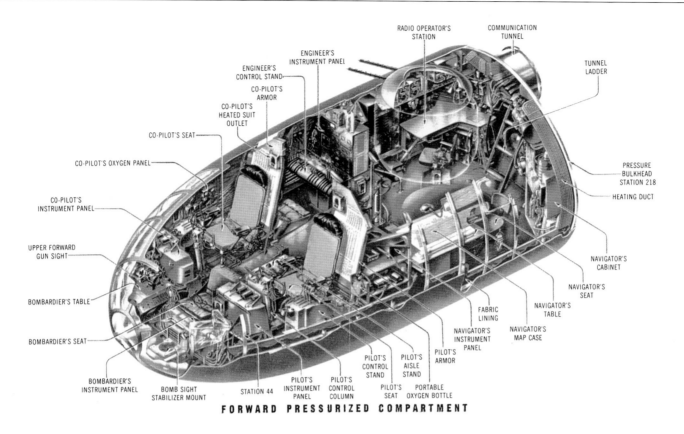

RADIO OPERATOR'S STATION

COMMUNICATION TUNNEL

ENGINEER'S INSTRUMENT PANEL

ENGINEER'S CONTROL STAND

CO-PILOT'S ARMOR

CO-PILOT'S HEATED SUIT OUTLET

CO-PILOT'S SEAT

CO-PILOT'S OXYGEN PANEL

CO-PILOT'S INSTRUMENT PANEL

UPPER FORWARD GUN SIGHT

BOMBARDIER'S TABLE

BOMBARDIER'S SEAT

BOMBARDIER'S INSTRUMENT PANEL

BOMB SIGHT STABILIZER MOUNT

STATION 44

PILOT'S INSTRUMENT PANEL

PILOT'S CONTROL COLUMN

PILOT'S CONTROL STAND

PILOT'S SEAT

PILOT'S AISLE STAND

PORTABLE OXYGEN BOTTLE

PILOT'S ARMOR

NAVIGATOR'S INSTRUMENT PANEL

NAVIGATOR'S MAP CASE

FABRIC LINING

NAVIGATOR'S TABLE

NAVIGATOR'S SEAT

NAVIGATOR'S CABINET

HEATING DUCT

PRESSURE BULKHEAD STATION 218

TUNNEL LADDER

FORWARD PRESSURIZED COMPARTMENT

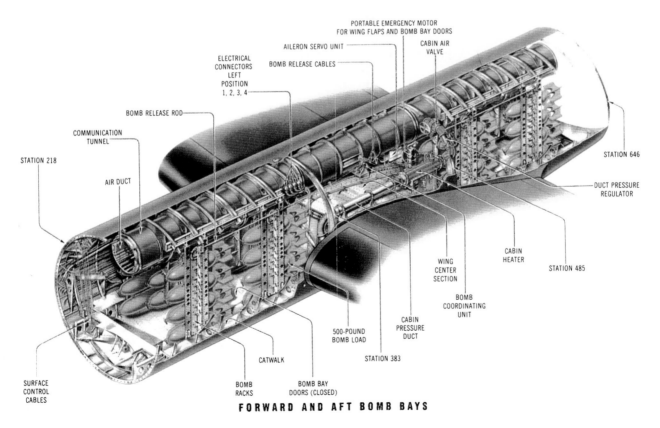

PORTABLE EMERGENCY MOTOR FOR WING FLAPS AND BOMB BAY DOORS

CABIN AIR VALVE

AILERON SERVO UNIT

BOMB RELEASE CABLES

ELECTRICAL CONNECTORS LEFT POSITION 1, 2, 3, 4

BOMB RELEASE ROD

COMMUNICATION TUNNEL

STATION 218

AIR DUCT

SURFACE CONTROL CABLES

BOMB RACKS

CATWALK

BOMB BAY DOORS (CLOSED)

500-POUND BOMB LOAD

STATION 383

CABIN PRESSURE DUCT

BOMB COORDINATING UNIT

WING CENTER SECTION

CABIN HEATER

STATION 485

DUCT PRESSURE REGULATOR

STATION 646

FORWARD AND AFT BOMB BAYS

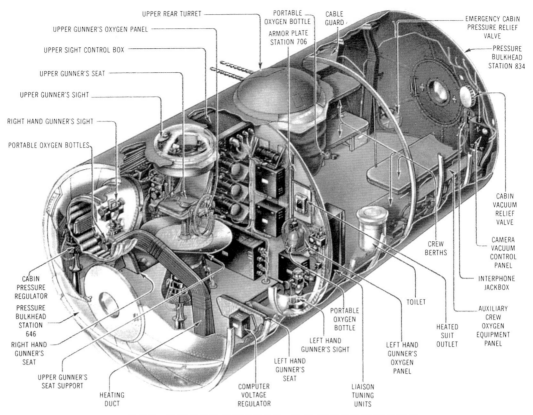

UPPER REAR TURRET
UPPER GUNNER'S OXYGEN PANEL
UPPER SIGHT CONTROL BOX
UPPER GUNNER'S SEAT
UPPER GUNNER'S SIGHT
RIGHT HAND GUNNER'S SIGHT
PORTABLE OXYGEN BOTTLES
PORTABLE OXYGEN BOTTLE
CABLE GUARD
ARMOR PLATE STATION 706
EMERGENCY CABIN PRESSURE RELIEF VALVE
PRESSURE BULKHEAD STATION 834
CABIN VACUUM RELIEF VALVE
CAMERA VACUUM CONTROL PANEL
INTERPHONE JACKBOX
CREW BERTHS
AUXILIARY CREW OXYGEN EQUIPMENT PANEL
HEATED SUIT OUTLET
TOILET
LEFT HAND GUNNER'S OXYGEN PANEL
LEFT HAND GUNNER'S SEAT
LIAISON TUNING UNITS
PORTABLE OXYGEN BOTTLE
LEFT HAND GUNNER'S SIGHT
COMPUTER VOLTAGE REGULATOR
HEATING DUCT
UPPER GUNNER'S SEAT SUPPORT
RIGHT HAND GUNNER'S SEAT
PRESSURE BULKHEAD STATION 646
CABIN PRESSURE REGULATOR

AFT PRESSURIZED COMPARTMENT

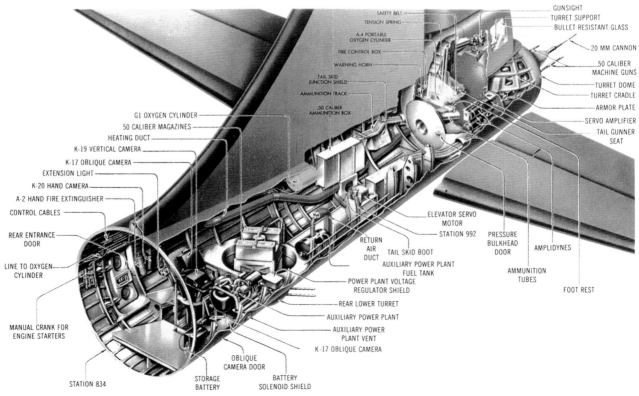

SAFETY BELT
TENSION SPRING
A-4 PORTABLE OXYGEN CYLINDER
FIRE CONTROL BOX
WARNING HORN
TAIL SKID JUNCTION SHIELD
AMMUNITION TRACK
.50 CALIBER AMMUNITION BOX
GUNSIGHT
TURRET SUPPORT
BULLET RESISTANT GLASS
20 MM CANNON
.50 CALIBER MACHINE GUNS
TURRET DOME
TURRET CRADLE
ARMOR PLATE
SERVO AMPLIFIER
TAIL GUNNER SEAT
G1 OXYGEN CYLINDER
50 CALIBER MAGAZINES
HEATING DUCT
K-19 VERTICAL CAMERA
K-17 OBLIQUE CAMERA
EXTENSION LIGHT
K-20 HAND CAMERA
A-2 HAND FIRE EXTINGUISHER
CONTROL CABLES
REAR ENTRANCE DOOR
LINE TO OXYGEN CYLINDER
MANUAL CRANK FOR ENGINE STARTERS
STATION 834
STORAGE BATTERY
BATTERY SOLENOID SHIELD
OBLIQUE CAMERA DOOR
K-17 OBLIQUE CAMERA
AUXILIARY POWER PLANT VENT
AUXILIARY POWER PLANT
REAR LOWER TURRET
POWER PLANT VOLTAGE REGULATOR SHIELD
AUXILIARY POWER PLANT FUEL TANK
TAIL SKID BOOT
RETURN AIR DUCT
ELEVATOR SERVO MOTOR
STATION 992
PRESSURE BULKHEAD DOOR
AMPLIDYNES
AMMUNITION TUBES
FOOT REST

TAIL SECTION (UNPRESSURIZED) AND TAIL GUNNER'S COMPARTMENT

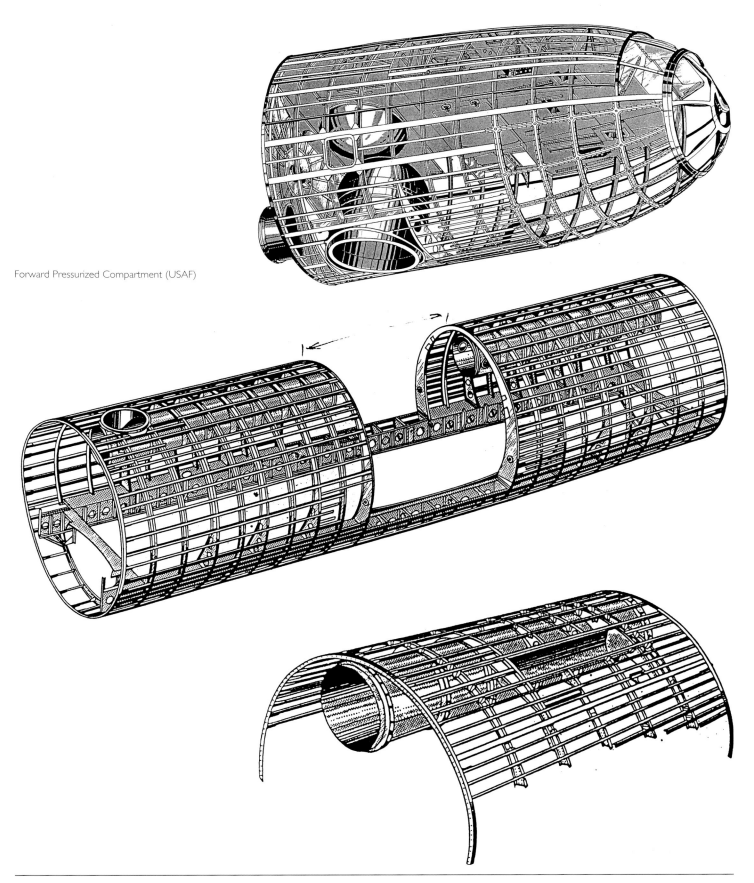

Forward Pressurized Compartment (USAF)

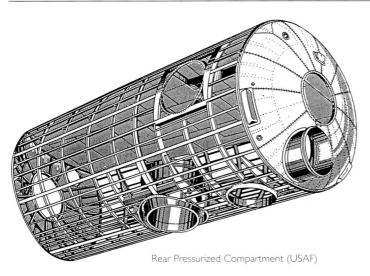

Rear Pressurized Compartment (USAF)

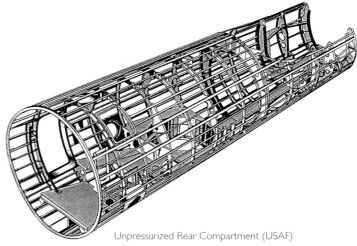

Unpressurized Rear Compartment (USAF)

Rear Pressurized Section

This compartment extended from station 646 to station 834, and was comprised of the upper rear turret and the side and upper Plexiglas sighting stations in the forward portion of this compartment. It was bolted to the bomb bay section and the rear unpressurized section around the circumference of the pressure bulkhead. Access to this section was through a door in each bulkhead. Early B-29s had crew bunks located in the rear of this section. The CFC gunner and two blister gunners occupied this compartment. Later one, and sometimes two radar operators operated their equipment here.

Rear Non-Pressurized Section

This section of the B-29 extended from the aft pressure bulkhead at station 834 to the mainframe station 1076, and was not pressurized. Located in this section were the lower rear turret, camera mounts, and auxiliary power unit (APU). It was used for general stowage. Its entrance was the main rear entrance door on the right side of the fuselage toward the front of the section, and an emergency escape hatch.

Tail Gunner's Section

This pressurized section extended from station 1076 to the end of the fuselage, and had the tail turret projecting from the rear. The controls for the operation of the tail turret were contained from pressure bulkhead at station 1110 aft to the armor plate at station 1144. Normal entrance and exit was through a door in the pressure bulkhead, and an additional emergency hatch. This section was bolted to the rear pressurized section at station 1076. All five fuselage sections are discussed in detail later.

Pressurized Cabins

History

For years aeronautical engineers had investigated pressurized cabins as the answer to anoxia and aeroembolism. Anoxia, the lack of oxygen, is one of the main problems of high altitude flying. At 12,000ft and above air pressure is less, and there is not enough pressure to force enough air into the lungs to supply the body with sufficient oxygen. The lack of oxygen causes sluggishness, fatigue, then unconsciousness, and finally death. Aeroembolism, called aviator's bends, occurs at high altitudes. At sea level pres-

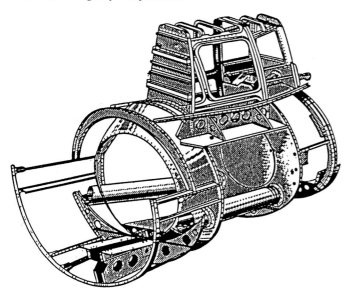

Tail Gunner's Compartment (USAF)

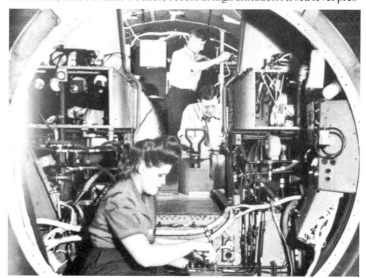

Final wiring and instrument installation in the forward compartment at the DeSoto, Warren, MI factory. (USAF)

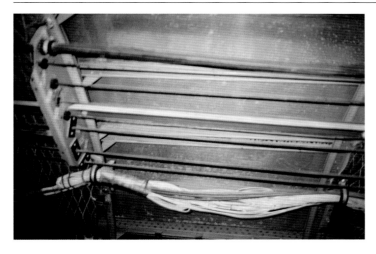

Bundled electrical wiring (top), rudder and elevator control cables (middle) and copper tubing on the sidewall of the rear unpressurized compartment. (Author/Pima)

sure oxygen and nitrogen both dissolve in the blood, but as an aircraft climbs higher the air pressure decreases, and oxygen is still absorbed, but nitrogen is released in bubbles that could block a blood vessel in the brain, causing permanent disability or death. The only remedy for aeroembolism is to return to a lower altitude, where the higher air pressure forces the nitrogen gas back into solution.

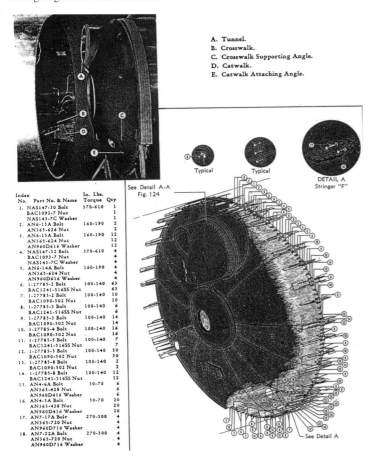

A. Tunnel.
B. Crosswalk.
C. Crosswalk Supporting Angle.
D. Catwalk.
E. Catwalk Attaching Angle.

Index No.	Part No. & Name	In. Lbs. Torque	Qty
1.	NAS147-30 Bolt	370-610	1
	BAC1093-7 Nut		1
	NAS143-7C Washer		1
2.	AN6-15A Bolt	160-190	2
	AN365-624 Nut		2
3.	AN6-15A Bolt	160-190	12
	AN365-624 Nut		12
	AN960D616 Washer		12
4.	NAS147-32 Bolt	370-610	4
	BAC1093-7 Nut		4
	NAS143-7C Washer		4
5.	AN6-14A Bolt	160-190	4
	AN365-624 Nut		4
	AN960D616 Washer		4
6.	1-27785-2 Bolt	100-140	63
	BAC1241-516SS Nut		63
7.	1-27785-2 Bolt	100-140	10
	BAC1090-502 Nut		10
8.	1-27785-3 Bolt	100-140	6
	BAC1241-516SS Nut		6
9.	1-27785-3 Bolt	100-140	14
	BAC1090-502 Nut		14
10.	1-27785-4 Bolt	100-140	16
	BAC1090-502 Nut		16
11.	1-27785-5 Bolt	100-140	7
	BAC1241-516SS Nut		7
12.	1-27785-5 Bolt	100-140	30
	BAC1090-502 Nut		30
13.	1-27785-8 Bolt	100-140	2
	BAC1090-502 Nut		2
14.	1-27785-8 Bolt	100-140	12
	BAC1241-516SS Nut		12
15.	AN4-6A Bolt	50-70	6
	AN365-428 Nut		6
	AN960D416 Washer		6
16.	AN4-5A Bolt	50-70	20
	AN365-428 Nut		20
	AN960D416 Washer		20
17.	AN7-17A Bolt	270-300	4
	AN365-720 Nut		4
	AN960D716 Washer		4
18.	AN7-22A Bolt	270-300	4
	AN365-720 Nut		4
	AN960D716 Washer		4

Typical   Typical   DETAIL A Stringer "F"

See Detail A-A Fig. 124

See Detail A

Joining Sections: This diagram shows the placement of nuts, washers and bolts required to join the rear bomb bay section to the forward rear pressurized compartment. (USAF)

In 1919, test pilot Lt. Harold Harris flight tested the first pressurized cabin in an aircraft. It was a large tub-like chamber covering the cockpit, with a wind-driven blower mounted on the wing that blew compressed air into the cockpit. The test failed when the pressure control device malfunctioned, as did the cockpit instruments that recorded a cockpit temperature of 150-degrees and an altitude of 9,000 feet below sea level! The early problem with pressurized cabins was that aircraft design was not sophisticated enough to seal the fuselage joints, doors, and windows, as well as around the instruments. In 1934, Wiley Post developed a high altitude pressure suit that was fabricated from rubberized parachute silk and an aluminum oxygen helmet. The bulk and weight of the suit made movement very difficult in the confines of an aircraft.

The XC-33, a modified Lockheed Electra airliner, was the first successful pressurized aircraft. Exhaust-driven turbo superchargers maintained the interior cabin pressure to approximately 10,000 feet when the XC-33 was flying at 25,000 feet. An auxiliary impeller operating on the same shaft as the engine supercharger furnished cabin supercharging. The main drawback of this system was that the cabin supercharger speed varied with the main engine output, and the cabin pressure decreased when the engine slowed down. The windows leaked, and frost would form on the inside of the window and ice on the outside. Instruments malfunctioned as their cases leaked. The problem was partially solved in the XC-35, when rubber cement was used to seal blisters, turret wells, and its green house nose. This rubber seal was not totally satisfactory, as it could not be used for duct sealing and on the larger structural joints that continued to leak.

Boeing led the way in pressurized cabin development in 1938 with its four-engine Model 307 production Stratoliner, in which the entire cabin was pressurized. The primary difficulty in designing a pressurized cabin was to select a fuselage shape that would best resist the internal cabin pressure at high altitudes. Engineers knew under pressure air tended to equalize, as demonstrated by the round bubble gum bubble. An airtight sphere would be the perfect pressure cabin, as it had no bending stresses, but a sphere was not an option for an aircraft design. Boeing engineers used the experience of the AAC, whose engineers found the circular cross section to be the optimum cabin configuration, being the strongest and lightest structure. The Stratoliner fuselage maintained a circular cross section, but was tapered at the nose and tail. It was partitioned by rounded bulkheads that would better resist the large pressures, instead of a flat bulkhead, which would need to be shored by heavy support beams. There was no pressurization in the tail section. Air leakage was a problem in sealing the pressurized compartments. The fuselage skin seams were riveted, and a tape saturated with zinc chromate, a sealing material that remained soft, was inserted between the joints. Control cables and wiring had to run through the bulkhead between the pressurized cabin and the unpressurized tail section, and between the pressurized lower cabin walk and the unpressurized wings. A synthetic rubber bushing was fitted in the bulkheads, and the cable or wiring was passed through it. The cable was held snugly enough to stop air leakage, but was allowed to move to operate the controls. Doors on the Stratoliner closed inward so that the internal pressure pressed them against the frame to create a seal. A mechanical compressor geared directly to the engine, rather than to the turbo supercharger, pressurized the 307 cabin. The constant speed propellers maintained constant engine rpm so that the geared compressor maintained cabin pressure during descents. The 307 could only be pressurized to 12,000 feet (2.5psi) at 20,000 feet.

The cabin pressurization innovations developed in the Stratoliner were used in the B-29 but the large B-29 was to create new problems. In the Stratoliner the entire aircraft except the tail was pressurized but Boeing used the "capsule" approach to pressurize the three compartments of the B-29. Shown is the forward pressurized compartment with the tunnel entrance (top) and bomb bay entrance (middle). (USAF)

Of course, the bomb bays weren't pressurized for obvious reasons so a means to connect crew members from the forward pressurized to the rear pressurized compartments was developed and this was via a tunnel. The tunnel opened on top of the cockpit bulkhead with a ladder leading up to it. Shown is the exterior tube as seen from inside the bomb bay. (Author/Pima)

The next AAC experimental pressurizing program was with the XB-28, a North American Aircraft Company medium, twin-engine bomber. A plastic compound was sprayed over the entire interior to seal the cabin, and thin rubber strips were placed between all riveted joints. The XB-28 used a mechanical engine-geared supercharger that maintained cabin pressure at 8,000 feet at 33,000 feet. Placing all turrets outside the pressurized cabins solved the problem of sealing the defensive armament positions. The guns were remotely controlled from pressurized sighting stations. Auxiliary heaters circulated heated air through ducts into the cabin.

B-29 Pressurization

The cabin pressurization innovations developed in the Stratoliner were used in the B-29. But the B-29 design was to create new problems, as Boeing used the "capsule," or "little Stratochamber" approach to pressurize only the crew-occupied areas. The entire cabin, except the tail, of the Stratoliner had been pressurized, but of the B-29's five sections (nose, bomb bays,

rear pressurized, rear unpressurized, and tail), three pressurized crew areas were built into the airframe (nose, rear, and tail). The unpressurized rear fuselage separated the pressurized rear compartment from the pressurized tail compartment, so the tail gunner was cut off from the rest of the bomber during pressurized flight. The aircraft had to be depressurized for the tail gunner to leave his position. Of course, the bomb bays were not pressurized for obvious reasons, so a means to provide a connection for crew from the pressurized nose to the rear pressurized compartments was developed, and this was via a tunnel.

Sealing the Cabin

Boeing engineers utilized two methods of structural sealing:

(a) Compression sealing compounds were used between all joints with conventional riveting. After cleaning the area with lacquer thinner, U.S. Rubber Co. rubber cement was applied and allowed to partially harden, and then was pressed into place. Adhesive tape was sand-

The nose contained 26 panes of glass and Plexiglas caulked with soft, green zinc chromate. Only the panels next to the airplane commander and co-pilot were movable. The distinctive B-29 forward nose section consisted of eight molded Plexiglas panes set in a cast aluminum frame that was bolted to the fuselage frame. (Both Author/Pima) NOTE: 2 photos/1 caption

wiched between all overlapping joints that were then riveted to produce an airtight seal. All rivets were dipped into the sealing compound before being placed.

(b) After conventional riveting all joints in normal construction were painted or sprayed, coating them with a sponge-like plastic compound.

Both methods still allowed about 10 pounds of air to escape, but cabin air blowers were able to pump four times that amount of lost air into the cabin every minute, and cabin pressure was maintained by the use of regulators that balanced incoming air and air leakage loss.

Windows and Pressure Doors

The nose contained 26 panes of glass and Plexiglas designed to withstand 10 pounds pressure, and was caulked with soft, green zinc chromate. Only the panels next to the airplane commander and co-pilot were movable. They could be opened by pulling a handle, and were latched open by sliding the windows upward. The distinctive B-29 forward nose section consisted of eight molded Plexiglas panes set in a cast aluminum frame that

The pressure door was single-hinged and sealed by a rubber circumferential gasket. The door shown opens from the rear pressurized compartment to the bomb bay. The window allowed the crew to check for bomb hang ups above 8,000ft and enter the bay below that altitude. (Author/Pima)

was bolted to the fuselage frame. Bullet resistant glass was incorporated above the airplane commander's and co-pilot's instrument panels. There also was a square fixed glass panel above the navigator's station on the port side behind the airplane commander, and a window for the flight engineer on the starboard side above his head. Modification centers later replaced several of the Plexiglas nose windowpanes with flat glass panes so that the navigator had some "good" glass to shoot through, as the astrodome proved insufficient and incorrectly placed. In later production B-29s the entire nose was converted to flat glass. Five windows made up the tail gunner's section, with the rear window and aft side windows that surrounded the gunner's head made of bullet resistant plate glass.

There was a pressure bulkhead door (station 218) connecting the aft of the front pressurized compartment to the front of the forward bomb bay. Exit from the front of the pressurized rear cabin could be through the pressure bulkhead door (station 646) leading to the rear of the rear bomb bay. The third pressurized bulkhead door (station 834) led from the back of the rear pressurized compartment to the front of the rear unpressurized compartment. The bomb bay pressure doors had small windows in the center so the bomb bays could be checked for hung up bombs. The small tail gunner's cabin had its entrance through a pressure bulkhead door (station 1110). These doors swung inward into the pressurized compartment, so the pressure would push the door into the seal.

Cabin Supercharging and Pressurization

Boeing engineers initially employed the mechanical supercharger used on the XB-28, but turned to the turbo-driven supercharger design of the XC-35, and developed engine-driven superchargers to pressurize early B-29s. These were a simplified and lighter system that bled off the compressed air from the turbo impeller into the cabin, as well as into the carburetors. Later model B-29s used two modified engine-driven cabin superchargers located in each inboard nacelle, and each supplied air and heat to an independent and separate system of ducts within the aircraft. The cabin superchargers were not directly geared to the engines, but operated to conform to the supercharging requirements for supplying the separate systems.

For maximum engine efficiency the superchargers were set to their lowest point that maintained the selected cabin airflow, and the optimal cabin airflow was the minimum flow that maintained the cabin altitude.

Under normal conditions pressurization was initiated at 8,000ft, as climbing from sea level to that altitude the cabin pressure remained the same as the outside pressure. At 8,000ft all windows, pressure doors, and the cabin relief valve (located under the flight engineer's seat) were closed. The cabin supercharger air intake regulator valves (located on the engineer's control stand) were opened. The most important part of the pressurized cabin design were the automatic cabin regulators manufactured by the Airesearch Manufacturing Company. The regulators bled off compressed air from the engine superchargers and pumped air inside the cabin at a constant rate and pressure. From 8,000 to 30,000ft the regulators maintained a constant 8,000ft cabin pressure by allowing pressure above that to escape. Not all the supercharged air sent to the cabin was needed at low altitudes, as the outside pressure was high, and the automatic regulator vent released a large proportion of the incoming supercharged air. The three pressurized crew areas were automatically maintained when flying at altitudes above 30,000 feet with a pressure of 6.55psi differential maintained between inside and outside: e.g. 10,000ft at 33,000ft and 12,500ft at 40,000ft.

After climbing to altitude and leveling off the airplane commander set a predetermined power for range or maximum endurance cruising. If the cabin airflow was then too low with the cabin air valves open full then the commander needed to provide the additional boost necessary to supercharge the cabin. He increased the turbo boost slightly (the inboard engines had to be run at 200rpm higher than the outboard engines), and also retarded the throttles to the desired manifold pressure. This procedure could necessitate a fuel transfer to the inboard engines that were using more fuel to maintain the pressure.

Combat procedures required that there be a progressive manual release of cabin pressure 30 minutes prior to entering a combat zone to prevent a rapid decompression if the bomber were damaged. At high altitudes, prior to the release of cabin pressure, crewmen were to wear and adjust their oxygen masks and, if equipped, plug in their electrically heated flying suits.

On descent, pressure was to be released slowly to prevent crew discomfort, but at low altitudes it could be released quickly without crew

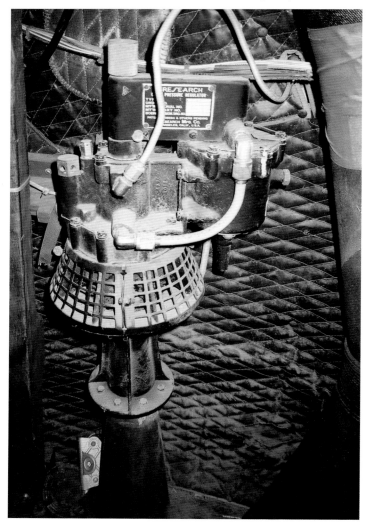

The most important part of the pressurized cabin design were the automatic cabin regulators manufactured by the Airesearch Manufacturing Company. The regulator bled off compressed air from the engine superchargers and pumped air inside the cabin at a constant rate and pressure. From 8,000 to 30,000ft the regulators maintained a constant 8,000ft cabin pressure by allowing pressure above that to escape. (Author/Pima)

discomfort by pulling either of the two cabin pressure release handles (one located on the pilot's control stand, and the other at the aft side of bulkhead 646). A vacuum relief valve was developed to prevent a vacuum from being formed inside a pressurized aircraft when it was not under pressure and in rapid descent. The outside pressure on descent would increase while the internal pressure would remain the same, and the fuselage would be in jeopardy of collapsing. The vacuum relief valve was designed to open at a certain point to let pressure equalizing air inside the fuselage. In case of the failure of one engine the compressed air supply from either nacelle was sufficient to pressurize the entire cabin. Compressed air was ducted from the superchargers of each inboard engine as a redundancy in case an engine malfunctioned, or was damaged in combat. In case of automatic pressure regulator failure the flight engineer could employ the manual pressure relief control. Cigarette smoking was allowed in the cabin, but the carbon monoxide reduced the oxygen-carrying capacity of the blood's hemoglobin. This airflow through the cabins provided some ventilation.

Heating and Ventilating System

Cabin heating was automatically maintained at a constant 70°F by two independent systems that either heated or cooled the air. The sources of heat were two gasoline heaters, one in each supercharging system, and from the heat of compression (when air is compressed it is heated) from the cabin superchargers. The output from these units was controlled automatically by two thermostats located overhead on the flight engineer's panel. The thermostats were of the compensating type (i.e. compensation being derived from the heater and aftercooler controls), and controlled the amount of heat output by positioning the heater throttle and aftercooler dampers, and adjusted immediately for the required temperature change. When the aircraft was climbing from sea level to 8,000ft there was little output from the cabin superchargers, and thus little heat from compression. In the climb the thermostat setting required heat, and would close the aftercooler dampers and start the gasoline combustion heaters. But as altitude increased there would be a concomitant increase in heat of compression from the cabin superchargers. As altitude further increased the heat of compression became sufficient; the thermostat shut down the gasoline heaters, and the aftercooler dampers would control the temperature. However, at very high altitudes the heat of compression could become inadequate, and in early B-29s electric flying suits were plugged in, but later in the war stored flight jackets and gloves were found to be sufficient.

Depressurization Tests

An unanswered question during development of the pressurized cabins was the consequences of an enemy AA shell or aircraft bullet puncturing the pressure wall. At 35,000ft the outside pressure is 3.5psi and the temperature less than 60°F below zero, while the bomber's cabin pressure would be 6.5psi and the temperature 65-70°F. Within seconds after a perforation the cabin would be depressurized to 3.5psi, and the cabin temperature would begin to plummet. It was known in deep sea diving that ascending too rapidly to the surface caused the bends, and although a diving ascent involved a much greater pressure differentiation, research at the time had not determined the effect of depressurization at high altitudes.

At the Wright Field Aero Medical Laboratory, Maj. H. Sweeney reproduced combat conditions by placing a P-38 cockpit in a large stratochamber. Sweeney sat in the cockpit, which was maintained at 10,000ft pressure and separated by a diaphragm from the surrounding stratochamber,

Cabin heating was automatically maintained at a constant 70F degrees by two independent systems that either heated or cooled the air. The sources of heat were two gasoline heaters, one in each supercharging system, and from the heat of compression from the cabin superchargers. When air was compressed it was heated and used to heat the cabins. If cooling was needed then cold air from the outside of the aircraft was passed to the air conditioning unit, cooling the air flowing through it. (Author/Pima)

and was depressurized to equate 35,000ft. A screwdriver was used to perforate the diaphragm, air in the cockpit rushed out, and almost instantaneously Sweeney's body was subjected to depressurization from 10,000 to 35,000ft. Motion picture records showed Sweeney's lips and cheeks to bulge and flap while his chest contracted in spasms as the air was sucked from his lungs. When he put on his oxygen mask the spasms ceased, and his lungs quickly adjusted to the new low pressure.

Boeing conducted its B-29 depressurization tests at its Seattle Plant #1, employing Maj. Sweeney, who was aided by John Christian, head of the Boeing armament unit. Sweeney and Christian entered a B-29 fuselage, and for safety from the test bullets sat near the rear pressurized compartment bulkhead. The cabin was pressurized to altitude, and the Boeing armament unit fired bullets into the middle of the cabin, which caused almost instantaneous pressure equalization. The only physical change the men noted was a sharp drop in the temperature due to the sudden expansion of the air in the compartment when the pressure was equalized. These tests demonstrated that there were no adverse affects to the body from rapid depressurization. Consciousness was not lost, there was no noise, and the ears cleared automatically and painlessly as air rushed from the lungs through the nose and mouth. Instantly, the crew was able to fully function and put on their oxygen masks.

There was no problem with a sudden increase in cabin pressure except above 30,000ft, which exposed the crew to temporary painful reaction to the bends.

There were several precautions to be taken for depressurization during flight:

1) The oxygen mask was to be kept attached to the left side of the helmet for instant emergency use
2) Safety harnesses were to be worn near the sighting blisters in case of explosive decompression.

3) One danger resulting from the explosive decompression caused by a large shell hole was that air accelerated at a high speed through the tunnel. The force was sufficient to propel a man caught in the tunnel out either end with serious consequences.

The first unexpected airborne incidence of depressurization occurred during a routine training flight over Texas, when a Plexiglas sighting blister blew out at 30,000ft. The alarm signal announced the loss of pressure, and the crew donned their oxygen masks and continued the flight uneventfully. In India an uncommon number of blisters blew out at high altitude, and an investigation determined that the cause was the large variations of temperature on the ground caused hairline cracks that weakened the blisters. Four times as many blisters blew out as were in stock in the CBI for replacement, and the engineering section had to repair the damaged blisters. The engineers used other damaged blisters to cut out a conforming undamaged section, and cemented and bolted it over the same section of the damaged blister. The problem was solved in production by strengthening the blister by using two layers of Lucite with a single ply of Butacite sandwiched between. These two transparent materials were somewhat soft and flexible, did not shatter, and had self-sealing properties that limited a bullet hole to a minimum size. If a bullet perforated a new Lucite/Butacite blister, disks of the strong material were placed nearby, where they could be easily placed over the hole and the higher inside pressure would tightly hold the disk in place. Nonetheless, the waist gunner was equipped with a new safety harness system. The gunners wore two safety belts, one to be used to hold them firmly in the seat, and another attached to the floor to allow greater freedom of movement when not seated. The belts were double-stranded and capable of withstanding forces of up to 5,800lbs. There is a famous photo of left blister gunner Sgt. James Krantz hanging outside his blister position on the B-29 *American Maid* at 29,000ft over Japan on 3 January 1945. During the mission Japanese fighters hit the bomber and the

Well-known photo of left blister gunner Sgt. James Krantz hanging outside his blister position on the B-29 *American Maid* at 29,000ft over Japan on 3 January 1945. During an attack Japanese fighters hit the bomber and the blister blew out, taking the gunner along. Krantz, a former machinist, had designed his own safety rig from a parachute harness, and was jerked to a stop at the end of its short tether. Krantz survived his ordeal and recovered from his injuries. (USAF)

blister blew out, taking the gunner along. Krantz, a former machinist, had designed his own safety rig from a parachute harness, and was jerked to a stop at the end of its short tether. His gloves and oxygen mask were torn off, and he banged against the fuselage in the freezing cold slipstream. The crew was too occupied to immediately notice the gunner's predicament, but the co-pilot and CFC gunners soon came back and tried to pull him back inside, but were unsuccessful. After several more harrowing minutes the bombardier came back to help, and the three were able to turn Krantz around, and after about 15 minutes outside Krantz was finally back in the bomber. He was given morphine and plasma to keep him from going into shock and he survived, suffering a dislocated shoulder and badly frost bitten hands.

Pressurization Developments by Other Nations

Luftwaffe

The German Luftwaffe introduced a pressurized crew cabin for the Ju-86, and later in the Ju-388. By the late 1930s the Ju-86 had been downgraded as a bomber, but in early 1940 the prototype Ju-86P V1 appeared with a pressurized nose cabin for a crew of two. Two 950hp Jumo 207 engines powered the P V1, and pressurization was provided by bleeding off of air from one of the engine superchargers. The P V1 could only reach a modest 32,000ft, but soon the improved P V3 was able to reach nearly 40,000ft, and a successful reconnaissance mission was flown over England, far out of the range of RAF interceptors. An order was issued to convert a small number of Ju-86Ds into the P variant. The bomber version was to carry 2,200lbs of bombs, and the photo-recon version was equipped with three automatic cameras. Neither had any defensive armament, as they flew above interception. The reconnaissance versions flew regular operational missions over England, pre-invasion missions in preparation for Barbarossa, the invasion of Russia in June 1941, and over North Africa and the Mediterranean in 1942. The JU-86P remained unchallenged until August 1942, when a specially equipped Spitfire shot one down at 42,000ft. Two more were shot down before they were withdrawn from operations in May 1943. The bomber version flew about a dozen sorties over the Western Front for 14./KG 6 in August 1942, bombing unsuccessfully (inaccurately) from about 30,000 to 40,000ft. The bombers were (mis)used as transports, and destroyed in the desperate attempt to resupply the encircled German troops at Stalingrad. Work continued upgrading the Ps to the R variant, which was able to reach 47,000ft by increasing the wing area, adding the GM-1 (nitrous oxide) boost to supplement the superchargers, and adding new four-blade propellers. Only a small number were converted, and their operational fate is unknown.

By 1943 the Luftwaffe was losing its superiority in aircraft performance, and looked to modifying and improving existing models. The Ju-188J (night fighter), K (bomber), and L (reconnaissance) models, descendants of the prolific Ju-88, were chosen for high altitude development, and were redesignated as the Ju-388. A pressurized nose section was developed, and the Model J reached 42,600ft. Only 75 models of all versions were built, the majority for reconnaissance, as developmental problems and then Allied bombers attacking the Junkers factory delayed large scale production.

RAF

Wellington Mark V

In 1938, the Vickers Company was asked to investigate developing a high altitude bomber equipped with a pressurized cabin. The first order for two prototypes based on the Wellington bomber was issued in May 1939. The Mark V prototype program was to use the 1,425hp Hercules VIII and XI engines and the 1,600hp Merlin 60 engine. The specifications called for a crew of three to be housed in a pressurized cabin providing a ground pressure of 10,000ft, and a bomb load of 1,000lbs (4,000lbs was projected to be carried) that was to be carried over 9.6 hours. The long (18ft, 3in), narrow (5ft, 5in) cylindrical crew compartment was very cramped, and could only be entered through a small (3ft, 2in) pressure door at the rear of the cylinder that made an emergency exit difficult. The pilot's seat was mounted on a shelf with the navigator/bombardier in front of him, and the radio operator located behind him. The pilot's head protruded into a dome that had very limited forward and downward visibility, but to facilitate landing vision the dome was offset to the left. Engine problems were encountered with freezing grease and oil due to the intense cold at high altitudes, and also with the internal air-conditioning and heating, but these problems were overcome. However, the turbosupercharged Hercules VIII and XI engines did not yield enough power, and the English pressurization agenda concentrated on the Mark V/Merlin 60 program. Two Mark V/Merlin 60 prototypes were completed, and 10 Mark IV/Merlin 60 production versions were ordered, but only one was built (and nine were canceled). The Mark Vs provided test data for the development of the pressurized cockpits for the Spitfire and Westland Welkin.

Wellington Mark VI

The Wellington VI was designed to investigate high altitude bombing using the top secret Norden bombsight. The Mark VI was structurally similar to the Mark V, except it carried a crew of four: pilot, navigator, bombardier, and radio operator. This model also met similar lubrication and air conditioning/heating problems that were remedied. Although the Merlin engine performed adequately, by the time the Mark VI was ready for operations, the superlative Mosquito had been introduced and was able to carry a similar two-ton bomb load at almost the same altitude, but without a pressurized cabin. There were 120 Mark VIs ordered, including the prototype, but only 64 were built. The Mark VIs conducted high altitude re-

Women workers installing the sound dampening and temperature insulating Fiberglas blankets developed and produced by Owens-Corning. (USAF)

search and special radio tests, including "Oboe" blind bombing experiments and training. Reports indicate that the Mark VI was used in at least two daylight bombing missions.

Cabin Soundproofing

To reduce the incessant roar of the four 2,200 horsepower engines, Boeing acoustic engineers and Harvard's Cruft Laboratory working under the backing of the National Research Council Committee on Sound Control developed a system that would make the B-29 the quietest of the heavy bombers. An olive-colored blanket made from equal quantities of animal hair, cotton, and kapok was developed to line the fuselage. The outside face of the blanket was coated with a doped fabric that was airtight, and to reduce heat loss was silver coated. The inside face was covered with a strong, porous fabric. The thickness of the blanket depended on its location, and ranged from one-half to one and a half inches, and the total blanket installation weighed 398lbs. They were installed with special fasteners that fa-

cilitated their removal for repair, replacement, or reconditioning. After Pearl Harbor the Japanese captured the major sources of kapok, and new soundproofing material needed to be developed. The Harvard Electro-Acoustic Lab demonstrated that the surface of fibers used in sound insulation should be large in comparison to their weight, leading to the development of Fiberglas produced by Owens-Corning. With a plastic binder these synthetic fibers were formed into a blanket one half inch thick. An asbestos sheet was sewn between two blankets and mounted three inches from the sides of the fuselage walls. This kapok substitute was found to be superior, as it reduced the total blanket installation from 398 to 167lbs, and was so effective that normal conversation could be heard between the airplane commander and co-pilot. The panel fasteners were of the "Mae West" spring snap type attached to the panels, and snapped into holes drilled into the supporting structure. The blanket material was also placed in the tunnel between the pressurized nose and rear compartments, where it not only served its soundproofing function, but also was a thermal insulator and cushioning carpet for the knees of the crawling crewmen.

Fuselage Exits/Entrances

The pressurized nose cabin had three exits. Normal entry and exit was through the nose landing gear wheel well via a hatch in the floor beside the flight engineer. This hatch could be used as an emergency exit. The pressure bulkhead door (station 218) afforded an emergency exit through the bomb bay. The flight engineer's window was removable and could be used in an emergency, but only on the ground or in the water. There was a removable emergency hatch located on the right side of the cabin at the flight engineer's station. It could be opened from the inside or outside by pulling either of its two ring handles to lift the door inward. It was not to be used in flight due to the proximity of the inboard propellers. In the center of the forward cabin bulkhead was a circular pressurized door with a window in the center, appearing much like a commercial clothes dryer window that looked into the bomb bay.

Exit from the pressurized rear cabin could be through the pressure bulkhead door (station 646) leading to the bomb bay, or through the pressure bulkhead door (station 834) leading to the aft unpressurized area.

Close-up of an insulating blanket fitted around a control panel. Using a plastic binder synthetic fibers were formed into a blanket one half inch thick. Two blankets were sewed to the opposite ends of an asbestos sheet and mounted three inches from the sides of the fuselage walls. The synthetic fibers were substituted for the dwindling supplies of Asian kapok and was found to be superior as it reduced the total blanket installation weight from 398 to 167lbs. (Author/Pima)

Nose wheel well entrance to forward pressurized compartment. (Author/Pima)

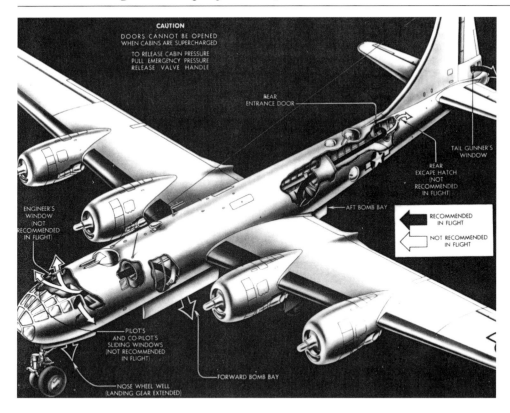

B-29 entrances/exits with exits recommended in flight. The exits could not be opened when the cabins were pressurized in flight. To released cabin pressure the emergency pressure release valve handle had to be pulled. (USAF)

Exit from the rear unpressurized area was via the rear entrance door, or through an escape hatch located on the upper left side of the fuselage, and could be used only while on the ground or water.

The small pressurized tail gunner's cabin (between pressure bulkheads at stations 1110 and 1144) had its entrance through a pressure bulkhead door (station 1110). Emergency exit was made through a window to the tail gunner's right (aircraft port) side.

The tail gunner and the crew of the rear pressurized compartment enter through the fuselage entrance via a ladder. (USAF)

Fuselage Colors, Decals, and Signs, National Insignia, and Unit Markings

Exterior Fuselage Colors

In photographs the B-29 was mostly seen in its natural aluminum finish, but a small number—possibly 55 early B-29s—were painted in standard AAF Dark Olive Drab (OD/shade 41) with Neutral Gray (shade 43) undersides. The propeller bosses and blades were painted Black (shade 44), and the final four inches of the blade were painted Identification Yellow (shade 48). The identifying data for the model and serial numbers and fuel and weight requirements were in one or two-inch block capital letters and numbers located on the left side of the fuselage, just below the airplane commander's window. There was a small oval black metal plaque fastened near the ceiling, on the upper forward turret structure to the right of the engineer's station. It listed in natural metal lettering the manufacturer, model, serial number, and the engine maker and type. The only large individual marking was the four-figure radio call (designator) number that was painted on both sides of the fin.

Of the first XB-29s, the first (s/n 41-002) was OD, the second, (s/n 41-003 - the Allen crash aircraft) was silver, and the third (s/n 41-18335) was unpainted aluminum. The 14 service test YB-29s were furnished in OD and gray, and the ninth flew combat in OD with the 462nd Bomb Squadron in the CBI as a "Hump" fuel transport. The first 40 Boeing-Wichita production B-29s (s/n 42-6205 through 42-6254, minus five s/n each in this batch that were assigned to Martin and Bell) were OD. Photos of subsequent Boeing-Wichita (BW) production blocks show silver aircraft. Photos of all production blocks of Bell (BA) and Martin (MO) aircraft are all silver aircraft. However, there is a photo of a Boeing-Renton (BN) B-29 of production block B-29A-1-BN in OD being transported on a barge. That BN production block numbered 20 aircraft, and it is unclear if the other 19

The B-29 was mostly seen in natural aluminum finish but a small number, possibly 55 were painted in standard AAF Dark Olive Drab (OD/shade 41) with Neutral Gray (shade 43) undersides. Shown is the third XB-29 that was still in natural aluminum and ready to be painted and join the two olive drab camouflage XB-29s in the background. (USAF)

were finished in OD. In December 1943, it was decided not to paint any American heavy bombers, saving not only many man-hours of painting labor and the cost of the paint, but also increasing the performance by deleting the weight and drag of the paint. Other AAF heavy bombers had anti-dazzle paint patches on their engines or near the front cabin, but the B-29 crew did not have a sun reflection problem in the Plexiglas nose of the bomber. The propeller blades remained black with yellow tips, but the bosses were left unpainted. The rubber deicer boots on the fin and tailplane were black, as were the radio call numbers.

After March 1943 night bombing missions over Japan increased, and the natural metal finishes proved to be good reflectors of Japanese searchlight beams. On the Marianas bases, all groups were scheduled to have the undersides of their bombers painted, but ultimately the groups of the 314BW that were selected for night missions against the Japanese oil industry were given painting priority. Jet #622—high gloss paint developed for night fighters—was applied about half way up the sides of the fuselage and engine cowlings. Later, replacement bombers arrived from U.S. depots already painted with black undersides.

Decals and Signs

The B-29 was known for its nose art, but close examination of the bomber showed it to be a veritable bulletin board of decals, stencils, and signs both inside and out. The bomber carried hundreds of signs and diagrams to direct pilots, crew, and maintenance men with explanations and warnings. All maintenance instructions were in black, and all warning markings and fire extinguisher location panels were in red.

In the days before computers, the layout of the decal was developed from a blueprint by hand, and the letters and numbers were hand cut from stock printed sheets of alphabets and numbers. They were glued into place on a piece of rigid paperboard and laid out on a piece of glass as they were to appear on the decal. A custom-built camera designed for photo-templates then photographed the paperboard sign. The film was processed on

In December 1943, it was decided not to paint any U.S. heavy bombers, saving not only many man hours of painting labor and the cost of the paint, but the decision also increased aircraft performance by deleting the weight and drag of the paint. (Author/Pima)

After March 1943 night bombing missions over Japan increased and the natural metal finished were good reflectors of the Japanese searchlight beams. Jet #622, high gloss paint, developed for night fighters, was applied about half way up the sides of the B-29 fuselage and engine cowlings. Shown is a B-29A-50-BA of the 314BW with AN/APQ-13 radar radome antenna between the bomb bays. (USAF)

special transparent paper with black lettering. The stencil was cut by a photochemical technique into a thin gelatin sheet with the lettering on it. The stencil/gelatin sheet was then fastened to a piece of porous silk and stretched over a wooden frame that was placed over a special paper covered with glue. A rubber blade moved paint over the silk screen/gelatin sheet, causing the paint to seep through onto the paper. The first paint layer was the background color, after which the lettering paint was run through the silk screen and superimposed on the background. The wood-framed stencil racks were placed on shelves to dry, with steam sprayed on them to keep them from curling. The final decal was made up of layers of paint on paper that was covered by a layer of clear lacquer to seal the paint. Many of the decals were subcontracted, but the Boeing-Renton paint and photo-template shops produced more and more of their own decals as the war progressed. The completed decals were organized into envelopes corresponding to the section of the bomber to which they were to be placed. Every boy who has built a model airplane is familiar with the method of applying the decals. The backing (paper) was soaked for 10 to 30 seconds in lukewarm water that dissolved the glue coating holding the paint on the paper, and then the paint could be separated from the paper. The loosened

The B-29 was known for its nose art, but close examination of the bomber showed it to be a veritable bulletin board of decals, stencils, and signs, both inside and out. (Author/Pima)

decal was moved slightly off the edge of the paper and applied to the bomber's surface, and the paper was then slowly pulled away, laying the paint portion flat to stick on the surface when it dried.

National Insignia

The National Insignia was established on 1 January 1921 with an Insignia Blue circle with white five-pointed star, with an Insignia Red circle inside the star. A change in the National Insignia was ordered on 18 August 1942 for it to become a blue circle with a white five-pointed star inside. The red circle inside the star was removed, as it could have been confused for the Japanese "meatball." The National Insignia on the XB-29s was an Insignia White (shade 46) five-pointed star, super imposed on an Insignia Blue (shade 47) circle. A 60in diameter National Insignia was located on the upper surface of the port wing, and on the lower surface of the starboard wing, and 50in diameter National Insignias were also placed on both sides of the fuselage slightly aft of the sighting blisters. On 29 June 1943, there was another change ordered for the National Insignia, with an Insignia White rectangle added to both sides of the white star inside the blue circle, and the entire National Insignia outlined in Insignia Red. The YB-29s received these markings at the factory, and the first and third XB-29s (the second was lost in the Eddie Allen crash) had these markings changed in the field. From this time forward the B-29 National Insignia was standardized in size to 60in diameter on the wings and 50in diameter on the fuselage. Its location on the wings remained the same, but there were slight variations on the fuselage on aircraft from the various factories (the Boeing-Renton B-29s were placed at station 762, while the Boeing-Wichita, Martin-Omaha, and Bell-Atlanta Insignias were at station 756). On 17 September 1943, there was another National Insignia change ordered (the substitution of the Insignia Red for the Insignia Blue outline), but by this time only a few B-29-1-BWs had been produced with the old National Insignia and had to have them modified.

Unit Markings

All B-29s of the 20th Air Force were identified by their large tail markings that mostly followed a system of labeling.

58th Bomb Wing/CBI

Initially, seven B-29s were to outfit a very heavy Bomb Squadron, and four squadrons comprised a Bomb Wing (28 B-29s). This compared to 56 aircraft in the B-17 or B-24 Bomb Groups that were able to carry the same bomb load as the 28 B-29s. The B-29 Bomb Groups were organized into a bombardment wing (BW) composed of four Bomb Wings. The first Bomb Wing was the 58th BW, which broke the rule and had five groups assigned to it: the 40th, 444th, 462nd, 468th, and 472nd (the 472nd was later transferred to become the nucleus for a training unit). The remaining four 58BW groups were sent to India via Africa in March 1944 to fly under XX Bomber Command.

When the 58BW arrived in India it carried no unit or identification markings, and continued to be unmarked as it ferried equipment to forward bases being readied in China. For radio communication the radio call letter system was used, and the black call numbers were painted on the vertical tail to be used for visual identification. Soon the individual groups added other markings to identify the aircraft in their group. The 444BG painted two-foot black plane-in-group numbers below the radio call number, and then painted 30in numbers that were the repeat of the last three

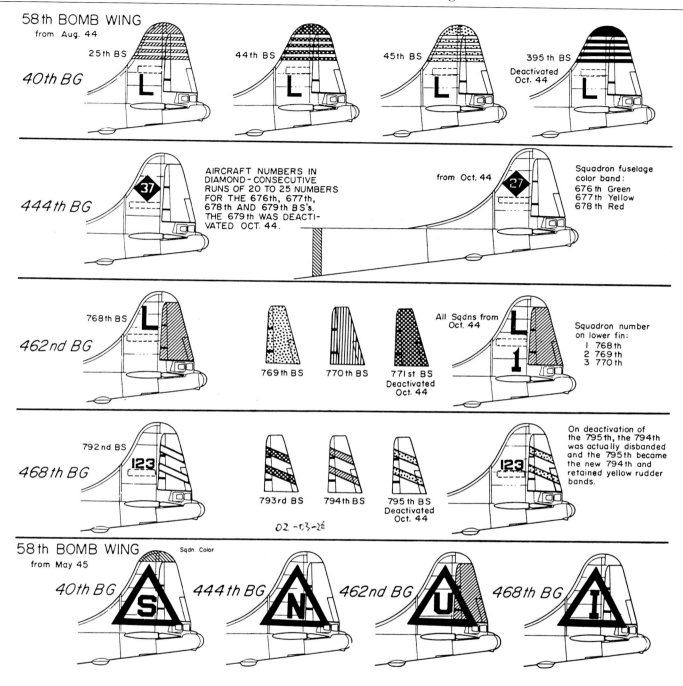

58th BOMB WING
from Aug. 44

40th BG

25th BS L

44th BS L

45th BS L

395th BS
Deactivated
Oct. 44 L

444th BG

37 AIRCRAFT NUMBERS IN DIAMOND - CONSECUTIVE RUNS OF 20 TO 25 NUMBERS FOR THE 676th, 677th, 678th AND 679th BS's. THE 679th WAS DEACTIVATED OCT. 44.

from Oct. 44 27

Squadron fuselage color band:
676th Green
677th Yellow
678th Red

462nd BG

768th BS L

769th BS

770th BS

771st BS
Deactivated
Oct. 44

All Sqdns from Oct. 44 L 1

Squadron number on lower fin:
1 768th
2 769th
3 770th

468th BG

792nd BS 123

793rd BS

794th BS

795th BS
Deactivated
Oct. 44

123

On deactivation of the 795th, the 794th was actually disbanded and the 795th became the new 794th and retained yellow rudder bands.

02-03-26

58th BOMB WING
from May 45

40th BG S

Sqdn. Color

444th BG N

462nd BG U

468th BG I

numbers of the radio call number above the radio call number. A black five-foot block group identification letter was painted by the 40BG under the radio call number, and by the 462BG over the radio call number. In summer 1944, as group missions of 12 to 24 bombers were being assembled, the groups decided to inaugurate the use of bright markings on the vertical tail to facilitate assembly, with the colors of these markings identifying the four squadrons in the individual group. The 468BG painted two dark blue, red, white, or yellow diagonal bands to the rudder. The 40BG painted four horizontal black, dark blue, red, or yellow bands across the top of the fin and rudder, and also painted the tip of the tail. The 462BG painted the entire rudder blue, green, red, or yellow. The 444BG painted a large black

diamond above the radio call number, and on the diamond the white plane-in-group number was superimposed. The need to assemble a formation quickly required that the flight leader's aircraft be easily and quickly identified. The lead bombers of the 58BW were identified as follows: the 444BG by black diagonal bars on the squadron bands, and the 40BG and 462BG by a broad black band painted vertically on the dorsal fin.

Early Markings of the 73rd and 313th Bomb Wings/Marianas

The 73BW, composed of the 497BG, 498BG, 499BG, and 500BG, each with three squadrons, was the second Wing to complete its training, and began operations in late October 1944. The 73rd instituted a basic system

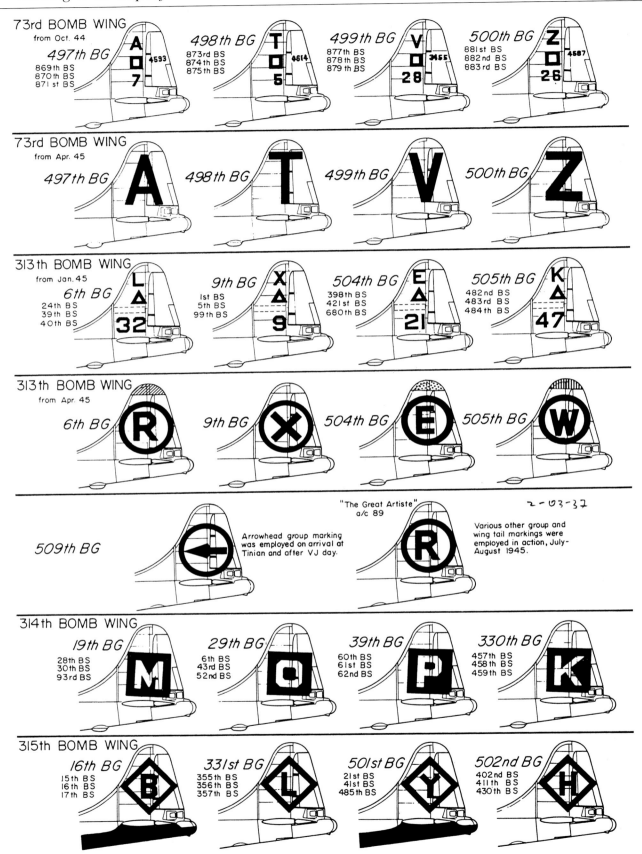

Marianas-based Bomb Wing Bomb Group Markings (Author/Pima)

using the large letters on the rudders and tail of its B-29s. Each group was allocated a letter that was painted in a 36in block capital letter towards the top of the fin. The assigned letters were "A"-497BG, "T"-498BG, "V"-499BG, and "Z"-500BG. The marking of the Bomb Wing was the outline of a 15in square painted below the 15in group letter. Each bomber of the group was assigned a 30in number from 1 to 20 for the first squadron, 21 to 40 for the second, and 41 to 60 for the third. This black aircraft number was painted below the Bomb Wing marking, and its base was located on the level of the rudder. To place these markings the radio call numbers were removed, and the last four call numbers were repainted as black 6in numbers above the top of the rudder trim tab.

When the 313BW arrived at Tinian in early 1945 it adopted the 73BW marking system, using a triangle as its Bomb Wing designation (vs. the 73BW's square). The 36in group letter remained at the top of the tail, and the 30in to 36in aircraft number below the Bomb Wing triangle. However, the radio call numbers remained on the tail between the triangle and aircraft number.

Standardization of Markings/Marianas

The third Marianas Bomb Wing, the 314BW (the 19BG and 29BG arrived at the same time as the 313BW, and then was followed by the 39BG and 330BG), became operational, and the 315BW was scheduled to follow soon behind, along with the transfer of the 58BW from the CBI. With this glut of 20 bomber groups under its control, the XXI Bomber Command authorized the standardization of unit identification marking schemes. The markings of the 73BW and 313BW were found to be too small to be seen over 4,000ft in good visibility. The most significant markings while the bombers were trying to assemble were those that identified the group and wing, so the new marking system had the large vertical tail to use as a billboard. The wing symbols were to be 10 to 12ft high and wide, with the 5 to 6ft group letters inside the symbol with each letter, number, or marking to be 12in to 18in wide. The symbols assigned were a triangle for the 58BW, a circle for the 313BW (formerly a triangle), a square for the 314BW, a diamond for the 315BW, and the 73BW (formerly a square) would have a letter without a symbol. The group letters used by the 73BW were preserved, but were now 12ft high. The black outline (i.e. unfilled) was used by the 313BW for its circle, the 58BW for its triangle, and the 315BW for its diamond. However, the 314BW used a solid black square (the center group letter was created by taping out the letter on the bare metal and then spraying on the square, leaving the letter when the tape was removed). A broad vertical solid black band on the forward upcurve of the tail fin identified the flight leader's flash. Under the new marking standards, new groups were to use consecutive aircraft identification numbers of 20 to 25 numbers per each squadron that were to be painted on the rear fuselage in 36in black numbers. Also, the radio call numbers were removed. The application of the new letters and numbers took many hours and then weeks (mid-April to early May 1945), and often individual bombers would fly into combat with a combination of old and new markings.

B-29 Group Markings

Personal Markings and Nose Art

Initially the tone of the names and art were left to good taste, but it seemed that the more remote and distant from Headquarters and civilization, the more bold and indiscreet the nose art became. This is evident when comparing ETO bomber and fighter nose art in very proper England with that in the "uncivilized and amoral" Pacific islands. As the war went on there were occasional outcries and movements to eliminate or, at least, control personal markings, mostly initiated by civilian visitors to the front, the base clergy, and PR-conscious HQ brass. Photos of aircraft nose art made their way into Stateside publications, also causing a hue and cry amongst the righteous. In June 1944 Charles Lindbergh accompanied Gen. Paul Wurtsmith to Topline Airstrip in New Guinea. In his *Wartime Journals* he wrote the following: "The cheapness of the emblems and names painted on the bombers and fighters nauseates me at times—mostly naked women or 'Donald Ducks'—names such as '*Fertile Myrtle*' under a large and badly painted figure of a reclining nude." In 1943, renowned novelist and champion of the "illustrated literature on aircraft fuselages," John Steinbeck, defended the practice in the following dispatch to the *New York Tribune*: "The names must not be changed. There is enough dullness in war as it is." But "boys will be boys," and the markings became increasingly more risqué, especially in the Pacific.

73BW and 313BW Tail Markings before April 1945

Wing Symbol	Group Letter	BG	Wing Symbol	Group Letter	BG	Wing Symbol	Group Letter	BG
Plain	A	497	Triangle	L	6	Triangle	X	9
Triangle	E	504	Square	T	498	Square	Z	500
Triangle	K	505	Square	V	499			

Tail Markings from April 1945

Wing Symbol	Group Letter	BG	Wing Symbol	Group Letter	BG	Wing Symbol	Group Letter	BG
Plain	A	497	Diamond	L	331	Plain	T	498
Diamond	B	16	Square	M	19	Triangle	U	462
Circle	E	504	Triangle	N	444	Plain	V	499
Plain	F	3*	Square	O	29	Circle	W	505
Diamond	H	502	Square	P	39	Circle	X	9
Triangle	I	468	Circle	R	6	Diamond	Y	501
Square	K	330	Triangle	S	40	Plain	Z	500

* = PRS (photo-reconnaissance squadron)

In August 1944, the Air Force issued Regulation (35-22) that stated in part:

1) *Policy:* The custom of decorating organizational equipment of the Army Air Force with individual characteristic design is authorized by the Secretary of War and is encouraged as a means of increasing morale.

2) *Definitions:*
   a) "Equipment" as used herein means operating equipment, i.e. airplanes.
   b) "Design" or "Organizational Design" as used herein refers to the markings applied to organizational equipment, and does not refer to group or other unit coat of arms, not to uniform insignia, or shoulder or sleeve insignia.

This military double speak placated the protesters, but made no dictates on the type or method of nose art in the field. Generally nothing changed, unless there was to be a very official inspection, at which time the indecent female figures had clothing painted over offending areas, and especially offensive language was deleted, but all only temporarily. By the time the B-29 became operational these restrictions, never really enforced in the Pacific, were ignored. The large, unmarked areas on the nose of the B-29 under the airplane commander's and co-pilot's windows was an ideal canvas for amateur, but often very talented artists, to embellish the bomber with varied nicknames and artwork that grew increasingly more and more

Intricate nose art drawing on the *Phoney Express*, a B-29 of the 58BW/462BG/769BS based on Tinian. (USAF)

ribald. Most of the nudes, copied from "Vargas Girls" calendars or masterly done from memory, were bare-breasted and provocatively posed. Full frontal nudity did exist, but for the most part was avoided by a lifted leg, a turned back, or panties. By May 1945, the Marianas nose "art" was deemed so suggestive that the 20th Air Force Command took steps to control it. The 73BW command issued orders to remove all nose art but the mission symbols. Nicknames could be retained in an "approved" form: black capitals

A beautiful full color hand-painted aluminum panel reproduction of the nose art on the *Bockscar* atomic bomber. Fighter and bomber nose art is fabricated and sold by Gary Velasco (www.fightingcolors.com) of Velasco Enterprises. (Author's collection)

The Pima Air Museum's B-29 *Sentimental Journey* that flew with the 458BS/330BG/314BW took the 330BG emblem, consisting of a circle around a map of North America and the designation of a specific city was placed on the right side. (Author/Pima)

Camel Caravan was the first B-29 to reach China and is shown here after it had completed all of its 47 Hump missions. This cargo B-29 flew three Hump missions in four days during October 1944. (USAF)

on a standardized wing motif (a yellow flash with the nickname on it over a winged black ball). In the 313BW each group had its individual nose motif, but consisting of a white streamer with the nickname printed on it. For example, the 6BG that had served in the Panama Canal Zone in the 1920s and '30s had a bust of the pirate Jean LaFitte inside a triangle (the group symbol) as its group motif. The nickname of the aircraft was painted in red inside the white streamer streaming aft from the triangle. The four groups of the 314BW adopted the map of North America (the USA in red) in a blue circle with a white outlined pennant with the name of a chosen city on it as Wing motif. The wing motif was carried on the right side, and the left side was allowed to carry an "unofficial" name, which meant the nudes and nicknames continued. The 315BW largely ignored the edict, and uncensored nose art continued on many of its aircraft until the end of the war.

Mission Markings

It was customary for bomber crews in all theaters to post a record of their missions on the left side of their aircraft's noses. Among the mission markings were bomb shapes for bombing missions (dark-colored bombs for night missions and light-colored bombs for day missions), slanted mine shapes for mining missions, CBI ferry missions by camels, supply missions by pack mules, and enemy aircraft shot down by Japanese "Rising Sun" flags.

Many aircraft crews had the names of each member stenciled under his station (i.e. tail gunner under his window, the top turret gunner next to his turret, etc.) Also, the name of the Crew Chief and the ground crew were often stenciled somewhere on the nose.

A 3PRS F-13-A-40 BW is showing 20 cameras indicating 20 photo recon missions. (USAF)

4

Wing

Background and Design

Boeing engineers aspired to design a wing that exhibited low drag both during cruising and at high speeds, had a high lift coefficient, and had good stall characteristics. A major design consideration was that most of a Long-Range bomber's gross weight was made up of fuel, and the wings had to serve as fuel tanks. At the time a major premise of aircraft design was to keep wing loading (the weight carried by each square foot of wing area) to a minimum. Designers thought that a high wing loading was dangerous, as it would lead to take off problems and produce very high landing speeds. However, high wing loading after take off was advantageous due to its lower drag and greater range. The Boeing design department decided to refocus from the thicker wings the company favored for its bombers. The laminar flow, high aspect ratio wing developed by David R. Davis for Consolidated's XB-24 Liberator bomber was considered to be the most effective design for Long-Range bombers. Boeing followed that developmental direction for its proposed Model 334A, which came off the drawing boards in July 1939 with a wing very similar to the XB-24, but had a higher wing loading. The Model 334A was never built, and only reached the wooden mockup stage, but Boeing designers were on the right track, and set out to develop a wing flap to negate the drawbacks of highly loaded wings.

Eddie Allen, Head of Boeing Flight Testing and Aerodynamics, and George Schairer, Boeing Chief Aerodynamicist, led Boeing engineers in continued testing of the "Davis Wing" concept in their wind tunnels. Schairer had been with Consolidated before coming to Boeing in 1939, and was definitely influenced by the work there. He suggested that the Davis concept of the Model 334A be retained, but decided that a different approach would be needed for the Model 345. They kept the long narrow taper of the Davis wing and developed the Boeing 115 wing for the Model 345. The Boeing 115 Aerofoil had the potential of increased range due to its lower drag. The AAF was unconvinced about the wing, as it was concerned that because of its high wing loading its operational ceiling would be reduced, and would affect its take off and landing characteristics. After comprehensive wind tunnel tests Boeing engineers developed a wing flap that would offset the high wing loading and alleviated the Air Force's worries. The wing had an unusually high aspect ratio of 11.5, but was of a laminar flow type that gave it a good lift/drag ratio. Compared to conventional wings the 115 was deep between the main spars, giving it greater strength, increasing the space for fuel tanks, and gave the bomber more gradual stalling characteristics.

Boeing continued its wing research, and the end result was the superlative 117 Wing, whose primary advantages were:

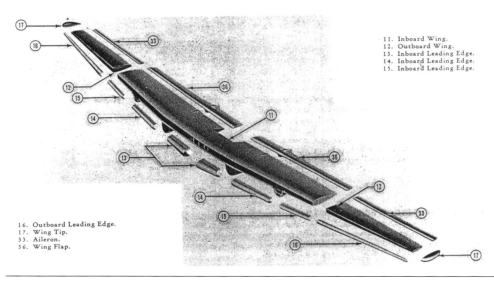

11. Inboard Wing.
12. Outboard Wing.
13. Inboard Leading Edge.
14. Inboard Leading Edge.
15. Inboard Leading Edge.

16. Outboard Leading Edge.
17. Wing Tip.
33. Aileron.
36. Wing Flap.

Major Components of the Wing Section (USAF)

Leading edge wing assembly at the Martin, NB factory. (USAF)

Trailing edge wing assembly at the Murray factory, Scranton, PA. (USAF)

1) Decreased drag per pound of lift.
2) Gave better stall warning and more gradual stalling characteristics.
3) Increased the thickness of the interspar area, which gave greater strength to the primary structure, and increased the area to place fuel tanks.

The wingspan of the 117 was 141ft, 3in, with an area of only 1,736 square feet. The long, thin, narrow wing not only supported the entire aircraft, but also four engines, nacelles, and the fuel tanks and fuel load. At maximum gross weight the wing loading was a huge 69lbs/square feet, and was more than double that of the B-17. To give the B-29 maximum range, maximum space had to be provided in the wing to accommodate the fuel tanks, and yet the wing had to have the necessary internal structures to provide maximum strength with minimum weight. The wing could not flutter, needed to have high torsional (twist-resistant) strength, and also needed to resist bending up to 100in under maximum load and maneuvers. The flexibility of the wing was later demonstrated in flight with a full combat load when the airplane commander looked out of the cockpit and saw that the wing tips were well above the fuselage. The wing had a 4.5-degree dihedral angle and a 7-degree leading edge sweep that, along with the large vertical fin, gave the bomber stability both in direction and roll, controlling any tendency to skid or slip. The high aspect ratio resulted in high wing efficiency because a lower percentage of air loss occurred at the wing tips, and so induced drag was kept low.

Each wing was constructed of five sections, with each section being a torque box made up of a front and rear web spar connected by solid chordwise ribs (bulkheads) to create rigid cells. All Boeing aircraft since the Monomail had used the bridge-type truss construction that had riveted tubular spars. But George Martin, the assistant head of the Boeing structure team, felt that web spars constructed from flat plates of sheet metal, with flanges bent up for rigidity, were stronger and better suited for larger aircraft. The basic web spar construction design had been conceived by John Northrop in 1928, and subsequently used in the Douglas DC series of aircraft when Northrop formed his new company in 1932 that was 51% owned by Douglas. Northrop's wing spar design became the aircraft industry standard, and Boeing abandoned its Warren truss wing/bolted tubular spar construction it had used on the B-17 and used the fundamental Northrop design for the B-29. However, Boeing's wing panels were at-

tached to the fuselage by a totally different means than the Northrop design. The wing consisted of two heavy extruded duralumin web spar flanges weighing 255lbs, which was the largest extrusion ever utilized in a production aircraft to that time. This beam was positioned just outside the two outboard nacelles, and connected at the centerline inside the bomb bays.

The 117 wings were of the all-metal, stressed-skin type (i.e. the aluminum alloy skin was considered part of the wing structure and carried part of the wing stresses). The heavy upper wing skin and the lower under surface skin were riveted to these spars. The skin at the wing roots was the heaviest at the time, being 3/16th inch thick. The skin was reinforced with stringers that provided additional strength (stiffness) to the spar structure. The ribs or bulkheads served the dual purpose of providing contour and shape to the wing, and of adding rigidity and strength to the structure. The ribs were spaced spanwise at intervals of about three feet to form a long, tapered, cambered box that allowed room for individual self-sealing fuel tanks. Nose and trailing edge ribs made up the airfoil sections for the wing, and flush-riveted, butt-jointed aluminum alloy skin covered the wing structure. To give the wing maximum strength, three-inch hat-section stiffening

At the Boeing Wichita plant the entire inboard wing and center section were manufactured in one piece and carried by cranes to final assembly where they passed through the fuselage and were installed as a single unit and bolted at the center line of the aircraft. There was a major difference in the Renton wing installation. The B-29A had short stub wing center section installed a short distance into the fuselage. (USAF)

members ran spanwise of the wing. They were called hat-section because they were shaped like top hats in cross section. These stiffeners were positioned at eight-inch intervals, and the skin and ribs were riveted to them. The hat-stiffeners were so large that they could correspond to spars on the wing of an ordinary aircraft. The inboard wing panels housed the nacelles, flaps, and landing gear. The outboard panels contained the fabric-covered ailerons. The B-29 and B-29B had their entire inboard wing and center section manufactured in one piece and carried by cranes to final assembly, where they passed through the fuselage and were installed as a single unit, bolted at the centerline of the aircraft.

The B-29A Renton Wing

There was a major difference in the Renton wing installation. The B-29A had a short stub wing center section installed a short distance into the fuselage that increased the B-29A wingspan by 12in over the B-29 and B-29B, and thus brought about its "A" designation. The stub mount simplified construction, but had a few undesirable effects on the performance, as the heavier structure increased the aircraft weight by 706lbs and reduced the gasoline capacity by 213gals in the center wing tank (1,333gals vs. 1,083gals).

The Renton wing structure was built in Seattle and trucked to Renton for installation. Once on the Renton "Wing Line," instead of attaching body sections to the wing, the wing structure went through 19 successive stations (#19 to #1), at the end of which the completed wing was equipped with nacelles, engines, and landing gear, and only required propellers and wing tips. The Renton Wing Line measured 225ft wide by nearly 600ft long. A powerful electric motor, rated at a half million pounds, moved the Wing Line forward at six feet per minute at predetermined times. It took approximately six minutes for a wing to move from one station to the next. The "Wing Line" was actually two distinct but identical lines. Each line had a central dolly that held the port and starboard wings at worker level by a unique cantilever support. The 20 to 30 workers at each station were on a precisely determined schedule of man-hours required to complete each station procedure. By the time the wing reached position #11 it had all its internal components installed (e.g. V-board, fuel cells, fuel valves, and booster pumps), and many external components installed (e.g. nacelles,

The Renton wing structure was built in Seattle and trucked to Renton for installation. Once on the Renton "Wing Line," instead of attaching body sections to the wing, the completed inboard wings went through 19 successive stations (#19 to #1) at the end of which the wing was equipped with nacelles, motors and landing gear and only required propellers and wing tips. (USAF)

wiring and tubing, and harness assemblies). At the remaining stations completed assemblies were added (e.g. engines at station #8, the landing gear at station #7, and the cowl flaps at station #6). At each station inspections and functional testing were undertaken. Final inspection was done at station #3. At station #2 the dolly was removed, and at #1, the end of the line, there was a crane that lifted the completed wing off the line to be joined to the fuselage.

Wing Flaps

Actually, the Boeing 117 wing improved aircraft aerodynamics by about only 10%, and it was the development of the Fowler wing flap that led to the great achievement of the 117 wings. To get enough lift when the bomber was flying slowly on take off and landing, reversible electric motors extended and retracted large track-mounted flaps from the rear of the wings. The flap that formed the trailing edge of the inboard wing was constructed of a single tubular spar, and aluminum alloy ribs covered with a heavy aluminum alloy skin. Five carriages were bolted to the spar of each flap. Each carriage was provided with seven relatively small roller bearings that rode on arc-shaped tracks extending aft from the rear wing spar. The center carriage of each wing flap had two additional rollers that rode on the sides of the track to prevent lateral movement of the flap. Two actuating screws transmitted the controlling power to each flap.

The flap control switch was located on the airplane commander's aisle stand, and the flap position indicator was located on the co-pilot's instrument panel. The airplane commander was warned not to lower the wing flaps or fly the airplane with full flaps down at a speed in excess of 180mph, or with the flaps half down (25-degrees) above 225mph. To reduce the take-off distance and speed the flaps were set at 25-degrees for take off, and lowered to 45-degrees to reduce landing speed and distance. The flaps increased the bomber's lift by two-thirds on take off and landing, and more lift provided slower speeds. Without using flaps and using the wing alone, the plane would stall at the slow speeds required to maneuver reliably close to the ground. The B-29 flap gave the aircraft the same landing speed as the smaller B-17. The B-29 flap was larger than the entire wing of many fighter aircraft, and increased the overall wing area by 19% (332 square feet) when fully extended, increasing the downwash angle of air leaving the wing. The great efficiency of the flap can be illustrated by comparing it to the small two-seat Piper Cub liaison aircraft. The B-29's weight was 94 times that of the Cub, and with only 9.4 times the wing surface the bomber landed at only 3.5 times the speed of the Cub!

Emergency Flap Operation

A portable emergency motor in the bomb bay allowed both for emergency lowering of the flaps, or the emergency operation of the bomb bay doors. It was normally stowed in the flap socket in the center wing section of the inboard wing, approximately at the centerline of the bomber. The motor was engaged with a torque connection on top of the midwing section between the bomb bays. Its electrical receptacle was located adjacent to the torque connection.

Ailerons

Boeing developed ailerons that were statically and aerodynamically balanced. A tab was located on each aileron hinged to the outboard panels, and acted as both a trim tab and servo tab. Small control wheels on both the airplane commander's and co-pilot's control stands actuated the tabs. These tabs were an adjustable servo type that reduced the aileron operating loads, as well as providing a means of correcting wing heaviness, and reduced control effort to a minimum. The larger B-29 was much easier to roll than the B-17.

Fuel System

The fuel system on the B-29 was similar to that on the B-17. Each engine received its fuel supply from a system that was independent of the other three engines. It consisted of self-sealing fuel tanks, an electrically-driven boost pump, a shut off valve operated by a solenoid valve, a fuel strainer, an engine-driven fuel pump, and a carburetor that incorporated a solenoid-operated primer valve.

Fuel Cells

The normal fuel supply was carried in 22 individual self-sealing cells located between the wing interspar ribs in the inboard wing. Seven of these cells on the outboard side of each wing were interconnected to form the tank assemblies for engines No. 1 and No. 4 (outboard engines), with a total capacity of 1,367.5gals and 42gals expansion space. Four inboard cells on each side of the wing were interconnected to form the tank assemblies for engines No. 2 and No. 3 (inboard engines), with a capacity of 1,436.5gals and 67gals expansion space. Four jettisonable auxiliary tanks could be installed, two in each bomb bay in place of the bombs, adding 2,560gals to the total fuel carried (8,168gals). The fuel in the auxiliary tanks was transferred to the main engine tanks when needed, as it could not be used directly from the auxiliary tanks

The self-sealing fuel cells that comprised the wing tanks were installed in the wing cavities between the interspar wing ribs. Cells for the normal system were numbered successively, #1 through #11, from inboard out, with the suffix L or R added to designate left or right hand cells. The

fuel cell ribs were identified by their tank numbers, and were located in the cell from fore to aft in the sequence of their dash number, a –1 rib being the furthest rib foreword. The ribs were interchangeable between right and left hand fuel tank cells of the same number. Each engine received its fuel from a system separate from the other three engines, thus eliminating the possibility of failure of all four engines in case of fuel line problems. All fuel cells were constructed of three parts: lining, sealant, and outer retaining covering, all of which consisted of seven plies. The inner, two-ply liner was the gasoline-resistant layer that acted as the container. It was made of Buna-N, a synthetic rubber with excellent adhesive qualities, and was backed by rayon or nylon fabric. The sealant layer was made of three plies sealed with compound rubber. Two of the sealant plies were made from Buna-S, which was a synthetic rubber with good mechanical and bonding properties, could blend with natural rubber, and most important, swelled when it came in contact with aromatic fuels (eg gasoline when released by a bullet puncture). The third sealant ply was a cord fabric impregnated with natural and Buna-S rubbers whose cords ran lengthwise down the cell. The two-ply outer retainer gave the fuel cell its strength and support, and increased the efficiency of the mechanism that restored the punctured area to its original shape. One outer covering ply was a cord fabric similar to the third sealant ply but applied at a 45-degree angle to the cell. The outer sealant ply was similar to the third and sixth plies, except that it was impregnated with Buna-N instead of Buna-S.

Bomb Bay Fuel Tanks

In combat in the CBI, gasoline supply was a problem for the XX Bomber Command. The XXI Bomber Command in the Pacific could receive its fuel by sea in large gasoline tankers, but to get gasoline to China the XX had to fly numerous trips across the "Hump." The early B-29s had an improvised fuel system with an off-loading manifold to allow the bombers to

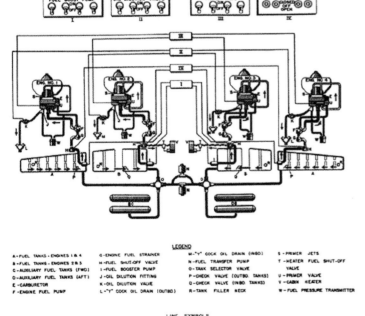

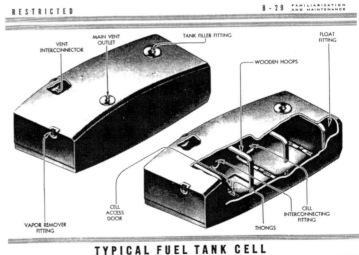

TYPICAL FUEL TANK CELL

The normal fuel supply was carried in 22 individual self-sealing cells located between the wing interspar ribs in the inboard wing. Seven of these cells on the outboard of each wing were interconnected to form the tank assemblies for engines No. 1 and No. 4 with a total capacity of 1,367.5gals. Four inboard cells on each side of the wing were interconnected to form the tank assemblies for engines No. 2 and No. 3 with a capacity of 1,436.5gals. (USAF)

Fuel System Flow Diagram (USAF)

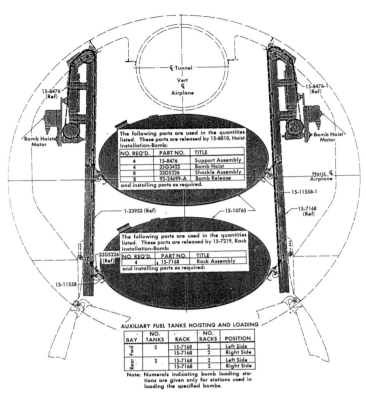

Bomb Bay Auxiliary Fuel Tank Hoisting and Loading (USAF)

not directly to any specific engine. The tanks could be jettisoned in case of an emergency.

Fuel Tank Capacity (U.S. gallons)

Tank Location	Number of Tanks	Expansion Space (gals)	Capacity (gallons)	Total (gallons)	Total (gallons)
Outboard	2	43	1,324	2,648	
Inboard	2	67	1,459	2,918	
Normal Supply		5,566			
Bomb Bay	4	20	640	2,560	
Auxiliary Supply		2,560			
Maximum Capacity		8,126			

Aviation Fuel

Aircraft engines could not use the anti-knock fuel used in automotive high performance engines without damage resulting from overheating, pre-ignition, and/or detonation. Aviation fuel was a special high-octane, low viscosity fuel rated on a performance number scale as 100/130. Fuel was delivered by either the 2,000gal "bowsers," or 4,000gal "gas wagons" with four dual tires, and pulled by a 6 x 7.5 ton F-1 tractor.

Fuel Pump

A type AN-4102 rotary, four-vane, positive displacement fuel pump was mounted on a pad on the left side of the accessory case of each engine. The pump consisted of a cast aluminum alloy housing containing a sleeve with

be used as makeshift air tankers. The early bomb bay tanks were temporary and difficult to install and remove.

Later the Good Year 2FI-6-4562 self-sealing 640gal (with a 20gal expansion capacity) auxiliary fuel tanks, supported internally by fiber hoops, were mounted two in each bomb bay (2,560gals total). For loading into the bomb bays the auxiliary tanks were supported underneath by two special slings that were attached to the 500lb bomb racks by B-7 bomb shackles and A-2 bomb releases on each side of the bomb bay. The bomb hoist motor lifted the two tanks, one above the other, into each bomb bay. Fuel in the auxiliary bomb bay tanks could be transferred to any wing tank, but

A 610-gallon bomb bay fuel tank on trailer. In combat in the CBI gasoline was a problem for the XX Bomber Command as numerous fuel ferrying trips had to flown across the "Hump." The early B-29s had an improvised fuel system to allow the bombers to be used as makeshift air tankers. The early bomb bay tanks were temporary and difficult to install and remove. (USAF)

The Good Year 2FI-6-4562 self-sealing 640gal (with a 20gal expansion capacity) auxiliary fuel tanks were mounted two in each bomb bay. The tanks were supported internally by fiber hoops. (USAF)

an eccentric bore, in which a rotor with four vanes was driven by a drive shaft coupled to the engine drive gear. The pump was equipped with an integral, disc-type, spring-controlled, adjustable relief valve and bypass that maintained constant fuel pressure. When the fuel pressure was greater than the tension on the relief valve spring the valve was forced open, and the fuel was bypassed from the discharge side of the relief valve back to the intake side.

Supplemental Fuel Boost Pumps

Fuel pressure was maintained through conventional engine-driven fuel boost pumps. If the engine pump failed there was an electrically driven G-10 fuel boost pump at the outlet of each gasoline tank. These pumps were powered directly from the fuel pump drives on the engine. The G-10 pump was used to furnish pressure to move fuel in case of engine driven pump failure. It was also used to supplement the engine fuel pumps at starting and take off to prevent vapor lock at high altitudes. A switch on the flight engineer's switch panel controlled the boost pumps at low speed and a fixed pressure of 8psi. Four rheostats on the flight engineer's panel provided additional control, giving a range of 12 to 18psi.

Fuel transfer

Two reversible, electric motor-driven pumps controlled by the flight engineer were located under the mid-wing section between the bomb bays, and could transfer fuel from one tank to another via a self-sealing hose. The transfer rate was 1,500gals per hour at sea level, and decreased as the altitude increased (at 30,000ft the rate was 500gals per hour). The selection of tank transfer was by two cable-controlled selector valves that could be adjusted by levers on the flight engineer's station. The fuel could only be transferred across the centerline of the aircraft. Thus, it was necessary when transferring fuel from one adjacent wing tank to another, to first transfer the fuel to the opposite side of the aircraft and then back to the desired tank.

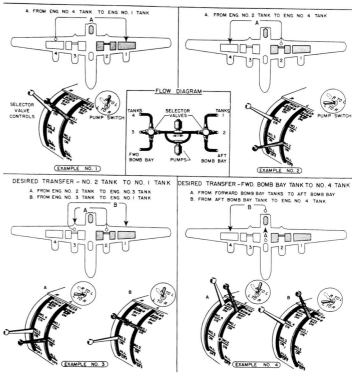

Fuel transfer Diagram. (USAF)

After flying for a number of hours, fuel needed to be switched from bomb bay tanks to wing tanks. There was one fuel transfer valve at the rear bomb bay tank position, and another at #4 wing tank position. The flight engineer turned the fuel transfer switches to ON, which transferred fuel from right to left. He watched the fuel tank gauge, and when the needle showed that the #4 tank was FULL he turned the switches OFF. However, when the fuel was transferred, the full wing tank caused that wing to drop. To compensate the flight engineer moved the right transfer valve to the #1 wing tank position, then pushed the switches forward, this time to pump fuel from #4 to #1. When the tanks were evened up (each to about 3/4 full) the plane would again be in balance. The flight engineer would then turn all switches OFF. Tanks #2 and #3 would be filled the same way.

Some B-29s and early B-29As used a fuel transfer system, while later models used the manifold system. In the fuel transfer system each engine had an independent fuel transfer from designated wing tank fuel cells. If one engine shut down, fuel from its tank could be transferred to the other tanks via the transfer pumps controlled by the flight engineer. In the manifold system, each engine removed fuel from its own tank, but was also connected to a spanwise manifold that was filled from each of four wing tanks. Each engine could draw fuel from the manifold or from its own tank.

The B-29 carried 5,566 gallons of special high-octane, low viscosity 100/130 aviation fuel in its wing tanks plus 2,560 in its four bomb bay tanks. The fuel was delivered by either the 2,000-gallon "bowsers" or 4,000-gallon "gas wagons" pulled by a 6 x 7.5 ton F-1 tractor. (USAF)

5

Nacelles and Engines

Nacelles

Once Materiel Command accepted the Wright R-3350 engines, Boeing aerodynamic and project engineers could proceed on comprehensive design work on the nacelles and mountings for the engines. Of all the B-29 components, the nacelles caused the most design problems, but ultimately the Boeing Aerodynamics Department designed a superb small, clean nacelle that reduced drag to a minimum. The problem with designing the B-29 nacelle was that the project engineers needed to house not only the engine in it, but also two superchargers, inter-coolers and, importantly, the main undercarriage legs and wheels. The engineers also needed to position these components to provide adequate space for maintenance, and to provide large air intakes to eliminate the need to place air intakes on the leading edge of the wings. Scaled-down clay models were made for wind tunnel tests at the University of Washington, the California Institute of Technology, and the National Advisory Committee for Aeronautics (NACA). Clay model after clay model was reconfigured until finally an aerodynamic shape was found to accommodate the landing gear and engine and accessories, and the placement and shape of the air intake. To eliminate the placing of numerous air inlets on the leading wing edges, one large air duct was placed in the nacelle nose that gave the nacelle an oval shape. During wind tunnel testing it was discovered that the nacelles adversely deflected airflow over the wings. To remedy the situation a small spoiler was added to the trailing edge of the wing between the inboard nacelles and the fuselage. Boeing engineers named the spoiler after the "Yehudi," who was "the little man who did it all." Once the aerodynamic shape was proved up, lightweight materials that were adaptable to mass production had to be designed and developed. It took over a year to reach what was a superb compromise, and the design was so efficient that once the gear was retracted onto the nacelles the total drag on the bomber was halved!

The outboard and inboard nacelles were of stressed skin, monocoque construction, and designed to be removed from the wing as a unit for repair and overhaul. Each nacelle was attached to the wing by two fittings provided on the front spar, and by a series of bolts that attached the nacelle fairing "skate" to the wing upper camber skin. All four nacelles were of similar construction, and with a few exceptions contained similar internal installations. A corrosion-resistant steel firewall was located at the back of the nacelle, just forward of the wing front spar, and was part of the engine oil tank shell. The rear section of the inboard engine nacelles were attached to the flaps and lowered with them. Because the flap moved back before moving down, it was not necessary to do the same with the out-

Nacelle cowling manufacture at the DeSoto, Warren, MI plant. (USAF)

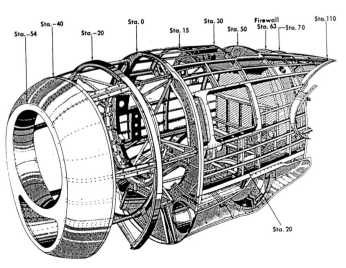

Inboard Nacelle Structure (USAF)

All four nacelles were of similar stressed skin, monocoque construction and designed to be removed from the wing as a unit for repair and overhaul and with a few exceptions contained similar internal installations. (Author/Pima)

board nacelle. A large air duct in the lower nacelle structure extended from the nose ring cowling into the aft portion of the nacelle to supply all the air required for use in engine and cabin supercharging, as well as nacelle ventilation.

Engines

Wright Cyclone 18 R-3350

Four 18-cylinder, Model R-3350 Wright Cyclone engines that were of the standard radial design, with two staggered banks of nine cylinders each, powered the B-29. The specifications of the engine were:

Model	711C18BA2 (B series)
Type	18 cylinders, 2-row radial, air-cooled, geared drive, Supercharged, 4-cycle
Construction	3-piece steel crankcase, Cylinders with steel barrels with W-type aluminum alloy fins and cast aluminum alloy heads, one inlet valve and one exhaust valve (sodium cooled) per cylinder actuated by push rods, 2-throw 3-piece counterbalanced crankshaft supported in 3 roller bearings, Planetary reduction gear, ratio 0.44:1 or 0.56:1
Supercharger	G.E. Gear-driven, 2-speed supercharger, ratio 6.61:1 and 8.81:1
Carburation	One Chandler-Evans 58CPB4 variable venturi pressure-type down-draft carburetor with automatic mixture control
Ignition	One Bendix-Scintilla DF18LN-1 dual magneto and one 18-point distributor. Two 28mm long reach spark plugs per cylinder. Shielded ignition system
Lubrication	Pressure feed, 60-70 lb/sqin Dry sump
Starter	Optional. Eclipse E-160 or 1416 direct cranking or Series 48 inertia and direct cranking, starter

WRIGHT CYCLONE 18BA (R3350BA) SERIES AIRCRAFT ENGINE
Exploded View of a Typical Engine

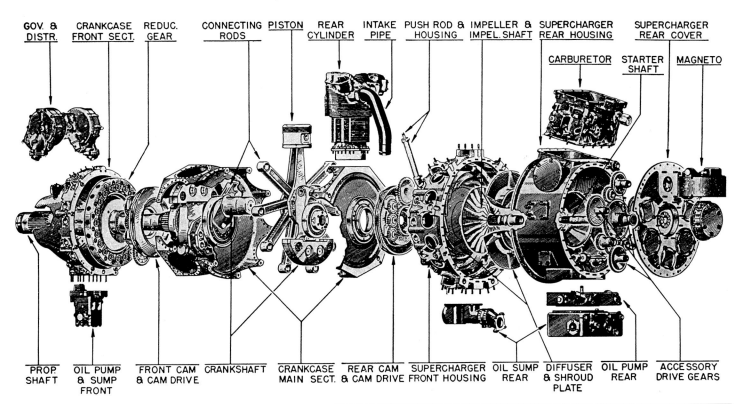

Bore	6.125in
Stroke	6.3125in
Displacement	3.347cuin
Compression Ratio	6.85:1
Diameter	55.8in
Length	76.2in
Frontal area	17.0square feet
Weight	2,670lbs
Weight/hp	1.21lb/hp
Fuel consumption (cr)	0.46lb/hp/hr
Oil consumption (cr)	0.020lb/hp/hr
Gasoline grade	100/130 octane
Oil grade (viscosity)	120 S.U. secs
Output/displacement	0.66hp/cuin
Output/piston area	4.15 hp/sqin
Piston speed (max.)	2,946 ft/min
Rating (take off)	2,200hp/2,800rpm/ at sea level
Rating (normal, low)	2,000hp/2,400 rpm/4,500ft
Rating (normal, high)	1,800hp/2,400rpm/14,000ft
Rating (cruising)	1,300hp/2,100rpm/no specific altitude
Military	2,200hp/2,600rpm /25,000ft
	(for maximum of 5 minutes)

Temperature Limits (Degrees F)

Conditions	Cylinder Head	Oil
Ground Operation	500F	203F
Take Off Power	500F	203F
Military Power	500F	203F
Rated Power (1hr)	478F	185F
Rated Power (continuous)	450F	185F
70% Rated Power (cont.)	450F	185F

Engine Costs

Chicago-Dodge's initial estimated for the R-3350-23 was $25,314 per engine, plus a fee of $1,519. By the end of 1944 this figure was lowered to $14,500 plus a fee of $580, and further decreased for late model B-29s to $11,537 for the -23 engine and $12,954 for the -57 fuel injected model, despite its numerous engineering changes.

Boeing's Engine Responsibility

Boeing was responsible for the installation of the engine, its cooling, control, and supply of lubricating oil and fuel, but not for its structural safety or capability to function. During the XB-29 preliminary design phase, the Boeing Power Plant Design Unit initiated a thorough inclusive survey of engine problems relating to cooling, controls, superchargers, fuel, oil, exhaust, and fire. When the basic problems were identified they were delegated to specialist engineers that took their assigned problems back to their group to be analyzed and solved.

Engine Sections (Nose, Power, Supercharger, and Accessory)

Nose Section

The nose section housed a planetary-type reduction gear that reduced the propeller shaft rpm to 0.35 of the crankshaft speed. A propeller governor was mounted on top of the nose section. Wright engineers analyzed 82 engine failures occurring between October 1942 to February 1943, and the reduction gear was found to be a major cause; several changes were made,

Side View

Front View

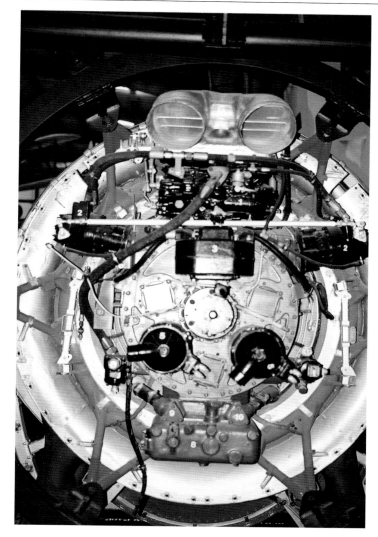

Rear View
Note: Previous and following engine photos were taken of the demonstration cutaway of Pima Air and Space Museum's R-3350.

especially to the pinion gears. A slowly responsive governor caused overspeeding that was corrected by increasing the size of the oil galleries in the nose, and increasing the size of the scavenge pump, which increased oil flow.

Starter

In early model B-29s, each engine was equipped with a combination inertia and direct cranking Jack and Heintz JH4E starter that was mounted on the engine accessory drive cover. The engines on later model aircraft were equipped with combination, inertia-direct cranking starters that could be of the Eclipse E-160 (or 1416) or Series 48 direct cranking type, which were powered by the P-2 generator. An Eclipse No. E93231 portable external energizer driven by the auxiliary power plant applied power to an Eclipse E-95996 starter gearbox through the flexible shaft to a connector located on the lower side of the nacelle skin.

The starter allowed either manual or electric cranking of the engine. The starter was operated electrically by a double-throw, momentary contact toggle switch on the flight engineer's switch panel. The starter switch was held in the ACCELERATE position until the flywheel had gained sufficient speed (in about 15secs), to approximately 22,000rpm. When the starter switch was moved to START, the starter jaws and engine jaws engaged. A disc clutch in the starter functioned as a shock absorber and as a torque limiter, preventing excessive loads from damaging the starter or engine. The starter motor was in operation with the starter switch in either the ACCELERATE or START positions, and was able to maintain rotation of the engine after the energy of the flywheel had been expended. Engine cranking without the use of an electric starter motor was brought about by manually accelerating the flywheel with a hand crank. The hand crank operated in a gearbox on the crank support, where the rpm was stepped up and then transmitted to the flywheel gearbox by a flexible shaft.

Power Section
Cylinders:

There were two staggered rows of nine cylinders each. The cylinders had a 6.125in bore, 6.312 stroke, and a displacement (capacity) of 3,347cuin. The cylinder head temperatures were measured by thermocouples at the #1 cylinder in the rear bank, and the readings were sent to the airplane

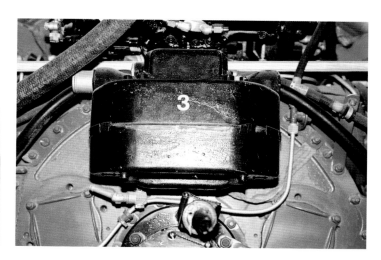

#1 Fuel Master Control (replaces carburetor on fuel injected engines) #2 Fuel Injection Pumps

#3 Magneto

#4 Starter

#5 Generator (two on each outboard engine), #8 Rear Case Oil Sump, #9 Oil Inlet Line, #10 Oil Outlet Line.

commander and flight engineer. The R-3350 cylinder design was similar to the R-2600 engine being forged of a nitralloy barrel, with Wright's aluminum "W" finned muff rolled into the outside diameter. The barrels were machined from nitralloy steel forgings and had their inner surfaces nitrated and screwed, and shrunk into aluminum alloy heads. The cylinder head had a hemispherical combustion chamber with two inclined valves operating in bronze bushings shrunk into the head. The heads were cast, which would cause acute operational problems later.

On the R-3350-5 engines used on the XB-29s the front and rear cylinders were staggered. To save weight the cylinder heads were integral aluminum castings with a lacework of W-type cooling fins cut into grooves on the exterior of the steel barrel as deep as four inches, and as little as 1/16-inch thick, spaced five per inch. The next nitralloy forged steel cylinder barrel had 40 cooling fins about 1/32-inch thick, and 5/8-inch deep machined on the outside surface. Wright soon developed a better barrel design on its R-3350-13, -21, and -23A (war engines). Instead of cutting fins into the barrel, 54 thinner, deeper, aluminum fins were rolled into slots that increased the cooling area of the barrel by 45%. By rolling instead of machining the barrel fins the wall thickness of the barrel was reduced by half, saving 24,000,000lbs of the scarce nitralloy. The total cooling surface on the 18 cylinders was 5,850square feet, or 3,900sqin per cylinder, which equates to the surface area almost equal to a 60 x 100ft parcel of land! Although this number seems to be impressive, it was not enough to keep the R-3350 cool under high power climbs.

Valve rocker arm and springs were enclosed in housings cast integrally with the head. The combustion chambers were hemispherical, with two valves per cylinder. The exhaust was sodium cooled, with the exhaust ports on the front row of cylinders facing forward, rather than rearward, and this exhaust port positioning would later cause problems in the service life of the engine. The front cylinders exhausted forward into the front collector ring, while the rear cylinders exhausted into the rear collector ring. The front collector ring sections directed their exhaust through flexible couplings into the rear collector ring. The combined exhaust was then directed into the exhaust transition ducts on each side of the engine. The

Fuel Pump

Wright developed a better barrel designs on its R-3350-13, –21, and -23 (the combat engine). Instead of cutting fins into the barrel, 54 thinner, deeper, aluminum fins were rolled into slots this increased the cooling area of the barrel by 45%. The total cooling surface on the 18 cylinders was 5,850sqft or 3,900sqin per cylinder almost equal to the surface area of a 60 × 100ft lot! (Author/Pima)

exhaust then passed through the left or right supercharger turbine wheels before exiting the flight hoods on each side of the nacelles. The pistons were Wright "Uniflow" full-trunk, heat-treated aluminum alloy die forgings. Half-dome heads were used to obtain the correct compression ratio. The pistons were cut for six piston rings (the sixth on the bottom); the top three were of the wedge type, and the next three were square cut. The piston pins were case hardened with beveled ends, and were retained by coiled spring retainers held in small annular grooves at the ends of piston-pin holes. The Wright Engine Committee set up a program to test different types of piston rings. Because the early R-3350s had little flight time, the choice of the best piston ring was delayed, and then it was further delayed by the demand for millions of rings for all the engines used in World War II. The single piece H-section master rods and eight articulated rods were machined from solid forgings. The main crank pin bearings were silver lead indium plated with steel backings, and fitted loosely in the large bore of the master rod. Master rod bearing and knuckle pin lubrication was improved via a bearing oil seal on each master rod. The chrome steel knuckle pin had nitrided bearing surfaces, and was center-drilled and tapered at one end to accommodate a locking screw. The chrome nickel steel articulated rods had split bronze bushings pressed into both ends. An Engine Test Stand Program was established to enable component transfer from one engine source to another either at production, modification, or overhaul.

The top three cylinders in the rear row (numbers 1, 3, and 5) were particularly exposed to exhaust valve seat erosion, with ensuing erosion of the valve guide boss at about 175 hours. A schedule was established to inspect the exhaust ports after 140 hours, and every 15 hours thereafter. If any evidence of erosion was found the engine was changed. The leaking of the exhaust ball joint for the front cylinders allowed the white-hot exhaust to be blown over the cylinder heads, causing overheating. Redesign of the ball joint mitigated the problem.

Exhaust Collector Assembly

The exhaust collector assembly was fabricated from stainless steel sheet sections consisting of a forward collector ring and two connecting pipes. Exhaust from the front row of cylinders was collected by a ring located forward of the engine in the nose ring cowl. Exhaust from the rear cylinders was collected by a ring located aft of the rear cylinders. Two connecting pipes connected the front and rear rings. Stub sections branched from the collector rings and attached to each of the 18 exhaust ports.

Crankcase

The three-piece (front, center, and rear) crankcase was originally an aluminum forging, but later was replaced by forged steel. The three pieces were machined and divided at the centerline of the front and rear cylinders, and were bolted together internally. Steel retainers were installed on the inside diameter of the bearing support sections, except the rear, which contained the rear main bearing, oil seal, and oil distributor.

The forged chrome-nickel alloy steel crankshaft was of the two-throw split-clamping type, allowing the use of a single-piece master rod. The shaft was hollow throughout its length, heat-treated to withstand high loading and speed. Oil was transferred to the hollow crankshaft at the rear main bearing distributor for lubrication. The crank pins were nitrited to decrease wear.

The three-piece clamping-type crankshaft was braced by three main roller bearings fastened on the shaft and in the crankcase diaphragm. Two very large dynamic damper counterweights, one per row, were located adjacent to and directly opposite each crankpin. They were used to dampen vibrations, but in early models were insufficient, as crankshaft vibration was transmitted to the propeller shaft, causing the shaft to fatigue and fail. To remedy the problem, eight (four front and four rear) counterweights, running at twice the crank speed, were placed radially around the crankshaft axis and driven by the cam drive. The forward section was splined to accommodate the reduction driving gear and the front cam driving gear splines. A journal for the rear main roller bearing was formed by an extension on the rear section. It carried internal splines for the accessory and starter drive shaft coupling. The crankcase was consisted of five main sections that were (from rear to front):

1) Front section: Constructed of magnesium alloy and housed the propeller reduction gear assembly, the driving gears for the front lubricating oil pump, gearing for the distributors, propeller governor pump, and valve tappets and guides for the front row of cylinders.
2) Main section: Made up of three steel forgings that were bolted together internally.
3-4) Supercharger front and rear housings: Were fabricated from magnesium alloy and provided room for the impeller, diffuser, induction passage to the impeller, supercharging drive gears, and all engine accessories.
5) Supercharger rear housing cover: The rear engine housing cover was machined from a magnesium alloy of the typical Cyclone pattern and covered the engine accessories.

<cap>2-05-14 Crankcase drawing

Valves

The small, one pound nickel steel valves were an engineering feat. They opened ports through which millions of cubic feet of intensely hot gases were vented, and then closed these ports instantly to allow more gasoline and fresh air to be drawn into the cylinder. During the compression and explosion of this mixture the valves kept the ports tightly closed. At 2,800

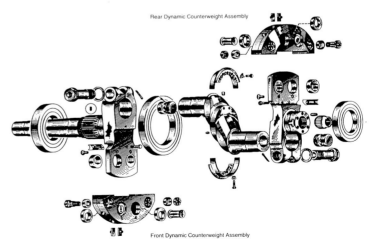

Rear Dynamic Counterweight Assembly

Front Dynamic Counterweight Assembly

The three-piece crankcase was originally an aluminum forging, but later was replaced by forged steel. The crankshaft was of the two throw clamping type allowing the use of a single piece master rod. The three-piece clamping-type crankshaft was braced by three main roller bearings fastened on the shaft and in the crankcase diaphragm. Two very large dynamic damper counterweights, one per row, were located adjacent to and directly opposite each crankpin. (USAF)

Bendix Carburetor (Author/Pima)

engine revolutions per minute these valves opened and closed 1,400 times per minute. In the closed position the wide ends of the valves were part of the combustion chamber wall, and had to withstand the considerable force of the engine's power stroke.

There were two valves per cylinder. The intake valves had tulip shaped heads and solid stems, and the exhaust valves had mushroom shaped heads and hollow sodium cooled stems. The stem of the exhaust valve was hollow in order to contain liquid sodium to act as a cooling medium against the extremely intense heat of the exhaust. This hollow design had to be engineered to be strong enough to withstand the staggering forces hammering against it. The cam rings were driven off both ends of the crankshaft through intermediate gearing at one-eighth engine speed. The push rods were totally enclosed. One of the major R-3350 problems was valve failure due to high cylinder head temperatures and inadequate lubrication. Wright Field engineers corrected the problem with a revised system of oil crossover tubes that connected the cylinders in the same bank. Valve adjustment was critical, and compression checks were scheduled for every 50 hours, but some Bomb Wings did them after every mission. Valve guides were inspected every 10 hours.

Ignition System

The dual Scintilla DFL18N-1 magneto was geared to turn 1.125:1 in a clockwise direction. It provided a double ignition from a single unit employing the rotating magnet principle and stationary coils. Two radio shielded high-tension ignition cables conducted the current from the magneto to the two distributors mounted on top of the crankcase front section. Current from the distributor was conducted by radio-shielded ignition cable to the 36 spark plugs. The engine firing order was 1, 12, 5, 16, 9, 2, 13, 6, 17, 3, 14, 7, 18, 11, 4, 15, and 8.

Carburetors

The front cylinders of the early Wright engines were inclined to run leaner than the rear cylinders due to poor carburetor mixture distribution, causing engine overheating and heavy valve wear. These carburetors were also in-

clined to induction system fires. Bendix was the initial supplier for the downdraft carburetion units for the R-3350-21 "combat engine." But Bendix also was the major vender for many other types of engines, and the Chandler Evans Company (Ceco) was contracted to supply its Model 58-CP-4 downdraft, fully automatic non-icing unit, which was mounted on top of the supercharger rear section. Initially the Chandler Evans carburetor had many production problems.

The flow of air delivered to the engine was controlled by the carburetor throttle, and was measured by an air meter. The air meter consisted of a rectangular parallel venturi with suction holes and impact tubes throughout their entire length to measure the flow of the entire airstream. The flow was indicated by the pressure differential between the impact tubes and venturi. The amount of fuel delivered to the engine was controlled by the fuel metering system, which operated as a function of the pressure differential obtained from the air meter. Since the air meter pressure differential was a relatively small force that had to be translated into fuel pressure variations in the fuel metering system, the venturi forces were amplified by a hydraulically actuated mechanism. The carburetor automatically compensated for the varying density of the air and special fuel requirements for acceleration. To the basic carburetor jet system an additional jet system was provided for idle, cruising lean, and take off conditions, where special fuel mixtures were required.

The fuel was pumped to the carburetor inlet chamber at a pressure of 16 to 18psi. The inlet chamber was equipped with a vapor trap that automatically freed all vapor by allowing it to escape in small quantities through a weighted valve to the fuel tank. The fuel flowed through the strainer to the diaphragm operated fuel regulator valve. The fuel flowed from the regulator valve to the mixture control. Holes in the mixture control disc led to the jets. If the engine used a constant mixture for all operating conditions one jet would be sufficient, but since it does not, it is necessary to arrange the system using four jets. This system consists of the "A" jet for minimum requirement (Automatic Lean); the "C" jet that was for manually opened in parallel with the "A" jet to supplement the fuel flow for Normal rich operation (Automatic Rich); and the "B" jet, also in parallel, which is spring loaded to automatically enrich the mixture for full throttle or take off conditions. The "B" and "C" jets were in series with the "D" jet, which limited the amount of fuel added for maximum power conditions and controlled their combined output.

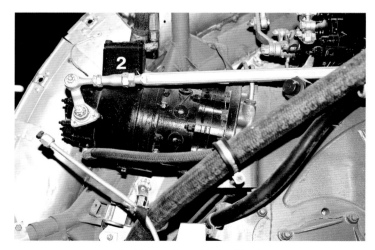

Fuel Injector Pump (Author/Pima)

The power output of an engine was determined by the air consumption, therefore the fuel flow through the carburetor had to be proportional to the airflow. A variable hydraulic force located on top of the fuel regulator diaphragm accomplished the increase in fuel flow with increases in airflow. The pressure meter valve controlled this hydraulic force.

Fuel Injection

Throughout the war the AAF requested that fuel injection replace carburetors for better fuel distribution and extended valve life. Near the end of the war direct fuel injection solved the carburetor's problem of having some cylinders tending to run lean (low on gasoline content) due to poor mixture distribution. Fuel injection was made possible with the introduction of new steel alloys and machining techniques for producing plungers to tolerances of ten-millionths of an inch. The introduction of fuel injection involved a significant tooling problem, and the engineering and procurement sections at Wright Field did not want to interfere with factory engine production during the change over. The introduction of fuel injection was to start by November 1944, but there were the inevitable production setup difficulties that delayed its installation until late in the war. In all, there were 6,427 engineering changes in adopting fuel injection. Once the fuel injection unit was ready, to facilitate its installation the engine and nacelle had to be removed, requiring up to 400 man-hours, as the fuel lines were to be routed to accommodate the engine design. Engineers redesigned the routing of the fuel lines so that the fuel injection unit could be installed in two hours without removing the engine.

Fuel Injection gave a more even fuel distribution at lower temperatures, better acceleration, and there would be no carburetor icing at high altitudes (lessening the risk of fire). Fuel was injected into the late war R-3350-57 engine cylinders by two Bendix-Stromberg nine-plunger units directed by a master control unit that monitored the airflow entering the supercharger. The first unit supplied fuel to the front cylinders, and the second to the rear cylinders in accurately metered portions of fuel every twentieth of a second at 2,500psi through stainless steel tubing and atomizers into the combustion chambers. This arrangement enabled the fuel mixture to be adjusted if one row was running leaner than the other row. Again, Bendix was unable to meet the demand, and Bosch was contracted to manufacture fuel injection units for the R-3350-59 engines. There was an interchangeability problem between the two companies' fuel pump control units and the air scoop, and Boeing, Bendix, and Bosch engineers had to collaborate to solve this problem.

Master Fuel Injector Control (Author/Pima)

Turbosupercharger Section

Description

At sea level the weight of the earth's atmosphere is 14.7psi, but at 25,000ft it decreases to 5.5psi. The greater the air pressure, the greater the air weight (density = pounds per cubic foot), and vice versa. As an aircraft flies higher the pressure becomes less, and the density becomes less. If an engine is to maintain its power at higher altitudes, it has to take in a higher volume of air from the outside to keep the weight of airflow from decreasing. By using a supercharger the weight of airflow can be maintained at the rated power output of the aircraft. This is done mechanically by pumping air into the engine carburetor at the required pressure, causing the carburetor to add more fuel to keep the air/fuel mixture at the proper ratio. This increased amount of fuel and air, under greater than normal pressure, goes through the intake manifold, and provides a greater charge to the cylinder, and increases the force of the piston's power stroke. The mean effective pressure in the cylinder determines horsepower.

Development

The need to increase power output at high altitudes, where atmospheric pressure is lower, led to the development of the supercharger. During World War II America was the only combatant to utilize the supercharger on a series production basis. Dr. Sanford Moss of General Electric was credited with designing the first practical aircraft turbo-supercharger, improving on a French idea. Early systems broke down after a few flights due to turbine or bearing failure from high mechanical and thermal loads. Research and development continued in the 1920s and '30s, and culminated in reliable designs that could be placed into production. General Electric produced the majority of American superchargers in World War II with their Type B and Type C models. GE designed their superchargers to "maintain sea-level pressure at the carburetor from deck up to the rated altitude of installation."

The Mechanics of Supercharging

Supercharged engines were able to develop their take off power to an altitude determined by the maximum allowable speed of the turbine. At the critical altitude the waste gate would completely close, causing a maximum backpressure working against the engine. The result was the engine ran at sea level efficiency. Engine exhaust gases passed through the collector ring and tailstack to the nozzle box of each supercharger, and expanded through the turbine nozzle and drove the bucket wheel at high speed. A ramming air inlet duct supplied air to the impeller, which increased its pressure and temperature. However, in order to avoid detonation at the carburetor, the air supplied to the carburetor passed through the intercooler, where the temperature was reduced. The internal engine impeller, driven by the engine crankshaft, again increased air pressure as it entered the intake manifold. High intake manifold pressure resulted in greater power output. The amount of turbo boost was determined by the speed of the turbo bucket wheel, and the speed of the turbo bucket wheel was determined by the difference between the atmosphere and the exhaust in the tailstack, and by the amount of gas passing through the turbine nozzles. If the waste gate was opened, more exhaust gas passed to the atmosphere via the waste gate pipe and decreased the tailstack pressure.

Two Types of Superchargers and Intercoolers and Aftercoolers

Internal Supercharger

The internal supercharger was the one that was located between the carburetor and the intake manifold and forced a charged mixture into the cylinder. The internal supercharger provided a uniform distribution of the fuel/air charge to the cylinder, and increased the density of the charge. It was built into the engine, and obtained its power by being geared to the crankshaft.

External Supercharger

The external supercharger was one that was located between the outside air and the carburetor, and forced an increased amount of air or compressed air into the carburetor. The external supercharger was a turbine (turbo supercharger) that was turned by the engine's exhaust gases.

Intercoolers and Aftercoolers

In using a supercharger with sufficient compression capacity to provide the full weight of air at high altitudes, it was necessary to cool off the air or mixture after it had been compressed. This was accomplished by using special radiators called intercoolers or aftercoolers, depending on their location in relation to the carburetor. Both methods, with their large radiator equipment, not only increased weight and drag, but also increased aircraft vulnerability, as it added another vital system that could be hit by enemy fire.

B-29 Superchargers

The B-29 mounted eight General Electric B-11 superchargers, two for each engine, enabling each engine to maintain sea level horsepower up to 33,000ft. The two engine superchargers operated in parallel, as a single supercharger was unable to handle the volume of air required for a single engine. There were provisions to shut down one supercharger when cruising at low power, where they were known to operate erratically. The turbo superchargers were mounted vertically, one on each lower side of the nacelle, behind the firewall. The B-29 nacelles were recessed into the wing in an extremely clean installation, and in normal turbo supercharger installations the turbine wheel was exposed. But the B-29 supercharger installation had only the exhaust stack protruding from the nacelle, and a panel called a shroud covered the remainder. The supercharger unit consisted of a single speed blower with a 6.06-to-1 impeller-to-crankshaft gear ratio. The front cylinders exhausted forward into a collector ring that was located inside the leading edge of the cowl, which then directed the exhausted air under the engine to the turbo superchargers. The turbo compressor released the air into an intercooler, and then into the down draft carburetor, or master control unit, if the bomber was equipped with direct fuel injection. This supercharged air was then directed through a Chandler Evans Type 58 CPB-4 pressure carburetor mounted on top of the supercharger. The unit could maintain a pressurized fuel-to-air mixture of about 17in of mercury at 2,400rpm.

The supercharger system was extensively tested in B-17s, and was operational when it was installed in the B-29. Later the R-3350 was the

Turbosupercharger flight hood with nacelle shroud in place. (Author/Pima)

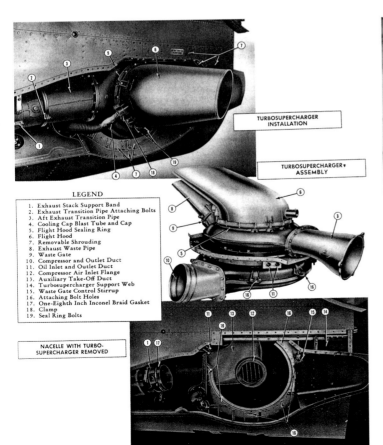

TURBOSUPERCHARGER
INSTALLATION

TURBOSUPERCHARGER
ASSEMBLY

LEGEND
1. Exhaust Stack Support Band
2. Exhaust Transition Pipe Attaching Bolts
3. Aft Exhaust Transition Pipe
4. Cooling Cap Blast Tube and Cap
5. Flight Hood Sealing Ring
6. Flight Hood
7. Removable Shrouding
8. Exhaust Waste Pipe
9. Waste Gate
10. Compressor and Outlet Duct
11. Oil Inlet and Outlet Duct
12. Compressor Air Inlet Flange
13. Auxiliary Take-Off Duct
14. Turbosupercharger Support Web
15. Waste Gate Control Stirrup
16. Attaching Bolt Holes
17. One-Eighth Inch Inconel Braid Gasket
18. Clamp
19. Seal Ring Bolts

NACELLE WITH TURBO-
SUPERCHARGER REMOVED

first Wright engine to be fitted with a Wright-designed gear-driven super-charger, replacing GE designs (GE continued to manufacture the impellers for the Wright supercharger), and the Wright design proved to be equal to the superlative Rolls Royce supercharger. During the war GE, aided by subcontractors Ford and Allis-Chalmers, manufactured 303,000 turbo-supercharger units.

B-29 Supercharger Construction
The supercharger consisted of three sections: the turbine, the compressor, and the oil pump bearing assembly. A single knob on the airplane commander's aisle stand controlled all the turbosuperchargers. The Type B and C units used single-stage, centrifugal compressors driven by a single-stage axial-flow turbine. A common shaft supported on two bearings mounted the turbine wheel and impeller. Lubrication was provided by a two-section dry pump system that pumped oil through bearings. One dry pump section supplied pressurized oil to the bearings, and the other section returned the oil to the oil reservoir.

Turbine: Exhaust from the engine was directed to the nacelle or fuselage mounted turbine to aid in cooling it. A nozzle box (exhaust collector ducting) directed the exhaust gases through the nozzle blades, and then against the turbine blades, popularly called "buckets." The waste gate unit was located on the nozzle box, which bled off excessive exhaust gases. The rpm of the turbine depended on the position of the waste gate, which controlled the amount of exhaust gases bypassed from the turbine nozzle box. If all the exhaust gases were permitted to flow through the turbine the result would be excessive boost pressures, especially at lower altitudes. The waste gate was a butterfly bypass valve that was initially controlled manually. Later, the turbo governor automatically regulated the waste gate to open when the turbine accelerated too rapidly, or when maximum safe speed (26,400rpm at 35,000ft) was reached. Both exhaust waste gates on each engine were operated by a small reversible electric motor that automatically received power from the regulator system when a change in waste gate setting became necessary to maintain the desired manifold pressure. There were four amplifier units—one for each nacelle—and they were located two above and two below the navigator's table. This system encountered many problems, and required constant monitoring by the airplane commander or flight engineer, especially during descent, when the danger of overboosting was greater. Installing automatic oil or electric servomotors solved the problem. The waste gate did cause some problems, as it stuck and resulted in a runaway turbine that could explode, sending pieces through the fuselage. The main reason for sticking was frozen moisture in the sensing lines leading to the regulator control. The problem was solved by the introduction of electronic regulators. Generally supercharger reliability was good, with most units running 400 hours between overhaul.

Compressor: A single-stage centrifugal compressor was mounted to the opposite end of the shaft. The compressor discharged air through a diffuser that converted kinetic energy from the impeller to potential (pressure) energy. Some type of intercooler cooled the high air temperatures from the compressors in order to delay the start of detonation resulting from the high charge temperature.

The high temperatures of the turbine system called for innovation in the use of high temperature alloys. Inconel alloy (nickel-chromium) was used extensively in the turbine to withstand the high temperatures, particu-

larly in the vital nozzle box, which was fabricated from Inconel welded stampings. The turbine blades presented the greatest challenge because of the red-hot temperatures and centrifugal loads of 24,000rpm, under which they operated. Because of the differential in thermal and mechanical demands placed on each blade and the retaining wheel, they were initially attached by a bulb-root attachment until methods of welding them to the wheel were perfected. The blade metal was vitallium-type alloy (Haynes Stellite 21), which was previously forged, and often failed until they were manufactured by the lost wax casting method.

Electronic Turbosupercharger Control
The B-29 electronic supercharger control system consisted of separate regulator systems, all simultaneously adjusted by a single turbo selector dial located on the airplane commander's aisle stand. Each system controlled the induction pressure of the particular engine through a Pressuretrol unit connected directly to the carburetor intake. The 115-volt, 400-cycle inverter supplied the electric power for the system. Each regulator included a turbo governor that prevented turbo overspeeding, both at high altitude, and during rapid throttle changes.

Accessory Section
In the accessory engine section there was a succession of gear trains that operated the fuel, vacuum, oil and hydraulic pumps, the generators, and the starter. The rear supercharger housing cover contained the components of the engine accessory section: tachometer, accessory gasoline pump, hydraulic and vacuum pump, dual magnetos, starter, two generators, and provision for a spare accessory drive. Spur gearing drove all accessories, and were powered either directly from a gear on the rear of the accessory drive shaft, or indirectly through the pinion gears. All gears were machined from steel forgings, had hardened teeth, and functioned in bushings in the rear cover, allowing the entire unit to be removed with the cover. Bendix Scintilla dual-type magnetos were installed in each engine, and were individually controlled by switches by the flight engineer. They supplied ignition via a high-tension current to the distributors mounted in the nose.

Engine Lubrication
Engine lubrication was of the dry sump full pressure type, in which all moving parts were lubricated by oil under pressure, except the piston pins, piston rings, propeller shaft thrust and radial bearings, crankshaft main bearing, and the valve operating mechanism for the lower cylinders (all of which were lubricated by oil spray from oil jets, or by gravity feed). There was a pressure and scavenging pump contained in the same housing at the front and rear of the engine. The rear pump supplied the oil for the main bearings, the rear section, and part of the front section. The front pressure pump supplied oil to reduction gears, torque meter, and oil booster pump. Oil pressure pumps also provided oil to master rod bearings, knuckle pins, cam, supercharger drive mechanism, and accessory drives. All sections of the valve gear were lubricated automatically. Oil pressure operated the hydraulic, constant speed, full feathering propeller. Oil filters were included both in the front and rear oil sumps to remove dirt and foreign particles from the oil before it entered the lubrication system.

Oil System
Each engine was supplied oil from an 85gal self-sealing tank located behind the firewall of each nacelle. The filler necks on the oil tanks were

placed on the side of the nacelle, which made it impossible to overfill them, and also left space for expansion. On some models a 100gal reserve oil tank was located on the port side of the center wing section, near the oil transfer pump and the oil selector valve. Oil was drawn from the oil tanks by two gear pumps, one located in the rear sump, and the other in the front sump. The sumps were machine-finished from magnesium alloy castings. The rear oil pump (rear sump), attached to the rear supercharger housing, was driven by a bevel gear that was integral with the spare accessory drive gear, and meshed with the oil pump drive shaft. Oil was supplied to the pump by an external line leading from the rear sump. After passing through the rear oil, pump oil passed through an oil filter, pressure relief valve, and check valve. The front oil pump (front sump) was attached to the lower rear side of the crankcase front section, and passed through a similar filter to the check valve system. Excess oil from all sections of the engines drained into the front and rear sumps, where it was collected by two oil scavenge pumps in the rear sump, and a single scavenge pump in the front sump. Each sump had a drain plug, and a small magnet was incorporated in each plug to pick up metal chips from the oil. An oil cooler was located on the OUT line between each engine and its oil tank. The flight engineer operated it automatically or manually. The airflow through the oil cooler was controlled automatically by a temperature regulator, or could be manually regulated by the flight engineer by means of switches on his panel. In addition to engine lubrication, the oil system served to operate the propeller governor and propeller feathering.

The standard 1100 (60wt) aircraft lubricating oil was a high viscosity fluid that was easily affected by cold. This property of the oil limited its use in high power engines in high altitude flight, and made engine design more difficult. At increasing altitude the high air content in the oil and the

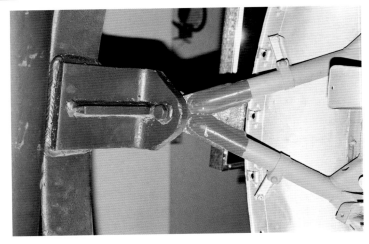

Engine Mount: front view (Author/Pima)

cavitation (i.e. choking) of the pumps limited the altitude the aircraft could attain. When the outside pressure became so low at high altitude the pumps ceased to operate. To remedy the situation Boeing engineers supercharged the oil tank and redesigned the line leading to the pump to reduce all possible pressure loss. In effect, this reduced the altitude inside the oil tanks so they could operate.

Oil Dilution Solenoid

An electrically-operated remotely-controlled oil dilution solenoid, 37D6210-Rev E, was installed on the right side of each nacelle, and located on a line leading from the fuel supply to the Y-drain valve. The purpose of the oil dilution solenoid was to allow gasoline to flow into the lubricating oil supply to give the lubricating oil fluidity in cold weather.

Engine Mounting

Vibration is a normal characteristic of every aircraft engine, and it is the principal source of vibration in an aircraft. In and of itself vibration is not damaging to an engine, but can adversely affect the propeller and nacelles. Aircraft instruments are very sensitive to vibration and need shock absorbing mounts. Vibrations could eventually loosen bolts, rivets, and fittings on the hydraulic or fuel lines, causing leaks. Fuel pumps could fail, causing the engines to shut down, while hydraulic pump failures could affect

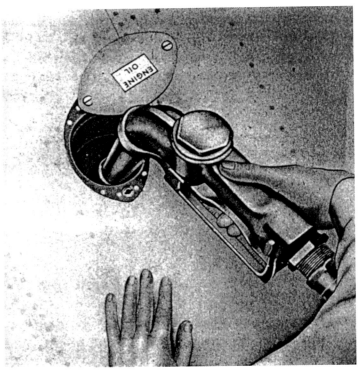

Each engine was supplied oil from an 85gal self-sealing tank located behind the firewall of each nacelle. The filler necks on the oil tanks were placed on the side of the nacelle that made it impossible to overfill them and also left air space for expansion. (USAF/Pima)

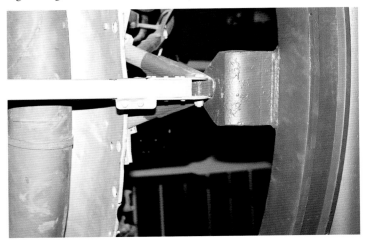

Engine Mount: rear view (Author/Pima)

gear, flaps, and brakes, causing take off and landing accidents. The great vibration of the Wright engine caused the small resistors and resister clips of the propeller governor used in the engine feathering system to fracture and malfunction at the current rpm. Wright engineers redesigned and improved the resistors and clips to solve the problem.

It was job of the Vibration Unit to locate and eliminate vibration, and Boeing estimated that its Vibration Unit eliminated about 70% of engine vibration. In the preliminary design stage of B-29 development, vibration engineers examined engine-propeller combinations, their installation in the nacelles, and the shock mounts cushioning the engine in the nacelles. Engine vibration was caused by the rpm of the turning engine, but not always in a direct relation. Also, the engine was geared so that the propeller did not rotate at the same speed as the engine. The four propellers were each a source of vibration, and each engine had the internal vibration of its many moving parts. R-3350 mounting was unusual, in that it was suspended from the rocker boxes. The loads were transmitted through the rocker shaft and rocker box, and then through the cylinder head. This suspension system was effective, but made cylinder changes difficult.

Spark Plugs

The four engines of the B-29 contained 144 spark plugs, and to change the 36 on each early engine, the propeller, cowl ring, and side panels had to be removed. Later cowls had removable side panels to make plug change easier, and these panels were retrofitted on the earlier engines. Early spark plugs used mica as an insulating material, and its major source was in northeast India, which was being threatened by the Japanese. Champion Spark Plugs developed the ceramic insulating material that is standard in today's plugs. The spark plugs tended to foul at lower rpms, and condensation formed in the humid weather conditions, so the engines had to be run up briefly after starting to clear it. Champion continually redesigned and improved its plugs, and found remedies to meet theater conditions.

Engine Cooling

The major problem with the R-3350 from early XB-29 testing and the loss of Eddie Allen and his crew was in flight fires and overheating, which would subsequently cause numerous B-29s to abort takeoffs, or to return to base prematurely. Engine cooling was such a problem in the early B-29s that airplane commanders quipped they had as much tri-motor time on the bomber as four motor!

The cowling was composed of a fixed cowling ring, a set of side panels and ten movable cowl flaps. The cowl flaps were installed on each nacelle to electrically regulate the cooling of the engines via toggle switches on the flight engineer's panel. (Author/Pima)

The Wright R-3350 Cyclone 18 was the largest engine ever built, weighing 2,595lbs "dry weight" (e.g. without accessories), and measuring 55in in diameter and 75in long. The large bulk of the air-cooled radial engine needed to have outside air flow over it for cooling. The induction system of an aircraft was the large system of ducts that was to supply and regulate air for the engine "to breathe." Air from the front of the cowl inlet was to be inducted to the carburetor, and while progressing through the induction system, air passed through filters, inter-coolers, and a number of openings to provide air to all portions of the engine requiring air-cooling. The primary design problem of the XB-29 was to provide the required airflow to cool the engines and to eliminate unneeded airflow. Wright had several other engines, notably the R-1820s used in the B-17, in production, and several others were being built under subcontracts; thus, the Wright engineering department was unable to devote its full attention to the R-3350's early problems.

In the CBI and Pacific the bombers operated from bases where the ground temperatures radiating off the hot taxiways was often well over 120°F. This temperature exceeded the minimum carburetor air temperature for the engine and caused the engines to strain and overheat. Normally 20 minutes of ground running time was the maximum, but when the weather became hot, to avert long taxi times B-29s occasionally had to be towed to the end of the runway before starting their engines. Overheated cylinders reduced the available power by 200 or more horsepower on takeoff. The lower rpm tended to foul spark plugs, which caused the bomber to taxi at a high rpm, causing the engines to heat to dangerous levels. Shorter taxiing times and take offs during cooler times of the day were the obvious remedies, but often were not viable. Champion worked on improved spark plug designs for theater conditions that were specially shipped and installed.

Early operational B-29 engines were severely tested when they ferried very heavy loads of fuel across the Himalayan Hump from India to their new bases in China. Boeing designers had anticipated that heavy loads were to be carried, but expected that the planes would fly the first several hours at low altitude, gradually burning off fuel, becoming lighter, and gaining altitude (which they would do flying from the Marianas to Japan). But for the Hump flights the B-29s had to climb immediately to 20,000 feet because of the chronic cloudy weather, and to avoid the heavy Air

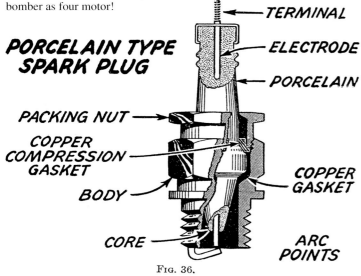

PORCELAIN TYPE SPARK PLUG

TERMINAL

ELECTRODE

PORCELAIN

PACKING NUT

COPPER COMPRESSION GASKET

BODY

COPPER GASKET

CORE

ARC POINTS

FIG. 36.

Generally, the cowl flaps were open for start, warm up and taxiing and were fully closed if the engine were feathered. In all other operating conditions the cowl flap position was determined by maximum or minimum cylinder head temperature permitted for prevailing conditions. (Author/Pima)

Transport Command air traffic, primarily C-47s that had to fly at lower altitudes.

Engine overheating remained a problem throughout the war, and the cowl flaps were a major cause and answer to the overheating problem. The cowling was composed of a fixed cowling ring, a set of side panels, and 10 movable cowl flaps and two immobile flaps on the top of the cowl. The cowl flaps were installed on each nacelle to electrically regulate the cooling of the engines via toggle switches on the flight engineer's panel. There was a thermocouple on each engine that was connected to the flight engineer's panel, and indicated the cylinder head temperature of each engine, allowing the flight engineer to regulate the cowl flaps for the desired temperature. Cowl flap position was indicated on a gauge on the flight engineer's panel. The cowl flaps and intercooler flaps were operated by means of flexible drive shafts interconnecting electrically driven jackscrews controlled by momentary contact (i.e. open-close) switches.

The cylinder heads overheated partially due to the Boeing engine cowling design. During taxiing, the cowl flaps were set to their widest opening of 26-degrees, while during landing they were set to 8-degrees. Cowl flaps were set for the highest permissible cylinder head temperature: 470°F for take off and 418°F for cruising. Cowl flap position was critical. If it were opened too wide drag was increased, and the bomber would drop behind the formation. If it were not opened wide enough the engine would overheat. Recommended cowl flap settings did not allow for discrepancies in instruments and in thermocouples that were often out of calibration. As a remedy, it was recommended that the cowl flaps be shortened, and that the top two fixed flaps on each nacelle could be opened. More cooling air was circulated when the cowl flaps were shortened, which effectively rendered the cowl openings as larger, and exposed the engine to cooling air even when the flaps were closed.

The B-29 induction system had only one large air inlet located at the leading edge of the cowl to distribute air to positions behind the engine. The conventional induction system used separate ducts running up to the leading edge of the cowl, as their oil coolers were positioned at the front of the cowl. A duct then divided and supplied the carburetor and inter-cooler. Early R-3350 engines were difficult to cool, which resulted in internal engine failures and induction system fires. Boeing heat and airflow special-

ists built a mockup of the XB-29 induction system to reproduce all the flight conditions that the aircraft might encounter. To reproduce these flight conditions electric motors were installed in the mockup to drive the turbines, and to replicate their behavior in flight. Calibrated tubes were attached everywhere, as each accessory and part of the induction system was to have the airflow to and through it measured and evaluated. The distribution of airflow, examination of the air eddies, and abnormalities of the airflow in the duct system were thoroughly investigated. From these tests changes were made in the induction system.

There were other overheating fixes. To improve cooling, cuffs were installed on the root of the propeller blades. With the award of large engine contracts Wright was forced to direct attention to the R-3350. It improved cylinder baffle designs and added seals to increase air flow to the cylinders, modified collector ring installation, improved valve cooling by designing inter rocker box lubrication lines to flood the valve stem, upper guide, and spring with oil to carry away the excess heat. Alterations were made to the engine and cowling ducting, and reduced the potential for backfiring and induction system fires. Finally, the changes to the cowling and cowl flaps, the induction system improvements, and the engine modifications by Wright overcame the engine overheating problems.

In the early B-29s the airplane commanders had problems maintaining their engines on the right side of the power curve. Under ideal conditions a B-29 flew at 200 mph with the cylinder heads at normal temperatures and the cowl flaps closed. If the flight engineer observed that the engine temperature had increased five degrees he opened the cowl flaps three degrees to bring the temperature down. However, the drag from the opened cowls caused the airspeed to drop, and the airplane commander then had to increase the power to regain speed, but this correction caused the engine temperature to rise again. Then, in a vicious cycle, the flight engineer would open the cowl flaps wider to lower the temperature, and the bomber would again slow down. To correctly adjust this situation, the airplane commander had to dive the bomber to get it back "on step." The "step" is that position of the airfoil at which the aircraft flies the fastest with the minimum power output. As the bomber increased its speed in the dive the airplane commander had to reduce power and close the cowl flaps. The increased airspeed and lower power setting cooled the engines and put the bomber on the proper side of the power curve.

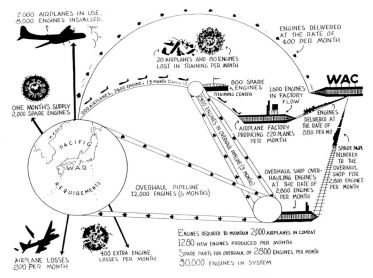

Engine Production and Overhaul (USAF)

Engine Failures and Overhauls

Engine failures in the B-29 were responsible for half of the aborts in training and operations in 1944, and for about half of the causes for loss or serious damage. When matched for reliability with the B-24's Pratt & Whitney R-1830 Twin Wasp and the B-17's Wright R-1820 Cyclone, the B-29's Wright R-3350 did not compare. In March 1945 the B-29's R-3350 was averaging only 170 hours in training and combat, as compared to the B-17's 400 average hours. During training in December 1944 the B-29s had a 32% abort rate, with 44% of those due to engine problems, while the abort rate for the B-17 was 10.5% (only 2.7% due to engine problems), and 23.4% for the B-24 (7% engines). Engine failure was the cause of 28% of the accidents in the first 500 B-29s, as compared to only 4% for the first 500 B-17s.

The time between engine overhauls of an engine was supposed to be 400 hours, but the average time in early combat was 152 hours before the engine had to be removed and rebuilt. Engine changes occupied the ground crews day in and day out, but July 1945 the time between overhauls averaged 265 hours

Wright vs. Dodge 3350 Engine-Causes for Removal

Cause	Wright	Dodge	All
Low Compression	43.2%	8.1%	29.2%
Valves	13.8%	25.4%	18.9%
Cylinders	9.1%	15.1%	10.5%
Metal in Sump	8.0%	16.7%	12.8%
Tech Order Time	12.6%	15.2%	9.2%
Combat & Accident	3.3%	4.4%	3.4%
All Others	15.1%	10.0%	16.0%

Above and following: The standard production model propeller was the 16ft, 7in Hamilton-Standard (a division of United Aircraft Corp.) hydromatic, constant speed, full-feathering propeller. The steel blades were painted flat black with Hamilton Standard decals at mid-prop. There was a stencil near the hub end of the blade with the propeller specs and there was a 6in yellow tip. (Author/Pima)

Both the XB-29s and the YB-29s had three-bladed, 17ft diameter propellers that provided good take off performance but were inadequate at altitude. (USAF)

Propellers

The three XB-29s and the first YB-29s had three-bladed, 17ft diameter propellers that provided good take off performance, but were inadequate at altitude. Propeller gear ratio was between 34 and 43 revolutions of the propeller for every 100 revolutions of the engine crankshaft. The B-29 design demanded very large propellers in order to reach maximum speed and cut through the greatest amount of air. The large diameter propeller produced very high blade tip speeds that could approach the speed of sound (750mph). At this speed phenomena, known as "compressibility burble," was created, and its sudden high drag dramatically affected the aircraft's performances. As the majority of propellers turned 43 times for every 100 engine revolutions, a way had to be found to make the propeller turn more slowly. The 43/100 ratio would be too high for the B-29, and would reduce its climb rate, high altitude performance, and its speed. A new propeller gear ratio was designed that would turn the props 35 times for each 100 revolutions of the engine, making it one of the slowest turning propellers, resulting in lower tip speed with lower noise and higher efficiency.

To achieve this ratio, Boeing engineers added a blade and shortened the prop 5in in diameter. Thus, only the three XB-29s and the next YB-29s mounted three-blade props.

The four Hamilton-Standard (a division of United Aircraft Corp.)16.67ft electric four-bladed hollow hydromatic, constant speed, full-feathering propeller (type C-644S-A22 and A24) were the largest fitted to an American production aircraft. The steel blades were painted flat black, with Hamilton Standard decals at mid-prop. There was a stencil near the hub end of the blade with the propeller specs, and there was a 6in yellow tip. Boeing investigated using the electrically controlled Curtiss prop, but chose the Hamilton-Standard for production reasons, although the Curtiss props would have been a better choice in the long run. Reversible propellers were also considered, as they decreased the landing distance by over 50%, but their reliability was low and maintenance high. At the end of the war a few B-29s of the 509CG/313BW—the atomic bombers—were fitted with the Curtiss reversing props. These propellers were reversible, and synchronized simultaneously with a single control. They had different hubs and domes, and had cuffs added to increase cooling.

Propeller Components

The propellers consisted of five major components: the hub, blades, gear assembly, power unit, and the brush and slip ring assemblies.

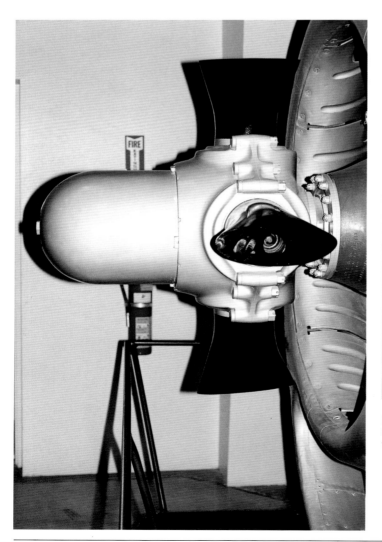

Boeing investigated using the electrically controlled Curtiss prop but chose the Hamilton-Standard for production reasons although the Curtiss props would have been a better choice in the long run. (USAF)

1) Hub Assembly

The hub was spider-machined from a solid steel alloy forging. It served as a mount for six bronze slip rings, one of which was bonded to the hub and insulated from the remaining five rings. The other five rings, four blade assemblies, and a slinger ring were insulated from the hub and each other. The hub assembly was drilled and insulated to carry electric power conduits from the slip rings to the power unit. Five insulated brass connector rods carried electric current from the slip rings through passages in the hub to the contact rods at the front face of the hub. The contact rods were seated in a bushing assembly that transferred the current to the power unit to complete the electrical circuits to the electric motor. Seals were placed around the insulators to prevent grease from leaking through. A slinger ring and tubes for anti-icing were part of the hub assembly.

2) Blade Assemblies: The four hollow steel propeller blades contained shanks that were threaded inside to accommodate the bevel gears. Installed on the shank of each blade was a bearing assembly consisting of a stack of four individual angular contact type ball bearings, a seal, and a blade retaining nut that secured the blade in the hub socket. The bearing assembly allowed the blade to freely rotate in the hub under high centrifugal loads. A plug was installed in the blade gear to prevent hub lubrication from getting into the blade, causing an out-of-balance condition. A seal placed in the blade nut prevented the hub lubricant from escaping. The blade nut was slotted to take balance weight and the blade nut locking key. Aluminum alloy cuffs around each blade shank improved engine cooling. Collectors attached to the shank of each blade collected the anti-icing fluid along the leading edge of the blade.

The brake assembly consisted of two solenoid-operated brakes that stopped the electric motor armature when the blades reached the selected angle. During increased rpm operation, one brake acted as a drag to prevent the rpms from increasing too fast. The brakes held the rpms constant when the propellers were operated at a fixed pitch. If the electric current failed, the brakes held the props at that angle.

3) Power Gear Assembly: The power gear, mounted in a steel adapter, was a spiral bevel gear that meshed with the blade gears. It was splined internally to engage with the splines of the low speed movable ring gear of the rear speed reducer. An angular thrust bearing absorbed the power gear thrust. The power gear assembly transmitted the torque force from the speed reducer through a system of bevel gears to the blade assembly to bring about a change of blade angle.

4) Power Unit Assembly: The power unit assembly consisted of a small reversible motor, brake, and a speed reducer, divided into two parts (the front and rear housings). The two stages of the planetary gearing were contained in these housings, while gaskets between the housings and seals at each end made the unit oil-tight. The unit was partially filled with oil having an extremely low pout point, which assured operation at high altitude and low temperatures.

a) Cut Out Switch Assemblies: The power unit cut out (or limit) switches were located in the rear housing. These closed circuit, spring-loaded switches were opened by cams that were tripped by cam segments.

The cams controlled the low (17 degrees), high (57 degrees), feather (84.7 degrees), and the reverse blade angle (-15.7 degrees) limits. The cams opened the cut out switches according to the degree of rotation of the movable ring gear at specified blade angle limits.

b) Electric Motor Assembly: The reversible electric motor, bolted to the speed reducer front housing, was of the series type, and had two field windings that provided for rotation in either direction. It received its power from the aircraft's power supply through the brush and slip ring assembly. The reverse feature allowed the increase or decrease of rpm, depending on the direction of the motor's rotation.

c) Magnetic Brake Assembly: The brake assembly was mounted on the front of the electric motor, and consisted of the inner and outer brake cage assembly.

d) Speed reducer converted the relatively high rpm and low torque of the electric motor into high torque and low rpm to produce the necessary force to change the blade angle.

5) Brush and Slip Ring Assemblies: The slip ring brush assembly was mounted in an aluminum housing bolted to the nose section of the engine.

Propeller Balance

To demonstrate the delicate balance of their propellers, manufacturer demonstrations placed a four-ounce handkerchief on a prop blade at 3 o'clock, and it would move the whole propeller. To balance a prop, grains of lead were added to the hub end until balance was reached.

Propeller Feathering

The B-29 propeller feathering system was installed in each nacelle, with the pump and motor units located in the lower rear section just forward of the firewall (at the left side of the inboard nacelles and right side of the outboard nacelles). Feathering was initiated by closing the throttle, and pushing the magnetic push button switch, which operated a solenoid switch. This switch started an electric motor driven pump that pumped oil into the propeller dome and governor. The oil was forced under pressure through the constant speed governor to the propeller, where it overrode the constant speed governing action and caused feathering. When the prop was fully feathered the hydraulic pressure rose quickly, and the pressure cut out switch on the control head opened the magnetic coil circuit when a specified pressure was reached.

If the damaged engine lost oil so that there was a drop in oil pressure, a three-gallon oil reservoir tank (in later models), located directly below the main oil tank, supplied enough oil for feathering and unfeathering. In early model B-29s without reserve oil tanks, or if this reserve tank was damaged, it was recommended that an engine be feathered before oil pressure fell to nil. Once the oil was lost the propeller governor no longer functioned, and the prop windmilled at a low pitch due to centrifugal force. The rpms at which it rotated depended on altitude and airspeed. At high altitudes, high windmilling speeds could produce a centrifugal explosion of the propeller or destroy the engine, and a reduction of power and loss of altitude was requisite to reduce the windmilling speed. Once at a lower altitude the airplane commander could resume safe cruising, as the windmilling prop would not exceed normal rpm limits. The feathering procedure was:

1) CLOSE the throttle.

2) Push the feathering button and inform the flight engineer to prepare for feathering. The button did not have to be held down as it popped up when the propeller was fully feathered.

3) Fuel OFF (mixture, fuel boost and fuel valve).

4) Auxiliary equipment OFF (generators, cabin air valve, vacuum pump) or transferred to another engine.

5) Cowl flaps and oil cooler doors CLOSED.

6) Ignition OFF when propeller stops turning.

7) Re-trim the aircraft for balance and power.

The unfeathering procedure was:

1) Propeller switch in low rpm until limit light lights.

2) Push feathering button and hold until propeller reaches 800 rpm and not more than 1,000rpm.

3) Ignition ON.

4) Fuel valve and fuel boost on mixture AUTO RICH.

5) Warm to 200F at 1,200rpm then advance rpm and throttle.

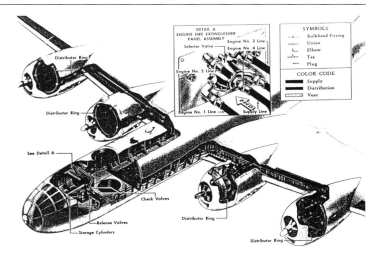

Engine Fire Extinguisher System (USAF)

Engine Fire Fighting Equipment and Procedure

Equipment

Of all the concerns of the B-29 crews fire was preeminent, as was demonstrated by the high number of aborts for any minor engine malfunction. Once started fires were difficult to extinguish, and firewalls were ineffective, and were contemptuously called "tin pans." The B-29 was equipped with a CO_2 system fed by two high-pressure 1,200psi CO_2 bottles charged with 12.6lbs of liquid CO_2. The bottles were located in the nose wheel well, and had lines running to all four-engine nacelles; they could be used individually or together. The gas was discharged through a rigid siphon tube inside the gas cylinder that extended from the release valve to within a short distance of the bottom of the cylinder, assuring the discharge of all the liquid. The main discharge line from each cylinder was fed through a common line through a T-connection. Check valves prevented the gas from entering one cylinder when the other was being discharged. The common discharge line led into a selector valve, where it was directed to the correct nacelle by the flight engineer. The CO_2 entered the nacelle from the wing leading edge through the fire-seal bulkhead fitting. The clamped tubing extended forward inside the nacelle, and attached to the distributor ring by a T-connection on the inboard side at about the nacelle centerline. The distributor ring was 0.5in aluminum alloy tubing attached to the engine mount by six clamps, and circled the front of the engine. One-sixteenth inch holes were spaced three inches apart, and located 90-degrees around the tube from the preceding hole. Another reason the CO_2 extinguishers were ineffective was that engine fires burned intensely because of all the magnesium parts. It was reported that CO_2 extinguishers put out only seven of 52 fires reported through June 1945.

Procedure

If a crewman spotted a nacelle fire, he was to call its position over the interphone. The procedure was for the airplane commander to feather the propeller, and instructed the flight engineer, "Use engine fire procedure." The flight engineer would move the fuel mixture control to idle cut-off, and shut off the fuel valve and boost pump as the airplane commander increased the air speed to try to blow out the fire. The cowl flaps were set to no more than 15-degrees, and the throttle was closed. The fire extin-

guisher controls were located on the left-hand side of the flight engineer's instrument panel, and consisted of a selector knob and two release knobs. The selector knob controlled the selector valve that directed the CO_2 to the proper nacelle. It was a five-way valve with a single inlet and four outlet ports, one to each engine. The two release handles designated FIRE PULL were connected to the valves on top of the CO_2 cylinders by cables. When the handle was pulled, a valve on top of the cylinder was released, and the gas pressure inside the cylinder forced the valve open, letting the gas escape through the lines to the nacelle. The flight engineer turned the selector knob for the proper engine and pulled the CO_2 release handle for whichever bottle he needed to activate and, if necessary, the second handle was pulled. To keep smoke from entering the cabin the flight engineer closed the cabin air valves, and the radio operator made sure that the forward pressure door was closed. If smoke entered the cabin, the co-pilot opened his window, or the bomb bay doors if necessary (the forward pressure was opened to the bomb bay). If the fire became out of control the bomb bay doors were opened, and the airplane commander called for abandoning ship. If the fire became so bad that there was danger of an explosion from the gas tanks the emergency bell was sounded to alert the crew to prepare to abandon the aircraft. Only when the airplane commander gave the order could any crewman leave the aircraft.

De-icing Equipment

Wing De-icers

De-icer boots were first used in 1933 on the Model 247 transport. The B-29 de-icer system used a set of conventional Goodrich pulsating reinforced rubber boots that consisted of four sections for each wing, two for the horizontal stabilizer, and one for the fin. The front, or expanding side, of each boot was constructed of a soft, thin rubber cover that was backed by a rubber-impregnated fabric, and five to nine tubes were placed between the rubber cover and fabric. The number of tubes depended on the thickness of the leading edge the boot was covering. This soft outer cover could be easily damaged by dragging a fuel hose over it, or by placing a ladder against it. The de-icing system was controlled by a toggle switch at the flight engineer's switch panel. The boot tube pressure was controlled by two solenoid-operated valves that distributed the pressure supplied by four engine-driven vacuum pumps mounted on the accessory section of each

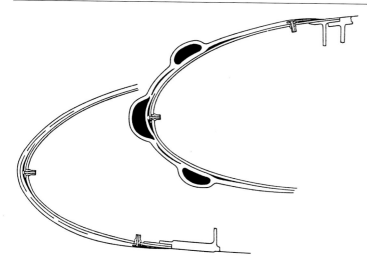

Figure 366—Cross Section of Deicer Boot During Deflation and Inflation

engine. These valves allowed symmetrical alternating pulses of vacuum (deflation) and pressure (inflation) through the tubes of the boot to pulsate and crack off any ice that formed. De-icing boots were later eliminated, because if they were damaged in combat they would interfere with the flight controls. They were deleted in production by Boeing-Wichita with the B-29-50-BW, by Martin with the B-29-20-MO, by Bell the B-29-20-BA, and with Boeing-Renton with the B-29A-5-BN. Several post-war winterized B-29 versions were equipped with de-icing boots, and some flew combat over Korea.

Propeller De-icers

The propeller de-icing system consisted of a 24gal tank of isopropyl alcohol (plus three gallons for expansion), filter, two 24-volt Eclipse electric pump motors, two pumps, fluid check valve feeder tube, slinger ring, and nozzle tubes to each propeller. The tank was located below the floor in the forward end of the rear pressurized compartment, and was held in place by straps. The propeller blades were de-iced by pumping liquid isopropyl alcohol into the slinger ring on the propeller hubs by two electric pumps, also located below the aft cabin floor. The inboard and outboard propellers were supplied by separate pumps that distributed the alcohol onto the base of the blades, which then flowed along the blade tips by centrifugal force, deicing as it moved. A toggle switch on the flight engineer's switch panel energized the two electric pumps that directed fluid at the slinger rings at two to five gallons per hour.

6

Landing Gear

The components of the B-29 landing gear system were the tricycle landing gear, made up of the dual nose wheel and the two dual main wheels, and the tailskid. Previously the tricycle gear was used in the Consolidated B-24, North American B-25, and Martin B-26 bombers, and only a handful of other bombers in the world.

The nose, main, and tailskid all used air-oil shock absorbers, and were electrically actuated and driven by a screw mechanism. Early model landing gear was operated by two electric circuits—one for normal operation, and one for an emergency. Soon it was decided that if the electrical system failed even the emergency landing gear would not function, and a manually operated system was installed.

Tires

Normally 100-150 landings could be made on the main wheel tires, and more on the nose wheel tires, which hit the ground after the main wheels. The use of comparatively small dual tires had several advantages:

1) The wheel wells could be smaller and shallower.
2) Their contact force on the runway was much less, and thus removed the need for reinforced runway surfaces for the heavy bomber.
3) Also, if there was a blow out, especially on a nose wheel, the bomber would continue to roll straight and not swerve. The tires are described with their landing gear wheels.

Nose Gear

The nose gear, manufactured by A.O. Smith, was a dual wheel, single oil-air strut, electrically retractable self-centering caster type capable of 136-degree total swivel. The tricycle landing gear involved engineering the correct correlation of the nose wheel and the main wheels to assure good handling and steering qualities. The nose gear operated simultaneously with the main gear, and was made up of a trunnion, a compression strut, two torsion links, a retracting mechanism, a universal assembly, and a single air-oil shock strut. A cam and roller mechanism could return the gear to the center position from the full 68-degree side movement. A shock absorber was mounted on the shock strut to prevent a wheel shimmy. The dual, smooth contour 36in wheels mounted 36in smooth contour, 10-ply nylon cord tube tires inflated to 44psi. The dual nose wheel configuration had never been attempted, as the B-24, B-25, and B-26 had single nose wheels.

Nose Gear: Front View

The B-29 nose gear needed dual tires, due to the bomber's heavy weight, and were designed for a vertical load of 50,000lbs. The nose gear did not have steering, and turns on the ground were brought about by the use of power variations on the outboard engines, and by differential braking.

Main Gear

The main gear, also manufactured by A.O. Smith, was a cantilever-type, dual wheel, single oil-air shock strut, electrically retracted gear. The width (tread) between the two wheels was 27ft, 11in. The heavy duty, smooth contour cast dual wheels were 29.5in in diameter, and were interchangeable with later model B-17s and B-24s. The wheels mounted 56in smooth contour, 16-ply nylon cord casing tube tires with puncture-proof inner tubes that were inflated to 70psi. These tires were the same as those on the B-17F and G and the B-24. The wheels were secured to the axle with a thrust bearing, the brake assembly torque-flange, and a locknut. The wheels were retracted electrically, and an alternate motor was provided for emergency operation. In the B-17 main gear design the wheels protruded when retracted, but for aerodynamics in the B-29 Boeing engineers needed to retract the wheels forward and up, entirely into the nacelles behind closing doors. To test the design a scaled-down model was built and installed on a

The nose gear had smooth contour 36in wheels mounting 36in smooth contour, 10-ply nylon cord tube tires inflated to 44psi. (Author/Pima)

Nose Gear: Rear View

Main Gear: Rear View

Douglas A-20 at Wright Field. The tests were successful, even though a tire did blow out. Each main gear was designed for a vertical load of 160,000lbs, and weighed approximately 3,000lbs. The left and right assemblies, without fairings and electrical connections, were identical and interchangeable. The main wheels were equipped with expander tube-type hydraulic brakes, operated conventionally from the rudder pedal.

Tailskid

The tailskid was an oil-air shock strut, electrically retractable type manufactured by A.O. Smith. A retractable tailskid was installed because of the B-29's length and low profile. It functioned in conjunction with the landing gear to protect the lower rear turret during high angle take offs and landings.

Emergency Landing Gear Procedures

Experience demonstrated that if only one gear failed to extend, better results were achieved if the emergency landing were made on any combination of two gears extended. However, if two gears failed to extend, then the remaining gear was to be retracted, and a belly-landing attempted. If either of the main gears failed to extend, the procedure was to continue a normal approach and land as slow as possible, keeping the unextended gear wing up with aileron adjustment for as long as possible. If the nose wheel failed to lock a normal landing was made by holding the nose in the air as long as possible, but not so long that it crashed down on the runway. To prevent fires all switches were to be cut as soon as the aircraft was on the ground.

Portable Emergency Motor

The portable emergency motor in the bomb bay that was used for the emergency lowering of the flaps, or the emergency operation of the bomb bay doors, was also used for emergency lowering of the main gear. It was normally stowed in the flap socket in the center wing section of the inboard wing, approximately at the centerline of the bomber. The motor was plugged into a power receptacle, and its cord could reach each gearbox. After checking the direction of turn (noted on the motor handle)—and that the clutch had been shifted—it was inserted into the lower position of the gearbox. It was run until the stops were engaged, indicated by a jarring sound, and the slipping of the motor's clutch was heard. It took about one minute to retract the gear, and 40 seconds to extend it.

Main Gear Assembly with Shock Strut (Photos taken by author of Pima Air & Space Museum's B-29)

The main gear wheels mounted 56in smooth contour, 16-ply nylon cord casing tube tires with puncture-proof inner tubes that were inflated to 70psi. These tires were the same as those on the B-17F and G and the B-24. (USAF)

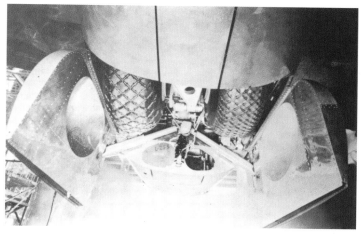

The wheels were retracted electrically and an alternative motor was provided for emergency operation. In the B-17 main gear design the wheels protruded but for aerodynamics in the B-29 Boeing engineers needed to retract the wheels forward and up entirely into the nacelles behind closing doors. (Author/Pima)

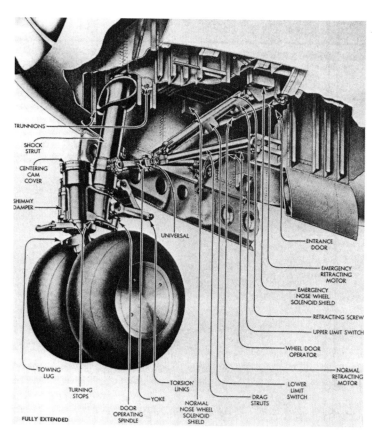

Nose Gear Retracting Mechanism (USAF)

The nose gear was a dual wheel, single oil-air strut, electrically retractable self-centering caster type capable of 136-degree total swivel. The nose gear operated simultaneously with the main gear and was made up of a trunnion, a compression strut, two torsion links, a retracting mechanism, a universal assembly, and a single air-oil shock strut. (Author/Pima)

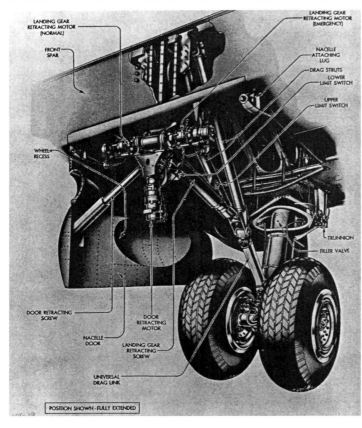

Main Gear Retracting Mechanism (USAF)

The main gear was of the cantilever-type, dual wheel, single oil-air shock strut, electrically retracted. The width (tread) between the wheels was 27ft, 11in. The heavy duty, smooth contour cast dual wheels were 29.5in in diameter and were interchangeable with later model B-17s and B-24s. (Author/Pima)

Manual Landing Gear Procedures

If the gear did not retract—or worse, did not extend—there also was a manual backup system available to the portable emergency motor. The system was comprised of a hand crank for each main gear and the nose gear, which was connected to torque tubes and gearboxes to move the landing gear screws. Cable-operated clutch handles disconnected the normal motors from the gear during emergency operation and engaged the manual system. The handles (the same ones that operated the emergency nacelle door release) for these clutches were located at station 485, within easy reach of the crew manning the crank handles. There were operating instruction decals located above each gearbox at the cranking stations for the main gears, and another instruction decal on the back of the airplane commander's armor plate for the nose gear.

Main Gear Manual Emergency Procedures

The main landing gears were each operated manually by a hand crank inserted into a gearbox located just behind the main wing spar, and above each catwalk in the rear bomb bay at station 520 (above the rear spar bulkhead in B-29As). A torque tube projected from each gearbox outboard through the wing trailing edge ribs to a right angle gearbox near wing sta-

tion 137. From this gearbox another tube projected forward to a gearbox on the rear side of the front wing spar, from which a short tube connected to the gears that actuated the landing gear screws. To raise the gear manually it had to be turned clockwise on the upper position on the gearbox (12

Tail Skid (Author/Pima)

to 1 ratio) for 774 turns, which took about 30 minutes. To lower the gear it was necessary to insert the handle on the lower position on the gearbox (6 to 1), turning clockwise until stop for 387 turns, and taking about 12 minutes.

Nose Gear Manual Emergency Procedures
The entrance hatch on the floor was opened, and the upper end of the support beam was swung down to a horizontal position and secured to the airplane commander's armor plate stanchion. A hand crank located under the entrance hatch was inserted into the gearbox socket. The gearbox (3 to 1) required 257 turns to raise or lower the nose gear in two to three minutes.

Towing, Parking, and Mooring
A bomber crewman or ground crewman was to be present in the airplane commander's seat when the bomber was to be towed. His duties were to be sure that the hydraulic system was operating, to release the parking brake, and operate the brake pedals when the bomber was being moved.

Clark tow tug with tow bar attached to towing lug placed near the center of the nose wheel axle. (USAF)

Forward Towing: There was a towing lug attached near the center of the nose wheel axle. Although the nose wheel could swivel 136-degrees, it was recommended that the towing direction should be as close to straight forward as possible, slowly and without jerks or sudden stops to avoid stress on the gear.

Rearward Towing: The lugs for rearward towing were attached to the rear of each main gear strut. Ropes or cables of equal lengths were attached, and the tow tug would try to keep the towing force in line with the aircraft centerline. Change of direction was made through the use of a tow bar attached to the nose wheel towing lug that was turned. The airplane could also be pushed backward by using the nose towing lug on smooth ramps and runways.

Parking and Mooring
Before mooring the aircraft the parking brake was set, and chocks were placed on both sides of each pair of wheels on the main and nose landing gear. The rudder pedals and ailerons were to be in the neutral position, the elevators in the down position, the throttles closed, and the controls locked. All hatches and doors were to be closed, but the bomb bay doors were left open in case there was a fire on the ground. The mooring lines were tied to nose wheel well eyebolt fittings, two eyebolts on the wings, the nose and main gear towing lugs, and a hole in the tailskid assembly. The bomber was to be headed into the wind with 18 to 24in. of slack on the mooring lines. If high winds, dust, rain, or snow were predicted the engines, turbo-superchargers, turrets, sighting blisters, and pitot tubes were to be covered. The covers were stored under the floor in the rear pressurized compartment.

Hydraulic System and Brakes
The B-29 was an all-electric aircraft, as hydraulic systems were very vulnerable to combat damage, which could shut down many important pieces of equipment and shower inflammable hydraulic fluid into the fuselage. The only hydraulic system on the B-29 was the braking system for the four wheels of the main gear. The normal brakes were controlled by toe pressure on the rudder pedals. The parking brake was a button pull handle on the airplane commander's rudder pedal stand. After the brake was set the

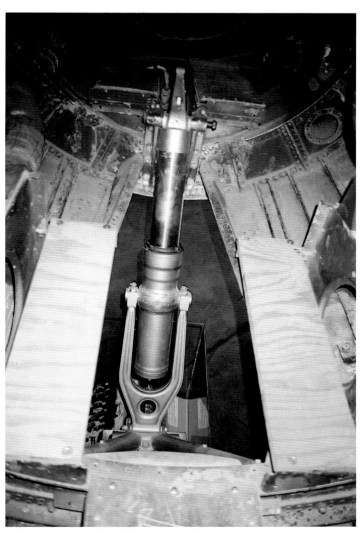

Tail Skid Oil-Air Strut (Author/Pima)

knob was to stay out. The parking brakes could only be set at the airplane commander's stand. The parking brakes were not to be set if the brakes were hot, as they would not cool properly.

The hydraulic panel was located under the floor of the forward compartment near bulkhead 218 (near the navigator's station), and contained:

a) Electric motor-driven pump.
b) Floating piston-type accumulator.
c) Filter.
d) Pressure switch.
e) Relief valve.
f) Shut off valve.

The panel was heated by a hot air outlet from the cabin heating system to prevent the hydraulic fluid from congealing during high altitude flight.

The hydraulic pump was operated by an electric motor that maintained a system pressure of 800 to 1,000psi, and was controlled by a pressure switch that closed the circuit and started the pump when the system dropped to 800psi, and opened it when the pressure reached 1,000psi. An amber warning light on the co-pilot's panel, and on the flight engineer's panel, lit when the main pressure fell below 800psi. The hydraulic pump ran continuously at pressures below 800psi (when the pressure fell below 200psi the pump cut out to prevent overheating if the hydraulic fluid was lost). A 3gal reservoir (earlier models had a 4.9gal reservoir) was situated in the forward compartment above the navigator's station. It had a half-gallon expansion space, and the tank gauge read approximately two gal-

A 3-gallon reservoir (earlier models had a 4.9gal reservoir) was situated in the forward compartment above the navigator's station. It had a half-gallon expansion space and the tank gauge read approximately two gallons when the parking brake was set. (Author/Pima)

lons when the parking brake was set. There were metering valves mounted on the airplane commander's and co-pilot's rudder pedal stirrup supports, which were controlled individually by toe pressure on either the airplane commander's or co-pilot's rudder pedals to apply braking.

For emergency use there were two brake levers on the aisle stand. The emergency system received pressure from the normal system, but was isolated by a check valve and emergency shut off valve (at the flight engineer's auxiliary panel) to prevent reverse flow. The flight engineer's panel had a hydraulic pressure gauge and warning light. The emergency system had to be recharged after five to seven applications of the brakes. There was a hand pump on the floor to the left of the co-pilot's seat to produce pressure when the electric pump was not working. There was a manually operated, dual-metering valve located on the aisle stand to meter emergency pressure to the wheel brakes. When using the emergency brakes a steady application of pressure of the brakes, not pumping, was required.

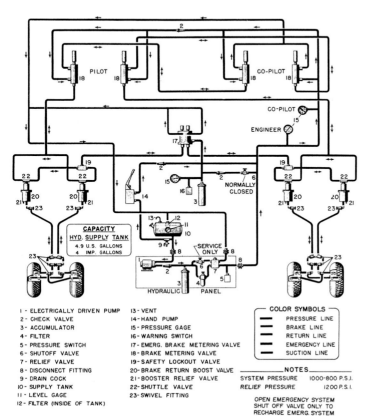

1 - ELECTRICALLY DRIVEN PUMP
2 - CHECK VALVE
3 - ACCUMULATOR
4 - FILTER
5 - PRESSURE SWITCH
6 - SHUTOFF VALVE
7 - RELIEF VALVE
8 - DISCONNECT FITTING
9 - DRAIN COCK
10 - SUPPLY TANK
11 - LEVEL GAGE
12 - FILTER (INSIDE OF TANK)
13 - VENT
14 - HAND PUMP
15 - PRESSURE GAGE
16 - WARNING SWITCH
17 - EMERG. BRAKE METERING VALVE
18 - BRAKE METERING VALVE
19 - SAFETY LOCKOUT VALVE
20 - BRAKE RETURN BOOST VALVE
21 - BOOSTER RELIEF VALVE
22 - SHUTTLE VALVE
23 - SWIVEL FITTING

COLOR SYMBOLS
PRESSURE LINE
BRAKE LINE
RETURN LINE
EMERGENCY LINE
SUCTION LINE

NOTES
SYSTEM PRESSURE   1000-800 P.S.I.
RELIEF PRESSURE   1200 P.S.I.

OPEN EMERGENCY SYSTEM
SHUT OFF VALVE ONLY TO
RECHARGE EMERG. SYSTEM

Hydraulic System (Author/Pima)

7

Bomb Bay Section

Development and Description

Boeing engineers designed the B-29 with forward and aft bomb bays that were separated by the wing center section, which placed each bomb bay on either side of the aircraft center of gravity. They were separated from the forward and rear pressurized compartments by bulkheads at stations 218 and 646. The bomb bay doors could thus be opened at any altitude without affecting the pressurization of the aircraft. Entrance to the bomb bays during flight was through the pressurized bulkhead doors to the catwalks, which extended down both sides of each bay. Exit from the pressurized compartments during high altitude flights could only be accomplished by depressurizing the cabins.

The initial bomb bay design was intended to carry only large size bombs, so to carry many smaller-sized bombs economically the bomb bay needed to be lengthened. Armament engineers at Wright Field redesigned the bomb bays, which meant the fuselage needed to be lengthened 62in. The new design gave the bomb bays the required space, doubling the number of 500lb bombs the bomber could carry, and also gave the tail gunner's position more room.

Catwalks

A catwalk was located on each side of the bomb bay, and provided a walkway between the forward and rear pressurized compartments. It added longitudinal fuselage strength, and the two main frames attached to the catwalks provided the terminal attachment for the inboard wing section. It provided attachment for the bottom of the side bomb racks.

Tunnel

A 34in diameter, 33ft long pressurized cylindrical communications tunnel provided access to the forward and rear pressurized compartments at all times. There is a story that portly Boeing engineer Wellwood Beall crawled through openings of various diameters until he became stuck, and this determined the diameter of the tunnel. It consisted of three sections. The first, or forward section (at station 247), extended from the forward compartment to a point directly over the front wing spar, where it was joined with the middle tunnel section that was part of the center wing section. The middle section extended aft to a point directly over the wing rear spar, where it joined to the third (aft) tunnel section. This third section extended

Rear Bomb Bay Doors with warning sign that the doors were air operated. If the bays were to be left open on the ground it was suggested that a guard be posted to be sure no one entered them. Crews did not trust the safety valves and switches and often wedged a 2 x 4 to be certain to hold the doors open. (Author/Pima)

Manufacture of the rear pressurized compartment by the Hudson Motor Co. of Detroit. The pressure bulkhead with the tunnel and bomb bay door openings are evident. (USAF)

Rear Bomb Bay (looking forward at the radome) with the tunnel leading from rear pressurized compartment across bomb bay. Above the yellow oxygen tank is the olive colored center wing attachment. (Author/ Pima)

Forward Pneumatic Bomb Bay Door Actuator (looking aft) The original electric doors were replaced with pneumatic doors that literally snapped open and closed when actuated by the bombsight. The air pressure for the system was provided by two compressors and was stored in the accumulators. (Author/Pima)

Above: Forward Bomb Bay (looking forward) with tunnel above and round door below tunnel leading from the forward pressurized compartment across the bomb bays into rear pressurized compartment. The sidewall bomb rack with a 500lb bomb is seen. (Author/Pima) Left: Manufacture of the bomb bay section. The tunnel can be seen at the top of the section. (USAF)

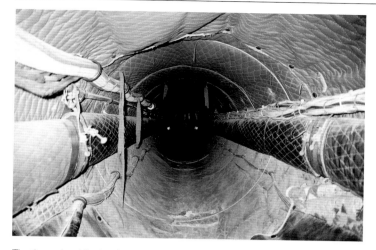

The thermal padding insulated the tunnel from the cold bomb bay and made crawling through it much more comfortable. Electric bundles and insulating ducting ran through the tunnel to the rear of the aircraft. (Author/Pima)

Bomb Bay Doors

Originally, the two doors in each bomb bay were operated by means of electric motors mounted in the aft right hand side of the forward bomb bay, and in the forward right hand side of the rear bomb bay within the catwalk. The motors drove retracting screws, two on each end of the bomb bay. Power for this mechanism was supplied through central gearboxes to which the retracting screws attached. Two solenoids—one for retraction and one for extension of the bomb bay door retraction screws—controlled each motor. During a bomb run, the bombsight controlled normal bomb bay door opening.

The electric doors opened slowly, increasing drag and decreasing speed, which increased the bomber's vulnerability to enemy interceptors and anti-aircraft fire. These doors were replaced with pneumatic doors that literally snapped open and closed. The air pressure for the system was provided by two compressors, and was stored in the accumulators. The doors were actuated by the bombsight, and snapped open immediately prior to bomb release. This made the bomber more stable on its bombing run, as there was no vibration, which was the case in the slowly opening electric doors. As well as the bombsight salvo switch, the bombardier had a bomb door selector switch that enabled him to open forward and aft doors together, or only the aft door. The bombardier's panel had two indicator lights showing which doors were open, and another light that warned when the

aft and connected to the station 646 pressure bulkhead. Above the entrance of the first section of the tunnel a Plexiglas dome was installed on all B-29s beginning with the serial number 42-24420 for use as an astrodome.

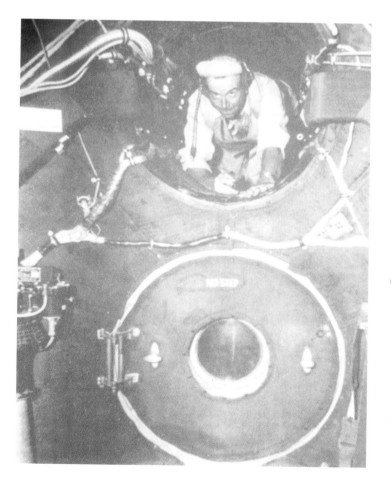

A 34in diameter, 33ft long pressurized, three section, cylindrical communications tunnel provided access to the forward and rear pressurized compartments at all times. Here a crewman enters the forward pressurized compartment. (USAF)

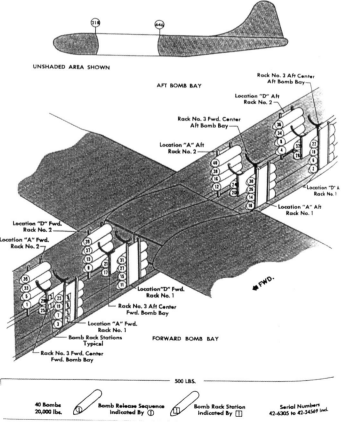

Bomb Bay Rack Stations (USAF)

doors were not latched. The airplane commander had two switches mounted on the aisle control stand that opened and closed both sets of doors simultaneously. There were two emergency pull handles for opening the bomb bay doors: one was located at the airplane commander's station, and the other just aft of bulkhead 218. In later models there were two emergency pull handles for closing the bomb bays. There were electrical safety shut off valves and safety switches to keep the doors opened or closed. The pneumatic doors were found to be hazardous to maintenance crews. If the bomb bays were to be left open on the ground, the valves were to be closed and the switches turned off. If the bay doors were to be tested on the ground, it was suggested that a guard be posted to be sure no one entered them. Crews did not trust the safety valves and switches, and often placed a 2 x 4 to be certain to hold the bomb bays open.

Turbulence Deflector

When the bomb bays were opened, air turbulence could cause the rear bombs in each bomb bay to hang up and dangle nose down, swinging out of control, possibly colliding with each other and perhaps exploding. When

The bomb racks could fulfill three purposes, to carry bombs, to carry auxiliary fuel tanks or to carry a cargo platform. The side racks were of web construction, consisting of two extruded aluminum alloy bomb rails, with quick release bomb rack attachment pins at each end to mate with the terminals on the catwalk and on the bomb rack support beam above the catwalk. (Author/Pima)

these bombs were released they tumbled dangerously out of the bomb bays. A deflector shield was developed and installed that reduced turbulence by about a third, enough to reduce bomb hang ups to a minimum.

Bomb Racks and Shackles

The bomb bays could stow bombs of several sizes to a capacity of 10 tons. The total bomb load depended on the amount of fuel required to reach the target. The normal bomb load was 40x500lb bombs, but four 4,000lb bombs could be carried internally. Late in the war B-29s were equipped with external wing racks to carry very heavy bombs, and a maximum of 20,000lbs of bombs could be carried. The following bomb loads could be carried: 80-100lb; 56-300lb; 40-500lb; 12-1,000lb; 12-1,600lb; 8-2,000lb; and 4-4,000lb. Late Silver Plate atomic B-29s could carry two 10,000lb atomic bombs.

Bomb Racks

The bomb racks could fulfill three purposes: to carry bombs; to carry auxiliary fuel tanks; or to carry a cargo platform. Three types of bomb racks were available on all B-29s: 500lb center racks; right and left 1,000lb racks; and right and left 4,000lb racks. Each rack was interchangeable on the same side of the bomber with others of its own size. The center racks were completely interchangeable. The cargo platform was a metal framework with wooden flooring; it was used in the rear bomb bay, and was mounted with eight bomb rack hooks. The platform was positioned in the bomb bay by the bomb hoist. There were fittings in each bomb bay for the installation of either two or three auxiliary fuel tanks.

The side racks were of web construction, consisting of two extruded aluminum alloy bomb rails, with quick release bomb rack attachment pins at each end to mate with the terminals on the catwalk, and on the bomb rack support beam above the catwalk. The center racks had two semi-circular collars to which the rails attached. The collars fit around the tunnel terminal fittings on support beams at each side of the tunnel. The center bomb rack was held in place by yoke fittings around the overhead pressurized tunnel.

There were eight or 11 side racks for the 1,000lb bombs, four side racks for the 1,600, 2,000, and 4,000lb bombs, four center racks for the 100 and 300lb bombs, and four center racks for 500lb bombs. However, center bomb racks were never installed in a bomber that had side racks for carrying 1,000lb or larger bombs.

Bomb Shackles

The B-29 had three bomb shackle sizes:

B-7: 100lb, 300lb, 500lb, and 1,000lb
D-6: 1,600lb or 2,000lb
D-7: 4,000lb

To hook the bomb shackle to the bomb suspension lugs, the release lever and the arming lever were pinched toward the center of the shackle, and a pull was exerted on the suspension lugs. The shackle hooks were threaded through the lugs on the bomb, and an upward pressure was applied to the test the strength of the connection by pulling up on the shackle.

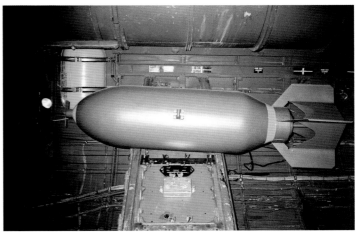

B-7 bomb shackle. To hook the bomb shackle to the lugs, the release lever and the arming lever are were pinched toward the center of the shackle and a pull was exerted on the suspension lugs. The shackle hooks were threaded through the lugs on the bomb and an upward pressure was applied to the test the strength of the connection by pulling up on the shackle. (Author/Pima)

500lb bomb attached to top shackle looking up toward tunnel. (Author/Pima)

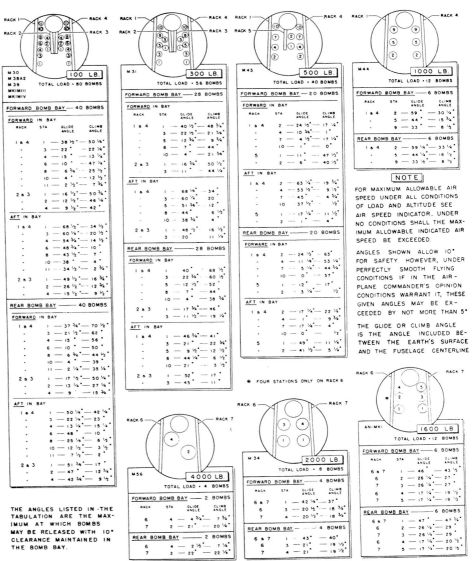

NOTE

FOR MAXIMUM ALLOWABLE AIR SPEED UNDER ALL CONDITIONS OF LOAD AND ALTITUDE SEE AIR SPEED INDICATOR. UNDER NO CONDITIONS SHALL THE MAXIMUM ALLOWABLE INDICATED AIR SPEED BE EXCEEDED.

ANGLES SHOWN ALLOW 10° FOR SAFETY. HOWEVER, UNDER PERFECTLY SMOOTH FLYING CONDITIONS IF IN THE AIRPLANE COMMANDER'S OPINION CONDITIONS WARRANT IT, THESE GIVEN ANGLES MAY BE EXCEEDED BY NOT MORE THAN 5°

THE GLIDE OR CLIMB ANGLE IS THE ANGLE INCLUDED BETWEEN THE EARTH'S SURFACE AND THE FUSELAGE CENTERLINE

THE ANGLES LISTED IN THE TABULATION ARE THE MAXIMUM AT WHICH BOMBS MAY BE RELEASED WITH 10° CLEARANCE MAINTAINED IN THE BOMB BAY.

* FOUR STATIONS ONLY ON RACK 6

Bomb Loading Diagram (USAF)

Right and following: This series of photos shows a 500lb bomb cradles on its hoist (left). The bomb being hooked to its shackle (center) and the fully loaded bomb bay with 20 500lb bombs loaded on both sidewall racks and center rack (right). (USAF)

Bomb Loading

The recommended procedure for loading bombs in the B-29 was to load the forward bomb bay first to keep the center of gravity of the bomber well forward of the main landing gear. The bombs were towed to the aircraft on a procession of bomb dollies carrying one bomb each. Care had to be taken to insure the proper setting of the bomb controls to prevent accidental release during loading operations. Once the bomb load to be carried was determined, the release sequence had to be decided and type A-2 release boxes installed only at stations where bombs were being carried. To load the bomb racks the bombardier's control lever had to be in the SELEC-TIVE position. A single length of strong copper wire was looped under the bomb, which was attached to a pulley-yoke motor assembly or special support bracket, depending on the size of the bomb to be loaded (all but 4,000lb bombs were hoisted by the pulley-yoke). The pulleys had to be installed in their proper position in the yoke, and the bomb shackles were snapped on the bomb suspension lugs, the arming wires for the tail fuses rigged, the release lever put in the LOCK position, and the arming lever in the SAFE position. The sling was placed under each bomb and was balanced, and the hooks on the hoist cable were attached to the sling hooks. The hoist motor was started, and the bomb was carefully raised to its station; the swaying bomb was guided by hand and latched on the bomb rack hooks. The type A-2 bomb release units were then plugged into each active bomb station to be loaded. After attaching the release unit, the bombardier returned the control lever to LOCK to prevent accidental release. The release units were held in place by plunger-type fasteners pressed in by hand into the corresponding holes in the bomb rack. Racks were to be loaded so that any empty stations were at the top. After the bombs were in position the armorer fused each bomb.

Modifications for Large Bombs

Several B-29s were outfitted with external bomb racks under their inner wing sections, between the fuselage and inboard engine nacelles. These special racks were designed to carry very heavy bombs, such as four 4,000lb bombs to be loaded two on each external bomb rack. The 12,000lb British "Tallboy" earthquake bombs were also to be carried on these racks. Several B-29s had bomb bay modifications to carry a single 22,000lb British

"Grand Slam" bomb. The Mk-1 "Little Boy" atomic bomb weighed 8,900lbs, and measured 10ft long by 2ft, 4in in diameter. It had a yield of 15 to 16 kilotons, and was a gun-type heavy uranium bomb. Five were built. The Mk-3 "Fat Man" atomic bomb weighed 10,300lbs, measured 10ft 8in long, and was 5ft in diameter. It was a plutonium implosion bomb with a yield of 18 to 49 kilotons. 120 were built. A "Thin Man" atomic bomb was designed but not built. It was to be approximately 17ft long and 2ft in diameter. The loading and carrying of these large conventional and atomic bombs will be discussed later.

Bomb Release

The bomb bays were arranged in tandem, with one located ahead of the center of gravity, and the other aft. However, one bomb bay could not be emptied before the other without temporarily altering the level flight of the bomber on its bombing run. To offset this situation a device called the intervalometer was designed to drop bombs alternately from one bomb bay to another (forward to aft sequence). The intervalometer could time the release of the bombs for one at a time so that they would impact in train, or they could be salvoed all at once. The bomb bay door electric circuit had a safety switch to prevent the bombs from being jettisoned before the doors were fully open.

Bomb Release Switch

The bombs could be released electrically or mechanically. The normal release operation was electrically, which allowed either automatic or manual control for individual, selective, or train bombing release of the bombs. In the all-electric system the A-2 bomb release unit was replaced by the A-4 release unit, and the control stand and all cable and mechanical controls were removed. The release circuit could be closed through either the bombsight switch or manual release switch. The bombs were carried on the racks by shackles that released the bombs electrically, and also retained or released the tail fuse arming wire. Earlier nose and tail arming wires were routed to the shackles, but electric arming solenoids were introduced for nose fusing to permit selective bombing.

Mechanical bomb release was done only in an emergency situation, and therefore in salvo by either of the two emergency release levers (at the airplane commander's control stands and at station 646), or by the bombardier's emergency release and rewind control. The mechanical systems were independent of the electrical system, and were coordinated by the bomb control unit. This system is discussed later in this section.

Bomb Door and Rack Control

The bombardier could control the doors and bomb racks by two control levers and an emergency release and rewind wheel to be used in case of control malfunction. The bomb door control lever operated switches that controlled the bomb bay door retracting motor and had two positions: OPEN and CLOSED. The lever could be operated independently of the bomb release control, but the bomb release lever was designed so that it could not be placed in the SALVO position without first engaging the bomb door control lever to open the bomb doors. The release lever had three positions:

1) LOCK: In the bomb LOCKED position the bomb racks were locked against any release of bombs by means of the emergency release levers and wheel.
2) SELECTIVE: In this position the bomb racks were prepared for single release by manual operation of the bombardier's release switch, or by automatic operation through the bomb interval release
3) SALVO: In the SALVO position the bombs were all released simultaneously and unarmed.

A mechanical lock, operated by the right hand door in the forward bomb bay and the left-hand door in the rear bomb bay, prevented the use of the bomb release mechanism until the doors were in the OPEN position. This prevented the accidental release of bombs when the doors were closed. A bomb door safety switch was attached to each bomb door, and prevented the use of the electrical bomb release circuit until the doors were fully open.

Emergency Bomb Release
Emergency Mechanical Release

The bombs could be released by winding the bombardier's hand wheel two and a half turns clockwise, or by pulling the emergency release handles 30in. There were two emergency release handles, one located on the airplane commander's aisle stand, and the other on the forward wall of the rear pressurized compartment, near the floor on the port side. The first part of the winding of the hand wheel or pull of the release handles released and opened the doors, and the final part operated the bomb release levers and dropped the unarmed bombs.

Emergency Electrical Release

There were three salvo switches: one located at the airplane commander's station; another at the bombardier's station; and the last at the right hand sighting station in the rear pressurized compartment. When any one of the salvo switches was CLOSED the bomb bay OPEN solenoid caused the bombs to be released unarmed.

Emergency Manual Release

If mechanical and electrical release failed, then actuating the emergency bomb door release on the airplane commander's control stand would open the bomb bay doors. The bombs could then be released singly by manually tripping the release lever on each bomb shackle.

8

Bombsights

Norden Bombsight M-7 and M-9

The Carl Norden Company was formed in 1929 in New York City, and by February 1931 the company delivered its illustrious Mark XV bombsight to the Navy. It was successfully tested against the obsolete heavy cruiser *Pittsburgh* soon after, and the results were so promising that the AAC also placed an order for the revolutionary bombsight. In tests over a dry lake at Muroc, CA, Army bombardiers were consistently placing their bombs within 50ft of their aiming point, resulting in its fabled "into a pickle barrel" accuracy. However, a long unvarying approach to target was necessary, and it was virtually impossible for any pilot to fly with the skill required to correct for wind drift, and maintain the constant altitude and speed that would guarantee bombing accuracy. As the bombing altitude increased these problems were magnified, and caused a decrease in bombing accuracy. The Norden Company improved its bombsight from the Mark XV to the M-7, and then to the M-9, which was introduced in late 1943. With the M-9 the closing speed of attack could be established at any time during the approach, and a fixed speed and altitude needed only to be maintained for 15 to 20 seconds by the use of the Norden produced gyro-stabilized automatic pilot, which was called the Automatic Flight Control Equipment (AFCE) by the Army, while the Navy named it the Stabilized Bombing Approach Equipment (SBAE). The AFCE was an internal computer consisting of an intricate system of numerable gears and cams and mirrors, lenses, and prisms that controlled the aircraft on the bombing approach and eliminating manual control.

The Norden bombsight weighed 45lbs, and was comprised of over 2,000 parts, many of which were manufactured to minute tolerances. The Norden sight was a two-part system, the sight proper, and the base unit, which contained the electronics and incorporated the AFCE. The Automatic Flight Control Equipment was connected to the C-1 autopilot, and allowed the bombardier to control the lateral movement of the bomber by his adjustments of the sight. The detachable upper half of the Norden contained the gyroscope for vertical stabilization of the instrument. The stabilizer consisted of the directional gyro, which was to detect deviations from the bomber's set course, and the flight gyro, which recorded any inclination for the bomber to either roll or to nose up or down. The sight was located on top of the stabilizer, and was equipped with a 2.5 power telescope that was driven by a variable speed electric motor with a gyro to keep the sight stable.

Norden Bombsight The Norden bombsight weighed 45lbs and was comprised of over 2,000 parts, many of which were manufactured to minute tolerances. The Norden sight was a two-part system, the sight proper and the base unit that contained the electronic and incorporated the AFCE. The Automatic Flight Control Equipment was connected to the C-1 auto pilot and allowed the bombardier to control the lateral movement of the bomber by the his adjustments of the sight. (Author/Pima)

In preflight, the bombardier had to enter basic data into the computer from precalculated tables. These tables provided data for the bomb trail (the distance the bombs would hit the ground behind the aircraft), and the time it would take the bombs to fall based on the scheduled speed and altitude of the approach. Approximately five minutes from the target the bomber's course was checked for drift from cross wind data that was entered into the computer. When the target came into view the bombardier trained the telescope on it and adjusted the telescope drive so that the bombsight maintained its course to the target. When the bombsight clutches were operated they immediately actuated the stabilizer-controlled autopilot. The flight and directional gyros both had electrical brushes fitted to them. If the bomber went off course the gyro maintained its orientation, and in response moved inside its case. The brushes would make contact with the solenoids, which engaged electric servo motors that then operated the aircraft's control surfaces and corrected the deviation. There was a link between the rudder and aileron servo motors to cause a bank in turns, but a designated switch could be operated that gave all directional control to the rudder and eliminated bank. The bombardier could control the stabilizer to take evasive action in case of heavy anti-aircraft fire, but these controls were limited by mechanical stops in the autopilot that eliminated steep banks. During the bomb run the bomber was kept extremely straight and level by the stabilizer. The telescope tracked the target until it reached the precise dropping angle when the bombs were released automatically.

An estimated 52,000 Norden bombsights were manufactured at an estimated cost of a half billion dollars. The major contractors were Carl L. Norden, Inc. (21,437 sets), Lukas-Harold Corp. (12,743 or 14,000?), Minneapolis Honeywell Regulator Co. (8,257), Victor Adding Machine Co. (7,000 est.), Burroughs Adding Machine Co. (6,041), and Remington Rand, Inc. (3,450). Honeywell and Victor were direct contractors to the AAF, the other companies were direct contractors to the Navy, and the additional AAF bombsights (all but about 6,500) were procured from the Navy contracts.

The entire American strategic bombing doctrine was based on the precision of the Norden bombsight, and although planners realized that it alone could not win a war, it could hasten its end. Gen. Ira Eaker, the first commander of the 8AF, summed up the initial Allied bombing philosophy in 1942 when he stated, "We should never allow the history of this war to convict us of throwing the strategic bombing at the man in the street" (i.e. unlike the indiscriminate bombing of Warsaw, Rotterdam, and then London by the murderous Luftwaffe). RAF Bomber Command tried precision daylight bombing, and took terrible losses while obtaining unsatisfactory results. Arthur "Bomber" Harris switched his RAF Bomber Command force to nighttime "precision" bombing, and was lucky to hit the target city, much less a target within the city, and became guilty of bombing the man on the street. The 8AF continued to espouse daylight precision "pickle barrel" bombing, but a study in early 1944 concluded that only 7% of all USAAF bombs fell within 1,000ft of their aiming point. The Norden bombsight in combat conditions was unable to hit the pickle barrel or the pickle factory, but more often hit the cucumber patch outside town! The original "pickle barrel tests" were conducted in good weather by very experienced bombardiers flying in the Douglas B-18A at 150mph at 12,000ft without flak or enemy fighters. The Norden-equipped B-17, B-24, and later the B-29 flew higher and faster, often in bad weather, facing disconcerting enemy AA and fighters. With the failure of precision bombing the USAAF concluded that area bombing, which was nothing more than the continuation

of inaccurate precision bombing, was justified because of "the contributions in numerous ways of the civilian population to the fighting strength of the enemy, and to speed securing of unconditional surrender." (USSBS)

AN/APQ-13

Once the B-29 was combat-ready, the AAF anticipated the use of the AN/APQ-13 radar set (nicknamed "Mickey") for its navigation and bombing. In the ETO the AAF had used both the British H2S and American H2X (designated the APQ-15) beginning in the fall of 1943. In August of that year, the AAF decided to develop another new X-Band bombing radar set from "off the shelf" components to be developed and built by Bell Laboratories and its Western Electric subsidiary, as well as MIT's Radiation Laboratory.

The new radar operator was stationed in the only space available in the B-29—the former bunk area in the aft of the rear pressurized compartment, a position that separated him from the navigator in the forward compartment. The first B-29 radar installations had one radar operator facing forward on the left side of the bomber, but later models provided for two operators facing outboard on the left side of the bomber. Initially, the radar operator and scope were mounted inside the aircraft, but the physical unit was mounted in the unpressurized rear compartment. However, difficulties with air pressure, cold temperatures, and electrical problems occurred at high altitudes. The main unit was then mounted at the radar operator's station in the rear pressurized compartment except for the inverter, which was located beneath the floor near the radar operator, and the radio frequency unit, which was located in the barrel-shaped enclosure just behind the radar antenna dome. The 30in AS-53/APQ-13 radar antenna was mounted in a hemispherical radome that was installed on the bottom of the fuselage between the bomb bays. Wartime photos were usually censored, and the radome was painted out. The antenna (called a "spinner") was dish pan-shaped, was mounted on edge, was rotated about its vertical axis, and could be tilted through a small angle about a horizontal axis while rotating.

The radar operator was stationed in the only space available, in the B-29, the former bunk area in the pressurized rear compartment but that position separated him from the navigator in the forward compartment. The first B-29 radar installations had one radar operator facing forward on the left side of the bomber but on later models provided for two operators facing outboard on the left side of the bomber. (USAF)

The radome could be extended or retracted by the radar operator by a retracting motor located under the wing. The APQ-13 consisted of:

Antenna Equipment	AS-53/APQ-13
Modulator	MD-12/APQ-13
Radio Frequency Unit	BC-1276-A
Synchronizer	SN-7/APQ-13
Indicator	ID-41/APQ-13
Control Box	C-71/APQ-13
Inverter	PE-218-D
Rectifier	RA-90-A
Voltage Regulator	TF-12-A
Phasing Unit	CN-6/APQ-13
Torque Amplifier	AM-19/APQ-13
Azimuth Control Box	C-72/APQ-13
Computer	CP-7/APQ-13
Range Unit	CP-6/APQ-13
Turn Control	GE 1027

APQ-13 radar was the most advanced bombing radar available when the B-29 became operational, and provided accurate fixes on the bomber's position when used with radar beacons. In November 1944 60% of the XXBC's sorties encountered radar malfunctions due to the inverters and lack of spares and inadequate maintenance by poorly trained personnel. However, in the early stages of the bombing offensive radar did make it possible for the bombers to reach their briefed landfall points by computing the winds at bombing altitude, in navigating the bombers over the initial point (IP), and getting it accurately aligned on the axes of attack.

APQ-13 radar was less accurate than conventional optical bombing, with less than 1% of its bombs hitting within 1,000ft of the aiming point. In early operations it was limited by the following:

1) The radar operators were hastily and insufficiently trained in the United States, which left them unable to evaluate the information depicted on their radarscopes in combat conditions. The radar operators also lacked sufficient navigation skills, and the aircraft navigator had to complete the computations required for bombing and navigation from his remote radarscope in the forward compartment.

2) In the early combat missions from the Marianas the bomber's routes avoided the Japanese-held islands south of Japan to prevent early warning, and thus the radar operator and bombardier were unable to use these landmarks for navigational checkpoints. The B-29s were then left to fly over open water for seven hours with no checkpoints between take off and landing.

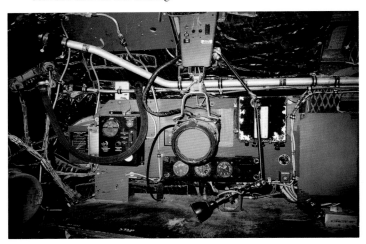

The main APQ-13 unit was mounted at the radar operator's station in the rear pressurized compartment except for the inverter (located beneath the floor near the radar operator) and radio frequency unit (located in the barrel-shaped enclosure just behind the radar antenna dome). The red bomb release switch, protected by a flap to prevent accidental release can be seen on the green panel above the screen. (Author/Pima)

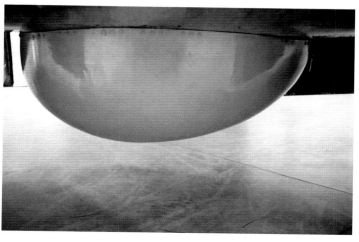

The 30-inch AS-53/APQ-13 radar antenna (arrow) was mounted in a hemispherical radome that was installed on the bottom of the fuselage between the bomb bays. Wartime photos were usually censored and the radome was painted out. The antenna (called a "spinner") was dish pan-shaped and was mounted on edge and was rotated about its vertical axis and could be tilted through a small angle about a horizontal axis while rotating. The radome could be extended or retracted by the radar operator by a retracting motor located under the wing. (USAF & Author/Pima)

3) The high bombing altitudes caused 25% of the airborne radar to malfunction, and the return signals at these altitudes were too weak to be of much use.

4) The strong jet stream winds at the high bombing altitudes limited the axes of attack to a downwind bombing run, which precluded the maximum use of the radar, as the target approaches with the more distinct radar markers were rarely used.

Dr. William Shockley, who was awarded the Nobel Prize for his invention of the transistor in 1956, developed a ground-based radar trainer. The complicated device was used at Smokey Hill AFB in early 1944 to train personnel for radar bombing in simulated bombing runs on Japanese targets. The radar operators were extensively trained in navigation and target identification utilizing clearly defined land-water contrast points. This improved intensive Stateside operational radar training, along with the initiation of low-level incendiary missions, led to conditions that were within the competence of the operators and capabilities of the equipment. Once Japanese defenses diminished over the more important targets the smaller, virtually undefended cities were attacked, and radar was given primary consideration in mission planning. As time passed there was a continuous

improvement in radar techniques when used in incendiary attacks. Improved target information and mission planning resulted in satisfactory radar bombing accuracy. This satisfactory accuracy was not of the "pickle barrel" standard by any means. Post attack analysis documented that 18% of the bombs fell within 2,000ft of the aiming point, 50% within 4,000ft, and 75% within 6,000ft, all of which were sufficient when using incendiaries to burn out large urban areas.

AN/APQ-7 Eagle Radar System

Early in the war combat bombing had demonstrated the pressing need for a precision high altitude radar bombsight. MIT's Radiation Laboratory began the project in November 1941 under the arrogant acronym EHIB, for "Every House in Berlin," In February 1943 the name was changed to AN/APQ-7, or "Eagle."

Both the APQ-13 and APQ-7 used the ground-scanning 3cm "X" band, but the Eagle used a new type of antenna that was fixed but electrically scanning, and produced much better resolution than radar using rotating antennas. The APQ-13 H2X "blind bombing" radar scanned 360-degrees, which made for poor definition. The beams on the Eagle sets scanned side-to-side, and narrowed to 60-degrees, generating excellent (10 times better)

The APQ-7 offered some significant upgrades over the APQ-13 the most important being a better level of target resolution on its radar scopes that give more accurate direct radar bombing. The APQ-13 radar scope showed a 360-degree picture and was thus the better navigational device. (USAF)

The large APQ-7 antenna (arrow) reduced the bomber's speed by 8mph and range by 412 miles compared to 3-4mph and 312 miles for the APQ-13. (USAF)

resolution (return beam definition). Initially the antenna was to be mounted to the wing, but instead it was housed under the fuselage in an aluminum vane that measured 40in wide, 36in long, and 8in high. Soon the antenna was lengthened to 18ft and ran parallel to the aircraft's wing, making it resemble a second shorter wing. In June 1943 MIT tested the Eagle using a B-24, and found it to be superior to the H2X. However, the tests discovered a number of problems with APQ-7. The size of the vane antenna produced drag that reduced the performance of the bomber, it was more difficult operate and maintain, and most importantly, was designed to scan 60-degrees forward, which limited its use as a navigational instrument. Nonetheless, the AAF ordered 650 sets in November 1943, and the first sets were sent to England in October 1944. The 8AF and 15AF equipped several B-17s and less than two dozen B-24s with the Eagle, and trained crews in its use. The set's resolution and accuracy was imposing, but its navigational capabilities were unsatisfactory, and VE-Day came before any of these bombers entered operations.

The Eagle had been specifically developed for the B-29, but did not enter that program until December 1943, and in January 1944 the AAF stipulated that a mockup was to be ready by mid-June. Problems with the bomber's development by Boeing further delayed the Eagle-Superfortress mating until mid-August. Meanwhile, the AAF increased its Eagle order to 1,650. By early November 1944 the AAF was becoming impatient, and set a 1 December deadline for the completion of all engineering, and a 15 December date for the start of testing, but as was usual with the B-29 program, neither deadline was met. The new radar was finally tested in B-29s at Boca Raton, FL, in February 1945, by which time orders had reached 2,650 sets for both the 20AF and the 8AF (the ETO orders were canceled in April).

In November 1944 AAF Chief Gen. H.H. Arnold authorized one B-29 wing to be equipped with the APQ-7 Eagle, and increased this order to two wings (315BW and 316BW) in late January 1945. These Wings were to fly stripped bombers for night and bad weather operations. The large APQ-7 antenna reduced the bomber's speed by 8mph and range by 412mi, compared to reductions of 3-4mph and 312mi respectively for the APQ-13. The established APQ-13 was scheduled for significant improvements, but the APQ-7 offered some significant upgrades over the APQ-13, the most important being that it had a much better level of target resolution on its radarscope that gave more accurate direct radar bombing. The APQ-13 radarscope showed a 360-degree picture, and was thus the better navigational device. Even though the APQ-7 only showed a 60-degree picture (30-degrees on each side of the bomber's heading), it could be effectively used in bombing. The average bombing run for the APQ-7 was 70mi, and the APQ-13 average was 33mi When the APQ-7 became operational it flew unopposed nighttime missions, so its increased bombing approach

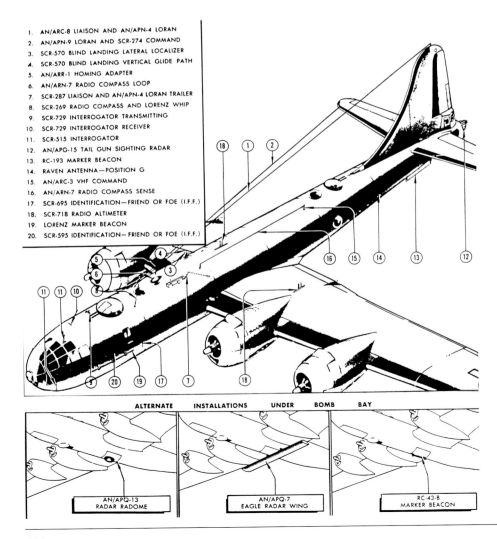

1. AN/ARC-8 LIAISON AND AN/APN-4 LORAN
2. AN/APN-9 LORAN AND SCR-274 COMMAND
3. SCR-570 BLIND LANDING LATERAL LOCALIZER
4. SCR-570 BLIND LANDING VERTICAL GLIDE PATH
5. AN/ARR-1 HOMING ADAPTER
6. AN/ARN-7 RADIO COMPASS LOOP
7. SCR-287 LIAISON AND AN/APN-4 LORAN TRAILER
8. SCR-269 RADIO COMPASS AND LORENZ WHIP
9. SCR-729 INTERROGATOR TRANSMITTING
10. SCR-729 INTERROGATOR RECEIVER
11. SCR-515 INTERROGATOR
12. AN/APG-15 TAIL GUN SIGHTING RADAR
13. RC-193 MARKER BEACON
14. RAVEN ANTENNA—POSITION G
15. AN/ARC-3 VHF COMMAND
16. AN/ARN-7 RADIO COMPASS SENSE
17. SCR-695 IDENTIFICATION—FRIEND OR FOE (I.F.F.)
18. SCR-718 RADIO ALTIMETER
19. LORENZ MARKER BEACON
20. SCR-595 IDENTIFICATION—FRIEND OR FOE (I.F.F.)

ALTERNATE   INSTALLATIONS   UNDER   BOMB   BAY

AN/APQ-13
RADAR RADOME

AN/APQ-7
EAGLE RADAR WING

RC-43-B
MARKER BEACON

B-29 Antenna Arrays After passing through modification centers there could be a number of antenna combinations depending on the time in the war and the unit's principal mission. (USAF)

was of little consequence. But since its targets were smaller the APQ-7's better target resolution produced a more precise bomb drop. Operations planners had long envisioned night operations for the B-29, and in September 1944 tests showed that removing turrets, blisters, and most armor diminished drag, reduced weight by 7,500lbs, and increased airspeed by 7 to 13mph (depending on altitude). Flame dampers were considered to reduce its visibility at night by enemy interceptors, but by March this idea was discarded, as the dampers increased weight and reduced engine power, and the Japanese night fighter force was found to be small and ineffective. The first production Eagle B-29 was stripped of 3,500lbs of equipment, and the drag of the deleted four turrets almost compensated for the loss of speed and range caused by its huge belly antenna. The stripped B-29 first flew from Seattle on 15 January 1945, and by the end of the month the 315BW was ready to receive their Eagle-equipped B-29s, but Bell-Marietta was delayed in its delivery of the bombers. In the meantime, the 315BW radar operators had to take their training in Eagle-equipped B-24s. It would not be until March 1945 that the Bomb Wing would acquire its first combat ready B-29B bomber from the Bell factory. The wing's aircraft finally reached Guam, in the Marianas, on 1 June under its excellent veteran leader from the ETO, Frank Armstrong, who made two changes. The bomber's underfuselage was painted gloss black to lessen searchlight detection. Training and tests had demonstrated that if the bombing altitude was halved from 30,000ft the demand on the engines was reduced, and the fuel efficiency increased to allow for a heavier bomb load, and also, at 15,000ft the APQ-7 was more dependable. The Eagle sets did not have the operational teething problems of the AN/APQ-13, as its operators had received extensive training with the set itself, and spent no time on formation flying or visual bombing. The 315BW did not enter combat until 26 June 1945, and its initial targets were the oil refinery and tank farms on the Honshu coast. The petroleum industry had proved to be the German war machine's Achilles' heel, and Japanese oil was a virgin target to test the viability of the APQ-7. The land/water disparity of these coastal targets made for excellent target definition on radar, and the results of the bombing could be more easily studied, as there were no previous bomb craters or damage to interfere with the assessment.

The 315BW flew 15 radar night missions before the war ended, and generally its results were as good, and sometimes better, than conventional visual Norden radar bombing. The Eagle radar could be coupled to the Norden bombsight in a configuration called the "Nosmeagle." The APQ-7 had a good degree of accuracy, as 10% of the bombs fell within 1,000ft of the aiming point, 30% within 2,000ft, and 50% within 3,500ft. However, the 315BW's attack on the Japanese oil industry was futile since it was not refining oil, as its imported oil source transported by shipping had been cut by submarines and the sea and aerial mining campaign. The radar unit was usually reliable, with about 10% failures, and with tweaking the set's range increased over 40% from 67mi to 96mi by the last mission. The antenna was exceptionally fragile, as the runway materials stirred up by the props and flying through rain damaged its leading edge, and it had to be replaced after approximately half a dozen missions.

By the time the Eagle was ready for more wide scale use the radar operators already using the AN/APQ-13 with other Bomb Wings had become very proficient with their sets, and the AN/APQ-23, an upgraded -13 system, was soon to be ready. After the war all Eagle sets were removed from operational B-29s. Despite being touted as a "radar bomber," during the war only 23% of the XXI Bomber Command's bombs were aimed by radar.

AN/APQ-30

This unit was a late war system that provided 360-degree scanning and a 3-degree beam width, and was an improved radar system over the AN/APQ–7, even though both had similar pulse widths.

9

Defensive Armament:
The Remote Control Turret and Central Fire Control System

Development

In the 1930s the defense of the bomber, based on current availability and experience, was by manually operated guns that were able to move through elevation and azimuth to cover the largest area possible around the bomber. At altitude a gunner—uncomfortable, cold, and breathing oxygen—could, mostly ineffectively, manage only one hand held gun. After Pearl Harbor, experience in Europe confirmed that multiple guns in power turrets were the most effective means of bomber defense.

The problem in designing the armament system for the B-29 was to furnish adequate protection against enemy fighter attack, but also not over arm the bomber, producing a deleterious weight and space problem that would diminish the bomber's performance. Because the B-29 was to operate at very high altitudes and over long distances engineers designed pressurized crew cabins, which meant the gunners were stationed inside the cabins at sighting stations (blisters), controlling small aerodynamic powered turrets via a computerized gunsight.

The remote control turret system had many advantages over the contemporary manned armament systems found on the unpressurized B-17 and B-24, whose gunners needed to use oxygen masks, and were exposed to freezing cold and to the noise and vibration of the firing guns. Since the remote turrets were unmanned they were smaller and created less drag, and a concomitant increase in aircraft performance. The turrets and gunners could each be placed in positions to afford the optimal protection against enemy fighter attacks, and also permitted the isolated placement of vital armament electronic operating equipment in protected areas, which also allowed easier servicing access, and expedited improved weight distribution and pressurization of the cabins.

Boeing and the Air Materiel Command engineers worked jointly to develop a remote armament system. In March 1940 Sperry, Bendix, and General Electric submitted remote turret proposals, and on 1 April the Air Materiel Command recommended that Sperry, with its periscope sight proposal, be given a contract to build a prototype system. The Sperry system placed the gunner and his periscope sight inside the pressurized fuselage and the turrets outside, where they could then be made smaller and retractable, resulting in a cleaner, more aerodynamic aircraft. The periscope aiming system allowed one gunner to control five guns by feeding data into a computer that calculated corrections for altitude, speed, temperature, ballistics, deflection, and parallax. The control of a turret could be transferred to other gunners who were in better firing positions. However, the Sperry periscope had the principal disadvantage of having a small field of vision. Other spotters on the bomber could inform the gunner of targets, but that would entail an involved communications system via the bomber's interphone. When the Sperry Automatic Fire Control System was being tested at Eglin Field, FL, it presented so many problems that there was a faction that opted for building the B-29 without pressurized cabins, and adding gun positions similar to the B-17. Because of these problems Sperry was unable to meet its promised delivery schedules. In December 1941 the Air Staff sent Col. Kenneth Wolfe, head of the Wright Field Armament Section, along with Colonels Leonard Harman and Roger Williams of Wright Field to Seattle with orders to abandon the remote sighting system and install conventional turrets, and to get the B-29 project moving forward. The trio met with Ed Wells and N.D. Showalter, who were adamant against installing conventional turrets, as they knew that these turrets would reduce the bomber's aerodynamic integrity that they had worked so hard to achieve, and the B-29 could not achieve the performance objectives the AAC had set. The bomber was so aerodynamically clean that lowering the landing gear caused as much drag as the rest of the aircraft! Over the weekend the Boeing engineers built wind tunnel models and demonstrated their turret position to Wolfe and Harman, who agreed, but asked Boeing to use retractable turrets similar to the Sperry ball turrets used on the B-17. Boeing engineers responded that the gunners could not be sustained in the freezing environment of these turrets, and that there was not enough room in the B-29 for them. Williams had heard that General Electric was developing an electronic remote armament system, and recommended it be investigated as a solution. In January 1942 both the retractable turret and the periscope concepts were abandoned, and the decision was made to use the General Electric Central Station Fire Control System, which was considered to be the only viable solution. In the meantime, the Sperry system was to be installed in the three XB-29s, and Sperry would continue to build 100 sets for the B-28 and B-32. It would take Sperry until November to correct the restricted periscopic field of view problem, but its system never entered combat. The Sperry system was only used in the XB-29, as the B-28 never went into production, and in January 1943 the B-32 was equipped with conventionally controlled turrets.

Studies found that the GE remote system could not fire accurately on concentrated frontal enemy attacks, which were the most prevalent Japanese attack mode on American bombers at the time. A possible answer was to add more forward firing guns by placing a new four-gun upper turret or a four-gun nose installation. (USAF)

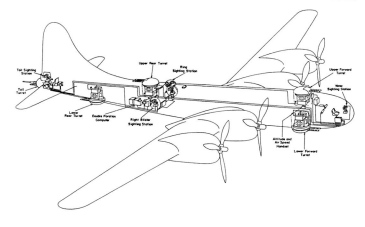

Turret and Sighting Stations (USAF)

Testing

Unfortunately, when the GE system was tested at Eglin Air Proving Ground, FL, it was found to be unsatisfactory to defend either the B-29 or B-32 due to its vulnerability, complexity, and inherent inaccuracy. It had many chronic maintenance problems that were impossible to correct during flight. However, the system did have the major advantage of making pressurization easier, and it weighed much less than a conventional turret system. Despite the optimism surrounding the GE remote system, in May 1944, only days before the B-29 was to go into combat, the final Eglin report concluded that the GE system was unsuited for unescorted missions where the airplane could be subjected to focused fighter attacks. A month later, another

Eglin report found the system "vulnerable" and "not functionally reliable," but held out hope that its problems would be solved. In tests it was found that the GE system could not fire accurately on concentrated frontal attacks that were favored by aggressive Luftwaffe fighters, and were the most prevalent Japanese attack mode on American bombers at the time. A possible answer was to add more forward firing guns by placing a new four-gun upper turret or a four-gun nose installation. Gen. Grandison Gardner of the Eglin Air Proving Ground suggested that the 20mm/twin .50 machine gun tail turret configuration be adapted to be mounted in the B-29 nose, but design proposals had to eliminate the bombardier's station to install the new turret and the project was dropped. The only logical

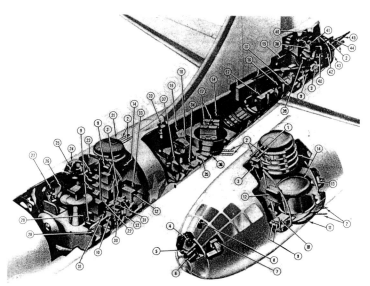

1. Gun Sight Aiming Point Camera.
2. Caliber .50 Machine Gun.
3. Servo Amplifier.
4. Nose Gun Sight.
5. Bombardier's Table.
6. Lower Forward Turret Control Box.
7. Camera Intervalometer.
8. Nose System Switch Box.
9. Amplidynes.
10. Dynamotor.
11. Lower Forward Turret.
12. Single Parallax Computer.
13. Altitude and Airspeed Handset.
14. Turret Safety Switches.
15. Selector Panel.
16. Caliber .50 Ammunition Track.
17. Caliber .50 Ammunition Boxes.
18. Vertical Camera.
19. Right Hand Oblique Camera.
20. Type K-20 Camera.
21. Upper Rear Turret.
22. Blister Station Control Box
23. Upper Sighting Blister.
24. Upper Control Box.
25. Upper Gunner's Sight.
26. Auxiliary Control Switch Box.
27. Right Blister Gunner's Sight.
28. Computer Voltage Regulator.
29. Switch Box Blister.
30. Left Blister Gunner's Sight.
31. Double Parallax Computer.
32. Auxiliary Control Switch Box.
33. Computer Armor Plate.
34. Left Hand Oblique Camera.
35. Camera Junction Box.
36. Lower Rear Turret.
37. Camera Shut-Off Valve Box.
38. Azimuth Drive Motor.
39. Elevation Drive Motor.
40. 20 mm Feed Chute Assembly.
41. 20 mm Gun Switch.
42. 20 mm Ammunition Box.
43. Tail Turret.
44. Gun Camera.
45. 20 mm Cannon.
46. Tail Gunner's Sight.

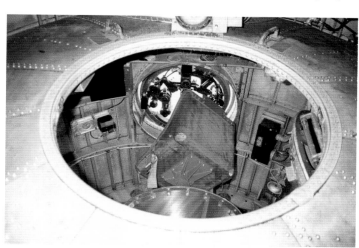

The top gunner, the Central Fire Control Gunner (CFC), was the key man in the system and sat in an elevated swivel-type chair that was sometimes known as the "Barber's Chair." (Author/Pima)

Gun and Camera Equipment Location (USAF)

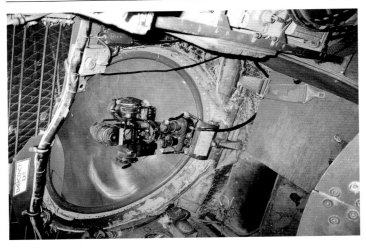

Right side sighting blister. There were five General Electric/Bell & Howell sights strategically located in the bomber that controlled the turrets through five electro-mechanical computers. This reflector type sight was mounted on a short pedestal and contained selsyn motors and rate gyros that operated in two planes. (Author/Pima)

Port sighting blister, top rear turret, and CFC sighting blister. (Author/Pima)

solution was to add two additional .50 machine guns to the twin guns in the existing dorsal forward position with contour followers and increased ammunition. The standard GE four gun P-61 Black Widow turret was modified by Emerson Electric and installed in both turret positions. Tests determined that the four-gun installation in the forward turret was preferred to the two-gun that, if it jammed, left the bomber vulnerable to frontal attack, but the installation added nearly a half-ton of weight, and decreased the range by 188mi (but the top speed by only 3mp). However, doubling the firepower did not necessarily double the new turret's efficiency, as it had a larger bullet dispersion, and had nearly half the hits per gun as the two gun turret (5% vs. 9%).

General Description

The defensive armament of the B-29 was the General Electric Model 2CFR55B1 Central Station Fire Control System. The system included two upper and two lower turrets, each mounting two .50cal machine guns, and a tail turret mounting two .50cal machine guns and a 20mm cannon and five sighting stations, together with the associated equipment.

Sighting Stations

Designing a Sighting Station

The primary consideration in designing a sighting station was to design and position its components in order to keep the blister size to a minimum to reduce drag. In designing the sight, its size was of primary importance, and parts of its design were compromised from ideal to meet this requirement. The sighting domes became chronically frosted at high altitudes, and various remedies were tried, such as fans, heaters, and pressure ducts that blew heated air over them, but none of these fixes were truly successful; the problem continued throughout the war, and was only alleviated when the XXBC began bombing at much lower altitudes.

Lower rear General Electric turret housed two .50 caliber machine guns that carried 500 rounds per gun in ammunition boxes and was controlled by the left and right side gunner's sight. (Author/Pima)

Gunner at sighting station and sight. (USAF)

Pedestal Sighting Station Parts

Azimuth Assembly

The azimuth assembly formed the base of the sight, and had two selsyn (self-synchronized) generators that were rotated by means of precise gearing. The selsyns transmitted an electrical signal matching the exact azimuth position of the line of sight. The azimuth assembly contained part of the auxiliary equipment of the sight, such as a rheostat for controlling reticle brightness, a switch for deleting the computer from the system, and a stow pin for locking the sight into azimuth.

Elevation Unit

The elevation unit also had two selsyn generators that rotated as the sight was moved in elevation, and transmitted an electrical signal matching the exact elevation position of the line of sight. The gunner controlled the position of the line of sight by manipulating handwheels on this unit. The gunner lightly rested the thumbs of each hand on a trigger, and a slight pressure on either one would fire the guns. The action switch located under the palm of his left hand had to be depressed to complete the circuit between the sighting action and the remote turret. If the gunner removed his hand from the left handwheel the switch was in the open position, and his

gunsight could no longer control his primary or secondary turret. The turrets under his control were transferred automatically to one of the other sighting stations. Superimposed on the right handwheel was a smaller wheel with which the gunner made more accurate range adjustments.

Retiflector Sight

The sight on the CFC system was called the retiflector sight, and was connected with a rudimentary computer mounted away from the sighting station. The sight and the computer calculated deflections for any attacking fighter. The navigator supplied part of the information the computer required via the interphone. The navigator's information included indicated air speed, pressure, altitude, and outside temperature, which allowed the computer to calculate the bomber's true air speed and the air density, all of which affected the speed of the bullet to the target. The remainder of the information was supplied by the gunner who:

1) Set the fighter's wingspan by turning a target size knob.
2) Tracked the attacker to give the computer its motion.
3) Framed the target by turning a range wheel or grip that supplied the data to the computer to calculate the distance to the fighter.

The two kinds of sights used on the B-29 were identical except for minor details. In the top sighting station, the sight was mounted on a ring and operated with two grip type handles, and all other stations had sights mounted on pedestals and operated with two hand wheels.

There were five retiflector sights strategically located in the bomber that controlled the turrets through five electro-mechanical computers. The General Electric/Bell & Howell sights were provided at these stations: bombardier station; upper gunsighting station; left hand sighting station; right hand sighting station; and tail gunner station. This reflector type sight was mounted on a short pedestal, and contained selsyn motors and rate gyros that operated in two planes. The selsyns connected the sight with the turret, and the rate gyros provided the computers with the target's speed and direction of movement. Pairs of course (1:1 ratio) and fine ratio (31:1) selsyns controlled the movement of the turrets in azimuth and elevation. Selsyn signals were corrected by single (tail gunner and bombardier) parallax or double parallax (all rear cabin stations) computers, and were am-

Sighting blister and sight. Stencil below the blister states: "Cut here for emergency rescue." (Author/Pima)

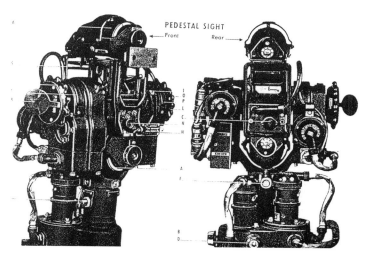

Pedestal Sight (USAF)

plified by servo amplifiers. This sight allowed the gunner to visually aim it, and also to provide an electrical signal that relayed the distance to the target. Range was obtained by utilizing the principle that, within some limits, the apparent size of an object was dependent on the distance to the object and on its physical size. In using the sight the gunner needed to know or estimate the wingspan of the target before it began to attack. When the gunner looked onto the 45 degree inclined, clear glass plate of the sight he saw the image of a circle of orange dots surrounding a center "pipper" that was reflected onto the screen from a concave spherical mirror. The projected image was focused to infinity, and allowed the gunner to sight through the glass with both eyes. The movement of the range control handle changed the size (diameter) of the circle of dots so that a range (distance) to the target was simultaneously furnished to the computer so it could make corrections. On the front of the sight cover was a wingspan setting dial that the gunner used to select the target's wingspan. The dial also illuminated a figure on top of the sighting screen that provided a visual manifestation of the selected wingspan. To use the sight the gunner aimed the center "pipper" directly at the target, and adjusted the size of the circle of orange dots so that the target's wingspan just filled its diameter. As the target neared, the gunner slowly turned the range control handle to keep the target constantly encompassed by the circle of dots. Micro-switch triggers mounted on the sight cover, one under each hand, fired the guns. The sights had flip down sunshades and a metal ring-and-post sight for use in case of electronics failure.

Computers

One General Electric Type 2CH computer was used for each of the five sighting stations. The computer design was divided into 17 components, and was placed into limited production without the usual development and testing. Of course, there were initial problems, but considering the advanced design of such an intricate piece of equipment, there were few modifica-

Computers beneath rear pressurized cabin floor. (USAF)

tions required, and General Electric sent out the components to its divisions and subcontractors for mass production. The five electro-mechanical computers, housed in the armored compartments under the cabin floors, were of two types that allowed for single and double parallax angles. The double parallax computers of the upper sighting station and the blister sighting station were located in the center of the airplane, and beneath the floor just aft of the upper rear turret. The double parallax computer for the right blister was located forward of the double parallax computer for the left blister. The tail sighting station single parallax computer was located beneath the floor, and just aft of the upper rear turret. The navigator's barometric altitude, indicated air speed, and temperature computer was located at his station. The production of the M-5 computer was licensed to the Singer Elizabethport works in September 1943 and reached 250 per week by the end of 1944, and over 500 per week by July 1945, by which time the factory had manufactured 20,794 computers.

Gunsights, which were placed at known distances from the turrets that they operated (the nose and tail), were controlled through single parallax computers, while gunsights that were operated at varying distances from their turrets (switching between the top and side gunners) were controlled by the double parallax computers.

The computers had to calculate parallax, ballistics, and deflection angles. The parallax angle resulted from the guns and sight being a distance apart, and a preset correction was programmed into the computer. The ballistics angle was a combination of gravity drop and bullet trail, which are the characteristics of bullets in flight. The deflection angle compensated for the distance traveled by the target during the flight of the bullets. To calculate the ballistics and deflection angles, the gunsight provided the computer with the necessary data: the target's speed, range, and direction. The navigator provided additional data, such as altitude (barometric), outside temperature, and IAS (indicated air speed) via interphone. Once the data was imputed, the computer calculated the sighting data and formulated a correction that was transmitted to the system between the gunsight and the turret via differential selsyns that adjusted the tracking of the guns in regard to the line of sight. The sighting was continually point blank (e.g. directly at the target), and if the gunner tracked the target smoothly through his sight and adjusted the range correctly as the target drew near, the computers took care of the other calculations needed for accurate aerial gunnery. The computer calculated and automatically corrected for:

1) Lead: Calculated the distance the target aircraft traveled during the time the bullet was to be in flight. (Much like the lead a hunter must allow to hit a flying duck).
2) Parallax: Calculated the distance between the sighting mechanism and the gun barrel.
3) Windage: Calculated the effect of the speed of the aircraft through the air on the bullet as it traveled to the target.
4) Bullet Drop: Calculated the pull of gravity on the trajectory of the bullet traveling toward the target.

If there was damage or malfunction of the computer system the gunner could operate the turret through his sight independent of automatic computing. The gunner would have to lead the target with the sight so that the guns that were following the exact direction of the sight would also lead the target.

Guns and Turrets

The five turrets were electrically controlled and operated. The guns were mounted within the turret assemblies so that they could move up and down in a vertical plane independent of the motion of the turret, which was sited in an azimuth direction. The two upper turrets and the lower forward turret extended into the pressurized compartments, but were sealed so that the guns were functioning under outside atmospheric conditions. The guns of the upper and lower turrets could be rotated continuously in an azimuth direction. The guns of the upper forward turret could be elevated or depressed through an arc from 2.5-degrees below horizontal to 90-degrees above horizontal. The guns of the lower turrets could be elevated or depressed through an arc from 5-degrees above horizontal to 90-degrees below horizontal. These four gun stations included a "dead man's switch," which if a gunner was out of action his turret assignment was automatically assigned to the secondary gunner. The tail turret could be rotated in an arc 30-degrees in any direction from straight aft. The guns were not accessible for hand charging during pressurized flight, but each .50 machine gun had an automatic gun charger attached to its side. The 20mm cannon was charged through cable action from the tail sighting station.

Central Fire Control Turrets:

Upper Rear Turret
> Location: Station 728
> Armament: Two .50cal machine guns
> Lower Limit of Fire: Horizontal

Upper Forward Turret
> Location: Station 177
> Armament: Two .50cal machine guns
> Lower Limit of Fire: 2.5-degrees below horizontal

Lower Rear Turret
> Location: Station 945
> Armament: Two .50cal machine guns
> Lower Limit of Fire: 5-degrees above horizontal

Lower Forward Turret
> Location: Station 192
> Armament: Two .50cal machine guns
> Lower Limit of Fire: 5-degrees above horizontal

Tail Turret
> Location: Extreme aft
> Armament: Two .50cal machine guns and one 20mm cannon
> Rear Limits of Fire: 30-degree angle above and below horizontal centerline and 30-degrees right and left of vertical centerline. There was a pyramidal cone of fire formed by these limits.

B-29 Gunners

1) The top gunner—the Central Fire Control Gunner (CFC)—was the key man in the system, and sat in an elevated swivel-type chair that was sometimes known as the "Barber's Chair." It was located under a clear plastic sighting dome located slightly forward of the upper aft turret, and in front of the rear tunnel entrance. The base of the chair contained slop rings to transmit electrical current from the power source to the sight. The sight could be moved 60-degrees on the horizontal without swiveling the stool, but further traverse of the sight without a corresponding rotation of the stool would break the electrical circuit. The CFC controlled the master gunnery panel that assigned turrets to each remote gunner. There were many combinations of turret control in this system, and the five gun positions were sited to cover every angle of attack with immediate concentrated fire-

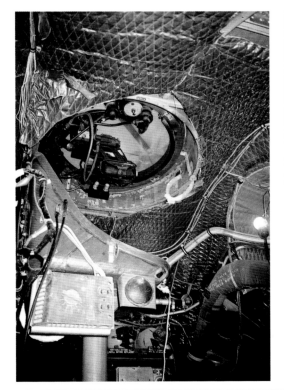

CFC position (left) and Barber's chair (right).

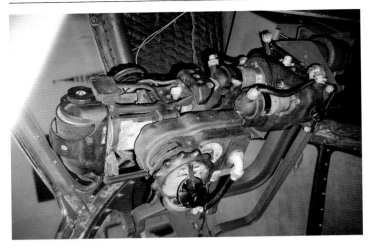

Bombardier's sight

power. In this system individual gunners (except the tail gunner) had primary control of a specified turret and secondary control of others. A gunner with control of a turret could hand over its control to gunners with secondary control. A system of signals was developed between gunners to allow quick hand off of turret control. The bombardier in the nose had the largest range of vision, and thus had primary control of both the upper and lower forward turrets, and could use them singly or together. The central fire control gunner, being located in the gunner's station amidships, had primary control of the upper rear turret and secondary control of the upper forward turret. The two waist gunners divided the primary control of the lower rear turret and secondary control of the lower forward turret. The tail gunner only had control of the tail guns.

2) The waist gunners, one on the port and one on the starboard, sat facing aft, and had a 180-degree horizontal traverse, and a converging angle of vision below the airplane. These sighting blisters were installed in the side of the fuselage, opposite each other, in the rear pressurized section. Stenciled somewhere around the outside of the blister were the words, "Cut

thru Glass for Emergency Rescue." In this system the gunner who had in his direct vision the incoming enemy aircraft could not only fire his primary turret, but could also "borrow" a second turret to increase his firepower.

3) The bombardier remained in his regular station in the nose, where he had largest range of vision, and thus had primary control of both the upper and lower forward turrets, and could use them singly or together.

4) Tail gunner was seated just behind the armor plate pressure bulkhead door at station 1110, and only had control of his guns.
The function and duties of the CFC gunners are discussed in depth later.

Turrets

Fuselage Turrets

The upper turrets were General Electric No. W8258272, and the lower turrets were General Electric No. W8258273; each housed two .50cal machine guns and carried 500 rounds per gun in ammunition boxes. For use on the B-29 the .50cal guns were mounted in Edgewater adapters, and held in place in the turret by a slider mount bolt on the rear trunnion, and by bolts holding the front trunnion mount of the adapter. The upper and lower turrets could be reloaded whenever the airplane was not pressurized, but the tail turret could only be reloaded from the outside (e.g. only on the ground). These turrets were equipped with cam-controlled cut off switches that protected the aircraft from its own fire. An AN-N-6 motion picture camera was located in each of the five power turrets, and was remotely controlled at the individual turret sighting stations.

Tail Turret

The tail turret was equipped with two .50cal machine guns and a 20mm cannon, and was the only manned gun station. Early B-29s had a tail turret mounting dual .50cal machine guns supplied with 1,000 rounds per gun, and a 20mm cannon with 110 to 125 rounds. The .50cal ammunition was carried in a pair of large boxes located forward of the horizontal stabilizer, and tracks carried the ammunition aft to the tail gunner. The cannon could

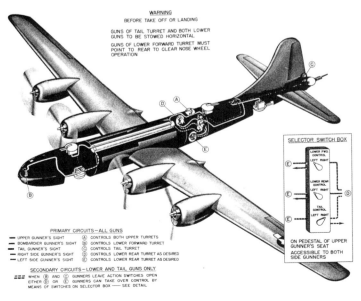

Turret Gun Circuit Control System. (USAF)

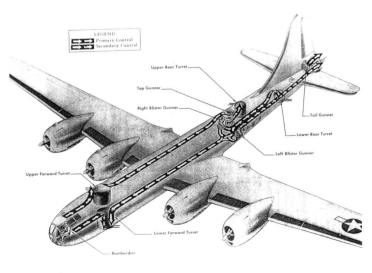

Primary and Secondary Gun Control Diagram. (USAF)

Control box for lower forward turret lower rear turret by the right and left blister sighting stations. (Author/Pima)

Top rear turret from rear pressurized compartment. (Author/Pima)

be fired separately or along with the machine guns. However, the cannon had a different trajectory than the machine guns, and only fired 7 to 11 rounds per minute; concurrent firing of the three guns was not effective, as the computer only calculated for the .50cal machine guns. It was recommended that the 20mm be fired only when the attacker was at close range (not more than 600yds), when the bullet drop of the machine guns and cannon were similar. Also, the 20mm cannon had feed mechanism problems. The cannon was later deleted in some models. The tail turret and guns were equipped with cut off switches and mechanical stops that limited its vertical and horizontal movement to 30-degrees in all directions.

AN/APG-15B
As the Japanese fighter defenses waned, and it was determined that their only effective mode of attack was from the rear, only the bomber's tail guns were retained, and the bomber was stripped of its upper and lower turrets and side sighting blisters. The armament revisions in the field did not change the bomber's designation, but the 311 Eagle (ANAPQ-7) radar-equipped B-29s modified at Bell-Marietta were redesignated as the B-29B. These bombers were equipped with the new AN/APG-15B radar fire control system that located and fired on an incoming enemy aircraft.

The AN/APG-15 was designed to detect enemy aircraft and give accurate range information to the gunner in the tail turret who controlled the

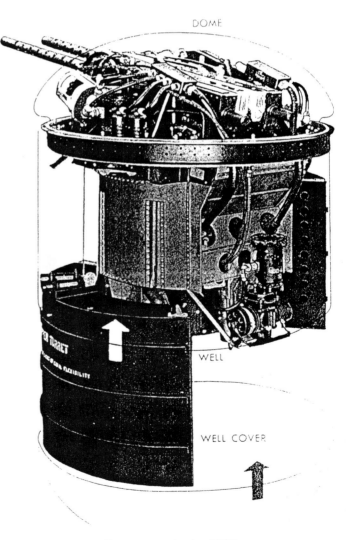

Top rear turret drawing. (USAF)

Top turret with port sighting blister and CFC sighting station. (Author/Pima)

Lower forward turret looking aft with bomb bay fuel tank in forward bay and bombs loaded in rear bay. (USAF)

Lower rear turret. (Author/Pima)

.50cal machine guns. This radar program began in February 1943 for use in the B-24 in the ETO, but by the summer of 1944 it was given priority in the B-29 program. The AN/APG-15 was a lightweight basic short-range radar unit designed by General Electric. It was mounted in the tail turret, and had a range of about 2,000yds. In tests the APG-15 was two and a half times more accurate than manual ranging, and scored three to four times the number of hits. It was to be used in the Eagle-equipped Bomb Wings, as their bombers were to be stripped of all armament except a tail gunner and two scanners. Ground personnel, lacking training, had problems maintaining the APG-15 in the field due to its complexity. The gunners also had insufficient training in its use, but its design caused the major problems. It had no IFF capabilities, making it unable to distinguish friend or foe, and its search-lock on ability was insufficient.

Turret Operation and Description
The control of the turret was initiated by turning ON the power turret switch, and slightly rotating the sight to energize the amplidyne generators. The turret was then under full control of the operator, and could be moved where desired. The turrets operated electrically by small self-synchronized selsyn A.C. motors that transmitted the position indicating signals. A dy-

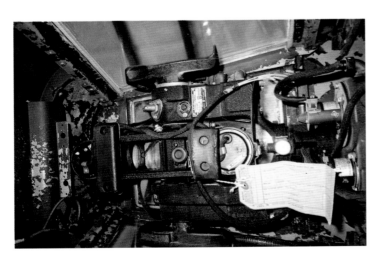

Tail turret sighting station. (Author/Pima)

Tail turret with twin .50cal machine guns and 20mm cannon. (USAF)

namotor (generator) provided 115 volt A.C. to the selsyns and a servo-amplifier. The set of selsyns on the gunsight was connected to a like set on the turret. The movement of the sight caused a disparity between the two sets of selsyns, which continually compared their individual alignments. When the turret selsyns detected this discrepancy, a signal was transmitted to the servo-amplifier that determined the direction of movement needed, and then furnished D.C. power to the turret drive motor by means of amplidyne motor-generators. The drive motors moved the guns and turrets in the requisite direction until the selsyns signaled that the sight and turret were aligned, the signal that indicated the discrepancy ceased, and the turret movement stopped.

The control system operated simultaneously in two planes: vertically for gun elevation and depression; and horizontally for turret rotation. In performance, the sight and guns moved instantaneously as a unit with a great degree of accuracy via electric signals. But in practice the gunners were unable to hit a target because the guns were located a distance away from the sight, and were aimed in parallel to the gunner's line of sight. To remedy this situation a method of adjusting the aim of the guns in relation to the line of sight was necessary. This adjustment had to be variable with

Tail turret with two .50cal machine guns. (Author/Pima)

Armorers of the 497BG loading ammo, (USAF)

The AN/APG-15 was designed to detect enemy aircraft and give accurate range information to the gunner in the tail turret who controlled the .50 cal. machine guns. (USAF)

the distance of the target from the turret, and was made by the means of computers as described previously.

Each turret initially carried 500 rounds per gun, but this figure was increased to 1,000rpg by using integral ammunition boxes and electrically powered feed assisters that drew rounds into the guns. Each gun had an automatic electro-pneumatic gun charger that fired the gun, and also allowed the gunner to remotely reload in case of a stoppage (early B-29s had CO_2 charged guns). The gun chargers were supplied by an integral pneumatic system made up of an electric air compressor, pressure regulator, and a storage cylinder. The lower turrets had small ejection doors located in the outer cover that opened automatically when the guns fired, and let spent cartridge cases and belt links fall out of the turret. In the upper turrets the cartridges and links were accumulated inside the aircraft and removed after returning to base.

Contour Follower and Interrupter

The contour follower and limit switch prevented the remotely sighted guns from firing into their own bomber. This device mechanically raised or lowered the guns to clear the fuselage or other obstructions. The contour interrupter prevented the upper guns from ever pointing at the top sighting station, and the contour interrupter used on the lower guns prevented them from firing at the curved fuselage.

Limit Stops

All turrets and the tail mount had mechanical limit stops that were built like rubber bumpers to prevent the guns from moving too far and striking the fuselage. They also had a set of automatic switches that cut off most of the power when the guns reached their limit stops, leaving just enough current to hold the guns firmly in place against the stops, and preventing the guns from firing. On the upper turrets there was a mechanical limit stop that kept them from traveling past 90-degrees straight up when the guns were raised. The lower turrets had stops that kept them from traveling below minus 90-degrees straight down when the guns were lowered. These stops were only bumpers, and had no switches to turn off the power.

Cameras

A Type AN-N-6 16mm-motion film gun camera was located in each turret or sighting station. When the camera switch on the control box was ON, the camera would start to take pictures as soon as the triggers were pressed. It could be set to stop operating as soon as the triggers were released, but it was usually set to continue to operate for three seconds after firing to show the fate of the intended target. With this extended running time there would not be enough film to last through a mission before all the ammunition was fired. So as not to waste film the gunner would turn off the camera switch when he test-fired the gun. When the gun switch was ON automatic heat-

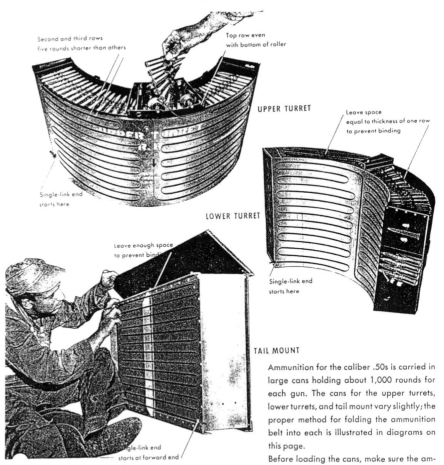

Ammo canisters for the upper turret (upper), lower turret (middle), and tail gun (lower). (USAF)

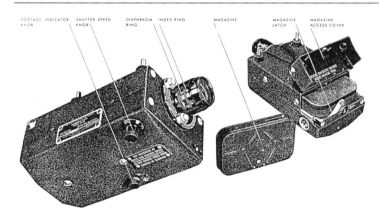

A Type N-6 16mm-motion film gun camera with a 50ft film magazine was located in each turret or sighting station. Before the mission a diaphragm ring on the camera was preset for the type of weather expected on the mission. (USAF)

In October 1944 Project S68 was initiated for manned turret evaluation. A B-29-20-25-BW (S/N 42-24441) was fitted with two remotely controlled Emerson Model 126 barbettes each mounting a single .50cal machine gun. The large egg-shaped barbettes were mounted on each side of the forward fuselage just above and adjacent to the forward tricycle gear. (USAF)

ers kept the camera mechanism warm. Before the mission a diaphragm ring on the camera was preset for the type of weather expected on the mission. It was set to "B" for bright weather, "H" for hazy, or "D" for dull weather. A film magazine containing 50ft of film was inserted in the camera, and the footage indicator dial was set at 50 (after the camera had been used, the dial showed how many feet had been exposed).

Stowing the Turret Guns

When out of range of enemy fighters the turret guns were to be stowed to decrease drag, and for safety when landing with loaded guns. The turret gun stowing positions were guns pointing straight forward for the upper turrets, and guns pointing straight aft for the lower turrets and tail mount. The lower forward turret was stowed in the aft position during take off and landing to prevent interference with the nose gear doors. To stow the guns the gunner pushed in the azimuth stowing pin of the sight to hold the turret in place. For both upper turrets and the lower forward turret the elevation stowing pin was also pushed in. For the tail mount the guns had to be held at about 10-degrees. The lower rear turret was also stowed to prevent the guns from hitting the ground, and the lower forward guns had to be clear from the aft position to allow the bomb bay doors to open. Automatic stowing occurred when the action switch operating the turret was released. The top turret guns were lowered as far as possible, and the lower guns raised as high as possible. If the power failed the lower two turrets could be stowed by hand using the slipstream. There were three warning lights (one for the two lower turrets, one for the upper turrets, and the last for the tail turret) mounted near the airplane commander's position. These lights were ON when these turrets were in use, and were OFF when the guns were stowed.

Gun and Turret Harmonization

Harmonization was a necessary obligation for the CFC system to operate efficiently; it was also time consuming, and required special training. Basically, B-29 gun/turret harmonization was the same as for conventional power turrets. An important part of harmonizing was to level the turrets, making sure that they were parallel to each other and at right angles to the bomber's centerline. The line of sight and the line of fire had to be adjusted so that they were parallel to each other, and remained that way when they moved. The B-29 CFC system caused special problems, as it had five turrets and five sighting stations, all at different levels, and at various dis-

tances from one another (up to 40ft from the sight). The line of sight from each sighting station had to be adjusted parallel to the line of fire from each turret. The CFC electrical system had to be carefully and exactly adjusted so that the guns would move exactly with the sights throughout their entire range of movement. The CFC was harmonized by the mechanical/electrical "Middle Distance Target Method," which used a group of target stands set up at various points about 500ft around the bomber. As Japanese fighter opposition decreased harmonization was given lesser attention. Consequently, when the infrequent fighter did attack the CFC did not function to maximum potential.

Effectiveness of the CFC System

By the end of the war the properly maintained, harmonized, and employed GE system became very reliable, and was effective against the diminishing Japanese fighter opposition. The infrequent problems that did occur were relatively insignificant (jams, accidental discharge, and overheating), and were caused by poor maintenance and improper handling in combat situations. The ejected shell cases and links dropped from the lower turrets could damage the radome and other trailing aircraft. A 20AF report showed that during June 1945, its bombers had fired nearly 1.1 million rounds of .50cal bullets from 30,000 guns, and only experienced 163 malfunctions, of which over half were blamed on the guns and not the system.

Since enemy fighters were much less of a problem in the Pacific than over Europe it is difficult to determine the true effectiveness of the B-29 remote gun system. According to the *Army Air Force Statistical Digest*, the total bomber losses over Europe and the Mediterranean of 44% and 31%, respectively, were credited to fighters, while only 21% of the 20AF B-29 losses were due to fighters (due to fewer Japanese fighters with inferior performance and poor pilot training). In the ETO each enemy aircraft destroyed in the air required 12,600 rounds of ammunition, and 11,900 rounds in the MTO. The B-29s of the 20AF needed only 9,800 rounds, but was it because the CFC system was better, or because the Japanese aircraft were far more fragile than their German counterparts? The turrets and guns were extremely reliable, with 94% turret reliability and 93% gun reliability in December 1944, and 100% turret and 97% gun reliability in January

1945. During 11,026 enemy attacks B-29 gunners claimed 714 enemy fighters destroyed, 456 probably destroyed, and 770 damaged for a loss rate of between 6.5% and 10.6%

German Remote Control Defensive Armament Systems
The Luftwaffe used its ill-starred He-177 Long-Range heavy bomber as a test bed for remote controlled gun mounts. In November 1941 a 20mm MG 151/20 cannon mounted in a FHL 151 Remotely Controlled Gun Mount equipped with a periscope was proposed, but only reached the mockup stage. In March 1942 the He-177 was approved to have remote controlled gun installations in its lower nose (one MG 81 machine gun) and forward top barbette positions. The barbette was to contain one or twin rear-facing MG 131s controlled by a remote system located under a Plexiglas dome behind the leading edge of the wing. The remote system never went beyond the developmental stage, and with the multiple problems that the He-177 design encountered during its development, the system was abandoned when it appeared that the Luftwaffe would never have a useful heavy bomber in its arsenal.

Experimental Turret Installations
In October 1944 Project S68 was initiated for manned B-29 turret evaluation. A B-29-20-25-BW (S/N 42-24441) was fitted with a Martin upper forward turret (at the rear of the forward pressurized compartment) and Martin upper rear turret (at the rear of the rear pressurized compartment) using twin .50cal machine guns. Two retractable Sperry A-13 ball turrets were installed mounting twin .50cal machine guns. The forward Sperry ball was fitted between the forward landing gear doors and the bomb bay doors, and the aft ball was mounted just forward to the tailskid, and was part of the tail gunner's pressurized compartment. The standard A-13 ball

A Martin upper forward turret (at the rear of the forward pressurized compartment) and Martin upper rear turret (at the rear of the rear pressurized compartment) were installed using twin .50cal machine guns. Two retractable Sperry A-13 ball turrets were installed mounting twin .50cal machine guns. (USAF)

turret was modified to have a shorter hanger than those used on the B-24 and the B-32, and thus did not retract entirely into the fuselage. The waist sighting blisters were replaced by hand-held .50cal machine guns like those used on the B-17 and B-24. Plywood boxes held the ammunition, and the spent casings were collected in a canvas basket on the floor below the gun. It was also fitted with two remotely controlled Emerson Model 126 barbettes, each mounting a single .50cal machine gun. The large egg-shaped barbettes were mounted on each side of the forward fuselage just above and adjacent to the forward tricycle gear. The project was probably the brainstorm from a higher echelon and was short lived.

10

Empennage

The horizontal stabilizer and trademark vertical tail of the B-17 had been exhaustively evaluated in wind tunnel and flight tests, and had served the Flying Fortress so well that Boeing engineers decided to test it to find if it could be adapted for the B-29. The tailplane and elevators on the B-29 were identical in shape and size to the B-17, but were of different section and construction. It was the B-29 vertical fin that was a problem that took two years to solve, in that it was to be four times larger dimensionally than the B-17 tail, and was to be the largest bomber tail ever used. The cantilevered vertical and horizontal stabilizers of the tail were constructed of ribs and spars covered by stressed sheet metal skin. Fabric covered the elevator and rudders. The B-29 tailplane section was modified with the use of a free elevator, so that its leading edge was turned up to give it the effect of an inverted airfoil. This configuration prevented stalling when the stabilizer was at a critical attitude.

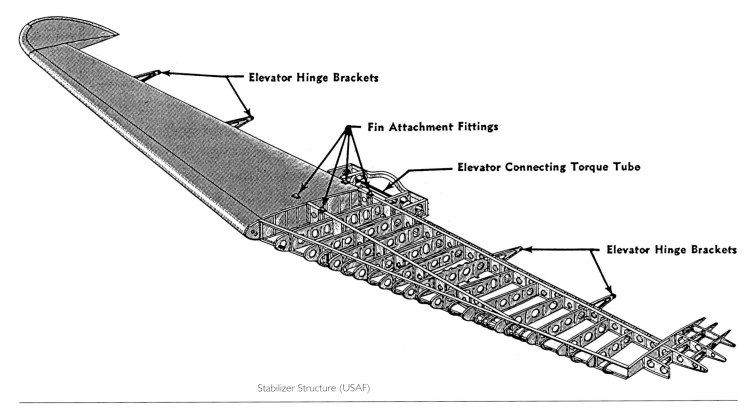

Stabilizer Structure (USAF)

Manufacturing the horizontal stabilizer at the GM Fisher Cleveland plant. (USAF)

The tailplane and elevators on the B-29 were identical in shape and size to the B-17 but were of different section and construction. (Author/Pima)

The B-29 vertical fin design had been a problem that took two years to solve in that it was to be four times larger dimensionally than the B-17 tail and was to be the largest bomber tail. (Author/Pima)

11

Armor

Heavy armor plate was built into both the B-17 and early B-29s, and placed in critical areas that would protect crewmen in areas vulnerable to enemy fire from the rear (e.g. the airplane commander and co-pilot had sheets of heavy armor behind their seats). But analysis of combat experience of enemy fighter attacks showed that attacks came from all directions. The armor protection, while still mainly directed from astern, was also then directed at 30 to 45-degrees off the aircraft centerline. The new armor was sheets of lighter dural aluminum placed on the sides and bottom of the fuselage, replacing the heavy rearward directed armor. The engines, along with the airplane commander/copilot area, were the most vulnerable areas of the bomber, and dural armor was placed in the engine nacelles. All armor was bonded electrically to the aircraft structure and flexibly mounted. Initially, these armor changes were done at the modification centers at Denver and the Continental Airlines Center, but later were incorporated at the factory production lines. Protective armor was provided to:

1) Two .25in face-hardened vertical steel panels were installed on aluminum stanchions mounted to the floor located directly behind the airplane commander and co-pilot seats. Bullet resistant glass was incorporated above the airplane commander's and co-pilot's instrument panels, and a .25in steel plate just forward of their instruments.

2) There were two rolled .25in steel plates aft of the forward pressure bulkhead 218, and on either side of the door to protect the radio operator, navigator, their equipment, and the bulkhead.

3) The rear pressurized compartment was protected by an armor wall approximately one third of the cabin's length back of the forward pressure bulkhead door at station 706. The wall consisted of four rigid rolled armor panels and a door panel that supported and protected the fire control equipment and personnel.

4) The computers were protected on three sides (right, left, and aft) by two rolled steel plates, and 0.25in 24ST aluminum deflecting plates.

5) The tail gunner's compartment was the most exposed and vulnerable crew area. It had a .375in face-hardened rolled steel panel fitting the fuselage contour immediately forward of the compartment at station

1144. There were three narrow steel panels around the sighting mechanism that were located below the three (aft and two side) bullet-resistant, laminated windows that surrounded the gunner's head. There was another armor plate behind the tail gunner's head.

"Flak curtains" developed for use over Europe were placed in crew areas to protect against chance anti-aircraft fire entering the fuselage near the crew stations. When the flak curtain was placed between the fuselage and a man wearing a flak vest, a bursting AA shell or fragment piercing the fuselage was stopped by the flak curtain, or slowed enough for the flak vest to stop the AA fragment. The flak curtain was a movable, semi-flexible piece of light armor that was similar to a flak suit in construction. The flak suit (see personal crew equipment section) was made from overlapping plates of .044 inch Hadfield steel plates sewed in separate cloth pouches. There were two types of flak curtains manufactured. One featured 2in x 2in .044 inch Hadfield steel plates (as in the M-1 vest) that overlapped enough to produce a thickness equivalent to two plates, while the second type had 4in x 8in .044 inch Hadfield steel plates that did not overlap as much as the first type.

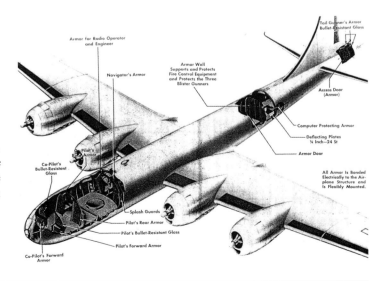

Armor Protection. (USAF)

12

Crew Oxygen System

The "Airplane Commander Training Manual" (AAF Manual 50-9) stated:

"The (oxygen) equipment provided is excellent, simple to operate, and safe for flights up to extremely high altitudes. But it is not safe unless you understand it thoroughly and follow the rules regarding its use strictly. You can't take shortcuts with oxygen and live to tell about it! The lack of oxygen, known as anoxia, gives no warning. If it hits you, you won't know it until your mates revive you from unconsciousness, if they can. Therefore, you must check the condition and operation of your equipment with extreme care, and continue to check it regularly as often as possible during flight."

Oxygen Systems
During the war there were two types of oxygen systems in use by the AAF: the demand system and continuous flow system. The demand system was automatic, and furnished oxygen on demand in the correct quantities for all altitudes. Every time the user inhaled, a volume of oxygen with the correct mixture of air was supplied. The continuous flow, as its name suggested, supplied a continuous oxygen flow. When the system was in use, the altitude dial on the regulator had to be manually adjusted to correspond with the altimeter reading to guarantee the correct amount of oxygen for the altitude being flown. The demand system was installed in all AAF aircraft in the last years of the war.

Oxygen Cylinders
Oxygen was necessary during unpressurized flight above 10,000ft, but was not needed when the cabin was pressurized to 10,000ft. At each crew station (there were 13 total oxygen outlets) there was an A-12 demand regulator, K-1 pressure gauge, A-3 flow indicator, low-pressure supply warning light and filler, and distribution manifolding. Eighteen C-1 2,100 cubic inch shatterproof cylinders supplied 29 cubic feet of gas to the low pressure A-12 oxygen demand Airco or Pioneer regulator unit. The cylinders were filled from one filler valve located on the outside of the fuselage, just forward of the left wing root. The 13 stations were supplied from two distinct distribution lines, and the loss of one line or its associated cylinders left each station with an alternate oxygen source. If there was damage to part of the system, all the functioning stations had equal access to the re-

maining oxygen supply. Two cylinders (one from each system) were to supply the tail gunner, and the other 16 bottles supplied the 12 other oxygen stations in the pressurized front and rear compartments. The airplane commander (four from the first system and two from the second), engineer, and radio operator stations (two from the first system and four from the second) were supplied by six cylinders, while the other stations were supplied by two (one from each system). The distribution lines of the forward compartment system were connected by a main line with a shut off valve at the engineer's station that was normally closed. The shut off valves were located in the forward end of the rear pressurized cabin, and at the

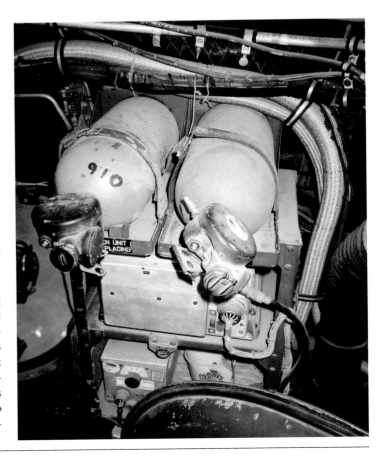

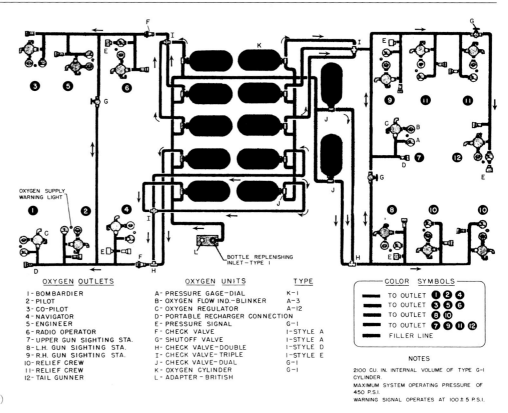

OXYGEN SUPPLY
WARNING LIGHT

BOTTLE REPLENISHING
INLET—TYPE I

OXYGEN OUTLETS		OXYGEN UNITS	TYPE
1 - BOMBARDIER		A - PRESSURE GAGE–DIAL	K–1
2 - PILOT		B - OXYGEN FLOW IND.–BLINKER	A–3
3 - CO-PILOT		C - OXYGEN REGULATOR	A–12
4 - NAVIGATOR		D - PORTABLE RECHARGER CONNECTION	
5 - ENGINEER		E - PRESSURE SIGNAL	G–1
6 - RADIO OPERATOR		F - CHECK VALVE	I–STYLE A
7 - UPPER GUN SIGHTING STA.		G - SHUTOFF VALVE	I–STYLE A
8 - L.H. GUN SIGHTING STA.		H - CHECK VALVE–DOUBLE	I–STYLE D
9 - R.H. GUN SIGHTING STA.		I - CHECK VALVE–TRIPLE	I–STYLE E
10 - RELIEF CREW		J - CHECK VALVE–DUAL	G–1
11 - RELIEF CREW		K - OXYGEN CYLINDER	G–1
12 - TAIL GUNNER		L - ADAPTER – BRITISH	

COLOR SYMBOLS

TO OUTLET ❶❷❹
TO OUTLET ❸❺❻
TO OUTLET ❽❿
TO OUTLET ❼❾⓫⓬
FILLER LINE

NOTES

2100 CU. IN. INTERNAL VOLUME OF TYPE G-1 CYLINDER.
MAXIMUM SYSTEM OPERATING PRESSURE OF 450 P.S.I.
WARNING SIGNAL OPERATES AT 100 ± 5 P.S.I.

Oxygen System Flow Diagram. (USAF)

right hand sidewall near the rear pressure bulkhead at station 834 to service the tail gunner's compartment.

The duration of the oxygen supply depended on the requirements of the individual crewmen, their activity, the temperature, and the charge of the system. The system pressurized at 400 to 450psi with the AUTO MIX ON lasted about six and half to seven hours for a crew of 11 at 25,000ft, and more than 10 hours at 15,000ft. Early B-29s had 14 oxygen cylinders that would supply four and a half hours of oxygen at 25,000ft. The zone between 20,000 and 30,000ft was the least economical altitude for oxygen

BREAKDOWN OF OXYGEN SOURCES

STATION	CYLINDER NUMBERS	
	First System	Second System
Pilot's	9, 10, 14, and 15	16 and 18
Copilot's	1 and 2	3 and 4
Bombardier's	1 and 2	16 and 18
Engineer's	1 and 2	9, 10, 14, and 15
Navigator's	3 and 4	16 and 18
Radio Operator's	3 and 4	9, 10, 14, and 15
Upper Gunner's	5 and 17	6 and 8
Left Blister Gunner's	6 and 8	11 and 7
Right Blister Gunner's	17 and 5	7 and 11
Raven Operator's	6 and 8	9 and 10
Radar Operator's	9 and 10	7 and 11
Relief Station	5 and 17	9 and 10
Tail Gunner's	12	13

Eighteen C-1 2,100 cubic inch shatterproof cylinders supplied 29 cubic feet of gas to the low pressure A-12 oxygen demand Airco or Pioneer regulator unit. The cylinders were filled from one filler valve located on the outside of the fuselage just forward of the left wing root. (Author/Pima)

use. Before entering combat the bomber was depressurized, and all crew plugged into the oxygen system. If the cabin was holed by enemy fire and could not be pressurized the crew continued the flight on oxygen, or descended to an altitude where oxygen was not necessary. A two-way check valve was located at the outlet of each cylinder to prevent loss of the total oxygen supply due to damage of an individual cylinder.

Regulator Panels

The regulator panel located close to each crewman's station consisted of an A-14 demand type regulator, a K-1 oxygen pressure gauge, a warning light, and an A-3 flow indicator. The regulator panels were found at 13 crew stations throughout the aircraft, providing one more station than the normal 12-man crew when the Raven was aboard. The panel for the CFC sighting station was mounted on the back of the swivel seat, and the oxygen line passed through the center post of the seat and attached to the regulator panel via a swivel joint. There were pressure warning lights to warn of low pressure.

A-14 Oxygen Regulators

The Type A-14 pressure demand regulator developed from the Aro Type A-12 demand regulator was standardized in November 1944, and was manufactured by Aro or Pioneer. A demand regulator (sometimes referred as the "diluter-demand regulator") was mounted at each station in the aircraft (two at the relief station). The demand regulator is one that furnishes oxygen on demand on inhalation, and no oxygen comes out on exhalation. It had an auto-mix mechanism controlled by a lever on the side of the cover, and automatically mixed the correct quantities of air and oxygen, the ratio depending upon the altitude. When the lever was on the ON posi-

The Type A-14 demand oxygen mask that entered service in mid-1943 was one of the best masks of the war. It was made up of a medium green rubber face piece and a corrugated hose that attached to the regulator. (USAF)

tion, oxygen furnished below 30,000ft was mixed with air. The quantity of the mixture depended solely on the breathing of the user. The dilution was controlled automatically by an aneroid to furnish the correct amount of oxygen that the body requires for a given altitude. Above 30,000ft the air inlet closed, and 100% oxygen flowed even though the regulator lever was in the ON position. With the lever on the OFF position, 100% oxygen was furnished at all altitudes. This wasted oxygen, and the lever was never to be at the OFF position, except in certain emergencies. The flow indicator on the oxygen panel blinked open and shut as the oxygen flowed, and needed to be checked during the flight, as it was the only indication that oxygen was flowing regularly. A pressure gauge on the panel was to read 400 to 450psi.

A-3 Flow Indicator

The A-3 flow indicator was connected to the regulator, and when oxygen flowed the eye-shaped blinker on the oxygen panel gauge winked open and shut.

K-1 Pressure Gauge

The K-1 pressure gauge was of the standard Bourdon tube construction, and read from 0 to 500psi. It read between 400 and 425psi with full pressure ON before take off check. All gauges were to be checked against all other gauges on board, and any discrepancy over 50psi was to be reported. While in the ON position the oxygen gauge was to be checked often. When the pressure fell below 100psi (the 100 to 0 portion of the scale was marked in red lacquer) the supply was getting low, and the airplane commander was to be notified. The regulator did not function accurately under 50psi, and the portable walk around cylinder was to be used.

Check Valves

Check valves were used throughout the oxygen system to prevent back flow, and the resultant loss of the entire oxygen supply due to damage to any part of the system. There was a dual type check valve on each cylinder that allowed each cylinder to be filled through the filler line without back

flow into the filler line. This dual valve also allowed the cylinder to empty into the system without back flow. There were check valves in the main supply line where it entered each crew station. If one or more cylinders were damaged or destroyed, only the oxygen from these cylinders was lost, as the check valves prevented the movement of oxygen from the undamaged cylinders to the damaged cylinders.

Low Pressure Warning System

Low oxygen pressures under 100psi at the affected station were indicated on both the pressure gauge, and by lighting of the warning light. The warning signal was activated by the increase or decrease of oxygen pressure on a spring-loaded diaphragm that opened or closed an electrical switch.

Oxygen masks

The Type A-14 demand oxygen mask that entered service in mid-1943 was one of the best masks of the war. It was made up of a medium green rubber face piece and a corrugated hose that attached to the regulator. An attaching strap ran along the bottom of the rubber face piece and held the mask to the face. There was a hook and tab on the right side of the mask for quick removal. Snaps and buckles on the right side of the helmet suspended the mask to the helmet. A microphone pocket was built into the mask just above the mouthpiece to accommodate the T-44 or ANB-M-C1 microphone. Excessive moisture accumulation from exhalation was a problem, and would condense and freeze inside the mask. A small electric heater was developed to be worn over the mask, and was used with the electric flying suit. The A-14 utilized the intermittent-flow principle, in which oxygen was supplied only when the wearer inhaled. With the inhalation there was a slight suction produced that caused the demand regulator to open and deliver oxygen to the mask. When the wearer exhaled the demand regulator automatically shut off, and the exhaled air passed out of the mask through a flutter valve. The A-14 was continually improved, and in January 1945 the A-14A was standardized, and remained in use until well after the war. There was an A-14 mask and regulator stored in a cloth bag at crew stations, and was to be suspended on the flying helmet for use when the bomber was depressurized.

The A-3 flow indicator was connected to the regulator and when oxygen flowed the eye-shaped blinker on the oxygen panel gauge winked open and shut. (Author/Pima)

The oxygen mask needed to fit perfectly, and each crewman had his personal mask fitted by the Personal Equipment Officer. It was stored in the supply room after each mission, where equipment personnel checked it for repair and cleaning. The mask check included looking over the mask and straps carefully for worn spots, loose studs, or deterioration of the facepiece and hose. The gasket was checked for proper seating on the male quick disconnecting fitting that was to fit snugly, requiring about a 10-pound pull to separate the two parts. The regulator hose was clipped to the flight jacket in such a way that the wearer was to be able to move his head fully without twisting, kinking, or pulling out the quick disconnects between the mask and regulator. Once this proper position was determined the PEO would sew a tab on the flight jacket on which to attach the hose. The mask was attached to the right side of the helmet. The knurled collar on the regulator was to be tight, and the diaphragm intact. The emergency valve was checked to see if the oxygen flowed, and then the valve was closed firmly. To check the function of the flow indicator the tester breathed from the regulator normally in the Auto-mix OFF position. The Auto-mix was then turned to the ON position, and the oxygen pressure was to be from 400 to 425psi. Checks were done on the walk-around bottles, mask function, and connections.

The helmet and mask were put on carefully, and the edges of the facepiece were slipped under the helmet. The mask had to fit tightly and have no leaks. The crewman was told to shave every day, as short beard stubble could affect the fit of the mask. The mask could be checked for leaks by three methods:

1) Mechanical leak detector: With the mask in place the crewman inhaled, held his breath, plugged the mask hose firmly into the leak detector, and released the bottom plate of the detector. If the plate descended in 10 seconds or less the mask had a leak.

2) Suction test: With the mask in place the tester's thumb was placed over the end of the hose, and the breath was gently inhaled. The mask was to collapse on the face, with no air entering.

3) Sniff test: The inhaler was filled with oil of peppermint. The mask was to be plugged into the regulator hose, Auto-mix was to be turned OFF (100% oxygen), and several breaths of pure oxygen were taken. Then, with the eyes closed, the inhaler was held close to the edges of the mask. If peppermint could be smelled then there was leak.

D-2 and A-6 Walk Around Equipment

Each station was equipped with a portable, walk-around oxygen cylinder with a regulator and a recharging hose. There were two types of portable, walk-around oxygen equipment available on the B-29. The large yellow D-2 cylinders with carrying slings were provided for each of these crew positions: airplane commander; co-pilot; flight engineer; navigator; radar operator; and upper and right gunners. The remainder of the crew used the smaller green A-6 portable oxygen units that clipped to the flight jacket, and were available to supply 6 to 12 minutes of walk around operation.

Before each mission the bottle was to be checked. The outlet of the bottle was to be sucked on to check if it gave an easy flow, then the outlet was blown on gently, then hard. Once the diaphragm was expanded there was to be positive and continued resistance. If there was only slight resistance the diaphragm was leaking, and was to be replaced with new bottle.

The small green A-6 portable oxygen units was clipped to the flight jacket and were available to supply 6 to 12 minutes of walk around operation. (Author/Pima)

Each bottle had pressure gauges and regulators that furnished 100% oxygen on demand. The pressure gauges had to be closely watched for refilling (at 50psi), and they could be refilled at one of the oxygen valves located at each crew station. To refill the hose fitting had to be snapped on the nipple of the regulator until it clicked and locked. When the bottle had filled to the pressure of the aircraft system the hose was removed, and the mask could be plugged into the bottle.

The walk around bottle was always to be used when disconnecting from the aircraft oxygen system, and the crewman was to hold his breath while switching bottles. The duration of oxygen supply varied, but did not last very long, and needed to be watched for recharging. It was always to be refilled after use.

Auxiliary Oxygen Unit

There was an auxiliary oxygen system with five G-1 storage cylinders mounted and interconnected on each side of the front and rear bomb bays for the use of 16 troops or crew being transported in them. There were four outlets on the front of the panel, each consisting of an A-12 demand regulator and a flow indicator.

Bailout Bottle

The bailout bottle was a small high-pressure (1,800psi) oxygen bottle with an attached gauge that furnished a continuous flow of oxygen. The cylinder was contained in a heavy canvas pocket with tie straps to attach it to the parachute harness. It had a bayonet connector to be plugged into the adapter on the oxygen mask. If the crew was to bail out at altitude, the mask was to be connected to the walk around bottle while heading for the emergency exit. Just before jumping the mask was disconnected from the walk around cylinder and attached to the bail out bottle, and the valve opened on the bailout bottle. In a free fall, to prevent the venturi effect from sucking oxygen from the mask the thumb was to be held over the end of the mask tubing.

13

Creature Comforts

Lavatory

A toilet was located across from the radar operator's station (ex-bunk bed area) in the central left section of the rear pressurized cabin. The toilet was an empty low drum with a sealed lid and plastic or paper liner. The crews had an unwritten rule that the first person to use the toilet had to empty it at the end of the mission. It often became a battle of wills, but once the toilet was used a line quickly formed. After the toilet's use the radar operator suffered, as his compartment was cramped, and the odor could become overpowering. Several inches of water with a covering layer of pine oil was added to the toilet to ameliorate the smell.

A relief tube was located on the navigator's cabinet in the forward compartment. During early Long-Range training missions a problem arose when brakes began to fail on landing. Investigation found a crystal-like material in the brake lines, and some discerning crew chief thought it smelled like "piss," and that solved the problem. The hydraulic system required a drain to dump excess fluid, and a designer—not wanting to add another hole in the clean fuselage—decided to connect the hydraulic vent line to the relief tube reservoir. On short-range missions this presented no problems, but on Long-Range missions, when the relief tube was used repeatedly, the urine level rose above the vent line opening, and urine was drawn into the hydraulic system.

Thermos Jugs and Vacuum Bottles

Two Stanley all metal heat-insulated thermos jugs were supplied; one located on top of the navigator's cabinet, and the other located on the rear compartment auxiliary panel. The jugs were one or two gallon capacity with a spigot at the bottom and screw top with a metal cup/cap combination. A cup dispenser was placed near the jugs. A smaller one or two quart Stanley vacuum bottle with a cork stopper and metal cup/cap combination was supplied for the tail gunner.

Food Warmers

Because of the long flight times to Japan it was necessary to feed the crews in order to maintain their efficiency. Since the cabins were pressurized and no oxygen masks were being worn, the cold sandwiches and juices that nourished the B-17 and B-24 crews could be replaced by more elaborate fare. The AAF established a test program at the 2nd Air Force's Smoky Hill base at Salina, KS, to determine menus, and a method to preserve the food

in flight. Eight volunteer B-29 crews ate different foods before entering pressure chambers, and also ate meals in the pressure chambers. The tests found that meals high in carbohydrates were best, as they supplied energy more quickly and increased efficiency up to three times. The tests also showed that the "carbed up" crews could go 5,000ft higher without oxygen. Any food that produced gases was deleted from the menu.

The Tappen Company developed a small food warming unit that was a small forerunner of the large aisle carts used on modern airliners. Two B-2 food warmer units (35lb empty, 40lb full) were provided to keep prepared meals at 160°F by electricity supplied by the 24-volt electric system,

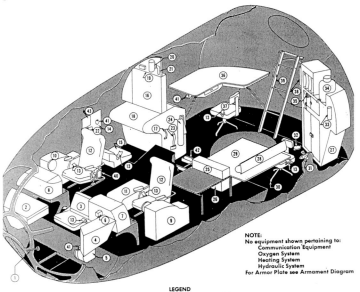

NOTE:
No equipment shown pertaining to:
Communication Equipment
Oxygen System
Heating System
Hydraulic System
For Armor Plate see Armament Diagram

LEGEND

1. Bombardier's Thermometer Inst.
2. Bombardier's Panel Inst.
3. Bombardier's Seat Inst.
4. Bombardier's Board Inst.
5. Bombardier's Control Stand
6. Intervalometer
7. Pilot's Instrument Panel Assy.
8. Copilot's Instrument Panel Assy.
9. Pilot's Stand Assy.
10. Copilot's Stand Assy.
11. Pilots' Aisle Stand
12. Pilot's and Copilot's Seat Assy.
13. Safety Belt (Type B-11)
14. Engineer's Equip. Panel Inst.
15. Engineer's Seat Assy.
16. Engineer's Instr. Board Inst.
17. Engineer's Stand Assist Handle
18. Engineer's Control Stand
19. Auxiliary Equip. Control Panel Assy.
20. First Aid Kit Assy.
21. Flashlight (Eveready)
22. Clip Board
23. Hand Axe
24. Fire Extinguisher
25. Navigator's Panel Inst.
26. Drift Signal Cabinet Inst.
27. Navigator's Cabinet Inst.
28. Navigator's Map Case
29. Navigator's Table Inst.
30. Navigator's Seat Assy.
31. Drift Recorder Inst.
32. Drift Signal Chute Inst.
33. Paper Cup Dispenser
34. Water Jug (Type III)
35. Sextant
36. Radio Operator's Table Inst.
37. Radio Operator's Seat Inst.
38. Waste Cup Receptacle
39. Front Tunnel Ladder Inst.
40. Check List and Holder
41. Ash Tray
42. Forward Entrance Ladder (Stowed)
43. Fuel System Diagram

Forward Pressurized Fuselage Furnishings. (USAF)

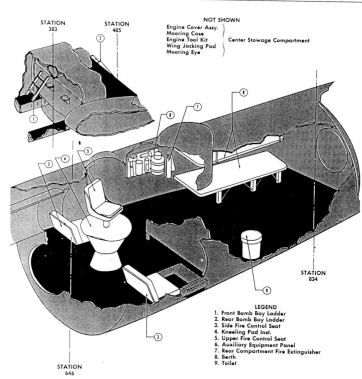

STATION
383

STATION
485

NOT SHOWN
Engine Cover Assy.
Mooring Case
Engine Tool Kit
Wing Jacking Pad
Mooring Eye

Center Stowage Compartment

STATION
834

STATION
646

LEGEND
1. Front Bomb Bay Ladder
2. Rear Bomb Bay Ladder
3. Side Fire Control Seat
4. Kneeling Pad Inst.
5. Upper Fire Control Seat
6. Auxiliary Equipment Panel
7. Rear Compartment Fire Extinguisher
8. Berth
9. Toilet

Rear Pressurized Fuselage Furnishings. (USAF)

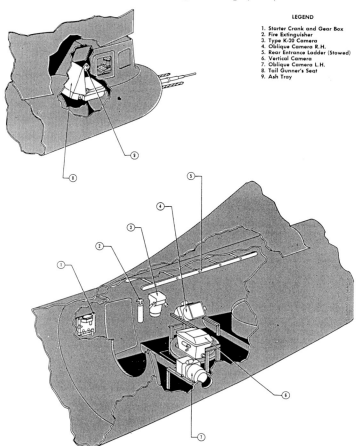

LEGEND
1. Starter Crank and Gear Box
2. Fire Extinguisher
3. Type K-20 Camera
4. Oblique Camera R.H.
5. Rear Entrance Ladder (Stowed)
6. Vertical Camera
7. Oblique Camera L.H.
8. Tail Gunner's Seat
9. Ash Tray

Tail Gunner Fuselage Furnishings. (USAF)

with each unit drawing about eight amps. Each warmer held six hot, full course meals contained in a four-compartment aluminum tray. It also held 12 one-pint aluminum cups for coffee or juices on a shelf on top of the unit. In the top of the cabinet was a drawer to hold silverware, condiments, and other foods that did not require heating, such as bread, cookies, cakes, and fruit. The aluminum cups and trays were replaced in April 1945 by the more sanitary stainless steel units, as the aluminum gave off an odor and affected the taste of the food.

A typical hot meal might include a soup, a meat like Swiss or Salisbury steak, mashed potatoes or potato cakes, buttered vegetables such as peas or carrots, a dessert such as a fruit cobbler, a hot roll, and coffee or tea. The only crewman to complain was the tail gunner, who could not be served until the aircraft was depressurized and he could move from his station.

Unfortunately, many of these food warmers were removed from the bomber, and the so-called "Air Crew Lunch" was brought on board, along with coffee in thermos bottles. The lunch consisted of snacks (typically sandwiches), candy, and chewing gum contained in a small rectangular box made of light cardboard.

Seats

All seats, except the upholstered navigator's and radio operator's seats, were of the bucket type. The type S-2 seat parachute packs often replaced

Two Tappen B-2 food warmer units were provided to keep prepared meals at 160F degrees by electricity supplied by the 24-volt electric system. The unit was a small forerunner of the large aisle carts used on modern airliners. Each 35lb (empty), 40lb (full) warmer held six hot, full course meals in a four-compartment aluminum tray. (Author/Pima)

The "Air Crew Lunch" consisted of coffee in thermos bottles and snacks, typically sandwiches, candy, and chewing gum, contained in a small light cardboard rectangular box. (USAF)

the cushions on these seats. All seats were equipped with Type B-14 lap seat belts and Type B-15 shoulder harnesses. When adjusting the seat belt, care had to be taken to put the belt over, not through, the parachute harness. An adjusting lever to the left of the seat locked the shoulder harness. The seat belt and the ends of the shoulder harness locked together at a quick release attachment in the center of the lap.

The airplane commander's and co-pilot's seats had vertical, horizontal, and reclining adjustments, and had a full-width back, removable head rest, and armrests. The bombardier's seat had only horizontal and vertical

adjustment, while the engineer's seat had no adjustments, and both had a half-back and no armrests. The radio operator and navigator had "posture-type" ("secretary") seats with no armrests, and a small pad for a backrest. The navigator's chair was on slides, and movable parallel with the aircraft centerline, while the radio operator's seat was fixed to the floor

The sighting blister chair was built into the structure and was not adjustable. The top gunner was provided with a stool mounted on a pedestal that could rotate 360-degrees to help in following targets. The tail gunner's seat was hinged above the gunner's entrance door—held by springs when not in use—and had to be pulled down after entry to the gun position.

Tables

The bombardier's table was located on the right front side of the forward pressurized compartment below the co-pilot's instrument panel, and was a plywood top that slid.

The rectangular navigator's table was on the left side of the forward pressurized compartment. The inboard side of the table was equipped with a folding leaf, and there was an ashtray on the aft side. The navigator's plywood map case was mounted on the overhead on the fuselage wall. The navigator's wooden instrument cabinet was placed in the corner of the pressure bulkhead and fuselage. Besides providing stowage of his equipment, including his sextant, it also held a water jug and cup dispenser. The drift signal cabinet was located under the navigator's table, and provided stowage room for 12 day or night drift signals.

The radio operator's L-shaped table was located on the aft right corner of the forward pressurized compartment. There was a control handle for the operation of the trailing antenna fairlead on the leg of the table directly under the ashtray, which was on the right front side of the table. Two legs angled from the front edge of the table and were clipped to the floor/wall junction.

Berths

In early B-29s, four berths were provided on both sidewalls of the rear pressurized compartment aft of the armor plate bulkhead. Later bunks were

B-29 Seats and Adjustments. (USAF)

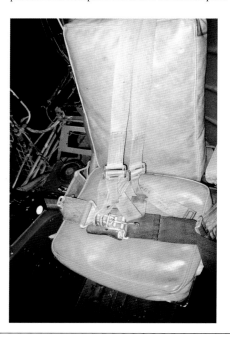

All seats were equipped with Type B-14 lap seat belts and Type B-15 shoulder harnesses. (Author/Pima)

The navigator's table was cramped between the port side wall, rear bulkhead and the upper forward turret (white area on left). (Author/Pima)

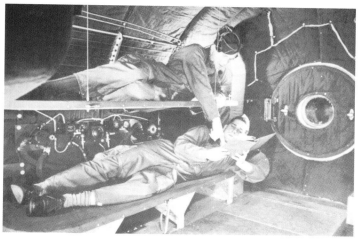

In early B-29s four berths were provided on both sidewalls of the rear pressurized compartment aft of the armor plate bulkhead. The berths were canvas-covered wooden frames and both the upper and lower berths could be folded up against the sidewall. Two could be used for seats for additional crew. Later bunks were removed from one wall and near the end of the war to make room for the new radar man and his equipment these berths were also removed. (USAF)

removed from one wall, and near the end of the war to make room for the new radar man and his equipment; these berths were also removed.

The berths were canvas-covered wooden frames, and both the upper and lower berths could be folded up against the sidewall. The lower two could be used for seats for additional crewmen by stowing the upper bunks in the up position against the side of the wall. The lower berth had three supporting legs, and vertical cables supported the upper berth. Two safety belts were provided when the lower berth was used as a seat.

Ladders

Forward Entrance Ladder: This ladder had fittings that slipped into two "Z" slots located on the right sidewall of the nose wheel well. The ladder was to be folded and stowed by strapping it to a plywood step cover on the navigator's floor.

Tunnel Ladder: This was a wooden three-step ladder that hooked onto a support bolted under the tunnel entrance. It provided an entrance to the tunnel from the forward compartment, and was stowed inside the tunnel when not in use.

Bomb Bay Ladders: There was a three-step ladder provided for each bomb bay that was fixed in place by straps from the catwalks to the top of the wing on the left side of the forward and rear bomb bays.

Nacelles Servicing Ladders: Two folding stepladders and a wooden platform for servicing the engine nacelles were stowed under the lower berth in the rear pressurized compartment.

Rear Entrance Ladder: This was a five-step wooden ladder used to enter the rear unpressurized compartment, and was stowed on the ceiling of that compartment.

Radio Operator's Table. (USAF)

Color Gallery

Forward Pressurized Compartment

Airplane Commander's Station

Airplane Commander's Instrument Panel

Airplane Commander's Control Stand

Co-pilot's Station

Co-pilot's Control Stand

Aisle Stand

Co-pilot's Instrument Panel

Bombardier's Station

Norden Bombsight

Bombardier's Instrument Panel

Flight Engineer's Station

Flight Engineer's Instrument Panel

Navigator's Station

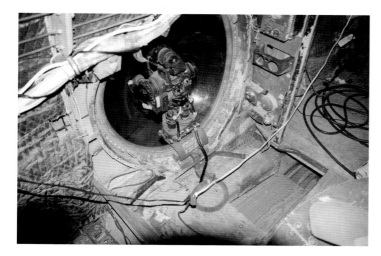

Starboard Sighting Station

APQ-7 Radar Operator's Station

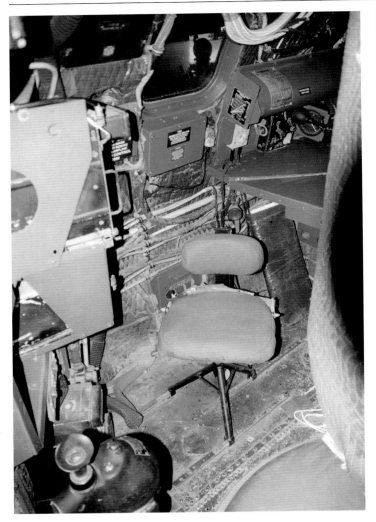

Navigator's Station

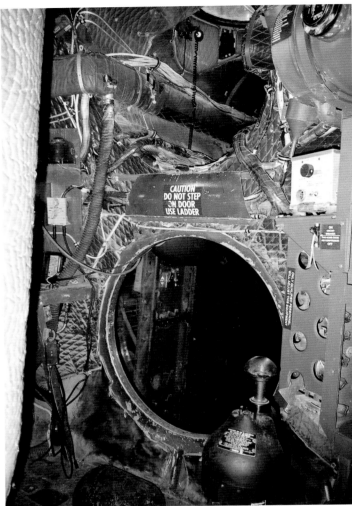

Rear of Forward Compartment

CFC Station

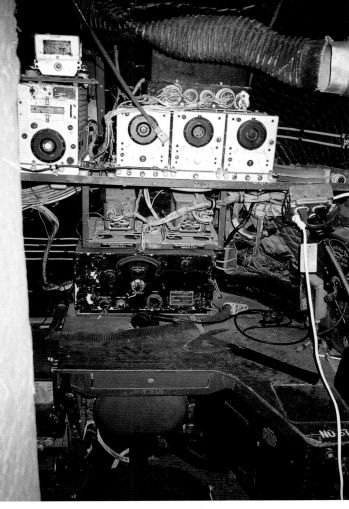

Radio Operator's Station

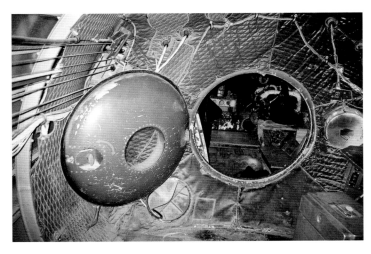

Pressure Door (from aft unpressurized to aft pressurized)

Oxygen Bottles and Tail Skid Shock

Rear Lower Turret

Tail Gun Compartment (looking over armored seat onto gunsight)

All photos were taken by the author of the Pima Aerospace Museum's B-29 *Sentimental Journey*.

14

B-29 Stations and Controls:
Description, Location, and Function

Flight Controls

In order to concentrate on flying procedure and combat tactics, the B-29 airplane commander and the co-pilot were relieved of the majority of the power plant controls, and most of the basic mechanical and electric system operations. This was accomplished by providing the flight engineer with a separate station, complete with all the required instruments and controls. The flight engineer was placed at the starboard side of the cabin behind the co-pilot, facing aft. In this position he was in direct communication with the airplane commander and co-pilot, and could visually check all four engines while seated at his station. The throttle levers were triplicated, with one set each for the airplane commander, co-pilot, and the flight engineer. The airplane commander was able to override the flight engineer's throttles to maintain sole control. A single knob on the airplane commander's aisle stand controlled all the turbosuperchargers. The primary flight controls, elevator, rudder, and ailerons were cable-operated. Secondary flight controls were electrically operated. To diminish vulnerability from combat, damage redundant systems were installed.

Boeing engineers considered control and stability so important that they sacrificed performance to arrive at an aircraft that was easy to fly, and had no adverse ground or flight characteristics. The result was a very large bomber that was easier to control with lighter control forces, and was more stable than the smaller B-17. During initial design considerations Boeing engineers thought that hydraulic boost of the flight controls would be required. Continued analysis and wind tunnel tests, and the incorporation of the Boeing control tabs led to controls that were light, simple, less expensive, less vulnerable, and more easily maintained than controls with hydraulic boost. The Boeing control system allowed the airplane commander to "feel the controls."

Control Stands
Airplane Commander's and Co-pilot's Control Stands

The airplane commander and co-pilot were each provided with a control stand that each mounted the power plant control levers and trim tab controls. Additionally, the airplane commander's stand mounted the landing gear power transfer switch and the releases for emergency cabin pressure, bombs, and landing gear. The co-pilot's stand mounted the throttle warning reset button.

Aisle Stand

The aisle stand was located in the aisle between the airplane commander and co-pilot, allowing each easy access to the controls. The controls mounted on the aisle stand were the control surface lock lever, emergency brake levers, wing flap control switch, propeller feathering switches, emergency alarm switch, interphone call switch, formation light rheostat, position light switches, identification light switches, propeller rpm, propeller pitch circuit breaker resets, AFCE (automatic flight control) system controls, and turbo boost selector.

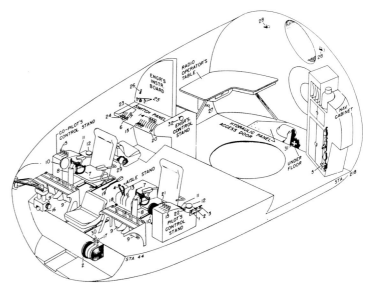

EMERGENCY CONTROLS	ENGINE CONTROLS	28 – LIFE RAFT (2)
		29 – CABIN PRESSURE RELIEF VALVE
1 – CABIN AIR PRESSURE RELEASE	14 – MIXTURE (4)	30 – BOMB DOOR RELEASE
2 – BOMB RELEASE	15 – THROTTLE (4)	31 – HYDRAULIC SHUTOFF VALVE (SERVICING)
3 – LANDING GEAR AND DOOR RELEASE	OTHER CONTROLS	32 – EMERGENCY OXYGEN VALVE
4 – METERING BRAKE VALVE		
5 – VACUUM SHUTOFF VALVE	16 – NOSE GUN SIGHT	REAR COMPARTMENT CONTROLS
6 – EMERGENCY CABIN AIR VALVE (2)	17 – BOMB RELEASE (BOMBARDIER'S)	(NOT SHOWN)
	18 – PARKING BRAKES	
FLIGHT CONTROLS	19 – HYDRAULIC HAND PUMP	A 1 – EMERGENCY BOMB RELEASE AT STA. 646
	20 – MIXTURE LOCK	A 2 – EMER. CABIN AIR PRES. RELEASE STA. 646
7 – AILERON	21 – THROTTLE LOCK	A 3 – CAMERA SYSTEM SHUTOFF VALVE
8 – ELEVATOR	22 – OVERCONTROL	A 4 – CAMERA SHUTOFF VALVE (3) STA. 834
9 – RUDDER AND BRAKE PEDAL	23 – VACUUM SELECTOR VALVE	A 5 – CAMERA REGULATING VALVE
10 – ELEVATOR TRIM TAB	24 – TANK SELECTOR (2)	A 6 – LOWER TURRET GUN SIGHT (2) AT STA. 686
11 – AILERON TRIM TAB	25 – FIRE EXTINGUISHER (ENGINE) (2)	A 7 – UPPER TURRET GUN SIGHT AT STA. 686
12 – RUDDER TRIM TAB	26 – FILLER VALVE (EMER. HYD. SYSTEM)	A 8 – TAIL TURRET GUN SIGHT
13 – SURFACE LOCKS	27 – TRAILING ANTENNA FAIRLEAD	A 9 – EMERGENCY OXYGEN VALVE AT STA. 646 AND STA. 834

Manual Controls Location. (USAF)

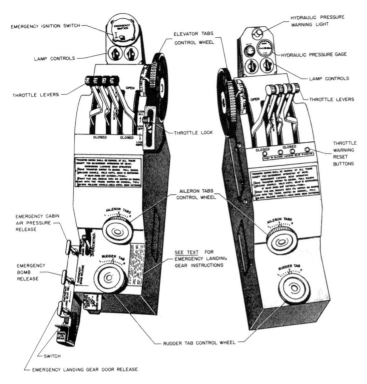

Airplane Commander's and Co-pilot's Control Stand (USAF)

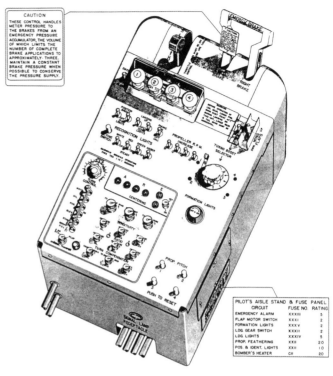

Aisle Stand (USAF)

The Flight Engineer's Control Stand

The flight engineer's control stand provided controls for throttles, mixture, fuel transfer, cabin supercharger, and vacuum selector. The flight engineer switch panel was located immediately behind the control stand.

The Navigator's Station

see page 193

Engine Controls

A)   Ignition Switches
    Description: Rotary levers, type B-5 ignition switches.
    Location: Flight engineer's instrument panel.
    Function: Provided individual engine ignition control, utilizing either or both circuits of the dual type magnetos.

1. Altimeter.
2. Turn Indicator.
3. Air-Speed Indicator.
4. Turn and Bank Indicator.
5. Rate-of-Climb Indicator.
6. Flight Indicator.
7. Pilot Directional Indicator.
8. Manifold Pressure Indicator.
9. Tachometer.
10. Radio Compass.
11. Turret Warning Lamps.
12. Remote Reading Compass.
13. Suction Gage.
14. Clock.
15. Static Pressure Selector Valve Switch.
16. Bomb Release Lamp.
17. Marker Beacon Lamp.

1. Altimeter.
2. Turn Indicator.
3. Flight Indicator.
4. Air-Speed Indicator.
5. Turn and Bank Indicator.
6. Climb Indicator.
7. Compass.
8. Clock.
9. Static Pressure Selector Valve Switch.
10. Landing Gear Warning Lamps.
11. Propeller Pitch Lamps.
12. Flap Position Indicator.

Airplane Commander's Instrument Panel (USAF)

Co-pilot's Instrument Panel (USAF)

B) Control Levers
  1) Throttle
     Description: Three throttle control levers for each engine interconnected by cables.
     Location: Airplane commander's control stand, co-pilot control stand and flight engineer's control stand.
     Function: Provided control of throttles.
  2) Supercharger Control
     Description: One dial knob on each turbo boost control.
     Location: Airplane commander's aisle stand.
     Function: Provided simultaneous control of all superchargers and turbo boost.
  3) Supercharger Synchronization
     Description: Four calibration screws.
     Location: Under four screw caps on pilot's aisle stand.
     Function: Adjust the correlation of four manifold pressures to a single dial setting.
  4) Mixture Control
     Description: Control levers connected to each carburetor mixture control by cables.
     Location: Flight engineer's stand.
     Function: Apply varying-degrees of friction.

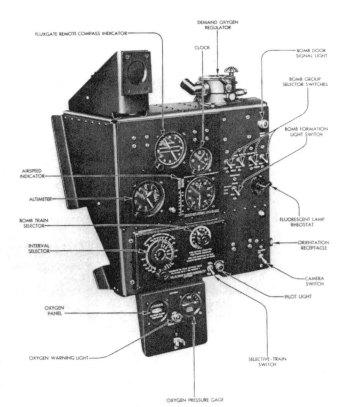

Bombardier's Instrument Board (USAF)

. Cabin Air Flow Gage.
. Cylinder Head Temperature Indicator.
. Oil Temperature Indicator.
. Nose Oil Pressure Gage.
. Rear Oil Pressure Gage.
. Oil Quantity Gage.
. Fuel Quantity Gage.

8. Cowl Flap and Intercooler Flap Position Indicators.
9. Tachometer.
10. Manifold Pressure Gage.
11. Fuel Pressure Gage.
12. Clock.
13. Cabin Air Temperature Indicator.

14. Deicing Pressure Gage.
15. Hydraulic Pressure Gage.
16. Air-Speed Indicator.
17. Cabin Differential Pressure Indicator.
18. Altimeter (Outside and Cabin).

19. Rate-of-Climb Indicator (Outside and Cabin).
20. Ammeter-Voltmeter Selector Switch.
21. D-C Ammeter.
22. D-C Voltmeter.
23. A-C Voltmeter.
24. Fuel Boost Control Rheostat.

Engineer's Control Stand (USAF)

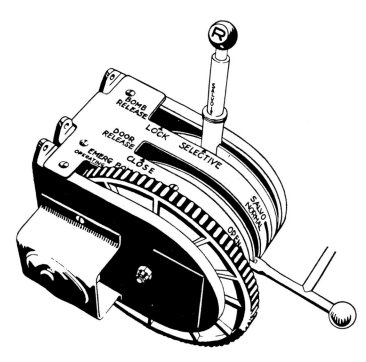

Bomb Controls (USAF)

5) Overcontrol
Description: Control lever.
Location: Pilot's control stand.
Function: In emergencies, allowed the airplane commander to assume control over the flight engineer's throttle levers.

C) Cowl Flap Switches
Description: Four, momentary contact switches.
Location: Flight engineer's panel.
Function: Provided control of the cylinder head temperature by operating the cowl flaps.

D) Intercooler Switches
Description: Four, momentary contact switches.
Location: Flight engineer's panel.
Function: Provided control of the carburetor air temperature.

E) Oil Cooler Switches
Description: Four, three position switches: OPEN, CLOSED or AUTO.
Location: Flight engineer's switch panel.
Function: Provided control of the oil temperature. A thermostat when in the AUTO position governed the oil cooler exit automatically.

F) Primer Switches
Description: Four, momentary contact switches.
Location: Flight engineer's switch panel.
Function: Directing fuel to the engine blower cases facilitating starting.

G) Oil Dilution Switches
Description: Four, momentary contact switches.
Location: Flight engineer's switch panel.
Function: Operated solenoid valves located in each nacelle to dilute the engine oil to facilitate cold weather starting.

H) Fuel Supply
1) Fuel Boost Switches
Description: Four toggle switches.
Location: Flight engineer's stand.
Function: Operated the fuel boost pumps that supplied fuel to the carburetors from each fuel system during starting. The boost pumps were also used to augment the fuel pumps during take off and operation above 15,000ft.
2) Fuel Boost Rheostats
Description: Four rheostats.
Location: Flight engineer's panel.
Function: Controlled the amount of fuel pressure from the boost pumps (not to exceed 18psi).
3) Fuel Shut Off Switches
Description: Four, momentary contact switches.
Location: Flight engineer's switch panel.
Function: Provided control of the solenoid fuel shut off valve. Two opposed solenoids were used, one for closing and the other for opening. Small dots near each switch indicated the direction in which the valve was last actuated. A transparent shield

protected the switches from accidental operation.
4) Fuel Tank Selector Levers
Description: Two control levers.
Location: Left side of the flight engineer's control panel.
Function: Operated by means of cables, the two selector valves located under the midwing section. Four positions were available on each selector valve to permit choice of tanks when transferring fuel.
5) Fuel Transfer Pump Switch
Description: Three pole, triple throw switch.
Location: Flight engineer's switch panel.
Function: Provided control of the fuel transfer pumps. Three positions, L to R, R to L and OFF were indicated. The pump switch was interlocked with the selector valves by a relay and prevented the pump from operating if the selector valve was off center.
6) Fuel and Oil Quantity Gauge Selector Knob
Description: Two, four position selector knobs.
Location: Flight engineer's instrument panel, one knob each for the fuel and oil gauges.
Function: Allowed the choice of indication of the quantities in any engine or oil tanks.

I) Propeller Controls
1) Pilot's Propeller Switches
Description: Four, momentary contact switches. These switches operated in lights indicated the limit of governor travel in either direction.
Location: Airplane commander's aisle stand.
Function: Provided individual control propellers.
2) Feathering Switches
Description: Four, magnetic, push button switches which when operated, were held engaged by the magnetic holding feature until feathering was completed.
Location: On aisle stand.
Function: Closed the circuit to the propeller feathering pump. The buttons could be pulled out manually if the action was to be stopped before completion. Propeller unfeathering required that the buttons be manually engaged, because the required oil pressures were more than that at which the magnetic holding feature stopped functioning. The button had to be engaged until the propeller attained sufficient rotation (200rpm) for the governor to assume control. A transparent, hinged guard protected the push buttons from accidental operation.
3) Propeller Anti-icer Switch
Description: Toggle switch.
Location: Flight engineer's panel.
Function: Operated the electrical pumps that supplied anti-icing fluid to the propellers.
4) Propeller Anti-icing Rheostat
Description: Two control knobs.
Location: Flight engineer's stand, lower inboard section.
Function: Varied the rate of the propeller anti-icer fluid from 2gal per hour to 5gal per hour. One rheostat controlled the flow to the outboard propellers and the other to the inboard propellers.

J) Starter Switches

Description: Four, momentary contact switches.

Location: Flight engineer's switch panel.

Function: Energized and meshed starters for engine start. Three positions—OFF, ACCELERATE, and START—were provided for each of the four starter switches.

K) Engine Fire Extinguisher

1) Selector Knob

Description: Manually operated, four-position knob.

Location: Flight engineer's instrument panel.

Function: Selected one of four of the engine to which to direct the CO_2 discharge. The capacity of a single CO_2 bottle was only sufficient for a fire in one engine.

2) Release Handles

Description: Two, manually operated pull handles, one for each of the two CO_2 charge bottles.

Location: Flight engineer's instrument panel.

Function: Released CO_2 discharge to desired engine.

Hydraulic System Controls

A) Brake pedals

Description: Standard rudder pedals.

Location: Airplane commander's and co-pilot's stations.

Function: Provided control in taxiing by tilting the rudder pedals forward for braking action. Each right and left brake could be operated independently. Repeated excessive use of the brakes without sufficient cooling between applications caused dangerous overheating and could cause failure of the brake structure or wheels and blowing out of the tires. Needless short stops especially from high speeds were to be avoided along with the dragging of the brakes while taxiing. The brakes were to be tapped after take off, before retraction to stop wheel rotation.

B) Emergency Brake Levers

Description: Two lever handles.

Location: Aisle stand.

Function: Provided individual or dual metering as conditions warranted. If the emergency brakes were used during landing care had to be taken not to drain the pressure in the accumulator to zero.

C) Parking Brake Handle

Description: Button-type pull handle.

Location: Airplane commander's rudder pedal stand (upper right).

Function: Set the parking brakes. Operate foot brakes then pull out the parking brake handle to lock metering valves in the depressed position. Parking brakes were not to be applied until drums cooled.

D) Pump Switch

Description: Toggle switch.

Location: Flight engineer's switch panel.

Function: For emergency of service override of the regulator.

E) Hand Pump

Description: Handle.

Location: Left of co-pilots seat, on floor.

Function: Provided pressure for setting the parking brakes.

F) Filler Valve Emergency System

Description: Two-way hydraulic valve.

Location: Flight engineer's instrument panel.

Function: Charge the emergency hydraulic accumulator. The valve was normally closed when the emergency pressure system was at its maximum.

G) Service Shut Off Valve

Description: Hand-operated screw-type valve.

Location: On hydraulic panel under the pilot's compartment floor

Function: Drain the service system pressure back to the supply tank.

Landing Gear Controls

A) Landing gear switch.

Description: Toggle switch.

Location: Aisle stand.

Function: Provided control of regular nose gear and landing gear (including nacelle doors) retracting motors.

B) Landing Gear Power Transfer Switch

Description: Toggle switch.

Location: Airplane commander's control stand.

Function: Disconnected the power from the normal landing gear operators and connected the emergency power bus to the main power system, should operation of the emergency landing gear, bomb door or wing flap motors with normal power be needed.

C) Emergency Landing Gear Switch and Door Release Handle

Description: T-type pull handle and toggle switch.

Location: Airplane commander's control stand (aft).

Function: Open nacelle wheel doors by mechanically releasing the screw and allowing the doors to fall open. Initial travel of the handle releases the nacelle doors. Subsequent travel engages a momentary switch that operated to lower out successively: the nose gear, left main landing gear and right main landing gear.

D) Warning Reset Buttons

Description: Four, plunger-type buttons.

Location: Co-pilot's control stand to the rear of the throttle levers.

Function: Shuts off the warning horn that sounded when the throttle was closed while the landing gear was retracted. Depressing the button for the throttle in question disengaged a spacer and allowed the switch to open the horn circuit.

Cabin Heating and Supercharger Controls

A) Cabin Airflow Valve Control Levers

Description: Two Levers.

Location: Flight engineer's control stand.

Function: Shut off the ventilating ducts by holding the vent check valves, located in the ventilating duct at the inlet to the communication tunnel, in the CLOSED position.

B) Cabin Heating Switches

Description: Two toggle switches.

Location: Flight engineer's control stand.

Function: Shut off ventilating ducts by holding vent check valves that were located in the ventilating duct at the inlet to the communicating tunnel, in the CLOSED position.

C) Manual Pressure Relief Valve

Description: Adjustable spring-loaded valve.

Location: Under the outboard edge of the flight engineer's seat.

Function: Allowed the flight engineer to manually control the cabin pressure regulators or to release the cabin pressure at high altitudes when combat conditions were anticipated.

D) Emergency Pressure Release Handles

Description: Two, T-type pull handles.

Location: One on the airplane commander's control stand and the other on the right sidewall of the rear pressurized compartment, near the forward bulkhead.

Function: Permitted the rapid escape of air from the pressurized cabin and allowed the pressure bulkhead doors to be opened in an emergency.

E) Pressure Warning Shutoff Switch

Description: Single throw toggle switch.

Location: Flight engineer's auxiliary switch panel.

Function: Disconnected the cabin warning horn should operation above 12,000ft cabin altitude be contemplated.

Vacuum System Controls

A) Vacuum Selector Valve

Description: Lever handle.

Location: Flight engineer's control stand.

Function: Permitted the selection of either the right of left inboard engine vacuum pump to provide suction for operating the gyro instruments.

1. Altimeter.
2. Gyro Flux Gate Compass Master Indicator.
3. Air-Speed Indicator.
4. Clock.

Navigator's Instrument Panel (USAF)

B) Emergency Shut Off Valve

Description: Two position, manually operated valve.

Location: Front of navigator's cabinet.

Function: Isolated the de-icing system and camera vacuum lines from the vacuum system in case of damage to the de-icer boots or lines.

C) Camera Vacuum Shut Off Valve (Master)

Description: Two position, manually operated valve.

Location: Camera panel (station 834).

Function: Isolated the camera vacuum system from the main vacuum system. This shut off valve had to be OPEN at all times to supply vacuum to the de-icers. Otherwise there was a danger that the de-icers could flutter due to the air flow over the leading wing edges.

D) Camera Shut Off Valve (Individual)

Description: Three, two position manually operated valves.

Location: Camera panel (station 834).

Function: Shut off the vacuum in each of the three individual camera vacuum lines.

Bomb Controls

A) Release Control

Description: Manually operated lever.

Location: Left of bombardier's seat.

Function: Allowed choice of the positions, LOCK, SELECTIVE, and SALVO, in controlling the individual bomb release units. A pin on the bomb door control lever projected in the path of the bomb release lever and prevented salvo release of the bombs with the door closed. Conversely, the doors could not be closed while there was any possibility of bombs being dropped.

B) Release Switch

Description: Momentary contact switch. A hinged guard on the switch panel provided protection against accidental release.

Location: Bombardier's instrument panel.

Function: Initiate the electrical release of the bombs.

C) Interval Release

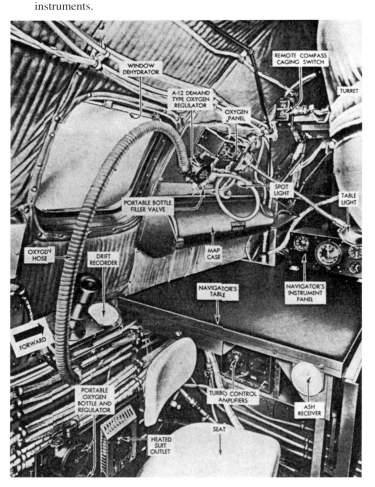

Navigator's Station (USAF)

Description: Control Box.

Location: Bombardier's instrument panel.

Function: Provided pulses for either selective or train release of the bombs. Controls were provided to vary the number and interval of bombs in a train.

D) Emergency Release

1) Bombardier's Release and Rewind Handle

Description: Hand wheel.

Location: Left of bombardier's seat.

Function: Caused the emergency release of the bombs and rewind the emergency system after release had been accomplished.

Operation: Two and a half turns clockwise are necessary to open the doors and release the all bombs. The same number of turns in the opposite direction completely rewinds the system.

2) Bomb Release Pull Handles

Description: Two, T-type cable pull handles.

Location: On the left aft end of the airplane commander's control stand and the other end at the forward bulkhead in the rear pressurized compartment on the left side near the communication tunnel.

Function: Caused the emergency release of all bombs.

Operation: Approximately 30in of travel was necessary to complete the release. By means of cables the pull handle operated the bomb coordinating unit that was a mechanism designed to transmit the first part of the pull to the bomb door emergency releases. Subsequent cable pull was directed to the bomb release levers that dropped the bombs unarmed. A safeguard against any bombs being released before the doors were fully opened was provided by an interlock system that locked the release levers until the doors reached their open position.

E) Group Selector Switches

Description: Four toggle switches

Location: Bombardier's instrument panels.

Function: Allowed the bombardier to remove any or all bomb groups from the normal (layer) release sequence.

F) Tank Safety Switch

Description: Two toggle switches.

Location: One switch on front left third of each bomb bay, above the catwalk.

Function: Opened the electrical release circuits as a safety feature when there were bomb bay tanks installed.

G) Bomb Bay Door Control Switch

Description: Manually operated lever.

Location: Bombardier's control stand.

Function: Provided for normal extension and retraction of the bomb bay doors. There was a portable motor for emergency operation of the bomb bay doors. This motor could be engaged into a screw mechanism in the right hand catwalk and the power receptacles were located adjacent to the motor engaging chuck.

Warning: Before opening or closing the bomb bay doors when the aircraft was on the ground the area under the doors had to be cleared to prevent personnel from becoming caught in or hit by the bomb bay doors.

H) Bomb Signal Switch

Description: Three position, toggle switch.

Location: Bombardier's instrument panels.

Function: Allowed the choice of BRIGHTLY OFF and DIM operation of the bomb formation lamp.

Turret Controls

A) Four Control Boxes

Description: Switch boxes.

Location: At each gunner's station. One control box served both side gunners.

Function: Provided control of power and power breakers. Operated the gun, computers and cameras.

B) Selector Switch Box

Description: Switch box.

Location: On pedestal on upper gunner's seat.

Function: Allowed side gunners to select secondary control.

Radio Controls

A) Liaison Set

1) Receiver

Location: Radio operator's table.

Operation: Direct control.

2) Transmitter

Location: Radio operator's table.

Operation: Direct control. Additional tuning units were stowed under the radio operator's table and in the rear pressurized cabin.

3) Transmitter Key

Location: Radio operator's table aft of the liaison set.

Operation: To key the transmitter when transmitting "CW" or "TONE."

Figure 73—Radio Operator's Station

1. Two of the Seven Transmitter Tuning Units	12. Compass Chart
2. Liaison Dynamotor	13. Inertia Switch (IFF)
3. Liaison Transmitter, BC-375-( )	14. Interphone Jack Box
4. Liaison Receiver, BC-348-H	15. Head-Set Disconnector Cord Plugged in Phones Jack
5. Antenna Transfer Switch	16. Microphone Disconnector Cord Plugged in Mic Jack
6. Antenna Tuning Unit, BC-306-A	17. Antenna Reel Control Box
7. Reading Light and Switch	18. Transmitting Key
8. Command Transmitters	19. Compass Indicator I-82A Mounted Beneath a Shield at This Point
9. Command Receivers	20. Trailing Antenna Fair-lead Control Lever
10. Radio Compass Control Box	21. Microphone Push-to-Talk Switch
11. Extension Trouble Lamp	

Radio Operator Station (USAF)

4) Monitor Switch
Description: Double throw, toggle switch.
Location: Radio compass relay shield located under the liaison radio transmitter.
Function: Allowed simultaneous operation of the liaison receiver and transmitter for test purposes.

5) Antenna Transfer Switch
Description: Handle.
Location: Shield above the radio operator's table.
Function: Allowed choice of antenna operation, using either the right hand wing skin or the trailing antenna.

6) Trailing Antenna Reel Control
Description: Control box.
Location: Radio operator's table.
Function: Provided control of the reel motor. A red signal lamp lit up of the landing gear was lowered while the trailing antenna was extended.

7) Trailing Antenna Fair-Lead Control
Description: Lever.
Location: Under the edge of the radio operator's table.
Function: Angularly retracted or extended the antenna fair-lead by a cable linkage.

B) Command Radio Set
1) Receivers
Description: Three receivers were controlled by a remote control box mounted on the base of the pilot's control stand.
Location: On the cabin sidewall above the radio operator's station.
Function: Interplane or air-to-air communication.

2) Transmitter
Description: Two transmitters were remotely controlled by a control box mounted on the side cabin wall at the pilot's station.
Location: cabin sidewall above the radio operator's station.
Function: Interplane or air-to-air communication.

C) Radio Compass
1) Receiver
Description: A "CW-VOICE" receiver remotely controlled from the control box mounted on the sidewall at the co-pilot's position or from the control box mounted above the radio operator's table.
Location: Upper left section of the forward bomb bay.

D) Interphone
1) Amplifier
Description: Automatic.
Location: Command radio modulator above the radio operator's table.
Function: Amplify interplane communication. The interphone amplifier had no switch and was in operation whenever the power circuits were energized.

2) Jack Boxes
Description: Selector switch knob and volume knob.
Location: At each active station in the pressurized cabins.
Function: Allowed selective reception or transmission by use of headsets and microphones.

3) Microphone Switches
Description: Thumb switches.
Location: All interphone stations had cord-type switches except at the pilot's stations where thumb switches were located on the aileron control wheels, and fire control where the switch was in the piston-shaped grip.
Function: Turned all microphones ON or OFF.

4) Voice-Range Filter Knobs
Description: Knob.
Location: Control boxes on cabin sidewalls beside airplane commander and co-pilot.
Function: Allowed selective reception of either the voice or range signals during their simultaneous transmissions.

5) IFF Radio (SCR 595 or SCR 695)
Description: Control box.
Location: On the pressure bulkhead at the radio operator's station.
Function: Aircraft identification.

6) ARR Radio (SCR 515A)
Description: Control box.
Location: On top of the airplane commander's instrument panel.
Operation: Remote Control was at the airplane commander's station by the means of the control box and the coder switch.

7) RC 103 Radio
Description: Control box.
Location: Oxygen panel at airplane commander's station.
Function: Lateral guidance during landing.

Lighting
A) Lighting
1) Identification Lights
Description: Push button and four toggles.
Location: Aisle stand.
Function: Identification and signaling.

2) Position Light Switches
Description: Two, three position toggle switches.
Location: Aisle stand.
Function: Allowed choice of BRIGHT, OFF and DIM operation of the position lights.

3) Formation Lights Rheostat
Description: Knob.
Location: Aisle stand.
Function: Control illumination of the formation lights.

4) Landing Light Switches
Description: Two, three pronged toggle switches.
Location: Flight engineer's auxiliary switch panel.
Function: Provided control of the retractable landing lights mounted in each wing. The lamps lit automatically when extended and could be extended down to 85-degrees.

5) Landing Gear Spotlight Switch
Description: Toggle switch.
Location: Flight engineer's auxiliary switch panel.
Function: Provided control of the wheel well lights employed to illuminate the landing gear when checking its extended position at night.

6) Fluorescent Lights
Description: Knobs.
Location: Airplane commander's auxiliary panel, co-pilot's auxiliary panel, flight engineer's auxiliary panel and bombardier's instrument panel.
Function: Start and operate fluorescent lights.
Operation: A starter-rheostat controlled each light and was provided with a OFF, DIM, ON and START position. To operate the lights, the knob had to be turned to the START position for about two seconds. The knob snapped to the ON position when it was released. Then the knob could be turned to the DIM position to reduce illumination.

7) Co-pilot's Compass Lamp Rheostat
Description: Knob.
Location: Co-pilot's auxiliary panel.
Function: Varied the illumination of the co-pilot's magnetic compass.

Miscellaneous Controls

A) Battery Switch
Description: Toggle switch.
Location: Flight engineer's switch panel.
Function: Disconnected the battery.

B) Generator Switches
Description: Toggle switches.
Location: Flight engineer's switch panel.
Function: Provided control of the generators through reverse current relays.

C) Generator Selector Switch
Description: Knob.
Location: Flight engineer's switch panel.
Function: Allowed the choice of current and voltage indications for any of the six generators of the main power plant. In addition this switch could select the voltage indication of the auxiliary power unit output.

D) Inverter Selector Switch
Description: Three-position toggle.
Location: Flight engineer's switch panel.
Function: Allowed the choice of either of the inverters as a power source of A.C. power.

E) Emergency Power Transfer Switch
Description: Two-position toggle.
Location: Battery solenoid shield near the auxiliary power unit.
Function: Transferred the battery and auxiliary power to the emergency power bus for emergency operation of the landing gear, wing flaps and bomb bay doors.

F) Pitot Heat Switch
Description: Toggle switch.
Location: Flight engineer's switch panel.
Function: Provided control of pitot tube heaters.

G) Surface De-icer Switch
Description: Toggle.
Location: Flight engineer's switch panel.
Function: Closed the air unloading valves and actuated the motor-driven distributor switch for progressive operation of the de-icer boots.

H) Camera Switch
Description: Toggle switch.
Location: Bombardier's instrument panel.
Function: Provided remote control of photographic equipment.

I) Alarm Bell Switch
Description: Toggle switch.
Location: Aisle stand.
Function: Permitted the airplane commander to operate the warning bells in the rear pressurized cabin and tail gunner's compartment.

Warning System

Horns, lights, and bells were used to warn the crew of dangerous conditions, both to them and the aircraft. Horns gave warnings regarding take off conditions and cabin pressure. A warning horn was located on the cabin sidewall above the airplane commander's seat, and warned him and the co-pilot of impending conditions that were dangerous due to the relative position of the wing flaps, throttles, and landing gear. There was a warning horn in each of the pressurized compartments to warn crewmen there if the pressure rose to 12,000ft or over. Warning lights were used to indicate unsafe landing conditions. There were four warning lights, three greens, and one red, on the co-pilot's instrument panel. Each green light illuminated only when its respective gear was extended, and the red light indicated if a gear was not fully extended or retracted. There were two alarm bells, each with one manual control switch located near personnel who were to signal the existence of dangerous situations. One bell was located on the right gunner's panel in the rear pressurized compartment, and the other in the tail gunner's compartment. There were warning systems for oxygen pressure, landing gear hydraulic pressure, turret stowage, and the IFF receiver.

15

Communications System

The communication equipment in the B-29 consisted of:

1) Radio and interphone equipment arranged to provide communication with ground stations and other aircraft.
2) In-plane communication between the crew.
3) Reception of range and marker beacons.
4) Automatic radio direction finding.
5) Recognition of friendly aircraft.

B-29 radios were used for communications, navigation, location, aid in landing, identification, and distress. The aircraft's radio call numbers were located on the pilot's and co-pilot's instrument boards, command radio set mounting, and on each side of the vertical stabilizer.

Each bomber was provided with a master communications wiring diagram and set of radio instruction books. The communications system consisted of 12 circuits that were identified by code letters and wire numbers. Every wire was tagged at both ends with a code number that designated the wire serial number and its particular circuit. The code numbers for each wire were shown in the master wiring diagrams, which illustrated only the

wiring supplied by the aircraft manufacturer, but no modification wiring.

Radio

USAAF radios and radars were originally identified with the prefix SCR (Signal Corps Radio), followed by a number designation. In 1942 a joint Army-Navy designation was adopted with the prefix AN, followed by a three letter classification and a number for each different design in that class (i.e. AN/APQ-7). In the three letter series the first letter "A" related to where the equipment was installed (A for aircraft), the second letter related to the type of equipment (I = Interphone, P = Radar, R = Radio, and S = Special), and the third letter denoted the purpose of the equipment (A = Assemblies or auxiliary equipment, B = Bombing, C = Communications, D = Direction finding, G = Fire Control, N = Navigation, Q = Special, S = Detecting Ranging or Bearing Indicating, T = Transmitting, W = Controlling, and X = Indication).

Early B-29 radio reception was a cacophony of interference due to the ignition of the 144 spark plugs, and from all the electrical equipment, motors, and generators on board. Communications engineers worked long

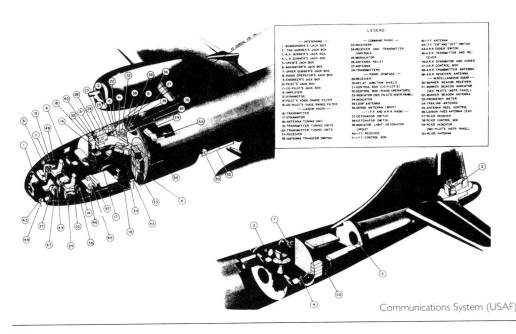

Communications System (USAF)

hours on solving this problem. Generator and motor interference was reduced, and engine ignition and spark plug noises were shielded and limited in range so as not to affect antennas. The placement of electrical wiring was studied to decrease disturbances passed from one bundle of wires to another. However, the answer to most radio noise reduction was through the use of condensers that stored an electrical charge. Depending on the radio equipment experiencing interference, a condenser was placed either at the noise source, or somewhere along the power line to the noise source.

Command Radio Sets (SCR-274-N /SCR-522)
The SCR-274-N

This set was a multi-channel receiving and transmitting set used for short-range voice communication with nearby aircraft or ground stations (within a maximum range of 30mi). The unit usually had three receivers (BC-453, BC-454, and BC–455-A), two transmitters (BC-457 and BC–458-A), an antenna relay switch, dynamotor and modulator, remote control boxes, and an antenna per set. It also had Morse transmission capabilities. The antenna extended from the lead-in insulator at bulkhead 218 to the horizontal tip of the horizontal stabilizer. It was used until mid-1943 in the XB-29, YB-29, and some early production B-29s.

SCR-522-A

The set was based on the Royal Air Force's TR1143 VHF (Very High Frequency) set, and consisted of the combination transmitter (BC-625-A) and receiver (BC-624-A) assembly housed together in a shock-mounted case under the floor of the rear pressurized compartment, a dynamotor unit, and a push button control box. There was a BC-602-A radio control box at the airplane commander's aisle stand that provided complete remote control of the communications function. The PE-94-A dynamotor located next to the transmitter-receiver provided the D.C. voltage for the SCR-522 and control circuits. The VHF antenna made up the rear support mast for the radio compass antenna.

The SCR-522 VHF Command Set provided two-way radio-telephone

SCR-274 Receiver (USAF)

SCR-274 Transmitter (USAF)

SCR-522-A (USAF)

line of sight communication with other B-29s in the formation, to rescue facilities, and to request and receive VHF D/F bearings within 100mi of home base. Its range was limited to line of sight transmission (i.e. at 5,000ft the line of sight is about 90mi, at 10,000ft it increases to 120mi, and at 20,000ft it is 150mi). When long distances were involved relay aircraft could be provided to retransmit messages. Unlike other aircraft radios, VHF did not suffer from fading at altitude, but was susceptible to interference if ignition and other electrical systems were not efficiently suppressed. Amplitude modulated radio frequencies operated on one of four preset crystal-controlled channels in the 100-156Mc range. Both transmitter and receiver were simultaneously switched to any one of the four channels by pushing the appropriate channel selector. Only voice communications were available, but interphone communication was possible between two or more stations. The use of the VHF channels was:

Channel "Nan" (B-134.10Mcs): Fighter-Bomber common channel that was used for any homing other than assembly at rally point and air-sea rescue.

Channel "Queen" (C-140.58Mcs): Air-Sea rescue communication and homing, if submarines or Dumbos gave homing other than the rally point.

Channel "Item" (C-127.68Mcs): Used as homing channel only between navigational B-29s and fighters.

Liaison Radio Set (AN/ART-13 transmitter and BC-348 receiver)
The Liaison Radio consisted of an AN/ART-13 transmitter and BC-348 receiver and antenna equipment. The set was controlled locally by the radio operator, but in later bombers could be remotely controlled from a control box at the co-pilot's position.

Liaison Transmitter (AN/ART-13)
This transmitter allowed automatic shifting of transmission frequencies from remote or local positions. Main components of the set were the transmitter, dynamotor, control unit, and a changeover switch. The liaison transmitter was located on the forward compartment right hand sidewall next to the radio operator's table. It had a frequency range of 200 to 500 kilocycles and 1,500 to 12,000Kcs that was covered by six interchangeable tuning units stored; two under the radio operator's table and four aft of the left

Receiver BC-348 (USAF)

gunner's armor plate. There were 11 preset frequencies, 10 in the 2,000Kc to 18,000Kc ranges, and one in the 200 to 1,500Kc ranges. A chart with the dial settings for desired frequencies was placed on the front of each tuning unit. The calibration of the frequency dial settings was close, but the exact transmission frequency had to be set by monitoring the incoming frequency with the receiver MONITOR switch. When the monitor switch was NORMAL the receiver was inactive, and then the transmitter could operate.

Liaison Receiver (BC-348)
The receiver was an eight tube, six band, superheterdyne set that was located on the radio operator's table.

Antennas
The liaison radio had fixed and trailing antennae, and either could be selected by using an antenna transfer switch on the cabin bulkhead above the radio operator. The fixed antenna extended from top of the vertical fin to the top of the fuselage just behind bulkhead 218. The trailing antenna was 250ft long, and was wound by a motor-driven reel through an insulated fair-lead located in the aft section of the forward bomb bay on the right hand catwalk. The RL-42 reel motor had a control lever that was located on the leg of the radio operator's table. A cable operated counter denoted the length of cable unreeled. A red signal light at the radio operator's station indicated that the landing gear was being lowered before the antenna was reeled in.

Interphone (RC-36 redesignated as the AN/AIC-2 in 1944)
The B-29 was so large and segmented by pressurized cabins that the interphone played an important role in the crew's combat efficiency. The interphone system provided communication between the crew at 14 stations throughout the airplane. In addition, the interphone allowed crewmen limited use of the radio facilities. The interphone equipment included a dynamotor, amplifier, filters, jackboxes, throat microphones, headsets, and extension cords. The interphone BC-1366 jack boxes were provided for the pilot, co-pilot, bombardier, flight engineer, navigator, radio operator, four gunners, and one relief crew. The jack box contained a microphone and earphone jacks, a volume control knob, and a five-position selector knob.

T-47/ART-13 Transmitter (USAF)

required that the speaker use a loud voice, but less than shouting. The speaker was to speak more slowly and precisely than normal. Because the interphone and its continued sequences of messages did not involve mistaken identity, the call up and sign off procedures were less rigid than with the R/T message. The use of procedure words and phrases that had clear and uniform meanings were to be used. For example, a few standard words in interphone communications were: "acknowledge," "roger," "over," "out," "request," "standby," "wilco," etc. Routine interphone phrases were "Request ETA," "Fighters at 10 o'clock," "Request ground speed (or air speed)," etc.

Ground Communications Facilities Available to the B-29
Air-Ground Station: Each Wing maintained an air-ground station under the Army Airways Communications System (AACS), which was the normal ground contact. These stations monitored all the strike frequencies and listened to every transmission. The air-ground stations and the Operations Control Officer coordinated all information received on the Bomber Command air-ground frequencies. They relayed important messages, such as distress calls to the Bomber Command Controller, for relay back to the Wing. Bomber Command frequencies, call signals, and all information regarding air-ground and air-air facilities along a particular route were given at the briefing. This information was listed in the SOI (Signal Operation Instruction, also known as a "flimsy"), and was to be thoroughly understood by the radio operator, and taken on board the bomber during the mission.

HF/DF Stations: Each base had HF/DF stations that were able to give a bearing within one minute. Bearings could be requested up to 150mi out by SCR-522 radio but were affected by the weather, especially atmospheric static.

VHF/DF Stations: Were able to give bearings within 100mi of home base.

Homers and ranges: The homer was a medium frequency transmitter that emitted a continuous coded signal in a 360 degree radius, and was picked up by a radio compass. It was the most common air-navigational radio device. The radio range was a normal four quadrant coded homing device.

OWI Station: These were continuously operating 50,000watt broadcasting stations that beamed signals from home base (Saipan) toward the Japan.

Radar Beacon (AN/CPT-6): Permitted an accurate fix on the bomber's position with its radar set as far as 150mi from base.

SUPRAD: A control station of the Pacific D/F Net that furnished the bomber with a D/F fix (latitude and longitude. It was reserved only for aircraft lost or in distress).

Early Warning Radar (MEW): Was a powerful ground station on Saipan that was able to pick up an aircraft from 150 to 200mi north of Saipan.

Emergency Radio Equipment
The SCR-578 was the famous "Gibson Girl," a hand-cranked transmitter used on life rafts that is discussed in detail in the aircraft the life raft section.

Interphone Jack Box RC-36 (redesignated as the AN/AIC-2 in 1944) (Author/Pima)

There were procedures for the use of the types of interphone equipment used:

a) Hand-held microphone was to be held touching the lips
b) Throat Microphone was to be worn snugly against the neck slightly above the prominence of the Adam's Apple with the words spoken distinctly in a normal tone.
c) Headset was to be worn with the headband spread as far apart as possible, and pressed firmly over the ears to insure the best possible seal.

The Type T-30 throat microphone was a vibration receptive carbon-type microphone that was activated by mechanical vibrations from the throat area during speech. A brown elastic strap with a snap at the end held the vibration-receiving unit in place against the Adam's Apple. A suffix at the end of the T-30 designation (i.e. T-30-Q) denoted the manufacturer: Q by Western Electric; R by Kellogg; S by Universal Microphone Company; and V by Shure Brothers. The T-30 throat microphone was furnished at all positions. "Push-to-talk" microphone switches were located on the aileron control wheels for the airplane commander and co-pilot, and in the ring sight of the top gunner. All other stations had the standard cord microphone push-to-talk switches that were located on the CD-508 extension cords to allow freedom of movement.

The HS-38 headset was the standard AAF set used in the war. It consisted of two adjustable brown leather-covered wire headbands to which the Type ANB-H-1 receivers were attached. The earphones were padded with black or brown sponge rubber cushions to reduce outside noise interference. The twisted connecting cord ended in a red plastic PL-354 jack.

Interphone procedure and discipline varied from crew to crew, but was generally based on R/T procedure, and the airplane commander was responsible for proper interphone discipline. Interphone communication

16

Electrical System

There are five methods that can be used to power the equipment of an aircraft ranging from the control surfaces, to bomb bays, to landing gear, to the superchargers, and so on. The methods are mechanical, pneumatic, hydraulic, and electrical, and combinations of the four. Combat experience, and the knowledge Boeing gained in developing the B-17, demonstrated that electrical wiring was more efficient, was less susceptible to combat damage, and was easier to install and maintain.

The B-29 was virtually an "all electric" aircraft, with 129 electric motors, 26 motor generators, seven generators, and an auxiliary engine, all connected by over three miles of wiring; all of which were effectively responsible for operating the aircraft. The motors were energized by a low voltage, 28.5-volt D.C. system run by six engine-driven P-2 generators connected in parallel rated at 300 amperes each at 5,000 to 10,000rpm, and turning at 2.8 times the engine crankshaft speed and supplying 1,800 amps. Two generators were installed on outboard engines #1 and #4, while single

generators were fitted on inboard engines #2 and #3, and all were driven by gears and shafts by the main engines. The main engines had to be turning at least 1,375rpms for the generators to put out their rated current. Two inverters converted the 28-volt direct current to 26-volt and 115-volt, 400-cycle alternating current.

Generators

The main electrical supply consisted of two 200 amp, 28-30 volt, engine-driven, direct current type P-2 generators on the outboard engine, and two 300 amp, 28-30 volt, engine-driven direct current type R-1 generators on the inboard engines. These generators were cooled by an "air blast" tube connected to the carburetor air inlet duct, and were regulated for both voltage and equal load. A two-speed generator overdrive was built into the generators on the two outboard nacelles in order to maintain correct engine driven generator speed over a wide range of engine speeds. It was mounted

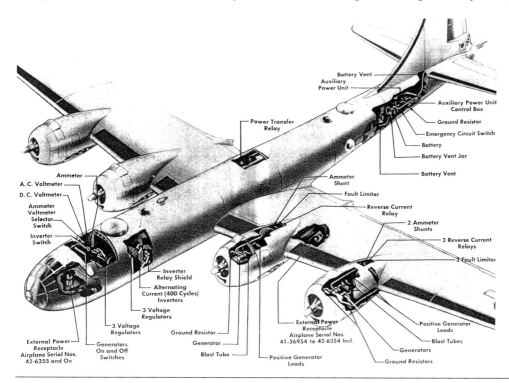

A-C and D-C Power Supply Diagram. (USAF)

between the pad and the generator. The overdrive had two gear ratios, and operated continuously to maintain the generator speed within its required limits while the engine ignition switch was on. When the engine ignition switch was off the power to the overdrive unit was also cut off.

D.C. Power (Direct Current)

D.C. power was a 24-volt single wire, ground return system provided by six 200 ampere, type P-2 engine-driven generators that supplied current to the distribution system. The generators were located one on each of the inboard engines, and two each on the outboard engines. They were cooled by forced air, and regulated for both voltage and equal load. There was an overdrive feature built into one generator drive of each engine that allowed the generator to produce full voltage when the engines operated at reduced rpm. Additional D.C. power was supplied by a type G-1, 34 ampere-hour, 24-volt battery that was placed near the APU, aft of the station 834 bulkhead. There were control switches for the generators and battery at the flight engineer's station. There was a 200amp, gasoline engine driven auxiliary power unit (APU) located aft of the battery. The auxiliary unit supplied power during starting, take off, and landing. In an emergency auxiliary motor and battery power could be transferred for emergency operation of the bomb bay doors, wing flaps, and landing gear. A third source of D.C. current was external power supplied by a portable generator through a standard three prong power receptacle located aft wall of the No.2 nacelle wheel well. When using the external power source, the battery and ignition switched had to be OFF.

A.C. Power (Alternating Current)

Two 750 V.A. inverters mounted on the navigator's cabinet supplied 400-cycle single phase, 26-volt alternating current for Autosyn instruments, and 115-volt, single phase alternating current for the radio compass, gyro flux gate compass, and the electric turbosupercharger control. The flight engineer could choose which inverter to be used by a switch on his panel.

Fuses

There were 17 fuse panels throughout the aircraft, and an additional fuse panel in radar-equipped aircraft. There was a list of fuse types and locations placed on the back of the co-pilot's armor plate, and another on the back of the CFC gunner's seat. Only five panels were accessible at any time: two flight engineer panels; a bombardier panel; the aisle stand fuse shield; and the turret junction shield. The four nacelle solenoid panels were inaccessible in flight, and the remaining eight were inaccessible in pressurized flight. Replacement fuses were placed inside or on the side of its fuse shield cover.

Electric Motors

The majority of the 129 motors were of the split field, reversing type with operating limits controlled by limit switches. Control of the motor operated equipment was generally in combination with position indicators or limit lights, and localized on the fight engineer's switch panels and the aisle stand.

Auxiliary Power Unit (APU)

When the main engines were not running, the Auxiliary Power Unit (called the APU, or "putt putt") was put in use for starting the engines, and for emergency power. It was located in the unpressurized port side of the aft fuselage opposite the rear entrance door. The 2-cylinder, 4-cycle, 7hp APU was either a horizontally opposed Lawrence Model 20A, or an Andover or Fairchild 90-degree V-type air-cooled gasoline engine. It was a permanent installation, and had its own cooling system, ignition system, and fuel and oil supplies. It was used separately, or in parallel with the normal electrical system from sea level to 10,000ft. The APU drove a 200 amp, 28.5-volt P-2 generator that fed a single 34-ampere/hour 24-volt battery, located forward of the putt putt. Starting the B-29 engines required that the putt putt be started to operate the P-2 generator, which supplied electrical power to operate the electric starter that started the engine. Once the bomber was in the air the putt putt was turned off, because the other six generators were being turned by the engines to supply electrical power. Before landing the putt putt was again started, and then turned off when the bomber reached its revetment.

Lighting

Exterior Lighting

Position Lights: As was the AAF standard, the B-29 was equipped with the Type A-9 red (forward port wing tip), Type A-9 green (forward starboard

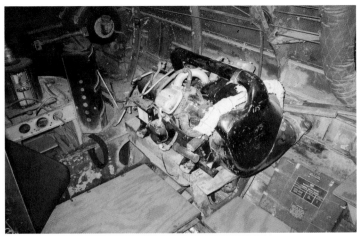

When the main engines were not running the Auxiliary Power Unit (called the APU or "putt putt") located in the unpressurized port side of the aft fuselage opposite the rear entrance door was put in use. The 2-cylinder, 4-cycle, 7hp APU was either a horizontally opposed Lawrence Model 20A or an Andover or Fairchild 90-degree V-type air-cooled gasoline engine. (Author/Pima)

wing tip), and Type D-1 white (below tail) position lights. The lights on the wing tips were contained in a transparent colored Plexiglas housing, and were controlled by a switch and fixed resistor on the pilot's aisle stand. The B-9A toggle switch gave choices of BRIGHT, OFF, and DIM. The white taillight had similar but separate provisions.

Recognition Lights: There were four recognition lights. The Type E-1 white recognition light was located on top centerline of the fuselage between the life raft hatches (at leading edge of wing). Three Type E-2 (fore to aft in sequence about two feet apart: red, green and amber) lights were located under the centerline of the lower fuselage forward of the bomb bay. These lamps could be set for any of several combinations by means of individual KEY-OFF-STEADY switches on the aisle stand. Lights positioned to KEY could be keyed simultaneously by a push button key switch installed next to the recognition switches.

Formation Lights: There were nine Type C-1 blue formation lights with T-3-1/4 3-candle power bulbs. Two lights were located on each inboard upper wing surface, one light on each outboard upper wing surface, and three lights were equally spaced on the centerline of the upper surface of the fuselage. A rheostat on the aisle stand with an OFF position controlled these lights.

Bomb Release Light: During mass or pattern bombing a bomb release formation light, located on top of the fairing above the tail gunner's window,

was used to signal bombers following in the formation that bombs were being dropped.

Landing Lights: The Type B-3A electrically operated; retractable landing gear light was mounted flush with the lower wing surface on the inboard end of each outboard wing. The eight-inch diameter all-glass 28-volt; 600-watt sealed beam was controlled by a reversible electric motor. Each lamp would light automatically when it was extended, and was controlled by a switch on the airplane commander's aisle stand.

Wheel Well Spotlights: Three small Grimes-type A2301 spotlights lit the landing gear at night when it was in the extended position. A switch on the flight engineer's auxiliary panel controlled them.

Night flares: For use with the drift meter during night flights.

Interior Lighting
Table Lights: The Type A-6 flexible gooseneck or Type A-11 three arm adjustable table lamp lit the bombardier, navigator, and radio operator's station tables.

Fluorescent Lamps: Type C-5 fluorescent lights were fitted with fluorescent ultraviolet bulbs and adjustable filters to vary or eliminate the amount of light that was projected on the airplane commander, co-pilot, bombardier, and flight engineer's instrument panels. Self-illuminating calibrations on the instruments fluoresced under ultraviolet light. These lights were controlled by a starter-rheostat that was provided with an OFF, DIM, ON, and START position. To operate the lights, the knob had to be turned to the START position for about two seconds. When it was released the knob snapped to the ON position, after which it could be turned to the DIM position to reduce illumination.

Cockpit Lights (Spotlights): The Type C-4 cockpit lights were small adjustable spotlights that supplemented the fluorescent lamps. They were contained in a cylindrical housing containing a 24-volt, T-3-1/4 bulb with a bayonet base. The light could be adjusted for either spotlight or floodlight effect by sliding the outer lens barrel. The C-4s were furnished for the tail gunner, upper gunner, the two waist gunners, radio operator, navigator, co-pilot, and airplane commander to provide optional instrument illumination.

Extension Lights: The Type B-7 extension light was provided with six feet of flexible cord on a self-winding reel, and an OFF-ON switch for a 3-candle power, 28-volt T-4-1/2 bulb. The housing was fixed at station 900 in the rear unpressurized compartment for operating the APU putt putt and cameras.

Dome Lights: Type A-9 and the Type A-7.
The A-9 was a reflector type lamp without a lens or cover glass. It used a 21-candle power, 28-volt, S-8 silver tip bulb with a single contact bayonet base. These lights were provided throughout the aircraft for general lighting: three in the forward pressurized compartment; two in the rear pressurized compartment; and three in the rear unpressurized compartment. The three dome lights in the forward, and one in the rear pressurized cabins were controlled by ON-OFF toggle switches that were integral with the

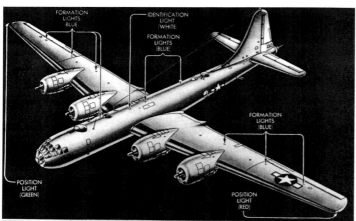
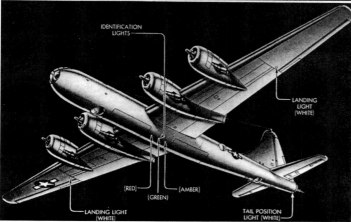

B-29 Exterior Lighting (USAF)

lights. The dome light on the face of the aft wall of the rear pressurized compartment close to the bulkhead was turned ON or OFF from either side of the bulkhead. Dome lights in the unpressurized rear section were operated either by a switch accessible by the tail gunner, or a switch near the rear entrance door.

The A-7 was a reflector, vapor-proof light whose socket was hermetically sealed, and its cover glass lens was airtight. It used a 21-candle power, 28-volt, S-8 clear bulb with a single contact bayonet base. This sealed light was used in the bomb bay, where there could be gasoline vapor from the bomb bay fuel tanks that could be ignited. There were four lights in each bomb bay, with a type B-5A switch for the forward bomb bay located on the aft leg of the radio operator's table, and another B-5A switch located on the aft side of the rear pressure bulkhead, near the door.

Compass Light: The co-pilot's magnetic compass was located on his auxiliary panel, and was illuminated separately by a small self-contained lamp whose brightness was controlled by a lamp rheostat located on the co-pilot's instrument panel.

Aldis Lamps: The Type C-3A Aldis Lamp was a portable signal lamp equipped with interchangeable filters, and was stowed on the top shelf behind the airplane commander's seat. It was plugged into the 24-volt receptacle located on any electric flying suit outlet. An Aldis lamp with a clear or white lens (colored lenses were too translucent to permit enough light transmission) was used for fast and easy communications between aircraft during radio silence. There was a trigger ON-OFF switch on the lamp to aid in signaling a sequence of light flashes. The lamp had to be held close to the sighting blister, and be pointed directly at the receiving aircraft, with the position of the sun being considered. A special set of slow, deliberate flashes was devised that used letters and single letters called "prosigns" to transmit messages. The sender received the prosign "K" for "Go ahead" before sending, and after each word sent waited for the receiver to send the prosign "R" for "I understand."

Wiring
For years electrical engineers bundled electrical wires in conduits of flexible metal tubing, but after the B-17 returned from battle it was found that when a conduit was struck by flak the whole conduit, and its many wires were torn away, requiring tedious, time consuming repair. It was found that wiring taped together in a "rope" when hit by flak had only the wires severed that were hit, and were much easier to repair.

Electrical wires were given distinctive colors on their outside insulation, and each wire in a circuit was stamped with a code number at its end for easier identification. But with the great number of bundled wires strung over long distances, many were the same colors, so the AAF ordered that individual wires be coded every six inches. But this could not be economically done by hand, and Chrysler modified a foil-stamping machine to automatically code the wires.

Emergency Electrical System
Two electrical buses or wiring systems were at hand: a normal bus and an emergency bus. The landing gear transfer switch and the bus selector switch (on the battery solenoid shield) allowed either power source—the engine-

driven generators or the APU and/or the battery—with either the normal bus or the emergency bus. Both could be used in combination.

The nose gear and main gear were provided with both normal and emergency motors. A portable motor could be used for the emergency operation of the flaps or bomb bay doors. The tailskid could only be operated by the normal electrical system, as it had no emergency motor.

C-1 Autopilot
The Minneapolis Honeywell C-1 Autopilot was an "electromechanical robot" that automatically flew the bomber in straight and level flight, or could maneuver it in response to fingertip controls by the airplane commander or navigator. The autopilot was powered by the rotary inverter, which was a motor generator unit that converted current from the aircraft's battery into 105-cycle A.C.

The autopilot control panel afforded the airplane commander with fingertip control, through which he could easily engage or disengage the system, adjust the sharpness or speed of its response to flight deviations, or trim the system for various weight and flight conditions. It consisted of various separate units interconnected electrically to operate as a system. The directional panel contained two electrical devices; the banking pot and rudder pick up pot, which signaled to the aileron and rudder section of the amplifier whenever the directional panel was activated by a change in course. The signals were amplified and converted by magnetic switches or relays into electrical impulses that caused the aileron and rudder servo units to operate the ailerons and rudder of the aircraft in the correct direction and amount to turn the aircraft back to its original heading.

Likewise, if the aircraft's nose dropped the vertical flight gyro detected the vertical deviation and operated the elevator pick up pot, which sent an electrical signal to the elevator section of the amplifier. This signal was amplified and relayed by electrical impulses to the elevator servo unit, which raised the elevators the correct amount to bring the aircraft back to level flight.

If a wing dropped considerably, the vertical gyro operated the aileron pick up pot, the skid pot, and the up-elevator pot. The signals from the operation of these units were transmitted to their respective aileron, rudder, and elevator sections of the amplifier. The electrical impulses to the aileron, rudder, and elevator servo units caused each of these units to operate its respective control surface just enough to bank and turn the aircraft back to level flight.

If a sudden cross wind turned the aircraft from its heading, the gyro-operated directional stabilizer detected the divergence and moved the directional panel to one side or the other, depending on the direction of the divergence.

If the airplane commander wanted to make a turn, he set the turn control knob to the degree of bank and in the direction of intended turn. His control command sent signals through the aileron and rudder sections of the amplifier to the aileron and rudder servo units, which operated the ailerons and rudder correctly to achieve a completely coordinated turn without slipping or skidding. As the aircraft banked the vertical flight gyro operated the aileron, skin and up-elevator pots. The signals from the aileron and skid pots canceled the signals to the aileron and rudder servo units, and streamlined these controls during the turn. The up-elevator pot sent signals that caused the elevators to raise just enough to maintain altitude. When the intended turn was finished the airplane commander turned the turn control back to 0, and the aircraft leveled off on its new course. The directional arm lock on the stabilizer was energized by a switch in the turn control, and prevented the stabilizer from interfering with the turn by carrying out its normal direction correcting function.

Engaging the Autopilot

Before take off the turn control was to be centered, and all switches on the control panel were to be OFF. When the temperature was between 10°F and 32°F, the autopilot needed to run up for 30 minutes before engaging. It could be warmed up on the ground prior to take off for immediate use after take off by turning on the master switch during engine run up. The autopilot had to be OFF during take off.

After take off the master switch was turned ON. After 10 minutes the pilot direction indicator (PDI) switch was turned ON, and the aircraft was trimmed for level flight at cruising speed. The PDI was a remote indicating device operated by the PDI pot, and when the autopilot was used the PDI indicated to the airplane commander when the system and aircraft were correctly trimmed. When engaging the autopilot, the aileron telltale lights were put out with the aileron centering knob, and then the aileron engaging switch was tripped. Once the ailerons were engaged on the autopilot, with the PDI centered, the autopilot could make aileron corrections automatically. The bombardier then disengaged the autopilot clutch, recentered the PDI, and locked it in place. The PDI remained locked and centered until the airplane commander had completed the rudder engaging procedure. The rudder telltale lights were put out with the rudder centering knob, and the rudder engaging switch was tripped. When the rudder was engaged the autopilot clutch was re-engaged, and the PDI lock released. The same procedure was then repeated for the elevator rudder. The final autopilot trim corrections were made, and if necessary, the centering knobs were used to level the wings and center the PDI.

In-flight Adjustments and Operation

After the C-1 was operating, the airplane commander was to scrupulously analyze the action of the aircraft to be certain that all adjustments had been made correctly for smooth and precise flight control. When the two telltale lights in any axis were out it indicated that the autopilot was ready for engaging in that axis.

Before engaging, each centering knob was to adjust the autopilot control reference point to the straight and level flight position of the corresponding control surface. After engaging, the centering knobs were used to make small attitude adjustments.

The sensitivity control was comparable to the human pilot's reaction time. When the sensitivity was set high the autopilot responded quickly to effect a correction for even the slightest deviation. If the sensitivity was set low, the flight deviations had to be relatively great before the autopilot made any corrections. There were three sensitivity increase knobs: one each for the aileron, the rudder and elevator, that were turned clockwise to increase and counterclockwise to decrease sensitivity.

The ratio control was the amount of control surface movement exercised by the autopilot when correcting a given deviation. The ratio control directed the speed of the aircraft's response to corrective autopilot actions. The correct ratio adjustment depended on airspeed. If the ratio was too high, then the autopilot overcontrolled and the flight corrections were too great. If the ratio was too low then the autopilot undercontrolled, and the flight corrections were too small. The ratio panel resembled the sensitivity panel with three increase knobs, one each for the aileron, rudder, and elevator.

The turn compensation was adjusted by having the bombardier disengage the autopilot clutch and move the engaging knob to the extreme right or extreme left. The aircraft then was to bank 18-degrees, as indicated by the artificial horizon. The recovery from this turn needed to be coordinated. If the PDI returned to center before the wings were level, the rudder ratio needed to be decreased or the aileron ratio increased, depending on the speed of recovery. If the wings were level before the PDI was centered the rudder ratio was to be increased, or the aileron ratio decreased, depending on the speed of recovery.

Bombardier's Autopilot Controls

The autopilot clutch was located on the directional gyro at the bombardier's station, and was used to disengage the directional stabilizer. When the clutch was engaged the pilot, navigator, and bombardiers steered the aircraft, but when it was disengaged, only the bombardier could steer the airplane using his turn control. The bombsight clutch on the directional stabilizer engaged the bombsight and autopilot, allowing the bombardier to steer the airplane by turning the bombsight. When the bombsight clutch was engaged the autopilot clutch was to be disengaged. The bombardier used his turn control knob to turn the airplane when he had control.

The Effect of High Altitude on the Autopilot

At high altitudes of 30,000ft and above there were several factors that affected the autopilot. High altitude affected the normal flight characteristics, and the pilot had to compensate for these changes. The aircraft flew tail low, especially when fully combat loaded. The controls became increasingly soft and the aircraft sluggish. Pilot control errors showed up more slowly and took longer to correct, and could take the aircraft far out of the formation before they were corrected. Low temperatures affected the autopilot, and it had to be properly warmed up and set up as soon after takeoff as practical. While in the climb the autopilot was to be adjusted with the necessary controls on the way up. At high altitudes the insulation of electrical wires lost efficiency and could affect the autopilot, and the generators needed to be checked periodically. The pilot had to know the characteristics of his aircraft under various conditions, be thoroughly familiar with the operation of the autopilot, and anticipate any correction the same as if he were flying the aircraft manually.

17

Navigation Equipment

Gyroscope and Gyro-activated Flight Instruments

A gyroscope was basically a flywheel that revolved so rapidly that its momentum of rotation resisted the change of direction of its axle. The gyro was usually housed in an airtight instrument case, and when used in aircraft instruments was a small heavy wheel (rotor) with its axle supported in a set of rings, and with the rings supported on a frame. The axle, rings, and frame that made up the gyro assembly were mounted with respect to each other, so that the rotor was free to maintain a constant attitude in space.

There were three gyro-activated instruments. The gyro-horizon and the directional gyro indicated what the aircraft was doing in relation to a bar or reference mark that the gyroscope stabilized. The third gyro was the turn indicator, in which the gyro caused the needle to indicate the occurrence of any change of direction or yawing (i.e. the rotation around the vertical axis of the aircraft).

The gyro-horizon provided a direct indication of the attitude of the aircraft. A freely mounted gyroscope rotating in a horizontal plane stabilized the horizon-bar through a linkage system. As the aircraft pitched and rolled, the instrument case and the index plane moved in relation to the horizontal bar. The movements of the index plane in respect to the gyro-stabilized horizon-bar corresponded at all times to what the airplane commander would see if he looked outside the cockpit, and saw the nose and wing positions in relation to the true horizon. This assuming, of course, that the index had been adjusted and the instrument was operating.

The directional gyro provided a directional reference that was stabilized by a freely mounted gyroscope rotating in a vertical plane. The calibration scale, which was a circular band with a compass rose printed on it, was mounted horizontally around the vertical gimbal ring of the gyro assembly. The gyro and the scale maintained their positions as the aircraft turned around the calibrated scale. When the direction as indicated on the calibrated scale was aligned with the direction as indicated by the magnetic compass, the directional gyro provided stabilized indications of headings and changes in headings.

The AN5735-1 turn indicator was the gyro-activated flight instrument, which provided a sensitive indication of changes in horizontal direction (turn) of the aircraft. Its gyro rotor was supported in a horizontal gimbal free to pivot about bearings that were located in the front and rear of the instrument. As the aircraft turned, the rotor processed laterally in proportion to the rate of turn. A linkage system transmitted the action of precession to the turn needle. The position of this turn needle accurately indicated the rate of turn, and with the aircraft in directional balance showed the approximate wing position.

Astrodome

The astrodome was not part of the original B-29, and was scheduled for the 265th production B-29. Once it appeared the navigator found it difficult to "shoot" aft with the astrocompass, and had to get partially into the tunnel to get a reading! It was recommended that the astrodome be moved at least 15in forward.

Astrocompass (*see* navigator)

Magnetic Compass

A standard pilot's compass was positioned at station 30 in the nose, where there was minimal deviation when the gunsight and bombsight gyros were shut off. This compass was used as an auxiliary instrument.

Radio Compass (SCR-269)

The radio compass was used for radio reception, homing, or for taking bearings on a radio transmitting station. The radio compass consisted of:

1) A receiver located in the upper left section of the forward bomb bay.
2) Two control boxes located at the radio operator and co-pilot's stations.
3) CW-VOICE switch located next to the co-pilot's control box.
4) A relay to switch control from one box to another.
5) An automatic loop antenna located on the fuselage above the bomb bay.
6) A retractable whip antenna aft of the forward upper turret.
7) Direction indicators located in the pilot's instrument panel and radio operator's table.

A 400-cycle 115-volt A.C. current from the aircraft's inverters powered the radio compass receiver. It had frequency range of 150 to 1,750Kc, and could be operated using either the loop or whip antenna, or both.

Gyro Flux Gate Compass (GFGC)

The gyro flux gate compass was developed to satisfy a void for an accurate compass in Long-Range navigation. At the navigator's station there were many magnetic components, such as armor plate and electrical circuits, so that there were no desirable locations for a direct-reading magnetic compass. To remedy the problem a remote reading compass with its magnetic component outside the navigator's area was designed. The remote unit was called the transmitter, and the unit used by the navigator was called the master indicator. An auxiliary unit called the repeater indicator was placed at the airplane commander's station and other stations. The GFGC converted the earth's magnetic field into electrical impulses that provided precise directional readings, which could be duplicated on instruments at all desired points in the aircraft. Unlike the magnetic needle the GFGC would not go off its reading in a dive, overshoot in a turn, hang up in rough weather, or become frenzied in the natural magnetism polar regions.

The flux gate consisted of a flux gate transmitter, an amplifier, and master indicator, and was powered by the aircraft's inverter that supplied 26 volt AC. The system provided an accurate direction reading up to 65 degrees with horizontal, and within this angular limitation the readings were accurate because of the electrically-driven gyro, which maintained the operation of the flux gate in a horizontal plane. The master indicator and amplifier were unaffected by local magnetic disturbances, but the transmitter was located in the left wing to remove it from the magnetic materials in the fuselage.

In training manuals the three units of the GFGC were compared to the human brain, heart, and muscles. The transmitter was the brain, the amplifier was the heart, and the master indicator was analogous to the muscles.

The Brain

The main component of the transmitter was a magnetic-sensitive element called the flux gate, which received the direction signal by induction, and transmitted it to the master indicator. The flux gate consisted of three small coils arranged in a triangle, and each coil had a special soft iron core. The coil was made up of a primary (excitation) winding and a secondary wind-

ing, from which a signal was acquired. Each leg of the flux gate coil triangle was positioned at a different angle to the earth's magnetic field, the induced voltage was relative to the angle, and each leg produced a different voltage. When the angular relationship between the flux gate and the earth's magnetic field changed, there was a relative change in the voltages in the three legs of the secondary winding. These voltages were the motivating forces for the GFGC master indicator, which supplied indications of the exact position of the flux gate in relation to the earth's magnetic field. Each coil had a direction sensitive component that could distinguish one direction from another (i.e. east from north, but not north from south). The combination of the three coils could combine their information to give a directional signal.

The Heart

The amplifier supplied different excitation voltages at a frequency to the transmitter and master indicator. It was mounted at the rear of the navigator's table, and a green light indicted that it was operating. There was a rheostat on the left side of the amplifier face for adjusting sensitivity. On long northerly flying missions the rheostat had to be adjusted more frequently to compensate for the increasing magnetic latitudes. The amplifier amplified the autosyn signal, which controlled the master indicator, and served as a junction for the entire compass system. Power for the amplifier was furnished by the aircraft's inverter, and was converted to usable power for other units. The amplifier input was 400-cycle A.C., and various voltages could be used depending upon the available power source.

The Muscle

The master indicator was considered the muscle of the flux gate system, as it provided the mechanical power to drive the pointer on the main instrument dial. It was located on the navigator's panel, and incorporated an adjustment dial, to which the navigator could dial in magnetic variations. The pointer was driven by a cam mechanism that automatically corrected the reading for compass deviation, so that a corrected indication was realized on all headings. The pointer shaft was geared to another small trans-

REMOTE-INDICATING COMPASSES

Remote-indicating compasses consist of a transmitter, a master indicator, and one or more repeater-indicators, located wherever necessary in the airplane. The transmitter is located in a spot in the airplane having very little surrounding magnetic disturbance. In this way, deviation errors are minimized. The indications of the master indicator are transmitted, through an electrical hookup, to all the repeater-indicators, so that their indications are synchronized with those of the master indicator.

121

No caption needed on drawing Remote Compass folder (USAF)

mitting unit in the master indicator that could operate as many as six re-peaters in other locations. The amplifier, master indicator, and repeaters were not affected by local magnetic influences.

The installation of the GFGC was initially very unsuccessful, because excessive vibration in the wing caused chronic shorting of the transmitter. The problem was referred to the builder, Pioneer Instrument Company, who developed a new shock-absorbing mounting bracket that solved the problem.

LORAN (AN/APQ-4)
The B-29 carried the Philco AN/APQ-4 LORAN (LONG RANGE) air-borne navigational equipment to determine the geographic location of the aircraft by picking up LORAN signals from a known position on a grid. The LORAN was relatively simple, and could be used in bad weather until nearing target when the more accurate airborne radar could make a fix. The relatively low frequency, 1.950MHz LORAN consisted of two units that together measured approximately 1ft x 2ft x 2.5ft, and weighed about 80lbs. One unit was the power supply, and the other contained the oscillo-scope display tube, receiver, and timing circuit. The oscilloscope screen

The B-29 carried the Philco AN/APQ-4 LORAN (LOng RANge) airborne long range navigational equipment to determine the geographic location of the aircraft by picking up LORAN signals from a known positions on a grid. (Author/Pima)

was about four inches in diameter, and would display both a stationmaster and associated slave signal. Shore-based transmitters operating in pairs, typically separated by 400mi, sent out pulsed and precisely synchronized radio signals. The receiver identified these signals by their radio frequency and repetition rate, with the time differential between the two signals mea-sured in microseconds. By consulting the LORAN charts for the area, the navigator identified from this pair of stations a line of position that located the aircraft. On these charts there were lines of constant time for every pair of transmitting stations. The operator needed two successive fixes to deter-mine ground speed, drift, and ETA. In February 1945 the navigator could use LORAN out to 800mi (1,000mi maximum) from the Mariana's bases, and when Iwo Jima and Okinawa were captured and stations built there this range was extended to 1,250mi (1,600mi maximum). The LORAN's nighttime range was more than its theoretical daytime range. An experi-enced operator could get a fix in three minutes, and on a 1,400 mile mis-sion from the Marianas to Japan have a minimum error of 28mi. Late war B-29s were equipped with the RCA APN-9, which weighed only 40lbs. By V-J Day there were 75 standard LORAN stations to support the 75,000 airborne and shipborne sets. The Japanese never attempted to jam any of the LORAN systems.

Air Position Indicator (API)
The API provided a constant plot of true heading and true airspeed, espe-cially to provide dead reckoning (DR) while the bomber was in evasive action or undergoing attack. It provided an accurate air plot of true air-speed for the navigator. To plot the dead reckoning position the navigator had to adjust the wind readings from the coordinates indicated on the API. The fluxgate compass was tied into the API on the B-29 to give the true heading to the API computer.

Soon after it was introduced the API was not considered to be much value, as it induced errors into the air speed meter and compass systems, and it was unable to incorporate the air speed calibration correction. Also there was a lack of Technical Orders or other literature on its use, and there were no maintenance personnel or spare parts for the API. The API was never intended for exclusive use for all DR navigation, and a complete and accurate log was to be maintained. However, after the operator used the API for some time he was able to keep the error to less than 3% of the actual distance flown.

IFF Radio Identification Set SCR-695
The SCR-695 IFF (Identification Friend or Foe), operating in conjunction with the fixed stub antenna installed on the lower surface of the fuselage, provided a means of identifying friendly aircraft. It consisted of a BC-958 power control box, BC-965 selector control box, BC-966A radio receiver, and indicator box BO-767. The battery side of the battery solenoid sup-plied power. The transponder, which was a beacon, beamed a coded re-sponse via the antenna when an aircraft came within range of a radar set. Aircraft emitting the proper IFF response were assumed to be friendly, but the reverse was not necessarily true, either because of equipment failure, or simply by not having its set turned on. The operation of the IFF was automatic. The ON-OFF switch was located on top of the pilot's instru-ment panel and in the IFF control box. The on and off of the IFF varied with a particular mission, and was dependent on other operations in progress and the dispersal of the U.S. Pacific Fleet. The SOI (Signal Operation In-struction) flimsies directed the operation of IFF equipment. The IFF used

secret codes that were changed daily. To keep the secret apparatus from falling into enemy hands the set employed a destructor unit that consisted of a destructor "D" plug, two remote push button switches, and a crash switch and indicator. Both destruct switches had to be pushed together to send power to the "D" plug, which was denoted by two red indicator lights at the radio operator's station. There was an automatic crash switch at the radio operator's table that was tripped on impact.

The IFF had several other functions besides the IFF. It enabled home base radio to transmit bearings to the bomber up to 100mi from that base. Generally B-29 radar operators would check the IFF from 500mi out from any friendly base while returning home from a mission. It also enabled submarines to shoot a bearing on the bomber, determine its range, and inform naval radar equipment if the bomber were in an emergency situation.

Marker Beacon (RC-43A)

The marker beacon receiver gave the airplane commander visual indications that the aircraft was flying through the radiation field of a marker beacon transmitter. These transmitters gave the location of radio range stations, and indicated range course intersections, boundaries, and positions that were especially helpful in making an instrument landing approach. The length of the visual indication depended on the type of marker and the altitude of the aircraft. A station marker indication lasted about one minute at 10,000ft with the aircraft flying at 150mph. The marker beacon transmitter locations and keying data were found on the Radio Facility Charts.

The aircraft marker beacon receiver (BC-357-B) was located on a shock mounting on the left sidewall, just forward of the left .50cal machine gun ammunition case. The receiver was fine-tuned to ultra high frequency 75Mc signals. Its purpose was to automatically indicate signals received from instrument landing markers, fan-type and cone of silence markers, and other facilities using 75Mc horizontally polarized radiation. The antenna was mounted below the fuselage between the bomb bays, and was coupled to the receiver by a coaxial transmission line. As the aircraft flew over the conical field of the beacon transmitter an amber indicator light on the pilot's instrument panel flashed in synchronism with the transmitter keying.

Airborne Landing Equipment (SCR-570)

The SCR-570 provided lateral and vertical guidance to the airplane commander during landing operations, and was particularly useful in blind landing operations. It consisted of two radio receivers (the RC-103-A and AN/ARN-5A) that were located in tandem on a shelf behind the pilot's head, and a BC-732-A radio control box at the airplane commander's station. While the two receivers could be operated independently, both were required for landings.

Radar Compass (AN/ARN-7)

The AN/ARN-7, operated by either the co-pilot or radio operator, was located in the forward bomb bay on the left side of the tunnel. It was used for homing on Homers, ranges, or long dashes from rescue facilities. It was also used for bearings and homing on OWI and other high-powered broadcast stations. It was an emergency receiver for 100-1,750Kcs.

Radar Navigation

All operational B-29s were equipped with some type of radar system, and many experienced some problems with the equipment, but throughout the war there were continual improvements in the performance of both the radar equipment and operators. Early airborne radar designers gave little thought to the effect of their antennas on the aerodynamics of the carrying aircraft. Boeing engineers were particularly concerned, as streamlining was the hallmark of their Superfortress design. The first radomes were partially retractable, and decreased the aerodynamics of the bomber. While attending a meeting of the National Defense Research Commission (NDRS) at MIT's Radiation Laboratories, Cambridge, MA, Boeing Engineering Vice-President Wellwood Beall opened his remarks with, "An airplane isn't a Christmas tree to hang decorations on." Beall went on to explain why new, more aerodynamic radar antennas and radomes were needed. Boeing engineers joined MIT engineers to take part in two six-week courses conducted by Dr. Herbert Wheaton. A new, smaller antenna that could be fitted inside a smaller, more aerodynamic radome was developed by Dr. W.M. Cady of MIT, and Drs. Krutter, Sichak, and Van Atta of Bell Labs, who worked with Boeing engineers William Cook, Charles Davis, and Reginald Watney. Five test radome antennas were built at Boeing Seattle #1's Shop #27 using aircraft sheet metal fabrication techniques that proved to be better than the previous Bell Lab designs. The antenna was three feet long and V-shaped, and could fit into a newly developed, smaller radome. The radome had to be carefully designed to allow the uniform emission of microwaves to pass through its surface. MIT, Bell Telephone Laboratories, and Wright Field developed the BTO radar sets that were smaller, and yet more powerful than previous versions. Boeing equipped the B-29 with the improved radar sets, antennas, and radomes in their Denver Modification Center. The radar required another crewman; a radar operator, who was positioned behind the aft top turret in the rear pressurized compartment. To make room for the new man and his equipment the berths were removed.

The various radar unit antennas for the B-29 could easily be installed in the field. The hemispherical "cans," or teardrop-shaped pods (high frequency antennas), could be fitted to the fuselage by simply removing a cover plate, without interfering with the pressurization or cutting through the aluminum skin, and connected to the radar station by coaxial cables.

AN/APQ-13

The AN/APQ-13 was the advanced navigational and bombing radar that the B-29 had to be redesigned around. As a navigational system it gave accurate fixes on the bomber's position when used with radar beacons. Its value in the solution of navigational problems was only as good as the accuracy of the fixes the radar operator obtained with it. This was true whether the operator was using the APQ-13 to determine the wind velocity, to stay on course, or to make briefed axis of attack. The bombing aspect of the APQ-13 is discussed elsewhere.

SCR-718C

The RCA SCR-718C provided the airplane commander with a visual indicator showing the position of his aircraft with respect to the height above the terrain below (from 0 to 40,000ft). A vertical needle indicated the localizer course, while the horizontal needle indicated the glide path course.

The Philco SCR-729 was self-contained airborne radar interrogator system that worked with beacons as an aid to navigation. The set was based on the British *Rebecca* Mk I and its successor the AN/APN-2 was the American version of the *Rebecca* Mk II. (USAF)

The indicator No. I-152A was located above the navigator's table, and the BC-778 radio receiver and transmitter was located at station 5.3, mounted on the fuselage framework above the catwalk. Two AT-4/ARN-1 antennas, one for transmitting and one for receiving, were located under the wing rear spar, with the transmitter located on the starboard side of the fuselage, and the receiver on the port side. It was used to determine the absolute altitude of the bomber for its bombing run and landing approaches, and was coordinated with the drift meter to determine ground speed and track. The 12 or 24-volt receiver was designed to operate at six fixed crystal-controlled frequencies, and when tuned to any one of them the receiver was capable of receiving continuous wave, radio frequency, and amplitude modulated at two frequencies. The type I-101 indicator provided a visual indication to the pilot of his lateral position in respect to the runway. When the receiver was tuned to the 90 to 150-cycle modulation of the field localizer transmitter it was audible in the headset, while the needle on the indicator produced a visual guide. If the aircraft were on course the needle was centered, but the needle deflected either to the blue (90-cycle modulation) or yellow (150-cycle) side of the dial. The modulations were received by a horseshoe shaped antenna that was located on top of the fuselage near the wing. The Weight Reduction Board recommended removing the SCR-718 against the strong objections of nearly every B-29 navigator, and after several were removed the valuable instrument was soon reinstalled.

SCR-729 and AN/APN-22

The Philco SCR-729 was a self-contained airborne radar interrogator system that worked with beacons as an aid to navigation. The unit consisted of paired reception antennas (left and right, mounted on the B-29 nose near the navigator's and flight engineer's positions), a double dipole transmitter/receiver, and a quarter-wave transmission aerial. The unit was used to determine the range and bearing of any aircraft. The transmitter was to broadcast a trigger impulse that activated a transmission from the nearest ground beacon. The beacon signal was received by the two reception aerials, and gave the airplane commander his bearing relative to the beacon. The SCR-729 was based on the British *Rebecca* Mk I, and its successor (the AN/APN-2) was the American version of the *Rebecca* Mk II.

18

Radar Countermeasures (RCM)

It was not until May 1945 that radar countermeasures (RCM) became widely used by the XXIBC against Japanese radar-directed searchlights. Previously RCM had been extensively used in the ETO in a leap-frogging high technology radar race with the Germans. Graduates from the basic officer communications course were selected for training at the RCM School, which required 15 weeks of instruction, and during the war about 500 graduates were assigned to special duty with B-29 units. In the Pacific the Japanese had almost primitive radar warning sets and gun laying radar equipment that were based on U.S. and British radar sets captured early in the war, so the Allies had data available to develop countermeasures. This early 1940s era Japanese radar utilized a narrow band of frequencies that made RCM much less difficult. In late 1944 B-29 RCM was slapdash at best. New radar jamming and signal analysis equipment was placed on "ferret" flights, and operated by specially trained officers called "Ravens." The early rudimentary RCM jamming equipment was installed in the rear unpressurized compartment, where it could not be tuned during flight by the Raven, whose "station" was on the chemical toilet! Initially Ravens

were in short supply, and there were only a few in each bomber formation, but by the end of the war most bombers in each formation carried at least one. The switch to night bombing had individual bombers make separate sorties over the target, and each bomber could become the center of several different enemy radar sets that used a number of different frequencies, and an additional Raven or auxiliary navigator was added to help out.

The small bundles of Chaff used over Europe were ineffective against the Japanese radar frequencies. On 9 January 1945 the XXIBC countered Japanese searchlight radar by using a type of aluminum jamming Chaff called "Rope." The 6in wide by 400ft long strips of foil were dropped by hand when the searchlights were encountered. The long strips floated down behind the bomber, and the searchlight radar homed on them. The only problem with Rope was that there was not enough of it.

Each Bomb Wing (except the 315BW) was assigned four B-29s that carried "barrage" jamming devices. The radar jamming transmitters included the AN/APT-1, AN/APT-2, AN/APQ-2A, AN/APQ-9, and AN/APR-4 *Carpet* systems, which were mounted on a rack just aft of the left gunner's

These jamming B-29s were called "porcupines" due to the abundance of antennas protruding over the fuselage or "Guardian Angels" due to their purpose. Fortunately, the installation of these antennas in the field was easy and did not interfere with the clean aerodynamics of the aircraft. (USAF)

station. The radar operator and auxiliary navigator operated the devices in the rear pressurized compartment. The transmitters sent radio "hash" over three different frequency bands. Each transmitter was pre-tuned on the ground to a frequency corresponding to the enemy radar. For example, one transmitter was tuned somewhere between 480 and 700Mc, where it would transmit "hash" over a band of frequencies two to three Mc wide. These jamming B-29s were called "porcupines" due to the abundance of antennas protruding over the fuselage, or "Guardian Angels" due to their purpose. Fortunately, the installation of these antennas in the field was easy, and did not interfere with the clean aerodynamics of the aircraft. The aerodynamic semi-circular "cans" were mounted on the fuselage through cover plates, and connected to the radar units inside by co-axial cables. The higher frequency radar systems were not as aerodynamic, and were covered with plastic teardrop envelopes.

The first four Bomb Wing porcupines flew a mission on 1 July 1945 by flying ahead of the main formation, and orbited the target in a "stacked racetrack" pattern for an hour and a half. When the main bomber force arrived at the target, each of its bombers, with a total of 10 operators, augmented the RCM onslaught by "spot" jamming with one or two jamming devices and dropping Rope. The American RCM effort was so successful

that by June the Japanese switched off their radar when jamming began from above. The World War II RCM B-29s were continued after the war, and the special RB-29s were used during the Korean War, as well as to snoop on Russian radar during the Cold War.

AN/APQ-9 and AN/APR-4 *Carpet III*
This unit was an improved, powerful (15 to 80 watt) jamming set that was available in mid-1944, and was used against tracking and gun-laying radars. The usual jamming unit consisted of one AN/APR-4 search receiver (with a semi-automatic sweep through the 300-1,000Mcs band) and three AN/APQ-9 transmitters, with distinctive fishhook like aerials enclosed in clear protective Plexiglas domes. It could be used as a barrage jammer (when used with the APQ-9) or a spot jammer (when used with the AN/APR-4 receiver).

AN/APT-1 Dina
The *Dina* was a more powerful development of the AN/APT-3 *Mandrel*, which was a development of a British jamming set. The *Dina* consisted of a transmitter with a modulator and power source built into a single unit. It was used against enemy early warning radars.

19

Pitot Static System

Early System

The pitot static system used on the B-29 differed from most standard contemporary designs, in that the pitot and static pressure sources were located in separate locations on the bomber. Early B-29s were built with two pitot heads on either side of the fuselage, just below the centerline of the forward crew compartment (station 94). Each of these two pitot (impact) pressure sources served two systems. The right hand pitot head served the airplane commander, bombardier, and navigator, and the left hand head the co-pilot and the flight engineer. Each of the two systems were furnished static (atmospheric) pressure from a regular and alternative source located side-by-side at station 175. The aft source in each system furnished alternate static pressure. Tubing from the pitot and static sources carried pressure to various instruments to the forward pressurized crew cabin. There were selector valves in the lines, one at the airplane commander's and co-pilot's stations, and one to the right of the bombardier (or the glide-bombing attachment) that permitted the selection of either regular or alternate static source.

The readings of the airspeed indicator, altimeter, and rate-of-climb indicator depended on two types of pressures: pitot and static. The airspeed indicator was the only one of the three instruments that depended on both types of pressure for a reading. The altimeter and rate-of-climb indicator depended only upon static pressure. The pitot supplied impact pressure to the airspeed indicators. Atmospheric pressure to the altimeters, air speed indicators, and rate of climb indicators was supplied from a static source in the bomb bay. An alternate source of static pressure was also provided, and could be selected by either the airplane commander or co-pilot by means of valves located in their panels. The right hand system provided:

1) Pitot pressure for airspeed indicators at the co-pilot's and flight engineer's station.
2) Either (as selected) alternate or normal pressure for co-pilot's and engineer's altimeters, rate of climb indicator, and airspeed indicator.
3) Alternate static pressure only (no selection) for engineer's de-icer and cabin pressure gage.
4) Either alternate or normal static pressure (as selected) to the bombardier's glide bombing apparatus.

The left hand system provided:

1) The pitot pressure for the airspeed indicators at the airplane commander's, bombardier's, and navigator's stations.
2) Either normal or alternate static pressure (as selected) for the airplane commander's, bombardier's, and navigator's altimeters and airspeed indicators, and the airplane commander's rate of climb indicator.

Later System

The B-29s were later modified to a system using three pitot heads and four static sources. The three Kollsman pitot heads of the modified system were located on each side of the pressurized forward compartment (at station 109). Two of the pitot heads were located on the left side of the fuselage, with the single head directly opposite on the right side. The heads were located on the lower quadrant to facilitate the drainage of condensed and trapped moisture. The single right pitot head furnished pitot pressure for the flight engineer and co-pilot. The upper left head furnished pitot pressure for the airplane commander only, and the lower left head to the bom-

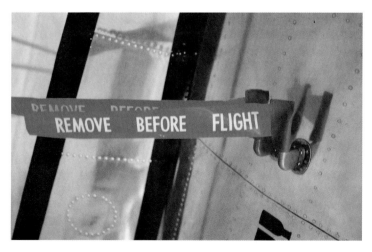

Two electrically heated Kollman pitot heads were located on the left side of the fuselage on either side of the crew compartment. Two of the heads were with the single head directly opposite on the right side. The upper left head furnished pitot pressure for the airplane commander only and the lower left head to the bombardier and navigator only. (Author/Pima)

bardier and navigator only. The pitot pressure opening was on the forward end of the tube, and the static pressure openings were located a short distance behind the forward head. The head was designed so that if any moisture or dirt was trapped it was prevented from reaching the instruments. A heating element inside the head prevented icing. The pitot static system pick up points were made up of two G-2 pitot probes and a set of 9/32-inch diameter holes.

The four static pressure source locations were incorporated: two on each side of the forward crew compartment at station 175, just below the aircraft centerline (the two left static sources were located immediately below the navigator's window and the right sources were directly opposite). These sources were semi-flush mounted fittings containing several small holes that passed inboard. The left forward source served the airplane commander's altimeter, airspeed indicator, and rate of climb indicator. The left rear source served the bombardier and navigator's airspeed indicators and altimeters. The right forward source served the co-pilot's rate of climb indicator, airspeed indicator, and altimeter. The right rear source served the flight engineer's de-icer pressure and cabin differential gauges, airspeed and rate of climb indicators, and altimeter. The engineer's source also had a tube that ran along the right side of the cabin to the bombardier's glide-bombing attachment.

Pitot Static Instruments
Airspeed Indicator Type F-2

Under standard atmospheric conditions at sea level, the airspeed indicator showed the speed at which the aircraft was moving through the surrounding air mass. A metal diaphragm housed in an airtight case was the actuating mechanism of the airspeed indicator. Pitot pressure was received inside the diaphragm, and static pressure was received into the case surrounding the diaphragm. The pointer on the instrument was activated by the expansion and contraction of a cell that was connected to the impact line of the pitot tube, and was measured in miles or knots per hour. The

difference between these two pressures was the indicated airspeed (IAS), and any change in either the pitot or static pressure caused a change in the IAS. Accurate true airspeed (TAS) calculations were to be made on a computer. However, a rough mental estimate could be made by adding 2% of the IAS for each 1,000ft of altitude (i.e. if the reading were 150 IAS at 10,000ft add 20% of 150 (30) to 150 to get an approximate reading of 180 TAS)

Rate-of-Climb Indicator (Vertical Speed Indicator) Type C-2

The rate-of-climb indicator measured the rate of change of altitude—either up or down—in hundreds of feet per minute, and was in reality a vertical speed indicator. The rate-of-climb indicator had the same actuating mechanism as the airspeed indicator. A diffuser valve restricted the flow of the air from the case to the inside of the diaphragm. Only static pressure was admitted to the inside of the case and to the outside of the diaphragm. A reading resulted when there was a difference in pressure between the inside and outside of the diaphragm. The difference resulted mainly in climbing or descending, when the pressure inside and outside the diaphragm tended to equalize. However, this took some time because of the restriction in the flow of air between the diaphragm and case. Due to this restriction there was a several second lag time in the readings. The instrument was to be used when establishing a constant rate of climb or descent in relatively smooth air, and then in conjunction with the altimeter, as it indicates the rate of change, not the amount of change in altitude. The rate-of-climb indicator was valueless in rough air.

Altimeter Type C-12

The actuating mechanism of the altimeter was the aneroid, which was an apparatus for measuring the outside static air pressure, and was calibrated in feet. A partially evacuated cell was surrounded by air from the static side of the pitot static tube. As the air pressure varied with changes in altitude the cell expanded, activating three pointers that rotated on a central shaft projecting through the face of the instrument. The longest pointer indicated hundreds of feet; the next longest indicated thousands of feet, and the shortest indicated tens of thousands. The calibration was usually subdivided into 20ft markings. Showing through a cutout at 3 o'clock on the faceplate was the barometric scale, which was a small scale used for adjusting the altimeter to different barometric pressures by turning a small knob at the edge of the instrument. The altimeter always registered the height above sea level, not the height above the terrain below!

PITOT
IDENTIFICATION
BAND
(BLACK)

PITOT MAST
MOUNTING HOLES

STATIC
OPENINGS
(11 HOLES)
(.046 DIA.)

STATIC
IDENTIFICATION
BAND
(BLACK-GREEN)

STATIC
(ATMOSPHERIC)
PRESSURE
IN

STATIC
PRESSURE
TO AIR SPEED
INDICATOR,
ALTIMETER, AND
RATE OF CLIMB
INDICATOR

PORT A
PITOT (DYNAMIC) PRESSURE
IN

PITOT PRESSURE
TO AIR SPEED
INDICATOR

THE ILLUSTRATION SHOWS THE STATIC PRESSURE FLOW DIRECTION WHEN THE AIRPLANE IS DESCENDING. WHEN THE AIRPLANE IS CLIMBING, THE STATIC PRESSURE FLOW IS REVERSED AND EXITS FROM THE STATIC HOLES.

BAFFLE

MOISTURE
DRAIN HOLE

NON-HEATED HORIZONTAL TYPE
PITOT-STATIC TUBE

20

Autosyn Instruments

Small, single aircraft were able to utilize direct-reading gauges and indicators on their instrument panels without a problem. However, large, multi-engine aircraft created a problem, as long braced spans of tubing and capillaries would be needed to connect direct-reading instruments (indicators) from a central instrument panel to the remote area where the monitoring transmitters of the direct-reading instruments were located. The remote areas mainly included the four engines and accessories, but also flap and shutters, landing gear, etc.

Autosyn instruments were basically a means of "reproducing, at an 'indicator,' motion introduced in the 'transmitter' by pressure, temperature, or otherwise sensitive mechanism at a remote location." An Autosyn transmitter contained a measuring device that was similar to the reading mechanism of a direct-reading instrument, but also had a linkage for converting the action of the measuring device into rotary motion via an Autosyn motor. Although the measuring devices varied depending on the individual equipment, the Autosyn motors were identical in all transmitters. The indicators also contained Autosyn motors, along with pointers and dials. All Autosyn motors, transmitter, and indicator were identical, resembling the small electric motors found in cake mixers. The most important parts of an Autosyn motor were the rotor—the turning part whose shaft was mounted on precision ball bearings—and the stator, the part that remained still. The basic principal of the Autosyn system was to duplicate the motion of one motor to another. Each Autosyn pair (indicator and transmitter) used a rotor, or "primary," that was energized by 400-cycle, 26-volt A.C., and the interconnected stator, "secondary." The transmitter rotor motion or position was translated into a combination of currents of varying strength, and then retranslated into indicator rotor motion or position. The rotor of one motor followed the slightest motion of the rotor of the other motor. Simple electric wiring between the transmitter and the indicator eliminated the need for any mechanical connections or tubing between them.

The mounting of Autosyn transmitters needed to be on special vibration-absorbing mountings due to the severe engine vibrations. Because of their small size, it was impracticable to mount individual transmitters on separate shock absorbers. The various transmitters for each engine were grouped and then mounted in a shock-mounted panel. The exceptions were the position indicator and fuel flow transmitters that were mounted on rubber, because their external connections were rigid. All pressure and mechanical connections to the transmitters had to be made by hose or flexible metal tubing, so that the anti-shock movement of the panel would not be impeded.

Four Autosyn transmitters located in the nacelles eliminated pressure lines between the engines and the indicators. These Autosyn instruments included:

1) Manifold pressure indicators that measured the pressure at which the fuel mixture was delivered through the manifold intake to the engine. It was basically an aneroid barometer registering the pressure in inches of mercury. It gave an indication of the power output of the engine, since power output was a direct function of the manifold pressure and rpm.
2) Fuel pressure indicators
3) Rear oil pressure indicators and front oil pressure indicators
4) Tachometers measured the rotational speed of the propeller. It was calibrated in revolutions per minute (rpm). There were two types of tachometers, centrifugal and electrical.

All these instruments were found at the flight engineer's station, and duplicate tachometers and manifold pressure indicators were located on the airplane commander's instrument panel. Beginning with aircraft 42-6205—the first production B-29—the Autosyn instruments were of the direct pressure type.

21

Ratiometer Instruments

These were instruments that transmitted readings by direct current and included:

1) Fuel and oil quantity gauges
2) Cowl flap position
3) Wing flap position
4) Landing gear position
5) Intercooler position

22

Vacuum System

The vacuum system furnished suction for the de-icer boots and the camera, and operated the turn and flight indicators at the airplane commander's and co-pilot's positions. The vacuum was supplied by one of the inboard engine-driven vacuum pumps in accordance with the setting of the vacuum, which was controlled by a cable system operated from the flight engineer's stand. A regulator maintained a vacuum of 4 to 6in Hg in the vacuum line. When the pressure differential between the cabin air and the outside air reached 4in Hg (about 13,000ft) the instruments were automatically cut off from the vacuum system, and the cabin differential pressure continued the operation of the gyros in the instruments.

Vacuum Pump

Each inboard engine was equipped with a Pesco No. 3P-207J rotary, four vane, positive displacement vacuum pump mounted on a pad on the left side of the accessory panel. The function of the pump was to operate air-driven gyroscopic instruments that required an air pressure lower than that of the atmosphere. The vacuum pump attained this pressure differential by creating a partial vacuum in the instrument.

Suction Relief Valve

The Pesco No. 3V-215-V suction relief valve maintained the constant pressure for the operation of air-driven gyroscopic flight instruments, as the change in the speed of an aircraft engine in flight resulted in a variation of the speed of the engine-driven vacuum pump, and thus there was a constant variation of the air pressure. When the vacuum on the suction side of the vacuum pump attained a preset force a diaphragm, held in place by a spring, opened and admitted air from the surrounding atmosphere.

23

Life Saving Equipment

Cabin Fire Equipment

For pressurized cabin fires during flight, whether electrical or otherwise, the emergency pressure relief handle was to be pulled immediately. If an electrical short caused a fire the flight engineer had to turn off all electrical power with the battery control and generator switches. The aircraft had three hand extinguishers for cabin use. One carbon dioxide (CO_2) extinguisher was located on the inboard side of the engineer's control stand, and another was in the rear pressurized compartment, aft of the auxiliary equipment panel. The third fire extinguisher—a CO_2 or carbon tetrachloride (CC_{14}) extinguisher, depending on the B-29 model—was located by the rear entrance door. The CO_2 extinguishers were the Type A-17 by Lux and the Type 4TB by Kidde, while the Type A-2 CC_{14} was manufactured by Fyr-Fyter. The carbon dioxide extinguisher was used on fires caused by gasoline, oil, or other inflammable liquids and electrical fires. The carbon tetrachloride extinguisher was used on so-called "Class A" fires, involving paper, cloth, wood, etc., because of its wetting action. While CO_2 could not be used on Class A fires, CC_{14} could also be used on inflammable liquid fires; however, CO_2 was more effective, as it deprived the fire of more oxygen. A disadvantage of the CC_{14} extinguisher was that it released a poison gas (phosgene) and dense smoke when directed at a fire, and needed to be ventilated as soon as the fire was put out. If the cabin became overly smoky or gaseous after using the fire extinguishers the bomb bay doors could be opened for ventilation. Any extinguisher that had been partially emptied had to be completely emptied and refilled after landing.

Life Raft and Accessories

Tests and combat experience had demonstrated that it was better to ditch the B-29 than to bail out from it. After ditching, larger rafts with much more survival equipment could be deployed, and would give the crew a much better chance of survival and discovery if they remained together.

The B-29 carried three A-3A six-man rafts: two were located in the left and right raft compartments atop the fuselage. A third raft was stowed inside the fuselage and thrown out the rear hatch by the crew, and inflated by pulling the CO_2 ripcord. After ditching a designated crewman pulled the raft releases located on each side of the tunnel opening in the forward pressurized compartment.

Release handles were located on the right hand side of the aircraft in both the forward and rear pressurized compartments. When the handle was pulled out about three inches, ball fittings on the end of the release cable forced the locks of the life raft doors open, and at the end of their travel fell free from the lock mechanisms. When the cable had been pulled out another three inches ball fittings on the CO_2 cylinders were pulled free, and inflation of the life rafts began. The inflation forced the rafts into the water. They were installed to land right side up, and were fastened to the aircraft by a safety rope that would sever when the aircraft sank.

Life rafts could be released manually from the top of the fuselage. Small access doors with flush spring catches were located over each door handle. The handles had to be completely turned in order to release the ball fittings. A Plexiglas window was installed in each life raft door over the CO_2 cylinder for visual inspection of the linkage of the cylinder to the release cable, and installation of the ball fitting in the cylinder neck.

The correct method to enter the raft was by stepping into it from the rear of the wing. If a man jumped into the raft he could tear out the bottom. The raft was to be fended off the wing, as often the flaps were torn loose in the landing and exposed jagged edges that could puncture the raft. If the raft inflated inverted it was to be pulled toward the wing, and two men should have been able to right it. If this could not be accomplished then a man was to jump into the water and climb up on one side, and pull the hand line attached to the opposite side and right it. When all the men were aboard the rafts they were to be tied together to keep them from drifting apart.

Each raft was equipped with an accessory kit that was contained inside the raft case, and the first rule was to keep the items of the kit inside the case, and to secure the case to the raft so it would not be lost if the raft capsized. Among the items in the accessory kit were:

1) Locomotion and flotation: three oars, sail, sea anchor, bailing bucket, and sponge.
2) Rations and water: Seven Type A rations, drinking water, water containers, fishing tackle, and a jack knife. The Type A ration kits were hermetically sealed in a tin container that contained six man-days of rations, including a dozen Charms candy rolls, chewing gum, and vitamins. There was only one can of water, as a solar still or chemical desalinization kit was included to provide water.
3) Health: first aid kit, sun lotion.
4) Repair: inflation pump, puncture plugs, and a repair patch kit,

5) Signaling: signal mirror, A-9 flashlight, whistle, sea marker, wrist compass, signal kit, a MX-138 radar reflector, and a SCR-578-A emergency Gibson Girl radio. The signal kit contained a M-8 pyrotechnic Very pistol, hand-held flares and smoke signals, and M-9 hand pyrotechnic projector. The MX-138 radar reflector was a collapsible reflector made out of a Monel (copper-nickel alloy) metal mesh, and was attached to an oar in a corner of the raft. The MX-138 could reflect radar signals sent from five to eight miles away.

"Gibson Girl" Dinghy Transmitter SCR-578-A & B

The hourglass shaped SCR-578-A & B (later the AN-CRT-3) was known as the "Gibson Girl," after the 1890's glamour girl with an hourglass figure created by the artist Charles Gibson. The self-contained radio set was water resistant, and could float for a while without damage. It automatically sent out a SOS signal followed by long dashes, and could also be used as a transmitter. It was stowed with the right side life raft, was accessible from the inside and outside of the aircraft, and was the responsibility of the radio operator after ditching. The 36lb radio was contained either in one canvas case, or two cases strapped together (the radio bag and accessory antenna bag). The carrying bag also contained a parachute in a compartment on top that would deploy when the ring was pulled as the bag was thrown out of the aircraft. The kit came with an instruction booklet for its operation and antenna deployment. Current for operating the radio was supplied by turning a hand crank that was dearly guarded, as there was only one. The antenna was raised either by a kite or hydrogen-filled balloon. The design was so successful that the Gibson Girl remained in service into the 1970s.

Gibson Girl Dinghy Transmitter (USAF)

"Walter"

Later in the war the radar beacon AN-CPT-2, known as "Walter," was put into service. Walter was a small (15in x 4.5in), three-pound, battery-powered distress signaling beacon that operated from a mast. Its range varied with the altitude of the search aircraft (18mi at the normal search altitude of 1,000ft and 25mi at 5,000ft).

Part Three

B-29 Training, Crews, and Equipment

1

Training of Flight and Ground Crews

B-29 Crews

B-29 crews were selected to be permanent teams, and their number varied from eight to 12, subject to the mission and combat situation, but usually was 11. There were six officers: the airplane commander (pilot); co-pilot; flight engineer; bombardier; navigator; and radio operator in the forward pressurized compartment. There were three enlisted men in the rear pressurized compartment: the central fire control (CFC) gunner, and the left and right gunner/scanners. The enlisted tail gunner was positioned in his pressurized compartment. Late in the war, as the B-29s were equipped with secret electronic apparatus, extra officers, called "Ravens," were onboard to operate this equipment in the rear pressurized compartment. The first crews were chosen from experienced four-engine crews, mainly from B-24 crews who had flown anti-submarine missions over the Atlantic and Mediterranean.

The crew and unit training were emphasized in B-29 training that initially was the shared responsibility of the AAF Headquarters and the Second Air Force. By the fall of 1944 pilot transition instruction was transferred to Training Command in order to accelerate the formation of B-29 units. Before the assignment of crews a specialized five-week training program was given to airplane commanders, co-pilots, and flight engineers to underscore the close teamwork required of these three crewmen in the handling of the B-29. Upon completion of this course these men were assigned to 2AF units for integration into complete crews. B-29 operational VLR bomber training then followed the conventional training phases, but took somewhat longer than heavy bombardment training. The AAF applied special standards with increased accent on high altitude, Long-Range navigation missions and the use of radar equipment. From the time the training program started in the fall of 1943 until the end of the war, it graduated 2,350 crews.

The B-29 training program emphasized that every crewman become an expert in his position and knowledgeable in maintaining his equipment, but also become interchangeable with other crew positions. Much of their knowledge was helpful to their short-handed ground crews, especially in the early CBI days. The nature of the bomber and its missions called for a closer integration of the crew, as their roles often were co-dependent. Examples were the interaction between the aircraft commander, co-pilot, and flight engineer during take off, during certain perilous portions of the flight

(e.g. bad weather), and during landing. Or between the navigator, the radar operator, and pilots for course setting, monitoring, and maintenance. Also during the bombing run, when the aircraft commander, navigator, and radar operator aided the bombardier. The left and right gunners were the scanners for the aircraft, watching the engines for problems, particularly for signs of overheating and fires; observing the landing gear before landing; and calling out flap deflections. Even though the B-29 was the first bomber to use pressurized cabins, the crew was instructed in the use of pressurized oxygen, heated flight suits, and procedures to be taken in case of cabin depressurization.

During a 3,600-mile round trip mission to Palembang, Sumatra, Maj. Ira Mathews 462BG/58BW and his crew made practical use of their knowledge of the B-29 and saved their lives and aircraft. The bomber lost an engine over the target, and soon lost another on the return. The crew jettisoned everything that was not bolted down, including their parachutes, to maintain altitude. However, the bomber continued to lose altitude, and the crew then began to strip the plane, unscrewing and loosening bolts. Gun turrets, guns, and instruments went out the bomb bay, and the bomber landed safely. When the ground crew looked inside they were amazed that such a thorough job could be done in the air, so good that the stripped bomber could have easily been converted to a tanker to fly gasoline over the Hump!

Training the crew as a team was emphasized, and making "teamwork their byword" was stressed in the training syllabus. It was not possible for the airplane commander to attend the crewman's training courses, but it was his duty to continually check their progress and classroom records. The crew was paired off, and was to train and quiz each other. Combat and emergency situations were to be simulated. The combat crew training requirements were (*The B-29: Airplane Commander Training Manual, AAF Manual No. 50-9, 1 February 1945*):

1) The airplane commander will complete a minimum of 20 hours formation flying above 25,000ft mean sea level.
2) The airplane commander will accomplish the instrument check prescribed by AAF Regulation 50-3.
3) The co-pilot will make a minimum of five landings from his own position.
4) The co-pilot will accomplish at least four hours instrument flying under the hood to include at least two instrument let downs on radio range.

5) The combat crew will complete a navigational mission of approximately 3,000mi. Cruise control will be emphasized.

6) The combat crew will complete a navigational mission by the use of radar alone, over a triangular course, for a minimum distance of 900mi.

7) The bombardier will drop a minimum of 20 individual bomb releases from above 25,000ft mean sea level.

8) The airplane commander, navigator, and bombardier will combine their efforts in performing a minimum of 12 camera bombing attacks on industrial targets, four of which will be above 25,000ft mean sea level.

9) The combat crewman, except the airplane commander, co-pilot, flight engineer, and radio operator, will accomplish a minimum of four camera bombing missions, exposing approximately 50ft of film on each, and aimed at an attacking aircraft. The errors in aiming will be discussed between the instructor and gunner prior to the next gunnery mission.

10) The combat crewman, with the exception of the airplane commander, co-pilot, and radio operator, will fire 200 rounds above 25,000ft mean sea level, divided between their primary and secondary gun positions.

Airplane Commander and Co-pilot Training

Unlike the B-17 and B-24, the pilot of the B-29 was referred to as the "airplane commander," while the co-pilot was often referred to as the "pilot." The organization and techniques for B-29 airplane commander training were similar to basic bombardment pilot training, but there were peculiarities in the B-29 program. When the B-29 program was initiated in mid-1943, because of its importance and the need for acceleration the customary procedure of selecting pilots from recent graduates of AAF schools was relinquished. Instead, airplane commander and other crewmen were conscripted from veterans who had comprehensive training in multi-engine aircraft. The Air Transport Command was expected to be the chief source of experienced pilots and navigators, but in practice only a few men were transferred from the ATC. Instead, instructors from Training Command's multi-engine school were the main pool for experienced pilots who could meet the early requirements of 400 hours of four-engine experience or training. By 1944 this standard was changed to 1,000 hours or more in other types of aircraft, or having been graduated from flight school with 300 hours flying time, of which at least 100 were on four-engine aircraft. On long missions the physical strain of formation flying was substantial, and the co-pilot needed to take over and have the qualifications of a first pilot, and was often a recent graduate of transition bomber school.

In August 1944 the B-29s were scheduled to fly to the Marianas in three months, and there was a shortage of B-29s that severely limited flying time during training. Much of the early crew training was done in well-worn B-17s, and the crews took turns flying the few available B-29s to Havana, Cuba, which was often the "target" for Long-Range training bombing missions. The Cuban capitol was chosen, as it was about the same distance from the fields in Kansas as were the distances from the future bases in the Marianas to Japan. Also, the over water approaches were similar to those to Japan. As these Cuban missions began in August 1944, B-29 flight engineers and airplane commanders—unfamiliar with the mysteries of cruise control and low on fuel—made emergency landings throughout the southeastern United States. The flight engineers were eventually indoctrinated in good cruise control technique: keep the manifold pressure at

high and the rpms low. While these Cuban missions familiarized the crews with Long-Range flying and navigating, they were flown without enemy opposition, and with good communications and weather information. Often bombs were carried and dropped on a bombing range in Texas during the return to Kansas.

Flight Engineer Training

In late 1942 the Air Technical Training Command directed Boeing to establish a "B-29 School" as soon as possible, as the AAF had 150 specially selected personnel ready to be trained as Flight Engineers. To expedite the request, Boeing used its Flying Fortress School and prepared a 600-page illustrated syllabus in only 10 days, and assembled an experienced teaching staff that turned out 150 trained flight engineers two months later. After initial semi-operational training, the Air Staff realized the importance of the flight engineer and decided to augment his training regimen. In April 1943 a flight engineer school was established, and accepted only officer graduates from maintenance engineering courses, as well as a small number of experienced enlisted mechanics. The flight engineer spent 12 weeks in officer training and maintenance engineering, 16 weeks in aircraft mechanics school, 12 weeks at the Boeing mechanics and electrical specialty school, and 10 weeks of flight engineering training.

By March 1944 the demand for flight engineers increased, and the school was compelled to accept more enlisted mechanics. However, many were found to be unqualified due to poor selection, and the number of qualified graduates remained inadequate. To fill the personnel deficit, many surprised pilots were inducted into the program, a move that did not make for many happy new flight engineers. In early 1945 the new flight engineer candidates were drawn from aviation cadets and students. Graduates from the program were equated to the bombardier or navigator, and graduated to become commissioned officers (1Lts.) or flight officers. However, during the war about half of the 7,800 graduated flight engineers in combat were non-commissioned officers (NCOs). The elimination rate varied during the war according to the qualifications of the various groups of candidates, but by 1945 the rate was about 9%.

Initially, flight engineer instructors were drawn from a school managed by Lockheed, but as the program expanded, graduates became the source of instructors. By March 1944 typically four weeks were spent at a general four-engine mechanics school at the Technical Training Command School at Amarillo, TX, which was followed by a 10-week electrical course at Chanute Field, IL, and finally five weeks concentrating on maintenance and inspection. The flight engineer then spent 10 weeks in a three-phase advanced course at the Boeing Aircraft School at Seattle. The first phase was designed to make the student a first-rate mechanic, able to manage in-flight glitches and emergencies; in the second phase the student learned to set the proper cruise control; and the third phase was four weeks of flight training. Since there was a shortage of B-29s, B-24s were modified to accommodate several flight engineer stations for the simultaneous training of multiple students. The B-24 substitution was sufficient until B-29s became available for flight engineer ground training in mid-1944. Finally, the flight engineer spent time at the Flight Engineer's School at Lowry Field, CO (this school was later transferred to Hondo Field, TX). The school went beyond aircraft maintenance and "nuts and bolts," and was called "Aircraft Performance Engineering." The concentrated course focused on transforming theory to paper figures, and then to actual flight plans that considered aerodynamics, such as lift/drag ratios, prop and engine efficiency, fuel consumption, and center of gravity. The course's most important function was to teach cruise control: "the method of carving the bomb load out of the fuel reserve." The main function of the flight engineer was to get the most miles for the least amount of fuel used while maintaining the engines at their most efficient power settings for fuel economy. For his calculations the flight engineer used an E-6-B circular navigation computer, a standard engineering slide rule, an engineer's scale, and a pair of dividers. Known figures for his calculations were contained in a book of B-29 test data that contained charts for temperature conversion, density altitude, climb and distance to altitude, nautical miles per gallon cruise charts, and descent charts with distance and time for range and time. With these tools he was able to calculate altitude, airspeed, and power settings to gain maximum range. But in conjunction with these figures he also had to accurately estimate the effect of the change in gross weight, altitude, and load factors on fuel consumption and aircraft performance. There could not be an error of over 100gal of fuel over a 3,000mi flight. Upon completion of the course the graduates were assigned to a B-29 transition school, where they learned to fly the bomber as part of the airplane commander/pilot/flight engineer team, after which the team began full combat crew training.

Navigator Training

It has been asserted that the navigator was the most intelligent and important member of the crew, and many intelligent prospective pilots were diverted to navigator training. Initially navigator training was 15 weeks, but later this was increased to 18, and then 20 weeks. It was a requirement for a Very Long Range bomber to have superlative navigation, and the Pacific Theater, with its long over water distances, unpredictable weather, and few navigational aids made that requirement even more imperative. There were two navigator roles (the lead and wing navigator), with the difference being in responsibility. The lead navigator was responsible for getting the formation to the target and back as directed in the field order. Wing navigators did the same navigation calculations as the lead navigator, except their method was to do DR (dead reckoning) based on follow-the-pilot procedures. A wing navigator had to be ready to take over as the lead navigator of the formation in case of emergency.

Radar Operator Training

The training of radar specialists began just before Pearl Harbor and continued throughout the war, and expanded in complexity. There were four types of radar specialists: those trained for sea search; for night fighter operations; for radar counter measures (RCM); and the most important, the "Radar Observer Bombardment," who was trained to bomb through overcast (BTO). In October 1943 the Boca Raton AFB, FL, began training the BTO operators, and that program became the foremost AAF radar program. In September the course was limited to pilots, but by November bombardiers and navigators, rather than pilots, were inducted into the BTO program. Bombardiers were given a 10-week course in radar techniques, and navigators received the same training, plus four weeks of non-radar instruction. The radar course consisted primarily of instruction and practice in the operation of standard airborne radar equipment, such as the AN/APQ-13, AN/APQ-15, and later the AN/APQ-7. The shortage of radar training aircraft was the main problem in the radar training program. During the war 7,600 radar operators were graduated, and most were sent to the Pacific.

Gunnery Training

In the primary phase of their training B-29 gunners attended the usual AAF gunnery schools, and then were assigned to the B-29 gunnery program to train them in the remote sighting system. B-29 gunnery testing was conducted at Eglin Field, FL, under Lt. Col. Paul Tibbets, and at Gulfport, MS. Because the B-29s were late off the production line, makeshift gunnery training was expedited by using artificial and mock up devices until early 1944. The remote sighting equipment was placed on fixed platforms on the ground, and B-29 gunners got experience with the remote apparatus by tracking aircraft flying overhead. War-weary B-24s were equipped with remote turrets and sighting stations, and gunners practiced gunnery routine. Once training B-29s became available gunnery tests showed that the new remote B-29 system scored three times as many hits as the conventional flexible and turret gunnery system. Initially there were some problems with the gun stop mechanisms, and several B-29s returned to base with self-inflicted wounds.

Ground Crew Training

Training ground crewmen became a problem when there were no B-29s, trained instructors, textbooks, and Boeing classrooms (they were occupied to capacity by B-17 students) available. Boeing engineers worked 24/7 to complete manuals, charts, and a comprehensive teaching syllabus. Since B-29 components were in short supply, wooden mock-ups for them were built for hands on use, and until these mock-ups were ready B-17 mock-ups were used. As the B-17 schools were occupied, the B-29 classes were taught at night. These Boeing B-29 school graduates were sent to bases to teach the thousands of ground crew needed to service the B-29s using Mobile Training Units.

When America entered the war most of the recruits for ground crews were mechanically inexperienced and needed to be trained as soon as possible to learn the operation, maintenance, and repair of the B-17, then in large-scale production, and entering combat in large numbers. To facilitate their training Boeing created Mobile Training Units, which were large trucks and trailers outfitted with large aircraft components, assemblies, and systems, such as engine cutaways, the hydraulic system, etc. Each component, assembly, and system was labeled with the names of its constituent parts and the function of those parts. When the B-29 came on line Mobile Training Units were assigned to facilitate its training program.

The B-29 ground crew trainees spent 112 days using the tried and true "learn-by-doing" instruction technique. Before graduation the trainee had to complete the renowned "100 hour inspection" of the B-29, and complete a "graduation field test." This field test entailed living for eight days under simulated combat conditions, where he had to demonstrate that he was able to change engines and make inspections with the minimum of tools and apparatus.

Aircraft and engine mechanics were trained by Boeing at Seattle, and by the Air Force at Amarillo, TX. Radio operators and mechanics were trained at Scott Field, IL, and radio technicians at Truax Field, WI. Armament personnel trained at Lowrey Field, CO.

Manuals

Five Manuals totaling 2,000 pages were prepared for the B-29:

1) *Preliminary Handbook*: Included operation, maintenance, and repair instructions.

2) *Pilot's Handbook*: Included flight and operation instructions.

3) *Erection and Maintenance Manual*: Included instructions for connecting the components of the bomber and maintaining it. Because this Manual was prepared as the B-29 was being produced the Air Technical Service Command sent writers and photographers to the various subcontractors to gather information and pictures for the Manual.

4) *Structural Repair Manual*: Included detailed instructions for the repair of the bomber

5) *Illustrated Parts Catalog*

These manuals were written in the style popularized by *Popular Mechanics* and *Popular Science* magazines, which reduced the technical information to a non-technical common denominator that could be easily understood. As a "picture is worth a thousand words," the text was well supplemented by specific drawings and photographs.

Soon the Air Force requested four new publications that were essentially storybooks well illustrated with line drawings. The books were: *Flight and Operations Manual, Inspection Manual, Familiarization Manual,* and the *Engine Change Manual.* Boeing composed the text and supervised its publication by Jordanoff, the well-known aviation publisher of the time, which provided the line drawings and published the book. The major textbook was the *Familiarization Manual for the B-29 Bombardment Airplane.*

B-29 personnel were kept up to date on the numerous changes through Technical Orders published and distributed by the Air Technical Service Command, Wright Field. Boeing also published the monthly *Field Service News*, which was issued to every military air base operating Boeing equipment. The *News* discussed recent problems of Boeing aircraft in the field, particularly the B-17 and later the B-29, and suggested remedies for their resolution.

58th Bomb Wing Training

The 58BW was activated on 1 June 1943 under Lt.Gen. Kenneth Wolfe, and for logistical reasons it was headquartered at Marietta, GA, near the Bell factory, but soon the groups of the 58BW were headquartered at four bases in Kansas. Wolfe had guided the B-29 through its development and was the top-ranking expert on the bomber, and Arnold rewarded him by naming him the commander of the newly formed XX Bomber Command in November 1943. But Wolfe was an administrative and research officer, and in March 1944 veteran combat officer Brig.Gen. LaVerne Saunders was assigned as Wolfe's deputy, and the two divided the command according to their strengths.

The AAF staffed the 58th with a small base of 25 each of highly experienced pilots and navigators, who were to be augmented by other experienced airmen gleaned from other heavy bomber training schools and ground personnel who were available in very limited numbers. The pilots were to have at least two years continuous experience with 400 four-engine hours, and the navigators were to have two years of continuous active duty or civilian service. Under the original table of organization the VHB crews were to have 14 men, but by 1943 this number had been reduced to 10 (later a radar operator was added). Two crews were assigned to each bomber, seven bombers per squadron, four squadrons per group, and four groups per wing, totaling 112 bombers (38 in reserve).

The first four 58BW groups scheduled for combat were created by splitting two former groups. In mid-November 1943 the 58BW was comprised of about 7,900 officers and men, which was much fewer than the 11,000 required under the table of organization. A most important impediment to the training program was the lack of B-29s, which were experiencing serious developmental and engine problems. The 58BW had received only a few B-29s between August and November, as once the bomber rolled off the assembly line it needed to be modified to the latest Boeing specifications. Each squadron had one B-29, three or four B-17s, and two B-26s to train 20 combat crews. The aircrews first used the twin-engine B-26 which, while appreciably different from the B-29, did have a tricycle landing gear, high aspect wing, and similar glide and landing characteristics. Soon it was replaced by the B-17, which permitted the entire crew to train together. Although this arrangement using other aircraft design was unsatisfactory and delayed training, it had to suffice, as in December 1943 the entire 58BW had only an average of 23 B-29s in inventory during the month. Due to engine problems, the lack of experienced mechanics, and the Kansas winter weather, serviceability was the underlying problem, as in November and December the 58BW had only an average of seven B-29s available for its four groups and 240 crews! Utilizing these few B-29s, the 58BW only averaged four hours of daily flying. By the end of the year the average crew had only 18 hours of B-29 flying time, and there were only 67 airplane commanders checked out. The 792BS continued to train its crews in its one B-29 until January 1944, when 58BW crews were suddenly sent to final assembly plants to ferry new B-29s to Air Depots at Kelly Field, TX, and Tinker Field, OK, for modification, and then ferry other newly modified B-29s back to their Kansas bases. But when these supposedly modified B-29s arrived in Kansas, it was found that often all the required modifications had not been completed, and that entirely new modifications were ordered. But with the new bombers the training situation improved somewhat by mid-February 1944, with the average crew flying time increasing to 35 hours; however, only 10% of the high altitude and 20% of the Long-Range mission requirements had been met. Gunnery was a particular problem, as only two B-29s with the CFC system were on hand, and thus only 10% of the gunners had been trained. Radar units had not been installed on any aircraft, and the radar operators had not arrived. When he visited Kansas on 9/10 March Gen. Arnold described the situation as "void of organization, management, and leadership." What followed was to be called the "Battle of Kansas," which has been described previously.

When the 58BW left for the CBI its aircrews had only completed half off its training requirements, averaging less than 40 of the required 80 training hours, and only one hour of the 20 hours required for formation flying above 20,000ft, and had not flown any radar missions. Just prior to overseas deployment 3,000 new ground personnel arrived and were split in two. Half of the 58BW ground crew was ordered to remain behind to train half of the new ground men for the next Bomb Wing, the 73BW. The untrained new 73BW half was to ship overseas and be trained by the other half of the 58BW ground men. In February 1944 the ground crews left Kansas for India, one group via ship crossing the Atlantic, and the other via ship to Hawaii and Australia. Both arrived in India by late March, then traveled by Indian railway and arrived at their bases in mid-April. Only the crews ferrying the B-29s remained in Kansas.

2

Combat Crews

Ratio of Crews to Aircraft

Once there were sufficient B-29s available, and the AAF ordered a sustained maximum effort during the second phase of the bombing campaign over Japan (9 March to the end of the war), the durability of the crews became the limiting factor. With better maintenance and supply the bombers could be flown more hours per month than could the crews. The planes could be flown 140 hours per month, whereas the crews could fly 100 per month for a few months; however, on a sustained basis it was determined that their limit was 75 hours per month. During bombing phase two the crew to aircraft ratio was 1.25 to 1, but the actual ratio was 0.94:1 when factoring in lead crew, shakedown training, and illness, yielding an actual monthly flying time of about 89 hours.

Combat Tours

In order to improve morale and give hope of survival the AAF adopted the RAF policy of implementing the "combat tour," which established a set number of missions to be flown, after which the crew would be rotated home. The 8AF bomber crews started with 25 missions, which was increased to 30 and then 35, while in the MTO this figure was set at 50 missions.

To establish the combat tour mission number in the Pacific different considerations from those in Europe had to be factored. The missions in the Pacific were longer than those over Europe, but enemy fighter and AA opposition was less; however, the consequences of mechanical failure were increased. A crew that ditched or bailed out had much less chance of survival and rescue than those in Europe, and it was much preferred to be captured by the Germans and put into a Luftwaffe-run POW camp than be captured by the Japanese. Also, the bomber bases in England were considered country clubs when compared to the bases first in India and China, and then in the Marianas. Nonetheless the Pacific tour number was set at 35.

The 58BW was the first wing to enter combat, and had already flown its aircraft in training and aircraft shakedown flights over Kansas, then had flown to Calcutta, India, via Maine, Morocco, and Egypt. The four Indian bases, particularly Charas, had primitive facilities, and were not within range of any worthwhile Japanese targets. Starting on 24 April 1944 its B-29s transported wing supplies over the Himalayan "Hump" to establish bases in China so it could begin bombing operations on Japanese targets.

These dangerous Hump missions—the aborted missions due to weather, or the B-29's chronic mechanical problems that caused turn arounds—were not counted as combat missions. The flying and living conditions in China were also difficult, and the crews of the 58BW did not fly as often as the crews in the Marianas, waiting for supplies to arrive, and for favorable weather conditions. By May 1945 most of the 58th's crews had over 500 hours of flying, and had been overseas for over a year, and morale had reached a low point. Finally, to circumvent the 35 combat mission policy a formula was devised that recognized that all flying hours in the CBI should be counted towards mission numbers. To determine the number of missions all combat mission hours, aborts included, were to be divided by 14, and the Hump transport hours by 28. A crew of the 468BG was rotated under this new policy in June, and by the end of July only a handful of 58BW's original crews were not back in America.

The 20AF in the Marianas based the initial combat tour mission number on a 50-50 chance of survival. The figures were based on the B-29 combat loss rate to November 1944, and established 600 hours of flying time as a tour. That figure meant if the average mission was 15 hours the combat tour should be 40 missions, although at that time the 8AF number was at 35. The 20AF set no definite official policy at the time, although its aircrews felt that 30 missions was a fair number. As the number of Marianas combat missions were increasing the 20AF finally set the tour number at 35 in the spring of 1945. This number did not delight the 73BW, which had been flying missions from Isley Field, Saipan, from the onset of the Marianas operations, and were approaching 30 missions. By the end of April three B-29 crews of the 497BG had reached 30 missions, and the 73BW command decided to temporarily waive the 35-mission number. On 12 May a crew of the 498BG was the first to reach the magic 35 number, and in June 435 men of the 73BW were rotated back home.

Accidents

During the war the B-29 accident rate inside the United States was 40 accidents per 100,000mi flown, as compared to the 35 for the B-24 and 30 for the B-17. Two thirds of the accidents were attributable to personnel errors. As the quality of the bomber was improved and the training and experience of the aircrew increased, the B-29 accident rate per 100,000 hours (overseas and stateside) also decreased from 158 in June 1944 to under 44 in October 1944, and to under 36 after January 1945.

3

Crew Clothing and Equipment

Personal Equipment Officer (PEO)

Through experience the AAF found that it needed a full-time officer to oversee the personal and emergency aircrew equipment. The Personal Equipment Officer was responsible for supervising the care and upkeep of this equipment, and for instructing personnel in its care and use. The PEO provided regular instruction in emergency procedures and the use of emergency equipment, and was available for personal consultation. The PEO worked in close association with the engineering and supply sections, and also with the Flight Surgeon.

The airplane commander had the ultimate responsibility for emergency equipment and procedures, and needed to check each crewman to be certain he knew the emergency procedures, as the safety of the aircraft and every crewman depend on the individual. Before each mission the airplane commander inspected the equipment of each man to see that he had everything required for the mission. The PEO gave the airplane commander a checklist of the required personal equipment.

Flying Clothing

The crews of the B-17s and B-24s over Europe were subjected to extreme cold during their high altitude missions, which required them to wear heavy flying or heated flying suits. The pressurization and heating system of the B-29 was so efficient in stabilizing the temperature in the crew compartments at 70°F that the most common flight uniform on the B-29 was shirtsleeves and khaki pants. However, when the cabin was depressurized on the high altitude approach over the target, or through damage or malfunction, the aircrews became subjected to the cold. They found that the B-11 jackets and gloves they carried onto the aircraft were sufficient to ward off the cold during the time over the target, or until the airplane commander dropped the bomber to a lower, warmer altitude.

Electrically Heated Flying Suits

Although it was impractical to adequately heat all B-29 crew stations, especially the tail gunner's position and the radar station in the aft of the rear pressurized cabin, even these positions did not require a heated flying suit. The majority of the electrically heated flying suits were used over Europe, and very few were issued to the B-29 crews after they left the cold Kansas winter of 1943-44.

There were two electrically heated flying suits. The F-2A electrically heated flying suit was worn over long-sleeved and long-legged woolen underwear and a woolen shirt, or under standard uniforms or shearling outerwear. The F-3 and F-3A suit was worn under the GI ground clothing normal for the theater (usually the intermediate flying suit), or over a uniform. A 24-volt flying suit heater receptacle and rheostat was available at each crew station in the B-29.

RESTRICTED

COMBAT CREW PERSONAL EQUIPMENT

CHECK LIST

TIME:_____
DATE:_____
AIRPLANE MODEL AND NO. _____
PILOT'S NAME:_____

	Pilot	Co-pilot	Engineer	Bombardier	Navigator	Radio Operator	Upper Gunner	Right Gunner	Left Gunner	Radar Operator	Tail Gunner	Other
( ) Jacket, electrically heated												
( ) Trousers, electrically heated												
( ) Gloves, electrically heated												
( ) Shoes, electrically heated												
( ) Jacket, intermediate												
( ) Trousers, intermediate												
( ) Jacket, winter flying												
( ) Trousers, winter flying												
( ) Gloves, summer or winter												
( ) Mittens												
( ) Shoes, flying												
( ) Helmet, flying												
( ) Headset												
( ) Oxygen mask												
( ) Microphone												
( ) Bail-out cylinder												
( ) Parachute												
( ) Parachute first-aid kit												
( ) Parachute emergency kit												
( ) Life vest												
( ) Flak helmet												
( ) Goggles												
( ) Sun Glasses												
( ) Pistol, cartridges, clips												

NOTE: Only checked ( ) items received this mission.

Combat Crew Personal Equipment List. Before each mission the airplane commander inspected the equipment of each man to see that he had everything required for the mission. The PEO (Personal Equipment Officer) gave the airplane commander this checklist of the required equipment. (USAF)

F-2 Electrically Heated Flying Suit (USAF)

There was a 24-volt suit heater receptacle and rheostat (arrow) at each crew station. (USAF)

F-2A Suit

The F-2A was a two-piece (jacket and trousers), two-layer, front zippered suit made up of an outer shell of brown wool, and could be separated and worn as a cloth uniform-type jacket. The trousers were the standard waist-level type held up by a belt and suspenders. The thermostatically controlled 24-volt wiring was arranged in a web inside the lining of the outside jacket. A short "pigtail" connected the suit to a six-foot extension cord that was to be plugged into the aircraft's electrical system rheostat. On the F-2A there were snap (press stud) fasteners on tabs on the jacket and trouser cuffs that acted as electrical connections to electrically heated gloves and shoe inserts. There was a small electrical connection on the front of the jacket to connect to the oxygen mask heater, or to the heated lens in the B-8 goggle. Some of the suits had a fleece collar, and others had the standard uniform collar.

F-3 and F-3A Suits

The F-3 was developed from the F-2A suit, which was found to be inadequate in tests, and it was made the standard electrically heated flying suit in late February 1944. The two-piece suit was made up of an olive or green cotton and rayon twill short "bolero-style" jacket that zippered in front, and "bib-type" overall trousers with adjustable suspenders. The F-3 was an improvement over the F-2A, as it was sturdier, roomier, and more comfortable for sitting and movement. The suit was supplied by a 24-volt multi-ciruit system with two circuits supplying the jacket, three for the trousers, and two each for the heated shoes and gloves. It was connected to an extension cord by an 18in "pigtail." The electrical circuitry was more reliable, and was efficient down to -60°F. A rheostat at each crew station in the aircraft controlled the suit's temperature. During aircraft warm up the electric suit extension plug was plugged into the heating outlet on the left side of the suit. The left outlet operated on a rheostat, and the right was a full current outlet. To test the suit the rheostat was to be turned on to check heating and then turned down. The heated glove and felt liner plugs were to be checked for proper connection to the outlets on the heated flying suit that supplied the current. The F-3A had the standard electrical chest receptacle for connection to the electrically heated lens for the B-8 goggle and oxygen mask. The F-3 suits were used over Kansas on a trial basis, and a few F-3A suits were available in later 1944 for flying the Hump in the CBI.

Gloves

Winter Gloves

The A-9 winter glove was standardized in mid-1935, and the improved A-9A was introduced in April 1944, and remained in service until the end of the war. The type A-9A was a gauntlet mitten-type with a thumb and forefinger that could be worn with rayon inner gloves if the electrically heated gloves were not needed. It had a goat, pony, and later deerskin outer shell, and a lamb shearling lining and large cuff. The A-9A could be worn over the electrically heated gloves if they were large enough. These gloves were issued to crews when they flew in Kansas and the CBI, but they were not needed in the Pacific.

Rayon Liner Glove

Thin rayon (or rarely silk) gloves were to be worn under winter gloves or the electrically heated gloves for extra warmth, and to protect fingers from freezing to metal when the heavy outer gloves had to be removed temporarily to do more exacting manipulations. These gloves were often taken along with the B-11 flying jacket during missions from the Marianas.

Electrically Heated Gloves

Electrically heated gloves dated back to the heated glove inserts devised by the French and used by the U.S. Air Service in WWI. The Type E-1 electric glove was a five-finger glove with a goatskin or pony hide leather outer shell and a knit wool lining. The 24-volt system had wire heating elements sewed between the shell and lining, and was designed to be worn with the F-1 heated flying suit. The E-1 was not sturdy or reliable, and was replaced with another heavier five-finger leather gauntlet with a woolen lining to be used with both the new F-2 and F-3 electric suits. This glove had its wiring placed over the back of the hand and fingers, and was sand-wiched between two layers of the knit lining. The early gloves were connected electrically to the arms of the suit by snap or stud fasteners, and in October 1944 the improved bayonet-type fasteners were introduced, and the Type F-3 suit was redesignated as the F-3A. By November 1944 there were over 280,000 pairs of these gloves on procurement, and modifications were made to the durability, flexibility, and heating wiring throughout the war.

Footwear

The stock low cut, rubber sole, leather shoe was usually worn in the Pacific, but the following shoes and boots were on the equipment list.

A-6 Shearling Shoe

It was found through experience that a flying shoe not only needed to be warm, but also durable if a pilot was shot down over enemy territory and had to escape on foot. Along with the coveted Type A-2 leather flying jacket and the Type A-6 flying shoe and its modifications were the most well known pieces of personal flying equipment of WWII. The shoe was first introduced in 1937 as a 10-inch high shearling shoe, zippered in front, with a rubber sole, and basically did not change much throughout the war. It could be worn alone as an intermediate temperature range boot, or for wear over electric shoe or inserts. Among the modifications was the addition of straps (A-6A) to improve its retention while parachuting, and in sticky muddy conditions, and to cut off cold from entering through the top of the boot. The shoe was waterproofed by adding a rubberized area around and above the sole and weatherproofing the upper.

F-2 Electrically Heated Shoe Insert

The A-6 shoe was found to give inadequate warmth during high altitude missions, and the answer was the development of the F-2 type shoe insert, which was designed for use in combination with the F-2 and F-3 heated flying suits. The F-2 was worn over stockings, and when worn in combination with the A-6 shoe allowed the feet to breathe and not perspire, a condition that could be dangerous in low temperatures. The insert was made of gray felt whose seams were reinforced by webbing, and had an elastic front section so it could be easily slipped over the foot. Four wires were fastened to the F-3 or F-3A flying suit at bayonet connections at a point above the inside top of the insert. These wires were sewed to the outside of the insert, and two separate circuits ran parallel to each other around and under the insert. A double layer of felt protected the wiring in the sole.

Q-1 Electrically Heated Shoe Insert

In late 1944 the Q-1 was developed for use with the variations of the F-2 and F-3 electric suits and the A-6 and A-6A shoes. The Q-1 was made of an inner and outer layer of nylon cloth that sandwiched a layer of cotton cloth. It had a nylon outer sole and a cotton duck insole. The foot entered the insert through an opening in its back, and then was closed by a flap that was secured around the ankle and then tied tight with laces. The insert had four improved, more flexible electric heating wires that were sewed in two separate, parallel circuits into the cotton layer. The Q-1's wiring disbursement was an improvement over the F-2 insert, giving better heat supply to the vital toe area as well as the heels. The Q-1 would be worn over the standard QMC issue leather shoes and woolen socks, and then slipped into a pair of A-6 or A-6A overshoes.

Headgear

The standard B-29 headgear in combat was a baseball-type cap or officer's hat; however, the A-11 Intermediate Helmet was on the equipment list.

A-11 Intermediate Helmet

The A-11 helmet was introduced in August 1943, and was one of the most common U.S. flying helmets of the war, with 207,000 being manufactured. The outer shell was made from cape leather (later earth brown sheepskin leather), with chamois (later a more uniform doeskin lining) and a quick-release chinstrap. It was conspicuous for its large "donut" earphone receptacles made from black rubber, and kapok-filled cushions that were designed for the ANB-H-1 radio receiver. A silk or woolen scarf was worn to cover the area between the collar and helmet.

The A-11 helmet was introduced in August 1943 and was one of the most common U.S. flying helmets of the war, with 207,000 being manufactured. (USAF)

Flak Suits and Helmets

M-1 and M-2 Flak Vest

The M-1 armored vest was standardized in October 1943. It was a full vest, having front and rear armor fastened together at the shoulders by quick release dot fasteners. The vest was fabricated of overlapping two inch (20-gauge) .045 Hadfield manganese steel sewed into pockets attached to a nylon canvas backing. The vest weighed 17lbs, 6oz, and covered 3.8 square feet. It was designed to be used especially by gunners and also by navigators, bombardiers, and radio operators, who did not have armor-protected seats, or would move about the fuselage and thus be exposed to the danger of front and rear AA fire. It was normally worn with the M-4 flak apron.

The M-2 was designed for pilots and other crewmen who sat in armored seats and were protected from the rear. It also was standardized in October 1943 with the M-1 vest. The M-2 was similar in construction to the M-1, but had an unarmored nylon back panel. The M-1 weighed 7lbs, 13oz, and covered 1.45 square feet. It was ordinarily worn with the M-3 apron. The vests were delivered to the bomber before the mission and put on as the plane approached the target.

Well-dressed and well-protected airplane commander wearing a M5 steel helmet over a standard leather helmet, M5 armored vest with M5 groin armor and multi-layered winter electric suit. (USAF)

M-3 to M-5 Flak Aprons

The M-3 and M-4 aprons had the same construction as the M-1 vest. The M-3 weighed 4lbs, 14oz and covered 1.15 square feet. The M-4 weighed 7lbs, 2oz and covered 1.66 square feet. The vests and aprons were worn over all other flying equipment, and were attached to one another by quick release fasteners. The M-3 attached to the front of either the M-1 or M-2 vest by three quick release fasteners. Tapes attached each section, and connected the fasteners to a red strap placed at the wearer's waist. A quick tug at the strap released the vest and aprons to separate from each other and fall off the body. The M-5 apron was first developed as the T-12 in December 1943, and was made up of 10 steel plates that had improved shapes and were hinged. The T-12 was modified into the T-13, which weighed about 14lbs and covered 1.63 square feet, and was standardized as the Armor, Flyer's, Groin M-5 in March 1944. The M-5 was made in three sections so that the center section could be drawn up between the legs, and the side sections were to lie over the thighs. It weighed 15lbs, 4oz and covered 3.72 square feet. The M-5 was attached to the vest by three dot fasteners, and tapes connected to a quick release strap. The airplane commander, co-pilot, and flight engineer generally wore it.

M3, M4, and M5 Flak Helmets

In December 1943 the M3 airman's flak helmet was basically a direct development of the standard infantryman's M1 "steel pot," with the steel structure of the helmet cut away over the ears to accommodate the earphones. The main difference was that there was no separate liner, as the suspension was attached to the steel shell, and a hinge was welded to the helmet shell, and a steel earflap was attached to cover the earphones. A web chinstrap was attached to the lower edge of the earflaps to hold them down. The olive drab M3 was fabricated from Hadfield manganese steel and weighed 3lbs, 3oz. The earphones were integrated into the regulation leather or fabric flying helmet to fit under the M3 shell.

The M4 was a product of the development of body armor, and was standardized in December 1943. It was a quick release skullcap made from unjoined Hadfield manganese steel plates sewed into a fabric foundation. The helmet was covered by taut brown leather, and had a chamois skin lining and a brown leather chinstrap with a buckle/dot fastener to hold it in place. It advantages were it weighed a pound less than the M3, and was trimmed out over the ears to accommodate the unimpeded use of the earphones and radio headsets, and so could be worn over the summer or winter flying helmets and oxygen masks. The M4 was well suited for gunners and for crew positions where space was limited. The M4 continued to be modified during 1944, and continued until it was replaced by the M5 in January 1945.

The M5 was an independent development in the search for "the" armored steel aviator's helmet. The M4 was difficult to manufacture because of its overlapping steel plates, and new research emphasized the development of a one-piece Hadfield manganese steel bowl with long hinged cheek plates riveted to the helmet. The cheek plates accommodated the earphones, and had a fully adjustable "one size fits all" head suspension. The olive drab M-5 weighed 2lbs, 12oz and was the standard helmet for all crewmen, except the top gunner station.

B-8 Goggles

The B-8 goggle, manufactured by Polaroid, was the last flying goggle to be standardized (October 1943) in the war. The "Polaroid" had a one-piece frame that was fabricated from heavy black rubber instead of metal, and had a single large lens that accommodated both eyes. The B-8 was furnished with a kit with several interchangeable tinted (four green and two amber), and three clear plastic lenses that could be worn singly or in combination. Later an electrically heated lens to eliminate fogging and frosting was included, and was integrated with the Type F-3 heated suit by a connection on the suit's front. Goggles were to be worn at all times, as they protected the eyes against the cold, and in an emergency against flash burns and solid fragments.

Sunglasses

The signature "aviator look" came from these glasses, and the style remains popular to this day. The classic "Glasses, Flying, Sun (Comfort Cable)" were standard at the beginning of the war, but were replaced by the "Glasses, Flying, Sun, Rose Smoke, Type 2" by the time the B-29 came into service. The Type 2 maintained the same face form nickel-silver metal frames, adjustable (i.e. bendable) "comfort cable" temple and bow, and the

traditional "aviator-shaped" lenses. It differed in slightly different adjustable nose rocking pads and replaceable anti-glare lenses that were rose colored. The rose color was chosen for their minimal color distortion, maximum brightness and contrast, and reduced glare. The glasses were carried in an aluminum or leather carrying case.

Life Vests (B-4 and B-5)

B-4 Life Vest

The life vest was commonly known by the RAF originated nickname "Mae West," as when inflated it was thought to resemble the well-known and well-endowed Hollywood film actress. At the start of WWII it became evident that the natural rubber sources from Southeast Asia would be severed, and the manufacturers of the Type B-3 life vest then in service would have material shortages. The four-pound AN-V-18 pneumatic vest tested by the Navy met specifications and used less rubber, as it was constructed into two pneumatic air compartments made of rubber-coated yellow fabric. An automatic system of two CO_2 cylinders or a separate mouth tube could inflate the two compartments. A head strap was provided, extending from the back of the collar to the rear of the belt, to prevent the wearer's head from slipping out of the collar opening. Later most vests were modi-

E-1 DARK ADAPTATION GOGGLE

GLASSES, FLYING, SUN, ROSE SMOKE TYPE 2

The signature "aviator look" came from the WW-II glasses, and the style remains popular to this day. The classic "Glasses, Flying, Sun (Comfort Cable)" were standard at the beginning of the war, but were replaced by the "Glasses, Flying, Sun, Rose Smoke, Type 2" by the time the B-29 came into service. (USAF)

In December 1944 the AAF standardized the Type B-5 Life Vest, which was a divergence from the conventional pneumatic B-4 vest. The B-5 more resembled a collar; it was shorter and wider, and had an improved strap design. (USAF)

fied in the field to include a dye marker. In May 1942 the AAF standardized the vest as the Type B-6, and in February 1944 it changed the nomenclature to the AN-V-18, AN6519. Therefore, a vest imprinted with "AN-18-V" was originally requisitioned by the Navy, one imprinted with "AN6519" or "AN6519-1" was requisitioned by either the Army or Navy, and those marked "Type B-4" were only Army issue. All three were identical, but were manufactured at different times.

B-5 Life Vest

In December 1944 the AAF standardized the Type B-5 Life Vest, which was a divergence from the conventional pneumatic B-4 vest. The B-5 more resembled a collar, as it was shorter and wider, and had an improved strap design. Like the older Type B-3 it had black neoprene bladders enclosed in a yellow cotton vest. The two air compartments were fitted with separate mouth inflators as a backup to the CO_2 cylinders. It weighed three pounds—one pound less than the B-3s or B-4s—and was more comfortable and buoyant when inflated due to the wider collar that supported the wearer's head. Modified versions of the B-5 remained in AAF service into the 1960s.

When the life vest was issued it was to be inspected and tested. It was worn over the flying clothing and tested by inflating it by mouth, so as not to waste the CO_2 cartridge, and the straps were then adjusted. With the vest inflated the waist straps were pulled fairly tight, and the crotch and back straps snug. After adjusting the back strap it was attached to the waist strap. The mouth valves were then opened, deflating the vest. After the inflation check both CO_2 cartridges were to be removed and inspected for a perforation of the end seal, which meant it had been used. The cartridge puncturing needle was checked by looking into the cartridge receptacle, and was to be pointing vertically. The light safety wire was checked, and the CO_2 cartridges were reinserted narrow ends down into the receptacle, and the receptacle cap screwed on tightly. The mouth inflator was tightly closed, as if it was partially open the CO_2, if released, would flow through when the emergency cords were pulled. Life vests were to be thoroughly inspected every six months. The date of last inspection was stenciled on the vest.

In combat the collar of the flight jacket was to be worn over the collar of the life vest and, of course, the life vest was to be worn under the parachute harness. The ends of the mouth valves were to be bent down or cut flush with the retaining loop so they would not poke the wearer in the eye when inflated. The parachute first aid packet was to be attached to the vest strap (not the parachute harness). The sea marker tab and release were checked. When rescue planes approached the dye was to be released by pulling the tab down. The dye was to be stirred with the arms to color as large an area of water as possible.

Life Raft (One-man)

There were two types of life rafts for use in the B-29: those for individual use after bailing out, and the A-3A six-man life raft for use after ditching, which is discussed in the aircraft equipment section.

Type C-2 One Man Life Raft (Bail Out Raft)

The C-2 one-man life raft, standardized in April 1944, was developed by the Equipment Laboratory, and was a huge improvement over its predecessor, the AN-R-2A. The raft pack measured approximately 15x14x3.5in, and weighed 16lbs with the accessories. The C-2 was about 66in long, and

was made up of a fabric floor that was cemented to a rubberized two-compartment fabric flotation tube, and had a rated capacity of 250lbs. It was more stable than the AN-R-2A, and was equipped with a spray shield that covered the legs to the waist. It was to be propelled by two small but useless hand paddles, and was supplied with a sail. There were pockets for additional survival supplies that included a sea anchor, bailing cup, one can of drinking water, a first aid kit, rubber repair patches and bullet hole plugs, a three foot cotton cord, and a can of marker dye.

When the bail out warning was given by the airplane commander, each crewman removed the individual raft pack from its stowage near his position and snapped it to his parachute harness. The corner of the raft pack cover was opened, the end of the lanyard was pulled out, and it was run under the parachute harness and snapped onto the D-rings of his life vest waist strap. The raft packs for the airplane commander and co-pilot were located immediately behind the armor plate of their seats. The flight engineer's raft was strapped to the cabin roof between the front upper hatch and aisle dome light. The raft packs for the bombardier, navigator, and radio operator were located on the floor between the lower forward turret and the wheel well step. The waist gunners' and top gunner's raft packs were fastened to the floor in the left forward section of their compartment. The radar operator's raft was strapped to the left wall immediately aft of and level to the rear hatch. The tail gunner had to leave his pressurized compartment—using oxygen, depending on the altitude—to retrieve his raft pack, which was strapped to the right wall just aft of the rear lower turret in the rear unpressurized compartment. When attached the raft pack looked like a seat parachute pack.

Once landing in the water and releasing the parachute the raft pack was opened by pulling the webbing strap. Depending upon the design the raft was inflated by unscrewing the valve handle or pulling the ripcord. The man either crawled in as the raft was inflating, or pulled himself in over the narrow end by the handles. The life vest was not to be removed at any time.

Type C-1 Emergency Vest

The one-man life raft accessory kit was the ingenious Vest Emergency Sustenance Type C-1. It was worn over the flying clothing, but under the life vest, flak vest, and parachute harness. This OD twill vest weighed 11lbs (with all its contents), had three front buttons, and was adjustable by three back ties. It had 16 numbered pockets that were each filled with a variety of survival equipment that had a specific pocket in the vest. The top pockets contained personal articles, while among the articles in the other pockets were: a first aid kit in a plastic box; a clever combination compass-matchbox-flint; a combination fishing and sewing kit; two-bladed folding knife; two cans of emergency rations, emergency signaling mirror and flares; gloves and hat; and a survival manual. A waterproof plastic holster for a .45cal pistol was provided under the left armpit, and a three-pint water canteen was hung on the belt. To eliminate the necessity of wearing the vest in flight the standard B-4 flap musette bag was adapted to carry the C-1 vest attached to the left side of the parachute harness. The C-1 vest was often customized in the field. B-29 crews in the CBI included the "Pointie Talkie" Chinese phrase book, paper "Blood Chits," Chinese money, and rayon cloth maps.

Parachutes

The B-29 Training Manual (Manual No. 50-9) describes the parachute:

"In lots of ways, your parachute is like the Ideal Girl Friend. Take care of her, treat her right, and she's steady, safe, and dependable—you'd be a fool to go out without her! If you ever have a falling out, she lets you down easy! But if you've been kicking her around and treating her like dirt, don't expect her to come through just because you happen to need her!"

The B-29 carried three different types of chutes: seat, chest type, and back. Consideration for the type of chute used was: first, the type of the mission; second, maximum safety while on the mission; and finally, to be as comfortable as possible during the mission. The PEO was responsible for recommending the proper chute for each crewman.

Type A-4 and A-5 Chest Type
The chest type parachute was often called the QAC (Quick Attachable Chest) due to its characteristic of having the parachute pack separate from the harness. The QAC was to be used where it was impossible or impracticable to wear the back type parachute. The harness was worn in flight, and the pack was stowed in a location that permitted quick access, but had to donned immediately at any sign of an emergency. Extra QACs were stowed in the pressurized compartments of the aircraft. The A-5 QAC replaced the A-4 in January 1945.

Type B-9 and B-10 Back Type
This parachute was recommended for use in all positions where it did not hinder the duties of the crewman. The back type parachute restricted the turning of the body, and thus limited the view to the rear. The development of the backpack parachute progressed with the development of quick release back type parachutes. The B-10 succeeded the B-9 in early January 1945.

Type S-6 Seat Type
The seat type parachute afforded a greater amount of turning and flexibility than the back type, and thus gave better all around visibility. But it was difficult to move around the aircraft wearing the unwieldy, protruding parachute packs. The airplane commander, co-pilot, and flight engineer, who did their duties sitting down and rarely left their positions, wore the seat type parachute.

Quick Release Mechanism
Combat experience in the early war demonstrated the need for a quick release device to free the parachute after landing. Tests were done to adapt the British Irving mechanism that had, in turn, been copied from the German quick release design. The Type A-4 Irving mechanism was put into extensive use, but proved to be unsatisfactory, and was replaced by the single point Type A-5 in January 1945. Just before landing the locking cap on the box was turned 90-degrees to set the release mechanism for instant operation. Immediately upon landing the safety clip was pulled, and the cap had to be pressed hard to release the lock, and the parachute harness would then slide off.

Watches
The type A-11 was a secondary, so-called "Hack" watch that was set off a master watch. It was a 15-jewel movement wristwatch with a black face, sweep second hand, and usually a brown fabric band. The watch came into service in May 1940 and was produced by Bulova, Elgin, and Waltham. The Hamilton AN5740 was the master navigator's watch used by both the Army and Navy (AN designation), with the AAF standardizing it at the beginning of 1942. The AN5740 was a pocket watch with a black face and a 24-hour dial; it was carried in its own metal case, and was cushioned against jarring and vibration by springs inside the case. The navigator was responsible for synchronizing all aircraft clocks and crew watches.

Flashlights
The Type A-6B flashlight was a penlight used for illuminating maps and apparatus inside the aircraft. The most well known flashlight of the war was the ubiquitous Army TL-122-B two-cell olive drab plastic type that could be carried in a belt or pocket by a metal clip. It was recognized by its characteristic right angle head.

ATTACHABLE CHEST-TYPE PARACHUTES

Group 1 Assemblies

Type QAC (AN6513-1). Quick attachable chest-type parachute with square pack. Harness has snap fasteners on chest and leg straps. It has D-rings for attachment of pack.

Type QAC (AN6513-1A). Quick attachable chest-type parachute with barrel-type pack. Harness has snap fasteners on chest and leg straps. It has D-rings for attachment of pack.

Note: On both AN6513-1 and AN6513-1A parachute assemblies the snaps are on the pack and the D-rings are on the harness. Either of these packs can be used with the harness shown.

Group 2 Assemblies

Type A-3. Quick attachable chest-type parachute with barrel type pack. Harness has bayonet type fasteners.

Type A-4. Quick attachable chest-type parachute with barrel-type pack and single point Quick Release harness.

Note: On the A-3 and A-4 parachute assemblies the rings are on the pack and the snaps are on the harness. This pack can be used with either of the harnesses shown.

Part Four

B-29 Crewmen/Flying the B-29

The B-29 had the largest crew of any bomber of war, numbering 10 to 12. The crewmen were the airplane commander, co-pilot, flight engineer, bombardier, radio operator, and navigator in the forward pressurized compartment, and the central fire control gunner and two blister gunners and tail gunner—and later one and then two radar operators—in the rear. The B-17 carried 10 crewmen: pilot, co-pilot, bombardier/nose gunner, navigator, engineer/top turret gunner, radio operator/top gunner, ball turret gunner, two waist gunners, and a tail gunner. The B-24 carried 10 crewmen as well: pilot, co-pilot, bombardier/nose gunner, navigator, radio operator, engineer/top turret gunner, ball turret gunner, two waist gunners, and a tail gunner.

The Avro Lancaster—Britain's largest bomber—carried a crew of only eight: the pilot, co-pilot, bombardier/nose turret gunner, navigator, radio operator, mid-top turret gunner, mid-lower turret gunner, and tail gunner. Germany's largest bomber, the Heinkel He-177 carried a crew of six, while the Focke-Wulf Fw-200 carried eight, including a flight engineer. The Japanese Mitsubishi G4M2 Betty, which was essentially a medium bomber, carried six or seven crewmen.

1

Airplane Commander

Airplane Commander's Responsibilities
More than any other American bomber, the B-29 combat crew manuals emphasized teamwork and air discipline, beginning with the airplane commander. The *B-29 Combat Crew Manual* described the responsibility of the airplane commander as:

"The airplane commander must be an outstanding personality, a skilled pilot, and a well-disciplined officer. He must possess an adequate knowledge of the duties of all crewmen and of their responsibilities before he can successfully direct their efforts into smooth functioning teamwork.

Too many pilots consider themselves pilots alone and forget that they are responsible for an intricate and very expensive piece of machinery run by eleven men as a team. The failure of any one of the crewmen to perform his assigned duty correctly might easily prove disastrous. The way in which you, as the airplane commander execute your power of command to weld a highly trained group of men into a closely-knit team will be reflected in the efficiency and capabilities of your crew. The airplane commander must truly be a versatile person. Among other things he must:

(a)   Be a pilot and a commander
(b)   Analyze each crewman and guide relations with him accordingly.
(c)   Analyze himself and his relations with each crewman and act accordingly.
(d)   Be a specialist on six different subjects pertaining to successful operation of a heavy bomber. These include piloting bombing, navigation, engineering, gunnery and radar.
(e)   Set the example in order to command the respect of all crewmen.
(f)   Promote a team feeling among his crewmen.
(g)   Not show favoritism.
(h)   Stand up for his crew, individually and collectively.
(i)   Compliment when compliments are due.
(j)   Reprimand and discipline when necessary.
(k)   Delegate routine duties to insure smooth operation and no slip-ups.
(l)   Insist upon constant training for all crewmen.
(m)   Consult his crew as a commander consults his staff.

The airplane commander must bear in mind that the members of his crew are working not for him, but with him in a concerted effort to accomplish their mission. Every crewman must have the confidence in, and the trust of, every other crewman. It is the airplane commander's responsibility to foster and develop that confidence and trust. Finally, the airplane commander must develop and expand the confidence of his crew in such a manner as to include the ground crew as an integral part of the team.

As an airplane commander, you are responsible for the daily welfare of your crew. See that they properly quartered, clothed and fed. See that they are paid when they should be paid. Away from your home situation, carry your interest to the point of financing them yourself, if necessary. You are he commander of a combat force all your own-small but specialized army-and morale is one of the biggest problems in any army, large or small."

Air discipline was stressed with complete interdependence of all 11 crewmen. Air discipline was to start on the ground, and the airplane commander was to be sure that each of his crewmen was competent in his job. Daily "bull sessions" were held with the crew; hypothetical emergency situations were discussed, and a plan of action was made. The airplane commander was to be sure that his crew attended scheduled training classes, and to correct any weaknesses in the crew as individuals and as a team. He was to "organize (his) crew and practice working as a team. In the air put into practical application and continued training those lessons learned on the ground." The airplane commander was to train his crew in fire control, interphone procedure, ditching procedure, and abandoning ship, so that "clock like precision can be reached and maintained."

Airplane Commander and Co-pilot Checklist
Walk Around Visual Checklist
The first step in a flight check was the visual inspection, called the "walk-around." The movable parts were inspected, and the ground around the aircraft was inspected for fluid leaks. The airplane commander literally "walked around" the aircraft in a routine prescribed by the *B-29: Airplane Commander Training Manual for the Superfortress*, AAF Manual No.50-9:

1) Condition of tires should be examined carefully for cuts and slippage.
2) Wheel chocks should be 2in in front of inboard tires and 2in behind outboard tires.
3) Oleo struts should be 13.25in between pin centers on main gear and 10in on nose gear.
4) Hydraulic lines should be checked for leaks.
5) Shimmy dampener oil level should be checked. Top of pin should be even with groove.
6) Engine fire extinguishers should be inspected for red disk at end of line running down from each CO2 bottle (nose wheel well). If the bottle has been accidentally discharged, the red disk will be missing.
7) Gear motor and door motor cannon plugs should have each plug checked for looseness. If the rotation collar was not screwed tight, engine vibration could shake loose the cannon plug connection.
8) Cables on main wheel well doors should be on pulleys and free of obstructions.
9) Pitot tube covers should be off.
10) All fastenings on inspection plates and engine cowlings should be tight.
11) Engines and nacelles should be free of grease and oil that is a fire hazard. Have it cleaned off before the flight.
12) Control surfaces and trim tabs should be inspected for dents or damage.
13) Windows and blisters should be inspected for cracks and dirt.
14) All seams and connections should be checked for fluid leaks.

Engine Pull Through

After the walk around the airplane commander would go inside the aircraft to be sure that all switches were OFF, and instructed the crew to pull the

The airplane commander instructed the crew to pull the propellers through in preparation to starting. If the aircraft had been standing for more than 30 minutes, each prop was to be pulled through at least 12 blades with no more than two men per blade. (USAF)

propellers through in preparation to starting. If the aircraft had been standing for more than 30min, each prop was to be pulled through at least 12 blades, with no more than two men per blade. If the propeller stuck the plugs were to be removed from the bottom cylinders, the prop pulled through to remove excess oil from the cylinders, clean plugs installed, and the prop pulled through again. The oil pressure was never to be relieved by pulling the propeller backwards.

Crew Inspection and Form 1A Checks

After the propellers were pulled each of the crew was to be personally inspected. After this inspection the airplane commander was to check and sign Form 1A and inspect the loading list, weight, and the center of gravity figures that had been prepared by the flight engineer, and were to be ready at inspection. The C.G. figures were to fall between the allowable limits of 18% minimum and 24% maximum.

Before Starting Checklist

After the walk around, crew inspection, and Form 1A checks the airplane commander and co-pilot entered the forward pressurized compartment cockpit through the wheel well. The airplane commander and co-pilot were seated side-by-side, and began their interior visual inspection from a printed checklist. Their first inspection was of their personal equipment:

1) Parachute OK. At this time the airplane commander and the co-pilot put their parachutes on (harness over life vest) and checked their seat-type dinghies.
2) Clothing OK. Airplane commander and co-pilot checked their clothing, adjusted their helmets and throat microphones, and attached their oxygen masks to the left side of their helmet. If the airplane commander was wearing a heated flying suit he turned the rheostat on his suit to OFF before plugging the push jack into the suit's socket, and then turned the rheostat to the ON position to warm up the suit.
3) Life vest OK. On all over water flights the airplane commander and co-pilot checked that their life vests were fitted with CO_2 cartridges and did not interfere with the parachute.

Next came the aircraft check:
1) Parking brakes and chocks SET. The airplane commander depressed the rudder pedals and pulled out the parking brake lever. He and the co-pilot looked out their respective windows to check to see if the chocks were in their proper positions as per the walk around.
2) Emergency landing gear door release in place. Pulling this handle would release the nacelle doors. (a T-shaped handle on airplane commander's control stand)
3) Emergency bomb release in place. (a T-shaped handle on airplane commander's control stand)
4) Emergency cabin pressure in place. (a T-shaped handle on airplane commander's control stand)
5) Landing gear transfer switch normal (located on the airplane commander's control stand). In this position, the landing gear switch operated the main landing gear and nosewheel. When the landing gear transfer switch was in the EMERGENCY position, power from the engine driven generators went to the emergency bus, and the emergency landing gear switches could actuate the emergency landing gear motors.

6) Landing gear switch NEUTRAL and fuse check (located on the airplane commander's aisle stand). The switch was to be in NEUTRAL, and the fuse in the aisle stand was in place and not burned out.

7) Battery switch ON. The flight engineer flipped the battery switch to ON and notified the airplane commander. Either the battery or APU, or both, energized all electrical circuits. Both were used for normal ground operation on loads up to 200 amps. For additional power an external power source of electric-driven generator was used.

8) APU started. Co-pilot instructed the tail gunner to start the APU.

9) Hydraulic pressure OK. The co-pilot asked the flight engineer to check the emergency hydraulic pressure on his panel (900-1,075psi), and then checked it on his own panel (800-1,000psi). A fluctuating needle indicated a faulty pressure regulator. If the hydraulic pump overheated and smoked, the flight engineer would remove the fuse on his aft fuse panel. The pump had to be stopped when the pressure reached 1,000psi to prevent overheating.

10) Flight controls checked. The airplane commander pushed down the locking lever, located at the forward end of the airplane commander's aisle stand. This action also unlocked the throttles, which had been

After the propellers were pulled each of the crewmen was to be inspected, but this formality was mostly ignored in combat theaters. (USAF)

held closed by a lock bar when the control lock was on. This lock bar was connected to the control lock in such a manner that a strong forward pressure on the throttles would be required to force the control lock off, eliminating the possibility of locked controls after take off. The co-pilot was to make his flight control check. In his check the co-pilot would alert the waist gunners over the interphone that he was about to check the controls. The gunners would look out their windows as the co-pilot pulled back the control levers for the elevator check. The left and right gunners would report that their respective elevators were UP. The co-pilot would then push the control column forward to check the down position of the elevators. The ailerons and rudder were checked in a similar fashion.

11) Radios checked. While the co-pilot was checking the flight controls the airplane commander turned on his command set and asked for taxi information. After checking the flight controls, the co-pilot turned on his radio compass and checked it for proper operation and then turned it off. The co-pilot then stood by on the interphone to be in continuous communication with the crew.

12) Altimeters SET. The airplane commander and co-pilot set their altimeters with the tower altimeter reading. They checked the altitude reading against the known elevation of the airfield. If the altimeter setting given by the tower indicated a different altitude from the known field altitude a note was made of the difference in height so that it could be used in correcting the reading when landing.

13) Turrets STOWED. Airplane commander checked the three turret warning lights on his instrument panel to see if they were unlit, showing that all three were properly stowed.

14) Adjust seats and pedals.

15) Lights checked. If the flight involved night operation, all the lights were to be checked: fluorescent, identification, landing, and position lights. Wing position lights were not visible from the aircraft in flight, and could be inspected at night from the aircraft by their reflection on the ground under the wing.

16) Oxygen check. The airplane commander and co-pilot checked their oxygen pressure gauges for proper pressure (400-425psi) and their walk around bottles (same pressure as the system). Auto mix should be ON, emergency valve OFF.

17) Propellers high rpm. The co-pilot pushed the switches on the aisle stand to INCREASE RPM, and held them there until the propeller limit lights on his instrument panel flashed ON, indicating that the props were in high rpm.

18) Turbos OFF. The airplane commander checked that the turbo selector dial was set at 0. The turbosupercharger regulators were then ready for instant operation at any time, as the amplifier tubes remained on even with the selector dial at 0.

19) Flight engineer's report. The flight engineer reported that his check list was complete, and the aircraft was ready to start engines. If the flight engineer had not completed his checklist the airplane commander would wait until he was ready before starting engines.

20) Stand clear. When they were ready to start the engines, both the airplane commander and co-pilot gave the command "Stand clear" to the ground crew ("clear right" and "clear left"). When the fireguard was ready, the co-pilot announced over the interphone "Stand by to start engines."

Starting Engines

Investigation had shown that incorrect engine starting procedures were the cause of many engine failures during take off and in flight. The airplane commander had to work with the flight engineer to be certain that he had completed his checklist, and was using the recommended starting procedures. The flight engineer was instrumental in starting each engine, and used the following procedure (abbreviated here but expanded in the flight engineer's start checklist):

1) Activate fire extinguisher stand by to the engine being started.
2) Turn master ignition switch ON.
3) Turn boost pump ON.
4) Energize starter for 12 to 16secs.
5) Move starter switch to START position.
6) After propeller made one revolution turn the ignition switch ON and hold the primer down as needed to start and smooth out the engine at 800 to 1,000rpm.
7) Move the mixture control to AUTO RICH.

The number of fingers held up by the airplane commander referred to starboard engines #1 and #2, and by the co-pilot to port engine numbers #3 and #4. These finger signals indicated the number of the engine to be started. The engines were started in the sequence of #3 then #4 to allow the fireguard outside the engine to back away and escape the prop wash from the started engine. Next #2 engine, then #1 engine was started. When the engine started, the flight engineer reported if the engine was operating normally and announced that he was ready to start the next engine.

When they were ready to start the engines, both the airplane commander and co-pilot gave the command "Stand clear" to the ground crew ("clear right" and "clear left"). (USAF)

To prevent engine overheating during ground time it was recommended that all the engines be started as quickly as possible, in no more than three minutes. The cowl flaps were to be in the full open position (27-degrees), and the engine run up was to be made immediately after starting. The engine was to be held at low rpm (700-800rpm), and when possible the bomber was to be turned into the wind for the engine run up. If the cylinder head temperatures rose above the allowable maximum the engines were to be shut down without blocking the runway, and under no circumstance was a take off to be attempted.

During engine run up the throttles were to be advanced smoothly and steadily, and each engine was to be checked individually for proper operation. The flight engineer handled the throttles throughout the starting procedure, maintaining the rpm between 1,000 and 1,200. When the engine was running, the flight engineer set the throttle at 700rpm (1,000rpm if the cylinder head temperature was below 300°F). Thereafter the airplane commander controlled the throttles, except when asking for the engine-driven generators and during engine run up. If either the flight engineer or co-pilot saw that the engine was "loading up" (black smoke or rpm drop, or both) he would inform the airplane commander. The started engine was not to be idled below 700rpm.

Magnetos were checked, and running the engine at full power for a few seconds cleared moisture condensation on the spark plugs. Proper engine function was important, as the critical period during take off at the high gross weights was immediately after leaving the ground, before the wheels and flaps were retracted. There were five "Don'ts" for starting an engine:

1) Don't start an engine until the before starting checklist has been covered item by item.
2) Don't start the engines until the propellers have been pulled through to eliminate the possibility of fluid locks.
3) Don't jam the throttles forward at any time, especially during the starting procedure.
4) Don't start engines until a fireguard was standing nearby.
5) Don't continue to run an engine if the nose oil pressure and rear oil pressure did not build up within 30 seconds after starting.

Before Taxiing

Before taxiing the duties of the airplane commander and the co-pilot were to check the following:

1) Vacuum. The co-pilot asked the flight engineer to check the vacuum reading for both pumps. The gauges on the instrument panel were to read 3.8 to 4.2in Hg. The only time the vacuum selector valve on the engineer's control stand was to be moved was during this check, as it was prone to wear.
2) Gyros. The airplane commander and co-pilot checked their gyro instruments for correct readings, and to be sure that they were uncaged and operating correctly. At this time they set the directional gyros to agree with the magnetic compass reading.
3) Instruments. The airplane commander and co-pilot checked their respective instrument panels for proper readings and operation of all instruments.
4) Bomb bay doors closed. The co-pilot instructed the gunners and radio operator to check that all ground crew were clear of the bomb bay

doors. He then asked the engineer if the generators were on, and instructed him to close the bomb bay doors. The flight engineer had previously set the throttle on the coolest engine to 1,400rpm and turned the generators on. The radio operator and one of the gunners checked visually through the windows on the bomb bay pressure bulkhead doors of their compartments to see if the bomb bay doors were closed. The flight engineer returned the throttle to 700rpm and turned off the generator at the co-pilot's instruction. Later B-29s were equipped with the pneumatic snap-opening bomb bay doors that eliminated the generator procedure.

5) Alarm bell, phone call signal light, and combat station inspection were dealt with by one interphone call check. The airplane commander switched on the alarm bell (aisle stand) and phone call signal light (aisle stand), and then called for a combat station inspection. The co-pilot repeated this command on the interphone and received acknowledgment in the following order: bombardier, navigator, flight engineer, radio operator, top gunner, left gunner, right gunner, and tail gunner, that they had completed a check of their station by replying bombardier OK, Navigator OK, etc.

6) Chocks out. The airplane commander and co-pilot visually checked that the chocks had been pulled on their side of the aircraft.

7) Parking brakes off, stand by to taxi. After releasing the parking brakes, the airplane commander gave the order "Stand by to taxi," and the co-pilot repeated the order over the interphone.

Taxiing Procedure

The B-29 was easy to taxi, as was typical of an aircraft with a tricycle landing gear. The four expander type tubes per wheel gave the bomber good braking, but because of its large size the aircraft could gain momentum quickly, and the side and top gunners were on alert to warn the airplane commander and co-pilot of any obstacles. Often with the 141ft wingspan a ground crewman walked at each wingtip to guide the bomber.

For all ground operations the rpm was to be set at 700 (after the cylinder head temperatures reached 300°F), and the mixture was to be set at AUTO RICH (never AUTO LEAN) to keep the bomber moving. With properly set carburetors the engines could idle as low as 500rpm without loading up. When taxiing uphill or in hot weather, the 700rpms would often not be sufficient to keep the bomber moving. To remedy this situation all throttle settings needed to be increased, but only to a point to continue taxiing and not to risk overheating. Like most aircraft the B-29 would weathervane into the wind. In a strong cross wind the airplane commander was to set the upwind outboard throttle at more than 700 rpm to prevent excessive use of the down wind brakes.

The airplane commander checked main and emergency hydraulic pressure before starting taxiing, as considerable braking would be needed to stop the heavily loaded aircraft. The bomber was to taxi slowly and keep a safe distance from the bomber ahead. It was recommended that the aircraft be taxied with its brakes alone, controlling both the speed and direction with the brakes, and not by increasing the engine rpm. This braking procedure would insure maximum engine cooling and prevent backfiring. However, excessive braking would cause the brakes to overheat and lose their effectiveness, and a judicious use of engine power blended with braking was then in order. All turns were to be made smoothly, with the wheel on the inside of the turn kept in motion. A quick, sharp turn could dislodge a tire from the rim, and at the high gross weights cause the landing gear to

collapse. To save their brakes airplane commanders were tempted to enter the taxi turn with extra power from the outside throttle. But this maneuver could cause the aircraft to accelerate quickly, and it then had to be slowed down with the brakes. If the aircraft gained too much speed the airplane commander was to bring it almost to a stop, pointed straight ahead, permit the brakes to cool, and then allow the bomber to roll slowly ahead.

Before Take Off

The duties of the airplane commander and co-pilot before take off were to check the following:

1) Emergency Brakes Checked. When starting to taxi, after the parking brakes were released the co-pilot would say "Emergency brakes." The airplane commander then pulled the emergency brake hand metering levers (aisle stand) to check if the emergency brakes on each side were operating properly. The co-pilot then asked the flight engineer to recharge the emergency system. Normal brakes could be used safely while recharging the emergency system because the electric hydraulic pump recharged both systems with the hydraulic serving valve on emergency.

2) Nose wheel straight. The co-pilot checked through the cockpit floor observation window to be sure that the nose wheel was straight before engine run up.

3) Engine run up. The airplane commander gave the command "Stand by for engine run up," and the co-pilot repeated the command over the interphone. Engine run up was in the following sequence:

a) Airplane commander increased all throttles to 1,500rpm and commanded "Check generators." The co-pilot started to move the flaps down (aisle stand), and asked the flight engineer to check the generators. The co-pilot held the flap switch DOWN until the flaps reached their full down position, and then returned them to 25-degrees (the flap movement was checked by the waist gunners). In the meantime the engineer would have checked the generators.

b) The airplane commander put all four propeller switches from full decrease then to full increase (warning light to warning light) to test the propeller governors. At full decrease the tachometers were to have stable uniform readings of 1,200 to 1,500rpm. When they were returned to full increase they were to read 1,500rpms.

c) After the generator and propeller check the airplane commander pulled the throttles back to 700rpm and ordered the flight engineer to check the magnetos. The flight engineer advanced the throttles to 2,000rpm, checked the magnetos of all engines, and called out "Right, both, left, both," and returned the throttles to 700rpm. The allowable rpm drop at 2,000rpm was 100. If the rpm drop on any engine was more than 100 and caused by fouled plugs, a full power check was run on that engine. Then the magnetos were checked on the bad engine (turbo off). If the rpm drop continued above 100 the aircraft was to be returned to the line. The magnetos were not to be checked with the turbos on, as a backfire could damage the turbo and waste gate assembly.

d) Simultaneously, the manifold pressure for each engine was checked in reaching 2,000rpm. The airplane commander set the turbo selector on No.8 and advanced the throttles one at a time to full OPEN to check the manifold pressure and rpm. The ground check gauges should read between 2,500 and 2,600 rpm and 46.5 and 47.7in of manifold pressure (deduct 0.5in manifold pressure for each 50rpm). Excessive manifold pressure indicated a bad cylinder, valve, or some other engine problem.

4) Wing flaps 25-degrees. If the flaps were not lowered to 25-30-degrees before take off a warning horn would blow when the throttle was opened to 3/4 or more. Gunners had checked the lowering of the flaps.

5) Trim flaps set. The airplane commander checked all trim tab controls: rudder and aileron neutral, and elevator as needed according to the calculated position of the center of gravity.

6) Autopilot off. The airplane commander made certain all switches (his aisle stand) were OFF with the turn control centered.

7) Windows and hatches closed. The airplane commander and co-pilot closed and secured their widows. The co-pilot also checked the forward entrance compartment hatch, and checked with the tail gunner to be sure that the rear entrance door and rear escape hatch were closed.

8) Turbos on No.8.

9) Propellers on high rpm.

10) Crew ready as co-pilot announced, "Prepare for take off."

11) Radio call completed, as airplane commander called tower and requested permission to take off.

Take Off Procedure

The cylinder head temperatures (CHT) were to be kept at a minimum before takeoff, and not to exceed 430°F. The takeoff with heavy gross weight was the most critical time of the entire flight. Some pilots preferred to hold the brakes at the end of the runway to get a power check before beginning the roll, while others preferred to make rolling takeoffs. The airplane commander had to be careful on rolling takeoffs so as not to overshoot the turn onto the runway and throw a tire off its rim.

With either method the airplane commander had to gain control of the direction of the aircraft by use of the rudder as soon as possible. When the aircraft began to roll down the runway, the airplane commander walked the throttles forward slowly until there was rudder control at 60 to 65mph. The throttles were then moved steadily forward to the full open position. This allowed the airplane commander to maintain directional control, first with the throttles, then with the rudder. If the throttles were advanced to 40-degrees at a standstill for a power check or moved forward too quickly at the beginning of the roll, there would not be enough reserve power necessary to hold the aircraft straight with the throttles. The brakes were not to be used to hold the plane straight on the runway except in emergencies, as this practice increased the take off distance and the time needed to attain rudder control, as well as overheating the brakes. By not using the brakes the aircraft would gain speed continuously from the point of run up to the point where the wheels left the runway.

The co-pilot was to make continuous power checks as the throttles were being advanced during the initial take off roll. Full power (47.5in and 2,600 rpm) was to be achieved during the roll down the first third of the runway. During his power checks, if the co-pilot noticed any irregular power readings he was to notify the airplane commander, who would have time to cut the throttles if he deemed that continuation of the take off was inadvisable. Care had to be taken when adjusting the propeller rpm so that none of the propeller rpm switches stuck at the full rpm position (both metal tabs were to be used when operating these switches). Take off was never to be attempted at less than full power, as take off at reduced power

increased the time for the bomber to reach 195 mph, and flying the aircraft below this speed was dangerous and did not cool the engines sufficiently. Full power was not harmful to the engines if the CHT remained within normal limits.

At the beginning of the takeoff roll the airplane commander closed the cowl from 15-degrees to 7.5 to 9-degrees (at wide open the aircraft could not leave the ground). As the takeoff speed increased the engines were cooled by the increased airflow. The airplane commander watched that the cylinder head temperature did not exceed the maximum, as higher temperatures resulted in reduced power. The intercooler shutters were wide open (15-degrees) for takeoff, then half open after the gear and flaps were retracted, and thereafter closed as required. If the turbos were used on takeoff very high carburetor temperatures resulted, with a large reduction of power if the intercooler shutters were closed.

A speed of 100mph was reached very quickly, but thereafter the acceleration was comparatively slow. When 110 to 120mph was reached the airplane commander raised the nose wheel two to six inches above the ground and held it there until 130 to 140mph was reached, and the bomber was in very good control. Care had to be taken not to lift the nose wheel too high off the ground, as stalling and engine failure could occur. At 140mph the airplane commander called for power condition 2 (43.5in and 2,400rpm). At 150mph the airplane commander called for flaps up easy, about 5-degrees at a time. The co-pilot had to wait for the aircraft to settle before raising the flaps another 5-degrees. When the flaps and gear were full up, airplane commander called for power condition 3 (39in and 2,300rpm at under 115,000lbs gross weight). The manifold pressure was then reduced with the turbo selector dial until the turbos were off, at which time the co-pilot informed the flight engineer that the turbos were off. The ensuing manifold pressure reductions were made with the throttles. As soon as the aircraft left the ground the landing gear was retracted, as its drag was very large in relation to the aerodynamic cleanliness of the aircraft, and was equivalent to adding more power. Engine power needed to be maintained until the gear was fully retracted. Flaps were retracted when the indicated airspeed (IAS) was 40mph greater that the takeoff speed. The power off stalling speed with the flaps up was 15 to 20mph IAS higher than the lowest takeoff speed with 25-degrees flaps at any weight. Therefore, it was necessary to maintain a margin of 20 to 25mph IAS above flaps up stalling speed when retracting the flaps. The wheels were to leave the ground at about 70% of the total runway length. As soon as the aircraft was safely airborne, the wheel brakes were to be applied to stop them from spinning, and the gear was to be retracted, further cleaning up the aerodynamics and effectively adding more power.

Emergency Take Off

Before take off all engines were completely warmed up, and it was necessary to dilute the oil to lower its viscosity to a point where there would be no danger of the hose connections being blown loose in case an emergency take off became required. All flight controls were to be checked, the fuel boost pumps were ON, and the mixture controls were AUTOMATIC RICH. The supercharger selector was to be set to "8" (47.5in HG, military power), and the propellers set at 2,600rpm.

Engine Failure During Take Off

If an engine failed during take off, its propeller was to be feathered immediately, and the fuel valve and mixture control shut off. The landing gear was to be retracted as soon as possible, and the trim tabs compensated for an unbalanced condition.

Climb and Cruising

Climb

The airplane commander worked closely with the flight engineer during climb, keeping in constant contact with him on cowl flap opening and cylinder head temperatures (to be kept at 478°F). The intention of the climb was to reach a predetermined altitude as soon as possible, and any opening of the cowl flaps decreased the rate of climb and increased the time high power settings were used which, in turn, deceased engine longevity. Rated power climbs for gross weights under 115,000lbs was to be at 39in, 2,300rpm, and 195mph, while at higher gross weights the climb was to be at 43.5in, 2,400rpm, and 195 to 205mph. Rated power climbs used less fuel than climbs at 39in and 2,300rpm, provided the CHT could be maintained within limits during a sustained climb. If all CHTs ran high during a sustained climb the airplane commander was to hold the climbing power and level off until the CHTs returned to normal, and afterward start to climb again. For each rpm setting, whether climb or cruising, there was a definite manifold pressure setting. Using more manifold pressure led to detonation, causing less wasted fuel. The aircraft commander was trained to use related power settings at all times and control the CHT with airspeed. For take off the intercooler flaps were at full open. For climb and cruise they were to be opened just enough to obtain the lowest possible carburetor air temperature. If in conditions that were to produce ice the intercooler flaps were to be regulated to maintain the carburetor air temperature to 77°F to 100°F. With the turbos off the intercooler flaps were to be completely closed.

Before the airplane commander leveled off the bomber he was to climb 500ft above the designated altitude, and then maintain rated power until the airspeed was increased to 220 to 230mph. He then decreased the power to predetermined settings, leaving the cowl flap openings in the same position until the cylinder head temperatures started to decrease. The cowl flaps were then closed as much as possible, maintaining 414°F for the cylinder head temperature. The airplane commander adjusted the altitude until he got the aircraft "on step," and stabilized the airspeed and cylinder head temperatures on cruise settings.

Cruising

Before going into cruise, the aircraft commander was to climb above the designated mission altitude: 500ft above for altitudes below 10,000ft; 1,000ft above for altitudes between 10,000 and 20,000ft; and 1,500ft above for altitudes over 20,000ft. He was then to hold his climbing power settings at zero rate of climb until the airspeed reached 210mph, at which time the aircraft would "go on step." The B-29 did not reach its maximum airspeed for a given power setting unless it was flown on step. For the predetermined cruising power to be set the aircraft was nosed slightly down, the cowl flaps opened to 10-degrees, and then the bomber descended to the desired altitude at 210mph. When the altitude was attained the cowl flaps were closed to 3-degrees, and the elevators were used to hold the predetermined cruising airspeed. The power settings were varied slightly to maintain this altitude. After the airspeed was established the cowl flaps were opened or closed individually to maintain CHT within safe limits.

The climb to high altitude did not begin until the bomber was in the air for several hours at lower altitude. As fuel consumption was highest at high altitudes, the air commander was to fly at minimum altitudes as long as possible.

Cruise Control

To enable the airplane commander to operate his aircraft at maximum range, and in combat missions drop the maximum bomb load on the target, he had to rely on the flight engineer. The flight engineer was thoroughly familiar with the cruise control charts, power curves, "Form F" (that determined the center of gravity and gross weight), and the standard operating procedures that had been worked out in tests. The Cruise Control Chart determined the power settings (for gross weight and cowl flap corrections), and took into consideration power correction for altitude, and an altitude correction for power and fuel consumption. The cruise control tenets were:

(a) Remain at minimum safe altitude as long as possible at heavy gross weights.
(b) Get into automatic lean as soon as possible.
(c) Beware of the backside of the power curve.
(d) Keep a close watch on the cylinder head temperatures and cowl flap settings.
(e) Be sure to fly "on step" at all times.
(f) Be on the look out for the "vicious circle" of cowl flaps and indicated airspeed.
(g) Fly the indicated airspeed for specific gross weights.
(h) Take advantage of descent from altitude, as it was one of the factors governing the economy of fuel used. The flight engineer and navigator helped to determine the point to begin descent. The descent was to be made at the slow rate of 200fpm, thus the required air speeds could be maintained at greatly reduced power settings.

The original cruise control charts worked out in the States were not applicable to combat, and after much experimentation a combat cruise control chart was evolved based on the average operation of all bombers within each group.

Maximum Endurance

Flying at a speed where the engines used fuel at the lowest possible rate achieved maximum endurance (e.g. using the least amount of engine power to keep the aircraft in the air). The Long-Range cruising speed of the B-29 was much higher than the B-17. To get good performance the aircraft had to be flown at a constant indicated airspeed (e.g. the power adjusted to maintain altitude). The less the aircraft weighed and the lower the altitude it was flown meant longer time in the air. Maximum endurance was obtained by trimming the aircraft for the best speed (slightly nose down), and dropping below the normal cruising power by reducing the rpm and holding the manifold pressure at 28in (plus or minus 2in). The absolute minimum rpm was to be 1,400rpm, so as not to lose current from the generators on the engines.

Maximum Range

Maximum range was flown at a speed and altitude that produced the maximum miles per gallon of fuel consumed. This was at a higher speed than for maximum endurance. By increasing the power a small amount to the minimum power needed to stay in the air (which increased fuel flow) a somewhat larger increase in speed, and consequently an increase in the miles traveled for each gallon of fuel consumed was attained. When the power was subsequently increased step by step, both the speed and fuel consumption was increased. There was a somewhat wide range of speed (called a speed band) in which the aircraft could gain the maximum miles per gallon, and this range was normally at least 15mph (indicated) wide in terms of indicated air speed. Flying the bomber within this speed band gave it its maximum range. However, there was a range of speeds in this power increase where the speed increased to its maximum while the rate of fuel consumption did not increase as much. The middle of this band was about 15mph (indicated) above the minimum power speed, and going above this speed the miles per gallon of fuel would decrease.

The lower part of this speed band was difficult to fly in formation. However, there was no need to fly at a low speed when a higher speed took the bomber just as far in a shorter time. A head wind decreased the range by its velocity per hour and, conversely, a tail wind increased the aircraft's range. Flying at the higher end of the speed band (the upper 5mph) could attain a greater range against a head wind. From a gross weight of 80,000 to 90,000lbs it was recommended to increase the flying speed 5mph from 180 to 185mph for every 10,000lbs gross weight increase. The weight of the aircraft could significantly affect speed, but altitude had no affect upon the indicated speed at which the aircraft flew at maximum range.

When flying for maximum range, the airplane commander had to keep the speed in one of these speed bands. He increased power by adjusting the rpm while maintaining the manifold pressure to 35in (plus or minus 2in) in AUTO LEAN at 2,200rpm (and below). When flying in formation the formation leader was to maintain the speed at the lower end of the speed range to allow the other bombers in the formation (which had to make some changes in speed to stay in formation) to stay within the economical speed band.

The richer mixtures at high powers, and the larger cowl flap openings that were required to cool the engines at high altitudes caused a great loss of range. Maximum range, like maximum endurance, was obtained at lower altitudes. However, flying at low altitude at powers of 35in and 2,200rpm in AUTO LEAN (or less) at the desired speed band did not increase the range. The B-29 was very aerodynamically clean, and every degree of cowl flap opening above that which was required to cool the engines increased the fuel consumption by at least 15gals per hour. Generally, there was no loss in range up to 15,000ft, and the range losses at the higher altitudes occurred almost entirely at the heaviest gross weights. To avoid the loss of range, the airplane commander flew at low altitudes until fuel had been consumed, putting the bomber at a more moderate weight, and then he would climb to a higher altitude. Maximum range depended on the aircraft's weight and drag. For every six pounds of fuel consumed, one gallon of gasoline (e.g. six more pounds) less was needed to travel as far. During the return leg of a Long-Range flight, making descents using the recommended Long-Range cruising speeds and the lowest recommended power settings, the maximum range could likewise be extended.

Engine Failure During Flight

If engine failure occurred during flight, the AFCE (automatic flight control) master switch was turned off, the throttle and cowl flaps were closed, the mixture was cut off, and the booster pump controls for the affected engine were shut off. The propeller was feathered, and the aircraft was trimmed to correct any unbalance. The AFCE master switch could then be turned back on. In case of multiple engine failure only one propeller at a

time was to be feathered, as feathering used excessive amounts of current. If the engine was not to be operated again during flight, the remaining fuel was to be transferred to the other engines, as desired.

Flying the B-29: Flight Characteristics

Despite its large size and weight, the B-29 had the flight characteristics of a much smaller aircraft. Even though large aircraft were usually slow in responding to the controls because of their large inertia, the control surfaces of the B-29 were surprisingly light. Even at low speeds, when the flying forces were low and inertia was high, its controls were responsive. In the critical periods (just after take off and while landing), the ailerons and rudders, although slow, continued to be responsive.

Elevators

The B-29 elevators were of an aluminum alloy frame construction and were fabric covered. The elevator control of the B-29 has been compared to that of the B-17. The horizontal stabilizer was almost the same size of the Flying Fortress, except that the Superfortress elevators had somewhat more balance. On the B-29 the front of the tail airfoil section was turned up so that the tail did not stall when making a power-on approach to a landing with full flaps down. The elevator trim tab was very responsive in high-speed dives, and the airplane commander had to be careful not to over-control the aircraft when flying with the trim tab.

Ailerons

The large ailerons could be utilized through a great angle (18-degrees up or down), and gave the aircraft good control. The travel of the control wheel was greater than the B-17, and this added control was essential if an engine failed just after take off, or if the fuel used on one side of the aircraft was more than the other. The aileron trim tabs were geared to move when the ailerons were moved. The shape of the wing airfoil was such that the part covered by the ailerons was hollow on top, and was full on the bottom. If the cables were cut during combat, the ailerons would trim down because of this configuration. This negative effect was counteracted by rigging the trim tabs down one inch at the trailing edge to trim the ailerons to more nearly neutral.

Rudder

Despite not being power-boosted, the rudder gave maximum control and stability. The diamond shape of the rudder was derived from extensive tests, and produced a rudder that performed normally during all flight conditions. The rudder could be moved with a small amount of effort, and did not become unbalanced or locked. The rudder forces of the B-29 were so light that it was sometimes difficult to judge what influence it was having on the aircraft. When the rudder was trimmed it was to be trimmed to get uniform pedal pressures.

Stability

The longitudinal stability of the B-29 was standard under all conditions, but the center of gravity needed to be maintained within recommended limits. The structural strength, and the elevator control that fixed the forward center of gravity limits were good under all conditions. The rearmost center of gravity was determined by the longitudinal instability that occurred at climbing power. Any rearward movement of this center of gravity limit made flying not only difficult, but also dangerous. It was essential

Part Four, Chapter 1 - Airplane Commander

that the center of gravity be maintained within design limits, and that the gross weight be kept at an absolute minimum for the mission to be flown. The flight engineer was responsible for these computations, and used a weight and balance slide rule to calculate them.

Stalls

The stall characteristics for the B-29 were normal. As it neared stalling there was a noticeable lightening of the elevator loads, and just before a full stall was reached there was shuttering and buffeting. During a stall there was rudder and elevator response, but no aileron response. Reduction of power reduced the stalling speed, but did nothing to affect the stall. In most aircraft it was possible to achieve a high rate of descent by applying power during a power-off stall without dropping the nose. But to recover from a stall in the B-29 the procedure was to first drop the nose and then increase the power. To bring the bomber out of a stall there needed to be a sizable movement of the controls. The power was never to be applied without first dropping the nose. The bomber recovered normally with no inordinate bias to drop off on one wing when the stall was properly controlled

During cruise the airplane commander had to be careful not to fly below the power-off stalling speed, as any loss of power when flying below this speed would cause a violent stall. For the same reason, on landing the airplane commander had to be very careful not to allow the speed to fall below the power-off stalling speed. Power was not to be used to reduce landing speed.

Prohibited Maneuvers

It was prohibited to fly the aircraft at any time with the center of gravity behind 34% of the mean aerodynamic chord (MAC), or with the CG ahead 24% of the mean MAC, except at low gross weights (under 120,000lbs). The restricted maneuvers were loops, spins, Immelmanns, inverted flight, rolls, vertical banks, and dives in excess of the red line speed for altitude.

Dives

The B-29 was limited in allowable diving speed by its strength limitations and control characteristics. When the speed increased the loads on every part of the aircraft increased rapidly, especially the horizontal tail surfaces. The red line was 300mph indicated, and was sufficiently above the level flight top speed to be adequate for most diving requirements. At high altitudes the red line speeds caused compressibility effects, such as wing and

tail buffeting, control ineffectiveness, and large elevator changes. At high altitudes the red line speed was reduced to conform to the "altitude-in-thousands-maximum airspeed" table fixed beside the airspeed indicator.

Dead Engine Characteristics

With one engine feathered and power balanced the straight and level flight of a B-29 was little different from normal four-engined flight. With a feathered engine the airplane commander was to turn into the dead engine at more than 150mph (indicated), and at least 20 to 25mph greater than the power-off stalling speed of the aircraft. If two engines were out on the same side the bomber was disposed to yaw and roll. To maintain lateral trim the airplane commander applied aileron that then caused the aircraft to crab, which in turn required the use of the rudder. It was necessary to maintain a speed of at least 10mph (indicated) above power-off stalling speed. At 100,000lbs it was just possible to maintain level flight with two engines feathered and the landing gear down, but at 130,000lbs level flight was possible with only one engine feathered and the gear down.

Formation Flying

There were four basic prerequisites for all types of B-29 formations to bomb successfully and evade enemy defenses:

1)	Develop a bombing pattern that envelops the target.
2)	Develop maximum defensive firepower against enemy fighter attack and mobility to evade flak.
3)	In case aircraft in the formation are lost, the formation leader would be able to close up the formation rapidly, and to its most efficient configuration.
4)	The formation should be easy to fly with the least pilot fatigue.

The XX and XXI Bomber Commands each had different formation doctrine. The XXIBC flew two flights of 11-bomber squadrons in a group formation, while the XXBC used the modified 12-plane staggered formation that had been successful over Europe.

The XX Bomber Command flew the ETO modified 12-plane stagger. Each element of three bombers flew in a "V," and four elements in the squadron also flew in a larger "V." In the three-plane element "V" the two wingmen were nose to tail and wing tip to wing tip behind the leader. The vertical distance between the right wingman was 50ft above the lead bomber, and the left wingman 50ft below it. The four elements, flying in a "V,"

The XX and XXI Bomber Commands each had different formation doctrine. The XXIBC flew two flights of 11-bomber squadrons in a group formation while the XXBC used the modified 12-plane staggered formation that had been successful over Europe. (USAF)

were separated vertically by 150ft, and the three following "Vs" flew nose to tail on the lead bomber. There were two elements behind and on the right of the lead element, and one behind and on the left. The minimum XXBC strike force was three 12-plane squadrons in trail spaced two minutes apart.

The XXI Bomber Command tactical doctrine required the following formation procedure:

The lead element of three bombers flew in a very tight diamond, ideally with the two wingmen flying level and slightly behind, nose to tail, the lead bomber. The wing tips of the two wingmen neither cleared nor overlapped the lead (unlike the slight clearance allowed in XXBC formations). The remaining eight bombers of the squadron were made up of two elements of four in a diamond. In order to avoid the prop wash of the lead bomber, the right bomber in each diamond flew just above his leader's vertical fin, nose to tail, while the left bomber flew just below, nose to tail. The last bomber in the diamond (following the lead bomber) flew just above the leader's vertical tail, nose to tail, with the two lateral bombers in the diamond. The squadron of three elements (the lead "V" and two lateral diamonds) formed a large "V." The vertical distance between the three elements in a squadron was 150ft, with the right element 150ft below and the left 150ft above the lead "V." The lateral distance was 400ft from the lead "V." The lead bomber of the second squadron flew 1,200ft to the right, 1,000ft above, and just behind the last bomber of the lead squadron. The two squadrons of a group were separated by two minutes. On long over water flights the XXIBC flew in looser formation that was better for fuel economy and weather penetration. Once the B-29s reached Japan the formation tightened up for mutual fighter defense. Former B-17 and B-24 pilots flying with the XXIBC found the B-29 as easy to fly in tight formation as the B-17, and easier than the B-24.

To assure that assigned mission range was achieved assembly was to be carried out in all cases as briefed, and as quickly as possible. There were three types of assembly: normal, in darkness, and above overcast.

1) The normal assembly plan followed a predetermined set of headings, and the airplane commander was to be sure that the time intervals were kept track of. After takeoff the airplane commander gained sufficient flying speed before he maneuvered into formation. It was best to fly a collision course with the formation leader than to use excessive power. The airplane commander had to anticipate the turns and relative speed of the bomber in front of him.
2) The assembly after darkness was challenging, as it was difficult to judge distances at night. The aldis light in the tail of each bomber aided the cautious approach for assembly. Once assembled the bombers flew in loose formation.
3) Assembly above overcast was made to briefing plans. Predetermined headings, air speed, and rate of climb were to be strictly followed as the bombers climbed through the overcast and assembled at a preassigned altitude above the overcast, usually over a homing beacon or radio range.

Maintaining Formation
Flight leaders had to be sure never to place their formation in the prop wash, nor maintain such high or low airspeeds that the rest of the forma-

tion would have trouble maintaining their proper position in the formation. The element leaders and their wingmen determined the depth of the formation with 30 to 50ft between aircraft, allowing the best defensive turret spread against enemy fighter attack. All airplane commanders were to maintain their position in the formation with a minimum of movement, so as not to force nearby aircraft out of position. Each movement of a lead aircraft was magnified as it traveled to the rear of the formation, causing abrupt throttle changes, and thus trim changes that meant constant and fatiguing fighting of the controls and the possibility of engine and supercharger failure. Close formations were easier to fly than loose ones, as it was easier to notice changes in relative positions, and any corrections were minor. In long missions the co-pilot was required to aid in the flying.

Formation flying required that the airplane commanders in the formation act as a team, and anticipate the movements of the formation. Each aircraft's movement in the formation depended on the changing speeds of the others in the formation. To do this the airplane commander had to overcome the tendency to over-run or fall behind by anticipating the movement of his aircraft and the others in the formation by remaining alert and operating the controls smoothly, increasing or decreasing speed. The airplane commander used two methods to increase speed: one was to increase power, and the other was to dive slightly. For decreasing speed he could reduce the power or put the bomber into a climb. The cowl flaps, wing flaps, or landing gear were never to be used to increase the drag for slowing down. To change speed, a change in altitude was beneficial only when the change was needed momentarily. For example, when a large formation made a turn in which the inside aircraft had to slow down and the outside aircraft had to speed up, the outside aircraft could gain speed by diving slightly, and the inside aircraft could lose speed by climbing slightly. If, when coming out of the turn the outside aircraft continued to have too much speed it could climb a little more. A gain or loss in altitude of 100ft momentarily dropped or gained aircraft speed from 3 to 5mph.

An aircraft's response to changes in power varied greatly with different loadings and different altitudes. For example, in a formation of B-29s with an average weight of 105,000lbs, cruising for Long-Range at 25,000ft after a maneuver, one bomber fell 300ft behind its assigned position. In order to regain its position in the formation the airplane commander increased rated power, and it would take him 35 seconds to do so. At 5,000ft the similar maneuver would take 25 seconds, because there was more power available for accelerating at low altitudes, as less of the available power was required to cruise at low altitude than at high altitudes. A 130,000lb bomber at 25,000ft had much more difficulty accelerating back to position.

In formation flying, the lead aircraft had to set up cruising conditions conforming to the operating charts. The bottom end of the Long-Range speed band (explained previously) was the proper position for the lead plane. The aircraft on the wing were to set their rpm at 100 to 200 rpm higher than the lead plane at manifold pressures recommended for those rpm, then reduce their manifold pressure with the desired boost control to obtain the desired speed. In high altitude formation flying, turbo reduction boost was limited by the amount of boost required for cabin pressurization. The airplane commander set the boost and the inboard throttles to gain the desired power, and then used the outboard throttles to stay in formation. The mixture control was to be set the same for all aircraft in the formation.

Formation Signals

Assume Normal Formation

Signal: Rock the wings in a slow, repeated rocking motion of the aircraft around its longitudinal axis (more than aileron flutter).

Meaning: Assume normal formation. From any other formation, go into normal closed-up formation.

Open Up Formation

Signal: Fishtail or yaw by rudder control, causing the aircraft to move alternately and repeatedly left or right.

Meaning: Open up formation. Where applicable, this signal may be used to order a search formation.

Attention

Signal: Flutter ailerons. Repeated and fairly rapid movements of the ailerons.

Meaning: Attention. This signal was used in the air (and on the ground for "ready to take off") to attract the attention of all aircraft. Airplane commanders were to stand by for radio messages or further messages.

Change Formation

Signal: Dip right or left wing.

Meaning: Change formation:

1) From any formation other than echelon, go into echelon of flights to the right or left.
2) If in echelon of flights, right or left, go into echelon of individual aircraft to the same side.
3) If in echelon of individual aircraft, go into echelon of flights on the same side on which the aircraft are echeloned.
4) If in echelon of flights or individual aircraft and wing is dipped on the side away from echelonment, form the same echelon to the opposite side.

Prepare to Land

Signal: Series of small dives or zooms.

Meaning: Prepare to land. This signal was an order to each airplane commander in the formation to take the requisite procedures preliminary to landing. A normal landing was to be made unless the radio or Aldis lamp announced a change.

Night Flying

Obviously, night flying was different from day flying, as vision and visibility were dramatically diminished. Night flying was instrument flying, and was much more disorienting than daytime instrument flying through clouds. At night an airplane commander had a tendency to rely too much upon his vision and other senses, rather than upon his instruments. The airplane commander had no horizon to depend on, but only isolated points of light that his senses told him were in a certain position in relation to the aircraft when, in fact, they were in a completely different relation. For example, he could mistake a star for a light on the ground, or for lights moving past the aircraft, when really the aircraft was moving around the lights. When the airplane commander reacted to the lights, his first inclination was to react to his senses, rather than rely on his instruments, and his aircraft would not respond as he expected, and he would become totally confused.

Night vision was important, and there were several techniques to improve it. Before the flight the airplane commander and co-pilot would avoid bright lights, and when entering the cockpit turn out all unnecessary lights and dim the instrument panel. When reading instruments, maps, and charts it was best to look at them rapidly and then look away. Goggles, side windows, and windscreens were meticulously cleaned, as scattered light from dirty surfaces reduced the contrast of faint lights and their background. Other night flying precautions were to check that all exterior and interior lights were in working order, along with the radio set operation and frequencies. The airplane commander, co-pilot, and flight engineer were supplied with flashlights in case of emergency. The layout of the home field and the relationship of the taxi strips to runways were thoroughly studied so they were easily recognized on a night approach.

Night Take Offs

Before taking off, day or night, it was necessary to get clearance from the tower before taxiing to the runway. To reduce the load on the electrical system when taxiing the landing lights were used alternately as needed. When taxing close to obstacles or parked aircraft it was necessary for ground crewmen to walk ahead of the tips of both wings and signal directions with flashlights. The airplane commander lined up on the center of the runway and selected a distant point of light as a reference point or, if visibility was poor, he would prepare to take off on instruments. The airplane commander had to pay careful attention in judging his speed and the distance to the aircraft ahead, as sudden closure was difficult to determine at night. On all night take offs the aircraft was to first climb to 500ft above the ground before leveling off to build up speed. Until the aircraft reached sufficient altitude for a turn, the airplane commander had to maintain a constant heading. The waist gunners were to look out for any aircraft in the path of a turn.

Night Landings

For night landings it was necessary to fly compass headings on the different legs of the traffic pattern. When the runway lights on the final approach seemed to separate it was necessary for the airplane commander to begin a medium turn to line up properly, and to avoid over or undershooting. On the down wind and base legs, the runway lights appeared to be a single row. As the aircraft flew closer to the runway on the base leg the lights began to separate into two rows, and this marked the time for the airplane commander to start the turn into the approach. On the final approach it was necessary for the airplane commander to remain high, and maintain a constant glide, airspeed, and rate of descent by making slight changes in power and attitude. The landing lights were turned on at their effective height of 500ft. The airplane commander was not to sight down the landing light beam, but instead try to use the entire lighted peripheral area ahead for reference, and also use the runway lights as a secondary source of reference. Using the landing lights alone could cause the airplane commander to level off too late for landing, while using the runway lights alone could cause the airplane commander to level off too high, especially if there was a haze or dust present. If the airplane commander was unsure of his final approach he was to carry a little more power to prevent stalling out high. The power was carried until the airplane commander was sure of making contact with the ground.

Landing

During let down it was desirable to maintain cruising speed with a large reduction in power, which resulted in fuel economy. Let down was to be executed at standard rates, and was to be initiated at the proper time in order to obtain maximum range. Excessive power settings and rates of descent were to be avoided to conserve fuel.

When entering the traffic pattern, eight to 10 minutes before landing the airplane commander went over his checklist:

1) Announce "Prepare for landing," and the co-pilot repeated the command over the interphone; the crew acknowledged the message in the following order: bombardier, navigator, flight engineer, radio operator, top gunner, left gunner, right gunner, and tail gunner. The tail gunner then started the putt putt.

2) The airplane commander called the tower for landing information.

3) The airplane commander and the co-pilot set their altimeters to the altimeter setting relayed by the tower.

4) Trailing antenna reeled in.

5) Autopilot OFF.

6) Turrets STOWED.

7) The co-pilot metered the brake pedals until the pressure fell below 800psi, and checked to see that the pressure returned to 1,000psi. Any difference in the final pressure was reported to the flight engineer. The co-pilot asked the flight engineer to check the emergency hydraulic pressure.

8) The APU was put on line, and the co-pilot checked with the tail gunner to be sure that he did this.

9) The co-pilot adjusted the props to 2,400rpm before the airplane commander reduced power.

10) The co-pilot, on the command of the airplane commander, lowered the landing gear. The IAS had to be less than 180mph before lowering. The side gunners checked the main landing and announced in order "Left gear down and locked," and "Right gear down and locked." The co-pilot checked the nose wheel through the observation window in the floor of the cockpit and checked the landing gear lights on his instrument panel. The red warning light and green gear down and locked lights (and the landing gear warning horn on early models) all operated from the gear motor limit switches. Since these switches were limit switches they indicated that the gear motors stopped, but it was possible that the gear could only be partly lowered due to some failure, and therefore the visual check was vital. The co-pilot then announced "Nose wheel down and locked."

11) The flight engineer reported the weight and CG figures to the co-pilot.

12) The co-pilot determined the stalling speed based on the current aircraft weight by referring to the table on his instrument panel and informed the airplane commander.

13) At the airplane commander's command, the co-pilot extended the wing flaps 25-degrees just before turning into the base leg. Later, on the final approach, and at the airplane commander's command, he extended full flaps, and the airplane commander retrimmed the elevators. The side gunners checked the position of the flaps and informed the co-pilot over the interphone.

14) The airplane commander called for the turbos on the base approach leg. The co-pilot announced "Turbos ON" to the flight engineer and turned the dial selector to 8.

Landing Procedure

The correct landing approach made landing easy. The airplane commander entered the landing pattern with the gear down at 180mph, 2,400rpm at 1,500ft from the direction opposite the end of the runway, passing about a two or three miles to port. He continued past the landing end of the runway for two or three miles, continuing at 1,500ft, reducing speeds to 160mph, and dropping the flaps to 25-degrees, and further reduced speed to 150 to 160mph. He then made a 90-degree left turn, flying another two to three miles, reducing speed to 150mph, moving the turbos to No.8, and lined up with end of the runway, which was two to three miles away.

Even though the B-29 was a large aircraft, the proper use of flaps in the traffic pattern enabled a slow pattern and a short approach. Flaps were not to put full down until the aircraft was lined up with the runway, had dropped down to 1,000ft, and was maintaining a speed 30mph above stalling speed. Go-arounds were much more difficult with full flaps. The final approach was to be 30mph IAS above the power off stalling speed with the flaps all the way down. After the flaps were full down, the airspeed was to be maintained at 30mph (indicated) above the power off stalling speed. Power was not to be chopped at any point in the landing approach. Long approaches were not essential even when the runway was narrow, but the base leg was normally started farther out than the B-17 or B-24. Boost was to be on, and the rpm set at 2,400. Power was not to be reduced rapidly on any part of the approach. The speed was never to fall below the power off stalling speed, even when landing. The landing gear was not to be lowered until the landing was a "sure thing," and one minute was to be allowed for the gear to be fully extended. The gunners checked the extension of the landing gear and the condition of the tires (no flats). On touch down the main wheels were to touch first, and then the nose wheels were allowed to settle as the airspeed dropped off. If the nose wheel was held up too long it would hit with great force when the airspeed dropped, and could cause damage or collapse. The aircraft was able to withstand inadvertent three-point landings on the main wheels and nose wheel simultaneously. The tailskid was never to touch first, except in a short field landing. Any landing in excess of 130,000lbs gross weight was to be made without drift, and without "dropping the aircraft in," as otherwise the touchdown strain would cause the gear to fold.

Cross Wind Landings

Landing under cross wind and gusty conditions was less critical for this airplane with its tricycle landing gear than for bombers having the conventional type gear (e.g. the B-17). Even though the B-29 had good aileron, rudder, and elevator control, it responded slowly due to its size and weight, and as much caution as possible was to be exercised in operating the aileron controls, trimming the ship for perfect balance and heading into the wind. In cross wind landing conditions a longer approach was recommended to provide enough time to correct drift. Just prior to the actual landing, the airplane was to be turned to head in the desired direction, the wing on the upwind side lowered just before the wheels touched, raised by employing a little throttle to the outboard engine on the low side. The bomber was to be brought to a stop as promptly as conditions permitted.

Go-around

The normal B-29 go-around procedure was not overly complicated. The airplane commander quickly informed the flight engineer of the go-around. With the drag and reduced acceleration of the flaps down landing attitude the airplane commander could not wait for safe flying speed. He had to raise the flaps from the full down position to 25-degrees all in one fluid movement (important). He increased the power gradually and continued the same approach angle until safe flying speed was regained. The airplane commander could then raise the gear as soon as he was sure that the runway would not be touched again. He then gently lifted the nose and continued, as he would with a normal take off.

Landing Roll

It was recommended that the brakes be used as little as possible once on the ground. On a long runway the aircraft was to roll until it lost speed, lowering the nose gear gently at 90mph and then braking smoothly and evenly. Near the end of the landing roll the co-pilot set the turbo to 0, set high rpm, and the throttles at 700rpm in preparation to taxi.

After Landing

The post-landing checklist included:

1) The co-pilot checked normal hydraulic pressure gauge for a reading of between 800 and 1,000psi.
2) Turbos OFF..
3) Propellers HIGH rpm.
4) Near the end of the landing roll and at the order of the airplane commander, the co-pilot raised the flaps all the way. The side gunners were to report on their position on the interphone.

5) Parking brakes set.
6) The co-pilot announced on the interphone, "Open bomb bay doors." The flight engineer set the throttle on 1,400, the coolest engine rpm. The radio operator and one of the gunners checked through the pressure doors and reported to the airplane commander that the doors were open. The flight engineer then returned the throttles to 700rpm and turned off all generators. With pneumatic snap-opening bomb bay doors the generator procedure was unnecessary.
7) Magnetos checked by the flight engineer at 2000rpm.
8) The airplane commander gave the order, "Cut engines" to the flight engineer who cut the engines simultaneously by:
   a) Running the engines at 700rpm until all CHT dropped (to 375F was optimal). While the engines were cooling at 700rpm, the flight engineer flipped the master ignition switch to the OFF position momentarily to check that all magnetos were grounded out.
   b) The engineer increased the throttle settings to 1,200rpm and ran each engine for at least 30 secondsat that rpm.
   c) Moving the mixture controls to IDLE CUT-OFF.
   d) Cutting the switches after the propeller stopped.
   e) Ordered the tail gunner to stop the APU.
9) The airplane commander turned off the command set and the co-pilot switched off the radio compass.
10) Controls LOCKED.
12) Wheel chocks in place and brakes off.
13) Forms 1 and 1A completed by the flight engineer and checked by the airplane commander.
14) The crew left the aircraft and lined up to be checked by the airplane commander (this procedure was dispensed with in combat theaters). Any defects or malfunctions not already noted were reported.

2

Flight Engineers

Background

The flight engineer position was not new to Boeing aircraft, as Pan American had a flight engineer on their Boeing Clippers, as did the Boeing 307 and 314. There also was a flight engineer on the early PBY Catalinas, B-15, the Lockheed Constellation, and the Navy's Mars seaplane. Although they were often considered "throttle jockeys," the flight engineer should be likened to the engineer on a sea-going ship. The flight engineer was often confused with the aerial engineer on other bombers, who was also a gunner. The aerial engineer offered advice to the airplane commander on the mechanical characteristics of the aircraft, watched the function of the aircraft in the air, and reported any mechanical problems to the ground crew after landing. The flight engineer, however, was a jack-of-all-trades, and had to understand, operate, and maintain every system in the bomber, and be able to do repairs in the air in case of an in-flight emergency. The B-29 was the first bomber where the pilots did not have a complete set of instruments or controls, and the flight engineer was in actual control of the mechanical function of the aircraft.

Flight Engineer's Role in the Mission

Flight Plan

Once the target information was available the flight engineer and the navigator began flight planning for the mission. The navigator determined the route and distances, and together with the flight engineer produced a basic flight plan using "0" wind. Using this basic framework the flight engineer augmented the flight plan to the target utilizing his predictions on the aircraft's gross maximum weight at take off. He then planned the lowest economical altitudes at which to fly to the target, taking into consideration the weight reduction of the aircraft as its fuel was consumed. A point along the flight path was then determined where the aircraft was light enough (due to fuel use) to climb to bombing altitude, and then its gross weight was determined at the Initial Point (IP) and over the target.

The next phase in flight planning was to formulate a reverse flight plan that started after the bomber had landed and was parked and empty of expendable fuel, and had a minimal reserve fuel. The reverse flight plan then positioned the bomber back to descent, and then back along its return route to the target. The flight engineer added the fuel used until the bomber was back to the bomb release point. At this point the difference of the

bomber's weight at bomb release minus ground weight was the maximum bomb load that could be carried.

An adjusted flight plan was configured using the predicted winds along the route in relation to the planned altitude and speeds. When the winds were calculated in the flight plan adjustments were made in the fuel required, and also the times and distances due to the true airspeeds and expected ground speeds. The flight engineer's adjusted flight plan included the expected power settings and fuel consumption for each segment of the

The B-29 was the first bomber where the pilots did not have a complete set of instruments or controls. The flight engineer was in actual control of the mechanical function of the aircraft. (USAF)

flight, and speeds to be flown for Long-Range cruise control. He calculated the weights for climbs route altitude, bombing altitude, return route altitude, and descents and applicable data for fuel consumption on the mission.

Mission day

On the day of the mission the flight engineer was responsible for carrying his clipboard, which held the following:

1) Forms 1, 1A, and F (later 2AF Forms #334 & 334A were used), and the Flight Engineer's Log and Report (later called the Flight Engineer's Log).

2) 41B Aircraft Discrepancy Log. The flight engineer was responsible for any repairs, and upon arrival at the aircraft the flight engineer met with the maintenance crew chief who, with his crew, had prepared, and possibly repaired the bomber. The two reviewed the 41B Aircraft Maintenance Discrepancy Log and discussed the general condition of the aircraft, the parts that had been replaced, and those that did not function or could not be relied on.

3) Weight and Balance (CG) Form (AN 01-1-40)
The balance, or center of gravity (CG), of any aircraft was just as important as its gross weight, and on the B-29 it was even more important. A relatively small difference in the location of the center of gravity could make a substantial difference in the bomber's flying characteristics. The aircraft was to be flown as near 25% MAC (Mean Aerodynamic Chord) as possible, or it would not get on step and would mush along in flight. The Weight and Balance book was used to determine the CG as closely as possible. The current weight of the bomber was determined by adding the weight of the loaded fuel, ordnance, and crew, along with anything else that had been added or removed. The loads in all compartments that were not part of the basic aircraft also needed to be calculated in the load computations. A "load adjuster" slide rule was used to mathematically calculate the CG by placing each added or subtracted weight in the bomber at its location; then the load adjuster could locate the CG. The landing CG could also be calculated by removing the ordnance and expended fuel to predict the weight and CG at touchdown. The Weight and Balance form was ready to pass on to the pilots for flight clearance.

Walk Around

The flight engineer inspected the entire aircraft, beginning at the nose wheel, examining the wheels, tires, struts, wheel well, and all visible wiring and tubing. Next he moved to the starboard and inspected the #3 and #4 engines, their cowlings, engine dome, governor pad, and the propeller blades and hubs looking for any damage, leaks, or other possible malfunctions. The leading edges of the wings, landing and navigation lights, and wing tips were inspected next. Continuing around the wing he looked at the trailing edge of the wing, the flight controls and landing flaps, and the fuel lines that ran along the back of the wing spar. When he came to the main landing gear he looked at the wheels, tires brakes, and all the tubing and fittings in the wheel well. Next he looked into the aft bomb bay (if the loading had been completed) and the right aft fuselage, sighting blisters, aft entry door, stabilizers, rudder, elevators, tailskid, tail gunner's hatch, and the tail light. The flight engineer repeated this inspection process on the port side of the aircraft, finishing at the nose wheel well, which was his

entrance hatch to the front crew department. The flight engineer was responsible for supervising the propeller pull through, but first he had to enter the plane to be sure the ignition switches were off. Later in combat the propellers were pulled through as the last procedure before entering the bomber.

After the engine pull through the flight engineer entered the aft cabin to check on the tail gunner's inspection of the putt putt, and to recheck its gasoline and oil, as well as to set the emergency switch at NORMAL to be sure that it was ready to deliver 200amps. While in the aft cabin he was to check the sealed tool kits under the top turret. The seals were placed to show that the tool kit had not been used and all the tools were inside. Next the flight engineer moved forward to the rear pressurized compartment to check that the two cabin pressure control regulator locks were OFF, indicating that the regulators were in the AUTOMATIC position. He then checked that the cabin pressure emergency release valve was in the CLOSED position and removed any loose objects that might interfere with it.

The flight engineer left the aircraft again to check that the portable emergency motor in the bomb bay was in the flap operating position. He then checked all turbosuperchargers, inspecting the waste gate axle, and to check that there was no ballooning in the nozzle box. He saw to it that the fire extinguisher carts and personnel were in their proper position around the aircraft for engine starting.

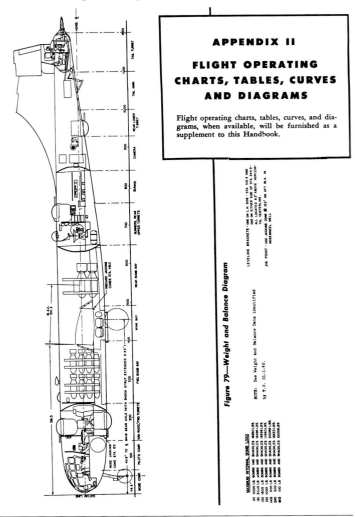

APPENDIX II

FLIGHT OPERATING CHARTS, TABLES, CURVES AND DIAGRAMS

Flight operating charts, tables, curves, and diagrams, when available, will be furnished as a supplement to this Handbook.

Figure 79—Weight and Balance Diagram

Personal Equipment Inspection

Like all crewmen, he checked his oxygen mask, parachute, life preserver, and flight gear. He made sure that he had his brief case containing the flight plan, logs, and charts, and his tools of the trade: slide rules, dividers, and pencils.

Pre-taxi and Starting

Once the flight engineer was at his position he connected to the oxygen mask, headset, and heated suit (if worn). Despite all his papers and implements, the flight engineer's position was a small, cold nook behind the co-pilot next to the wheel well. He had no desktop, and stowed the clipboard and briefcase in the foot well under his control board. The flight engineer was always on the look out for a wider clipboard to act as a makeshift desk.

After the crew was in position and their equipment stowed the aircraft commander would call the crew for their checklists, and before engine start the flight engineer would go over his checklist. First he would quickly run over his weight and CG calculations, and next he would get to the physical checks: the battery switch and master ignition switch were turned to ON. He then checked the oxygen equipment: the mask and regulator (auto switch ON and pressure at 425psi), and checked the emergency valve. He inspected the portable "walk around" oxygen bottle for a full pressure of 400psi. After he moved up to the navigator's station to check the first voltage regulator vent valve, he then looked at the other vent valve, which was located directly behind his panel, and made sure that both handles were in the UP position. The emergency motor was checked, and then the cabin pressure relief valve was turned all the way to the HIGH pressure position. He plugged into the interphone circuit, the jack in one socket and the microphone in the other. He then called the tail gunner to start the APU. The putt putt start sequence was to: 1) turn on ignition switch; 2) hold generator switch in the START position; 3) move control lever to RUN; 4) let it warm up for 2-3 minutes and snap generator switch to RUN position; and then 5) snap the equalizer switch ON. After the putt putt was running the flight engineer checked the voltage by setting the selector switch so that the voltage read 28 volts, and with the APU running electrical power was available.

He switched on the three fluorescent lights at his station, and twisted the lens to the open position have the desired amount of light shine on the gauges. Once the co-pilot received the correct barometric pressure from the tower he passed the figures to the flight engineer, who then set the two altimeters so that the outside and cabin pressures were the same. The aircraft commander reported the time on his chronometer watch so the flight engineer could set the clock on his panel. The flight engineer was then to test the power plant controls and instruments on his panel (the airplane commander had the master throttle controls, and could override the flight engineer's throttles). First he turned the mixture lock to OFF and checked the mixture controls, four throttles, vacuum pump selector valve, and emergency cabin air valves for ease of movement. The hydraulic system was next on the checklist. The two hydraulic gauges were to read around 1000psi. He set the push hydraulic pump switch to EMERGENCY and held it there until it reached about 400psi, then released the switch (that went back to AUTO). The hydraulic shut off valve was then opened, and the pressure on each gauge would rise to 1000psi. The hydraulic pump switch was again set on EMERGENCY, which caused the pressure to climb above 1000psi and showed the flight engineer that the pump would charge both systems; he then turned the shut off valve back to CLOSED. The flight engineer set

the parking brakes, and asked the airplane commander (left) and co-pilot (right) to look out their windows to check that the wheels were chocked fore and aft.

Using Form 1A, which showed how much fuel and oil was onboard, he checked these figures with the panel fuel and oil gauge readings. He checked the two autosyn inverter switches for readings of 26 volts, being certain that the first stopped running before trying the other. The four cowl flaps switches were spring loaded, and all four were to be held OPEN together via a hinged flip up plate until indicator, which was at the last line. The flight engineer looked directly at the cowl flaps through his window to be sure they moved. The oil cooler shutters were put into the AUTO position by four switches. The intercooler flaps were moved to the all OPEN position by pushing four switches at once by a hinged plate, and held there until the pointers on the indicator were all the way to the all OPEN position.

The airplane commander directed that the turbos be switched to OFF and the props put into HIGH rpm. The flight engineer snapped the four fuel shut off valves (a guard positioned in front of the switches prevented accidental closure) to OPEN. He turned on the cabin pressure warning switch, and the aircraft was ready for engine starting. The engines were started in the sequence of #3, #4, #2, then #1. The engine starting sequence was:

1) The #3 engine fire extinguisher selector was set to ON.
2) The #3 mixture control was cracked open.
3) The fuel booster rheostat was set to give about 16lbs fuel pressure.
4) The mixture control was then closed so that it temporarily knocked out fuel pressure to zero. The pressure would return to the correct pressure when the engine was running.
5) The flight engineer told the airplane commander to start #3 engine. (Engine pull through should have been about 30 minutes previous). The airplane commander warned of the start by hand signal through his window.
6) The flight engineer cracked the throttle to about the 1000rpm position.
7) The flight engineer pushed the starter switches to ACCELERATE for 15-30 seconds while watching the load on the APU ammeter. Later the starter was energized for 12-16 seconds instead of 15-30secs. The starter switch was then turned to START. After the prop had made two revolutions, the magneto switch was turned to BOTH, and the engine was primed. When the engine fired and was turning at 800rpm the mixture control was moved to AUTO RICH, and the starter switch was released at once, but the flight engineer continued to prime the engine intermittently until it was running smoothly. The fuel and oil gauges were checked:

1) Nose oil pressure needed to go to 30-50lbs in 30secs.
2) Rear oil pressure had to be 60-80lbs.
3) Fuel pressure was to fall between 15-18lbs.

Sometimes the engine would begin to start but then would stop. The restarting procedure was to turn off the magneto, then move engine mixture control back to idle cutoff. If this was not done quickly enough gasoline would spill out of the "gurgle tube," and the excess fuel would have to be blown out of the engine before restarting. The flight engineer needed to reset the mixture control and switch off the ignition, then open the throttle to wide and turn the engine over twice with the starters alone. Once the excess gasoline was expelled the flight engineer would begin the starting procedure over again after allowing the starter to cool off for several seconds.

If there was a fire in an engine nacelle the flight engineer would move the involved engine's mixture controls to IDLE CUT OFF, close its fuel shutoff valve, stop its booster pump, and set its fire extinguisher to ready. The cowl flaps were OPEN to allow the ground crew to attempt to extinguish the fire. If the ground crew were unable to extinguish the fire the cowl flaps were CLOSED and the fire extinguisher charges were pulled, as directed by the airplane commander. The flight engineer continued the checklist:

1) Turn ON cabin air conditioning switches
2) Check cylinder head temperatures, oil pressure, and fuel pressure
3) The aircraft commander was then ready to turn the generators ON, and the bombardier closed the bomb bay doors with the flight engineer and gunners looking through their windows to make sure bay doors closed.

Taxiing and Pre-take Off
The flight engineer informed the airplane commander the aircraft was OK to taxi, and he taxied the aircraft to the end of the runway, where the engines need to be rechecked:

1) The airplane commander increased all throttles to 1500rpm and moved the props to full gate race, then to full increase.
2) The flight engineer checked all generators for output voltage and amperage.
3) The airplane commander pulled back the throttles to 700rpm, had the flight engineer check the magnetos, and advanced the #3 throttle to 2000rpm and right magneto switch to the right (rpms dropped a little, anything less than a 100rpm drop was OK). The flight engineer then moved the throttle back to FULL and tried the left magneto (again rpms dropped a little), then set both magnetos back to BOTH and returned the throttle to 700rpm. The procedure repeated for the other three engines (#4, #2, and then #1). The flight engineer used his check list to recheck all other gauges for proper readings.

Take Off
The airplane commander released the parking brake and set the engines for full military power, turbos at position 8, and started to open the throttles. As the airplane commander rolled the aircraft onto the runway, he increased the engine power to maximum and asked for takeoff power. The flight engineer followed the airplane commander's throttle movements with his set, monitoring engine intake manifold pressure limits and propeller rpms. At this point the flight engineer got busy. He started closing the cowl flaps to maintain engine cylinder head temperatures to prevent them from overheating. He turned the fuel booster pumps ON, and started each of the six generators as soon as the engine reached 1,400rpms. Since no power checks had been made the co-pilot and flight engineer kept a close eye on the rpms and manifold pressure during the first third of the take off. If there were any abnormal readings the flight engineer would call the airplane commander to cut off the engine(s). While watching the Wright R-3350

engine's most important gauges—the cylinder head temperature and oil pressure gauges—the flight engineer had to keep the cowl flaps open as wide as possible as long as possible for cooling, but yet they had to be closed to around 7 1/2-degrees before leaving the ground. This was a difficult and sensitive procedure that required experience.

Initial Climb
After the bomber had lifted off the airplane commander made sure to apply the wheel brakes before retracting the gear to stop their spinning. A loud whine signaled the nose wheel retraction, and the blister gunners reported on the main gear retraction. As soon as safe flying speed was attained the cowl flaps were to be opened as much as 10-degrees, unless the cylinder heads were getting hot. After two minutes of climbing the aircraft commander would reduce power, and the flight engineer turned off the fuel booster pumps, making sure that there was no drop in fuel pressure. Once the gear and wing flaps were reported up the flight engineer called the tail gunner to shut down the APU.

Climbing
The climbing power setting (and any rpm changes) required the airplane commander to reduce the engine rpms. To do this there were four toggle switches (spring loaded to neutral), one for each propeller, with increase-decrease rpm positions that had to be held while the rpm was set. There were no synchronizers, and synchronization had to be done by ear after using the tachometer to get it as close as possible. At night a side gunner could shine an Aldis light on the spinning props, and the flight engineer used the shadows as a strobe and synchronized visually. After the rpms were set the manifold pressures and turbosuperchargers were set.

The climb was also a busy period for the flight engineer. He adjusted the cooling flaps on each engine to get every engine temperature into the optimum range. He adjusted cylinder head temperatures by using the cowl flaps; the carburetor inlet air temperature by adjusting the intercooler flaps, and kept the oil from getting too thin by using the oil cooler flaps. The flight engineer set the cabin pressurization to 8,000ft, and the cabin heat was furnished by the turbosuperchargers and controlled by the aftercooler flaps. Fuel system management began in the climb as the auxiliary tanks were used first. Every rpm and manifold pressure temperature had to be continuously monitored and adjusted, as the outside temperature was constantly changing. In addition, all data was to be recorded in the Flight Engineer's Log and the Fuel How Goes It Log (the planned actual fuel use chart that showed how much fuel remained).

First Cruising Altitude
The airplane commander leveled the bomber off at 10,000ft and set up cruising conditions. Cruising power was 2,100rpm and 31in of manifold pressure, and the flight engineer checked these settings on his panel. All cooling flaps had to be reset due to the change in airspeed and exterior temperature, and this was a continuous procedure. The cruise drag factor had to be calculated for cruise control purposes in order to set the power to fly at the correct speed for the weight and altitude being flown. The flight engineer turned the turbos OFF so that the intercooler flaps could be closed slowly without raising head temperatures. The flight engineer informed the airplane commander that he was about to set the mixture controls to AUTO LEAN and then did it. He made sure that the controls were put into the DETEN position and then locked them. The flight engineer needed to

continuously watch his panel gauges: nose oil temp at 30-50lbs, rear oil temp at 60-70lbs, and fuel pressure at 15-18lbs; cylinder head temps not more than the maximum limit; and oil temp under 91°F. The checklist prescribed that the flight engineer look at the six generators every 30min: output voltage was not to exceed 28 volts, and the ammeter should kick over the same amount for each generator and charge evenly. In addition to these duties, the flight engineer also had to fill out the flight engineer log record every 30 minutes for: percent of power used, airspeed, rate of climb, free air temp, pressure altitude, and most importantly, fuel consumption.

After a predetermined number of flying hours, fuel needed to be switched from bomb bay tanks to wing tanks. There was one fuel transfer valve at the rear bomb bay tank position, and another at #4 wing tank position. The flight engineer pulled the fuel transfer switches toward him to the ON position to make the fuel transfer from right to left. He watched the fuel tank gauge, and when the needle showed that the #4 tank was full he turned the switches OFF. However, when the fuel was transferred the full wing tank caused the wing to drop. To compensate the flight engineer moved the right transfer valve to the #1 wing tank position, then pushed switches forward this time to pump fuel from #4 to #1. When the tanks were evened up (each about 3/4 full) the plane would again be in balance. The flight engineer would then turn all switches OFF. Tanks #2 and #3 would be filled the same way.

Secondary Climb to Bombing Altitude
The secondary climb to the bomb run altitude was the same procedure as the climb after take off procedure, adjusting all the cooling flaps and temperatures to prepare the aircraft for high altitude flight over 10,000ft. The flight engineer depressurized the pressurized compartments, and the crew donned their oxygen masks and donned heavier clothing (or plugged in their heated flight suits). The tail gunner moved from the rear pressurized cabin to his tail gun position as the bomber climbed to 25,000ft.

Descent
After the bombing run the airplane commander began a Long-Range type cruising descent, losing altitude slowly as the bomber leveled off and cruised at lower altitudes for better mileage per gallon on the back to base leg.

Preparing to Land
The flight engineer ordered the tail gunner to start the putt putt and shifted the mixture controls to AUTO RICH. The de-icers and anti-icers were set to OFF. The cowl flaps were OPEN to 7 1/2, and the intercoolers were OPEN. As the bomber was coming into the down wind leg of the landing pattern the flight engineer had to coordinate his actions with the airplane commander. He gave the airplane commander the new gross weight and new CG. The plane entered the traffic pattern at an IAS of 180mph, and the co-pilot lowered the landing gear. The flight engineer checked the voltage and amperage on all six generators, and turned the fuel booster pumps ON. The airplane commander turned the turbo booster control up to 8 and set the props to 2,400rpm. The airplane commander informed the flight engineer that the turbos were now ON, and the flight engineer opened the intercooler flaps. The flight engineer checked the hydraulic pressure, and set the cowl flaps to keep the cylinder head temperature between 300-320°F. The co-pilot lowered the wing flaps 25-degrees to slow the aircraft's landing speed. During the entire landing approach the flight engineer closely monitored cylinder head temperatures on the overheating-prone Wright

engines.

The air speed needed to be reduced to between 150 and 160mph, and altitude be at 1,000ft just before lowering the wing flaps all the way. After the flaps were down the air speed had to be maintained at 30mph above stalling speed. Just before touchdown the flight engineer checked his primary gauges again: hydraulic pressure (which would be needed soon for the hydraulic brakes); cylinder head temperature; and oil pressure.

Landing
The B-29 landed at 90-110mph, and as soon as the plane was down the flight engineer started opening the cowl flaps to cool the susceptible engines. When the wing flaps were up the generators were turned OFF; next the fuel booster pumps were turned OFF. The intercoolers were OPEN, and the cowl flaps were OPEN to their widest position. While taxiing and braking the hydraulic pressure was monitored.

At the parking area the airplane commander's last function was to turn the turbos OFF and set the props to the FULL INCREASE position. The engines were still running, and the flight engineer who had started the engines was to stop them. He started by throttling them back to 700rpms. After the head temperatures dropped to 190°F he made a complete magneto test, opened the bomb bay doors, and then set the mixture controls to IDLE CUTOFF. When the engines stopped he opened all the throttles to WIDE. The flight engineer ordered the putt putt auxiliary power plant stopped, then turned OFF all the switches: master ignition, inverter, and battery. All controls were in LOCK. Once the brake drums were cool he set the parking brake.

Back on the Ground
After leaving the aircraft the flight engineer checked the fore and aft wheel chocks. With the airplane commander he conducted an after-flight walk-around, and then met with the crew chief to go over "discrepancies" (e.g. components that malfunctioned). Often the flight engineer would assist the crew chief in repairing any problem, especially engine problems, as he had intimate knowledge of the engine and could start and run them up during repair. Early B-29 post flight procedure included a personal inspection of the crew, but it was dispensed with in combat theaters. The Flight Log and Forms 1 and 1A were completed, and the flight engineer would go to the Intelligence debriefing.

The flight engineer and airplane commander conducted an after-flight walk-around, and then would meet with the crew chief to go over "discrepancies" (e.g. components that malfunctioned). After meeting with the crew chief they would go to Intelligence debriefing. (USAF)

3

Navigators

Navigator's Position

The navigator's position was located on the port side behind the airplane commander, and because the well of the top turret intruded into the forward compartment the navigator's station was cramped. He sat on a swivel chair in front of a green plywood table with a small drawer with an ashtray at the right end that extended lengthwise across the cabin. The table was hinged to allow easy movement around the turret. Located in front of the navigator were his navigational equipment, along with the altimeter, clock, and air speed indicator. A long, cylindrical map case was mounted on the fuselage wall above the table. There was a square window for the navigator on the port side of the fuselage with an oxygen tube hanging nearby. On a few later B-29s the navigator was located in the rear pressurized cabin, and shared a table with the radar operator to facilitate their dual functions.

Standard Navigation Procedures

The navigator's daily duties were to conduct checks on the astrograph, astro compass, drift meter, sextant, instrument calibrations, and the lighting system. Before every mission it was essential to have a flight plan containing as much information as possible. After the field order for a mission had been issued, the first objective for the group navigator was to analyze the order and determine what types of navigation and navigational options he could use to best advantage under the circumstances described in the field order. All navigators in the group also had to completely understand the order. The navigator had to know the route to the targets and all checkpoints along the way. The advantageous use of the sun in daylight missions was considered, and at night knowledge of the position of the stars would allow the navigator to quickly and accurately shoot three star fixes. The navigator had to study the enemy coastline and the area in the vicinity of the target in order to orient himself quickly and accurately. He had to be able to coordinate his radar, radio, and LORAN apparatus with other information to be able to fix his position immediately. The weather was the most important and variable factor affecting navigation, and the navigator needed to understand "weather navigation" in order to assess the weather and utilize the various methods of navigation and apparatus effectively. He had to collect and check route and target area forecasts, especially the winds aloft, as the most important weather variable was wind, especially in the Pacific with its jet stream winds. The navigator's mission folder contained all the data needed for the mission: the flight plan; charts;

It has been asserted that the navigator was the most intelligent and important member of the crew and that many intelligent prospective pilots were diverted to navigator training. It was a requirement for a Very Long Range bomber to have superlative navigation and the Pacific Theater with its long over water distances, unpredictable weather and few navigation aids made that requirement even more imperative. (USAF)

weather data; radar bombing data; emergency procedures; position reporting procedure; communications data; and maps showing the islands along the route that were held by the Japanese. The navigator read and then organized the folder so that all information could be found quickly and easily. He then prepared the master chart, on which he plotted the course and emergency landing fields and rescue data, and set the radio aids and pertinent intelligence data. After he completed the flight plan the navigator briefed the crew on take off time, rendezvous, and the ETAs in and out of enemy territory and at the target, and also escape routes. The navigator was responsible for keeping the correct time ("time tick frequency"), and once in the aircraft he synchronized all aircraft clocks and crew watches.

Because of the great distances involved and the limited reporting sources the navigator had to:

1) The navigator made continuous checks and cross checks of all navigation instruments: the astro, magnetic, and flux gate compasses. The IFF was checked to see that it was on and off at the proper times. He continually entered correct data into the CFC Gun Computer. Every 10 minutes he did an altitude (within 500ft), indicated air speed (within 5mph), and temperature (within 5-degrees) check, and completed the navigator's log.

2) The logbook was the main record of the bomber's movement on a mission, and needed to be complete and clear so that it could be understood at once in case of an emergency. The log was to record every important occurrence during the mission, and SOP was to record an entry every 15 minutes of the flight from that current position to the next. It was to include takeoff time, time and position of the assembly, time and position of the rendezvous, control points, turning points, and the bombing run data, time, and position of the IP, record of the IFF on and off, and a record of enemy surface and/or aircraft encountered. If enemy aircraft were encountered, then the type of aircraft encountered, methods of attack, and damage sustained were to be documented. The 15 minute log entries were to include the compass heading, calibrated airspeed and altitude, and recorded wind and temperature data.

3) Enroute to the target area rendezvous the navigator saw to it that the control points were met in time, location, and altitude. The gunners were informed when they could test fire their guns, and he constantly briefed the crew of being over enemy territory.

4) While over the target area the navigator was to record enemy anti-aircraft and aircraft activity, and any information on their formations and methods of attack and any damage inflicted to them.

5) Navigating back to home base was considered more difficult than inbound navigation, as it was easier to reach the large landmass of Japan than the small island airbases in the middle of the large Pacific Ocean. The failure to find radio and directional aids, danger of running out of fuel, suffering engine failure, and apparent damage from the enemy caused the navigator to be constantly vigilant and prepared to fly directly to an emergency field, or to be able to give an accurate position in case of ditching.

Navigation Instruments

1) Astro Compass (Type A-1) and Astrodome: The astro compass was an astronomical instrument that provided the navigator with a means of determining the true heading of the aircraft by reference to the sun,

moon, or stars. It mechanically solved the celestial triangle for azimuth or true bearing of a celestial body using hour angle, declination, and latitude. The astro compass required alignment with the fore and aft axis of the bomber in order to be used accurately. The astrodome sighting station was not scheduled to be placed until the 265th production B-29, and when it was installed it was placed 15in. too close to the rear compartment wall, and made celestial shooting to the rear difficult. There were times the navigator had to actually partially enter the tunnel to shoot. The optics of the Plexiglas astrodome were poor, and several panels of the Plexiglas nose of the bomber were replaced with flat glass so the navigator could shoot through its good optics. Later production models had the astrodome and entire nose converted to glass.

2) Gyro Fluxgate Compass (GFGC): The GFGC was a remote indicating magnetic compass that provided directions that were as unimpeded as possible from the influence of motors, armor plate, and other distorting factors of the earth's magnetic field. The GFGC has been previously discussed at length.

3) B-3 Drift Meter: The drift recorder made accurate readings of wind direction and velocity, and was used for calculating true ground speed.

4) Magnetic Compass: The magnetic compass was the basic navigational instrument. It consisted of a fluid-filled airtight case in which the compass card system was pivoted. The magnetic compass was susceptible to many errors—mainly deviation—and the errors created by the turning, accelerating, and decelerating of the aircraft and any outside turbulence.

5) Air Position Indicator (API): The API provided an accurate plot of true heading and true airspeed, and was especially important to provide dead reckoning while the bomber was in evasive action. The API was integrated with the fluxgate compass to supply the true heading to the API computer.

6) Sextant: The sextant was one of the most important navigational instruments. Basically, it was a kind of telescope for measuring the height of a celestial body (i.e. sun, moon, or star) above the horizon. The height was measured in angular-degrees on two or more celestial bodies, and knowing these angles the navigator could determine his position with great accuracy. There are several types of sextants, and the "bubble" type was the most practical for aircraft use. The bubble in this sextant provided the navigator with an artificial horizon from which to measure his angular altitudes. An artificial horizon had to be used if the natural horizon was obscured because of clouds, darkness, or haze.

Celestial Navigation and Dead Reckoning (DR)
Celestial Procedure
Celestial procedure was the most important navigational aid, and was the highest expression of the art of navigation. A three star fix was one of the most accurate positioning aids. The navigator had to be able to immediately and without uncertainty combine his celestial abilities with all the other navigational aids.

Dead Reckoning (DR)
Dead reckoning was the basic form of navigation, with all the other navigational methods being contributing factors to the successful use of DR. The value of other navigational methods was directly proportional to the

quality of the navigator's dead reckoning ability. Every bit of information available to the navigator had to be analyzed and then used properly. The navigator had to concentrate on air speeds, temperatures, and compass headings, as the smallest error was accumulative, and could soon become a 5% error. Each correction was to be made as soon as it occurred because of the high speed of the bomber, and often, because of this, the navigator overcorrected.

The navigator required a complete set of navigational equipment for celestial and dead reckoning navigation anywhere in the planned mission area: sextant and accessories; all calibration cards for gyro-fluxgate compass; E6B computer; Weems plotter; dividers; triangles; parallel rule; A-13 chronometer; A-11 hack watch; A-3 stop watch; current Air Almanac; H.O. 218 tables; Ageton or Dreisonstok; and Rude Star Finder. The navigator gathered a complete set of AAF Aeronautical Charts (scale 1:500,000) for anywhere in the general target area, along with necessary AAF Long-Range Air navigational Charts (scale 1:3,000,000) covering the entire operational area, 1:3,000,000 Mercator plotting charts, and LORAN charts.

Navigator/Crew Coordination
It was important for the navigator to coordinate with the other crew:

(a) Navigator-Airplane Commander: An airplane commander needed to have absolute confidence in his navigator, and the cooperation and mutual decisions between the two were essential for the airplane commander to fly a correct course, to climb and fly let downs according to plan, and to fly while on the C-1 autopilot.

(b) Navigator-Bombardier: The bombardier provided the navigator with pilotage information, drift checks, ground speed, and wind direction and velocity, and the navigator provided the bombardier with the same cross checks, along with target identification.

(c) Navigator-Radio Operator: The radio operator provided QAMs (meteorological information), QTFs (station bearings), OUJs (true course), and relative and true bearings from the radio compass.

(d) Navigator-Radar Operator: The radar operator could provide ground speed, wind direction and velocity, coastline landfalls, drift checks, and fixes according to azimuth and ground range. The navigator was to inform the radar operator of possible targets and their general bearing and distance form the flown course.

(e) Navigator-Flight Engineer: The two men integrated fuel consumption and mission distance remaining.

(f) Navigator-Gunners: The gunners sighted landmarks along the mission route through their sighting blisters. The navigator informed the gunners of areas of possible enemy fighter contact.

After landing the navigator checked all switches and stowed all equipment, and proceeded to debriefing and interrogation with his completed log sheets, maps, and charts.

4

Bombardiers

The bombing run from the Initial Point (IP) until the bombs were dropped lasted only a few minutes, but that was the point of the entire B-29 program and its mission. The group lead bombardier not only aimed his bombs, but also all those of his group. The wing bombardiers had the responsibility of dropping their bombs at the proper moment to augment the bomb pattern determined by the lead ship. But the bombardier's duties went beyond bombing, as he had to be able to take over the duties of the navigator in case he was disabled, and he also manned a gunsighting station, and had to be proficient in its operation. Another duty of the bombardier was as photographer to take strike photos.

The bombardier carried out a number of pre-mission checks of the bombs, bomb racks and bomb fuses, bomb formation lights, the electrical fuses and circuits, camera equipment, and his nose gunsighting station. He checked the bombing instruments (altimeter, SCR-716 absolute altimeter), and pre-flighted the Norden bombsight. He also helped the airplane commander in checking the C-1 Autopilot. The bombardier's kit contained a target folder that included aerial photographs of the target and approaches, target charts, the bombardier flimsy, weather data, and a sectional map of the area. Also included in the kit were bombing tables for the bombs to be carried, computers (E-6B, G-1, and C-2), stopwatch, tachometer, and Weems plotter.

Bombardier's duties after takeoff were to assist the airplane commander in looking for other bombers during turns and assembly, and assist the navigator in his dead reckoning by taking drifts and determining ground speeds with the bombsight. He checked his guns, cameras, and bombsight, pulled the bomb pins at 5,000ft, and watched for aircraft (friendly and enemy), shipping, and possible ditching survivors. In between he studied target area maps and photographs.

As the mission neared the target the bombardier became even busier. He had to recompute the bombing altitude and check it against the SCR-718 altimeter, and when the navigator gave him the wind, ground speed, and drift axis of attack these were entered into the bombsight computer. He turned on the intervalometer and chose an IP. The C-1 Autopilot was set, and several gentle turns were made with the course knob to check its operation. The level stabilizer was checked, and the aircraft was to fly straight and level.

The bombardier turned camera master switch ON at the IP and directed the radar operator to open the camera doors. After the bomber completed its turn and passed over the IP on the briefed bombing run, the lead bomber opened its bomb bay doors six minutes before the release point, and the wing bombers opened their doors three minutes later. He rechecked the C-1 Autopilot and altimeter, and then looked for as many checkpoints on the run in as possible to help locate the target. He turned ON all bomb switches, the bomb rack selector switches, and nose arming switch.

On a combined Radar-Bombsight bombing run the bombardier preset the latest drift reading from the navigator. The radar operator said "ready on seven zero-degrees, be prepared for the 'Ready, Mark' signal." At the command "Mark," the bombardier turned ON the rate motor switch. The bombardier kept his hand on the displacement knob, and when the radar operator said "ready on six eight-degrees," he prepared for "Ready, Mark." At the command "Mark," the bombardier turned the displacement knob to set the telescope index on six eight-degrees. Then the radar operator said "Ready on six five-degrees, be prepared for "Ready, Mark." At the command "Mark," the bombardier first turned the displacement knob to put the telescope index on sixty-five-degrees, and quickly rotated the rate knob a slight amount in the same direction as the displacement knob. This procedure was repeated at sighting angle intervals of five-degrees until the value five-degrees before the dropping angle was reached. At this point only a displacement correction was made. If at any time during the bomb run the target could be seen visually the bombardier would say "I see it," and proceeded with a normal visual bomb run. If the target again became obscured the bombardier would ask the radar operator to take over again, and the radar synchronization would continue.

Usually B-29s carried a single bomb camera to record the bombing results. The camera was mounted behind a flush door located in the rear unpressurized compartment. It was the responsibility of the bombardier to have the radar operator open the camera doors when the target was approached. A handle in the radar compartment, immediately forward of the bulkhead door, remotely opened the camera doors by the means of the B-1 or B-2 intervalometer mounted in the bombardier's compartment. The camera could be preset to automatically operate the shutter by electric remote control at specific intervals of time. After the bomb release the cameras were immediately started. The lead bomber in the formation continued on its bomb run for 45 seconds after its drop to get photos of the hits of the early bombers in the formation. Once the target was hit and began to burn it would disappear for hours, and even days, until the smoke and dust cleared away.

After the bombs were jettisoned the navigator LOCKED the bomb racks, the rack selector switches were turned OFF, the bomb bay doors were CLOSED, and the airplane commander was informed of these proce-dures. The bombsight was turned OFF, and as soon as the bombs impacted the cameras were turned OFF, and a strike report was given to the radio operator for transmission.

With the advent of pattern bombing the navigator had little to do. Immediately after takeoff he had to pull the bomb pins, but thereafter he was the nose gunner. All the bombs were toggled when the lead bomber released its bombs, so the wing bombardiers did not have to use their bomb-sights.

5

Radio Operator

Radio Telephone (R/T) Procedure

Because the XXI Bomber Command tolerated no "chatter," the radio operator had only two reasons for transmitting any message from the bomber: to tell something or ask something of importance; otherwise, he was breaking radio silence. Voice messages were to be spoken slowly and clearly, with an even emphasis on each word, and were to be kept short and to the point. Words were not to be run together, and messages were to be spoken in natural phrases and not word-by-word. The Phonetic Alphabet was used to spell words. The components of a voice message were:

(a) The call: For example, "Hello, William Six" (the call sign of the receiving station), "this is William One Two (the call sign of the calling station)."

(b) The text: Was the subject matter that was in plain language, code words or figures.

(c) The ending: Every voice transmission had to end with one of the following procedure words: "Over" meaning that the transmission had ended but a reply was expected, or "Out," meaning that the transmission was ended and no reply was expected.

When both stations were in good communication all parts of the transmission were made at once. When communication was difficult, phrase words or groups of words had to be repeated at the end of the message, or would be transmitted using the procedure phrase "words twice." The receiving station, before acknowledging receipt of the message, would repeat words that were missed or doubtful. The procedure phrases "say again" or "I will say again" were to be used in conjunction with "All before," "All after," "Word before," or "Word after." If a word needed to be spelled to insure correct reception the phrase "I spell" was to be used immediately before beginning to spell the word. The time of the transmission was stated in four digits and preceded by the words "time." For security purposes only necessary transmissions were to be made via R/T, as VHF transmissions were capable of being received as far away as 800mi from the transmitter.

The so-called "Q signals" were combined operating signals beginning with the letter Q, and were followed by two other letters. For example, "QUJ" meant "What is the true course to steer with zero wind to reach you?" "QFS" meant "Please place the radio beacon at __ in opera-

tion." As there were 350 Q signals in use the radio operator had to bring the Q Book (FM 24-13) with him on the mission.

Before take off the radio operator had a long list of checks to be completed: the command set; the liaison set; the interphone (and headsets and microphones); SCR-578; radar; radio compass; RC-103; IFF; antennas; marker beacon; and fuses and frequency meter. The radio operator also assumed flight surgeon duty, and was trained in first aid. He was responsible for the maintenance of the communications equipment, but was not adequately trained for first echelon maintenance.

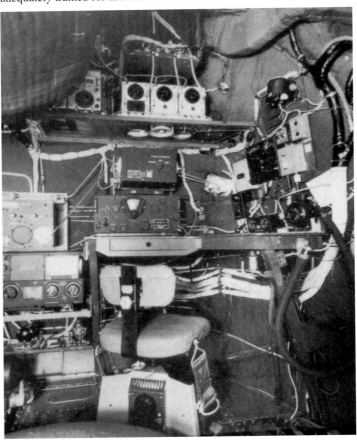

Radio operator's station (USAF)

6

Radar Operator and Radar Navigator

Radar Operator's Position

The radar operator's position was a makeshift position in the rear pressurized cabin that originally was designed for bunks. Conditions at the station affected not only the operator, but also the delicate radar equipment. The cramped, claustrophobic station became very hot, as the inverters under the floor produced considerable heat, and the odors of gasoline from the bomb bay tanks and from the nearby toilet were at times overpowering. The lighting of the station was also considered insufficient. Even though the cabin was pressurized, the maximum visual performance by the radar operator could be obtained only using higher levels of oxygen, but the radarscope shield would not allow wearing an oxygen mask.

Radar Navigator and Bombing

With the advent of instrument bombing the radar navigator assumed new importance. He was responsible for advising the airplane commander of navigational hazards, such as thunderheads and mountains. The navigator depended on radar for ground speeds and drift readings. Since an estimated 40% of the bombs were dropped through clouds the radar man was vital to the bombardier.

The APQ-13 radar returns from the Japanese coast were picked up from 50-60mi, and the coastline features were so distinctive that any radar operator could easily recognize the point he should make landfall from the terrain features he had studied in preparing for the mission. The standard radar bombing procedure required the cooperation of the radar operator, navigator, and bombardier. The wind speed and drift were determined as soon as landfall was made. The airplane commander was then to fly straight and level at bombing altitude to permit the navigator enough time for a precision turn onto the axis of attack before passing over the IP.

Scope interpretation was the radar man's most important job; no matter how well he operated his set and how well he knew the bombing procedure; if the radar operator and navigator could not orient themselves with what they saw on the set then the mission would fail. To make the mission successful the radar operator and navigator spent many hours studying the maps, charts, target folders, and PPI (Plan Position Indicator) Radarscope pictures of the route to the target and the target vicinity. Artist's drawings (based on maps, aerial photos, and topographical studies) of what the radarscope image might look like over the target were studied. Later, simula-

tors arrived that, by means of accurate terrain models of the area, allowed the missions to be flown to duplicate the actual scope presentation of the target. There were several factors, external and intrinsic, that affected the radarscope picture. Among the external factors were terrain and geographic factors, such as lakes, rivers, and islands, and man made factors, such as railway facilities, roads, and buildings. The inherent and operational characteristics of the radar set also affected the scope picture. Because of these influencing factors set tuning, the use of brilliance, tilt, and gain, and the constant study of the scope function and target area were important.

From the navigational standpoint, the APQ-13 Radar Set was a fixing apparatus. The set was only as good as the operator and the accuracy of the fixes he obtained from it, and then his accurate use of the computers and plotting equipment. Radar was not a substitute for standard navigation, but an aid and supplement. Experience showed that the APQ-13 had a range of only 40mi; radar resolution of landmasses was very limited, and the radar operator had to make use of experience and old fashioned "dead reckoning" in radar piloting.

"Offset bombing" was a technique that was developed against specific targets, such as buildings, refineries, and marshalling yards, which were often not easily made out on the PPI Radarscope. Like a golfer using the flag to aim at the cup, the radar operator would pick as his offset aiming point a nearby point that did show up clearly on the PPI. By predetermining the exact distance of this offset checkpoint from the unseen target, the radar operator was able to clock a time delay from the AP to the actual bomb release point.

Radar Mission by the Radar-Bombsight Method

As the bomber approached Japan the radar navigator divided his attention between two radarscopes. On his left was the LORAN, from which he obtained periodic fixes from powerful beacons located along his route. On his right was the PPI scope, which was an auxiliary "remote" scope that showed 360 degree scanned images of the earth's surface below. It operated in the same way as the parent scope on the radar operator's Bombing Through Overcast (BTO) unit, located aft of the tunnel. Both the radar operator and navigator closely watched their respective PPI scopes, looking for radar checkpoints (i.e. islands, coastlines, rivers, etc.) that were easily recognized on a radar screen. From these checkpoints the navigator could check and correct his position.

As the bomber approached the overcast target city it appeared as an irregular white patch at the edge of the PPI scope. The circular PPI scope was divided into compass headings, with a "lubber line" extending from the center of the circle (the true heading of the aircraft) toward the target. The PPI could be adjusted in range to enlarge the image of the area below on the scope, and to bring out the light and shadows on the scope that represented land and water, factories, docks, and other landmarks. As the bomber drew nearer the target the blurred images on the scope slowly moved nearer the center of the scope, which constantly represented the position of the bomber. The radar operator set his computers for the correct sighting angles, and a "bombing circle" was turned on the scope in the exact slant-range setting.

Meanwhile, the bombardier adjusted his Norden bombsight for the latest drift, speed, and altitude. At this point the bombardier was unable to see the target through the overcast to obtain the sighting angle, but the radar operator could see it electronically, and informed the bombardier over the interphones. Through training, experience, and the pre-mission briefing the radar operator was able to identify something in the irregular white patch on his scope as the target, which was nearing the center of the scope. There was a smaller circle inside the scope screen surrounding the scope center called the "bombing circle." The moment the outer edge of the white target touched the bombing circle the radar operator would inform the bombardier to insert the data. This procedure was continued through each new sighting angle as the bomber approached the target. When the target converged with the exact center of the scope the Norden bombsight automatically released the bombs.

Radar bombing, while never as accurate as visual bombing, allowed the 20AF to continue its bombing campaign through the chronic poor weather over Japan. Radar allowed the bombers to find and bomb urban areas with sufficient accuracy, and then through sheer quantity of aircraft and weight of bombs (25 times that required for visual bombing) cause heavy damage.

7

Gunners and the Central Fire Control (CFC) System

The Central Fire Control (CFC) System removed the guesswork out of "point of aim," but required practice to achieve skill in tracking, firing, and ranging to give the system enough accurate data to obtain a higher percentage of hits. Each gunner was personally responsible for his guns and turrets, but turret specialists repaired turrets and station ordnance personnel did gun repair.

Preflight Checks
Before boarding the bomber for the mission the gunners were responsible for the following preflight checks of their guns and turrets:

1) Check and harmonize guns using dummy rounds.
2) Check all equipment for safety wires where required.
3) Check ammunition carefully for excess corrosion, defective primers, position of links on rounds, round to round positioning, and for any bulges or burrs.
4) Load the ammunition cans, making certain the rounds were pointed in the right direction and did not bind in the can. Load guns as per group mission directive.
5) Check to see if the required spare gun parts and tool kit were on board.
6) Check CFC System and turret domes and latches.
7) Sight stowage.
8) Immediately before each mission all oil was to be removed and none applied, as the guns would perform better at high altitudes without any oil.

Once on board the bomber and before take off the gunners performed the following pre-flight station checks:

1) Check parachute and clothing.
2) Check oxygen system (pressure should be between 350 to 450psi)
3) Check to be sure that the cabin pressure valve was open.
4) Check heaters and lights.
5) Check interphones by putting on the headphones, adjusting the throat microphone, and then waiting for the interphone check. An alarm bell was rung by the airplane commander during combat station inspection, and the left and right fuselage gunners would inform the air-

plane commander that they had heard the alarm bell.
6) Each gunner would report to the airplane commander that he had completed his own checklist.
7) When the co-pilot called over the interphone, each gunner would observe and report the position of the rudder, elevators, and ailerons as the airplane commander operated each control. Before takeoff the airplane commander would say over the interphone "wing flaps," and when the flaps were down the left blister gunner would reply "left flap down 25-degrees," and the right blister gunner would make a similar reply. The blister gunners were responsible for checking that the bomb bay doors were closed.

Then the airplane commander would order "fasten you safety belt," and issue a "taxi alert." During taxiing the top CFC gunner was responsible for promptly reporting to the co-pilot the presence of any nearby aircraft that might interfere with taxiing.

Without the direction of the CFC gunner, and without gunner coordination the RCT System would lose its effectiveness and have blind spots. The CFC controller is shown here in an unusual exterior photograph of his sighting position. Note the camera port between the guns. (USAF)

After Takeoff

After take off the gunners:

1) Made sure the optic head was clean.
2) Pushed breaker switches IN and switched A.C. power to ON. The dynamotor then started, and the reticle lights went on (target size numerals, aiming dot, and range circle).
3) Turned the rheostat from DIM to BRIGHT and tested the reticle response.
4) Turned the rheostat lamp selector switch to check lamp's second (reserve) filament.
5) Turned the target size adjusting screw to check change of numerals and change of range dots. Made sure the reticle circle was clear.
6) Sighted at some distant object, moved his head, and made sure that the dot still seemed to be on the object, no matter where he held his head.
7) Turned ON the computer switch on the control box to start gyroscope and computer unit.
8) Turned the computer standby switch to IN to connect the computing mechanism into the circuits. Made sure the warning light that lit when the computer was on STAND BY had gone off when the action switch was closed.
9) Checked that the friction adjustments were just right for smooth tracking. If gloves were worn on the mission, the adjustments were tested with the gloves on.
10) Turned OFF all switches.
11) Moved the sight to the forward horizontal position and to LOCK.
12) LOCK pantograph.
13) The waist gunners were to inform the airplane commander that the flaps and gear were "FULL UP."

After these checks the gunner tried to settle into a comfortable position for scanning and tracking, but this was difficult, as his position in the blister was kneeling with his knees spread apart. The gunners played around with their parachute harnesses and padding, and tried to get their microphone cords and oxygen tubing out of the way; fortunately vigilant scanning was only required as the bombers approached Japan.

The aircraft generators were unable to start all the CFC equipment at once, and the airplane commander directed each turret to start up in turn:

1) Turn ON the switches in the power control box one at a time at 10-second intervals.
2) Turn the computer switch on the control box to IN. This supplied D.C. power to the computer and sight gyros. Check that the computer In-Out light was ON. This light was to be ON when both the computer switch on the control box was ON, and when the computer standby switch was at STANDBY.
3) Turn the computer standby switch on the sight to IN. The In-Out light then switched OFF.
4) Close the action switch and move the sight. Check to see that the primary control turret followed the sight. To check these turret movements: the top gunner could see the upper turret; the blister gunners could see the lower aft turret guns when the turret was pointing broadside; the tail gunner could see the tail mount; and the nose gunner could have the top gunner check the upper forward turret, and have

the navigator listen for the movement of the lower forward turret.
5) Check the secondary controls as per SOP. Check that the secondary turret followed the sight.
6) Adjust the brightness of the lights on the auxiliary control box in the blister sighting station to individual preference.
7) If he had not been informed previously, the gunner checked with the navigator to see if he had entered altitude, air speed, and temperature on the hand set.
8) Since an enemy fighter would be seen at a long distance, the range control was set for the smallest reticle, or maximum range.
9) If or when the airplane commander instructed the gunner to test fire, the gun switch was moved from SAFE to FIRE. The gunner would take a short burst, taking care not to fire into the formation. After the test the gun's switch was returned to SAFE.
10) On long missions the CFC would be put into STANDBY mode.

Engaging the Enemy

Once in the combat zone the gunner was assigned an area to scan, and would usually move the sight while scanning, but would leave the action switch OPEN so the guns would not follow. When an aircraft was spotted the gunner was to take four steps:

1) Report the target to the fire control officer by the o'clock system.
2) Identify the target as friend or foe. If it was an enemy, identify the type and wingspan.
3) Set the target size on the reticle. Some gunners found it helpful to set the target size previously to the wingspan of the aircraft most likely to attack.
4) Turn the gun switch to FIRE.

After the target was identified as the enemy, the gunner would move the sights on the target and follow it, and take the following steps:

1) Placed the reticle center dot right on the middle of the target and kept it there. The computer made all the necessary corrections for ballistics, parallax, and lead.
2) Kept the range set properly by carefully spanning the target with the reticle. The computer computations were only as good as the data fed into it, and range was very important.
3) It was important that the gunner had a comfortable hold on the grips so that he would not have to change it while tracking.
4) The gunner was to sight with both eyes, which was more natural and easier.
5) The target was to be tracked smoothly, as the computer calculated the amount of lead to give the gun from the rate at which the sight was turned. The range handle was to be adjusted continually so that the reticle just spanned the target's wingspan, or silhouette. If the sight was jerked or paused then the computer would jerk or pause the guns. If the gunner came off the target he then had to move the sight smoothly back to it. Even if the bomber was rolling or evading the gun tracking was to remain as smooth as possible, and the computer would make the necessary corrections. The gunner had to keep the center dot on the target and span its silhouette with the reticle.
6) If the gunner changed from one target to another, he was to swing the sight quickly with the action switch CLOSED. When a new target

was encountered the action switch was OPEN. This action switch open-closed procedure was to prevent the computer from entering erroneous corrections.

During combat it was estimated that 45% of enemy attacks were head-on attacks against the B-29's nose guns. Due to the high closing rates of a head-on attack the nose sighting station had to adopt the following procedure:

1) Set target size at 35ft.
2) Adjust the range hand wheel until the reticle (circle of dots) appeared (1,200yds).
3) When a single-engine target spanned three quarters of the reticle (1,600yds) the range wheel was to be spun to minimum, and tracking and firing was started. The same procedure applied to twin-engined fighters.
4) The gunner was to return to 1,200yds range as soon as the target left in order to have information in the computer ready for the next head-on attack.

It was important to begin firing before the enemy did. The gunners were to begin firing at 1,000yds, except for the nose gunner, who was to fire immediately because of the high closing speeds. All the gunner had to do was keep the target spanned in the reticle, track smoothly, and the computer would do the rest. Short bursts were to be fired, with a maximum firing rate not exceeding 30 rounds per minute per gun (two seconds of firing). The gunner was to release the trigger whenever control of his turret was transferred from one station to another so that bullets would not be fired when the turret was swinging around. It was important that the gunners listened over the interphones to keep current on the situation in the rest of the bomber.

Gunner's Duties Before Landing
Before landing the gunners had to take the following steps:

1) About two hours before landing the lower turret guns were to be cleared of ammunition by firing.
2) The gun switch on the control box was turned to SAFE.
3) The primary control gunners were to stow their turrets by stowing the sight and holding the action switch to CLOSED. The right blister gunner was also to stow the lower aft turret.
4) When the turrets were stowed the switches were turned OFF on the control box, and then the action switch was to be released. The stowing pins on the sight in both azimuth and elevation were to be pushed IN, and then the sight was to be covered.
5) When the airplane commander announced "Prepare for landing" over the interphone the tail gunner was to start the auxiliary power APU.
6) When the airplane commander announced "Wing flaps" the right and left blister gunners watched the flaps, and the left blister gunner reported "Left flap down 25-degrees," and then the right gunner reported likewise.
7) The landing gear was reported as "DOWN and LOCKED."
8) Safety belts were then fastened for landing.

Gunner's Duties After Landing

The blister gunner was to check that the bomb bay doors were OPEN. After each mission the gunner would first disarm and clear the guns, with another gunner standing by so no one would pass in front of them during clearing. Next he would remove the turret dome and open the gun covers and remove the ammunition belts, being sure that the last round was removed from the chamber. He would remove and empty the ammo cans, but did nothing with the receiver.

The guns were removed, taken to armament, and thoroughly cleaned with the prescribed cleaning fluid. The parts checked for full and free movement were: the ejector, the extractor switch, belt holding pawl, cover group, firing pin and extension, and the accelerator. While cleaning the gun each part was to be carefully inspected, and if there was a problem with any part it was to be replaced.

All gunners were to report all malfunctions of the CFC equipment to the CFC top gunner, who was to keep a record of the status of the equipment and then reported them to the flight engineer. After completing their after landing responsibilities the gunners reported to intelligence for debriefing.

Tail gunner
Before the mission the tail gunner would remove long belts of .50cal ammunition from their wooden boxes, and would stretch them out along the ground to make sure each round was clean and properly aligned. After the inspection he would return them to the boxes and haul the heavy boxes up the tall ladder of the rear entrance door, and then, stooping, he lugged them back toward the cramped tail gun position, which was very hot while the bomber was on the ground. He crawled and dragged the boxes to the ammunition containers located on each side of the fuselage just forward of the tail compartment, where he would feed the end of each ammunition belt into the tracks of rollers that led to the tail position and into the tail turret machine guns. He would then enter his 4x6ft tail compartment that was relatively spacious when compared to those on the B-17 and B-24. The tail gunner would check his bail out oxygen bottle, flak suit, and life raft. He then left the bomber, climbed up a ladder, and used a screwdriver to remove the outside covers on his turret. The gun lids were opened, the ammunition belts were slid along their tracks, the first round was loaded "hot" into the firing chamber, and the gun was actuated with a screwdriver and ready to fire. Before removing the ladder he closed the lids and cleaned the tail gun position windows.

At the start of the mission the tail gunner entered the fuselage through the rear entrance door and crawled through the tail section into the tail turret, closed the turret compartment door, and adjusted the seat and latched the lap belt. There was a chest parachute that was stored on the floor, and the gunner generally did not hook into it unless there was an emergency. The tail gunner wore a soft leather flight helmet and oxygen mask with a flak helmet over them, and wore a full flak suit that had a quick release, so it could be removed rapidly so the parachute pack could be strapped on. The tail gunner completed a preflight check similar to the forward gunners. The gun heaters were turned on during the flight, and the armorers generally did not oil the guns, as the oil would freeze and cause jams. The tail guns had a field of fire of plus or minus 30-degrees in azimuth and elevation. The tail gunner used his left hand on the "dead man's" grip that had to be held down to fire while his right hand worked the ranging control. The flight engineer entered the bomber's altitude, airspeed, and outside temperature into the computer, and all the gunner had to do was sight through the sight. There was bulletproof glass in the windshield, and a piece of armor plate on his seat back. The belt links and spent cartridges from the tail turret and the two lower turrets were ejected outside, while the links and cartridges of the other guns fell to the floor. To avoid hitting the gun debris of the lead bomber B-29 formations were flown in diamonds, and the last plane flew above the lead bomber (high enough to keep out of his slipstream but low enough to keep on the tip of his tail).

The tail gunner was responsible for the operation of the APU. Before starting the engines and when the battery switch was ON the tail gunner would switch the putt putt ON (see flight engineer section for starting sequence). When the co-pilot gave the "prepare for landing" order the tail gunner would stow the equipment, turn the switches OFF, start the APU, and notify the co-pilot when it was ON LINE. After landing the tail gunner would turn the put putt OFF when directed by the flight engineer. The tail gunner's post flight responsibilities were similar to those gunners in the forward compartments.

B-29 Gunnery

Areas of Search and Fire
Each gunner, in addition to controlling a specific turret combination, had also to keep a lookout over a specific and limited area of the sky, which was the area his guns would fire (except for the tail gunner, who fired into a smaller area than he searched).

In a study of 6,000 enemy fighter attacks to determine the levels and directions of attack during daylight missions it was found that they were almost evenly distributed: 32% Above; 34% Level; and 34% Low. On night missions (231 attacks) the enemy fighters were reported to come in at 53%

Level, 31% High, and 16% Low. However, these night figures could be in error, as many enemy attacks that originated at the High or Low positions could not be seen until they reached the Level position. On daylight missions High, Level, and Low attacks from the nose quarter were the enemy's preferred approaches of attack. On night missions the enemy tended to choose level or high attacks from the rear.

The Japanese preference for frontal daylight attacks was due to the difficulty of Japanese interceptors to overtake B-29s at high altitude (26,000 to 32,000ft), and also a frontal attack made the Jap fighter a difficult target because of the high rate of closure. The preference for nighttime tail attacks was due to the Japanese system of vectoring that placed their fighters on the tails of the B-29s. Nighttime B-29 attacks were made at low levels that enabled the Japanese fighters to overtake them. However, the Japanese never fully developed night tactics and lacked night fighters.

The Gunner's "How to Search and Fire"
Areas of Search and Fire for each gun position:
1) Nose Gunner:
Azimuth: Generally forward (10 to 2 o'clock) 150-degrees
Elevation: 60-degrees scaling up or down
2) Top Gunner:
Azimuth: Generally forward (9 to 3 o'clock) 180-degrees
Elevation: 60-degrees up from the horizontal
3) Waist Gunners:
Azimuth: One searched and fired to the outside of the formation, the other searched to the inside (1 to 6 o'clock right and 6 to 11 o'clock left) 150-degrees
Elevation: 60-degrees down from horizontal

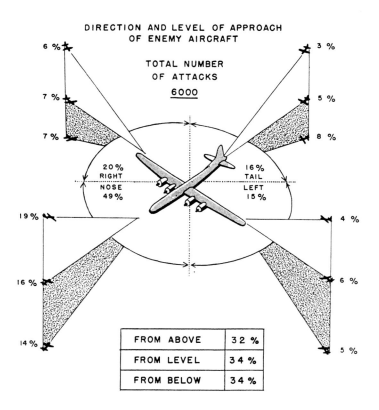

Daytime Direction and Level of Approach of Enemy Aircraft (USAF)

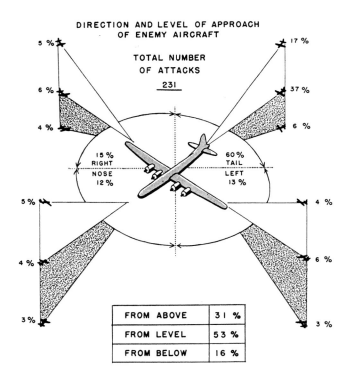

Nighttime Direction and Level of Approach of Enemy Aircraft (USAF)

4) Tail Gunner:
Azimuth: Searched over entire visual area (3 to 9 o'clock) 180-degrees
Elevation: 90-degrees divided evenly above and below horizontal

The main rule for search was:

"You've got to look with the expectation of seeing something. The man who doesn't expect to see something—doesn't. Focus your eyes at the outer range of your area and look to see. Don't look merely to be looking. Keep your attention focused and stay alert. A methodical system for hunting the sky may help:

1) Divide the area of the sky in your own mind into small zones.
2) Focus on the zone furthest forward, and don't let your eyes leave it until they have done a thorough job of searching in that zone.
3) Then shift to the next zone and do the same job.
4) Stick to your own area.
5) Always search the forward part of your area more frequently and carefully than any other. That's where attacks appear to start in relative motion, and that's where your hottest attacks come from. Search more often in the forward areas, rather than linger longer in them.
6) Always keep your guns pointing forward at standby—ready for the draw, to pick up targets swiftly and track them from front to rear."

While scanning the sky for enemy planes the gunner was not to move the sight, as every movement caused the computer to calculate deflections. The gunner did not want the computer to be calculating a non-existent deflection on a non-existent enemy when a real target was spotted. When a real target came into view then the sight could be swung quickly to line it up. The quicker the sights and guns were on the target, the less time it took the computer to start its computations.

Reporting the Target
Immediately after spotting any aircraft, friend or foe, the gunner got on the interphone and, speaking clearly, concisely, and in firm volume (not shouting) used the standard clock system, high, low, level to locate the aircraft. He then repeated the message once.

As soon as an aircraft was seen to be threatening (i.e. maneuvering, climbing, etc.) the gunner was to report them in the following fashion: number and type (pause); clock and elevation position (pause); and if enemy, what are they doing (repeat). For example:

"5 ZERO FIGHTERS (pause) TWO O'CLOCK HIGH (pause) OVERTAKING (repeat)"

As soon as the target was clearly attacking, the gunner reported (with his guns bearing) as follows: attack (pause); clock and elevation position (repeat):

ATTACK (pause) FOUR O'CLOCK HIGH (repeat)

In the breakaway phase of the attack gunners, other than those firing on the attack, could have a perfect shot at the target, providing they were forewarned. This was especially true for the side and tail gunners on nose

attacks that passed over or under the bomber to complete their breakaway. On a breakaway the report was:

attack (pause) clock and elevation position (pause) how breaking away ATTACK (pause) ONE O'CLOCK LEVEL (pause) BREAKING AWAY UNDER (repeat)

At the end of an attack the attacker could slide under a bomber to get itself in immediate position for another attack, and thus would offer itself as an easy target for the blister gunner toward whose side he was sliding, providing the gunner was forewarned. The report:

Attack (pause) clock and elevation position (pause) sliding under ATTACK (pause) THREE O'CLOCK LOW (pause) SLIDING UNDER (repeat)

Tracking the Target
"If you feed your computer the right information, it will come up with the right deflection. If you make a mistake, the computer will give the wrong answer and your bullets will miss every time. Your tracking and framing of the target must be absolutely on the nose" (from *Gunnery in the B-29*). The B-29 gunnery manual listed seven rules for tracking an enemy aircraft:

1) The body, especially the upper arms from elbow to shoulder, was to be braced. The hands were to remain steady and be supported on the sight, but the wrists and fingers needed complete freedom.
2) The sight had friction adjustments that were to be preset to individual preferences for tracking the target smoothly. If gloves were to be worn during combat then the adjustments were to be made with them on.
3) In glare conditions, the sky filter was to be used as little as possible, and the rheostat was to be turned up to maximum, and the filter used only enough to make the reticle clearly visible.
4) The gunner was to keep his eyes a few inches behind the optic head, with both eyes open while scanning.
5) Instant fighter recognition was important in order to dial in the wingspan without thinking.
6) The range wheel or grip was to be turned with a smooth, steady, easy motion to keep the target's wingtips framed accurately inside the reticle circle. If the target was seen from the side, where in most cases its fuselage was shorter than its wingspan, the gunner was to set in the wingspan, but keep the circle somewhat beyond the ends of the fuselage as seen in the sight.
7) The gunner was to maintain the dot of the reticle on the middle of the fighter and track it smoothly and continuously. Once tracking began the gunner was not to change his grip on the hand wheels or grips until the target was shot down or escaped. If the aim was off (e.g. failure to move the dot with the target or move past it) the gunner was not to jerk the dot back to place, but move it slowly and smoothly back. "If you get off target, get off the trigger."

The basic firing areas could be restricted or reduced to avoid hitting other bombers in the formation according to a prescribed safety rule:

"Every area of search and fire must stop one full clock angle (30-degrees) in azimuth away from any other bomber in the formation."

This rule for defining search and fire areas was slightly modified to act as a safety rule in firing if the gunner forgot the limits of his search and fire area during combat:

"You must withhold fire, in azimuth: 1 hour clock angle (30-degrees) away from another B-29 when tracking into it and a half hour clock angle (15-degrees) away from another B-29 when tracking away from it."

This rule allowed a safety margin for the gun computer leads and for parallax, when the guns could be pointing far ahead or lagging far behind the aiming point.

Firing on the Target
The remote system allowed the gunner to fire at any aircraft in range, and he did not have to wait for an attack. The rules for firing were:

1) Set the true wingspan of the target on the target dimension dial. At the start of the mission the gunner was to set the wingspan of the fighter most likely to be encountered, and turn the range handle until the reticle circle was as small as possible; the gunner then would be ready for quick action. If the enemy fighter encountered was not the one for the sight presetting, the setting could be quickly reset. If there was not time to change the wingspan size the gunner could make a correction as the target was framed. If the actual target wingspan was smaller than the dial setting he could keep the reticle a little beyond the wingtips. If the target was larger than the dial setting he could let the wingtips overlap the circle a little.
2) Place the center dot of the reticle on the target's fuselage at the leading edge of its wings.
3) Adjust the range so that the circle of dots in the reticle just touched the part of the target farthest away from the center dot.
4) Make sure that any friendly bombers were not hit.

5) Open fire and keep firing in bursts.
6) If, in tracking the target, the rounds came close to a friendly bomber the gunner was to invoke the safety rule and stop firing one full hour clock angle tracking toward, or stop firing a half hour if tracking away.

The tail gunner was to immediately report by interphone any aircraft within his search cone, and then was to continue a running report at 30 second intervals until the aircraft was identified as friend or enemy and, if enemy, until it had either been destroyed or escaped. To report the target's range, the gunner was to use the set words: SPOT, if the target were beyond 900yds; CLOSE, if the target were between 900 and 500yds; and the range in round number yards if it were under 500yds. The report sequence was:

target (pause) range information (pause) clock and elevation position (repeat)
TARGET (pause) SPOT (pause) SEVEN O'CLOCK HIGH (repeat)

Immediately after receiving this target report the radio operator was to issue the IFF challenge, and report back to the tail gunner if he detected if the aircraft was friendly. If the tail gunner did not receive a reply from the radio operator, or if his signal lights did not go on, indicating that the target was not another B-29, the tail gunner would assume that the target was hostile and open fire if its range decreased to 600yds. He was to fire long bursts, and continue to report on the interphone as long as the target was within 600yds, or until it was destroyed, evaded, or lost.

The US Strategic Bombing Survey report on the "Strategic Air Operation of Very Heavy Bombers in the War Against Japan (20th Air Force)" gave XXIBC B-29 gunners the following credits during 11,026 enemy attacks: 714 enemy aircraft destroyed, 456 probably destroyed, and 770 damaged. For every hundred enemy aircraft attacks B-29 gunners shot down or probably destroyed an average of 11. Japanese fighters shot down 58 B-29s, and 29 others were lost to combined aircraft and flak damage.

Part Five
Combat

Of all the aircraft of WWII, the B-29 probably had the most profound influence in the outcome of the war. Aerial strategic planning in the Pacific war hinged on the troubled development and deployment of this superbomber. Although the B-29 "A-bomber" will be forever given credit for ending the Pacific with the atomic bombings of Hiroshima and Nagasaki, it was the bomber's previous missions from the Marianas that had truly devastated the Japanese homeland.

1

Organization of the 20ᵗʰ Air Force

At the time the 20ᵗʰ Air Force was organized in April 1944, the XX Bomber Command was made up of the four groups of the 58ᵗʰ Bomb Wing that were on their way to the CBI, and the XXI Bomber Command's three Bomb Wings (73ʳᵈ, 313ᵗʰ, and 314ᵗʰ), each made up of four groups that were training in the United States and headed for the Marianas. The 20AF was under the command of the Joint Chiefs of Staff, with the theater commander having command of logistical support, except for that concerned directly with the B-29s.

In the Marianas the XXIBC and its subordinate units were organized differently than the usual overseas AAF organization. Because of the demand to deploy the B-29s into combat as quickly as possible, and the lack of base facilities, the number of air bases in the Marianas was to be limited. Normally, the operating entity in the AAF was the Bomb Wing or Bomb Squadron, but the XXIBC conceived the Wing headquarters to perform that function. Each Wing and its associated combat and service units

would operate from a single Wing base with 12,000 personnel, and could accommodate up to 200 bombers. Service responsibilities were centralized into Wing base functions due to the lack of equipment, supplies, and housing, as were the supply and maintenance functions of the separate service units. The tactical and strategic functions of the XXIBC were under the direct control of the 20AF. The Deputy Commander of the 20AF at Hickam Field, Hawaii, controlled supply and specific administrative concerns, but also was the CG of the Headquarters Army Air Forces, Pacific Ocean Area, and in this dual position was involved in the logistical support of the XXIBC. The Guam Air Depot was established to execute the required air depot functions for the XXIB, and was under the command of the Deputy Commander of the 20AF.

In early 1945 the XXBC (58BW) received orders to be transferred from the CBI to the Marianas, and be placed under the command of the XXIBC. In April 1945 the 58BW arrived in the Marianas, where it re-

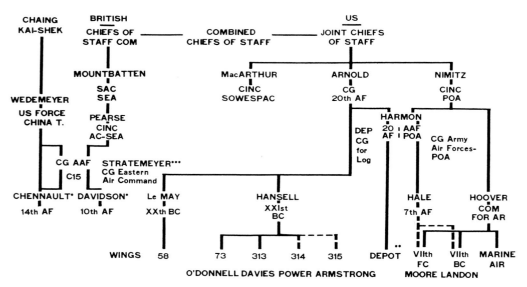

COMMAND, CONTROL, AND SUPPORT RELATIONSHIPS
TWENTIETH AIR FORCE
January 1945

*Responsible for Air Defense of B-29 bases
**Responsible for Depot Support of B-29s—Marianas
***Responsible for Depot Support of B-29s—XXth Bomber Command

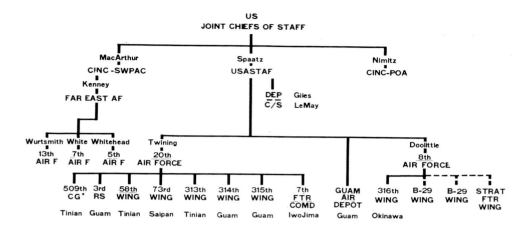

US ARMY AIR FORCES IN THE PACIFIC
US ARMY STRATEGIC AIR FORCES IN THE PACIFIC
AS OF 15 August 1945

*509th Composite (Atomic) Group

ceived an added Wing, and was followed by the 315BW in May. In July several significant changes were made when the XXIBC was redesignated as the 20AF. The VII Fighter Command on Iwo Jima and the Guam Air Depot, both under the command of the Deputy Commander, 20AF, were transferred to the 20AF, and the Deputy Commander, 20AF, was eliminated. The consequence of these changes was that the 20AF, with its headquarters on Guam, now had control of five VHB wings composed of 20 Bomb Wings, the VIIFC, and the Guam Air Depot. The U.S. Army Strate-

gic Air Forces, which was the next highest in the chain of command and acting under the direct control of the Joint Chiefs of Staff, was established on Guam. It was to act as an intermediate headquarters between the 20AF and Headquarters Army Air Forces.

As the XXIBC experienced combat it discovered that it was necessary to add a fourth Bomb Squadron to the three squadrons of each Bomb Wing, and also to revise the tables of organization of Wing headquarters and the XXIBC, but the war ended before these changes could be implemented.

20th AIR FORCE TACTICAL UNIT HISTORY

	1944 JUN	JUL	AUG	SEP	OCT	NOV	DEC	1945 JAN	FEB	MAR	APR	MAY	JUN	JUL	AUG
58th BOMB WING															
40th Bomb Group	▨	▨	▨	▨	▨	▨	▨	▨	▨	▨	▨	▨	▨	▨	▨
444th Bomb Group	▨	▨	▨	▨	▨	▨	▨	▨	▨	▨	▨	▨	▨	▨	▨
462nd Bomb Group	▨	▨	▨	▨	▨	▨	▨	▨	▨	▨	▨	▨	▨	▨	▨
468th Bomb Group	▨	▨	▨	▨	▨	▨	▨	▨	▨	▨	▨	▨	▨	▨	▨
73rd BOMB WING															
497th Bomb Group				▨	▨	▨	▨	▨	▨	▨	▨	▨	▨	▨	▨
498th Bomb Group				▨	▨	▨	▨	▨	▨	▨	▨	▨	▨	▨	▨
499th Bomb Group					▨	▨	▨	▨	▨	▨	▨	▨	▨	▨	▨
500th Bomb Group					▨	▨	▨	▨	▨	▨	▨	▨	▨	▨	▨
313th BOMB WING															
6th Bomb Group							▨	▨	▨	▨	▨	▨	▨	▨	▨
9th Bomb Group							▨	▨	▨	▨	▨	▨	▨	▨	▨
504th Bomb Group								▨	▨	▨	▨	▨	▨	▨	▨
505th Bomb Group								▨	▨	▨	▨	▨	▨	▨	▨
509th Comp. Grp.													▨	▨	▨
314th BOMB WING															
19th Bomb Group									▨	▨	▨	▨	▨	▨	▨
29th Bomb Group									▨	▨	▨	▨	▨	▨	▨
39th Bomb Group										▨	▨	▨	▨	▨	▨
330th Bomb Group										▨	▨	▨	▨	▨	▨
315th BOMB WING															
16th Bomb Group												▨	▨	▨	▨
331st Bomb Group												▨	▨	▨	▨
501st Bomb Group												▨	▨	▨	▨
502nd Bomb Group													▨	▨	▨
ATTACHED UNITS															
3rd Photo Recon Sqdn					▨	▨	▨	▨	▨	▨	▨	▨	▨	▨	▨
4th Em. Rescue Sqdn															
41st Photo Recon Sqdn															▨
55th Recon Sqdn (LRW)							▨	▨	▨	▨	▨	▨	▨	▨	▨

Structure of the 20ᵗʰ Air Force

20ᵗʰ Air Force

Activated: 4 April 1944

Bases: Washington D.C.: 4 April 1944

Harmon Field, Guam: 16 July 1945

Commanders: Gen. Henry Arnold: 4 April 1944

Maj.Gen. Curtiss LeMay: July 1945

Lt.Gen. Nathan Twining: 2 August 1945

XX Bomber Command

Activated: 20 November 1943

Bases: Kharagpur, India: 28 March 1944 to 17 June 1945

Sakugawa, Okinawa: 7 July to 16 July 1945

Commanders: Brig.Gen. Kenneth Wolfe: 20 November 1943

Brig.Gen. LaVerne Saunders: 6 July 1944

Maj.Gen. Curtiss LeMay: 29 August 1944

Brig.Gen. Roger Ramey: 20 January 1945

Brig.Gen. Joseph Smith: 25 April 1945 to XXBC

deactivated: 16 July 1945

Brig.Gen. Kenneth Wolfe: 20 November 1943 (USAF)

Gen. Henry Arnold: 4 April 1944 (USAF)

Brig.Gen. LaVerne Saunders: 6 July 1944 (USAF)

XXI Bomber Command

Activated: 1 March 1944

Bases: Harmon Field, Guam: 4 December 1944 to 16 July 1945

Commanders: Brig.Gen. Haywood Hansell 28 August 1944

Maj.Gen. Curtiss LeMay: 20 January 1945

Maj.Gen. Curtis LeMay: July 1945 (USAF)

Brig.Gen. Haywood Hansell 28 August 1944 (USAF)

Brig.Gen. LaVerne Saunders: 5 March 1944 (USAF)

Brig.Gen. Roger Ramey: 24 April 1945 (USAF)

58ᵗʰ Bomb Wing

Activated: 1 May 1943
Bases: Chakulia, India: 2 April 1944
                      Kharagpur, India: 23 April to 12 October 1944
                      Hijli Base Area, India 8 February 1945 to 24 February 1945
                      West Field, Tinian: 29 March 1945 to 15 November 1945
Commanders: Brig.Gen. LaVerne Saunders: 5 March 1944
                      Col. Dwight Montieth 8 February 1945
                      Brig.Gen. Roger Ramey: 24 April 1945
Voice Call: "Loyal"

40ᵗʰ Bomb Group

Activated: 1 April 1941 as 40BG(M), then May 1942 as 40BG(H),
                      then 40B(VH) November 1943
Assigned 20AF: June 1944
Squadrons: 25BS, 44BS, 45BS and 395BS (disbanded October 1944)
Training: Pratt, KS, 1 July 1943 to 12 March 1944
Bases: Chakulia, India: 2 April 1944 to 25 February 1945
                      Hsinching (A-3), China: Forward base

West Field, Tinian: 4 April 1945 to the end of the war
Commanders: Col. Leonard Harman: 10 April 1944
                      (to U.S. as Gen. Wolfe's assistant)
                      Col. William Blanchard: 4 August 1944
                      Col. Harry Sullivan: 16 February 1945
                      Col. William Skaer: 27 February 1945
First Mission: 5 June 1944 vs. Bangkok railway yards
DUCs: 20 August 1944 vs. Yawata
                      5-14 May 1945 vs. Kure naval a/c factories, Oshima oil
                      facilities, and Nagoya industrial area
                      24 July 1945 vs. Osaka light metals industries
Voice Call: "Robust," and later "Actor"

444ᵗʰ Bomb Group

Activated: 1 March 1943 as 444BG (H), then November 1943
                      as 444BG(VH)
Assigned 20AF: 29 June 1944
Squadrons: 676BS, 677BS, 678BS and 679BS
                      (disbanded October 1944)
Training: Great Bend, KS: 29 July 1943 to 1 March 1944
Bases: Charra, India: 11 April 1944
                      Dudhkundi, India: 1 July 1944 to 1 March 1945
                      Kwanghan, China (A-3) Forward base
                      West Field, Tinian: 7 April 1945 to the end of the war
Commanders: Col. Alva Harvey: 5 August 1944 (to 58BW
                      as Deputy Commander)
                      Col. Henry Sullivan: 22 April 1945
                      Col. James Selser: 3 June 1945
First Mission: 5 June 1944 vs. Bangkok railway yards
DUCs: 20 August 1944 vs. Yawata
                      10-14 May vs. Oshima oil facilities, Kobe a/c factories,
                      and Nagoya incendiary raid
                      24 June 1945 vs. Osaka
Voice Call: "Mashnote," and later "Ogre"

462ⁿᵈ Bomb Group

Activated: 1 July 1943 as 462BG(H), then November 1943
                      as 462BG (VH)
Assigned 20AF: June 1944
Squadrons: 768BS, 769BS, 770BS and 771BS
Training: Smoky Hill, KS: 1 July 1943
                      Walker, KS: 18 July 1943 to 12 March 1944
Bases: Piardoba, India: 7 April 1944 to 26 February 1945
                      Kiunglai, China (A-5): Forward base
                      West Field, Tinian: 4 April 1945 to end of the war
Commanders: Col. Richard Carmichael 26 August 1943
                      (shot down over Yawata)
                      Col. Alfred Kalberer: 20 August 1944
First Mission: 5 June 1944 to Bangkok
DUCs: 20 August 1944 vs. Yawata
                      23, 25, 29 May 1945 vs. Yokohama and Tokyo
                      industrial areas
                      24 July 1945 vs. Takarazuka a/c factory
Voice Call: "Wicked"

468th Bomb Group
Activated: 1 August 1943 as 468BG(H), then November 1943
                as 468BG(VH)
Assigned 20AF: June 1944
Squadrons: 792BS, 793BS, 794BS and 795BS
Training: Smoky Hill, KS: 1 August to 12 March 1944
Bases: Kharagpur, India: 13 April 1944 to 24 February 1945
                Pengshan, China (A-7): Forward base
                West Field, Tinian: 6 April 1945
Commanders: Col. Howard Engler: 8 September 1944
                Col. Ted Faulkner: 3 August 1944
                (shot down over Singapore)
                Col. James Edmundson: 5 November 1944
First Mission: 5 June 1944 to Bangkok
DUCs: 20 August 1944 vs. Yawata
                23, 25, 29 May 1945 vs. Yokohama and Tokyo
                industrial areas
                24 July 1945 vs. Takarazuka a/c factory
Voice Call: "Mingtoy," and later "Skookum"

Brig.Gen. Emmett O'Donnell 15
March 1944 to the end of the war.
(USAF)

73rd Bomb Wing
Activated: 20 November 1943
Bases: Isley Field, Saipan: 24 August 1944 to 20 October 1945
Commanders: Brig.Gen. Emmett O'Donnell 15 March 1944
                to the end of the war
Voice Call: "Husky"

497th Bomb Group
Activated: 20 November 1943
Assigned 20AF: July 1944
Squadrons: 869BS, 870BS, and 871BS
Training: Pratt, KS: 13 April to 18 July 1944
Bases: Isley Field, Saipan: 17 October 1944 to November 1945
Commanders: Col. Stuart Wright: 26 April 1944
                Col. Arnold Johnson: 26 February 1945
First Mission: 24 November 1944 vs. Japanese Homeland
DUCs: 27 January 1945 vs. Hamamatsu while under heavy attack
                after primary closed in

                26 July to 2 August for strategic attacks
Voice Call: "Happy," and later "Shyster"

498th Bomb Group
Activated: 20 November 1943
Assigned 20AF: July 1944
Squadrons: 877BS, 878BS, and 879BS
Training: Great Bend, KS: 13 April to 13 July 1944
Bases: Isley Field, Saipan: 6 September 1944 to November 1945
Commanders: Col. Wiley Ganey: 14 March 1944
                Col. Donald Saunders: 10 August 1945
First Mission: 24 November 1944 vs. Tokyo
                (flew several shakedown missions before)
DUCs: 13 December 1944 vs. Nagoya Mitsubishi engine plant
                1-7 June 1945 vs. Osaka and Kobe urban areas
Voice Call: "Mascot," and later "Waxwing"

499th Bomb Group
Activated: 20 November 1943
Assigned 20AF: July 1944
Squadrons: 877BS, 879BS, and 880BS
Training: Smoky Hill, KS: 1 December 1943 to 22 July 1944
Bases: Isley Field, Saipan: 18 September 1944 to November 1945
Commanders: Col. Samuel Harris: 14 April 1944
                Col. Morris Lee: 17 March 1945 (to CS of 73BW)
                Col. Walter Chambers: 13 August 1945
First Mission: 24 November 1944 vs. Japanese Homeland
DUCs: 23 January 1945 vs. Nagoya Mitsubishi engine plant
                22-28 April 1945 vs. Kyushu airfields
Voice Call: "Sandy," and later "Nordic"

500th Bomb Group
Activated: 20 November 1943 (B-17s)
Assigned 20AF: July 1944
Squadrons: 881BS, 882BS, and 883BS
Training: Walker, KS: 16 April to 23 July 1944
Bases: Isley Field, Saipan: 18 September 1944 to October 1945
Commanders: Col. Richard King: 5 May 1944 (lost Tokyo mission)
                Col. John Dougherty: 3 December 1944
First Mission: 24 November 1944 vs. Tokyo
                (flew several shakedown missions before)
DUCs: 23 January 1945 vs. Nagoya Mitsubishi engine plant
                15-20 June 1945 vs. Kyushu, Osaka, and Hamamatsu
                incendiary bombing
Voice Call: "Pluto," and later "Wisdom"

313th Bomb Wing
Activated: 23 April 1944
Bases: North Field, Tinian: 24 December 1944
Commanders: Brig.Gen. John Davies 23 April 1944 to end of war
Voice Call: "Goldbug"

6th Bomb Group
Activated: 1937 as 6BG, 1939 as 6BG(M), 1940 as 6BG(H),
                and 19 April 1944 as 6BG(VH)

Brig.Gen. John Davies 23 April 1944
to end of war. (USAF)

Assigned 20AF: April 1944
Squadrons: 24BS, 39BS, and 40BS
Training: Grand Island, NB: 19 May to 18 November 1944
Bases: North Field, Tinian: 28 December 1944
Commanders: Col. Kenneth Gibson: 28 December 1944
First Mission: 19 February 1945 vs. Japanese Homeland
DUCs: 25 May 1945 vs. Tokyo low-altitude night attack
               1-19 July 1945 mining operations on harbors in
               Japan and Korea
Voice Call: "Daredevil," and later "Cuckoo"

9ᵗʰ Bomb Group
Activated: 1935 as the (BG, 1939 as the 9BG(M), 140 as 9BG(H),
               and March 1944 as 9BG(VH)
Assigned 20AF: November 1944
Squadrons: 1BS, 5BS, and 99BS
Training: McCook, NB: 19 May 1943 to 18 November 1943
Bases: North Field, Tinian: 28 December 1944
Commanders: Col. Donald Eisenhart: 1 May 1944 (to CS of 313BW)
               Col. Henry Huglin: 6 March 1945
First Mission: 5 February 1945 vs. Japan
DUCs: 15 April 1945 vs. Kawasaki industrial area
               13-28 May 1945 for mining operations on Inland Sea
Voice Call: "Domino," and later "Crosstown"

504ᵗʰ Bomb Group
Activated: 11 March 1944 (B-17s)
Assigned 20AF: December 1944
Squadrons: 398BS, 421BS, and 680BS
Training: Fairmont, NB: 12 March to 5 November 1944
Bases: North Field, Tinian: 23 December 1944
Commanders: Col. James Connally: 6 April 1944
               Col. Glen Martin: 6 February 1945
First Mission: 19 February 1945 vs. Japanese Homeland
DUCs: 29 May 1945 vs. Yokohama industries
               27 July-14 August 1945 for mining operations on

Inland Sea, Korea, Shimonoski
Voice Call: "Albatross," and later "Gulfbird"

505ᵗʰ Bomb Group
Activation: 11 March 1944
Assigned 20AF: December 1944
Squadrons: 482BS, 483BS, and 484BS
Training: Harvard, NB: 1 April to 6 November 1944
Bases: North Field, Tinian: 19 December 1944
Commanders: Col. Robert Ping: 3 May 1944
               Col. Charles Eisenhart: 1 July 1945
First Mission: 6 February 1945 vs. Japanese Homeland
DUCs: 10 February 1945 vs. Ota a/c factories
               17 June-1 July 1945 fir mining operations on
               Inland Sea and Shimonoski Strait
Voice Call: "Skeezik," and later "Skyblue"

509ᵗʰ Composite Group (A-bomb unit)
Activated: 9 December 1944
Assigned 20AF: April 1945
Squadron: CG (received 15 modified B-29s from 393BS)
Training: Wendover, UT: 17 December 1944 to 26 April 1945
Bases: North Field, Tinian: 29 May 1945
Commanders: Col. Paul Tibbetts
First Mission: 20 July 1945 vs. Tokyo
Voice Call: "Dimples"

314ᵗʰ Bomb Wing
Activated: 23 April 1944
Bases: North Field, Guam: 16 January 1945
Commanders: Brig.Gen. Thomas Power: 29 August 1944
               Col. Carl Storrie: 23 July 1945
Voice Call: "Rampage"

19ᵗʰ Bomb Group
Activated: 1932 as 19BG, 1939 as 19BG(H) (B-10s, B-18s)
               1941 (B-17s)
               1 April 1944 as 19BG(VH)

Brig.Gen. Thomas Power: 29 August
1944 (USAF)

Assigned 20AF: December 1943

Squadrons: 28BS, 30BS, and 93BS

Training: Great Bend, KS: 1 April to 7 December 1944

Bases: North Field, Guam: 16 January 1945

Commanders: Col. John Roberts: 16 January 1945

First Mission: 25 February 1945 vs. Tokyo

DUCs: 9-19 March 1945 vs. Tokyo, Nagoya, Kobe, and Osaka
                       low-altitude incendiary
                       5 June 1945 vs. Kobe industries

Voice Call: "Kingbird," and later "Curious"

29th Bomb Group

Activated: December 1939 as 29BG(H) (B-18s and B-17s),
                       1 April 1944 as 29BG(VH)

Assigned 20AF: December 1944

Squadrons: 6BS, 43BS, and 52BS

Training: Pratt, KS: 1 April to 7 December 1944

Bases: North Field, Guam: 17 January 1945

Commanders: Col. Carl Storrie:28 May 1944 (to 313BW CO)
                       Col. Robert Mason: 23 July 1945

First Mission: 25 February 1945 vs. Tokyo

DUCs: 21 March 1945 vs. Omura airfields
                       19-26 June 1945 vs. Shizuoka industries, Tamashima
                       Mitsubishi a/c engine, and Nagoya Chigusa arsenal

Voice Call: "Dracula," and later "Toby"

39th Bomb Group

Activated: January 1941 as 39BG(H) (B-17s and B-24s),
                       1 April 1944 as 39BG(VH)

Assigned 20AF: February 1945

Squadrons: 61BS, 62BS, and 63BS

Training: Smoky Hill, KS: 1 April to 8 January 1945

Bases: North Field, Guam, 18 February 1945

Commanders: Col. John Fowler: 22 February 1945
                       (to 314BW as deputy Wing CO)
                       Col. George Mundy: 16 March 1945
                       Col. James Roberts: 16 August 1945

First Mission: 12 April 1945 vs. Koriyama Hodogaya chemical factory

DUCs: 10 May 1945 vs. Otake oil plant
                       23-29 May 1945vs. Yokohama industries and docks,
                       and vs. Tokyo industries

Voice Call: "Blackjack," and later "Miser"

330th Bomb Group

Activated: July 1942 as 330BG(H) (B-24s),
                       1 April 1944 as 330BG(VH)

Assigned 20AF: February 1945

Squadrons: 457BS, 458BS, and 459BS

Training: Walker, KS: 1 April 1944 to 7 January 1945

Bases: North Field, Guam, 18 February 1945

Commanders: Col. Elbert Reynolds: 18 February 1945
                       Col. Douglas Polhamus: 12 August 1945

First Mission: 12 April 1945 vs. Koriyama Hodogaya chemical factory

Brig.Gen. Frank Armstrong: 18 November 1944 to end of war. (USAF)

DUCs: 3-9 July 1945 vs. Tokushima and Gifu industrial incendiary
                       attacks and Kofu hydroelectric power center
                       8 August 1945 vs. Tokyo Nakajima a/c industries

Voice Call: "Baldeagle," and later "Mizpah"

315th Bomb Wing

Activation: 17 July 1944

Bases: Northwest Field, Guam 5 April 1945

Commanders: Brig.Gen. Frank Armstrong: 18 November 1944
                       to end of war

Voice Call: "Hyena"

16th Bomb Group

Activated: 1 April 1944

Assigned 20AF: March 1945

Squadrons: 15BS, 16Bs, and 17BS

Training: Fairmont, NB: 15 August 1944 to 7 March 1945

Bases: Northwest Field, Guam 14 April 1945

Commanders: Col. Samuel Gurney: 11 July 1944
                       Col. Andre Castellotti: 11 July 1945

First Mission: 26 June 1945 vs. Japanese Homeland

DUCs: 29 July to 6 August 1945 vs. Shimotsu oil refineries,
                       Kawasaki oil refineries and installations, and Ube
                       coal liquefaction factories

Voice Call: " Blueplate," and later " Abie"

331st Bomb Group

Activated: 6 July 1942 as 331BG(H) (B-17s and B-24s),
                       12 July 1944 as 331(VH)

Assigned 20AF: April 1945

Squadrons: 355BS, 356BS, and 357BS

Training: McCook, NB: 14 November 1944 to 6 April 1945

Bases: Northwest Field, Guam 12 May 1945

Commanders: Col. James Peyton: 12 May 1945

First Mission: 9 July 1945 vs. Japanese Homeland
DUCs: 22-29 1945 vs. Ube, Shimotsu and Kawasaki vs. bad weather and heavy enemy opposition
Voice Call: "Baywood," and later "Slicker"

501ˢᵗ Bomb Group
Activated: 25 May 1944
Assigned 20AF: April 1945
Squadrons: 21BS, 41BS, and 485BS
Training: Harvard, NB: 22 August 1944 to 7 March 1945
Bases: Northwest Field, Guam 14 April 1945
Commanders: Col. Boyd Hubbard: 14 April 1945
First Mission: 27 June 1945 vs. Japanese Homeland
DUCs: 6-13 July 1945 vs. Shumostu Maruzen refinery, Yokkaichi Utsobo refinery, Kawasaki oil installations
Voice Call: "Pathway," and later "Bailiff"

502ⁿᵈ Bomb Group
Activation: 25 May 1944
Assigned 20AF: May 1945
Squadrons: 402BS, 411BS, and 430BS
Training: Grand Island, NB: 26 September 1944 to 7 April 1945
Bases: Northwest Field, Guam 12 May 1945
Commanders: Col. Kenneth Sanders: 12 May 1945
First Mission: 15 July 1945 vs. Japanese Homeland
DUCs: 5-15 August 1945 vs. Uge coal liquefaction plant, Amagasaki tank farm, and Tsuchizaki oil refinery
Voice Call: " Stopwatch," and later "Temper"

Photo-reconnaissance Squadrons
1ˢᵗ Photo-reconnaissance Squadron, Flight C
Activated: October 1944: As the Photo Recon Detachment of the XXBC
13 February 1945: Redesignated as Flight C,
1ˢᵗ Photo-reconnaissance Squadron
19 July 1945: Attached to 8AF and left Guam
Bases: Hsinghing (A-1), China: October 1944
Harmon Field, Guam: May 1945
Commanders: Maj. Harry Allen: October 1944
Capt. George Alfke: May 1945
Capt. Daniel Forbes: 9 July 1945

3ʳᵈ Photo-reconnaissance Squadron
Activated: 19 May 1944
Bases: Isley Field, Saipan: 18 September 1944
Harmon Field, Guam, 11 January 1945
Commanders: Lt.Col. Patrick McCarthy: September 1944
Maj. Robert Hutton: 21 June1945

20ᵗʰ Air Force Wing and Group Staff Personnel

Unit	BW/BG /BS Commanders	Chief of Staff/ Deputy Commander
58BW	Brig.Gen. Roger Ramey	Col. Dwight Montieth
40BG	Col. William Skaer	Lt.Col. Oscar Schaaf
25BS	Lt.Col. William Kingsbury	
44BS	Lt.Col. Neil Wemple	
45BS	Lt.Col. Marvin Goodwyn	
444BG	Col. James Selser	Lt.Col. Alvin Moore
676BS	Maj. Robert Root	
677BS	Lt.Col. Gilbert Lassiter	
678BS	Maj. Charles Miller	
462BG	Col. Alfred Kalberer	Lt.Col. Richard Randolph
768BS	Lt.Col. Robert Rosebush	
769BS	Lt.Col. Cecil Durbin	
770BS	Maj. John Bagby	
468BG	Col. James Edmundson	Lt.Col. John East
792BS	Lt.Col. Theodore Watson	
793BS	Lt.Col. Douglas Hatfield	
794BS	Maj. Clarence McPherson	
73BW	Brig.Gen. Emmett O'Donnell	Col. Morris Lee
497BG	Col. Arnold Johnson	Lt.Col. Neil Van Sickle
869BS	Maj. Earl Kimbell	
870BS	Lt.Col. Fred Trickey	
871BS	Maj. John Carroll	
498BG	Lt.Col. Donald Saunders	Lt.Col. Jack DeWitt
873BS	Maj. William Clark	
874BS	Lt.Col. Boris Zubko	
875BS	Lt.Col. Gerald Robinson	
499BG	Lt.Col. Walter Chambers	
877BS	Maj. Colin Anderson	
878BS	Maj. James Coates	
879BS	Maj. Charles Fishburne	
500BG	Col. John Daugherty	Lt.Col. W.L. McDowell
881BS	Maj. Horace Hatch	
882BS	Lt.Col. Joseph Brannock	
883BS	Maj. John Van Tright	
313BW	Brig.Gen. John Davies	Col. Donald Eisenhart
6BG	Col. Kenneth Gibson	Lt.Col. Theodore Tucker
24BS	Lt.Col. Charles Blankenhorn	
39BS	Lt.Col. Henry Osborn	
40BS	Maj. Harry LaTourette	
9BG	Col. Henry Huglin	Lt.Col. William Hall
504BG	Col. Glen Martin	Lt.Col. Howard Hugos
398BS	Lt.Col. William Mullins	
421BS	Lt.Col. R.I. Barrowclough	
680BS	Lt.Col. Robert McBride	
505BG	Col. Charles Eisenhart	Lt.Col. Robert Blauw
482BS	Maj. Julian Dendy	
483BS	Maj. Cyrus Lewis	
484BS	Maj. William Gibson	
314BW	Col. Carl Storris	Col. Elbert Reynolds
19BG	Col. John Roberts	Lt.Col. George Chadwell
28BS	Maj. George Ulrich	
30BS	Lt.Col. Robert Irwin	
93BS	Lt.Col. Leon Lowrey	
29BG	Lt.Col. Robert Mason	Lt.Col. Loran Briggs
6BS	Maj. Gerald Jorgenson	
43BS	Lt.Col. Joseph Perry	
52BS	Maj. Thomas Abbott	

(Left to Right) "Rosie" O'Donnell, "Jake" Harmon, and "Possum" Hansell. (USAF)

Maj.Gen. Curtiss LeMay meets with his Bomb Wing commanders (Left to Right) Brig.Gen. John Davies (313BW), Brig.Gen. Thomas Power (314BW), LeMay and Brig. Gen. Emmett O'Donnell (73BW). (USAF)

39BG	Col. George Mundy	Lt.Col. Robert Strong		357BS	Lt.Col. Gerald Crossen	
60BS	Lt.Col. Woodward Carpenter			501BG	Col. Boyd Hubbard	Lt.Col. Aron Campbell
61BS	Lt.Col. William Crum			21BS	Maj. John Kunkle	
62BS	Maj. Harold McNeese			41BS	Maj. Robert Orr	
330BG	Lt.Col. Polhamus	—		485BS	Lt.Col. Frank Cochrane	
457BS	Maj. Virgil Kinnard			502BG	Col. Kenneth Sanborn	Lt.Col. Frank Pancake
458BS	Maj. Elmer Ambrose			402BS	Maj. Rex Dowtin	
459BS	Lt.Col. Robert Ryder			411BS	Lt.Col. Rudolph Seymor	
315BW	Brig.Gen. Frank Armstrong	Col. Leland Stranahan		430BS	Maj. Robert Booth	
16BG	Lt.Col. Andre Castellotti	Lt.Col. Collier Davidson		**509CG**	Col. Paul Tibbetts	—
15BS	Maj. Richard Kline			393BS	Maj. Charles Sweeney	
16BS	Maj. Coleman Stripling			VIIFC	Brig.Gen. Ernest Moore	Col. E. Mussett
17BS	Maj. Richard Levin			15FG	Lt.Col. John Mitchell	Lt.Col. Elmer Booth
331BG	Col. James Peyton	Lt.Col. Roland Barnick		21FG	Lt.Col. Charles Taylor	—
355BS	Lt.Col. Willard Wilson			414FG	Col. Henry Thorn	Lt.Col. Charles Gayle
356BS	Maj. Andrew Gordon			506FG	Col. Byron Harper	Lt.Col. Harley Brown

2
B-29 Airfields in World War II

CBI

Matterhorn (as discussed previously) was a plan prepared by the Air Staff for the use of B-29s from bases in China constructed by the Chinese under Chiang Kai-Shek. *Matterhorn* was the only possibility to test and use the B-29 against Japan prior to the future capture of the Marianas. However, the logistical requirements of the scheme were enormous, and the plan to expedite it was dreadful. The B-29s were to be based in India, and then were to stage through advanced bases in China. First the Chinese had to be coerced into building these advanced bases, and then it would be necessary to support the operations from these bases by air supply from India over the Himalayas. The B-29s would have to ferry gasoline and bombs over the "Hump," supplemented by a fleet of B-24s converted to tankers (C-87s). The plan under the best of circumstances had a low potential for large success. However, it offered the only means of attacking selected critical Japanese industries, especially the vulnerable Japanese coking (used in steel production) facilities, which had 73% of its capacity within range of the B-29s from China. In the plan was the provision for advanced bases to be provided by the Chinese, and rear bases to be provided by the British in the Calcutta area of India. Ten B-29 groups with 28 bombers per group were to be deployed to the CBI by October 1944, and 2,000 B-24s converted to transports were to be available to support the movement of gasoline, ordnance, and supplies from India to China. Stillwell's command was stretched thin, with 11,000 engineers (5,000 more were scheduled to arrive in the next few months) working with poor equipment and inadequate supplies. Ninety percent of Stillwell's men were working on the Ledo Road and pipelines, while the remainder were charged with building and maintaining 45 airfields in India and 25 in China.

India

With the cooperation of Britain and India, five existing airfields on the flatlands west of Calcutta were to have their facilities improved and runways extended. Adm. Lord Louis Mountbatten had been the motivating force behind the Indian government's agreement to take part in the airfield construction. In December a Topographic Battalion began surveying for the extension of the fields. The five fields were to be constructed at Kharagpur (command base), Dudhkundi, Chakulia, Kalikunda, and Piardoba by Indian and American engineer units under the direction of Lt.Col. Kenneth Madsen. In order to finish the fields it was agreed that

temporarily they were to be 1,000ft shorter than projected and stopped at 7,500ft, and were only 150ft wide. The first aviation engineer battalions had not arrived from America by late 1943, and to expedite construction the British Eastern Command provided local civilian contractors to begin work on the sites. Also, in late January the 382nd Engineer Construction Battalion had to be temporarily transferred from important work on the Ledo Road to rush the work on the XXBC HQ at Kharagpur, which had been the site of a former Indian Government political prison. When the 382nd arrived it met the unexpected and chronic problems that would plague the construction of the Indian airfields: total lack of modern transportation; communication and construction facilities; shortages of everything except high humidity and temperatures, wind, and dust; insects; and bad food, water, and sanitation. The Indian labor pool was unskilled, and the work was backbreaking in 100°F plus temperatures. The Indian railway system, overloaded in peacetime, ran on narrow gauge tracks, with antiquated locomotives pulling small cars that could only bring in small amounts of supplies that, after a while, finally began to accumulate.

At last, the 879th Airborne Aviation Battalion, 382nd Construction Battalion, and the 853rd, 1875th, and 1877th Aviation Battalions arrived to begin work on the Calcutta fields with borrowed equipment. In mid-April the 1888th Aviation Battalion arrived to increase Madsen's force to 5,000 and work progressed. Since India's rail system was already overburdened a 100mi pipeline was built from coastal Budge Budge to the five fields. In February 1944 the 22nd Air Depot Group arrived in India and was assigned

The Indian labor pool was unskilled, and the work was backbreaking in 100°F temperatures. Here Indian women are seen carrying crushed rock for the maintenance of Kharagpur. A 468BG B-29 is parked in the background. (USAF)

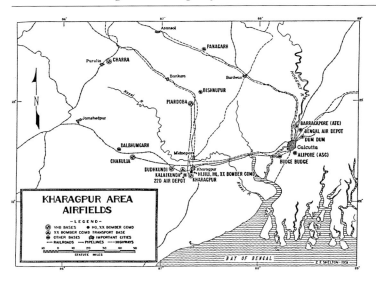

to Kharagpur, and four months later had established its warehouses and shops, and set up a system of receiving and distribution of parts and equipment. The 1875th Aviation Battalion arrived at the airdrome at Dudhkundi, which was a former RAF medium bomber strip about 70mi southwest of Calcutta. The 760 men of the Battalion moved into the existing buildings and, aided by 3,000 Indian laborers, began work to complete the runways. To produce cement, sand and gravel had to be trucked from railway sidings from eight to 12 miles away, and water was pumped from a stream two and half miles away. Once the cement was mixed it was carried by the Indian laborers on trays on top of their heads. The Battalion completed a 7,500ft runway, lengthened taxiways, and added 30 hardstands and facilities for 42 B-29s. The Battalion finished the field 10 days ahead of schedule, and moved on to work on Kalikunda, which was only a short distance away. This base was to be used by C-87 transports, and had an existing 5,000ft runway and a few steel mat hardstands. The 1875th again completed the base ahead of schedule, but by working in the midst of the summer monsoon.

Kharagpur, a former Indian Government political prison, was the site of the XXBC HQ. When 382nd Construction Battalion arrived it met the unexpected, and chronic problems that would plague the construction of the Indian airfields: total lack of modern transportation, communication and construction facilities, shortages of everything except high humidity and high temperatures, wind and dust, insects, bad food, water, and sanitation. (USAF)

The first B-29s arrived at Chakulia, India, on 2 April 1944 led by Col. Leonard Harmon, and closely followed by Brig.Gen. LaVerne Saunders. They had departed from Pratt Field, KS, on 25 March; proceeded to Presque Isle, ME; Gander Lake, Newfoundland; Marrakech, Morocco; then to Cairo, Egypt; and on to Karachi, India. On 24 April 1944 Col. Harmon flew the first Hump cargo mission across the Himalayas to China, landing at Kwanghan (the advanced base of the 444BG). On 25 April the first combat took place when two B-29s of the 676BS/444BG took off from Chakulia, India, on a gasoline ferry mission to China. Six Oscars attacked one B-29 piloted by Col. Alvin Clarke, and tail gunner Sgt. Harold Lanhan claimed the first B-29 aerial victory of the war. The first bombing mission was flown on 5 June against the Makasan workshops in Bangkok by Col. Alva Harvey's 444BG and Col. Harman's 40BG. The result was that the 350 tons of bomb did little damage; only 73 of the scheduled 100 bombers made the round trip, 23 failed to reach the target, six were destroyed, and 15 men were killed. The first attack on Japan since the Doolittle "Thirty Seconds over Tokyo" mission of 18 April 1942 followed 10 days later. The historic mission began between 13 and 15 June when 83 bombers flew over the Hump to the four staging bases in China. Of 75 B-29s scheduled for the mission Harmon led 68 B-29s of the 58BW on their heralded bombing raid on the Imperial Iron & Steel Works at Yawata. Despite much press hoopla the mission was a failure, except for its psychological effect on the Japanese and the American public. Of the 68 bombers 16 failed to reach the target, and most of the bombs hit nowhere near the factory—some exploded as far as 20mi away! Seven bombers were lost, and the mission so depleted the Chengtu gasoline supplies that the bombers could not return to India for several days.

China

Matterhorn called for the construction of four staging fields within a 50mi radius of Chengtu, in the Szechwan province, northwest of Chungking, and 1,150mi from Calcutta. The four airfields were located at Kwanghan (A-3), Pengshan (A-7), Kiunglai (A-5), and Hsinching (A-1). The 14AF under Gen. Chennault, of Flying Tiger renown, was responsible for the fighter defense of the bomber bases. The fighter bases were to be located at Fenghuangshan, Kwanghan, Shwanglui, and Pengchiachiang, and supplemented by an outer ring of smaller strips. Before construction on the Chinese fields could begin financial negotiations had to be worked out with Chiang Kai-shek for Chinese labor to help build the fields. Initially Chiang insisted on 20 Chinese for 1 U.S. monetary exchange rate to build the bases. Gen. Brehon Somervell, the head of Army supplies, told Chiang that he was prepared to stop construction, and offered him a 40 for 1 exchange rate, but both men were at an impasse; however, after typical Oriental negotiation a compromise was finally reached.

The construction was under the command of Maj. Henry Byroade, who had surveyed the Chengtu area in November 1943. The land was flat, and had a number of existing airfields that could be easily extended for the B-29s, while the area was also suitable for the proposed seven fighter strips. The Chinese Military Engineering Commission was to be responsible for construction, and the American engineers under Lt.Col. Waldo Kenerson would be primarily responsible for construction staff work, such as drafting, layouts, inspections, and the administration of the estimated 333,000 peasants that the Governor of Szechwan would eventually conscript over the next three months.

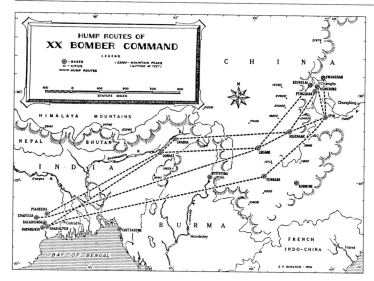

The problems of building air bases in China were the most difficult of any theater in the war. Compared to China, building bases in Europe was relatively easy. After D-Day only fighter and medium bomber strips had to be built on the Continent, as the Allied heavy bombers could continue to operate over Germany from their bases in the United Kingdom. The new

The problems of building air bases in China were the most difficult of any theater in the war. China had a vast pool of "rice-powered" manual labor, both men and women, from surrounding villages who were mainly farmers. They supplied their own hammers and picks and also their rice and shelter materials. (USAF)

bases on the Continent needed only to be 5,000ft long and 300ft wide, and dry, level areas of that size were not difficult to find. In Europe usually only about 30 cubic yards of earth had to be moved; portable PSP planking was quickly laid, and the fighters were ready to take off in a week or two. In China the runways were to be 8,500ft long, at least 200ft wide, and 2ft deep, with at least 30,000ft of taxiways, and all were to be completed in 90 days without modern equipment. Since the greatest portions of most fields were to be built over rice paddies, their walls were breached; the water drained into irrigation ditches, and then roads had to be built to the sites. Later, on the Pacific islands there was an abundant supply of coral to provide a firm base for runway construction, but in China this was a problem. In choosing the airfield sites primary consideration was given to their proximity to rivers, which would supply sand, gravel, and rounded stones for construction, but even then the material had to be transported miles, mainly by manual labor, as trucks were in short supply. Because the new fields were to be built by manual labor they were not expected to meet the required quality, but their length was to remain at 8,500ft, and not be reduced, as they were in India to accelerate their construction and get them onto operation. China had a vast pool of "rice-powered" manual labor, and each village in the vicinity of an airfield had a quota of 50 laborers, but labor saving devices could reduce this quota. A wheelbarrow counted as two men, a handcart as 10, and a mule or ox drawn cart for the full 50-man quota. The laborers—both men and women—from the surrounding villages were chiefly farmers who supplied their own hammers and picks, and their rice and shelter materials. Even though at the time the bases were scheduled to begin construction the Chinese New Year was a month away, and many peasants wished to celebrate in their villages, but it also was an idle period in the farming cycle, and the farmers could use the extra wages in those lean times. The peasants were paid 25 to 40 cents per day, and were housed in government controlled barracks. Propaganda units from Chungking were able to overcome rumors that were always rampant in large groups and quell any incipient unrest and mass defections by disgruntled workers who only wanted to return home, or who had not been paid promptly by the Chinese government.

Also, there were disagreements over ownership and value with the various Chinese whose property was to be appropriated for the airfields. Bargaining was an Oriental tradition, and the quick appraisal and disposition of their property without their input initially distressed the Chinese. However, the usually generous appraisals and the speedy payments prevented serious problems. Local graft and unreasonable demands by local politicians were also venerable Chinese institutions, but ordinarily could be controlled through negotiation and bribes. The materials required for construction of airfield buildings were in short supply in the Chengtu area, and a special board headed by the governor and consisting of the mayor of Chengtu and representatives of the local building supply organizations was convened to remedy the situation. Prices and material quotas were set, and the process then ran smoothly without much graft or price gouging.

Airfield construction began in mid-January 1945, but it was not long before Lt.Col. Kenerson found that the peasants had to be constantly supervised and prodded if construction were to progress. The lack of trucks to haul materials from the riverbeds slowed work, and the raw runway material often had to be carried several miles by laborers in twin baskets hanging from yo-yo poles. A press release stated that the Chinese had excavated enough material from the bases around Chengtu to "fill a 18in deep by 42in wide trench that ran from New York to Phoenix." Mechanical rock crushers were also in limited supply. On the sides of the runways were thousands of men, women, and children in their blue peasant apparel breaking rocks with hammers, and carrying thousands of tons of earth, gravel, and rock in baskets across their shoulders. The surface of the runways and hardstands was a caliche of hard clay and gravel that was wetted and rolled multiple times. There was the phenomenon of hundreds of Chinese chanting and grunting, pulling huge iron or concrete rollers weighing 20,000lbs that were, tongue-in-cheek, designated as "10-ton, 500-coolie power, rice-burning" rollers. The wheels of all the Chinese wheelbarrows squeaked, and when there were thousands of them it so irritated the Americans that the commander ordered the wheels to be greased. Upon hearing of the order the Chinese went on strike. The commander investigated the cause of the labor stoppage, and found that the Chinese did not like to hear the squeaking either, but it did keep away the evil spirits, who lived in silence!

By March construction was behind schedule; another conscription of laborers was ordered, and an additional 60,000 natives were put to work. On 24 April 1944 Kwanghan was officially completed and ready to receive its first B-29. That afternoon various American and Chinese officials, including Gen. Claire Chennault and 75,000 coolies, greeted the first

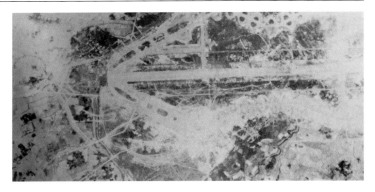

Aerial view of Kiunglai, home of the 462BG. The Chengtu area included four VHB bases: Kiunglai, Pengshan, Kienyang, and Kwangshan. (USAF)

B-29 flown by Col. Harman. The next day Pengshan was opened, followed by Kiunglai two days later (at Kiunglai Capt. Maynard Nichols and three enlisted men were in charge of 106,000 Chinese coolies), and Hsinching on 1 May. After the fields were finished the packed gravel surfaces needed continual maintenance, and a large number of Chinese were kept on hand. Occasionally a coolie would run out across the path of a B-29 that was taking off. The huge lumbering bomber could do nothing but move straight ahead, and a few Chinese were hit by the propellers and killed. Investigation into this strange behavior found that the Chinese believed that if they were having a streak of bad luck they could end it by leading the evil spirit that was following them into the path of the B-29.

The Bomb Wings that were to operate from the completed bases were: Hsinching - 40BG; Kwanghan - 444BG; Kiunglai - 462G; and Pengshan - 468BG. When the first B-29 groups arrived they faced daily temperatures of over 100°F that adversely affected the performance of both the men and the aircraft. The China bases had to be supplied by flying over the Himalayan "Hump," which adversely affected the quantity and quality of combat missions.

Ceylon

Although the bases in India and China put Japan's steel industry within range of the B-29s, the productive Palembang, Sumatra, oil fields remained out of range. The Pladjoe Refinery produced 20.5 million barrels of high-grade crude oil that furnished 22% of Japan's fuel oil and 78% of its avia-

Chinese farmers pull a 500lb roller to compact the gravel on clay runways. In the background a 4x4 plows gravel onto the clay runway in front of the roller. (USAF)

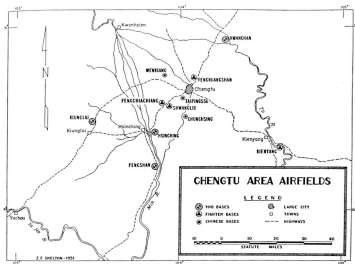

In the afternoon of 9 August 1944 56 B-29s of the 462BG of the 58BW staged into China Bay. The next afternoon, 54 B-29s headed for Sumatran oil fields at Palembang, but only 39 reached the overcast target. Thirty-one B-29s were forced to bomb by radar but eight B-29s assigned to mine Moesi were successful in visually laying their mines. After that one mission the base was abandoned. (USAF)

tion gasoline. The only bombing option was to stage the Chinese-based B-29s through Ceylon, and the British and XXBC engineers expanded the field at China Bay, on the large island's northeast coast. By mid-July 1944 the runway was extended to 7,200ft, and additional hardstands, taxiways, and fuel storage and distribution facilities were built for two B-29 groups totaling 56 aircraft.

In the afternoon of 9 August 1944 56 B-29s of the 462BG of the 58BW staged into China Bay. The round trip from China Bay to Sumatra was about 4,000mi, and because of the long range the fuel tanks were filled to capacity, only a ton of bombs or mines could be loaded for the mission. The next afternoon 54 B-29s headed for Sumatra, but only 39 reached Palembang, which was overcast. Thirty-one B-29s were forced to bomb by radar, but eight B-29s assigned to mine Moesi were successful in laying their mines visually. No post strike reconnaissance was done until 19 September, and it showed that little damage had been done to the oil fields. But even before this reconnaissance, despite the expense and effort in developing the China Bay base, the XXBC had decided to abandon China Bay, and Washington granted permission in early October.

Marianas

The Marianas Islands, codenamed *Gateway*, are located 1,500mi east of the Philippines, 3,400mi west of Pearl Harbor, and 1,260mi north-north-west of Tokyo. The 15 islands of the group are located in a 425mi long chain of hilly volcanic islands running north to south. Saipan (measuring 5.5x12.5mi) is the northern-most large island, Tinian (5x10.5mi) lays directly south of Saipan, and Guam (10x32mi) lays 100mi to the southwest of Saipan. Guam's weather was moderate to hot, averaging between 90°F days and 70°F nights with high humidity, and daily rains between July and December. Saipan and Tinian in the north were somewhat drier and cooler than Guam.

The islands were part of the 1920 Japanese Mandated Territories, and were heavily reinforced by the Japanese between February and May 1944 when it appeared that the Americans planned to seize the islands. Their capture would bring the B-29 within range of most of the Japanese Home-

land, and would eliminate the necessity of the Chinese B-29 bases and their logistical problems.

Operation Forager began in mid-June 1944 with the invasion of Saipan, then Tinian, and finally Guam. The Battle of the Philippine's Sea, called "The Great Marianas Turkey Shoot," occurred on 19-20 June, as the Japanese attempted its *A-Go Operation*, a naval counterattack on the American landing forces and navy. The ensuing combat was the largest carrier battle of the war, with the Japanese committing nine carriers and 470 aircraft, and the Americans 15 carriers and nearly 1,000 aircraft. The Japanese lost nearly all these aircraft and three carriers, and were unable to dislodge the Americans.

Marianas Base Organization

The Frank Report of 3 May 1944 approved five large airfields to be built in the Marianas, each to be utilized by a B-29 Wing. There were to be one base on Saipan and two bases each on Guam and Tinian. The XXIBC head-quarters, an air depot, and 20AF forward HQ were to be located on Guam. Later, a large air base was to be constructed on Iwo Jima for staging B-29s and basing Long-Range fighters for VLR missions. The Frank Report set completion dates for each field: 5 October-Isley Field No.1 (Saipan); 15 October-Isley Field No.2 (Saipan); 1 October-North Field (Tinian); 20 October-West Field (Tinian); 15 October-Depot Field (Guam); and 15 December-North Field (Guam). Isley Field was named after Cmdr. Robert Isely, but the misspelling in the Frank Report was perpetuated throughout the war. Three bombardment wings were scheduled to move to the Marianas, with the ground echelons of the 73BW to arrive at Saipan about 5 August, the 313BW at Guam about 5 October, and the 313BW on Tinian about 5 December. Their air units were scheduled to arrive on 5 October, 10 November, and 10 January, respectively.

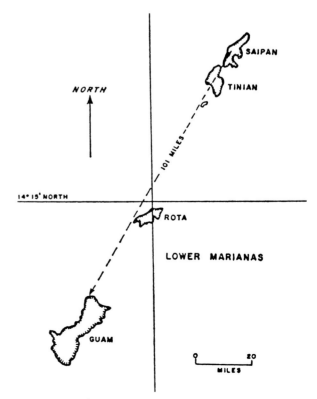

Southern Marianas Islands (USAF)

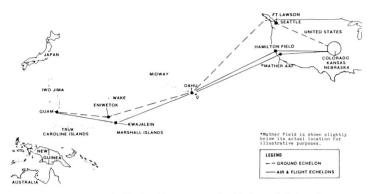

Ground and Air Echelon Movement to the Marianas (U.S. Army)

The stubborn Japanese opposition in the Marianas forced a change in the original base-building timetable. At Saipan the delay was minor, but on Guam and Tinian the ground and air echelons were put behind schedule about a month. On 9 August Adm. Chester Nimitz reported that Guam was to be the base for the Pacific Fleet, the forward HQ for CINCPOA, and the staging area for the projected invasion of Formosa. Nimitz gave the Navy priority for all construction, except for Depot Field, and the construction on B-29 facilities on Guam was to be postponed indefinitely. On 15 August the ground echelons of the 313BW were ready to move to California, and were due in Guam by 5 October to prepare facilities for the advanced air units expected on 10 November. Lt.Gen. Harmon visited the three Marianas Islands on 8-12 August and devised a plan to salvage the VHB airfield plan. Harmon's engineers had surveyed the Marianas airfield sites, and discovered one of the proposed Saipan sites was unsatisfactory for B-29 operations because of a 120ft ridge located about 6,000ft from the take off point. However, they reported that from five to seven 8,500 x 200ft runways could be built on Tinian, instead of the four planned. In order to neutralize the Guam VHB delays Harmon proposed that:

1) Isley Field No.2 (Saipan) be canceled, and substituted a 7,000ft field (Kobler) to be constructed for temporary storage of B-29 spares, and for the use of other aircraft.

2) Construction of two additional 8,500ft runways on Tinian.

3) All four groups of the 73BW were to operate from the two 8,500ft runways at Isley No.1 (Saipan) until the two additional runways at Tinian were completed.

4) A total of six runways were to be built on Tinian, with a priority of one on West Field and two on North Field to receive the first two groups of the 313BW (originally to fly from Guam) and the surplus from the 73BW.

5) The air depot and field on Guam was to be constructed as scheduled.

CINCPOA agreed to Harmon's suggestions, even though it had no cargo ship facilities at Tinian to bring in supplies and materiel to build the bases. The completion dates for the Marianas airfields were revised to 20 November-Depot Field (Guam); 1 December-North Field (Tinian); 1 January-West Field (Tinian); 1 February-North Field (Guam); and 1 April-Northwest Field (Guam).

Building an Airfield in the Marianas

The AAF decided to construct individual bases that would accommodate a

Wing Headquarters, four combat groups, and four service groups. For the first time a single airfield would serve 12,000 personnel, and would supply, maintain, and operate over 180 four-engined bombers. In the Pacific the logistics were mind boggling, as the islands were barren, had few roads, usable buildings, or storage facilities, and had no electric power, lumber, or drinking water. To build a B-29 base some 200,000 tons of equipment, material, and supplies were required. Everything had to be brought in by ship from depots thousands of miles away. When an island with a new airfield to be built was to be invaded, everything for the new airbase was loaded into about 40 LSTs and transports. Every item was carefully planned to fit into the finite shipping space, as was the manpower required to load and unload them, and the warships and airpower to protect them. The ships waited 1,000yds offshore while AAF engineers built facilities on the beach for unloading, and built roads inland to the prospective air base site. Once the onshore facilities were completed the prospective airbase was unloaded from the ships, reloaded onto trucks, and transported to a central supply center, where it was unloaded, sorted, and stored.

When selecting a site for a new airfield several factors were considered. Foremost was finding available space that permitted adequate runway length for take off and landings and dispersal areas, a low approach angle to the field, a finished graded runway slope of less than 1.5%, adequate drainage and foundation conditions, and the availability of coral for the foundation. The Pacific Division, Bureau of Yards and Docks conducted extensive soil tests at the site of each intended runway, and these tests were continued throughout construction by field parties. The method of construction was studied for each runway. When the bulldozers came ashore they plowed up the low undergrowth and small trees and removed the top soft layer of soil. The larger trees were dynamited, and this foliage was then pushed over to the side. Usually the topsoil layer was not deep, and once it was removed it was then necessary to remove the underlying coral to a foot below subgrade. The elevations that interrupted the runways had to be cut (flattened) by extensive dynamiting and scraping, and the depressions filled. Many large, very hard coral heads protruded in the process and were difficult to remove, and extensive blasting was required. In the cuts, large 10 to 16 cubic yard pans (scrapers), with one bulldozer pushing and another pulling, peeled off large areas of coral and transported it to nearby fills. Motorized pans called Turnapulls scooped up five cubic yards

Motorized pans called turnapulls, scooped up five cubic yards of material and carried it to a fill area. Scraping out a 500 x 8,500ft runway could mean a million of cubic yards to be removed and then refilled. Shown is a turnapull on Tinian as 313BW B-29s flew overhead. (USAF)

of material and carried it to a fill area. Scraping out a 500 x 8,500ft runway could mean a million cubic yards had to be removed and then refilled.

Once the runways were reasonably flat they required a foundation, and coral fill was chosen for its availability, and then for its hardness and the shape of its crushed particles. Coral for fill was removed from quarries called "borrow pits" that were of three types:

1) Push Pits, from which coral could be pushed by a bulldozer working down a slope to an area where it could be shoveled into trucks.
2) Bailing Pits, from which coral could be dug by power shovels without preliminary blasting and loaded into trucks.
3) Blasting Pits, in which dynamiting was necessary. The coral was soft and spongy and difficult to blast, as it absorbed much of the blast, requiring double charges.

Although it was advantageous that the borrow pits were located as near as possible to the construction site to minimize hauling time, the ease of extraction from a good bailing pit was more beneficial even if transportation time was very long. Construction required as many as 275 trucks hauling coral out of Tinian's pits. Choice coral would feel slightly sticky when properly mixed with water, "like lime mortar," and would have the slight odor of rotten eggs from the decomposing animal and vegetable matter that was mixed with it. Often small test batches were tried, but good coral

usually was easy to find in the Pacific. Runway coral fill was higher in clay content (more densely compactable) than that used for road foundations, which carried much more traffic that compacted the foundation sufficiently during use. Airfield runways were to support much heavier loads, and their foundations had to be well compacted before use. For the foundation layer a heavy fill coral was needed, and it was supplied by the blasting pits. This coral was transported by heavy trucks, and was crushed, graded, and compacted as a foundation. Next a wet mix called "live" coral was put down and "activated" by the crushing and grinding action involved when it was worked into the surface using seawater and rollers. A pipeline and pumping network, salvaged from captured enemy sources, was built from the ocean to the airfield site as a source of salt water for compacting of the new runways. The coral fills were to be ideally made in successive 8in layers that were compacted down to 6in, but often the entire depth was dumped and compacted at one time if time was short (additional resurfacing would be necessary later when the surface settled). The surface of the top 12in of the coral runway was preferably laid on a well-drained subgrade and a well-compacted three-layer fill. In finishing the surface seawater was sprayed on it to cement the coral particles and further compact them. For best results a coral runway would have to set for three days, and ideally for five days. The final procedure was to surface the runways and taxiways with an asphalt and coral mix 200ft wide. Liquid asphalt could not be shipped by sea, so drums of hardened asphalt were shipped. The problem

Once the runways were reasonably flat they required a foundation and coral fill was chosen for its availability and then for its hardness and shape of crushed particles. The coral for fill was removed from quarries called "borrow pits" that were of three types. (USAF)

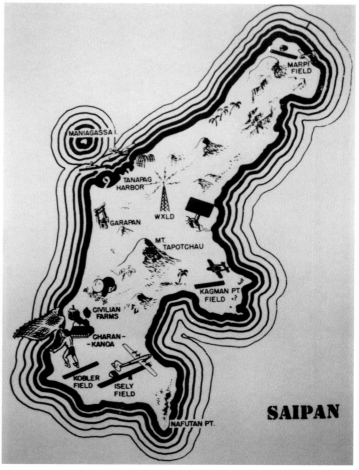

Saipan Airfields (USAF)

was to melt the asphalt, and the engineers jury-rigged the sugar boilers that were found in the many sugar cane plantations in the Marianas by adding smokestacks made from welded steel drums. On Saipan 700-tons of asphalt were produced using this method. The mixture was laid to a thickness of 2.5in, and then rolled to two inches. Nearly 700ft of 36in corrugated metal pipe were laid for runway drainage. In the 36 days it took to build the first runway on Tinian the Seabees moved 700,000 cubic tons of earth and coral, and drove 900,000mi doing it.

Saipan

Saipan (code-name *Tattersalls*) was invaded on the morning of 15 June 1944, and was declared secure on 9 July after savage fighting, during which the Japanese lost 23,800 of their 31,600 troops, with thousands more missing, buried in the island's caves and bunkers. A further 14,000 civilian laborers (Japanese, Korean, and Okinawan) were captured, and 22,000 more either committed suicide (rather than be captured), were killed in the battle, or were murdered by the Japanese to prevent their surrender. American losses were heavy at 3,325 dead and 13,000 wounded. With the loss of Saipan the Japanese Defense Zone had been breached; the Japanese suffered a naval aerial loss from which it would not recover, and the Americans secured a base for the B-29 armadas to strike the Homeland. The southern third of the island is a rolling plateau 200-300ft above sea level, with the 4,500ft Aslito Air Field located on a plain at the base of the Nafutan Peninsula. Sugar cane covered over 70% of the island.

Rebuilding Isley Field (Aslito) Saipan

Five aviation engineer battalions (805th, 806th, 894th, 1878th, and 1894th) carried out the primary construction on Saipan. The 805th Engineer Aviation Battalion was the first to arrive at Saipan, but since their objective, the Japanese Aslito Airfield, had not been captured the Battalion waited until 20 June (D+5) for American troops to capture the field so they could move on shore to rebuild the existing runway, build a new runway, and also build another runway nearby to be called Kobler. When they moved toward shore a barrage of Japanese 120mm fire greeted them, and their LSTs had to move back out of range. That same afternoon, while they were anchored off the coast of Charan-Kanoa, they were subjected to a two-hour enemy bombing and strafing air attack. A survey and reconnaissance party went on shore to survey and map the area for the new parallel 8,500ft runway and the refurbishing of the existing runway. First Aslito Airfield had to become operational for AAF P-47 fighters to protect the island from enemy air attack. On D+6, to get their equipment and supplies on shore a passage had to be blasted through the coral reef that surrounded the island, and once on shore a road had to be cut through a 50ft rock bluff by blasting and bulldozing thousands of tons of coral and rock. A platoon of men and a grader arrived at Aslito Airfield, cleared the rubble, and filled the bomb craters, and then they used a captured Japanese roller to compact the filled holes. The next day the bulk of the battalion arrived with more equipment and PSP (pierced steel planking) to extend the existing 3,700ft Japanese runway. By D+10 800x150ft of plank had been laid, an additional 400ft were cleared, and two 75ft shoulders were built; the field was operational for fighters. Work continued on the Aslito field to extend it to 6,000ft so B-24 bombers could neutralize the nearby Japanese bases in the Marianas, Bonins, Yap, and Truk, and it was completed by 6 August.

Meanwhile, on D+9 the surveyors had determined grades and lines for the first new 8,500x500ft runway. On D+12 a platoon began construc-

tion on a fuel tank farm that was operational two days later. The prefabricated tanks were bolted in place, with their lower section partially underground. The gasoline was piped from offshore tankers to the tanks, which were dispersed over several acres to protect them from each another in case of an enemy attack. Another platoon found that the existing Japanese fuel dump was undamaged and built tanks to transfer its 45,000gals of aviation fuel for Marine and Navy fighter aircraft that were now based at Aslito's shorter refurbished strip.

The Battalion met many delays in building the airfields. Their work was temporarily suspended when a 300-man Japanese banzai suicide attack broke through Marine lines on the Nafutan Peninsula and reached the airfields. The Battalion and Headquarters Service Company personnel picked up their rifles and .45s, beat off the attack, and continued their work. Occasional enemy snipers harassed the Battalion, and during the initial days the Japanese flew nightly attacks that hindered work and disrupted the sleep of the day shifts. Then the heavy daily tropical rains arrived and made the area a quagmire, and the engineers alternately battled dust and mud. There was no time to build housing, and there was no fresh food. Construction vehicles were used continuously, and broke down on the rough coral roads leading from the coral pits.

Work on the runways required fills of up to 20ft and cuts through solid limestone coral mounds of up to 17ft. Turnapulls were used to fill depressions, and rooters, jack hammers, wagon drills, carryalls, and caterpillars were used in the cuts. Despite the hardships, on 24 July the first 4,000ft of runway had been completed; by 27 September 7,000ft of runway were completed, and the first B-29s were operational from it, and by 15 October the entire 8,500ft was completed. In four months, the Battalion had excavated and moved almost a half million cubic yards of rock and earth from the runways, and quarried and moved two and half miles of coral to surface them. To attain a level runway the engineers used 600,000lbs of explosive to blast away the elevated limestone obstructions. The completed tank farms contained 525,000gals of fuel, and the repair of the Japanese fuel system added another 45,000gals capacity, while revetments were built to protect 2,000 fuel drums. The engineers constructed 44 Quonset

Isley Field. The coral on Saipan was harder than expected and the terrain was more rugged than shown by aerial reconnaissance. Lt.Gen. Millard Harmon decided that fewer bases were to be built on the island and it was decided that six runways would be built on Tinian. (USAF)

huts for Wing headquarters administration buildings and housing, and an additional 20 warehouses.

On 12 October 1944 the first B-29s to arrive at Isley were buzzed by four P-47 Thunderbolts as they approached. The first bomber to land was *Joltin' Josie*, flown by Maj. Jack Catton of the 498BG, with XXIBC commander Brig.Gen. Haywood Hansell on board. As the tired Hansell got off the bomber he was confronted by news cameras and commented, "When we got some fighting in, I'll do some more talking." On 20 October the 73BW under Brig.Gen. Emmett "Rosie" O'Donnell arrived at Isley.

The Saipan construction undertaking was more difficult than anticipated and cost twice the estimates at $63.3 million. The coral on Saipan was harder than expected, and the terrain was more rugged than shown by reconnaissance, and Lt.Gen. Millard Harmon decided that fewer bases were to be built on the island. All four groups of the 73BW were to use the two 8,500ft runways on Isley Field, and Kobler was to be used by spare bombers and transport aircraft. It had been decided that six runways would be built on Tinian.

On 12 October 1944 the first B-29s to arrive at Saipan were buzzed by four P-47 Thunderbolts as they approached. The first bomber to land was *Joltin' Josie* flown by Maj. Jack Catton of the 498BG with XXIBC commander Brig.Gen. Haywood Hansell on board. (USAF)

Isley Air Field

Runways	No.	Size	Surface
	2	8,500x200	Asphalt
Hardstands	**No.**		**Surface**
	179		Asphalt
Service Aprons	**No.**		**Surface**
	2		Asphalt *
B-29 Capacity	28		

* 4 asphalt aprons proposed with 25 B-29 capacity
216,000 barrels of aviation gasoline (256,000 barrels planned)

Tinian

Tinian (code *Tearaway*) was only three miles due south of Saipan, and was a relatively flat island that was virtually covered by commercial sugar cane. There were four Japanese airfields: the 4,700ft No.1 and No.3 near the north end at Ushi Point; the 5,000ft No.2 on the east shore at Gurguan Point; and the uncompleted No.4 northwest of Tinian Town (now named San Jose), the only sizable town on the island. The landings were made on 24 July, and Tinian was declared secure on 1 August after the Japanese lost over 5,000 troops (with thousands more buried in caves and bunkers), and 4,000 civilians who were killed in the pre-invasion bombardment. The Marines lost 330 dead and 1,570 wounded.

Before the invasion, plans for developing Tinian as a major air base had been prepared. Under these plans the two strips built by the Japanese—the 4,700ft strip at the north end of the island and the 5,000ft strip on the west coast—were to be extended to 6,000ft each so that medium and heavy bombers could begin to operate from them as soon as possible. After these were completed the northern runway was to be lengthened to 8,500ft, and then the other strip was to be lengthened to 8,500ft for the initial B-29 operations. The next phase was to build two more 8,500ft runways on the Japanese strip on the west coast near Tinian Town. The work was to be done entirely by the Navy's Sixth Construction Brigade, consisting of the 9th, 13th, 18th, 38th, 50th, 67th, 92nd, 107th, 110th, 112th, 121st, and 135th Battalions. The normal complement of a Seabee battalion was 32 officers and 1,073 men, but this figure varied widely, and eventually 15,000 Seabees

Isley had two 8,500x200 asphalt runways and 179 asphalt hardstands and 298 service aprons. All four groups of the 73BW were to use the two runways on Isley Field and nearby Field was to be used by extra bombers and other aircraft. (USAF)

were at work on Tinian. Immediately after the island was secured the plan was modified. The rehabilitated Japanese northern strip was extended by 1,000ft on the west end and 650ft on the east end (to 6,150ft), and it was widened to 300ft. This field was eventually to become the enormous Tinian North Field. In September the other Japanese strip there was lengthened to 6,000ft and designated North Field, Strip No.3. Meanwhile, the Japanese west coast strip that had been heavily damaged during the invasion was refurbished into a 4,000ft fighter strip. A site a mile east of this fighter strip was selected for the proposed third and fourth B-29 fields. A 6,000ft runway (designated West Field Strip No.3) was designated as a large Navy strip, and almost all work was stopped at North Field, and the equipment there was transferred to construct the Navy's West Field runway and facility.

Once the Navy base was completed work was restarted on the North Field complex to lengthen them for B-29 use, and also double the number of fields from two to four. The first phase of this project was the development of Strip No.1 to 8,500x300ft, and the construction of its taxiways, hardstands, and aprons, and it was ready on 22 December 1944. The second phase was the extension of Strip No.3 to the required 8,500x300ft.

The third phase was the construction of North Field No.2 between the two existing strips with its taxiways, hardstands, and aprons, and it was ready on 27 February. Instead of immediately beginning North Field Strip No.4 all effort was shifted to the construction of West Field, Strip No.1, the first B-29 strip there. Work on two 8,500ft strips, located north of the Navy's strip, was begun simultaneously on 1 February 1945. Both strips were parallel to each other, were 500ft wide, and included 10 miles of taxiways, 220 hardstands, two service aprons, sub-service aprons, and warm-up aprons, 251 buildings for administration, repair, and maintenance, and four personnel camps. On 1 April 1945 Strip No.1 was completed, followed by Strip No.2 on 20 April. Then, after these West Fields were completed work was restarted on North Field, and the fourth 8,500ft runway was widened to 500ft, and additional hardstands were built; on 5 May 1945 North Field Strip No.4 was completed. Construction on this strip was slowed, as the last 1,500ft extended over the edge of the Tinian Plateau, and extensive fills had to be made. After work was started a decision was made to reduce the maximum taxiway grade from 2.5% to 1.5%, because it was decided that the bombers were to taxi under their own power to the takeoff line, instead of being towed there by a tractor. This decision increased the amount of earth to be removed from North Field by a half million cubic yards. When it was completed North Field complex had four parallel 8,500ft runways 1,600ft apart with taxiways in between, eight taxiways totaling 11mi, 265 hardstands, two service aprons, 173 Quonset huts, and 92 steel arch buildings. To surface all six of Tinian's runways over a half million tons of asphalt had been mixed with coral, and then laid and rolled, and rolled again.

Despite the fact that the island, whose surface had been 90% cultivated with sugar cane and was virtually level, the movement of enormous quantities of earth was necessary for the construction of the new airfields. The construction of both North and West Fields required a massive earth moving enterprise involving deep cuts in hard coral and high fills. There were cuts as deep as 15ft and fills as high as 42ft. North Field excavations totaled 2.11 million cubic yards, and fill required 4.79 million cubic yards.

Tinian (USAF)

When it was completed North Field (looking south) had four parallel 8,500ft runways 1,600ft apart with taxiways in between, eight taxiways totaling 11 miles, 265 hardstands, two service aprons, 173 Quonset huts and 92 steel arch buildings. Note B-29 landing (arrow). (USAF)

The construction of both North and West Fields were a massive earth moving enterprise involving deep cuts in hard coral and high fills. There were cuts as deep as 15ft and fills as high as 42ft. North Field (shown) excavations totaled 2.11 million cubic yards and fill required 4.79 million cubic yards. At West Field cut was 1.72 million cubic yards and fill was 3.30 million cubic yards. (USAF)

Tinian Air Fields

Field	Runways	Size	Surface	B-29 Capacity
North	4	8,500x200	Asphalt	231
	4		Coral	
Hardstands	**No.**		**Surface**	
	56		Coral	
Service Aprons	**No.**		**Surface**	
	2		Asphalt	3
Field	**Runways**	**Size**	**Surface**	**B-29 Capacity**
West	2	8,500x200	Asphalt	232
	2		Asphalt	3
Hardstands	**No.**		**Surface**	
	2		Asphalt	3
Service Aprons	**No.**		**Surface**	
	48		Coral	

167,000 barrels of aviation gasoline storage (400,000 barrels planned)

At West Field the cut was 1.72 million cubic yards, and the fill was 3.30 million cubic yards. The great difference between cut and fill was made up from the huge borrow pits in the island's underlying coral. The April 1945 issue of *Fortune Magazine* compared New York Mayor Fiorello LaGuardia's proposed Idlewild Airport to Tinian's fields as the largest in the world. Idlewild's 14.5mi of runways fell short of Tinian's North Field with 20mi, and West Field, which was only slightly shorter. Besides, the Tinian runways were 500ft wide, as compared to LaGuardia's 300ft. The total cost to develop Tinian was $35.2 million.

After the invasion fuel was obtained from trucked drums until facilities were built at Tinian Town to collect bulk aviation gasoline from steel barges (called YOGL) to fill tanker trucks. Tank farm construction began in early September, and two months later a 25,000 barrel farm was completed, followed by a submarine pipeline that supplied gasoline from off-shore tankers to a 56,000gal barrel facility that was ready at the end of November. When the Tinian fuel system was completed in early March 1945 it consisted of a 14,000-barrel diesel oil storage farm, a 20,000-barrel farm for motor fuel, and a series of six farms for storing 165,000 barrels of aviation gasoline. All fuel was piped in via a submarine pipeline from a tanker moored just north of Tinian Town, where there were numerous pumping stations that distributed the fuel to West Field via two dispensing points, and North Field via six dispensing points through 16mi of pipeline. The aviation gasoline storage was at two main farms and four secondary farms near each of the two main airfields.

Bomb and Aerial Mine Dumps

In September 1944 the first ammunition storage dump of 11 revetments was completed. Mine Assembly Plant No.4 on Tinian was the aerial mines depot for B-29 mining operation, and assembled more mines than all the other mine depots combined.

Guam

Guam (code *Stevedore*) is by far the largest island in the Marianas (225 square miles, vs. the 177 square miles for all the other 14 islands combined), and is shaped like a figure eight, with a four mile waist. The average elevation is less than Saipan, but its foliage was more tropical, lush, and dense than Saipan and Tinian. The south end is covered with grass and scrub forest cut by fertile (rice and vegetables) river and stream valleys, and several swamps. The soil on the southern half is volcanic clay that turned into thick mud during rains. The northern half is rolling terrain atop a 400-500ft plateau covered with tropical forest and thick undergrowth. The Japanese built a 4,500ft airstrip on the Orote Peninsula on the west center coast, and another 5,000ft strip at Tiyan (Agana), which was 2.5mi east of Agana, the administrative center of the island. Another strip was cleared at Dededo, three miles northeast of Tiyan, near Tumon Bay on the west coast.

The United States gained control of Spanish-occupied Guam during the 1898 Spanish-American War, and on 10 December 1941 the Japanese captured it. The civilian population was treated harshly by the Japanese

Building North Field on Guam involved two 8,500x200 asphalt strips and 158 hardstands. (USAF)

B-29s of the 39BG of the 314BW taxi for a mission to Japan. (USAF)

occupation, and was forced to build the airfields and fortifications. Guam was invaded on 21 July and not secured until 10 August after much fierce fighting. The Japanese lost over 18,400 troops, with thousands more unaccounted for in caves, where they held out often for years (the last holdout surrendering in 1972!). The U.S. casualties were 1,700 killed and over 6,000 wounded. During the invasion Agana, Guam's capitol and largest city (12,000 population), was destroyed, as were the other important towns on Apra Harbor, along with all harbor facilities and installations. Before construction the airfields could begin the port had to be restored by dredging and building piers and other port facilities. The total cost to build Guam into a major supply, repair, and operational base was $280.8 million, by far the highest cost of any base in WWII (Leyte-Samar was second at $215.6 million).

Guam was in striking distance of the Japanese Homeland, and bordered the Japanese lines of air and sea communications and supply in the Western Pacific. For this reason the island was to be developed into the headquarters of the 20AF and Pacific Fleet, and to a huge supply depot in the final assault on Japan. Fifteen Seabee Battalions (4th, 23rd, 25th, 41st, 48th, 49th, 53rd, 56th, 59th, 72nd, 76th, 94th, 103rd, 109th, and 136th) were supported by seven AAF engineer battalions, all under Seabee command. Guam was different in B-29 planning from the other Marianas' bases. The airfields at Tinian and Saipan were operational fields. Guam, while also having operational fields, was to have Depot field, where all B-29s in the Pacific would go for major overhauling in the permanent machine shops and maintenance hangars, and it was to be the HQ of the XXIBC. Likewise, Navy harbor improvements on Tinian and Saipan were temporary short range developments to speed along the war, while on Guam Apra Harbor was to become one of the principal ports in the Pacific, and the HQ of the Pacific Fleet. Five airfields were proposed, with the three Japanese strips to form the nucleus of the first three fields, and two new fields were to be constructed on the northern end of the island. Orote Airfield had construction priority, as Marine and Navy fighter aircraft used it to fly ground support missions on the Japanese-held portions of the island. Orote, which was completed to 4,500ft by the Japanese, was completely rebuilt and extended to 5,500ft by Marine engineers, and was operational on 29 July. Navy Seabees constructed the hardstands, warehouses, shops, and administrative and living quarters. The second airfield was built on the former, nearly completed Japanese 5,000ft field near Agana. It was extended to

7,000ft field and paved with asphalt. A second 6,000x150ft strip was constructed nearby, and the two fields were ready for the Naval Air Transport Service and AAF freight and passenger traffic.

After the island was secure the AAF Engineering Battalions moved to the north, "B-29 end," of the island, and were assigned to be the lead construction battalions on the operational runways and Depot Field installations. The Japanese had nearly finished a third strip (Dededo, to the north of Agana), and this site was chosen for the establishment of Depot Field (later called Harmon Field). The orientations of the runways were altered to reduce flight interference from nearby hills. The initial runway was 7,000x150ft, covered by two inches of asphaltic concrete, and augmented by 12,000ft of taxiways and 42 hardstands. Eight 130x160ft superstructures and 160x190ft repair hangars were also constructed to form the largest air repair base in the Pacific. Harmon Field was to serve as the HQ of the XXIBC from early December 1944, and then the 20AF from July 1945 until well after the war, May 1949. During the Vietnam War, from 1965 to 1972, B-52 bombers flew missions from North Field, which had been renamed Anderson AFB in 1947. The first B-29s landed on 24 November 1944.

In early 1945 two new runways were built out of the dense jungles on the north end of the island. The 8,500x200ft North Field runways were built near Ritidian Point entirely by AAF Engineers, and were to be capable of handling 160 bombers. The first runway was commissioned on 3 February 1945, and the first Tokyo raid was sent from there three weeks later. By the end of April a second runway was ready for operations.

Northwest Airfield was built on Pati Point by the combined cooperation of Army Engineers and Navy Seabees. The construction of this field was slowed by 26ft cuts and fills through very hard limestone, but the south runway was finished two days ahead of schedule, and opened for operations for the arrival of more and more B-29s on 1 June 1945. To accommodate these bombers work was rushed to complete taxiways, hardstands, and operational facilities, and get the second north strip operational one month later.

As Guam was to be a major base, it was necessary that large stores of equipment, ordnance, supplies, gasoline and oil, spare parts, and food be available. By March 1945 a vast tank farm was completed that provided

Harmon Field was to serve as the HQ of the XXIBC from early December 1944 and then the 20AF from July 1945 until well after the war, May 1949. During the Vietnam War, from 1965 to 1972, B-52 bombers flew missions from North Field that had been renamed Anderson AFB in 1947. (USAF)

328,000 barrels of aviation gasoline, 130,000 barrels of diesel, 40,000 barrels of motor gasoline, and 448,000 barrels of fuel oil. At Guam an estimated million gallons of gasoline was used daily. On VJ-Day it was estimated that the supplies on hand at Guam could have filled a train 120mi long!

Guam Air Fields

Field	Runways No.	Size	Surface	Hardstands No.	Surface	Service Aprons No.	Surface	B-29 Capacity
Harmon	1	7,000x200	Asphalt	84	Asphalt	2	Asphalt	21+
North	2	8,500x200	Asphalt*	82	Coral	3	Coral	40 all
				76	Asphalt	2	Asphalt	
North-west	2	8,500x200	Asphalt^	27	Coral	5	Asphalt	30
				2	Asphalt	1	Coral	

+ Asphalt aprons parking for 75 B-29s
* Asphalt for 180ft of width Runway #1 the rest coral/Runway #2 Asphalt
^ Asphalt for 150ft of the width of both runways, the rest coral
309,000 barrels of aviation gasoline storage (436,000 barrels planned)

Daily Base Life

Once the airfields were built, construction battalions concentrated on an extensive complex of Quonset huts and barracks for personnel that made base life reasonably comfortable by Pacific standards. The occupants of the Quonset hut were separated by job category, such as huts for navigators or bombardiers. Generally, enlisted men were billeted in tents that were set on concrete or wooden floors. The island temperatures were quite mild, and the ocean breezes could make sleeping in tents more comfortable than sleeping in the enclosed permanent buildings. Initially the mess halls were tents, and everyone, officers and enlisted men, ate together. More permanent mess halls were constructed, along with kitchen facilities, and the quantity and quality of the food improved by early 1945, as the Navy was able to ship less building materials and more food. There were outdoor churches and movies, and audiences sat on wooden bomb crates. Movies were passed around between wings, but many were seen several times. Radios and pin up girls were a staple of every barracks. Bartering was the financial way of life, with whiskey and Japanese souvenirs the currency of the day. Sports, particularly baseball, were popular, and Bomb Wings formed teams that played in Wing leagues. Basketball and football

Quonset housing replacing tents on Isley for the 498BG in October 1944. (USAF)

Mess facilities being set up on Guam. (USAF)

were played, but were not as popular as baseball because of the heat and humidity. Rats were a problem on Guam, and a ritual was the "de-ratting contest" held between several Quonset huts. For every rat confirmed killed a rat was painted above the hut's door, and for every wounded rat that escaped a "probable" was awarded by painting a half rat credit. At the end of the rat campaign the losers rewarded the winners with a beer party. The men on Tinian remarked about the absence of bird life, and the frequent visits from tarantulas that ambled into their billets from the nearby banana and cane fields.

Iwo Jima

Iwo Jima (code *Rockcrusher*, later *Starlit* and *Workman*) meant "Sulfur Island" in Japanese, and was located halfway between Saipan and Tokyo at 670mi south of Tokyo, and 600mi north of Saipan. The 7.5 square mile pork chop shaped island is the largest island of the Volcano Island group, measuring 4.7mi by 2.5mi, with the famous Mt. Suribachi at the southern tip. The Japanese built three airfields on the island. Motoyama Airfield No.1 was completed in 1943 on a raised foundation with 5,025ft and 3,965ft runways, and to the northeast Motoyama Airfield No.2 was built in 1944, and had 5,225ft and 4,425ft runways. The third airstrip was to the northeast of No.2, and had an uncompleted 3,800ft runway. February is the driest month and May the wettest month, with accompanying high winds.

Invasion plans for Iwo Jima had been formulated as early as September 1943, but when the Marianas were captured its significance increased, as B-29s were about to begin their attacks on Japan. The island was to serve not only as an emergency field, but also as a fighter base that would permit Long-Range P-51 Mustang fighter aircraft to rendezvous with the B-29s flying north from their Marianas bases and escort them (starting 7 June 1945). Another psychological consideration was that the island would be the first of the Home Islands to be invaded.

The island was invaded (*Operation Detachment*) on 19 February 1945, and the last pocket of major resistance had been wiped out in late March, but it was not until late May that mopping up operations ended the ruthless battle that killed an estimated 20,000 Japanese. The Iwo Jima campaign was the costliest thus far in the war for America, as the Marines lost 6,000 dead and 17,300 wounded.

On 26 February Airfield No.1 was ready for use by observation aircraft, and on 3 March by transports that would bring in much needed supplies and evacuate the many wounded. By 16 March Airfields No.1 and No.2 were usable by fighters, but 50 damaged B-29s had already made emergency landings on them. Once fighting subsided, the Navy Ninth Construction Brigade (8th, 90th, 95th, and 23rd Special Battalions and 41st Regiment) was assigned to develop and expand all three airfields. No.1, No.2, and No.3 were renamed South, Central, and North Fields. South Field became a 6,000x200ft fighter strip, and work on additional taxiways and facilities continued after the field was in operation on 7 April, when the first fighter escorts took off for Japan. Central Field was expanded into a 6,000ft fighter strip and two 8,500ft bomber runways. By 7 July these bomber runways had been paved, and during that day alone 102 B-29s returning from Japan were forced to land there. One runway was extended to 9,800ft to give damaged B-29s more length on which to land (the second 8,500ft runway had been graded to 9,400ft by the end of the war but was never paved). The built from scratch 5,500x200ft North Field was completed as a fighter field.

Emergency Landings

By the end of the war 2,395 of the 25,005 B-29 sorties flown (9.2%) had made emergency landings on Iwo Jima, saving 24,761 airmen. A summary

By 7 July Iwo Central Field bomber runways had been paved, and during that day 102 B-29s returning from Japan were forced to land there. One runway was extended to 9,800ft to give damaged B-29s more length on which to land. (USAF)

of emergency landings showed that 1,872 (78.2%) of these landings were made for refueling or minor repairs, and 524 (21.8%) were made for major maintenance that included 311 (13%) for engine changes, 64 (2.6%) for battle damage, and 149 (6.2%) for other reasons.

Iwo Jima Air Fields

Field	Runways No.	Size	Surface	Hardstands No.	Surface	Service Aprons No.	Surface	B-29 Capacity
Central	1	9,800x200	Asphalt	25	Earth	1	Asphalt	14
	1	9,400x200	Earth*					
North+	1	5,500x200	Asphalt					
South+	1	6,000x200	Asphalt					

* 90% earth on runway, asphalt not completed
+ Fighter field
200,000 barrels of aviation gasoline (280,000 barrels proposed)

Kwajalein

The Kwajalein Atoll is located in the Marshall Islands, and consists of 80 islands that stretch 66mi in a chain that form a large lagoon. Only Kwajalein Island, on the far southeast end of the atoll, had enough area to support a large airfield. The Japanese had greatly developed the island with a 400x5,000ft airfield, and had a rock-crushing plant in place to supply crushed coral for road and airfield construction. The Seabees extended the field to 6,300ft, with two 80ft taxiways and 102 hardstands that could accommodate heavy bombers. A large 340,000-barrel petroleum tank farm was constructed on nearby Bigeji Island. The B-24s of the 11BG and 30BG flew from Kwajalein to stage through Eniwetok to bomb the large bypassed Japanese bases in the Marshalls and Carolines, and particularly the large base at Truk. When the Marianas were developed into the B-29 hub in the Pacific the Kwajalein runway was further improved. To transfer the B-29s to Saipan it was planned that the ATC ferry the bombers from Mather Field, CA (10 miles east of Sacramento), with stops at John Rogers Airport, near Honolulu, and then to Kwajalein. It was planned to deliver five B-29s a day from 20 October 1944 until the 73BW's authorized strength of 180 bombers was attained. However, bombers arrived at only two or three per day, and by 4 November there was a cumulative shortage of 17 bombers at Saipan and 30 at Mather. Despite Lt.Gen. Harmon's intervention the short-

Iwo Jima

Central Field looking toward Mt. Suribachi. By the end of the war 2,395 B-29s had made emergency landings, saving 24,761 airman. (USAF)

ages continued, and by 22 November, two days before the first combat mission, only 118 B-29s were available in the Marianas. The flights to Hawaii and then to Kwajalein gave the inexperienced B-29 crews a taste of long over water navigation they would soon encounter from the Marianas.

Okinawa

After Okinawa was secured at the end of July 1945 it was projected to become a massive air, sea, and army base for the invasion of Japan. In early April, soon after the invasion, the GHQ chief of the Army Forces in the Pacific (AFPAC) came ashore and proposed that very heavy bomber bases be added to the already imposing airfield construction program on

Okinawa. For the construction 26 aviation engineer battalions were sent to Okinawa from all over the globe, and their first duty was to themselves, as they built comfortable living quarters before starting the airfields. On 18 April 1945 a 500BG B-29 commanded by Capt. Robert Cordray with two engines out was the first B-29 to land on Okinawa. The B-32s of the 386BS/319BG flew eight operational missions from Yonton near the end of the war. By the time the war ended construction was well under way, and plans had been made for 96 aviation engineer units, many seasoned units from Europe, to work in the western Pacific. After the war work continued on the mammoth Okinawa air bases, but not by the aviation engineers, who were returned home after long service.

B-29 Bomb Group Combat Bases in World War II

Bomb Group	Combat Bases	Bomb Group	Combat Bases
6BG	Tinian (North Field)	472BG	Smoky Hill, KS (as OTU)
9BG	Tinian (North Field)	497BG	Saipan (Isley)
16BG	Guam (Northwest Field)	498BG	Saipan (Isley)
19BG	Guam (North Field)	499BG	Saipan (Isley)
29BG	Guam (North Field)	500BG	Saipan (Isley)
39BG	Guam (North Field)	501BG	Guam (Northwest Field)
40BG	Chakulia, India, Hsinching, China & Tinian (West Field)	502BG	Guam (Northwest Field)
330BG	Guam (North Field)	504BG	Tinian (North Field)
331BG	Guam (North Field	505BG	Tinian (North Field)
444BG	Charra & Dudhkundi, India, Kwanghan, China & Tinian (West Field)	509BG	Tinian (North Field)
462BG	Piardoba, India/Kiunglai, China & Tinian (West Field)		
468BG	Kharagpur, India, Pengshan, & Tinian (West Field)		

Maintenance and Supply

Maintenance

During training in the U.S. the B-29 units employed AAF routine maintenance procedures using the standard "crew system" that the AAF had been using for a decade. Each bomber had a crew chief, assistant crew chief, a staff of specialized personnel (armorers, mechanics, sheet metal men, radiomen, etc.), and a squadron supply sergeant. In America and Europe this system worked well, as there were sufficient experienced ground crew personnel and sufficient aircraft and parts to go around if an aircraft were grounded for repairs. But once the B-29s reached India the crew system did not work, as there were few experienced ground personnel and no extra aircraft or spare parts. In the Marianas each new Wing began operations without its maintenance facilities in place, and had to spend the first months organizing its maintenance scheme and completing its facilities, all the while maintaining its aircraft for combat operations.

In order to realize the maximum utilization of the tools and equipment and the maximum flexibility of personnel in the face of highly fluctuating workloads between groups the "Combat Maintenance System" was initiated. With the exception of a small, permanently assigned maintenance crew for each bomber the System combined squadron maintenance personnel on a group basis, and each group furnished personnel to each shop, which were organized on a Wing basis, rather than a group basis. The aircraft were serviced by an assembly line maintenance system of group specialists and centralized specialized shops. Everyone worked on aircraft that needed repair, and experienced personnel supervised and trained the less skilled personnel. When the ground echelons were shipped to the combat theater its mechanics were relatively inexperienced, especially with the highly complicated B-29. To remedy the situation mechanic training was an ongoing process, with an experienced mechanic being assigned a novice mechanic to assist and learn as an apprentice. The Wing Deputy Chief of Staff for Supply and Maintenance was in charge, but the Wing Maintenance Controller actually directed maintenance. Under the Wing Maintenance Controller were two Assistant Wing Maintenance Controllers, who were each responsible for the functioning of the maintenance personnel of four Bomb Wings that had been combined into two Service Groups, and a service center under each Assistant Wing Maintenance Controller. This combination of Service Groups was a further extension of the Combat Maintenance Organization.

An example of this integration was seen in the service groups of the 73BW on Saipan, which had four service groups with each set up to operate a base for 5,000 men. To prevent a duplication of work the personnel from the 65th and 91st Service Groups were integrated into Service Center A to service the 497BG and 498BG aircraft on the northern airfield. Personnel of the 303rd and 330th Service Groups were integrated into Service Center B to service the 499BG and 500BG bombers on the southern field. Salvage and reclamation shops, tire build-up, and engine build-up were centralized as Wing Projects. The Service Center operations were limited in the early months due to the lack of shop facilities and equipment, and the necessity of using service personnel to construct their own facilities. Once the facilities were completed, from 1 March 1945 to the end of the war these two Service Groups repaired 564 bombers, with 81% being repaired within three days. Every month the 600 men in these groups completed 100,000 man-hours of work, of which two-thirds was directed toward aircraft repair, and just over a quarter to shop overhead and maintenance. An example of the increased efficiency was that the time to change an engine decreased from three days to four hours.

Each group furnished personnel to specialized shops that were organized on a wing basis rather than a group basis. Maintenance personnel in the four service groups were combined into maintenance sections for each of two service centers. Shown is a combined engine service center. (USAF)

The Air Depot on Guam was activated on 1 October 1944 with only the air echelons of two air depot groups. On 19 November 1944 the first personnel were assigned to the Maintenance Division, and its growth was relatively slow until February 1945, at which time personnel were increased by two-thirds (to 983), and continued to increase monthly (March 1,313, April 1,837, May 2,173, June 2,337, and July 2,649). The rate of aircraft maintenance increased from a total of eight aircraft from November through February to an average of 128 bombers repaired per month from March 1945 until the end of the war. At the beginning of January 1945 the Maintenance Division's total facilities in the Marianas consisted of eight hangars, but by the end of the war it increased to 16 hangars and 23 shops.

The complexities of the B-29 airplane, and the large scale of the operations in the Marianas, demanded significant specialization by the headquarters personnel allocated to the Operational Engineering Section (OES). The OES standardized flight line and flight test procedures, and directed research into operational problems affecting maintenance. Among the problems they investigated were the correction of established power settings for the climatic conditions of the Marianas, the effect of center of gravity on performance, accurate determination of fuel flow, cruise control, and others.

After Iwo Jima was captured in mid-March 1945 emergency maintenance facilities were set up there to take advantage of the island's geographical position half way between the Marianas and Japan for B-29 emergency landings for refueling and maintenance. However, these emergency maintenance facilities were initially insufficient, and there was a large accumulation of grounded bombers by the end of May. Measures were taken to reorganize the Iwo Service Center and bring in specialized personnel, and the backlog disappeared within a month. By the end of June the Service Center was running smoothly, and the all-important Engine Build-up Shop was repairing 10 engines daily. In addition to the emergency maintenance on the hundreds of distressed bombers that landed weekly at Iwo, there was regular maintenance to be done on the B-29s stationed on the island for fighter navigation missions, photo and weather reconnaissance sorties, and staging missions.

Supply

The Air Force Air Depot worked closely with the XXIBC from the start of operations, but it was not assigned to the XXIBC until the 20AF was activated. On 9 November the ground echelons of the two air depots arrived in four ships loaded with supplies. The unloading and storage of supplies was very difficult due to the lack of docking, transport, and warehousing facilities. While warehouses were being constructed the supplies were constantly moved, but the rainy, muddy weather, shortage of transport, and the arrival of more supply ships confused inventory, transporting, and storage. The 20AF supply situation in the Marianas encountered critical shortages of many items, particularly parts essential for the operation of the B-29. By December 1944 B-29 maintenance was seriously slowed by inadequate parts inventories, and something had to be done. That month there was an average of 148 B-29s on base, and 11.3% were grounded for lack of parts (the average percentage of bombers out of commission was 5.7% for the first five months of Marianas operations). The maintenance organization initially in effect was four Service Groups assigned to each Wing to operate in two Service Centers. Each Center had its own flight line, with warehouses and inventory that were duplicated by the second center. After three months the Wing supply organization was modified to incorporate one Wing Supply Control Center with Supply Division Depots. Each stocked similar parts and supplies for all units in one place, and with a centrally located stock inventory locator. Firm controls for the delivery of critical items (especially those that would ground an aircraft) were instituted at Bomber Command, Wing, and Air Depot levels, and standard quantity lists were kept at 30-day levels. To meet on base supply demands the extensive use of local manufacture, improvisation, reconditioning, and cannibalization was initiated. In March 1945, the XXIBC established a system that projected the need for specific parts based on past demands and the requirements of future operations. The system worked so well that even when Marianas operations increased 75% in March 1945, subsequently there was never a lack of supplies through the end of the war. In July 1945, with an average of 925 B-29s on base only 0.2 were grounded for lack of parts. In July, the last full month of the war, the Service Centers and Supply

Signs lined the Saipan roads to remind personnel of the importance of maintenance. (USAF)

The chronic problems with the R-3350 meant that engines needed to be serviced and often replaced with new engines. The photo on the right shows problem engines being cast aside to be replaced by newly arriving engines (right photo) shown here having their protective shipping wrapping removed. (USAF)

Division Depots managed to stock 84,461 different items, of which 49,058 were requisitioned during the month. A total of 36,179 requisitions were made for 123,728 total items, as compared to the 2,205 requisitions for 10,626 items in December 1944, the first full month of operations. From November 1944 to January 1945, when the system was reorganized, it took an average of 4.2 days from requisition to the receipt of supplies. This figure was reduced to an average of 1.1 days from January until the end of the war. The under roof warehouse space totaled 953,000 square feet, located in 150 buildings, and the outdoor space measured 796,500 square feet. In December 154 aircraft were serviced (148 B-29s on base), and in

July this figure, including 7AF aircraft, had increased to 2,090 aircraft (952 B-29s on base).

An important innovation in the Marianas was the unique supply system set up by Col. C.S. "Bill" Irvine that bypassed the A-4 Supply Command in distant Hawaii. Through proper channels it would take the Navy six weeks to send the parts and supplies by ship. Irvine had previously been in the Air Materiel Command, and used his connections there and with the Air Transport Command to establish his "private" air cargo service. When he needed parts or supplies he radioed the Air Materiel Command depot in Sacramento and had "his C-47s" fly the parts directly to the XXIBC.

4

Summary of Operations
XX Bomber Command

In February 1944, the average airplane commander in the 58th Wing (XX Bomber Command) had less than 35 hours of flying time in the B-29 bomber, the program was behind schedule, and Gen. Arnold was most anxious to "commit the B-29 to combat as soon as possible." Aircraft were still being modified during March when the Command was ordered to move to the CBI. As a result of constant modification during the preceding six months, the tactical squadrons sometimes had only one aircraft available to them for training.

As previously described, the original Wright R-3350-5 engine was unreliable, and consequently was replaced by a later R-3355-23 type engine called the "war engine." Even this engine was unsatisfactory, and it was replaced just prior to going overseas with the R-3350-23A "combat engine." Estimates of bomber losses anticipated enroute to the CBI ran as high as 15%, primarily because of the unknown capabilities of the new engines. The movements overseas took place during the months of April, May, and June 1944, consisting of a move halfway around the world: Kansas, Maine, New Foundland, French Morocco, Egypt, and India. Fortunately, these engines were far superior to the original model; consequently, the aircraft lost on the way were well within the calculated "risk."

The first mission, called a "shake down mission," that was in range of B-29s taking off from bases in India was flown in early June against Japanese targets in occupied Bangkok, Thailand. However, the XXBC had not reached its bases of operations against targets on Japan proper until the aircraft of the Wing took off in the middle of June for the flights over the Himalayan "Hump" to China. From there it could stage for the first attack by land-based aircraft into the heart of the Japanese Empire. Undoubtedly the sight of these huge aircraft was an invaluable morale factor for the Chinese armies fighting into their eighth year of war, but because of the distances involved the Japanese Homeland did not feel the true power of the B-29. The tenuous aerial pipeline of supply extending 1,500mi from India over the "roof of the world" to Chengtu, China, could not logistically support the XXBC's operational capabilities. It is often forgotten that the beginning of this aerial pipeline in India was itself 15,000mi from the United States, where the supply of materials originated to be transported by ship across the Pacific.

The first effort of the XX Bomber Command was primarily individual medium altitude attacks at night. Then in August, because of the lack of accuracy achieved in that mode of attack, daylight four-ship formations were attempted. The accuracy immediately improved, although the bomb load was decreased. In September, the XXBC started flying 12-ship formations, again decreasing the bomb load, but showing an immediate return in more bombs actually placed on the target. This can be attributed to the use of selected lead crews for bomb aiming of their own bombs, and the loads of 11 other bombers. In October there was an increase in the bomb loads, as better cruise control and piloting ability were realized from the augmented training program established by Gen. LeMay. It was during this month that, for the first time, Bomber Command achieved total destruction of a target (the aircraft depot in Formosa).

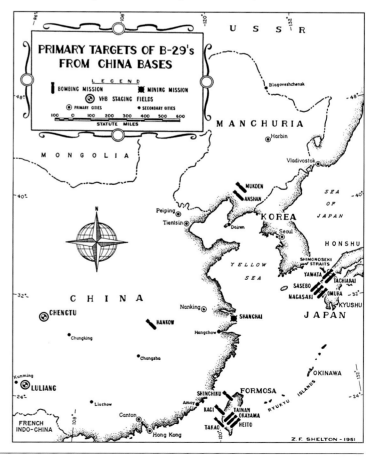

XX BOMBER COMMAND MISSIONS 1944-1945

MISSION NUMBER	DATE	TARGET	A/C AIRBORNE	BOMBED TARGET	BOMB TONS	A/C LOST	E. A/C CLAIMED
1	5 Jun	Bangkok	98	77	353	5	0-1-2
2	15/16 Jun	Yawata (1)	68	47	107	7	0-0-0
3	7/8 Jul	Sasebo, Yawata Omura, Nagasaki (1)	18	12	31	0	0-0-1
4	29 Jul	Anshan, Taku (1)	96	75	140	5	0-3-4
5	10/11 Aug	Palembang (2)	54	39	39	1	0-0-0
6	10/11 Aug	Nagasaki (1)	29	24	70	1	1-0-0
7	20 Aug	Yawata (1)	88	71	112	14	17-13-12
8	8 Sep	Anshan (1)	108	90	206	4	8-9-10
9	26 Sep	Anshan (1)	109	73	215	0	11-9-31
10	14 Oct	Formosa (1)	130	103	638	2	0-0-0
11	16 Oct	Formosa (1)	72	43	269	0	3-3-9
12	17 Oct	Formosa (1)	30	10	62	1	8-0-7
13	25 Oct	Omura (1)	78	59	153	2	7-5-18
14	3 Nov	Rangoon	49	44	417	1	0-0-2
15	5 Nov	Singapore	76	53	83	2	1-1-5
16	11 Nov	Omura, Nanking (1)	96	29	160	5	2-2-12
17	21 Nov	Omura (1)	109	61	199	6	27-19-24
18	27 Nov	Bangkok	60	55	382	1	7-3-6
19	7 Dec	Mukden (1)	108	80	276	7	20-10-30
20	14 Dec	Bangkok	48	33	181	4	0-1-0
21	18 Dec	Hankow (1)	94	84	511	0	1-3-10
22	19 Dec	Omura (1)	36	17	52	2	5-4-12
23	21 Dec	Mukden (1)	49	19	88	2	21-6-19
24	2 Jan	Bangkok	49	44	179	0	0-1-1
25	6 Jan	Omura (1)	49	28	91	1	4-6-10
26	9 Jan	Formosa (1)	46	39	293	0	0-0-0
27	11 Jan	Singapore	47	25	46	2	6-1-17
28	14 Jan	Formosa (1)	82	55	394	0	0-0-0
29	17 Jan	Formosa (1)	92	77	553	1	0-0-0
30	25/26 Jan	Saigon (M)	26	25	98	0	0-0-0
31	25/26 Jan	Singapore (M)	50	41	126	0	0-0-0
32	27 Jan	Saigon	25	22	65	0	0-0-0
33	1 Feb	Singapore	113	83	191	2	3-4-14
34	7 Feb	Saigon	67	33	175	1	0-0-1
35	7 Feb	Bangkok	64	58	354	0	0-0-0
36	11 Feb	Mingaladon	59	56	414	0	0-0-3
37	19 Feb	Kuala Lumpur	59	49	176	0	1-0-7
38	24 Feb	Singapore	116	105	220	1	0-0-0
40	27/28 Feb	Johore Straits (M)	12	10	29	0	0-0-0
41	2 Mar	Singapore	64	50	107	2	0-1-4
39	4/5 Mar	Shanghai (3) (M)	12	11	70	0	0-0-0
43	10 Mar	Kuala Lumpur	29	24	100	0	1-0-4
42	12 Mar	Singapore	49	44	98	0	0-0-1
44	17 Mar	Rangoon	77	70	591	0	0-0-0
45	22 Mar	Rangoon	78	76	519	0	0-0-0
46	28/29 Mar	Yangtze (3) (M)	10	10	65	0	0-0-0
47	28/29 Mar	Saigon (M)	18	17	63	0	0-0-0
48	28/29 Mar	Singapore (M)	33	32	65	0	0-0-0
49	29/30 Mar	Singapore	29	24	68	0	0-0-0

(1) Flown from Chengtu, China. (2) Staged through China Bay, Ceylon. 8 AC (462 BG) mined the Moesi River in the longest missio flown by the 20 AF in WW II, 4030 miles. (3) Staged through Luliang, China. (M) Mining mission.

From AAF, *Statistical Digest*, Office of Statistical Control, December 1945

During the last two months of 1944 the Hump lift had been increased to an extraordinary extent, and the XX Bomber Command's allocation of fuel and ordnance from this lift had multiplied greatly. As a result the XXBC was able not only to multiply its efforts against the Japanese Homeland, staging from China, but by utilizing the time that the aircraft spent in the rear area (India) was able to multiply its effort substantially on the Southeast Asia Campaign (Singapore, Burma, and China) from Indian bases.

In January 1945 the XX Bomber Command had reached an experience level in which the various commanders of its units understood crew and aircraft capabilities, and were able to confidently dispatch missions with knowledge that the mission planning rationale they used was correct. Weather forecasts had become more reliable, bombardiers' accuracy was greatly increased, and the ability of the ground crews to maintain the aircraft and load them on short notice had become proficient.

In the latter part of January 1945, a decision was reached that VHB aircraft would relinquish their China bases and operations against the home islands of Japan until they were able to move to Okinawa after its capture. During this month personnel and staging equipment belonging to the XX Bomber Command were evacuated from China back to India. Pending movement to its new Okinawan bases, the XX Bomber Command operated from India exclusively against targets requested by the Allied Supreme Commander Southeast Asia. These operations included mining of the water approaches to Singapore, and the mining of certain South China ports. The precision bombing effort of the Command was utilized in most part in HE and incendiary attacks on targets in the Singapore area. However, a few limited effort missions were dispatched against targets in Burma. On 30 March the last mission of the XX Bomber Command was flown to Singapore, and the 58th Wing, the only VHB Wing of the XX Bomber Command, prepared to move its base to Tinian under the command of the XXI Bomber Command.

5

Summary of Operations
XXI Bomber Command

The 73rd Wing was the first of five wings of the XXI Bomber Command, which were ultimately scheduled to go into combat. On 10 August 1944, the first service group arrived at Saipan to start preparation of the necessary facilities of the 73rd Wing base. The first B-29 of the Wing arrived at Isley Field, Saipan, on 12 October.

From the arrival of the first units, all efforts were intended toward getting the 73BW to bomb Japan as quickly as possible. However, problems of inadequate airfield and housing facilities, maintenance equipment, and limited supplies were to be overcome before the first mission could be conducted. The fact that the entire 73BW, including four Bomb Wings and four service groups, were stationed together at one airfield created unique problems of organization and administration. Never before in AAF history had a total of over 12,000 personnel been located at one combat base.

According to the target directive from headquarters, 20th Air Force, Washington, the XXIBC was given the primary task of destroying Japan's aircraft industry, and the secondary task of supporting Pacific operations. In accordance with this directive, the first mission to the Empire occurred on 24 November, when 111 aircraft were airborne against Nakajima Aircraft Company plant at Musashino, near Tokyo. Attacking from 30,000ft, only 24 aircraft bombed the primary target, which was partially obscured by cloud cover, while an additional 59 dropped their high explosive bombs on the secondary target, the urban area of Tokyo. This attack marked the opening of an air operation that would be unparalleled in military history.

The operations of the Marianas-based B-29s can be divided into two distinct phases:

1) 24 November 1944 to 9 March 1945: This phase was considered a period of tactical experimentation and adjustment. The XXIBC sought to verify the operational capabilities of the B-29 in an air offensive against Japan, and to establish the best method of utilizing the bomber, considering the enemy's vulnerability to air attack and defensive tactics.

2) 9 March 1945 to 15 August 1945: During this phase the effort of the XXIBC was devoted to the application of the tactical knowledge and experience previously acquired in phase one. This phase was marked by the beginning of low altitude incendiary attacks, and was characterized by intensive operations designed to maximize the effects of B-29 attacks on the enemy's economy

Phase 1: 24 November 1944 to 9 March 1945

The first attack on 24 November 1944 set the pattern for the missions that followed prior to 9 March 1945. Of the 22 major missions, 16 were against priority targets in the aircraft industry group, particularly aircraft engine plants, and four were against the urban areas of Tokyo, Nagoya, and Kobe. In addition, two strikes were against Iwo Jima in December to assist in neutralizing the enemy defenses prior to its invasion.

With the exception of a small harassing night attack against Tokyo, the planning during this period was substantially the same for all the attacks against the mainland. The B-29s were to take off in the early daylight hours from their bases in the Marianas, assemble in squadron formations,

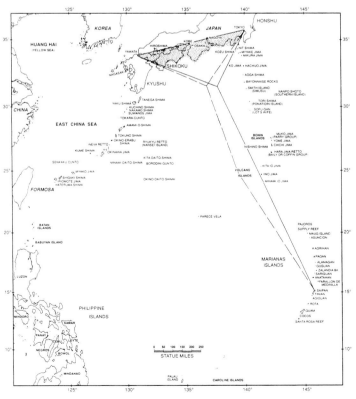

Primary Targets from the Marianas (USAF)

usually at Nashimo-Shima, and bomb Japan at 30,000ft (later reduced to 27,000ft). For the most part only high explosive bomb loads were carried, usually 500lb general purpose, although incendiaries were carried on the raids against urban areas, and both types were dropped on precision targets.

The chief factor preventing this high altitude precision bombing plan from being successfully executed was the weather. Severe weather fronts enroute to the target made navigation difficult, particularly since LORAN and other navigational aids were not yet operational. Formations became scattered, and minimal fuel reserves often forced aircraft to bomb targets of opportunity on the coast, rather than penetrate further inland to the primary target.

Moreover, once over Japan, the weather was often not as predicted. Weather forecasting was extremely difficult, with little or inadequate data from the important areas west and northwest of Japan (China, Russia, and Korea). The very high bombing altitudes added to the weather difficulties because of the accompanying strong winds, and the fact that it was possible for any one of several cloud layers to obscure the target. The experience with the weather is indicated by the fact that of the 16 high altitude precision attacks during the period against aircraft industry priority targets, four attacks completely failed to bomb the primary targets, while only seven bombed with three fourths of the airborne force, and five with less than three-fourths of the force. The extent of the target destruction accomplished by these high-level daylight precision bombing missions indicated that the combat capability of the B-29 units was not being exploited. So as a tactical experiment during this phase high-level precision bombing was interspersed with three high altitude daylight incendiary attacks. These incendiary attacks were executed against urban industrial areas, the results of which were not successful due to insufficient number of aircraft participating, low bomb load, and weather difficulties at high altitude.

Until 4 February, the XXIBC operations were conducted by the 73BW, with an average of 125 B-29s assigned. On 4 February the 313BW joined with the 73BW, and on 5 February two groups of the 313BW went into combat. The aircraft strength of the command increased from 119 aircraft on 24 November 1944 to 385 on 9 March 1945. During the entire period each Wing operated with inadequate airfield facilities, maintenance equipment, and supplies, and limited target information. A lack of experience and parts handicapped maintenance and supply personnel. The high fuel consumption required for assembling and climbing to bombing altitude limited the B-29's bomb load to about three tons. Missions were conducted every four to six days, depending on weather, and during the three months of December, January, and February missions were conducted on only 18 of 90 days, or one in five days. All these factors combined to produce a high non-effective rate of airborne aircraft, and a low rate of combat effort (three to four sorties monthly per assigned aircraft, and an average of 58 hours per aircraft and 44 hours per crew were flown).

The cost to the attackers on these operations was relatively high, rising to 5.7% of airborne aircraft during January. On several missions, over 500 attacks from 200 to 300 enemy aircraft were experienced. In addition, losses to other causes other than enemy action were high, while the absence of a friendly advanced base (Iwo Jima) forced crews to ditch aircraft that otherwise would have only been battle damaged. The high loss rate, coupled with what was considered poor bombing results, caused a drop in crew morale.

Phase 2: 9 March 1945 to 15 August 1945

Against the background of operations described in Phase 1, the Commanding General, Curtiss LeMay, decided to conduct low altitude night incendiary attacks against the urban industrial concentration of Japan's principal cities. Several considerations led to this decision. From the viewpoint of target selection, Japan's industrial system, including, as it did, a large number of small workshops scattered throughout the urban areas, was particularly vulnerable to incendiary attacks against these areas. In addition, it was hoped that the high intensity fires started by the various incendiary bombs would spread to the priority targets located within the large cities. However, these factors by themselves were not sufficient to cause the change. Rather, the most important consideration was the fact that this change made possible a concurrent change in bombing methods. Urban area attacks did not require the same degree of bombing accuracy as precision targets. Therefore, it was felt that the desired destruction could be accomplished by radar bombing methods even when cloud conditions obscured the target. Thus, the weather obstacles could be overcome. It was further decided to attack by night, with individual aircraft bombing at altitudes ranging from 5,000 to 8,000ft. The major advantages offered by this method were the following:

1) The elimination of flying formation and climbing to very high altitude, which consumed large volumes of fuel, meant that the bomb loads could be greatly increased.
2) There were fewer aborts and other losses when flying at low altitude, as the engines endured less stress and strain, and consequently there were more effective aircraft over the target for each mission.
3) Although the low altitude missions involved the increased risk of heavier AA fire, it was felt that the advantages of surprise and the weak enemy night fighter strength would outweigh this disadvantage.

Under this plan, five night attacks against major cities were launched within 10 days, commencing with the devastating attack on Tokyo on the night of 9/10 March 1945. In this 10 day period three wings, one of which (the 314BW) was just beginning combat operations, dispatched 1,595 B-29 sorties against Japan, dropping 9,365 tons from an altitude averaging 7,000ft on four major urban areas, and destroyed 32 square miles of densely populated and highly industrialized quarters. The cost of 14 aircraft for the mission over Tokyo and eight aircraft on the other four targets (1.4% of sorties) was not considered disproportionate, especially considering the damage, both physical and psychological, to the enemy.

Although the March incendiary attacks effectively marked the end of very high altitude precision bombing, the operations of the XXIBC from that time were not confined to the low altitude mission. Rather, the Command attempted to keep its operations as flexible as possible, in order to take advantage of changes in the weather over the target. Throughout the spring and early summer, weather over Japan became progressively worse. The plan of the XXIBC was to schedule daylight attacks against pinpoint targets when weather forecasts indicated a reasonable certainty that daylight visual bombing conditions would exist; otherwise, night low-level incendiary attacks were planned against urban industrial areas. Moreover, when daylight missions were conducted, it was found possible to lower the bombing altitude substantially from previous levels, thereby obtaining the advantage of greater bomb loads, fewer non-effective aircraft, and increased bombing accuracy. Photo-reconnaissance and bombing analysis made it apparent that the B-29 attacks were seriously affecting the enemy's industrial complex, and it was decided that every effort would be made to intensify these operations in an attempt to destroy the overall Japanese economy and knock the enemy out of the war. In general, the operations of the XXIBC fell into the following categories:

1) Urban industrial areas
2) Priority targets
3) Tactical Support
4) Mining
5) Atomic Bomb

These categories of operation cannot be separated chronologically, since two or more were conducted each month, and at times during the same day. All the operations during this period were affected by a number of important factors that require further explanation.

The size of the XXIBC was continually increasing, with the 314BW flying its first mission on 9 March. The 58BW was scheduled to transfer from the CBI to West Field, Tinian, and an advanced echelon of 16 bombers and crews arrived at Tinian on 21 March, and were attached to the 313BW until the balance of the Wing began arriving on 21 April. The 315BW began arriving on 27 May, and flew its first mission on 26 June.

Iwo Jima was secured, and the island was used as a daylight assembly point enroute to Japan; it also allowed individual B-29s to fly there and save fuel, rather than assemble over the Marianas. The Iwo emergency field reduced losses, and provided a base for staging for the longer missions to northern Honshu, Hokkaido, and Korea. It also provided a base for the fighters of the VII Fighter Command (which was later merged into the 20AF). The fighters provided VLR escort for the B-29s and flew fighter-bomber strikes on the mainland.

Another important factor influencing the XXIBC's operations since March was the changing aspect of enemy opposition. Enemy fighter strength was declining, and although on several occasions the B-29s met strong opposition over the target, these were exceptional cases. The Japanese night fighter force was very weak, and this factor contributed to the very low loss rate on all night attacks. Flak and searchlight defenses were strong in the Tokyo area, but were comparatively weak, particularly in most of the secondary cities attacked in June to August.

The better flight training of combat crews, both in the Marianas and the United States, the adoption of the lead crew principal, and increased theater experience lead to improved bombing accuracy and air discipline, and fewer accidents. Maintenance personnel became more experienced and facilities improved, and at no time after the Marianas maintenance scheme was reorganized did it interfere with missions that were initially scheduled

DESTRUCTION OF URBAN AREA TARGETS

NOTE. — These pages list primary targets only.

Urban area targets	Population	Square miles built-up area	Square miles planned target area	Square miles destroyed	Percent built-up area destroyed	Percent planned target area destroyed	Missions	A/C bombing	Losses	Tons delivered
Akashi	47,751	1.42	0.8	0.9	63.5	101.0	1	123		975.0
Amagasaki	181,011	6.9	(1)	.76	11.0	(2)				(2)
Aomori	99,065	2.08	1.8	.73	35.0	40.5	1	63		551.5
Chiba	92,061	1.98	1.2	.86	43.4	72.0	1	125		892.3
Choshi	61,198	1.12	1.0	.48	43.0	37.9	1	104		779.9
Fukui	97,967	1.9	1.7	1.61	84.8	95.0	1	128		960.4
Fukuoka	323,217	6.56	4.0	1.37	21.5	34.3	1	221		1,525.0
Fukuyama	56,653	1.2	1.0	.88	73.3	88.0	1	91		555.7
Gifu	172,340	2.6	1.8	1.93	74.0	107.0	1	129	1	898.8
Hachioji	62,279	1.4	1.2	1.12	80.0	93.3	1	169	1	1,593.3
Hamamatsu	166,346	4.24	1.5	2.97	70.0	162.6	1	130	4	911.7
Hameji	104,249	1.92	1.0	1.48	71.7	121.0	1	106		767.1
Hiratsuka	43,148	2.35	.8	1.04	44.2	130.0	1	133		1.162.5
Hiroshima	343,968	6.9	(3)	4.7	68.5		1	4		45.5
Hitachi	82,885	1.38	1.2	1.08	78.2	73.3	1	128	2	971.2
Ichinomiya	70,792	1.28	1.0	.97	76.0	96.0	2	247		1,640.8
Imabari	55,557	.97	.8	.73	76.0	97.0	1	64		510.0
Isezaki	40,004	1.0	.5	.16	16.6	33.0	1	87		614.1
Kagoshima	190,257	4.87	2.0	2.15	44.1	105.0	1	171	2	1,023.1
Kawasaki	300,777	11.3	3.0	3.7	32.8	94.0	1	250	12	1,515.0
Kobe	967,234	15.7	7.0	8.75	56.0	125.0	3	874	11	5,647.8
Kochi	106,644	1.9	1.8	.92	48.0	51.0	1	134	1	1,117.6
Kofu	102,419	2.0	1.5	1.3	15.0	87.0	1	133		977.9
Kumagaya	48,899	.6	.6	.27	45.0	45.0	1	82		593.4
Kumamoto	210,938	4.8	3.0	1.0	21.0	33.0	1	155	1	1,121.2
Kure	276,985	3.26	2.0	1.3	40.0	65.0	1	157		1,093.7
Kuwana	41,848	.82	.8	.63	77.0	79.0	1	94		693.0
Maebashi	86,997	2.34	1.3	1.0	42.0	77.0	1	92		723.8
Maysuyama	117,534	1.67	1.0	1.22	73.0	122.0	1	128		896.0
Mito	66,293	2.6	2.0	1.7	65.0	85.0	1	161		1,151.4
Moji	138,997	1.12	.8	.30	26.9	37.8	1	92		626.9
Nagaoka	66,987	2.03	1.2	1.33	65.5	110.8	1	126		928.3
Nagasaki	252,630	3.3	(3)	1.45	43.9		1	2		45.0
Nagoya	1,328,084	39.7	16.0	12.37	31.2	77.0	5	1,647	23	10,144.8
Nishinomiya	111,796	9.46	4.5	3.5	37.0	62.3	1	255	1	2,003.9
Nobeoka	79,426	1.43	.8	.52	36.0	64.0	1	126		876.4
Numazu	53,165	1.4	1.4	1.25	89.5	89.5	1	125		1,051.7
Ogaki	56,117	1.2	.8	.48	40.0	60.0	1	93		663.7
Oita	76,985	2.2	1.4	.55	25.2	39.6	1	131		801.9
Okayama	163,552	3.38	1.8	2.13	63.0	119.0	1	140	1	985.5
Okazaki	84,073	.95	.8	.65	68.0	81.0	1	128		857.4
Omuta	177,034	5.37	1.5	2.27	42.5	136.0	2	240	1	1,733.8
Osaka	3,252,340	59.8	20.0	15.54	26.0	81.5	4	1,627	23	10,417.3
Saga	50,406	1.2	1.0	(5)			1	63	1	458.9
Sakai	182,147	2.32	1.8	1.02	44.0	57.0	1	116	1	778.9
Sasebo	205,989	2.34	2.0	.97	42.0	48.0	1	145		1,070.9
Sendai	223,630	4.53	3.0	1.22	27.0	41.0	1	130	1	935.5
Shimizu	68,617	1.41	.8	.74	52.0	84.0	1	153	1	1,116.7
Shimonoseki	196,022	1.42	.8	.51	36.0	63.8	1	190	1	836.4
Shizuoka	212,198	3.46	2.0	2.28	66.0	112.5	1	158	2	1,022.3
Takamatsu	111,207	1.8	1.5	1.40	78.0	96.0	1	116	2	833.1
Tokushima	119,581	2.3	1.4	1.7	74.0	121.0	1	141		1,127.9
Tokuyama	38,419	1.27	.73	.68	53.5	64.3	1	107		789.5
Tokyo	6,778,804	110.8	55.0	56.3	50.8	86.0	5	1,699	70	11,472.0
Toyama	127,859	1.88	1.88	1.87	99.5	99.5	1	176		1,478.1
Toyohashi	142,716	3.3	1.5	1.7	52.0	113.0	1	160		1,026.1
Tsu	68,625	1.47	1.0	1.18	81.0	98.0	1	76		730.0
Tsuruga	31,346	1.13	.8	.77	68.0	96.0	1	94		692.2
Ube	100,680	1.8	1.0	.42	23.0	42.0	1	103		726.7
Ujiyamada	52,555	.93	.8	.36	39.0	45.0	1	119		839.5
Utsonomiya	87,868	2.75	1.4	.94	34.2	67.1	1	115	1	802.9
Uwajima	52,101	1.0	.9	.52	52.0	58.0	2	159		1,106.3
Wakayama	195,203	4.0	2.0	2.10	52.5	105.0	1	125		883.8
Yawata	261,309	5.78	3.55	1.22	21.0	33.0	1	221	4	1,301.9
Yokkaichi	102,771	3.51	1.0	1.23	35.0	123.0	1	95		591.6
Yokohama	968,091	20.2	8.0	8.9	44.0	111.2	1	463	7	2,590.8
Other								490		2,334.6
TOTALS	20,836,646	411.0	192.16	178.10	43.3	92.2	81	14,569	175	98,511.9

1 With Osaka.
2 See Osaka.
3 No planned area.
4 Atomic bombing mission. Bomb weight not included.
5 No damage.

SOURCE: Twentieth AF Statistical Summary of its Operations Against Japan.

at three to five day intervals. All these factors contributed to a conspicuous increase in XXIBC performance. The reports for each month showed improvements in the number of missions flown, bomb weight delivered, and bombing accuracy and effectiveness. In both June and July 10 major missions were flown.

Operations Against Industrial Urban Areas

The March "Blitz" revealed that the overall Japanese economy was vulnerable to low level incendiary attacks, and LeMay ordered that maximum force be applied in repeated attacks in the shortest period of time. Tokyo was attacked once in March and twice in April, and the four other principal Japanese cities were attacked in a series of day and night missions from 14 May to 15 June. The first daylight mission against a major urban industrial area was flown on 14 May against northern Nagoya when 529 B-29s destroyed 3.2 square miles of the city for the loss of only 12 bombers. Two days later this raid was followed by a large-scale night attack against southern Nagoya, and then two missions against Tokyo on 23 and 25 May; all for the loss of 46 bombers in exchange for another 22 square miles of Japanese cities destroyed.

At this time large areas of Osaka, Yokohama, and Kobe remained intact. It was not possible to attack these cities by radar bombing, as it was difficult to distinguish the damaged from undamaged areas on the radarscope. LeMay decided to bomb these targets by day at altitudes of between 18,000 and 20,000ft. These missions occurred between 29 May and 15 June, and completed the plan to destroy the industrial areas of Japan's five largest cities. After these successful raids the XXIBC preyed on smaller cities that were chosen for:

1) Congestion and flammability.
2) Presence of war industries.
3) Presence of land and water transportation facilities.
4) City size.
5) The ease of radar location an identification.

Once the cities had been selected there were other factors that had to be considered. Some of the cities were located too far north, and the B-29s

had to be staged through Iwo Jima to hit them (Aomori was the only such mission). The bombers were to bomb by radar from 8,000 to 15,000ft, but on nights of good visibility bombing was done visually.

Small city missions began with raids against four urban industrial areas on 17 June, and did not end until the end of the war, with 57 smaller cities being successfully attacked in 60 missions The three unsuccessful attacks against cities (Ichinomiya, Omuta, and Uwajima) were repeated. The results were 57 cities substantially annihilated, with a total of 178.1 square miles destroyed.

Industrial Priority Targets

Whenever weather forecasts predicted that there was to be a high probability of visual bombing conditions over the target the XXIBC flew daylight raids against specific targets, primarily the aircraft component industry. Targets previously bombed unsuccessfully were bombed again, and additional factories were added to the target list. Once the aircraft industrial complex was destroyed other target complexes were bombed.

In planning these missions, one of the major problems was to provide for alternate targets in case visual bombing was not possible against the primary target. If the primary target was suitable for visual and radar bombing, the target would be bombed. If the primary target was blocked by weather for visual bombing and was unsuitable for radar bombing; an alternative target, usually an easy to hit urban area, was designated as the primary radar target.

The magnitude of these attacks, and the importance of the weather component are implicit in the fact that, between April and August, 48 missions were flown on 16 days, involving 4,356 sorties, which was 19% of the total XXIBC endeavor for that period. Of these 48 missions, on only 19 missions (40%) did 75% or more of the attacking bombers bomb the primary target visually; on 13 missions (27%) 25% to 75% of the bombers bombed the target visually; and on 16 missions (33%) the primary target was bombed by radar. When weather conditions allowed visual bombing the results were usually very good to excellent. Due to experience and continual training, along with lower bombing altitudes and decreased enemy opposition, bombing accuracy improved significantly. As more B-29s arrived in the Marianas the XXIBC was able to attack more than one target

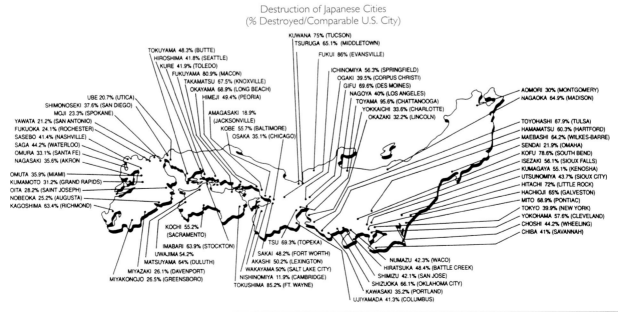

Destruction of Japanese Cities
(% Destroyed/Comparable U.S. City)

per day, and on 26 June nine targets were scheduled to be bombed. Fighters from the VII Fighter Command flew escort missions, but weather was again an intervening factor in the success of these missions.

In addition to the daylight attacks against priority targets, night missions against these targets were also flown. These night attacks were patterned after the success of the March urban incendiary missions. LeMay believed that by using a combination of radar navigation and flares to light the target area, visual bombing using HE bombs could be employed against precision targets that were not vulnerable to incendiary attack. Five missions on three nights were carried out using this procedure with poor results. Although the APQ-13 navigational radar took the flare ships over the target, the flares provided inadequate illumination of the target to allow the bombardiers to see the target through the optics of their bombsights. The remedy would be a reflex type bombsight, marker bombs, and improved flares, and no further missions of this type were scheduled until these remedies arrived.

The Japanese oil industry and related facilities were selected as a primary target, and the 315BW and its specialized bombers were conscripted for the task. The wing's B-29s were equipped with APQ-7 Eagle radar, which was designed for radar bombing, as it had 10 times the resolution of the APQ-13 sets. The Japanese oil complex was vulnerable, as many of the large refineries were located on or near the coast, which made them easy to identify on the new radar. Also, all armament except the .50cal tail guns were removed, allowing for a significant increase in bomb load, but dictated the attacks to be conducted during nighttime. The 315BW began operations on 26 June, and it carried out 15 missions to nine targets by the end of the war.

Tactical Operations

Tactical missions were conducted against Japanese airfields on Kyushu in conjunction with the invasion of Okinawa and are discussed later.

Mining Operations

Japan was dependent on water transportation for the movement of men and material, and the XXIBC began mining operations of the Japanese home waters on 27 March 1945. It had three main objectives:

1) To prevent the importation of raw materials and food to Japan.
2) To prevent the supply and movement of military forces.
3) To disrupt shipping in the Inland Sea.

The XXIBC mining campaign is discussed later in the chapter.

Atomic Bomb

By early August 1945 Japan was on the verge of defeat, as there few targets left without substantial damage, but the Japanese rulers refused to acknowledge their defeat. Sixteen hours after the atomic bomb was dropped on Hiroshima President Harry S. Truman announced, "If they (the Japanese) do not accept our terms, they may expect a rain of ruin from the air, the like of which has never been seen on this ear...." The defining event of the Second World War was the dropping of the atomic bombs on Hiroshima on 6 August and Nagasaki on 9 August 1945, as their specter shaped Cold War strategy for the next 45 years. The atomic bomb and missions are described later in the chapter.

SUMMARY OF TARGET DESTRUCTION

TARGET	ATTACKS	A/C BOMBING	TONS DROPPED	A/C LOST	SUMMARY OF RESULTS
URBAN AREAS					
NAGASAKI	1	24	87.0	1	.05 sq miles, or 1.5% of total area destroyed.
A/C INDUSTRIES					
MANCHURIA A/C MFG. CO., MUKDEN	2	99	348.3	7	Slight damage to A/C plant. Nearby arsenal suffered heaviest damage.
OKAYAMA A/C PLANT, FORMOSA	2	146*	1019.0*	2*	Of 80 bldgs, 43 destroyed and 12 damaged. Heavy damage.
ONURA A/C PLANT, KYUSHU	6	233**	669.5**	19**	287,300 sq ft, or 10.3% of total area destroyed.
OIL & PETROLEUM INDUSTRIES					
BUKUM IS. OIL STORAGE, SINGAPORE	2	46	114.5		Slight damage to surrounding bldgs based on strike photos only.
SAMBOE IS. OIL STORAGE, SINGAPORE	1	11	21.8		No post strike recon, damage unavailable.
SEBOROK IS. OIL STORAGE, SINGAPORE	1	11	23.2		No post strike recon, damage unavailable.
PLADJOE REF. PALEMBANG, SUMATRA	1	31	26.0	1	No post strike recon, damage unavailable.
IRON & STEEL PRODUCTIONS					
IMPERIAL IRON & STEEL WORKS, YAWATA	2	119	205.5	19	Slight damage; 1 bldg destroyed first raid, scattered hits on second raid.
SHOWA STEEL WORKS ANSHAN, MANCHURIA	3	249	562.8	6	Considerable damage; several direct hits; estimated 4 to 6 months out of commission after first raid.
RAIL FACILITIES, YARDS, STATIONS					
BANGUE MARSHALLING YARDS, BANGKOK	1	55	382.2	1	Heavy damage; both A.F.'s destroyed, including 90 items of rolling stock.
MALAGON R.R. YARDS, RANGOON	1	44	418.2	1	Considerable damage to roundhouse and other buildings.
CENTRAL R.R. REPAIR SHOPS & MARSHALLING YARDS, KUALA, LUMPUR, MALAYA	2	73	266.2		439,568 sq ft, or 57.5% of total area destroyed. (50% roundhouse destroyed and 3.1 mi of tracks, 631 items of rolling stock, 6 locomotives, and several buildings.)
RAMA VI R.R. BRIDGE, BANGKOK	3	135	701.0	4	Few direct hits & near misses scored. Center span nearly collapsed. Tracks heavily dam...
PORTS, HARBORS, NAVAL BASES					
HANKOW DOCK AREA	1	84	532.4		40-50% target destroyed.
KEELUNG WHARVES, FORMOSA	1	39	266.0		No post strike recon, damage unavailable.
SINGAPORE HARBOR AREA	5	321	655.0	9	1,722,600 sq ft - Includes damage done to docks and naval base.
SAIGON HARBOR AREA	2	55	240.3	1	Slight damage. Urban area suffered heavy damage.
MAIN QUAY, TAKAO, FORMOSA	1	13	84.8	1	Heavy damage to quay and shipping.
AIRFIELDS & AIRDROMES					
KAGI AIRFIELD, FORMOSA	1	54	361.8		353,700 sq ft, or 42% of total area destroyed. All hangars severely damaged.
SHINCHIKU AIRFIELD, FORMOSA	1	77	522.0	1	99,000 sq ft, or 16.2% of total area destroyed.
EINANSHO AIRFIELD, FORMOSA	1	10	62.5		Damage unavailable.
TACTICAL TARGETS					
RANGOON SUPPLY DUMPS AND MINGALDON	3	202	1362.2		At least 220 bldgs destroyed plus some adjacent barracks, 39 barracks & 5 admin bldgs
CANTONMENT AREA					damaged.
MISCELLANEOUS & OTHER					
HEITO ARSENAL, FORMOSA	1	1	6.0		Damage unavailable.
BANGKOK AREA	1	77	353.0	5	Damage unavailable.
SECONDARY & TARGET OF OPP.		402	1614.3		
TOTAL	46	2611	10925.5	80	

MINING			
MISSION NO.		A/C MINING	NO OF MINES
5 MOESI RIVER CHANNEL, SUMATRA		8	16
30 SAIGON AREA		25	184
31 SINGAPORE AREA		41	191
39 YANGTZE RIVER NEAR SHANGHAI TAISING REACH NEAR NANKING		11	132
40 JOHORE STRAITS, SINGAPORE		10	55
46 YANGTZE HARBOR AREA, SHANGHAI		10	120
47 SAIGON & CAM RANH BAY AREA		17	121
48 SINGAPORE AREA		32	125
TOTAL		154	964

NOTE: Number of attacks does not indicate number of missions as there were 2 or more primary targets on some missions.
* Includes data for Heito Airfield, Formosa, an alternate primary on one mission.
** Includes data for Sasebo Dock Area, Tobata Iron & Steel Co, Tsientsin-Pukow R. R. Yards, which were alternate primary targets.

XXI BOMBER COMMAND MISSIONS 1944-1945

MISSION NUMBER	DATE		PRIMARY TARGET	WINGS	A/C ABR	BOMB PRI	BOMB TONS	TIME OVER OVER PRIMARY	ALTITUDE OF ATTACK	TARGET WEATHER	A/C LOST	E/A CLAIMED	A/C IWO
302	28/29	Jul	Uwajima U/A	314	32	29	205	0116-0225	10-11230	4-6/10	0	0-0-0	2
303	28/29	Jul	Shimotsu I/O	315	82	76	658	2302-0123	10-12000	4-10/10	0	0-0-0	2
304	29/30	Jul	4 Targets M	313	29	24	161	0001-0156	7-12900	4-8/10	0	0-0-0	17
305	1/2	Aug	7 Targets M	313	43	37	242	0051-0223	8-12000	0-10/10	0	0-0-0	17
306	1/2	Aug	Hachioji U/A	58	180	169	1593	0145-0329	14-16000	0-8/10	1	0-0-0	36
307	1/2	Aug	Toyama U/A	73	182	173	1466	0136-0327	12-13600	0/10	0	0-0-0	8
308	1/2	Aug	Nagaoka U/A	313	136	125	924	2335-0058	12-13400	0-2/10	0	0-0-0	38
309	1/2	Aug	Mito U/A	314	167	160	1145	0142-0316	12-15200	8-10/10	0	0-0-0	6
310	1/2	Aug	Kawasaki I/O	315	128	120	1017	2314-0046	16-18600	0-10/10	0	0-0-0	7
311	5/6	Aug	9 Targets M	313	30	27	176	2332-0232	7-8600	0/10	0	0-0-0	11
312	5/6	Aug	Saga U/A	58	65	63	459	0041-0056	12-15500	0-9/10	1	0-0-0	16
313	5/6	Aug	Maebashi U/A	313	102	92	724	2328-0108	15-16900	0-9/10	0	0-0-0	15
314	5/6	Aug	Nishinomiya U/A	73/314	261	250	2004	0125-0201	12-16000	0-8/10	1	0-0-0	24
315	5/6	Aug	Ube I/O	315	111	106	938	2324-0131	10-12600	0-6/10	0	0-0-0	5
316	5/6	Aug	Imabari U/A	58	66	64	510	0105-0147	12-12800	0-5/10	0	0-0-0	5
317	7	Aug	Toyokawa Arsenal	58/73/313	131	124	813	1113-1139	16-23600	0-4/10	1	0-0-0	7
318	7/8	Aug	7 Targets M	313	32	29	189	2302-0132	1-12000	0-8/10	0	0-0-0	11
319	8	Aug	Yawata U/A	58/73/313	245	221	1302	1101-1136	19-24500	4-6/10	4	2-0-2	100
320	8	Aug	Tokyo I/A	314	69	60	289	1727-1744	19-22450	0-2/10	3	0-0-0	12
321	8/9	Aug	Fukayama U/A	58	98	91	556	2325-0035	13-13800	0-5/10	0	0-0-0	4
322	9/10	Aug	Amagasaki I/O	315	107	95	918	0129-0311	15-17300	0-8/10	0	0-0-0	14
323	10	Aug	Tokyo Arsenal	314	76	70	320	1050-1059	22-26200	5-7/10	0	0-0-0	8
324	10/11	Aug	5 Targets M	313	31	31	203	0032-0147	7-12900	0-6/10	0	0-0-0	2
325	14	Aug	Hikari Arsenal	58	167	157	885	1417-1518	15-17700	0-4/10	0	0-0-0	20
326	14	Aug	Osaka Arsenal	73	161	145	702	1416-1501	22-25000	0-5/10	0	0-0-0	4
327	14	Aug	Marifu M/Y	313	115	108	710	1225-1319	15-18500	0-5/10	0	0-0-0	40
328	14/15	Aug	Tsuchizaki I/O	315	141	132	954	0048-0339	15-11800	5-10/10	0	0-0-0	13
329	14/15	Aug	Kumagaya U/A	313/314	93	81	593	0123-0239	14-19000	0-5/10	0	0-0-0	5
330	14/15	Aug	Isesake U/A	73/314	93	86	614	0108-0315	15-18200	7-10/10	0	0-0-0	6
331	14/15	Aug	4 Targets M	313	39	35	224	0042-0308	8-12800	0-6/10	0	0-0-0	1

Abbreviations:

AA—Antiaircraft
ABR—Airborne
A/C—Aircraft
A/D—Air Depot
A/F—Airfield
Ch—Chemical
D/A—Dock Area
E/A—Enemy Aircraft
F/S—Fuel Station
I/A—Industrial/Aircraft factory
I/Ac—Industrial/Aircraft components

I/Ae—Industrial/Aircraft engines
I/Ar—Industrial/Area
I/Me—Industrial/Light Metals
I/O—Industrial/Oil Refinery
I/Os—Industrial/Oil Storage
M—Mining
M/Y—Marshalling Yard
PRI—Primary
S/B—Seaplane Base
U/A—Urban Area
U/B—U-boat Base

The time given over the primary target is local, Mariana time.

Source: Resume 20th Air Force Missions.

Above and following: *Statistical Digest,* Office of Statistical Control, December 1945

Weather and Jet Streams

During the early high altitude daylight visual bombing missions weather was the most serious problem, and missions were frequently delayed for several days awaiting favorable forecasts. Good forecasts did not mean that the weather would be good over the target. Only 30% of the bombers sent out with favorable weather forecasts were able to bomb their primary targets, and of these many bombed through broken clouds. The remaining 70% arrived at the target area to find it obscured by clouds, and were forced to bomb by radar, or move on to secondary targets.

The weather over the Japanese Homeland was unreliable, and long-range forecasting was vital to mission planners. Neither the Russians nor Chinese had the means or ability to provide data from the Asian continent, from which the future weather over Japan would flow. To forecast the weather on the 1,300-mile route from the Marianas and over Japan the XXIBC sent out three daily weather strikes. The primary purpose of the weather strike was to gather weather data, but to make the mission more beneficial these weather planes were loaded with nuisance bombs to be dropped on Japan.

In the winter large masses of cold air swept from Siberia and the Asian Continent towards the entire length of the Japanese island chain. When the cold, dry Siberian air mass approached Japan it picked up heat and mois-

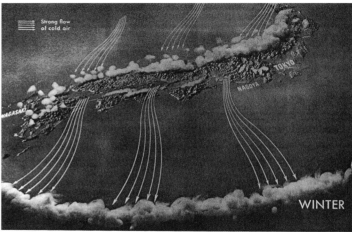

"Winter Weather" photo shows how Japan confronts a B-29 pilot approaching from Saipan, looking northwest.

XXI BOMBER COMMAND MISSIONS 1944-1945

MISSION NUMBER	DATE	PRIMARY TARGET	WINGS	A/C ABR	BOMB PRI	BOMB TONS	TIME OVER PRIMARY	ALTITUDE OF ATTACK	TARGET WEATHER	A/C LOST	E/A CLAIMED	A/C IWO
76	18 Apr	Tachiari A/F	73	23	20	80	0841-0854	15-15400	0/10	2	1-3-6	5
77	18 Apr	Kanoya East A/F	313	20	19	114	0850-0917	16-16800	0/10	0	0-0-0	
78	18 Apr	Kanoya A/F	314	33	30	86	0850-0858	18-19140	2-7/10	0	0-0-0	
79	18 Apr	Izumi A/F	73	23	21	82	0829-0858	15-16300	0/10	0	0-0-0	1
80	18 Apr	Kokubu A/F	313	22	19	137	0845-0901	15-17000	0/10	0	0-0-0	
81	18 Apr	Nittagahara A/F	314	11	11	33	1003-1023	18-18200	2-7/10	0	0-0-0	
82	21 Apr	Oita A/F	73	30	17	81	0755-0756	14-15300	0/10	0	0-0-6	1
83	21 Apr	Kanoya East A/F	313	33	27	179	0809-0901	16-17350	0/10	0	0-0-0	
84	21 Apr	Kanoya A/F	314	33	30	136	0804-0835	16-17800	0/10	0	0-0-0	
85	21 Apr	Usa A/F	73	30	29	136	0911-0922	14-15800	0/10	0	0-0-0	2
86	21 Apr	Kokubu A/F	313	35	34	219	0920-0953	12-14000	0/10	0	0-0-0	
87	21 Apr	Kushira A/F	314	31	28	133	0959-1007	17-17675	0/10	0	0-0-0	
88	21 Apr	Tachiari A/F	73	21	17	80	1003-1004	18-19200	0/10	0	0-1-1	2
89	21 Apr	Izumi A/F	313	16	13	89	0814-0949	14-14500	0/10	0	1-3-5	
90	21 Apr	Nittagahara A/F	314	23	22	97	0925-0934	15-16500	0/10	0	0-0-0	
91	22 Apr	Izumi A/F	73	21	19	81	0852-0905	16-18000	0/10	0	0-2-2	1
92	22 Apr	Kushira A/F	313	18	9	42	0858-0945	16-16600	0/10	0	0-0-0	
93	22 Apr	Miyazaki A/F	314	22	22	101	0834-1010	14-17500	0/10	0	0-0-0	
94	22 Apr	Tomitaka A/F	73	18	18	77	0926	16-17500	0/10	0	0-0-0	0
95	22 Apr	Kanoya A/F	313	25	19	86	0834-0936	15-15950	0/10	1	0-0-0	
96	24 Apr	Tachikawa I/Ae	73/313/314	131	101	474	0952-1006	10-14500	0/10	5	17/23/25	
97	26 Apr	Usa A/F	73	21	18	81	0816-0844	15-26500	10/10	0	0-0-0	
98	26 Apr	Oita A/F	73	22	19	81	0713-0807	13-24000	10/10	0	0-0-0	
99	26 Apr	Saeki A/F	73	23	19	81	0735-0818	20-25390	10/10	0	0-0-0	
100	26 Apr	Tomitaka A/F	73	22	21	102	0707-0845	13-24500	10/10	0	0-0-0	
101	26 Apr	Matsuyama A/F	313	37	15	77	0947-1032	22-26615	10/10	0	0-0-0	
102	26 Apr	Nittagahara A/F	313	23	18	101	0940-0958	13-25000	10/10	0	0-0-0	
103	26 Apr	Miyazaki A/F	313	21	19	95	1017-1119	13-19000	10/10	0	0-0-0	
104	26 Apr	Kanoya A/F	314	22	19	82	1052-1131	20-27000	10/10	0	0-0-0	
105	26 Apr	Kushira A/F	314	22	13	72	1104-1203	22-29000	10/10	0	0-0-0	
106	26 Apr	Kokubu A/F	314	22	17	88	1054-1139	20570	10/10	0	0-0-0	
107	26 Apr	Miyakonojo A/F	314	21	17	105	1107-1153	10-26100	10/10	0	0-0-0	
108	27 Apr	Izumi A/F	73	22	21	89	0946-1045	15-17700	0-2/10	1	1-1-1	1
109	27 Apr	Miyazaki A/F	73	21	21	89	1030-1034	11-12900	2/10	0	0-0-0	1
110	27 Apr	Kokubu A/F	313	22	19	117	0937-0958	10-12000	0/10	0	4-3-6	
111	27 Apr	Miyakonojo A/F	313	18	14	100	1017-1051	10-12000	0/10	0	0-0-1	
112	27 Apr	Kanoya A/F	314	21	20	107	0935-0955	16-17020	0/10	1	0-0-2	
113	27 Apr	Kushira A/F	314	19	17	83	0925-0931	15-17610	0/10	1	0-0-11	
114	28 Apr	Izumi A/F	73	24	23	144	0950-0958	15-17380	0/10	0	0-0-0	2
115	28 Apr	Miyazaki A/F	73	20	20	124	1052-1053	11-12800	0/10	1	0-0-0	1
116	28 Apr	Kokubu A/F	313	20	17	113	1012-1013	12-12250	0/10	1	2-2-6	
117	28 Apr	Miyakonojo A/F	313	19	17	122	0951-0952	11-12000	0/10	0	1-1-4	
118	28 Apr	Kanoya A/F	314	23	22	118	0935-0957	15-17000	0/10	1	0-1-0	
119	28 Apr	Kushira A/F	314	23	23	128	0925-0927	16-17800	0/10	2	10-7-10	
120	29 Apr	Miyazaki A/F	73	21	19	109	0858	15-15950	1/10	0	0-0-0	2
121	29 Apr	Miyakonojo A/F	73	23	22	127	0817-0820	14-16600	1/10	2	11-2-2	7
122	129 Apr	Kokubu A/F	313	22	22	157	0805-0806	12-13000	0/10	0	12-5-7	
123	29 Apr	Kanoya East A/F	313	15	14	81	0821-0822	14-14500	0/10	0	5-3-6	
124	29 Apr	Kanoya A/F	314	20	18	96	0925-0936	17-18500	0/10	0	0-0-0	
125	29 Apr	Kushira A/F	314	20	16	89	0954-0957	17-17600	0/10	0	0-0-1	
126	30 Apr	Tachikawa A/D	73/313	106	69	378	1122-1154	17-21500	6-10/10	0	1-0-4	15
127	30 Apr	Kanoya A/F	314	11	11	61	1140	18200	0/10	0	1-0-2	
128	30 Apr	Kanoya East A/F	314	11	10	59	1138	17100	0/10	0	2-1-2	
129	30 Apr	Kokubu A/F	314	10	5	26	1142-1144	17-17900	0/10	0	6-4-9	
130	30 Apr	Oita A/F	314	11	10	58	1113-1114	17-17900	9-10/10	0	0-0-0	
131	30 Apr	Tomitaka A/F	314	12	11	59	1114-1115	16-17550	0/10	0	0-0-0	
132	30 Apr	Saeki A/F	314	11	11	65	1113	17-17700	7/10	0	0-0-0	
133	3 May	Tachiari A/F	314	11	9	52	1607-1608	18-18800	0/10	0	10-4-2	6
134	3 May	Miyazaki A/F	314	11	11	66	1612-1614	17-17550	0/10	0	0-0-0	
135	3 May	Miyakonojo A/F	314	11	11	63	1557-1558	17-18100	0/10	0	0-1-?	
136	3 May	Kanoya A/F	314	11	8	43	1636	18000	0/10	0	0-0-0	2
137	3 May	Kanoya East A/F	314	11	11	59	1631	17400	0/10	1	0-1-0	1
138	3 May	Kokubu A/F	314	11	9	48	1634	18500	0/10	0	0-0-0	3
139	3/4 May	Shimonoseki M	313	97	88	577	0000-0335	4-8650	5/10	0	0-0-0	7
140	4 May	Oita A/F	314	22	11	55	1006-1007	17-18040	0/10	1	0-0-6	10
141	4 May	Omura A/F	314	10	10	43	0953-0956	18-18500	0/10	0	1-0-0	4
142	4 May	Saeki A/F	314	9	9	46	1008-1015	18-18450	0/10	0	0-0-0	1
143	4 May	Matsuyama A/F	314	21	17	90	0909-0925	18-18900	0/10	0	0-0-4	2
144	5 May	Oita A/F	314	17	17	105	1316-1320	17-17900	0/10	0	1-0-0	
145	5 May	Tachiari A/F	314	11	10	61	1325	18-18500	0/10	2	7-7-7	
146	5 May	Hiro I/A	58/73	170	148	578	1140-1211	18-24700	3/10	2	3-2-1	68
147	5 May	Kanoya A/F	314	11	10	55	2053	18000	0/10	1	0-0-0	
148	5 May	Chiran A/F	314	11	8	32	2111	17100	0/10	0	0-0-0	1
149	5 May	Ibusuki A/F	314	10	10	55	2038	17000	0/10	0	0-0-0	
150	5/6 May	Kobe, etc. M	313	96	86	548	0016-0419	5-8400	7/10	0	0-0-0	2

XXI BOMBER COMMAND MISSIONS 1944-1945

MISSION NUMBER	DATE	PRIMARY TARGET	WINGS	A/C ABR	BOMB PRI	BOMB TONS	TIME OVER OVER PRIMARY	ALTITUDE OF ATTACK	TARGET WEATHER	A/C LOST	E/A CLAIMED	A/C IWO
1	28 Oct	Truk U/B	73	18	14	42	0855-0900	25-27400	0/10	0	0-0-0	
2	30 Oct	Truk U/B	73	18	8	24	1100-1103	25-27400	5/10	0	0-0-0	
3	2 Nov	Truk U/B	73	20	17	43	1034-1135	25-27300	7/10	0	0-0-0	
4	5 Nov	Iwo Jima A/F	73	36	24	120	1623-1639	26-27500	9/10	0	0-0-0	
5	6 Nov	Iwo Jima A/F	73	17	6	30	1232-1234	27-29000	4/10	1	8-0-0	
6	11 Nov	Truk U/B	73	9	8	40	1355-1357	25-26000	2/10	0	0-0-1	
7	24 Nov	Tokyo I/Ae	73	111	24	58	1312-1532	27-32000	2-7/10	2	7-18-9	
8	27 Nov	Tokyo I/Ae	73	81	0	0			10/10	1	0-0-0	
9	29/30 Nov	Tokyo I/Ar	73	29	23	78	0050-0527	25-33200	10/10	1	0-0-0	
10	3 Dec	Tokyo I/Ae	73	86	60	141	0503-0630	16-33100	0/10	5	10-11-18	
11	8 Dec	Iwo Jima A/F	73	82	61	599	1020-1150	19-23400	7-10/10	0	0-0-0	
12	13 Dec	Nagoya I/Ae	73	90	71	181	1457-1638	26-32300	3/10	4	4-1-0	
13	18 Dec	Nagoya I/A	73	89	63	154	1400-1543	28-32000	5/10	4	5-11-12	
14	22 Dec	Nagoya I/Ae	73	78	48	130	1404-1558	28-32600	6-10/10	3	9-17-15	
15	24 Dec	Iwo Jima A/F	73	29	23	109	1424-1535	19-21800	7/10/10	0	0-0-0	
16	27 Dec	Tokyo I/Ae	73	72	39	103	1342-1503	28-33800	2/10	3	21-10-7	
17	3 Jan	Nagoya D/A	73	97	57	150	1545-1633	28-31500	6/10	5	14-14-20	
18	9 Jan	Tokyo I/Ae	73	72	18	42	1513-1535	29-34400	0/10	6	13-3-11	
19	14 Jan	Nagoya I/A	73	73	40	94	1540-1628	29-32000	7-10/10	5	16-7-26	
20	19 Jan	Akashi I/A	73	80	62	153	1450-1524	25-27400	2/10	0	4-4-8	
21	21 Jan	Truk A/F	313	33	30	165	1034-1108	25-26000	1/10	0	0-0-0	
22	23 Jan	Nagoya I/A	73	73	28	83	0535-0547	25-27200	9/10	2	33-22-40	
23	24 Jan	Iwo Jima A/F	313	28	20	120	1228-1330	26-28000	0-10/10	0	0-0-0	
24	27 Jan	Tokyo I/Ae	73	76	0	0			10/10	9	60-17-39	
25	29 Jan	Iwo Jima A/F	313	33	28	168	1428-1447	23-25200	0-3/10	0	0-0-0	
26	4 Feb	Kobe U/A	73/313	110	69	185	1557-1656	24-27000	5/10	2	4-20-39	
27	8 Feb	Truk A/F	313	31	30	150	1057-1133	29-30700	8/10	0	0-0-0	
28	9 Feb	Truk A/F	313	30	29	145	1119-1121	24-26000	2/10	0	0-0-0	
29	10 Feb	Ota I/A	73/313	118	84	248	1605-1641	26-29400	1/10	12	21-15-26	
30	11 Feb	Sea Search	313	9			1518	3000	10/10	0	0-0-0	
31	12 Feb	Iwo Jima AA	313	21	21	84	1211-1250	24-24500	3/10	0	0-0-0	
32	12 Feb	Sea Search	313	10			1643-2030	2000	1-10/10	1	0-0-0	
33	14 Feb	Sea Search	313	6			1415-1725	3000	4/10	0	0-0-0	
34	15 Feb	Nagoya I/Ae	73/313	117	33	91	1502-1555	25-34000	0-3/10	1	7-8-23	
35	17 Feb	Truk U/B	73	9	8	10	1646-1647	26-26900	0/10	0	0-0-0	
36	18 Feb	Truk A/F	313	36	36	171	1227-1340	24-25900	1/10	0	0-0-0	
37	19 Feb	Tokyo I/Ae	73/313	150	0	0			5/10	6	39-16-37	
38	25 Feb	Tokyo U/A	73/313/314	229	172	454	1458-1642	23-31000	10/10	3	0-0-0	
39	4 Mar	Tokyo I/Ae	73/313	192	0	0			10/10	1	0-0-0	1
40	9/10 Mar	Tokyo U/A	73/313/314	325	270	1667	0107-0400	5-9200	3/10	14	0-0-0	9
41	11/12 Mar	Nagoya U/A	73/313/314	310	285	1793	0119-0417	5-8500	2/10	1	0-0-0	
42	13/14 Mar	Osaka U/A	73/313/314	206	274	1678	0057-0425	5-9400	5/10	2	1-0-0	
43	16/17 Mar	Kobe U/A	73/313/314	330	304	2331	0338-0546	5-9000	1/10	3	1-0-0	18
44	18/19 Mar	Nagoya U/A	73/313/314	310	290	1863	0304-0548	4-9000	2/10	1	0-0-0	
45	24/24 Mar	Nagoya I/Ae	73/313/314	248	223	1526	0100-0217	5-9800	3/10	5	0-0-0	
46	27 Mar	Kyushu A/F	73/314	161	151	521	1140-1259	14-18300	1-7/10	0	1-2-4	
47	27/28 Mar	Shimonoseki M	313	102	94	571	2337-0142	5-8000	0-8/10	3	1-0-0	
48	30/31 Mar	Nagoya I/Ae	314	14	12	52	0046-0150	7-7900	7/10	0	0-0-0	
49	30/31 Mar	Shimonoseki M	313	94	85	513	0053-0348	5-8200	0-8/10	1	0-0-0	
50	31 Mar	Kyushu A/F	73/314	149	137	538	1140-1242	14-18100	0-3/10	1	11-5-3	
51	1/2 Apr	Tokyo I/Ae	73	121	115	1019	0301-0443	6-7960	0/10	6	1-1-0	7
52	1/2 Apr	Kure M	313	6	6	24	2302-2333	25-26460	0/10	0	0-0-0	
53	2/3 Apr	Hiroshima M	313	10	9	56	0116-0136	6-6100	3/10	0	0-0-0	
54	3/4 Apr	Hiroshima M	313	9	9	54	0010-0045	6-6150	1-10/10	0	0-0-0	
55	3/4 Apr	Shizuoka I/A	314	49	48	223	0230-0435	7-9000	10/10	0	1-0-0	
56	3/4 Apr	Koisumi I/A	313	68	48	274	0214-0341	7-7950	10/10	0	1-0-0	
57	3/4 Apr	Tachikawa I/A	73	115	61	503	0330-0534	6-7200	9/10	1	0-0-0	4
58	7 Apr	Tokyo I/Ae	73	107	101	490	1100-1106	11-15650	2/10	3	80-23-50	31
59	7 Apr	Nagoya I/Ae	313/314	194	153	680	1200-1354	16-25000	1/10	2	21-11-22	
60	8 Apr	Kanoya A/F	73	32	29	116	1129-1153	17-19300	10/10	0	0-0-0	2
61	8 Apr	Kayoya A/F	313	21	6	27	1132-1135	17-18800	10/10	1	0-0-0	
62	9/10 Apr	Shimonoseki M	313	20	16	94	0140-0216	5-6300	8/10	0	0-0-0	
63	12 Apr	Tokyo I/Ae	73	114	93	490	1208-1221	12-17500	2/10	0	11-2-10	32
64	12 Apr	Koriyama Ch	313	82	66	274	1220-1330	7-15000	0/10	0	0-0-0	
65	12 Apr	Koriyama Ch	314	85	70	172	1233-1328	7-9000	0/10	2	0-0-0	
66	12/13 Apr	Shimonoseki M	313	5	5	20	0146-0216	6-7110	0/10	0	0-0-0	
67	13/14 Apr	Tokyo Arsenal	73/313/314	348	327	2124	2357-0336	6-1100	0/10	7	6-0-2	
68	15/16 Apr	Kawasaki U/A	313/314	219	194	1110	2343-0156	6-10000	0-3/10	12	NA	
69	15/16 Apr	Tokyo U/A	73	118	109	769	2325-0055	8-10100	0-3/10	1	1-0-0	2
70	17 Apr	Izumi A/F	73	22	20	80	1528-1529	15-16100	0/10	0	0-0-0	0
71	17 Apr	Tachiari A/F	73	21	21	84	1551-1600	15-16000	0/10	0	1-6-2	2
72	17 Apr	Kokubu A/F	313	24	20	138	1530-1538	17300	0/10	0	0-0-1	
73	17 Apr	Kanoya East A/F	313	21	20	118	1547-1550	16-17300	0/10	0	0-0-0	
74	17 Apr	Nittagahara A/F	314	10	7	21	1610	18-18500	0/10	0	0-0-0	
75	17 Apr	Kanoya A/F	314	34	30	73	1538-1544	17-19400	0/10	0	0-0-0	

XXI BOMBER COMMAND MISSIONS 1944-1945

MISSION NUMBER	DATE	PRIMARY TARGET	WINGS	A/C ABR	BOMB PRI	BOMB TONS	TIME OVER PRIMARY	ALTITUDE OF ATTACK	TARGET WEATHER	A/C LOST	E/A CLAIMED	A/C IWO
227	26 Jun	Nagoya Ars., etc.	314	32	25	144	1010-1029	15-19910	0/10	1	4-2-1	4
228	26 Jun	Kagamigahara I/A	58	79	60	412	1012-1055	15-16900	0-3/10	1	6-3-3	11
229	26 Jun	Eitoku I/A	313	67	50	346	1013-1034	17-24700	0-10/10	2	0-0-0	15
230	26 Jun	Nagoya I/Me	314	33	29	150	0919-1034	17-25000	0-10/10	0	0-0-0	7
231	26 Jun	Kagamigahara I/A	314	35	25	143	1026-1100	14-17400	0/10	1	9-1-2	4
232	26/27 Jun	Yokkaichi I/O	315	35	33	223	2335-0150	15-16000	10/10	0	0-0-0	1
233	27/28 Jun	Kobe, etc. M	313	30	29	187	0051-0324	6-8700	0-10/10	0	0-0-0	2
234	28/29 Jun	Okayama U/A	58	141	138	982	0343-0407	11-13300	0-10/10	1	0-0-0	4
235	28/29 Jun	Sasebo U/A	73	145	141	1059	0137-0253	10-11700	90/10	0	0-0-0	8
236	28/29 Jun	Moji U/A	313	101	91	626	0111-0243	10-11600	10/10	0	0-0-0	2
237	28/29 Jun	Nobeoka U/A	314	122	117	829	0246-0417	7-12000	8/10	0	0-0-0	6
238	29/30 Jun	Kadamatsu I/O	315	36	32	209	0106-0137	15-16875	8/10	0	0-0-0	
239	29/30 Jun	Shimonoseki M	313	29	25	165	0121-0243	4-8500	0-10/10	0	0-0-0	1
240	1/2 Jul	Kure U/A	58	160	152	1082	0102-0305	10-11800	6/10	0	0-0-0	16
241	1/2 Jul	Kumamoto U/A	73	162	154	1113	0059-0230	10-11500	9/10	1	0-0-0	4
242	1/2 Jul	Ube U/A	313	112	100	715	0147-1312	10-11600	1-5/10	0	0-0-0	22
243	1/2 Jul	Shimonoseki U/A	314	141	127	833	0325-0400	7-19000	4-9/10	1	0-0-0	22
244	1/2 Jul	Shimonoseki M	313	28	24	161	0053-0233	7-8700	4-10/10	0	0-0-0	2
245	2/3 Jul	Minoshima I/O	315	40	39	297	0108-0207	15-16000	4-10/10	0	0-0-0	
246	3/4 Jul	Shimonoseki M	313	31	26	253	0037-0311	7-8900	0-4/10	0	0-0-0	5
247	3/4 Jul	Takamatsu U/A	58	126	116	833	0356-0542	10-11100	0/10	2	0-0-0	27
248	3/4 Jul	Kochi U/A	73	129	125	1061	0252-0352	11-11530	1/10	1	0-0-0	6
249	3/4 Jul	Himeji U/A	313	107	106	767	0050-0229	10-11500	4-7/10	0	0-0-0	4
250	3/4 Jul	Tokushima U/A	314	137	129	1051	0224-0419	10-16940	0/10	0	0-0-0	3
251	6/7 Jul	Chiba U/A	58	129	124	890	0239-0405	10-11500	10/10	0	0-0-0	14
252	6/7 Jul	Akashi U/A	73	131	123	975	0115-0227	7-8200	4-8/10	0	0-0-0	2
253	6/7 Jul	Shimizu U/A	313	136	133	1030	0133-0310	7-8300	4-10/10	1	0-0-0	2
254	6/7 Jul	Kofu U/A	314	138	131	970	0047-0235	11-17100	8/10	0	0-0-0	3
255	6/7 Jul	Maruzen I/O	315	60	59	442	0019-0118	10-11500	10/10	0	0-0-0	
256	9/10 Jul	Shimonoseki M	313	31	29	193	0102-0317	6-8800	0-9/10	1	0-0-0	9
257	9/10 Jul	Sendai U/A	58	131	123	909	0103-0305	10-10700	3/10	1	0-0-0	13
258	9/10 Jul	Sakai U/A	73	124	115	779	0233-0406	10-11350	1/10	0	0-0-0	2
259	9/10 Jul	Wakayama U/A	313	109	108	800	0058-0258	10-11600	1/10	0	0-0-0	1
260	9/10 Jul	Gifu U/A	314	135	129	899	0034-0220	14-17700	0/10	2	0-0-0	3
261	9/10 Jul	Yokkaichi I/O	315	64	61	469	2340-0038	15-16950	0/10	0	0-0-0	2
262	11/12 Jul	Shimonoseki	313	30	25	150	0032-0247	7-9400	4/10/10	0	0-0-0	7
263	12/13 Jul	Utsunomiya U/A	58	130	115	803	0019-0230	13-14600	10/10	1	0-0-0	27
264	12/13 Jul	Ichinomiya U/A	73	130	123	772	0154-0345	6-12200	10/10	0	0-0-0	3
265	12/13 Jul	Tsuruga U/A	313	98	92	679	0000-0207	12-13400	10/10	0	0-0-0	2
266	12/13 Jul	Uwajima U/A	314	130	123	873	0013-0226	10-16400	10/10	0	0-0-0	6
267	12/13 Jul	Kawasaki I/O	315	60	53	452	0106-0219	15-16700	8-10/10	2	0-0-0	
268	13/14 Jul	Shimonoseki M	313	31	30	199	0012-0327	6-8600	0-10/10	0	0-0-0	18
269	15/16 Jul	5 Targets M	313	28	26	172	2308-0325	8-8400	8-10/10	0	0-0-0	17
270	15/16 Jul	Kadamatsu I/O	315	69	59	477	0041-0201	10-11700	3-10/10	0	0-0-0	5
271	16/17 Jul	Namazu U/A	58	128	119	1036	0213-0352	10-11600	7-10/10	0	0-0-0	5
272	16/17 Jul	Oita U/A	73	129	124	790	0112-0232	10-11500	4/10	0	0-0-0	2
273	16/17 Jul	Kuwana U/A	313	99	94	693	0225-0340	10-11300	10/10	0	0-0-0	4
274	16/17 Jul	Hiratsuka U/A	314	132	129	1163	0032-0212	10-15200	10/10	0	0-0-0	11
275	17/18 Jul	5 Targets M	313	30	27	178	0048-0311	7-8500	4-10/10	0	0-0-0	7
276	19/20 Jul	12 Targets M	313	31	27	184	0003-0247	7-8400	0-10/10	1	0-0-0	11
277	19/20 Jul	Fukui U/A	58	130	127	953	0024-0145	12-14000	0-3/10	0	0-0-0	16
278	19/20 Jul	Hitachi U/A	73	130	125	963	0020-0153	12-13650	10/10	2	0-0-0	1
279	19/20 Jul	Chosi U/A	313	97	91	629	0131-0252	10-11400	3-10/10	0	0-0-0	3
280	19/20 Jul	Okazaki U/A	314	130	126	850	0152-0310	12-16300	0-9/10	0	0-0-0	4
281	19/20 Jul	Amagasaki I/O	315	84	83	702	0020-0100	15-16900	8-10/10	0	0-0-0	1
282	23/24 Jul	3 Targets M	313	29	23	156	0137-0257	7-8300	3-10/10	1	0-0-0	11
283	23/24 Jul	Ube I/O	315	80	72	620	0103-0240	12-15600	5/10	0	0-0-0	8
284	24 Jul	Osaka I/Me	58	90	82	488	1251-1322	19-22100	0-3/10	1	0-0-0	42
285	24 Jul	Takarazuka I/A	58	88	77	475	1133-1203	19-20600	0-4/10	0	0-0-0	40
286	24 Jul	Osaka & Kuwana	73	170	154	1010	1144-1227	19-23000	9/10	0	0-0-0	39
287	24 Jul	Eitoku I/A	313	74	66	451	1125-1152	20-23800	10/10	0	0-0-0	26
288	24 Jul	City of Tsu	313	41	38	280	1127-1154	15-18600	10/10	0	0-0-0	1
289	24 Jul	City of Tsu	314	81	75	298	1138-1154	18-22600	10/10	0	0-0-0	15
290	24 Jul	Handa A/I	314	81	77	537	1138-1156	15-19700	10/10	0	0-0-0	15
291	25/26 Jul	Kawasaki I/O	315	83	75	668	2323-0003	16-18100	0-4/10	1	0-0-0	3
292	25/26 Jul	6 Targets M	313	30	29	195	0050-0157	6-8400	6-10/10	0	0-0-0	8
293	26/27 Jul	Matsuyama U/A	73	129	127	896	0008-0218	11-12359	0-2/10	0	1-0-0	7
294	26/27 Jul	Tokuyama U/A	313	102	97	752	0122-0235	11-12500	3-10/10	0	1-0-0	12
295	26/27 Jul	Omuta U/A	314	130	124	965	0113-0231	13-16300	0-10/10	1	0-0-0	16
296	27/28 Jul	7 Targets M	313	30	24	161	0034-0211	7-10400	0-10/10	3	0-0-0	2
297	28/29 Jul	Tsu U/A	58	78	76	730	0047-0156	11-11600	8-10/10	0	0-0-0	7
298	28/29 Jul	Aomori U/A	58	65	61	547	2337-0048	14-14700	0-9/10	0	0-0-0	7
299	28/29 Jul	Ichinomiya U/A	73	127	122	869	2356-0148	13-16700	4-8/10	0	0-0-0	7
300	28/29 Jul	Ujiyamada U/A	313	99	93	735	0215-0324	12-13800	0-5/10	0	0-0-0	9
301	28/29 Jul	Ogaki U/A	314	95	90	659	0152-0350	14-16400	2-5/10	0	1-0-0	10

XXI BOMBER COMMAND MISSIONS 1944-1945

MISSION NUMBER	DATE	PRIMARY TARGET	WINGS	A/C ABR	BOMB PRI	BOMB TONS	TIME OVER PRIMARY	ALTITUDE OF ATTACK	TARGET WEATHER	A/C LOST	E/A CLAIMED	A/C IWO
151	7 May	Kanoya A/F	313	10	10	55	1333	14400	2/10	0	0-1-2	
152	7 May	Ibusuki A/F	313	11	10	58	1308	12000	2/10	0	0-0-2	2
153	7 May	Oita A/F	313	10	10	66	1329	12250	2/10	2	13-11-2	4
154	7 May	Usa A/F	313	11	11	73	1307	14100	2/10	1	21-5-0	4
155/6	8 May	Kanoya A/F	313	20	17	102	1222-1333	17-21200	10/10	0	0-0-0	
157	8 May	Oita A/F	313	12	12	82	1239-1325	17-20000	10/10	0	0-0-0	6
158	8 May	Matsuyama A/F	313	12	11	76	1236-1325	18-23000	10/10	0	0-0-0	3
159	10 May	Matsuyama A/F	313	22	16	109	0827-0835	18-18500	0/10	0	0-0-0	7
160	10 May	Usa A/F	313	22	15	78	0839-0906	18-19000	0/10	0	3-0-2	8
161	10 May	Miyazaki A/F	313	11	7	43	0906	19000	0/10	0	0-0-0	4
162	10 May	Kayoya A/F	313	12	4	25	0855-0857	18000	0/10	0	4-4-8	1
163	10 May	Tokuyama F/S	73	60	54	243	1052-1103	14-20000	2/10	0	0-0-0	2
164	10 May	Tokuyama Coal	73	63	56	262	1107-1120	18-21000	2/10	0	0-0-0	4
165	10 May	Otake I/O	314	132	112	549	1048-1114	14-19700	0/10	1	3-2-8	12
166	10 May	O'Shima I/Os	58	88	80	383	1105-1150	16-18700	0/10	0	0-0-1	6
167	11 May	Oita A/F	313	20	17	101	0900-0927	18-19000	1/10	0	0-0-0	1
168	11 May	Saeki A/F	313	11	7	45	0931	19400	0/10	0	0-0-0	1
169	11 May	Nittagahara A/F	313	11	5	29	1653-1715	15-22400	2-6/10	0	0-0-0	2
170	11 May	Miyazaki A/F	313	12	12	82	1610-1640	15-20000	0/10	0	0-0-0	3
171	11 May	Miyakonojo A/F	313	11	11	76	1615-1646	17-20000	10/10	0	0-0-0	2
172	11 May	Kobe I/A	58/73/314	102	92	460	1153-1211	15-20000	4-8/10	1	9-22-15	14
173	13/14 May	Shimonoseki M	313	12	12	70	0120-0229	5-8030	0/10	0	0-0-0	
174	14 May	Nagoya U/A	58/73/313/314	524	472	2515	0905-1025	16-20500	1-8/10	11	23-16-31	
175	16/17 May	Shimonoseki M	313	31	25	152	0148-0326	6-11000	4/10	0	0-0-0	
176	16/17 May	Nagoya U/A	58/73/313/314	516	457	3609	0305-0558	6-18340	3-9/10	3	2-0-0	16
177	18/19 May	Shimonoseki M	313	34	30	192	0152-0309	5-6700	3-6/10	0	0-0-0	2
178	19 May	Tachikawa I/A	58/73/313/314	309	272	1486	1151-1258	13-26640	10/10	4	0-0-0	20
179	20/21 May	Shimonoseki M	313	30	30	184	0148-0311	5-6600	6-8/10	3	0-0-0	4
180	22/23 May	Shimonoseki M	313	32	30	177	0207-0311	5-8100	4/10	1	0-0-0	3
181	23/24 May	Tokyo U/A	58/73/313/314	558	520	3646	0239-0438	7-15100	1-6/10	17	6-1-2	49
182	24/25 May	Shimonoseki M	313	30	25	172	0144-0359	6-8400	0/10	0	0-0-0	3
183	25/26 May	Tokyo U/A	58/73/313/314	498	464	3362	2338-0213	7-22000	1-9/10	26	19-0-4	
184	26/27 May	Shimonoseki M	313	30	29	200	0132-0330	5-8200	0-3/10	0	0-0-0	1
185	27/28 May	Shimonoseki M	313	11	9	62	0058-0126	6-7700	0/10	1	0-0-0	
186	29 May	Yokohama U/A	58/73/313/314	510	454	2570	1014-1129	17-21000	9/10	7	6-5-10	39
187	1 Jun	Osaka U/A	58/73/313/314	509	458	2788	1028-1200	18-28000	0-10/10	10	16-9-24	81
188	5 Jun	Kobe U/A	58/73/313/314	530	473	3079	0822-0947	13-18800	0-8/10	11	86-31-78	43
189	7 Jun	Osaka U/A	58/73/313/314	449	409	2594	1209-1328	17-23150	8-10/10	2	0-0-3	59
190	7/8 Jun	Shimonoseki M	313	31	26	159	0128-0239	5-8400	8-10/10	0	0-0-0	4
191	9 Jun	Naruo I/A	58	46	44	264	0930-1003	19-21200	5-10/10	0	3-5-15	8
192	9 Jun	Akashi I/A	313	26	24	144	1052-1054	16-17400	8-9/10	0	0-0-0	4
193	9 Jun	Nagoya I/A	313	44	42	265	1017-1023	19-20700	0/10	0	2-3-2	7
194	9/10 Jun	Shimonoseki M	313	28	26	171	0101-0243	6-8400	0-2/10	0	0-0-0	5
195	10 Jun	Kasumigaura S/B	58	29	23	123	1001-1012	17-20100	2-9/10	0	0-4-8	3
196	10 Jun	Tomioka I/Ac	58	33	32	173	1024-1029	21-22000	10/10	0	0-0-0	
197	10 Jun	Kaigan I/Ae	73	124	118	806	0957-1038	19-21200	2-3/10	0	NA	18
198	10 Jun	Chiba I/Ac	314	27	26	138	0845-0846	15-17200	10/10	0	0-0-0	2
199	10 Jun	Ogikubu & Kasu.	314	65	52	281	0837-0927	21-23000	10/10	1	1-4-9	9
200	10 Jun	Tachikawa A/D	314	34	29	164	0852-0857	20-22000	10/10	0	0-1-3	2
201	11/12 Jun	Shimonoseki M	313	27	26	182	0140-0239	7-8500	2-10/10	0	0-0-0	
202	13/14 Jun	Shimonoseki M	313	30	29	311	0119-0234	7-7700	0-10/10	0	0-0-0	
203	15 Jun	Osaka-etc. U/A	58/73/313/314	511	444	3157	0944-1155	16-26900	10/10	2	NA	43
204	15/16 Jun	Shimonoseki M	313	30	30	175	0155-0350	7-9000	0-10/10	0	0-0-0	1
205	17/18 Jun	Shimonoseki M	313	28	25	163	0024-0213	6-8550	0-8/10	0	0-0-0	2
206	17/18 Jun	Kogoshima U/A	314	120	117	810	0006-0149	7-9200	6-10/10	1	0-0-0	3
207	17/18 Jun	Omuta U/A	58	126	116	769	0200-0409	6-9000	10/10	0	0-0-0	7
208	17/18 Jun	Hamamatsu U/A	73	137	130	911	0159-0305	7-9010	3-9/10	0	0-0-0	1
209	17/18 Jun	Yokkaichi U/A	313	94	89	567	0246-0405	7-7800	6/10	0	0-0	
210	19/20 Jun	Toyohashi U/A	58	141	136	946	0158-0417	6-8800	7-10/10	0	0-0-1	4
211	19/20 Jun	Fukuoka U/A	73/313	237	221	1525	0011-0153	9-10000	1-3/10	0	0-0-0	10
212	19/20 Jun	Shizuoka U/A	314	137	125	868	0151-0354	8-12000	2/10	2	0-0-0	2
213	19/20 Jun	Shimonoseki M	313	28	28	180	0132-0218	8-10200	5/10	0	0-0-0	2
214	21/22 Jun	Osaka Sea M	313	30	25	158	0048-0239	6-8600	1-5/10	0	0-0-0	1
215	22 Jun	Kure Arsenal	58/73	195	162	796	1031-1143	18-26250	2/10	2	0-0-0	10
216	22 Jun	Tamashima I/A	314	123	108	603	0936-1030	15-18300	0-2/10	2	1-0-0	3
217	22 Jun	Himeji I/A	58	58	52	351	1046-1137	15-18000	0-5/10	0	0-0-2	11
218	22 Jun	Kagamigahara I/A	313	28	17	90	1016-1018	16-18400	5/10	0	0-1-2	11
219	22 Jun	Kagamigahara I/A	313	21	17	116	0019-0023	16-18200	5-7/10	1	0-3-4	
220	22 Jun	Akashi I/A	313	30	25	148	1051-1053	18-19600	3-10/10	0	0-0-0	
221	23/24 Jun	Fukuoka, etc. M	313	27	26	163	0132-0346	4-8700	1-10/10	1		1
222	25/26 Jun	Shimonoseki M	313	27	26	177	0111-0211	6-8700	0-7/10	0	0-0-0	2
223	26 Jun	Osaka I/Me	58	71	64	382	1026-1202	19-25300	10/10	0	0-0-0	8
224	26 Jun	Osaka Arsenal	73	120	109	758	1018-1116	17-29060	10/10	1	1-1-0	14
225	26 Jun	Akashi I/A	313	36	31	184	1001-1052	16-26200	10/10	0	1-0-1	8
226	26 Jun	Nagoya Arsenal	314	35	33	190	1007-1011	16-18400	0/10	0	6-0-1	2

ture from the Sea of Japan, forming heavy clouds that dumped rain on the slopes of the mountainous spine of the island, and along the entire northwest coast. Targets along this coast were not bombed in the winter. After dropping their rain the clouds dried out, and the lighter Siberian air then lifted over the mountains and arrived clear and dry over the southeastern coast that faced the Pacific. This weather condition made attacks on targets on the southeastern coastal plains of Honshu and Kyushu (including Tokyo and Nagoya) ideal winter bombing targets. However, this same cooler Siberian air continued to sweep out over the Pacific toward the Marianas, where it under cut warm, moist, tropical air, and produced a turbulent weather front with towering clouds. Bombers had to penetrate this front both flying from their bases to Japan, and then on their return. Once over their target at 30,000ft the bombers battled 200 mile an hour jet stream winds and icing. Bomber formations broke up and expended fuel, and navigation and bombing from high altitude became difficult.

In the summer, there was a weak flow of cool air circulating over the Sea of Japan to the northwest of the islands. Moving inland from the northwest Japanese coast, this cool air ascended over the central mountain chain and converged with the strong flow of warm Pacific air. A thick layer of towering clouds and heavy rains formed on the entire southeastern side of the mountains, covering the coastal plains of Honshu and Kyushu, and thus protecting Tokyo and Nagoya, but leaving the northwestern cities exposed to attack in the summer.

When the B-29s first flew over Japan at high altitudes they encountered previously unknown high winds of 120mph, usually flowing from west to east. These winds, that could reach speeds of over 200mph, are now known as the jet stream. Bombing runs with these high winds put the bomber's ground speeds at 400 to 500mph, which made the Norden bombsight ineffective. Bombing into the winds slowed the ground speeds so low as to put the bombers in jeopardy over areas heavily defended by antiaircraft guns. Bombing laterally to the winds was impossible due to the extreme drift. These winds also made second runs over a target difficult, as getting back to the target was a navigational problem and used too much fuel. On a mission to the Nakajima Musashino Engine Plant, near Tokyo, B-29s approached the target downwind in a 215mph wind which, when added to the bomber's airspeed, meant they attempted to bomb the target at 535mph!

The 2nd Weather Reconnaissance Squadron was activated in early 1944, and assigned to the CBI to work with the XXBC and the 14AF in China

"Summer Weather" photo, also from Saipan approach, shows clearest bombing area now northwest coast.

and the Eastern Air Command in Burma. In November 1944 the 17th WRS was consolidated into the 7th WRS, and was responsible for weather forecasting for the Pacific north of the Marianas, but was largely ineffective, due to insufficient numbers of aircraft and personnel. By late 1944 the AAF realized that accurate weather forecasting was required for the success of its bombing campaign over Japan, and formed AAF Weather Services, Pacific, and deactivated the 7WRS in February 1945. The Weather Service was given a wide range of forecasting responsibilities throughout the entire Pacific, including the B-29 routes to Japan from the Marianas. Because the Weather Service reconnaissance missions were not far ranging enough the 20AF trained and activated a small weather-observer unit, the 655th Bombardment Squadron (H), in August 1944. The squadron arrived in the Pacific in the spring of 1945, and was redesignated the 55th Weather Reconnaissance Squadron (VLR). It consisted of eight forecasters and observers who named themselves the "Fighting 55th." B-24 and B-29 weather reconnaissance aircraft were dispatched, with the Liberators flying within an 800mi radius of the Marianas, and the weather recon B-29s flying to Japan, Korea, Okinawa, and adjacent areas. A forecaster would fly on a weather strike mission to collect weather data over Japan during the planning phase of a future mission, making several trips across the islands, and out into the Sea of Japan to the west. Another important function of weather recon missions was to photograph the areas where ditchings might occur to facilitate future rescues.

Planning a Bombing Mission
In Washington, DC, the Committee of Operational Analysis (COA) and Joint Target Committee (JTC) compiled an initial list of 1,000 precision targets in Japan. From this list the Joint Chiefs of Staff (JCS) placed the targets into significant groups: aircraft production; the coke, steel, and oil industries; shipping; and the urban industrial areas. The COA further prioritized the target groups into significance: the aircraft industry; urban industrial areas; and shipping, with individual targets given priority in each group. The JTC gave these targets to the XXIBC to formulate a bombing strategy and then implement it.

Target specialists of the XXI Bomber Command's Intelligence (A-2) and Operations (A-3) divisions sent out photo recon aircraft of the 3rd Photo Squadron to collect a mosaic of photos of target areas in Japan. Photo Interpreters (PI) studied every detail of the photos, and assembled and catalogued target data for the A-2 and A-3 planners. These planners met with veteran operations officers and experts in targets, navigation and weather, enemy AA and fighter defenses, armament, ordnance, radar, and radio. The planners devised a basic mission plan, called the "fragmentary plan," that included the number of bombers and bomb load required, the routes and altitudes to and from the target, navigational checkpoints, aiming points, and the axis and altitude of attack. This plan and others were sent to the commanding general of the XXIBC for approval for future use. It was immediately sent to the A-2 at each Wing HQ as a heads up on probable missions in the three day to three week time frame. With this warning the Wing A-2s could study and gather the necessary mission data, such as maps, charts, route plans, etc., in a target file, and file it until more specific orders were issued. In this way the wings and aircrews would not have to depend on the pre-mission briefing alone. Also, XXI HQ was not committed to a specific mission at a specific time. If weather closed the scheduled target, then an alternate target on file could be substituted, and the bombers would not be grounded for lack of information.

The final orders from the CG of the XXIBC were issued in two stages. The "Intentions" stage was issued one or two days before the mission. It specified the target, and authorized the wings to have their groups prepare all material for briefings and ready the bomb load. The "Firm Decision" stage was issued to the wings 12 to 24 hours before the mission, after the final weather forecast, and was passed to the groups. It included the date and hour of takeoff and authorized bomb loading.

Each Wing issued its own field orders, which included the order of takeoff for each group. The group A-3 prepared a schedule called the Signal Operation Instruction (SOI), also known as a "flimsy," that was given to each airplane commander, giving the exact time and order of take off for individual group bombers. With the flimsy and target file in hand the airplane commander attended the briefing. First to speak was the Group CO, who announced the target. The operations officer discussed the size of the mission. The intelligence officer, using the large wall map, described the target, the route to and from the target, checkpoints, assembly point, aiming points, flak, and enemy aircraft status. The weather officer gave a weather briefing. Then the operations officer spoke again and gave the assembly procedure, bombing altitude, types of bombs, bombing procedure, formation briefing, and flak and fighter avoidance, along with radar jamming. The group briefing usually took half an hour. After the group briefing there were more detailed specific mission briefings for each crewman.

After these briefings the crew went back to their barracks to pick up some personal effects and visited the latrine. Before take off they ate a

Group Briefing. First to speak was the Group CO, who announced the target. The operations officer discussed the size of the mission. The intelligence officer (shown) using the large wall map described the target, the route to and from the target, checkpoints, assembly point, aiming points, flak and enemy aircraft status. (USAF)

breakfast of scrambled powdered eggs, fried potatoes, toast and butter, canned fruit, canned tomato or orange juice, and the all important cup(s) of coffee.

6

Ordnance Carried by the B-29

General USAAF Ordnance

Bomb Types

1) High Explosive (Demolition)
2) Fragmentation
3) Incendiary
4) Chemical
5) Practice
6) Drill and gauge

Only the first four were used in combat.

Bomb Markings

GP-TNT: Olive with yellow nose and tail bands
  Marked on nose: GP 500lb/AN-M64A1/TNT/S1HTA
GP-COMP B: Olive with double yellow nose and tail bands with inner
  bands marked COMP. B
  Marked on nose: GP/500lb/AN-M64A1/COMP/ B/S1HWA
GP-TRITONAL: Olive with triple yellow nose and tail bands with inner
  bands marked TRITONAL
  Marked on nose: GP/500lb/AN-M64A1/ TRITONAL/S1ICA
INCENDIARY: Silver-white with three red bands: top middle and bottom
  Marked on nose: INCENDIARY/500lb/AN M 76/PT 4
CHEMICAL: Silver-gray with green band(s):
  One green band: non-persistent gas
  Two green bands: persistent gas
  Marked on nose: CG GAS/xxlb/AN M 78
  All these bombs had dark lettering and the lot number marked on mid-
  section and all but the chemical bomb had the arsenal named on the
  mid-section
LEAFLET: Olive with no stripes
  Marked on long axis: BOMB LEAFLET/xxlbs Size M 105A1/LOT #
23lb FRAGMENTATION: Olive with yellow bands on the top of the
  first segment
  Marked on first segment: FRAG/AN M 81/Lot #
4lb FRAGMENTATION: Olive with yellow band on each side
  Marked on side M83

PWP SMOKE: Silver-gray with yellow band on middle and bottom
  section
  Marked in yellow lettering: 100lb/M47A4

Precision Bombing and Ordnance

On 12 October 1944 Brig.Gen. Haywood Hansell, the GC of the XXIBC,
arrived in the Marianas to initiate his enthusiastic strategic bombing campaign against the Japanese Homeland. In 1940 Maj. Hansell had helped
draft AWPD-1, the planning instrument of the American strategic bombing offensive in WWII. Hansell had commanded a Bomb Wing and air
division in Europe for the 8AF, and was Gen. Arnold's choice to direct the
B-29 bombing campaign from the Marianas. The goal of a strategic bombing campaign is to destroy the enemy's industrial capacity, and thus his
ability to make war. As in Europe, the enemy's aircraft industry was chosen as the first target complex in order to secure air supremacy. Precision
bombing theory selected a component of an industry that was highly concentrated in a few areas (e.g. the Schweinfurt ball-bearing complex in Germany, upon which much of Germany's rolling stock depended). In Japan
the comparable industry was the aircraft engine industry, as Nakajima (30%)
and Mitsubishi (33%) were the two major engine producers. Hansell selected the 73BW to fly the first Marianas based attack with the Nakajima
Musashino plant, near Tokyo, as the target. After 10 previous training missions (seven against the bypassed Truk naval base and three over Iwo Jima)
the 73BW left Saipan on 24 November 1944 with 111 B-29s, but only 24
succeeded in bombing the Musashino factory. The precision-bombing campaign of Japan by the B-29s continued to obtain unsatisfactory results that
were compounded by the strong jet stream winds and the chronically cloudy
Japanese weather, which lessened the effectiveness of the fabled Norden
bombsight. The purpose of a bomber was, of course, to drop bombs accurately on a target, and that was a primary problem for the B-29 and its
Norden bombsight, which was renowned for its accuracy. The bombing
accuracy in early missions was abysmal, as the best accuracy on any mission was on 25 October 1944 when only 16% of the 58BW's bombs falling
on Omura fell within 1,000 feet of the aiming point. A study of the average
accuracy of both the XX and XXI Bomber Commands estimated that visual bombing from 31,000ft averaged only 5% hits within 1,000ft of the

aiming point, 12% from 24,500ft, and 30% from 20,000ft. Radar aiming was even more inaccurate, with less than 1% of the bombs hitting within 1,000ft of the target (the average was two miles!). More troubling was that 22% of the bombers failed to bomb the target at all. Although the strategic bombing campaign established air superiority, it had minimal effect on the aircraft, petroleum, or transportation industries, and no effect on the determination of the Japanese military, government, or civilian population to continue the war. Thus the B-29, the most advanced precision bomber of the war, came to symbolize the ultimate failure of precision bombing.

Hansell's aircraft engine campaign continued to the end of January and was a discouraging failure. Hansell was inflexible; he firmly adhered to his bombing philosophy, and ignored Washington's directives to vary tactics and do more area bombing. Hansell believed that 8AF daylight precision bombing in Europe had a more significant effect on German industry than the British Bomber Command under Sir Arthur "Bomber" Harris, who expounded night area bombing. Something had to be done, and Gen. Curtis LeMay replaced Hansell. Although also a transfer from the 8AF European Theater bombing school, LeMay's bombing philosophy was not as rigidly tied to daylight precision bombing in formation, and he believed in varying tactics and changing target systems.

A new air strategy was needed, and target planners had known for some time that the Japanese cities were much more prone to fire and incendiary bombing than European cities. They also knew that incendiary bombing of Japanese cities would cause huge conflagrations that would inflict terrible civilian casualties. When LeMay decided to switch to area incendiary bombing he used the justification that, because of the predominately hilly terrain of Japan, Japanese industry and residential areas were commingled into the flat topography of its large cities, much more so than in Germany, where industry was concentrated into specific areas. Therefore, it was unavoidable that, while bombing the factories, the civilian population would be harmed. LeMay did not have sufficient bombers available to carry out the fire bombing campaign until March 1945, and was forced until then to continue the strategic bombing campaign using high explosive bombs. Once the fire bombing campaign began, it was only because incendiary bomb stocks ran low that strategic bombing with high explosive bombs continued.

Tactical Bombing Operations

During the invasion of Okinawa a number of B-29s from 73BW and 314BW were deployed to attack Japanese Homeland airfields on Kyushu and Shikoku that were resisting the American invasion, particularly with kamikaze attacks. These missions were flown from the relatively low altitudes of 13,000 to 21,000ft. The first two missions were full-scale attacks flown by the two wings on 27 and 31 March in support of the naval and landing operations. On 17 April further B-29 tactical missions were ordered against Japanese airfields that were staging kamikaze attacks against the U.S. Navy lying off Okinawa. The campaign began on 27 March and ended on 11 May after 2,104 sorties were flown in 93 missions, with 75% of the tactical effort against the Kyushu and Shikoku airfields, and the remainder against fuel reserves, especially in the Tokoyama area. Initially 250lb fragmentation bombs were used, but post strike photo recon determined that GP bomb loads, half with delayed fusing from one to 36 hours, would be more effective. These missions were generally successful, with 350 enemy aircraft destroyed or damaged on the ground, greatly reducing the number of ka-

mikaze attacks, and saving many American ships and sailors in the process.

The Bombing Campaign Against the Japanese Oil Complex

The B-29s of the 315BW were equipped with the new APQ-7 Eagle bombing radar, which had 10 times the resolution of the APQ-13 sets. The Japanese oil complex was vulnerable to bombing by radar, as many of the large refineries were located on or near the coast, which made them easy to identify on the new radar. Also, all armament except the .50cal tail guns were removed, which allowed for significant increases in bomb load, but dictated the attacks be conducted during nighttime. The 315BW began operations on 26 June when 35 bombers hit the Utsube River Oil Refinery at Yokkaishi, with an average of 7.3 tons of bombs dropped per bomber. The 315BW carried out 15 nighttime missions to nine targets by the end of the war, during which 1,200 sorties dropped 9,084 tons of bombs, mostly 500lb GP, on primary targets, 95% by APQ-7 radar. The average bomb load increased from 7.3 tons on the first mission to 10.3 tons on a mission to the Nippon Refinery at Amagsaki on 9 August. The major oil refining, synthesizing, and storage capacity (6.06 million barrels) of Japan was thought to have been destroyed. However, the success of the American submarine and aerial mining campaign against Japanese vessels carrying crude oil had drastically reduced the amount of petroleum that was delivered to the Homeland, and the B-29s destroyed an oil complex that refined or stored no oil. The B-29 loss rate was three aircraft lost, 66 damaged, and only 16 attacks by enemy night fighters were recorded.

Ordnance

High Explosive Bombs

A bomb is defined by the Ordnance Department as "a missile intended to be dropped by an airplane." Parts of a bomb are:

a) Casing
b) Suspension lugs
c) Tail fins
d) Fuses (nose, tail or both)
e) Primer detonator (fits into the adapter-booster)
f) Main explosive

Bomb dump. 500lb Bomb casings without tail fins or nose, and tail fuses with their shipping bands attached. (USAF)

Armorers attaching tail fins to 500lb bombs. (USAF)

Twenty-two 500lb bombs waiting to be loaded in a 444BG B-29. (USAF)

The explosive train is a series of actions that cause the bomb to detonate. It is made up of a fuse or fuses: nose, tail, or both, which act on a primer detonator, the detonation of which actually sets the explosive train in action by transmitting to an adapter booster that sets off the main explosive charge. The sensitivity of the train begins with the primer detonator, which is extremely sensitive, since it must react to the comparatively weak blow from the fuse(s), while the main explosive charge is more insensitive, and must be detonated by an intermediate charge contained in the adapter-booster.

A HE, high explosive bomb (earlier nomenclature: demolition bomb) was a package of high explosive carried in a aerodynamic bomb body or casing that needed to be light yet strong. Between 50% and 60% of the weight of the bomb was high explosive, and the remainder steel casing. The bomb needed to remain in one piece until it detonated, generally inside the target, instead of breaking upon the first impact. In order to achieve the penetration necessary for different targets and still contain the maximum amount of explosive, demolition bombs were constructed of several different metals of varying hardness and thickness.

Type	% of Explosive
General purpose (GP)	50-55%
Semi-armor piercing (SAP)	32%
Armor piercing (AP)	5-12%
Light case (LC)	77%
Depth bomb (DB)	70-75%

Bombs could be filled with various explosive compositions:

Explosive Ingredients

RDX (Cyclonite, Hexogen)	Cyclotrimethylene trinitramine
TNT (Trinitrotoluene)	Toluene, nitric acid
Torpex	TNT, RDX, aluminum
Amatol	TNT, ammonium nitrate

Fuses

Fuses on bombs were timed to give the attacking aircraft the ability to escape the explosion, and allow the bomb to penetrate deeper, making the explosion more effective. The bomb was pre-armed by screwing a fuse into the nose, or sometimes the tail of the bomb. All fuses were unarmed before the bomb release. While unarmed a mechanical restraint prevented the firing pin from moving and firing the primer. Both nose and tail fuses were unarmed after the bombs were hung on the shackles. An arming wire was secured to the shackles, and was run through a hole in the fuse, from which the tagged safety pin had been removed. When the bomb was released the arming wire was withdrawn from the fuse, making the bomb "live," and the arming vanes or propellers began to rotate loose and fell away after a few hundred feet, arming the bomb. If the need to release a bomb over friendly territory arose, the mechanical arming wire was released with the bomb, preventing fusing.

Simply, the fuse of a bomb consisted of two parts: the firing pin and detonator. The detonator—usually fulminate of mercury—exploded when struck by the firing pin. Lying between the detonating charge and the firing pin were safety devices that prevented the firing pin from hitting the deto-

Precision bombing was not so precise. A study of the average accuracy of both the XX and XXI Bomber Commands estimated that visual bombing from 31,000ft averaged only 5% hits within 1,000ft of the aiming point, 12% from 24,500ft, and 30% from 20,000ft. (USAF)

nator during shipment and handling. An intermediary charge (the primer detonator) located between the fuse and the main charge was used to produce the maximum explosive effect. Multiple fuses were sometimes fitted to insure detonation, and could be located in the nose, tail or, less often, the center body.

Fuses were classified according to their position on the bomb and their operating principle. The type of fuse installed depended on the type of target, the method of attack, and the type of explosive used. Bomb fuses were classified according to arming method:

1) Arming vane type
2) Arming vane type with mechanical delay
3) Arming pin type
4) Arming pin type with time delay
5) Time

Any of these fuse types could be used in the nose or tail of a bomb. Nose fuses, except time fuses, functioned on impact by direct action, e.g. the firing pin was driven into the primer at the instant the nose of the bomb hit the target. Tail fuses functioned by inertia, e.g. the plunger that carried the firing pin continued its forward motion as the bomb was slowed or stopped by the resistance of the target. Thus, the nose fuse was slightly faster than the tail fuse.

General Purpose (GP) Bombs

A new range of GP bombs became available in late 1943 in five sizes:

1) 100lb bomb would demolish a two-story building; destroy a gun position, locomotive, motor transport, or aircraft on the ground (damage it at 75 feet) if exploded within 10 feet of the target. Generally they were considered uneconomical for use in bombers, and also in fighter-bombers; could carry two or three 100lb, versus two or three of the more effective 500lb bombs.

2) 250lb bomb (replaced the M31 300lb bomb) would destroy the walls and floors of most buildings, and sink or severely damage shipping up to cruiser size within 20 feet. This bomb was considered less effective than the 500lb bomb in Europe, but was effective against the more lightly constructed Japanese buildings.

3) 500lb bomb would destroy steel bridges, underground defenses, most tanks, and light cruiser-type shipping when hitting within 25 feet. The 500lb GP bomb with an instantaneous fuse was effective against most military installations not protected by reinforced concrete or masonry.

4) The 1,000lb bomb would destroy or severely damage light concrete fortifications, and displace piers and the spans of the heaviest bridges. This bomb was not used extensively, as B-29 bomb bay design prevented economical loading.

5) 2,000lb bomb would destroy heavy concrete fortifications, and crack or burst a large hole in dams, or sink a heavy cruiser or battleship with a direct hit or nearby explosion in the water. The 2,000lb GP bomb was used against reinforced concrete and other massive structures and buildings containing heavy machinery. The bomb could penetrate the structure, crater the floors, and destroy the machinery.

6) The 4,000lb light case (LCVE) bomb was used only as a blast bomb, primarily against medium and long span steel structures. It was very successful, but limited supplies restricted its use.

Major U.S. Explosive Bombs (Pre-1943)

Type	Weight
M30	100lbs
M31	300lbs
M32	600lbs
M33	1,100lbs
M34	2,000lbs
M43	500lbs
M44	1,000lbs

Major U.S. High Explosive Bombs (Post -1943)

Type	Weight	HE Weight
AN-M30 GP	100lbs	54lbs
AN-M57 GP	250lbs	123lbs
AN-M64 GP	500lbs	262lbs
AN-M65 GP	1,000lbs	530lbs
AN-M66 GP	2,000lbs	1,051lbs

Other Bombs

Type	Weight	HE Weight
AN-M56 LC (Blast)	4,000lbs	3,245lbs
AN-Mk1 AP	1,600lbs	215lbs
M52 AP	1,000lbs	
M58 SAP	500lbs	
M59 SAP	1,000lbs	

Fragmentation Bombs

The destructive power of a fragmentation bomb resulted entirely from the fragmentation of the bomb, whose scored casing had been designed to break into 1,000 to 1,500 pieces weighing about three ounces that were projected outward at up to 4,000 feet per second. There were two types of fragmentation bombs:

1) Anti-personnel: Designed to burst on contact with the ground and spray fragments the size and speed of a .30 caliber bullet, or a finned model designed to explode in the air.

M27 bomb service truck delivers a M56 4,000lb LCVE bomb. (USAF)

M81, 260lb fragmentation bomb. The yellow bands at the end denote RDX explosive filler. (USAF)

T4E4, 500lb fragmentation cluster of 20lb M41 fragmentation bombs. (USAF)

2) Anti-material: Designed to burst on the ground, or above parked aircraft or light-skinned motor transport.

Over Japan one fragmentation bomb or fragmentation bomb clusters were usually dropped in combination with incendiary bombs (e.g. one or two M88 fragmentation bombs with 4,900lbs of incendiaries). Also, a number of lead bombers were loaded with fragmentation bombs with the intention of forcing the populace and fire fighters to take shelter, and the main bomber force would then drop their incendiary bombs. The T4E4, 500lb fragmentation cluster of 20lb fragmentation bombs and 260lb fragmentation bombs were dropped as anti-personnel bombs during incendiary attacks, and on airfields on Kyushu and Shikoku during the Okinawa campaign. Fragmentation bombs (name/weight) included:

M40A1	23lbs	AN-M83	3.5lbs
M41A	20lbs	AN-M86	120lbs
AN-M81	260lbs	AN-M88	220lbs
AN-M82	90lbs		

The fragmentation bomb was dangerous to handle. In January 1945, a fragmentation cluster broke loose from a 40BW B-29 and exploded on the tarmac, killing seven, and also destroying the adjacent bomber. (USAF)

Fragmentation bombs were considered very dangerous ordnance to handle, as they were fully armed and could detonate on impact. There were several serious accidents during early CBI operations, and they were withdrawn from service there.

Experimental Ordnance

Boeing-Wichita developed experimental external under Wing bomb racks that were fitted between the fuselage and inboard engines for use against designated targets in Japan. The racks were tested on a B-29075-BW (S/N 70060), and were designed to carry four 4,000lb bombs, or a combination of bombs, including two 12,000lb "Tall Boy" or 22,000lb "Grand Slam" bombs. The B-29 was able to carry its full complement of internal bombs or bomb bay fuel tanks. The installation never reached combat.

In tests at Eglin Field the 12,000lb Tall Boy, designated DP (Deep Penetration), was fitted into specially modified bomb bays that had their doors removed. To fit the large bomb into the bomb bay special loading pits were dug, and special bomb-hoisting dollies constructed to allow the bomb to be raised into the aircraft. The same technique was used later to load the atomic bombs.

Pumpkin Bomb

The California Institute of Technology was responsible for the atomic bomb delivery system, and built a number of 10,000lb conventional bombs inside the casings of the Fat Man bombs, which were called the "Pumpkin" because of their color and shape. After testing at the Navy's Inyokern rocket range the Pumpkin bombs were shipped to the Marianas to be used in Air Force Special Missions by the 509th Composite Group of the 313BW. The 509th used these bombs to practice for their atomic bomb attack on Nagasaki during 12 missions, involving two to six bombers dropping one pumpkin each: 20 July (4 missions/10 aircraft); 24 July (3/10); 26 July (2/10); and 29 July (3/8). After the Hiroshima atomic bomb mission of 6 August there were two pumpkin missions with six bombers on 8 August, and then on 14 August there were two final pumpkin missions with seven bombers.

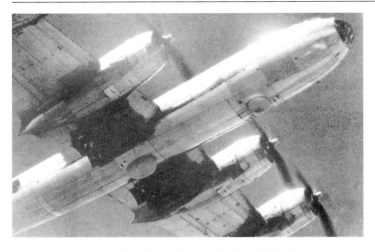

Boeing-Wichita developed experimental external under wing bomb racks that were fitted between the fuselage and inboard engines for use against designated targets in Japan. It was tested on a B-29-75-BW (S/N 70060) that was equipped to carry four 4,000lb bombs. (USAF)

Two 22,000lb "Grand Slam" bombs carried on external racks. The B-29 was able to carry its full complement of internal bombs or bomb bay fuel tanks. The installation never reached combat. (USAF)

Incendiary Bombing and Ordnance

Pre-Pearl Harbor studies of bombing effectiveness in Europe had shown that the Luftwaffe and RAF use of incendiary bombs was as effective pound for pound as high explosive bombs. The pre-war bombing strategy of the Army Air Corps was concentrated on the precision dropping of high explosive bombs on a target. Because of its inaccuracy, the AAC felt that the incendiary bomb was a bomb that attacked the civilian population, and was ineffective against hard industrial targets. This conviction continued after America entered the war, as the 8th Air Force dropped seven times more high explosive bombs as incendiary on European targets throughout the war. When Japan became a target, war planners found that the construction of Japanese cities differed from those in Europe, as 95% of German cities were constructed of brick and stone, while 80% of Japanese cities were built from wood and paper products. The construction of many of the Japanese roofs was wood or thatch, and easily penetrable by incendiary bombs. The dwellings in Japanese cities were densely populated and crowded together along narrow streets, making multiple fires difficult to control. It was estimated that 15 primarily German urban areas targeted by

In tests at Eglin Field the 12,000lb "Tall Boy" designated DP (Deep Penetration) was fitted into specially modified bomb bays with their doors removed. (USAF)

the RAF Bomber Command for area bombing contained about 12% of Germany's labor force. Studies indicated the 15 major Japanese urban area targets contained nearly 45% of the enemy's labor force. There were thousands of "home" industries crowded in city centers that were particularly vulnerable to concentrated incendiary attack (30% of the Japanese labor force was employed in factories with less than 30 workers). Key Japanese military industries were far more concentrated. For example, 40% of Japanese aircraft engines were produced in one city, 30% of aircraft assembly in two cities, 50% of machine tools in four cities, 45% of ordnance in seven cities, and 90% of electronic tubes in three cities. While the key industries in the priority target systems would not be destroyed in a concentrated area incendiary attack, they would be greatly affected by the destruction of the component and subassembly factories that supplied them, and the loss of life of the work force and their housing. Another major consequence of incendiary attacks was the collateral disruption to utilities, transportation, and storage. The destruction of these key industries would have to be left to precision bombing.

From early 1943 the AAF no longer followed its prewar Norden bombsight precision bombing philosophy, and radar (non-visual) bombing was used 60% of the time; it had accounted for 50% of the bombs dropped by the 8AF, and had been used in three successful and deadly high altitude non-precision attacks on Germany (Berlin, Dresden, and *Operation Clarion*). By mid-February 1945 XXIBC planners decided that combustible urban areas were only second to the Japanese aircraft industry as a target, and wanted to achieve successes comparable to the 8AF, which was beginning to run out of worthwhile targets in Germany. In February the XXIBC bombed three urban areas in high altitude incendiary bombing missions. Daylight attacks on Tokyo (at 22,000ft) and Nagoya (at 30,000ft), as well as a nighttime attack on Kobe (at 24,000ft) under new XXIBC commander Curtis LeMay were relatively unsuccessful. LeMay sent out a larger XXIBC force on a daytime incendiary mission on Tokyo on 25 February at 27,000ft. The raid scored the best XXIBC results ever, but LeMay was not satisfied. He decided to decrease operational bombing altitudes from their previous average of 30,000ft (under Hansell) to 5,000 to 10,000ft. The reason for high altitude missions was to evade enemy flak, but photo recon showed the Japanese had relatively few AA guns as compared to Europe, and their medium Army 20mm and 40mm flak was only effective up to 4,500ft, and only their limited numbers of medium Navy 25mm guns could reach to 8,000ft. Bombers flying at low altitude should have been exposed to Japanese heavy flak, but these batteries were unable to track the fast-moving B-29s. Japanese fighters would also have had an advantage, but LeMay made another bold decision, deciding to fly the incendiary missions at night to diminish the threat from AA fire and fighter interception. The Japanese had only two of its four night fighter units stationed in Japan, and their radar-controlled searchlight/AA batteries were mostly inferior, and could be easily jammed. Formation flying during night missions was hazardous, but celestial navigation was easier at night (if clear), and LORAN had a much greater range at night. Also, night missions meant returning and landing in the daylight, and a daytime ditching or bailout meant a better chance of search and rescue. Low altitude missions did not change the troublesome Japanese weather and cloud conditions that remained unpredictable and changeable, even while the bombers were over the target. However, the winds at lower altitudes were generally 25 to 30 knots, as compared to the jet stream winds of 120 knots or more prevailing at high altitudes. Attacks at lower altitudes would allow greater bomb loads because of decreased gasoline consumption, and aircraft maintenance would be less, as there was less wear and tear on engines at lower altitudes.

The Incendiary Mission

Two homing aircraft from each Wing took off 20 to 30 minutes before the main force. They carried no bombs, but carried additional fuel and radio equipment, as well as the standard defensive armament. They were to orbit the target at 25,000ft, and expert radio operators were to direct the oncoming bombers. Three marker bombers from each group, modeled after the RAF Pathfinder bombers, also flew ahead. They were manned by the outstanding crews of the group, and would set fires in a large "X" across the target area to mark four points in the 10 square mile target area. A number of lead bombers were loaded with fragmentation and HE bombs with the intention of driving the populace and fire fighters to take shelter and prevent fire fighting. The fragmentation bombs were the T4E4, 500lb cluster of 20lb fragmentation bombs, 260lb fragmentation bombs, and the HE

The statistical effect of the incendiary bombing was staggering. Raids on 68 cities destroyed 2.5 million housing units (with 614,000 being razed by the Japanese for firebreaks) which left 30% of the population homeless and 806,000 civilian casualties. (USAF)

	AN-50A2 AN-M50xA3	AN-M69	M47A2	M76
Filling and weight (lbs)	Mg. 1.3 Th. 0.62 Tetryl 38g (in M50xA3)	IM 2.8 or NP 2.8	IM 40 lbs or NP 40 lbs	PT-1 180 lbs
Method of functioning	Intensive: Filling stays near bomb	Tail ejection: Burning sock of mixture is ejected up to 75 yrds	Scatters over a 50' radius	Scatters over a 150' radius
Bomb fuze		M1	AN-M126 AN-M126A1	AN-M103 nose AN-M101A2 tail
Burning time	5–7 min	4–5 min	10 min (approx)	20 min (approx)
Bomb weight (lbs)	3.7 (4-lb type)	6.2 (6-lb type)	69 (100-lb type)	473 (500-lb type)
Terminal velocity	420'/sec	225'/sec	825'/sec	1000'/sec
Penetration at T.V.	4" reinforced concrete (heavy construction)	2"–3" concrete (light to medium construction)	5" concrete from 25,000'	15" concrete from 25,000'
Aimable 500-lb clusters (symbol, weight, contents, adapter, fuzes, burster)	AN-M17A1: 490 lbs 110 bombs M10 adapter T55 nose fuze Primacord	M18: 350 lbs 38 bombs M9 adapter T55 nose fuze T53 tail fuze Primacord	M12 or M13	M14 Adapter-Booster M115
Altitude recommendations	Quick-Opening: from 8000' or less Aimable: Medium to high, with cluster burst set for 5000'	Quick-Opening: from 1000' to 8000' Aimable: Medium to high, with cluster burst set for 5000'	Min safe release: 200' Penetration good from 15,000' and higher	Min safe release: 300' Penetration good from 15,000' and higher

Incendiary Bomb Types

bombs were the 500lb and 4,000lb bombs, instantaneously fused or with proximity fuses. The main force flew to the target aided by LORAN, and at about 65mi from the Japanese coast the radar operators took over. The Bomb Wings climbed to their assigned bombing altitudes (specific 1,000ft bands for each wing) at about an average altitude of 7,000ft. When they neared the pathfinder fires they dropped their 500lb firebomb clusters, not on the fires, but adjacent to them. Each cluster was made up of 38 M-69 incendiaries fused to separate at 2,000 to 2,500ft. The intervalometers were set to space the release of the bombs, and thus the impact point, so that the clusters exploded at 50ft intervals. The bomb load of each bomber covered a rectangular area of 350 by 2,000ft (about 16 square acres). The attack plans took into account the wind direction, so that smoke would not cover the next areas to be bombed.

Fifteen major Japanese cities had more than 70% of their built up areas destroyed. The 20AF flew 6,960 sorties, dropping 41,592 tons of bombs on Japan's five largest cities. These cities (Kyoto was off limits) suffered 133,000 killed, 117,000 injured, and 1.4 million homeless, and had 102 square miles burned out. Tokyo had 51% of its city area damaged and 87,000 killed and 60,000 injured, and almost 750,000 homeless. By August there were no more strategic targets remaining, as Japan's largest cities had virtually been burned to the ground, and then its secondary cities had been attacked, and an additional 76 square miles of their built up areas were devastated. The fire bombing campaign certainly caused great destruction and suffering on the civilian population, and lowered their will to resist. However, the Japanese kamikaze/samurai psyche made surrender impossible, and despite the debate that rages to this day the atomic bombs were necessary, and gave the Japanese government the reason to end the suffering.

Incendiary Bombs
100lb Gelled Gasoline Bomb M-47
It was not until 1940 that the AAC developed its first incendiary bomb, the 100lb, 4ft long, 8in diameter M-47 incendiary bomb. The Army Chemical Warfare Service filled a stock chemical bomb case with a gelatinous mixture created by the British that consisted of rubber, coconut oil, and lye blended with gasoline. The heavy M-47 easily penetrated most enemy roofs,

M47 Incendiary Bomb (USAF)

500lb M69 Incendiary Cluster Bomb (USAF)

and just after penetrating a burster charge would detonate, exploding the case and scattering a cone of flaming globs of gasoline downward and outward, scattering them over a 50 square feet area to burn for about 10min. The resulting small fires were relatively easy to put out if they ignited surrounding structures. This bomb was used mainly by pathfinder forces, as it had a high "appliance fire value," and lit up an area quickly, especially in congested, highly inflammable areas. This bomb was also filled with white phosphorous as an anti-personnel bomb. The M-47 was initially used, as it was in stock, but after the M-69 clusters became available, it became the incendiary of choice.

Cluster Bombs

M-69 Clusters
The M-69, initially designated the M-56, was developed by the newly formed National Defense Research Committee (NDRC), the military branch of the Office of Scientific Research and Development (OSRD). There was a shortage of magnesium and a threatened shortage of rubber (a filler material), and substitutes had to be found. The NDRC's various divisions employed many of the foremost scientists and engineers from industry and academia. Their research resulted in the development of two gasoline gels

Fusing a mixed load of 500lb M69 clusters (side racks) and 6lb oil bomb clusters (center rack). (USAF)

that did not necessitate rubber. One was napalm (a combination of *nap*thenic and *palm*itic acids combined in gasoline), that was to become the standard incendiary gel filler. The bomb itself was designed to be small so that a large number could be dropped at once and start more fires in more places, making fire fighting more difficult. Its case had to be light and thin, but strong enough to penetrate the roof, while not bursting prematurely on hitting the roof, and be able to propel its incendiary filling throughout the room in which it settled.

The M-69 was 6lbs, 3oz, and its steel casing was about 20in long and 3in in diameter. The bombs were bundled in clusters in the bomb bay, and the clusters separated and the bombs fell free when released. The bomb's casing was without stabilizing tailfins, and a 3ft cloth streamer, much like a kite tail, was released after separation and stabilized the bomb, controlling the rate of descent. Once the bomb had penetrated the roof it had either come to a stop on its side, or had embedded its nose in the floor. A delay fuse was activated, and after 3 to 5 seconds it detonated an ejection ignition TNT charge. The TNT explosion would cause the magnesium to ignite the gasoline gel contained in a cloth sock. The explosion of the ignited gel would blow the burning gel out the tail of the casing as far as 100ft. The gel would burn for 4 to 5 minutes, and when in contact with combustible material would burn fiercely and tenaciously.

Oil Cluster Bombs
The 500lb cluster of 6lb oil bombs was very successful against light, inflammable construction. These bombs had cloth tails to slow their descent, to prevent them from penetrating heavy structures. The clusters, containing 10lb of oil and white phosphorous bombs, were used against medium construction. These bombs did not have cloth tails, but had reinforced heads that permitted deeper penetration than the oil-filled bombs. The white phosphorous was often used as an anti-personnel feature to inhibit fire fighting.

M-50 and M-52 Clusters
In early 1941 the Army Chemical Warfare Service purchased the 4lb British Mark-II incendiary bomb, made some modifications, and redesignated it the M-50. It was nearly 3ft long and 3in in diameter, with a magnesium body, and filled with powdered iron and aluminum oxide. The light M-50 was dropped in clusters of 34 bombs strapped together with metal bands. After the cluster was dropped an arming wire released the bombs from the

cluster, and they separated in descent. The bombs would penetrate a roof and lay on the floor, where its filler would ignite and burn intensely, igniting the magnesium casing; the resulting fire would burn at 2400°F for 5 to 7 minutes, and was very difficult to extinguish. The M-52 was a 2lb version of the M-50. After the M-50 was developed it virtually replaced the M-47. After the M69 was chosen for the bombing campaign on Japan, the M50 and M-52 were used mainly in the ETO in 500lb clusters of 110 M50s.

Thermite-Magnesium Clusters
Clusters containing 4lb thermite-magnesium bombs were used against heavily industrialized areas that contained machinery or machine tools. These bombs could penetrate heavy structures and produce intense heat that could fuse metal. Some of these bombs also contained tetryl explosive heads to discourage fire fighting.

500lb Gasoline Gel-Magnesium Bomb
This bomb had ballistics that were similar to a GP bomb, and was sometimes used with mixed loadings. It was utilized against soundly constructed buildings containing heavy machinery, and because the magnesium burned very brightly it was also dropped by pathfinders in built-up areas of poor inflammability as a marker. The bomb was not used very extensively.

Testing the Incendiary Bombs
To test the M-50, M-52, and M-69 incendiary bombs, the NDRC built an exact replica of a section of a Japanese city at Dugway Proving Ground, Utah. Tests began in mid-May 1943, and continued to the first of September. Bombers in formation dropped clusters of quick-opening incendiaries from various altitudes, and detailed records were made for each bomb hit. The results demonstrated that the M-69 was the most effective of the three incendiaries. The M36 was a 220lb cluster of 36 M69s, and was the most devastating incendiary cluster dropped in WW II.

The success of the incendiary missions depended on two factors. A pattern density of 600lbs of M-69 incendiaries per square acre (roughly 100 of the 6lb bombs) was considered necessary, but no guarantee of success. Area density was the concentration of aircraft bomb loads, their location, and the accuracy with which the incendiaries were delivered. The bombs had to be laid quickly in compact areas so that the fires could merge, and also to prevent the firefighters from gaining control. Surface winds were found to be very important, as they quickly spread and merged the fires, but rain and snow had little effect, as the incendiaries burned so hot that they were able to set wetted combustibles aflame, and even fire-resistant buildings were damaged. Firebreaks were ineffective, as bombs fell on both sides, but the breaks did allow an avenue of escape for Japanese civilians. As mentioned previously, incendiary bomb loadings were mixed with high explosives and fragmentation bombs to obstruct firefighters and civil defense personnel.

Strike Reports
A strike report was referred to as the "Bombs Away Message," and was to be sent by each bomber that had bombed individually or, if it was done by a formation, by the Formation Leader only. The strike reports were to be made immediately after the bombs had been dropped on the primary and secondary targets. If the bombers had bombed the last resort target or target of opportunity, their strike reports were delayed for at least one hour to allow a clear radio channel for those bombers attacking primary or second-

ary targets. Normal radio procedures with codes were used. There were two types of Strike Reports: the Normal Strike Report #1, and the Incendiary Strike Report #2. The Normal Strike Report #1 included:

(a) Target bombed
     P = Primary Target
     S = Secondary Target
     L = Last Resort Target
     O = Target of Opportunity
(b) Method of Bombing
     V = Visual
     R = Radar Bombing
     N = Navigation
(c) Bombing Results
     1 = Excellent; meaning pattern centered on aiming point
     2 = Good; meaning few hits on aiming point
     3 = Fair; meaning hits in target area
     4 = Poor; meaning missed the target area
     5 = Unobserved
(d) Fighter Escort
     A = Friendly fighter escort present
     B = No friendly fighter escort
(e) Number of planes in Bomber Formation
     1 = One plane
     2 = Two planes
     3 = Three planes
Etc. Etc.

The six-character message was repeated three times to insure reception, and a sample message would be:

PV3A11 PV3A11 PV3A11, which would mean:
"Primary target was bombed visually, and the observed results were that hits were made in the target area, but no hits were observed on the aiming point. Friendly fighter escort was present, and there were 11 bombers in the formation."

The Incendiary Strike Report #2 included:
(a) Target bombed
     P = Primary Target
     S = Secondary Target
     L = Last Resort Target
     O = Target of Opportunity
(b) Method of Bombing
     V = Visual
     R = Radar Bombing
     N = Navigation
(c) Cloud Coverage
     1 to 9 for tenths, x for 10/10ths
(d) Situation to Target
     A = General conflagration
     B = Several large fires
     C = Many fires
     D = Few scattered fires
     E = Unobserved

(e) Fighter Opposition
   1 = Heavy
   2 = Moderate
   3 = Meager
   4 = None
(f) Flak
   A = Heavy
   B= Moderate
   C = Meager
   D = Slight
   E = None

The six-character code message was repeated three times, and a sample message would be:

PR8E4D PR8E4D PR8E4D, which would mean:
"Primary target was bombed by radar, 8/10ths cloud coverage over the target, the situation over the target was unobserved, there was no fighter opposition, and flak was slight."

XXIBC Bombing Totals and Results
During the war the 20AF's B-29s dropped 159,862 tons of bombs, 91% of all the bombs dropped on Japan by all services. At the end of the war the 20AF used the following bomb ratio:

HE Bombs:
40%   500lb GP
30%   2,000lb GP
20%   4,000lb LC
5%   1,000lb GP
5%   Miscellaneous and special purpose

There were no HE bomb shortages during the war, but the 4,000lb bombs were not initially ordered in sufficient quantities.

Incendiary Bombs:
40%   100lb gelled gasoline M-47
40%   500lb clusters M-69 (6lb oil and 10lb oil WP)
20%   500lb clusters M-50/M-52 (4lb magnesium)

There were times when the stocks of incendiary bombs were exhausted, and incendiary missions were curtailed until supply could catch up with demand. Often an available bomb was chosen for the mission, rather than the best bomb type. Frequently incendiary bombs were unloaded from the arriving ships and transported directly to B-29s waiting on their hardstands for loading.

In March 1945 the ratio between percent incendiary and percent HE was 72/28, in July 74/26, and 80/20 in August. For the entire B-29 bombing campaign (June 1944 to August 1945) the bomb ratio was 61% incendiary (as compared to 14% in Europe), 33% HE and fragmentation, and 6% mines. (20AF, *A Statistical Summary of Its Operations Against Japan*, June 44-August 45)

A brief synopsis of the destruction caused by the 159,862 tons of bombs (1,193 tons per day during the last three months of the war):

65 major cities were severely damaged or almost totally destroyed.
178 square miles of industrial urban areas were destroyed.
602 major factories were destroyed.
83% of oil production was destroyed.
75% of aircraft engine production was destroyed.
330,000 killed and 476,000 wounded (Direct civilian casualties in the concentrated 10 month span of B-29 attacks were more than Japanese military forces suffered in three and half years of war).
2.3 million homes were destroyed.
8.5 million civilians were homeless, and 21 million were displaced.

At the end of the war the 20AF had dropped almost 160,000 tons of bombs in 37 weeks, but had another 160,000 tons stocked and ready to drop in the next 11 weeks if the atomic bombs had not ended the war.

Aerial Mining and Mines
On 10/11 August 1944, the XXBC conducted the first B-29 mining mission as part of its China Bay/Palembang raid, but then did not carry out another one for five months, when it sent 76 bombers to mine Singapore harbor on 25/26 January 1945. Japan was very exposed to an air and sea blockade, as its Merchant Marine imported 90% of its coking coal, 86% of its iron ore, 80-90% of its oil, 24% of all coal, and 20% of its food. Particularly vulnerable was Japan's Inland Sea, which carried 80% of the nation's commerce. In October 1944 the Committee of Operation's Analysts (COA) issued an ambitious three-phase plan that called for 15,000 mines to be laid between 1 December 1944 and 31 August 1945, which would sink an estimated 500 ships totaling two million tons. Adm. Chester Nimitz strongly "suggested" that an initial 150 monthly B-29 mining sorties laying 600 mines in the crucial Shimonoski Straits and four major ports would be the minimum effort to secure an adequate blockade. Nimitz went on to ask for 250 monthly B-29 sorties to be conducted between April and September 1945. The XXIBC objected that the training for the mining missions would interfere with their primary strategic bombing mission. The AAF was between the proverbial rock and a hard place, as it did not want to divert its B-29s from their strategic bombing campaign, but also did not want the Navy to ask for Long-Range aircraft (i.e. B-29s) to conduct its own mining campaign. The AAF felt that they had no choice, and drew up a mining plan to begin April 1945 involving 150-200 sorties per month for three months. With this plan the XXIBC could conduct mining sorties when bad weather prevented the strategic bombing on socked in primary targets. A Navy task force arrived on Tinian in mid-January and set up a mine depot that was ready in a month. A detachment of aerial mining experts under Cdr. Ellis Johnson instructed the 313BW on the intricacies of aerial mining. Six trial missions were planned to test equipment and formulate mission tactics. The 504BG (313BW) began the trial missions on 27 January over the bypassed Japanese Islands of Rota and Pagan. Mine laying tests were conducted at altitudes ranging from 1,500, 2,000, 3,000, 10,000, and 25,000ft. The training of the 504BG was followed by training of four crews from each of the other three Bomb Wings of the 313BW, which flew two test missions. These tests determined that low altitude solo mine drop sorties conducted at night with radar were optimal. Bombing altitudes of 5,000 to 8,000ft were chosen for the same reasons as city bombing. Japanese AA was ineffective at these altitudes, barrage balloons were moored below 4,000ft, the majority of the Japanese hills were below 5,000ft, and nearly

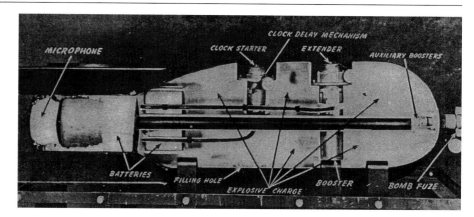

The Mark 13 acoustic mine had a battery-supplied microphone in its tail section. It rested on the bottom at no more than 150ft, and was detonated by the noise of ship's propellers or engines that passed directly overhead. (USAF)

double the bomb load could be carried. The mines were dropped by parachute to decrease the effect of the impact on the water. High altitude drops by parachute were basically inaccurate, as the lower the drop altitude the less the parachute drift, and the higher the accuracy. When dropped from 25,000ft the mine floated for a minute and a half, and landed with an "accuracy" of one mile. The low-level night missions with the increased mine loads were determined to be 20 times more effective as daylight high altitude mining sorties, and 10 times more effective as nighttime high altitude mining sorties. The skill of the radar operator was paramount, as all mines were aimed by radar. The 313BW became the "mining wing," and by the time its first mission was flown on 27 March it had 182 of its 205 crews trained for mining.

Operation Starvation

The mining campaign was appropriately code named *Operation Starvation*, and was a five-phase campaign designed to play a part in the blockade of the Japanese Homeland with the objective of:

Aerial view of Shimonoski Straits. The mining campaign was appropriately code named *Operation Starvation* and the first phase was to block narrow Shimonoski Straits, the major waterway between Honshu and Kyushu Islands. 80% of the Japanese merchant fleet passed through these waters and blocking them would deprive the Japanese from resupplying their forces during the battle for Okinawa (USAF)

1) Blockading the Shimonoski Straits, through which 80% of the Japanese merchant fleet passed.
2) Blockading of the industrial and commercial ports in the Inland Sea, and Tokyo and Nagoya.
3) Stop shipping between Korea and Japan by mining Korean ports, and those on the northwestern coast of Japan.

The first phase of *Starvation* was to block narrow Shimonoski Strait, the major waterway between Honshu and Kyushu Islands, to deprive the Japanese from resupplying their forces during the battle for Okinawa. The first night of mining missions (27/28 March 1945) was to be the largest of the war, as 94 313BW B-29 sowed 924 mines in the Shimonoski Strait, and three nights later 87 B-29s dropped 825 mines in the Strait and near three ports. The mines used were magnetic and acoustic, as these were the only detonators available.

A total of 21,389 mines were laid in the mining campaign against Japan, of which the Navy laid 3,000. There were a total of 4,323 aerial mining sorties, of which 2,078 were flown by the USAAF, 1,128 by the RAAF, 631 by the RAF, and 486 by the USN. The 20AF flew 1,529 sorties and laid 12,135 mines in 26 designated minefields in 46 missions. While the 20AF's 1,529 sorties represented only 35% of the total aerial mining sorties, these sorties dropped 58% of the mines (the other mines were dropped mostly by PBY Catalinas that had a mine load capacity of two to four mines each). The result of mining on the total blockade was difficult to separate from the other factors of submarine and direct aerial attacks on Japanese shipping. The *US Strategic Bombing Survey Summary Report* stated that during WWII in the Pacific 8.9 million tons of enemy merchant shipping had been sunk or damaged, and credited 54.7% to submarines, 30.8% to direct air attack, 9.3% to mines, and the remaining 5.2% to accidents and gunfire. Though the 9.3% attributed to mines seems small, it was accomplished in the last four and a half months of the war, as compared to the 44-month submarine campaign. The 20AF flew 40 mine laying B-29s and lost 15 (103 crew), as compared to the 40 other mine laying aircraft lost by other services, while the USN employed about 100 submarines and lost 52 (approximately 4,000 crew) during the entire war. Not included in these figures are the millions of yen, and the estimated 20,000 men and 350 vessels that the Japanese assigned to counter the mining campaign. Also not considered are the number of searchlights and AA guns that were drawn away from the Japanese cities that were beleaguered by B-29 bombing attacks. Mining comprised only 5.7% of the 20AF's missions, as compared to the 94.3% for bombing and incendiary raids, but this small percentage had a comparable economic impact. The destruction of the Japanese merchant fleet prevented food, raw materials, and oil from reaching the Homeland. Thus, it had a direct effect on civilian morale (food) and the war industry, which had no fuel or raw materials for its factories that had been abandoned, and were being fruitlessly bombed in the strategic bombing campaign.

Aerial Mines

Mines are classified by their means of positioning and detonation. Bottom mines rested on the sea floor, moored mines were anchored to the bottom at a specified depth, and drifting mines floated near or on the surface. The other method of classifying mines was by their detonation mechanism. The only firing mechanism used before WWII was the mine that exploded on contact when a ship struck it and bent one of the protruding contact "horns." During WWII the intricate "influence" mines triggered by a ship's physical "disturbance" were developed. The magnetic mine was the first influence mine, and was actuated by a vessel's steel hull, and was followed by the acoustic mine, which detected propeller or machinery noise, and lastly by the pressure mine, which detected movement through the water. In a last mine development designers combined firing mechanisms to make the mines more lethal.

Aerial Mines

Designation	Abbrev.	Actuating Mechanism	Availability	% Usage
Mark 9, Model 1	M-9	Magnetic	—	48%
Mark 13, Model 5, A-3	M-13 A-3	Acoustic	03/45	17%
Mark 25, Model 1, A-5	M-25, A-5	Subsonic	03/45	10%
Mark 25, Model 2 A-6	M-25 A-6	Pressure-magnetic	04/45 —	25%

Based on *Mines Against Japan* Johnson, E.A. & Katcher, D.

Mine Use: 1,000lb Mark 26>53%
2,000lb Mark 25>47%

Mark 25 and Mark 26 Aerial Mine

The most adaptable and prolific aerial mine of WWII was the U.S. Navy's Mark 25, which weighed 2,000lbs, including its 1,250lbs of explosive, and its smaller 1,000lb Mark 26, with 625lbs of explosive. The Mark 25 looked much like a conventional bomb, except for the half-slant to the nose that gave it improved underwater trajectory, and the circular parachute pack at the tail. After the mine left the bomber a static line opened the parachute, which decreased the impact when the mine entered the water. A pair of arming wires passed through small lugs that were recessed in two areas 90-degrees from the two bomb suspension lugs. Mining B-29s were equipped with AN/APQ-13 navigational radar for night and bad weather mine laying over featureless waters. The B-29 required only minor modifications to carry the 12 1,000lb Mark 26 or seven Mark 25 mines, or any combination of the two types. The Mark 25 could be dropped from any altitude above 200ft at a maximum speed of 230mph into waters of 16 to 150ft depth. After the mine came to rest on the sea floor it armed itself, conforming to the preflight settings, and then waited for an enemy vessel. The different Mark 25 models were distinguished by particular detonators

The most adaptable and prolific aerial mines of World War II was the US Navy's Mark 25 that weighed 2,000lbs including its 1,250lbs of explosive. (USAF)

for magnetic, acoustic, or pressure actuation, by clock starters and delays, by ship counters, and by redundant safety attributes. The minefield planner would select a Mark 25 model considering the water depth, types of ships, and traffic frequency in the area, as well as enemy minesweeping capabilities. Aerial mines could be adjusted so that a number of ships, usually mine sweepers, were allowed to pass so that the mines could explode under the transports. All mines were equipped with "sterilizing" devices that disarmed them after a specific time.

Mark 13 Model 5 Acoustic Mine and Mark 9 Model 1 Magnetic Mine

The Mark 13 acoustic had a battery-supplied microphone in its tail section. It rested on the bottom at no more than 150ft, and was detonated by the

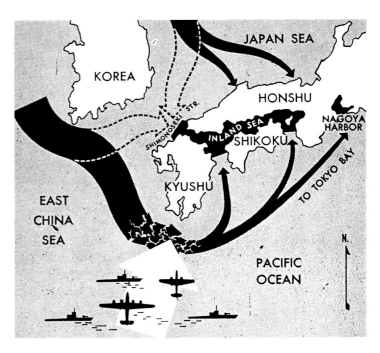

Mining of the Japanese Homeland. (USAF)

noise of ship's propellers or engines that passed directly overhead. The microphone electrically influenced the mine's timing mechanism, which then operated the firing relay. The Japanese swept these mines by sending artificial noise into the surrounding water, where they were easily detonated, and one explosion could also cause the other nearby acoustic mines to detonate (acoustic mines often just detonated without reason). The Mark 9 magnetic mines were set off by the change in the earth's magnetic field produced by the iron in the hull of a passing vessel. These mines were cleared by sweeping the area with a wire supplied with an electric current that set up a magnetic field that fired the mines. In areas where there was limited mine sweeping the older type acoustic or magnetic mines were used, while the more sophisticated pressure magnetic mines were used in the Shimonoski Straits.

Minefield Planning and Mine Laying

Minefield planning depended on many details. All mining missions were radar controlled, with the radar IP and AP points having to be selected, taking into account the location of the minefield, the surrounding terrain, and any nearby AA opposition. The width of the channel determined the sensitivity of the firing mechanism, and the time between each mine release. The type and effectiveness of Japanese countermeasures determined the proper mix of detonators.

The mine laying procedure was for bombers to fly at low altitudes between 5,000 and 8,000ft to drop mines at night. This scheme eliminated the need for large defensive formations, as bombers flying at night were less likely to be detected by enemy defenses, and to be intercepted by enemy fighters. Also, more bombs could be carried, and could be dropped more accurately, and the dropped mines were more likely to remain undetected. Another consideration for night drops was if a B-29 did not return to base, there were 12 hours of daylight for search and rescue (SAR). AN/APQ-13 radar made the identity of initial and aiming points easy, and the bomber would drop its mines in a string. These individual strings of mines created a broad area of water that was dangerous to enemy shipping.

Atomic Bomb Missions—the Bombs
Background and Rationale

The XXBC B-29s began their operations against the Japanese Homeland in August 1944, when the 58BW bombed the Yawata Steel Works. The XXBC overcame overwhelming logistical problems while operating from bases in India and advanced bases in China. Bombs were dropped on Manchuria, Korea, and Thailand, and 800 tons on Japan—a small amount in the future bombing scheme, but a portent to the Japanese. In late November 1944 the B-29s of the XXIBC operating from the Marianas began a large-scale offensive against Japan. The offensive was based on the AAF's traditional daylight visual precision bombing ideology, and mainly against the Japanese aircraft industry, particularly engine manufacture. The offensive continued until early March with mixed results, but Japanese fighter production did begin to decline from Fall 1944. On 9 March 1945 LeMay made his significant decision to shift to low-level firebombing, and in 10 days 9,373 tons of incendiaries decimated four of Japan's largest cities and 31 square miles of urban and industrial area. In April and early May the XXIBC moved on to a tactical role in supporting the invasion and fierce fighting on Okinawa, and disrupting the destructive kamikaze attacks at their bases on Kyushu. Once Okinawa was secured the bomber offensive was continued, utilizing mostly incendiary attacks, but also precision bombing, depending on the target. During May and June six more of Japan's largest cities were written off, and the target lists included the enemy's secondary cities. By the time the atomic bombs were ready the B-29s delivered 91% (147,000 tons of 160,800 total tons) of all bombs dropped on Japan, and 66 urban areas and 178 square miles were unlivable. This total bomb tonnage was one ninth that dropped on Germany, but caused equivalent damage in terms of the effect on Japan's ability to wage war. Before the atomic bombs were dropped, statistically Japan was thoroughly beaten and unable to effectively wage war. Whether it was necessary to drop the atomic bombs remains an unending ethical and political question that is more easily raised after the fact by today's revisionists of WWII history. In the context of August 1945 was the specter of invading the Japanese is-

The aerial mine laying procedure was for bombers to fly at low altitudes between 5,000 and 8,000ft to drop mines at night. The Mark 25 looked much like a conventional bomb except for the half-slant to the nose that give it improved underwater trajectory and also by the circular parachute pack at the tail. After the mine left the bomber a static line opened the parachute which decreased the impact when the mine entered the water. (USAF)

lands with colossal casualties, and of the Russian army that was about to enter the war, over running Manchuria, and then taking easy spoils in Asia. After Hiroshima and Nagasaki the collective Japanese military and civilian psyche changed, and the Emperor was forced to stop the bleeding and end the war.

The Atomic Bombs

In general usage, the atomic bomb refers to the type of bombs used on Japan, but to be accurate, the hydrogen bomb is also an atomic bomb, as both use the energy released from the nucleus of atoms. The earlier atomic bombs released energy by nuclear fission (the splitting of the atom), while the hydrogen bomb worked by nuclear fusion (the joining of small atoms together to make larger ones).

The force of nuclear fission results from the forces holding each individual atom of a material together. Atoms are made up of three kinds of particles: protons and neutrons, which form the nucleus of an atom; and electrons that circle the nucleus. Most naturally occurring elements have very stable atoms, and are virtually impossible to split, but the metal uranium has atoms that are relatively easy to split, because it is an extremely heavy metal, with the largest atoms of any element. There are two isotopes (a form of an element defined by the number of neutrons in its atom) of uranium. Natural uranium consists mainly of the isotope U-238, but also contains about 0.6% of the isotope U-235. Unlike U-238, the atoms of U-235 can be split. Both isotopes of uranium are naturally radioactive (i.e. their large, unstable atoms slowly disintegrate over long periods of time). The atoms of U-235 can be forced to break up much faster in a chain reaction by having its atoms forcibly split by neutrons traveling at speeds near that of light. The U-235 atom is so unstable that the impact from another neutron is able to split it. As U-235 splits it gives off energy in the form of heat and harmful gamma radiation, and also two or three extra neutrons are thrown out and split other atoms to start a chain reaction. The chain reaction occurs within a millionth of a second to create an atomic explosion.

Theoretically, only one split U-235 atom should be needed to yield enough neutrons to split other atoms to create a chain reaction. But in practice, there has to be a certain weight of U-235, called the "critical mass," present to produce a chain reaction that will maintain itself. If there is less than this amount there will be too few atoms to ensure that the neutrons from every other atom that had split will hit other unsplit atoms. The weight of pure U-235 required 110lbs, but U-235 is never quite pure, and more is needed. Uranium is not the only substance used in manufacturing atomic

bombs; the other is the man-made element plutonium in its isotope form, U-239. Of course, building an atomic bomb is far more complicated than placing a piece of uranium larger than critical mass inside a bomb casing, as it would explode at once. Two pieces of fissionable material are placed safely apart inside the bomb casing, and intricate mechanisms place the two together by either "shooting" them together or "assembling" them to start the chain reaction.

Hiroshima Mission
"Little Boy" Bomb

The simplest atomic bomb is the "gun-type," in which the atomic portion of the bomb was encased in a lead shield container. At one end of the barrel is a "target" piece of U-235 that is slightly smaller than the critical mass. This piece of U-235 is spherical, with a conical wedge removed from it. This conical wedge cut extends into the center of the sphere and faces toward the other end of the barrel. At the other end of the barrel there is another conical wedge of U-235 that is exactly the same size as the target conical wedge, and is covered by a neutron reflector. This piece has its pointed end facing toward the conical cut in the target, and the two pieces are just over critical mass. The smaller piece has a high explosive charge behind it that, when discharged, shoots the cone into the sphere, and the force of the collision joined the two pieces solidly together, and the bomb exploded instantly. The bomb was estimated to have a potential yield of 15-16 kilotons of TNT.

The cast bomb casing was fitted with a box-frame tail cone and stabilizing fins, and had airstream deflectors on the casing forward of the tail cone. Little Boy measured 10ft long by 29in in diameter and weighed 8,900lbs. It was encased in an armored, blackened dull steel jacket with a flat, rounded nose. Telemetry monitoring probes and associated batteries were placed on the outside of the forward bomb casing.

Loading

The bomb was transported on a detachable cradle on a special dolly covered with a concealing tarp, and wheeled to a protective 13x16ft pit for temporary storage. When the bomb was ready to be loaded it was transported along tracks and positioned over a nine-foot pit, where a hydraulic lift took it from the dolly that was then removed, along with the tracks. The lift rotated the bomb 90-degrees and lowered it into the pit. The B-29 was towed next to the pit with the wheels of its main landing gear nearest the pit, positioned on a turntable that rotated the bomber 180-degrees until it was over the pit. The hydraulic lift raised the bomb to a point directly under the open forward bomb bay doors. The next step was an exacting procedure, as there was little clearance in the bomb bay and the catwalks. A plumb bob was dropped from a bomb shackle as a guide to line up the bomb cradle jacks, which then lifted the bomb to the single shackle. Adjustable sway braces were attached to the bomb, and after 20 to 25 minutes the bomb was loaded.

Fusing

The bomb had a triple fusing system to arm it. Outwardly there were short trailing radar whip antennae, clock wires threaded into holes in the bomb's upper casing toward the tail, and a hole in the tapered tail end that admitted external air for the barometric readings. The main fuse was a radar unit adapted from a tail warning IFF device, "Archie," developed to warn of aircraft approaching from the rear. Both Little Boy and Fat Man carried

Little Boy (USAF)

Loading Little Boy into the *Enola Gay*. (USAF)

four Archies as a redundant safety measure. Instead of warning of an approaching aircraft, this radar unit would transmit signals off the approaching ground. At a pre-determined altitude, agreement by any two of the four units would send a firing signal to the next stage of fusing. This phase consisted of a number of clock-activated switches that were activated after 15 seconds by arming wires that were pulled out of the clocks when the bomb was dropped out of the bomb bay. Their function was to prevent detonation in case the Archie units were activated by signals that were reflected from the bomber. A second arming device was a barometric pressure switch that was pre-set to close at a pressure corresponding to 7,000ft. After this barometric arming a firing signal was sent directly to the primers, which lit the cordite charges that initiated the "atomic gun" and shot the conical wedge into the sphere to start the chain reaction.

The Mission and the Bomb

On 6 August 1945, seven B-29s of the 509th Composite Group were scheduled to take part in the mission, with three bombers in the strike force. Col. Paul Tibbets was the Group Commander and airplane commander of the lead B-29, the *Enola Gay*, which he named after his mother. The two other B-29s—the *Great Artiste*, piloted by Maj. Charles Sweeney, and *Necessary Evil*, piloted by Capt. George Marquand—were assigned to the mission as photographic and scientific blast measurement escorts, respectively. Three other B-29s were to fly over three targets to determine which had the best weather for the mission. These were the *Full House* (Pilot: Capt. Ralph Taylor, Target: Nagasaki), *Jabbitt III* (Maj. John Wilson/Kokura), and *Straight Flush* (Maj. Claude Eatherly/Hiroshima). A spare B-29 (*Big Stink*) was stationed at Iwo Jima (note: *Big Stink* later would drop the atomic bomb in the *Crossroads* Bikini tests in 1946). The 12-man *Enola Gay* crew:

Col. Paul Tibbets: Group Commander/airplane commander
Capt. Robert Lewis: co-pilot
Capt. William "Deak" Parsons (USN): weapons officer
Capt. Theodore Van Kirk: navigator
Maj. Thomas Ferebee: bombardier
1Lt. Jacob Beser: electronic countermeasures technician
2Lt. Morris Jeppson: electronics officer/assistant weapons officer
S/Sgt. Robert Caron: tail gunner
S/Sgt. Wyatt Duzenbury: flight engineer
Sgt. Robert Shumard: assistant flight engineer/mechanic

Sgt. Joseph Stiborik: radar operator
Pvt. Richard Nelson: radio operator

Despite the previous great secrecy of the atomic bomb project, there were dozens of photographers and reporters on hand to record the 0245 predawn takeoff of Air Force Special Mission No. 13 (see Pumpkin bombs). Ten minutes after takeoff the *Enola Gay* climbed to 5,000ft, and the two weapons officers, Parsons and Jeppson, climbed into the cramped and unpressurized, but relatively warm (at low altitude in the tropics) bomb bay. They placed green plugs into the bomb that blocked the firing signal and prevented accidental detonation. Then they removed the rear plate and the armored plate underneath and revealed the gun breech. A plug in the breech was unscrewed with a wrench and carefully stored on a rubber pad. Four sections of cordite were placed one at a time in the breech, the plug was replaced, and a firing line was connected and the two plates replaced. This procedure required about a quarter hour, and another 15 minutes were then spent checking the monitoring equipment at the panel at the weapons officer's station in the forward compartment. The bomb now only needed to be armed. At daybreak, just off Iwo Jima the bomber climbed to 9,300ft to rendezvous with the two observation aircraft, and flew on automatic pilot toward Japan. After about another hour and a half, just before the B-

Enola Gay Crew: Kneeling (L-R) Stiborik, Caron, Nelson, Shumard, and Duzenbury. Standing (L-R) Porter, Van Kirk, Ferebee, Tibbetts, Lewis, and Beser. Not pictured Parson and Jeppson. (USAF)

Fat Man (USAF)

29 began its climb to bombing altitude, Parsons returned to the bomb bay to arm the bomb. He removed the green plugs and installed red plugs that activated the bomb's internal batteries. The bomber then began its 45 minute climb to the bombing altitude of 31,500ft after being informed that Hiroshima was all clear. As the *Enola Gay* approached Hiroshima the two escort bombers dropped back, and the crews donned their protective goggles. At 12mi from the drop point, bombardier Ferebee took control of the aircraft for a visual bomb run, with Van Kirk giving him radar course corrections. Ferebee released Little Boy and immediately unclutched his bombsight. Once dropped the bomb fell forward and exploded several miles ahead of release point. If the B-29 continued to fly in the same direction it would fly too close to the explosion, so it had to turn away quickly, banking at 155-degrees to the rear to escape the shock wave. The 155-degree bank was determined as optimal, as it pointed the tail of the bomber directly to the shock wave and not the side of the bomber, which was considered dangerous. The first atomic bomb would explode 1,900ft above the center of Hiroshima at 0816—43 seconds after it fell from the belly of the *Enola Gay*. The explosion was equivalent to 15 to 16 kilotons of TNT; it killed 75,000 people and destroyed 48,000 structures. The *Enola Gay* returned to Tinian without incident after flying for 12 hours, 13 minutes (0815 local time).

Nagasaki Mission
"Fat Man" Bomb

The U-239 plutonium atomic bomb was somewhat less complex and more fissionable than the U-235 bomb. It had a lower critical mass weight of 35.2lbs. This weight could be further reduced to 22lbs by forming a sphere of this weight of U-239, and then surrounding it with non-fissionable U-238. The outer U-238 shell would rebound neutrons back into the center of the fissionable U-239 sphere, and reduced their loss to the outside. Plutonium was not easily exploded by the gun-type mechanism, and needed to be "assembled" with much greater speed than U-235, or it would not explode. The plutonium atomic bomb was assembled by a procedure called "implosion." The plutonium was shaped into a number of wedge-shaped pieces that, when placed together, would form a sphere. These wedges were grouped in a ring at equal intervals around a source of neutrons. Explosive charges of exactly equal weight were positioned behind each wedge. When the charges were detonated they fired each wedge towards the cen-

ter of the ring, and they collided at exactly the same instant to start the chain reaction and explosion. "Fat Man" was 10ft, 8in long, but was a rotund 60in in diameter and weighed 10,300lbs.

The Mission and the Bomb

"Fat Man" was originally scheduled for assembly by 11 August, but this date was advanced two days, as good weather was forecast for 9 August. On 8 August the bomb was loaded into the forward bomb bay of *BOCKSCAR*, named after its usual commander, Capt. Frederick Bock. The primary target of Air Force Special Mission No. 16 (there were two Pumpkin Special Missions on 8 August) was to be Kokura Arsenal, and the secondary was Nagasaki. The *BOCKSCAR* bombing crew for the mission was Maj. Charles Sweeney's *Great Artiste* crew with three additional members. The usual *BOCKSCAR* pilot, Capt. Frederick Bock, was flying the *Great Artiste*, which was the scientific aircraft on the mission. A third B-29 (*Big Stink*) piloted by Capt. James Hopkins was also assigned to the mission as the high-speed photo aircraft. *Full House*, piloted by Maj. Ralph Taylor, was the *BOCKSCAR* backup on Iwo Jima. Two weather B-29s (*Up n'Atom*, piloted by Capt. George Marquand to check Kokura, and *Laggin' Dragon*, with Capt. Charles McKnight/Nagasaki) were sent out to recon the weather over the primary and secondary targets. Because a typhoon

Bockscar Crew: Kneeling (L-R) Buckley, Kuharek, Gallagher, DeHart, and Spitzer. Standing (L-R) Beahan, Van Pelt, Albury, Olivi, and Sweeney. Not pictured Ashworth, Barnes, and Beser. (USAF)

was threatening off the coast of Iwo Jima the rendezvous was to be off the Japanese coast of Kyushu. The 13-man *BOCKSCAR* crew:

Maj. Charles Sweeney: squadron commander/airplane commander
1Lt. Charles Albury: pilot
2Lt. Fred Olivi: co-pilot
Capt. James Van Pelt: navigator
Capt. Kermit Beahan: bombardier
Capt. Frederick Ashworth (USN): weapon officer*
1Lt. Jacob Beser: radar counter measures*
2Lt. Philip Barnes: weapon test officer*
M/Sgt. John Kuharek: flight engineer
S/Sgt. Edward Buckley: radar operator
Sgt. Abe Spitzer: radio operator
Sgt. Albert DeHart: tail gunner
Sgt. Raymond Gallagher: assistant engineer/mechanic/scanner
*additional members

The second A-bomb mission was not to duplicate the smooth Hiroshima mission. Shortly before takeoff, the flight engineer (Kuharek) discovered that one of the fuel pumps was not functioning, and 600gals of gasoline in the bomb bay tank were unavailable. This would have been reason to cancel a normal mission, but the Japanese had to be shown that Hiroshima could be quickly repeated, and the weather after the ninth was to be socked in for at least five days. Again with great press fanfare, Capt. Sweeney barely lifted the overweight *BOCKSCAR* off from Tinian at 0347. All the aircraft on the mission ran into bad weather inbound, but both weather aircraft reported good weather over the primary and secondary targets. Then the weapons officers, Ashworth and Barnes, discovered to their dismay that the red arming light on the black box connected to the bomb indicated that the firing circuit had closed. For a half-hour the two calmly traced the problem to a switch malfunction, and the crew could breathe easier. The *BOCKSCAR* and *Great Artiste* rendezvoused off Kyushu, and after waiting 40 minutes for the *Big Stink* the two B-29s continued on toward Kokura. When they reached Kokura the huge army arsenal was obscured by smoke and haze, and after three unsuccessful runs the prescribed visual bombing accuracy could not be attained. Also, the city's heavy AA fire was ranging in, fighters were seen in the distance, and fuel

was becoming a concern. Sweeney decided to head toward Nagasaki, and against orders would use radar if visual bombing were impossible. The weather over Nagasaki was not much better, and 90% of the bombing run was made by radar. At the last second the bombardier (Beahan) saw a break in the clouds and dropped the bomb at 10:58 local time. Sweeney banked the *BOCKSCAR* out of danger and concentrated on returning to base. He had only 300gals of fuel left, which was not enough to get them back to Tinian, and Okinawa or ditching became the alternatives. Sweeney tried to contact the ASR units who did not answer, presuming the three B-29s had already returned to Tinian, so Sweeney turned toward Okinawa. When he reached the island he tried to contact the tower without success. Running very low on fuel he could not afford to circle the field, and as a last resort dropped flares and was given clearance to land at 1400 (local) with only seven gallons of fuel remaining. *BOCKSCAR* was refueled and landed at Tinian at 2330 that night to little fanfare.

"Fat Man" had exploded at 1,650ft above the hilly city with an estimated force of 22 kilotons. However, these steep hills confined the larger explosion of this atomic bomb and caused less damage and loss of life than "Little Boy." The next morning the Japanese Inner Cabinet learned of the Nagasaki attack, and heard a report on the extent of the Hiroshima damage, and that the Russians had invaded Manchuria. However, the Samurai code of the Cabinet members would not allow them to surrender, but Divine Emperor Hirohito intervened, and Japanese Foreign Minister Togo contacted the Allies for surrender terms. Togo qualified the surrender, demanding that the Emperor remain Japan's Sovereign Ruler. President Truman and the Allies agreed, but the Emperor's rule would be subject to the Allied Commander in Japan, and eventually the Japanese people would be free to choose the type of government they wanted as per the Potsdam Agreement. For three more days the Japanese military and civilian regimes could not agree to these surrender terms, and finally, on 14 August, the Emperor acted again, and commanded the divided factions to "bear the unbearable and accept the Allied reply." He also agreed to personally inform his subjects of his decision over the radio the next day. Before noon on the 15th, the Japanese people heard their Emperor for the first time. Despite the fact that the Japanese people had previously only received propaganda that they were winning the war, and that the Emperor's speech was so formal and ambiguous, and that he had not used the word "surrender," the Japanese people understood, and were shocked that Japan was defeated and had surrendered.

B-29 Tankers

The *Matterhorn* plan to bring B-29s to the CBI involved transferring B-29 bases in India to China so that targets in Japanese occupied areas, and even

Since seven gallons of fuel were burned for every gallon delivered it was decided to convert one B-29 of the 40BG into a dedicated tanker (B-29-1-BW/42-6254). The bomber was stripped of all protective armor and armament except the tail guns and the sighting blisters were removed and covered over with aluminum. The converted transport was unofficially designated the "C-29." (USAF)

Japan itself, could be bombed. This involved transferring equipment and supplies, particularly fuel, from India to China. The logistical problems were daunting, and the supply system soon fell behind schedule. It had been decided to use the B-29 as a transport, and even though this would shorten their combat lives, Lt.Gen. K.B. Wolfe and Arnold knew this and the expediency of delivering supplies outweighed the wear and tear on the aircraft. On 24 April 1944 Col. Jake Harman flew the first cargo mission to China, flying 1,200mi in five and half hours from Kharagpur, India, to Kwanghan, China, the advanced base of the 444BG. The distance was not the problem, but crossing the Hump—the towering spine of the world's highest mountains, the 20,000ft+ Himalayas, and their treacherous weather—forced continuous high altitude flying until the bombers could descend to the huge Chengtu Plain.

Since seven gallons of fuel were burned for every gallon delivered it was decided to convert one B-29 of the 40BG into a dedicated tanker (B-29-1-BW/42-6254). The bomber was stripped of all protective armor and armament except the tail guns, and the sighting blisters were removed and covered over with aluminum plates. The converted transport was unofficially designated the "C-29." Four bomb bay tanks increased the fuel capacity to 8,050gals, and with its reduced weight it could carry more fuel by weight, and consumed only 2.25gals of fuel per each gallon delivered. The delivered load to China was 2,410gals of gasoline, 100gals of oil, and 3,290lbs of dry cargo. Early that month several more 40BG B-29s were converted to tankers, which had been christened with such appropriate names as *The Gusher* and *Esso Express* (468BS), and the *Petrol Packin' Mama* (462BS) and *Hump-Happy Pappy*, *Hump-Happy Mammy*, and *Hump Happy Jr.* In July, *Hobo Queen* of the 58BW/462BG, with a crew of seven, set a record for gasoline delivered. The veteran YB-29 carried over 4,000gals in six bomb bay tanks, 60 five-gallon cans stowed in the tail, and an additional ton of general cargo for a gross weight of about 137,000lbs. The bomber was the only YB-29 in the CBI, and was the same YB-29 that had flown to the United Kingdom in March as a ruse to have the Germans think that the B-29 was about to be deployed to the ETO. *Camel Caravan* was a 468BG B-29 that had been flown to the CBI by Gen. LaVerne Saunders, and was the first B-29 to reach the forward bases in China. The bomber was converted to a tanker, and flew 47 tanker missions under Maj. Jack Ladd, including three missions in four days.

The combat B-29s continued to be pressed into service as tankers, and Arnold worried that these B-29s were becoming too worn for combat, and ordered that the number of their gasoline transport missions be reduced. These supply missions decreased in August and in September, when the C-109, B-24 transport versions, flown by Liberator-trained B-29 crews, took over the fuel transport duties. The C-109 was a Ford-modified B-24 J or L with turrets deleted, and carrying seven non-jettisonable bomb bay tanks and one tank in the nose to transport 2,900gals of gasoline. In October 11,000 tons, the most monthly supplies of the CBI air campaign, were carried. With the appearance of the C-109 the transport B-29s were sent back to the States in November. The B-24 was never the easiest bomber to fly, and there was a lack of maintenance and parts; consequently, in December the C-109 fuel tankers were withdrawn from service and also were sent back to the States. In 1945 the transports of the Air Transport Command (ATC) carried the bulk of the supplies.

From February 1944 to February 1945 the Hump airlift transported approximately 45,000 tons of supplies, with the ATC carrying 76%, combat B-29s 13%, B-29 tankers 9%, and the C-109s only 3%. Aviation fuel accounted for almost 90% of the supplies carried. The 5,000 ton monthly requirement (to support 225 combat sorties) was only met for three of the months during the campaign. The XXBC had originally estimated that, with the required supplies delivered, it could fly 432 sorties per month from Chinese bases. But in September it flew 217, in October (the record supply ferrying month) it flew 310, November 205, 287 in December, and 269 in January (the 58BW flew its last operations from China on 17 January).

Leaflet Mission and Leaflet Bombs

While not thought of as a weapon, millions of leaflets and hundreds of thousands of newspapers were dropped on the Japanese Homeland in the final months of the war. Leaflet sorties were begun in February 1945, but it was not until May that LeMay ordered 100 tons to be dropped monthly. The 73BW conducted the first leaflet drops in June 1945, when it combined leaflet bombs with conventional bombs during their weather missions. Soon leaflet bombs were only dropped as part of weather missions, as the efficacy of the dropping "mental" and "physical" bombs together was questioned. The first leaflets, approved by LeMay, were dropped on a city that was one of 10 listed in the leaflet that was scheduled to be bombed within 72 hours. The leaflets began by stating:

"This advance notice will give your military authorities ample time to take the necessary defensive measures to protect you from our inevitable attack. Watch and see how powerless they are to protect you."

It continued by warning that:

"the systematic destruction of city after city will continue as long as you blindly follow your military leaders, whose blunders have placed you at the very brink of oblivion. It is your responsibility to overthrow the military government now and save what is left of your beautiful country."

They ended by warning the population to evacuate. In June the 73WB dropped 508 bombs, dispersing 15,200,000 leaflets and 101,000 newspapers over Japanese population centers.

The first leaflets, approved by LeMay, were dropped on a city that was one of 10 listed in the leaflet that was scheduled to be bombed within 72 hours. Shown is an actual leaflet warning that B-29s would drop incendiaries on its recipient. (USAF)

In July the 313BW and 314BW joined the 73BW in the combined weather-leaflet missions. The 313BW combined its mining activities with leaflet drops, with their emphasis on the starvation that would result from the mining blockade of Japanese ports. In July more cities were listed as potential bombing targets, and of 31 listed on 5 August 14 were fire bombed by the last day of the war. These forewarnings concerned the B-29 crews, but the Japanese were so defenseless that any opposition was negligible. In July 1,001 leaflet bombs were dropped, dispersing 33,000,000 leaflets and 200,000 newspapers. These figures pale in comparison to six billion leaflets dropped on Europe, 57% by the AAF. After D-Day the Special Leaflet Squadron dropped 1,577,000,000 leaflets, and the 8AF dropped 1,176,000,000 leaflets over Europe.

There were several ways to disperse leaflets. One was the olive drab Mark II 500lb leaflet bomb, which was used for accurate spot bombing in tactical situations, such as persuading defenders of a small area to surrender. The M-26 and M-16 bomb cases were the main leaflet bombs. These bombs had a tail fin and a two-piece casing that was joined longitudinally, and separated after the bomb was jettisoned by a fused detonation. Another method was simply to pack the tied bundles of leaflets onto a pallet into the bomb bay. When they were dropped the ties on the bundles would break open in the wind stream, and they would disperse over the countryside.

The M-26 and M-16 bomb cases were the main leaflet bombs. These bombs had a tail fin and a two-piece casing that was joined longitudinally and separated after the bomb was jettisoned by a fused detonation. (USAF)

POW Supply Missions

When the Japanese surrendered on 15 August 1945, they held 70,000 Allied POW in 150 camps, with two-thirds in Japan, and the remainder in China, Formosa, Manchuria, and Korea. Until they could be liberated by occupation troops it was imperative that the sick and starving prisoners were supplied with food, clothing, and medicine. But first the locations of the camps had to be plotted, the logistics sorted out, and the supplies gathered. The 73BW, based at Isley Field on Saipan, was to administer the operation, but B-29s from the other wings flew in supplies to be packed at Saipan from sub-depots at Guam and elsewhere. The B-29s participating in these missions had large capital letters spelling out "P.W. SUPPLIES" on the under surfaces of their wings. These were black letters on natural finish, and white letters on B-29s painted with anti-glare black undersurfaces. The 315BW flew airlift missions to the Philippines to bring in 24,000 supply parachutes, but an unsuccessful test drop was made on Isley Field, and some chutes failed to open, and all 24,000 of the chutes had to be opened and repacked. The Air Service crews, who called themselves "Saipan Samaritans," worked three eight-hour shifts to weld two barrels together to supply enough barrels for the drops. They welded 1,800 supply drums, which looked like little blockbuster bombs, and were hung from the bomb bay bomb shackles. More supplies were packed on pallets stacked on special bomb bay cargo platforms with parachutes on top. Everyone, including flight crews, helped to load the supplies. The B-29s carried sufficient supplies for 200 prisoners in 18 bundles or drums loaded in the bomb bays to be dropped at 1,000ft. The camps were identified by "POW" painted on the roofs of the buildings, or by panels on the ground.

The B-29s lined up in long rows called "Conga Lines" to be loaded and then for take off. The first drop on each camp contained sufficient supplies for three days. If the camp was not liberated by that time then a second drop was made with supplies for seven more days. If a third drop was necessary then food for 10 more days was dropped. The first POW supply drop was made on 8 August on the camp at Weisien, on the Shantung Peninsula, China. All five Bomb Wings participated in the POW supply missions: the 58BW and 313BW on Tinian; the 314BW and 315BW on

In July 1945 1,001 leaflet bombs were dropped on Japan dispersing 33,000,000 leaflets and 200,000 newspapers. These figures paled in comparison to six billion leaflets dropped on Europe. (USAF)

The B-29s lined up in long rows called "Conga Lines" to be loaded and then for take off. All five Bomb Wings participated in the POW supply missions, the 58BW and 313BW on Tinian, the 314BW and 315BW on Guam and the 73BW on Saipan. B-29s flew into Isley to be loaded for these missions but sometimes also brought in additional supplies from sub depots at Tinian and Guam. (USAF)

The B-29s participating in these missions had large capital letters spelling out "P.W. SUPPLIES" on the under surfaces of their wings. There were black letters on natural finish and white letters on B-29s painted with anti-glare black undersurfaces. (USAF)

Guam; and the 73BW on Saipan. B-29s flew into Isley to be loaded for these missions, but sometimes also brought in additional supplies from sub depots at Tinian and Guam. The 315BW flew three of the longest missions of the war when it flew 4,000mi round trips to Mukden, Manchuria. After a month there were only three camps that needed further supplies, and the final drop was made on 20 September 1945. There were cases of Japanese civilians intercepting errant supplies, but by and large the drops were accurate and timely, and there were instances of these civilians returning the supplies to the camps. The wings flew 1,010 sorties, dropping 4,104 tons of supplies on 154 camps to 63,500 POWs. Seven B-29s were lost in these mercy missions.

The last B-29 shot down in WWII was lost on 29 August 1945, during a POW supply drop on a camp near Hamhung, Korea. *Hog Wild* of the 500BG, piloted by 1Lt. Joseph Queen, was in the area of the camp when a pair of Russian Yak fighters approached and signaled Queen to follow them. The B-29 followed, and was led to a small landing strip about 10 miles from the camp. Queen turned back toward the POW camp, but the Soviets fired across his nose and motioned him to land. Instead Queen turned to-ward Iwo Jima, but after he reached the Korean coast the Yaks attacked and set the bomber's #1 engine on fire. Queen ordered the crew to bail out, but after six had jumped the engine fire subsided somewhat, and Queen decided to land on the Soviet strip. He landed safely, and the Russians were able to extinguish the fire, and took the remaining crew captive. Queen explained that their mission was a POW supply drop, and were allowed to return to *Hog Wild* to pick up personal belongings. While they were in the aircraft they noticed that it had been stripped of papers, as well as the aircraft commander's handbook and some equipment. At the end of the war the Russians were interested in duplicating the B-29, and *Hog Wild* was a late factory model. The next day Queen and his crew began to walk toward the bomber and were forcibly detained. On 31 August the six crewmen who had bailed out were returned, and Queen was allowed to contact Saipan by his aircraft radio. He asked for spare parts to repair the bomber, and on 11 September a C-47 flew in. Queen decided to salvage the bomber rather than repair it, and all flight instruments, gunsights, bombsight radar, and other sensitive equipment were removed, loaded in the C-47, and flown back to Saipan with the crew.

1,800 supply drums were welded together to look like little blockbuster bombs and were hung from the bomb bay bomb shackles. More supplies were packed on pallets stacked on special bomb bay cargo platforms with parachutes on top. (USAF)

7

Japanese Defenses

B-29 Vulnerability

During the war the 20AF flew 31,387 bomber sorties (3,058 by the XXBC and 28,329 by the XXIBC), with 29,153 effective and 25,410 reaching the primary or secondary target. B-29 losses (including operational losses on combat missions) totaled 360. Operating from the CBI, the XXBC lost 38 bombers over Japan and 18 over Manchuria. The XXIBC lost 304 B-29s: 50 from November to February 1945; 24 in February 1945; 28 in March 1945; 39 in April 1945; 23 during April-May 1945 attacks on Kyushu; 98 in May-June 1945; 33 in July-August 1945; and 9 during the March-August 1945 mining missions. Losses on combat missions averaged 1.3% of sorties airborne, and 147 bombers were lost as the direct result of combat: 50% to enemy fighters; 36% to anti aircraft fire; 13% to a combination of both; and 1% to collisions. A further 260 B-29s were lost in the United States. B-29 crew losses were 576 killed in action, 2,406 missing in action, and 433 wounded and evacuated. In a AAF School of Applied Tactics study of 129 downed B-29s, it was found that engine failure accounted for 25%, combat (flak and fighters) 21%, navigational error 21%, mechanical failure 13%, fire 6%, weather 6%, and others 6%.

Compared to Europe the enemy fighter opposition was light. There were 11,026 fighter attacks reported by 31,387 sorties, or one in three sor-

Japanese fighter opposition reached it zenith on 27 January 1945 when 56 B-29s were assaulted by 984 fighter attacks that destroyed nine B-29s. The last effective enemy fighter opposition was met on 5 June 1945 when 483 B-29s endured 672 fighter attacks with nine B-29s being lost to the fighters and flak. (USAF)

ties met fighters, but the bombers in the early missions were attacked more often. B-29 gunners claimed 714 enemy fighters destroyed, 456 probably destroyed, and 770 damaged for a loss rate of between 6.5% and 10.6%, vs. a 1.4% loss rate (approximately 450 B-29s) to all causes.

The XXBC in the CBI drew the heaviest fighter opposition, as its 3,058 sorties drew over 2,200 enemy fighter interceptions, or about 72% of the bombers met enemy fighters. The XXIBC examined its first 25 (all daylight) missions (ending with the 6 January 1945 Omura mission), and reported that its bombers had encountered over 2,200 interceptors, mainly over Kyushu and Anshan-Mukden (XXBC: *"Enemy Tactics: 25 Mission Summary,"* 6 Feb.1945). The majority (87%) of the combat occurred over the target area, and mostly (58%) after bombing. Only 11% were reported as coordinated attacks, a figure that was credited to the B-29 formations operating at high altitudes and its high speed, but also to the inadequate high altitude performance of the Japanese fighters, and the poor training and limited skill of the Japanese pilots available to defend the Homeland. The study showed that 41% of the attacks were on the nose (56% from above), and only 16% were from the rear (60% from below), with the frontal attacks being much more successful. On these 25 missions gunners were credited with downing 130 enemy aircraft, or an estimated 17% of the attacking force. With the prevalence of nose attacks the bombardier and CFC gunners claimed about 25% each of the aerial victories, while the tail gunner claimed 19%, and the remaining 31% were about equally divided between the waist gunners.

The XXIBC B-29s drew approximately 8,800 fighter attacks on their 28,000 sorties, or approximately one in three of its bombers met enemy fighters. The XXIBC found that its missions flown at lower altitudes drew more Japanese interceptors and suffered more casualties. Of 64 bombers lost, 46 were lost to interceptors, 17 to unknown causes, and only one directly to AA fire (the loss of four additional B-29s was partly attributed to flak). However, Japanese AA fire did cause 47% of the damage to bombers that returned to base.

Japanese Early Warning System

The Japanese early warning system was made up of a rudimentary system of picket boats, air-warning stations, land-based radar, and visual observation.

Japanese Navy picket boats operated in pairs as much as 300mi south and east of Japan at intervals of 50 to 60mi. Although a few picket boats were equipped with radar, most relied on visual and auditory spotting. They communicated to shore via radio by a naval code, and in urgent situations by voice. The Japanese Army was also able to obtain this early warning by monitoring the Navy channel. VII Fighter Command fighters sank many of these boats by the end of the war, and their effectiveness was nil. Small patrol boats, converted from fishing boats, were also positioned only about 50mi off the Japanese coast, and sent radio warnings of the approaching bombings, but these warnings were not early enough to be of much use.

The Japanese located offshore air warning stations in the Nanpo Shoto Islands, which extended 670mi south of Tokyo, and terminated with the Volcano Islands (Iwo Jima). These warning stations depended on visual and auditory spotting that would be transmitted to Japan, and only a few of the islands close to Japan were equipped with radar. B-29s were routed around these outer islands despite their usefulness as navigation points.

The early Japanese Type A warning radar was of the Doppler-type, utilizing a radio transmitter operating on 40-80Mc that sent out continuous radio beams with a superimposed audio beam to a receiving station from 40 to 100mi away. When a bomber crossed the beam a tone was heard at the receiving station that only indicated that an aircraft was somewhere between the transmitter and receiver. A Japanese technical legation returned from Germany in 1940, and work was started on pulse-type radar. By 1942 the Army and Navy had both built the short-range Radio Detector No.12 and 13, Mark I Model II and III sets, culminating in the Radio Detector No.14 MKI, Model IV operating at 50Mc. The Japanese had a chain of the Model 12 and 13 sets—supplemented by the newer Model 14 sets—ground radar stations on the south coast of Honshu, Shikoku, and Kyushu, and on the islands near the coast. There were numerous gaps in the coverage, but the approaches to important targets were well covered. Many Army and Navy radar stations operated virtually side by side, which was another example of the failure of these two services to cooperate. The usual radar setup was two stations, although several had as many as five. There were three lines of radar defense at 10, 30, and 60 minutes flying time from the target area. Radar data was relayed for plotting to control centers operated by various Military District Armies that coordinated the fighters, AA, and civilian defense. Both the Army and Navy radar provided disparate ranges, and neither was able to determine the altitude, or whether fighters escorted the formation.

The Japanese Army and Navy both used civilian and military observers organized into an Air Defense Observation Corps. Army observers were divided into Air Reporting Regiments that were, in turn, split into smaller groups that reported by a direct landline to a section HQ that had land communication with the operations center of the local District Ground Army. The Navy had a similar organization reporting to a Navy District HQ. These observers were especially useful in areas where the topography prevented accurate radar function, and in reporting the formation size, escort, and target probability.

Four Army District Ground Armies in Japan were responsible for the collection of early air raid warning information from the Army warning system, and its distribution to the various air force, AA, ground, and Navy commands (after April 1945 the four District Armies were replaced by six Area Armies). Of the four District Armies only three, Tokyo, Osaka, and Fukuoka, had to be concerned with defense, as Sapporo, on the northern island of Hokkaido, was not a target area. Each District Army had opera-

tions centers that were to act as a conduit for all air raid information. The data was transferred to plotting boards, and the conclusions drawn were sent to air, AA, and ground units. The air units in each district were located at the operations centers, and directed their operational aircraft from there. In April 1945 the six Area Armies operated under the same warning system. The warning system was limited by the deficient radio communications system, and the slower telegraphic systems had to be used. The Nagoya area, which contained many important targets, was not the headquarters of a District Army, and only had a Flying Brigade assigned to it. The Brigade was subordinate to the Flying Division located at Osaka, and all information and orders had to channel through Osaka, which delayed any response. In April 1945 Nagoya became the headquarters of a new Area Army, but the Army instituted an air defense comparable to the original three Districts. The Flying Divisions usually made the decision when to intercept, but tactical control of the fighter units was under unit commanders. These commanders received abridged reports of the information collected by the District operations centers, and had to act with this limited, often late, information. Four main Naval District Headquarters located at Kokosuka, Maizuru, Kure, and Sasebo collected the Navy early warning information. The Navy system was very similar to the Army system, with operations centers located in the four headquarters. Unfortunately, the Navy unit commanders also were distanced, and received belated abridged information. The Army and Navy exchanged early warning information via liaison officers, monitoring radio messages and direct landlines between the two services. In lieu of a single integrated warning system these communications options should have been adequate; however, the unfortunate war-long Army-Navy rivalry prevented comprehensive use of the system.

Japanese Fighter Opposition

Three Phases of B-29 Bombing Operations from the Marianas and Japanese Fighter Opposition:

Phase 1) High Altitude Precision Daylight Missions
(24 November 1944 to 25 February 1945)
The bombing strategy for this period was limited by a relatively small number of B-29s, and by their range and target options. The Japanese were able to consolidate their fighters to protect these key targets, and put up their most effective defense, which improved over the period. Japanese fighter opposition reached its zenith on 27 January 1945, when 56 B-29s were assaulted by 984 fighter attacks that destroyed nine B-29s.

Phase 2) Low and Medium Altitude Daylight Missions
(25 February to 14 August 1945)
The last effective enemy fighter opposition was met on 5 June 1945, when 483 B-29s endured 672 fighter attacks, with nine B-29s being lost to the fighters and flak (69 Japanese fighters were claimed to be shot down). The diminished Japanese fighter interception was caused by:
a)   Increasing numbers of B-29s arriving in the Marianas from February 1945.
b)   The B-29s flew at lower altitudes, giving them longer ranges, and put more targets into danger; the Japanese had to stretch their constantly diminishing fighter forces to meet this new threat, and could no longer concentrate its forces.
c)   The Japanese lost a large number of aircraft during the battle for Okinawa, and during the B-29 interdiction bombings on Kyushu and

southern Honshu.

d) Japanese aircraft assembly and engine production were decreased by the B-29 bombings.

e) When Okinawa was captured the Japanese decided to conserve their air forces to be used against the threatened invasion of the Homeland.

f) Long-Range P-51 fighter escorts for the B-29s became available, and destroyed Japanese fighters in the air and on the ground.

Phase 3) Night Missions (9 March 1945 to 14 August 1945)
The Japanese night fighter force was never very numerous or effective, as without airborne radar they had chronic problems in locating and maintaining contact with the B-29s at night.

Japanese Fighter Control
The inadequate Japanese early warning system gave the Japanese no accurate track of the approaching B-29s until they were less than 150mi (30 minutes) off the coast of Japan. The bomber's over-water approach to within such close range of a wide area of coast prevented the Japanese from effectively channeling the bomber's approach routes by deploying their limited number of AA guns. When the XXIBC was able to attack more widely dispersed targets at once with their increased number of bombers, the Japanese were hesitant to commit their fighter forces. It was not for some time after the bombers crossed into Japanese territory that the controllers were able to determine the target and commit their aircraft, by which time it was too late to reinforce the target with fighters from other areas. For this reason there were few or no interceptions of the bombers along their route before they dropped their bombs. As described, the Japanese fighter control stations were divided into large Districts (later Areas) corresponding to important industrial and urban areas. In each District there was a central control station, and smaller sub-districts that communicated with each other and their central District. There was District-to-District communication, with each district controlling its own fighter net. However, each central control District was reluctant to relinquish its fighters to another control District. The smaller District sub-stations were assigned to direct fighters for the protection of their target area. Ground control of the fighters was under unit commanders, rather than the larger Flying Divisions. This system put only 10 to 50 planes from several units into the air, and each unit under different ground control. The amount of fighter opposition (with the weather constant) was in direct proportion to the number of fighters based within 100mi of the target. The fighters were sent to assemble over an area supposedly in the path of approaching bombers. But once in the air the interceptors had no current information on the location of the bombers, and had to rely on visual sightings, as radar stations could not vector them.

Deployment of Japanese Fighter Forces
Japanese Army Air Forces (JAAF)
Following the New Guinea campaign in 1943-44, the Japanese Army Air Force lost 30-40% of its combat strength, and the JAAF fell back to the Philippines, where they had 2,100 aircraft transferred from Burma, China, Manchuria, Formosa, the Ryukus, the Kuriles, and the Japanese Homeland. The JAAF was decimated in the Philippines, and the remnants were transferred back to the Homeland at the start of the B-29 raids from the Marianas. Since the Japanese Naval Air Force was committed to Okinawa from bases in Kyushu and southern Honshu, the JAAF was assigned to defend the Homeland against the B-29s, and was supplied with the re-

maining defensive fighters that could be manufactured under bombing duress. However, to supplement their defensive forces the Japanese employed their training aircraft and their neophyte pilots.

Japanese Navy Air Force (JNAF)
In late 1944 the JNAF was reorganized into a series of Area Air Groups to consolidate the remains of its battered combat air units, which suffered huge losses defending the Marianas. However, the Okinawa campaign forced the Japanese to commit almost all their combat naval air, and a few army units (mostly medium bombers) to the defense of Okinawa. The Japanese realized that if Okinawa was captured it would provide another base from which to attack Japan. Therefore, the JNAF would have little use for offensive aircraft, and their medium, torpedo, and dive-bombers were thrown wholesale into the battle. Once Okinawa was lost in mid-June the JNAF converted its Kyushu based fighters from the suicide and bomber attack forces to an interceptor force, which effectively doubled the Japanese Homeland fighter strength against the B-29 attacks. Also, the Japanese were able to almost double fighter production from May 1945, as they had dispersed production, phased out bomber production, and concentrated on fighter production. However, there was not a concomitant increase in fighter attacks, as the Japanese appeared to be conserving their fighter forces for the forthcoming invasion of Japan.

Japanese Fighters
The Japanese fighters were divided into two classes: first line fighters (comparable to the P-51 and P-47) Ki-84 Frank, JM-2 Jack, N1K5J George, and A6M5 Zeke 52; and second line fighters (comparable to the P-40) Ki-61 Tony, Ki-44 Tojo, J1N1-S Irving, Ki-45 Nick, and A6M3 Zeke 32. To meet the B-29 threat, the first line fighters were armed with the 40mm cannon or two 25mm to 35mm machine cannon. The Japanese always had a problem with inadequate radio equipment, with their standard radio only having a range of 50mi at 10,000ft. At the end of the war a newer version radio with a range of 70mi was fitted in the Franks and Tonys. Because Japanese defensive fighters no longer needed extreme range defending Japan they attempted to place more armor protective plate, ranging from crude to so-

Generally, the entire JNAF was based in the Kyushu area in the south while the JAAF was concentrated in the Tokyo area leaving the remainder of Japan either undefended or defended by a token force. Throughout the war the JAAF and JNAF never pooled their resources and the divided their responsibilities unrealistically with the JNAF covering all oceans and naval bases and the JAAF everything else. (USAF)

phisticated. Self-sealing fuel tanks were developed and fitted, but were ineffective against .50cal machine gun fire. In an attempt to produce front line fighters, the Japanese fighter industry converted from the German Daimler-Benz inline type to the 18-cylinder radial 2,000hp type, which was similar to the U.S. Wright types.

As the Japanese attempted to increase front line fighter production to counter the B-29, it was ironic that the B-29 attacks drastically decreased all fighter production (except the Zeke 52, which was considered the least effective of the front line fighters). By March 1945 Japanese fighter production was unable to replenish losses, and the entire Japanese front line fighter strength at that time was committed with no reserve. The paper strength of the Japanese fighter force was constantly far different than what could be put into the air. Japanese maintenance was chronically sub-standard, and by 1945 even more so, with the loss of many experienced maintenance personnel. With the destruction of their airfields it was estimated that the Japanese serviceability rate dropped as low as 25%.

The number and types of Japanese fighters able to intercept the B-29s decreased when the bombers flew over 21,000ft. But as the mission altitudes decreased, all first line and most second line enemy fighters could climb to intercept, and could also stay up longer, as they did not consume fuel climbing to the high altitudes. Thus, the XXIBC flew daylight missions at high altitudes and night missions at low altitudes (6,000-10,000ft), because the Japanese night fighter force was ineffective.

Ineffectiveness of the Japanese Air Forces

Generally, the entire JNAF was based in the Kyushu area, while the JAAF was concentrated in the Tokyo area, and the remainder of Japan was either undefended, or defended by a token force. Throughout the war the JAAF and JNAF never pooled their resources, and they divided their responsibilities unrealistically, with the JNAF covering all oceans and naval bases, and the JAAF everything else. Each service had its separate warning system, with insufficient exchange of information. During the entire 14 month period of the B-29 attacks on Japan the JAAF and JNAF never committed more than 27% of their total fighter strength to the defense of Japan. The U.S. Strategic Bombing Survey (Pacific War) *"Japanese Air Power"* published the following table:

Average Number of Japanese Fighter Attacks per XXIBC Sortie

Nov. 1944 1.1	Feb. 1945 2.2	May 1945 0.3
Dec. 1944 5.1	Mar. 1945 0.2	June 1945 0.3
Jan. 1945 7.9	Apr. 1945 0.8	July 1945 0.02
	Aug. 1945 0.04	

The best month JAAF fighters had against the B-29s was facing the XXBC from China in August 1944, when 1.75% of the bombers were lost, and from then on losses exceeded 1% only in November 1944 (1.47%) and January 1945 (1.29%). At the height of 20AF operations from May to August 1945, losses were less than 0.2%. On 20 August 1944 88 B-29s raided targets in northern Kyushu and lost 14 aircraft to all causes. The 8AF loss rate to Luftwaffe fighters throughout the war was about 0.6%, and in the worst month (April 1943) was 6.1% (vs. the 1.75% over Japan). The proof of the poor showing of the JAAF was the immense damage done to Japanese cities.

Koji Takaki, in *B-29 Hunters of the JAAF* (Osprey, UK, 2003), credits Capt. Fujitaro Ito of the 5th Sentai with 17 B-29 victories and 20 dam-

aged, and Capt. Nagao Shirai of the 244th Sentai with 11 victories. Takaki lists 14 JAAF pilots who shot down five or more B-29s. The top JNAF aces flew the two-seat J1N1-S Gekko, mostly as night fighters. Lt. Yukio Endo shot down eight B-29s and damaged eight others before being shot down in mid-January 1945. CPO Juzo Kuromoto shot down eight B-29s, with five (and one damaged) downed on the night of 25 May 1945

Training

One of the main reasons for the diminished Japanese fighter effectiveness was the shortage of trained pilots through combat losses, and the loss of training facilities in the Philippines, Burma, and Formosa in late 1944. The JAAF lost many air units, and their experienced flying and ground personnel, who could not be evacuated by submarine, ship, or air back to Japan. A further reason was ineffective command and inferior equipment. With the loss of foreign training bases the demand shifted to the overburdened Homeland facilities, where weather and American air attack were not conducive to training. New pilots were inadequately trained and thrown into air defense, where they quickly became casualties, and were replaced by even less adequately trained pilots; a vicious cycle. By the end of March 1945 Japanese Homeland air strength decreased due to the B-29 raids on the aircraft assembly and engine manufacturing plants, and also due to the U.S. Navy carrier raids of February and March that destroyed many Japanese fighters in the air and on the ground. At that time the Imperial General Headquarters decided to conserve its air power for suicide attacks on enemy surface vessels during the attack on Okinawa and the anticipated invasion of Japan. The only time Japanese fighters took off was to intercept unescorted B-29s, and then only under very favorable circumstances (except in July 1945, when B-29 attacks on the small cities were at their height). At the end of the war the Japanese had 10,700 aircraft and 18,000 pilots available for combat. These pilots had only about 100 hours of flying time, and a very few with 600 hours, staff officers, instructors, or veteran pilots were assigned to escort the suicide aircraft.

Japanese Fighter Attack Classification

"Belly Button"

Single Japanese fighters favored a climbing approach on the belly of the B-29 originating from any direction, but commonly the attack was made from the front or rear quarters, was pressed as close as possible, and was broken off by a dive. B-29 gunners began to fire at very Long-Range to encourage the Jap to break off early before he came into effective firing range.

"12 o'clock Express"

The Jap fighter would dive at top speed from 12 o'clock high and open fire from 1,000 to 500yds, and pressed the attack as close as possible to fire as many rounds as possible in the short firing time. Gunners were to be vigilant and place the reticle at maximum range, and wait until the fighter approached to within 1,300yds, then move the reticle to minimum range and encompass the attacker and continue firing until he broke off or dove below out of range. The pilots of single B-29s were to turn away from this attack to force the enemy pilot to make a more difficult deflection shot.

"Side Wheeler"

This attack was made from 3 or 9 o'clock, as the Japanese preferred right-side attacks. The Jap pilot positioned himself to the rear of the formation, out of range, and then flew ahead and in a medium banking turn made his firing run at the beam of the bomber and turned away. Gunners fired short bursts at the enemy fighter on his overtaking run before his turn, and then fired continuously on his firing approach.

"Tail Pecker"

This infrequent attack was a climbing attack on the rear of the bomber from 5 to 7 o'clock. The Jap closed slowly to get an easy, no deflection shot, and stayed low to stay out of range of the tail gunner's radius of fire. The tail gunner would report the enemy approach to the airplane commander, who would raise the nose and expose the enemy fighter to the tail gun's cone of fire.

Because of the high speed of the B-29, enemy attacks from the rear required too much time to close, and so frontal passes were favored, followed by a dive and a climb to gain a position to the rear and below. If the B-29 jinked to evade the Japanese pilots were instructed to feint a pass to the inside of the turn, and at the instant the bomber reversed direction he was to dive below and at the bomber, and hold his position and fire as long as possible.

Studies showed that 95% of all enemy attacks occurred after landfall, and 50% were made in and around the target area. By reducing the B-29 time over the Homeland the Japanese would have less time to organize their interceptions, and would have less time to attack the bomber formations. Of course, the time spent over the target depended on the location of the target and the bombing approach.

Ramming

After six months of operational investigation of the feasibility of ramming the B-29s, in April 1945 the JAAF undertook the training and indoctrinating of its pilots and aircraft. The pilots were thoroughly briefed on the B-29 formations and the bomber itself, including the most effective angles of attack and the vulnerable points of impact. To enable the fighter to climb and maneuver more quickly, all armament and expendable equipment was removed. The finest oxygen and radio equipment was installed and tested in ramming aircraft to give them the greatest chance of success.

Before an impending attack the ram fighters climbed to altitude and formed a "protective circumference" around the center of the strategic area where the bombing attack was expected. Each airplane commander was ordered to remain in his assigned position, and remain in radio contact with the ground and other fighters in the patrol. Once the bombers were located and their route determined the fighters were notified, and climbed to gain altitude superiority, looking for advantageous positions in the clouds and out of the sun. The nose attack was favored, as it was the most advantageous position for a surprise attack, and the fighter faced the least amount of defensive fire (as opposed to the heavy fire faced during an attack on the rear or flanks of the B-29). The fighter was to attack from above (1,000 to 2,000ft) and ahead of the bomber's line of flight. The Japanese pilot had to be alert; as if he was spotted the bomber would make an evasive maneuver to which he had to react. The fighter dove to a point about 300ft below the nose of the bomber, and then throttled back to gain time (lowering the combined closing speed), then pulled up from 300 to 1,000ft to crash into the bomber. The pressurized compartment was the best point of impact in the frontal attack, and the empennage was favored for side and rear ramming attacks. The collision was to be quick, and the wing of the ram fighter

was to be inclined vertically to increase the likelihood of a collision. Mass ramming attacks were the most successful, as opposed to individual attacks. About four times as many B-29s were damaged in ramming tacks than destroyed. Fortunately, by the time the Japanese had fully developed their ramming tactics the Japanese air forces had virtually disappeared from the air.

Inclined Guns

The Luftwaffe had made good use of inclined, upward-firing gun installations, and the Japanese copied them, but not with the same effect. The guns were used primarily on night fighters, and the installation mainly used was the 30-degree forward and upward firing type, but a few 70-degree installations were used. On the Ki-45 the Army used two upward HO-5 20mm cannons, and on the Ki-46 a 70-degree HO-204 37mm cannon. The JNAF Irving used two 30-degree upward and two 30-degree downward Type 99 20mm cannons, the Frances had four Type 99 20mm cannons 30-degree cannons, the Jack had two Type 99 20mm cannons, and the Zeke had one 20mm 30-degree cannon. The inclined guns were not widely installed, and documentation of their success is sparse.

Air-to-Air Bombing

In one air-to-air bombing attack technique the Japanese fighters approached the bomber formations singly or in pairs in frontal attacks from 2,000 to 3,000ft above the formation, and then made a slight 20-degree dive and leveled off at about 300ft above the formation. The first fighter dropped his bomb above the formation and broke off in a steep chandelle up and away to his left, while the other fighter did the same, but to his right. Sometimes the Japanese would send in a "feinter" aircraft to draw attention away from the air-to-air bombing fighters. The B-29 gunners were instructed to shoot at any approaching enemy aircraft from long-range, causing the Japanese fighter to chandelle and exposing his vulnerable belly.

In another air-to-air bombing method at least three or more enemy fighters would coordinate an air-to-air bombing and shooting pass. They would approach at 12 o'clock very close together, line astern. The first two approached high, released their bombs, and dove away, one left and one right. The other fighter or fighters would come in shooting, fast and straight on, immediately after the aerial bombs exploded. The first two fighters were to continue to draw fire, and the bombs were to distract the gunners from the approach of the follow up fighters. Again, the gunners were to open up at long-range on the first two fighters and continue firing, but were on the look out for the follow up fighter(s) that, despite their high speed, were relatively easy targets, as they were flying on a direct firing run.

"Ta-Dan"

Japanese Army fighters carried a 110lb "Ta-Dan" breakaway canister bomb that contained 36 high explosive 0.9lb bomblets (a 66lb Ta-Dan with 36 bombs was also used). The main bomb had an aerial burst fuse that opened the container after release. It was first used in 1943 with minor success in the South Pacific. Ideally the tail attack was the most effective, but the pilots were reluctant to approach the heavy tail armament, and employed the frontal diving attack to release the Ta-Dan. The fighters would climb above and ahead of the B-29 formations, and attempt to time their release by using a set of tables and their gunsight so that the bomblets would explode among the bombers. Because of the precise timing these bombs were

AIR-TO-AIR SCATTERING BOMBS

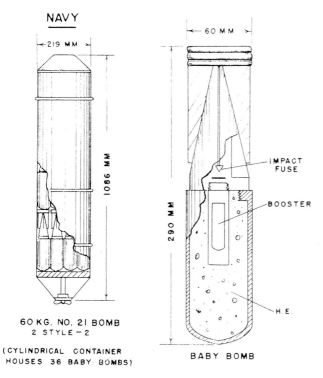

NAVY

← 219 MM →

1086 MM

60 KG. NO. 21 BOMB
2 STYLE-2

(CYLINDRICAL CONTAINER
HOUSES 36 BABY BOMBS)

← 60 MM →

290 MM

IMPACT FUSE

BOOSTER

H.E.

BABY BOMB

ineffective, and only a few bombers were downed. The JNAF counterpart of the Ta-Dan was the 108lb No.21 bomb that housed 36 2.2lb bombs, but was little used by that service.

"Ro-Ta"

When using the Ta-Dan, the interceptor needed to be in position above the bomber formation, but the Ro-Ta developed in 1945 allowed the Japanese fighter to attack from level or low attitude. This aerial bomb had 38 Ta

bomblets in the forward portion, and a time-fused expulsion charge carried in a rocket-propelled container. The weapon, though promising, was not fully developed before the end of the war.

Air-to-Air Phosphorous Bombs
Unlike the JAAF, which concentrated wholly on the Ta-Dan aerial HE bombs, the Navy focused on the incendiary type aerial bomb in operations. The JNAF nomenclature for this aerial burst incendiary shrapnel bomb was "Sango," while American newspaper reports popularized it as "balls of fire," or "fire bomb." There were three sizes: the 70.6lb, the 117lb, and the 551lb, with the 70.6lb, Type 99 Mr-3 being the most commonly used against the B-29 formations. The bomb was constructed of a timed bursting charge of picric acid and 198 phosphorous-filled steel pellets. The tail fin was bent to impart a spin and increase accuracy. The fighter flew about 500ft above an oncoming B-29 formation, and when the bombers closed to about 4,000ft the fighter dropped its bomb, which was thrown forward and exploded above the path of the bombers. The explosion threw out the phosphorous pellets at 1,000fps to create an "incendiary danger cone" into which the bombers would fly.

Parachute Bombs
The Japanese developed their first parachute anti-bomber weapon, the To-2, in 1935. The To-2 was a 4lb bomb usually carried in clusters of 10. After being dropped, each bomb swung suspended by a steel cable from its silk parachute. Two sizes of parachutes were used to give two rates of fall and greater dispersion. The weight of one 10 bomb cluster was only 110lbs, and allowed four clusters (40 bombs) to be carried by a single engine fighter. The method of attack was to have three fighters fly abreast above the formation and drop their bomb clusters into the formation. The chances of a hit were good, and a single hit could bring down a bomber that ran into the cable, which would swing up under the aircraft and detonate its all-ways fuse. The promising bomb ran into several problems. It was developed in the late 1930s when bomber speeds were relatively slow, but by 1945 the fast B-29 would cut its cable on impact. The B-29s flew at high altitudes, and the Japanese had no fighter that could fly above them to attack. Also, the Ta-Dan was more favored, which relegated the parachute bomb to a lower priority.

AIR-TO-AIR INCENDIARY BOMBING

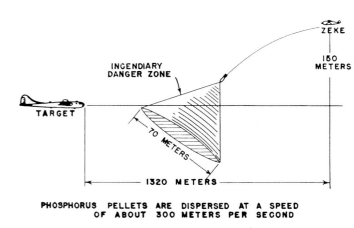

ZEKE

150 METERS

INCENDIARY DANGER ZONE

TARGET

70 METERS

1320 METERS

PHOSPHORUS PELLETS ARE DISPERSED AT A SPEED OF ABOUT 300 METERS PER SECOND

PARACHUTE BOMBING TACTICS

TO-2

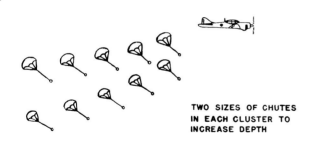

TWO SIZES OF CHUTES IN EACH CLUSTER TO INCREASE DEPTH

Cable Bomb

The Japanese and the Luftwaffe used the idea to drag an impact-fused bomb on a 3,300ft cable behind a fighter into a bomber formation. Unlike the Germans, who used a conventional demolition bomb (and abandoned it because of the high drag), the Japanese used a pair of lightweight bombs with a special release device. The heavier bomb (11lbs) hung 100ft below the lighter bomb (2.2lbs) in aerodynamic slings, and all bombs were fused by all-ways impact fuses. Again, the use of this weapon was precluded by the Japanese lack of a high altitude fighter.

Air-Launched Rockets

By spring 1944 the Japanese began the development of aerial rockets; the Navy concentrated on the fin-type, and the Army the spin-stabilized type, with the first type to be perfected to be put into production by both services. The Navy's fin-type was the first to be accepted, but the Army claimed it could not manufacture them with the equipment in their arsenal, and continued with its spin-stabilized version to the detriment of both. Although there were reports of air-launched rockets being used against B-29s, there are no Japanese records of their operational use.

Japanese AA Guns

Medium Flak

Army 20mm Field AA Model 98 Machine Cannon (1938)
This gun was a single mount with a rate of fire of 120rpm and an effective range of 5,000 to 8,300ft (tracer burn out altitude). It was the most effective and widely used of Japanese medium AA guns.

Navy 25mm Field AA Gun Model 98 Machine Cannon (1936)
This gun could be a single, twin, or triple mount firing 175 to 200rpm per barrel, with an effective range of 8,000 to 10,500ft. It was used on all the important islands of the Japanese perimeter defense and moved to the Homeland, but was not widely used there.

Army 40mm Field AA Gun
The 40mm gun was a single or twin mount firing 60 to 100rpm per barrel, with a range of 5,000 to 8,500ft. The Japanese Army captured 200 British 40mm Bofors guns during the capture of Singapore and continued to use them. The Japanese Navy used a twin-mounted copy of the 1931 British Vickers-Armstrong gun, but it was not used in large numbers

The fire control of medium guns depended on tracer observation (largely in the daytime, and entirely at night). The medium AA shells were not time-fused and exploded on impact, and failing to hit a target exploded at tracer burnout. Medium flak damage was characterized by a small entry hole and a large exit hole, and caused major damage. Medium flak was only a threat to the B-29s during the night attacks and over the large cities (Tokyo, Nagoya, Osaka, etc.), where effective medium flak was encountered up to 10,000ft; over smaller, less important cities the flak was generally ineffective at altitudes of 6,000 to 7,000ft, which indicated that the higher performance guns were used in the more important targets.

Heavy Flak

Army 75mm Field AA Gun Type 88
This gun was one of the most prolific of all Japanese AA guns. It was issued to most Japanese Army units in the field, but as the war went on many were withdrawn to the Japanese Homeland. The design originated in 1928, and was simply constructed from easily machined parts. The gun was mounted on a pedestal that attached to five outrigger legs. Compared to other WWII AA guns, this gun was a substandard performer, having a maximum effective range of 24,000ft, but it was the best Japanese high altitude flak gun.

Army 105mm AA Gun Type 14
The Type 14 was developed in 1925 as a mobile gun, but was too unwieldy, and was used for static AA defense. Like the 75mm Type 88, it was also was unexceptional, but also was another AA gun produced in any number.

Heavy flak was director-controlled and time-fused, and exploded with flying fragments that caused generally minor damage. The continuously pointed fire was the predominate type of heavy flak fire, but predicted concentrations, barrages, and "creeping barrages" were also used. Because their fire control equipment was inadequate the Japanese used the predicted concentration and barrage fire to greatest effect.

The Japanese deployed two, three, and sometimes four six-gun batteries (24 guns) concentrated in a small area, and received information from nearby gun-laying radar. This radar grouping was developed from the German "Grossbatterein" system. The Japanese placed light and medium AA guns on trawlers far offshore to fire on B-29s that were flying at low altitude to conserve fuel before climbing to bombing altitude.

Japanese Gun-Laying Radar

Japanese gun-laying radar first appeared in 1943, and was copied from captured British SCL, GL Mark II, and the U.S. SCR 268 sets. Because the American set was so complex to copy the Japanese chose the British sets as an example. The first two Army sets were the Tachi 1 and 2 developed from the SCL, and were superseded by the Tachi 4. These units had a transmitter and receiver on the same mount, but the set had poor accuracy and was too difficult to use. The 78Mc Tachi 3 was perfected from the British GL Mark II unit, and became the standard Army radar unit. The Navy developed the large and difficult to use S-set that was replaced by the smaller, simpler, and more accurate 75Mc S-24. During B-29 operations, intelligence found that the Japanese had few radar-controlled guns in use, as during raids in 8/10 to 10/10 overcast the AA fire was sparse and inaccurate, indicating that the guns were not radar controlled. Also, during night attacks the gun-laying radar was probably not used, as only B-29s caught in a searchlight beam were fired upon.

Flak explodes the fuel tanks of a B-29 over Japan, leaving the starboard wing and #4 engine behind. (USAF)

Despite losing most of its horizontal stabilizer to flak, this B-29 of the 504BG landed safely on Tinian in July 1945. (USAF)

Evasion of Flak

The XXI BC issued a Flak Intelligence Report entitled "*Evasion of Flak*" in its 12 April 1945 Air Intelligence Report. At the time of the study (early 1945) the XXIBC was flying high altitude missions with minimal losses to AA fire, with only one bomber in 20 hit by heavy flak being lost, and with four out of five bombers hit by flak receiving minor, non-threatening damage. However, the XXIBC was concerned that these losses would dramatically increase when the low altitude incendiary raids were begun, and decided to conduct these raids at night and at altitudes between the effective range of medium and heavy AA guns. It defined the evasion of flak "as any measure or maneuver by a single aircraft, a formation or whole force attacking a target, which leads to a decrease in loss and damage from flak." The report described two main principles for flak evasion. The first was to plan the mission so that the attacking aircraft would be within the range of the smallest number of flak guns for the shortest period of time possible to, over, and from the target. The second was to make the enemy gun-laying as difficult as possible through flight maneuvers and other counter measures (i.e. RCM). The report listed rules to minimize flak exposure:

1) The attack should be flown at the optimum altitude consistent with other considerations (e.g. "let the efficiency of a bombing operation be defined as the ratio of destruction of the target, the expected number of bombs on the target, to the cost of the operation in terms of expected loss and damage from all causes"). The optimum altitude for any mission was that altitude for which the efficiency was a maximum. Sometimes a mission had to be flown at a lower than optimum altitude for strategic necessity to insure a more complete destruction of a high priority target. Bombing strategists believed it was always a mistake to bomb from higher altitudes except when weather dictated.
2) Flak analysts were to determine the axes of attack and withdrawal, taking into consideration the target size, aiming points, navigation, and wind and weather.
3) When several axes of attack were used they were included in a narrow area, exposing the bombers to the minimum number of guns, and saturating the enemy AA defense in the area.
4) The time interval over the target between the first and last bomber over the target was to be as short as possible, saturating the enemy AA

defense. A study showed that flak risk was reduced by 88% by decreasing the time interval between formations from 2.6 minutes to 12 seconds (about a mile between formations).
5) Flying two or more formations in line abreast (consistent with target size and aiming points) further reduced flak risk by decreasing the time over the target, saturating the defense, decreasing the intensity of their fire, and making it more difficult for the enemy to set up an effective barrage zone.
6) The attack routine was to be varied, so as not to be stereotyped so the enemy could not set up his AA defenses.

Once the B-29s began to bomb individually, evasive action was only effective against continuously accurate fire or predicted concentrations of AA fire, and could not be used during the bombing run. Evasive action was achieved by a change in speed, altitude, or course, or a combination. Decrease in speed was not recommended, because it increased the time over the zones of fire. An increase in speed alone was not effective, as continuous heavy flak bursts occurred every four seconds. An increase in IAS from 200mph to 265mph in 15 seconds would correspond at the end of four seconds to an increase of only 15 to 20 feet from its predicted position. Likewise, a change in altitude alone meant that a bomber climbing at 500fpm would only deviate from its original line of flight at a rate of 8 to 9fps. A 30-degree dive would mean a loss of 180-200fps, and was a much more effective evasively than a climb, but only could be used with sufficient altitude, as decrease in altitude meant an increase in AA effectiveness. A course change was the single most effective evasive maneuver, as the amount of deviation from original course increased with the radius of turn. It was found that the most effective maneuver for a single bomber was a diving turn with an increase in speed.

Night AA

During night bombing missions the Japanese usually only fired on bombers illuminated by searchlights, and the XXIBC used evasive techniques developed by the RAF Bomber Command over Germany. It was found that the Japanese defenses (the searchlights) had to be saturated with a maximum force during a minimum time over target. Around the clock attacks with variations in attack altitudes confused and exhausted the Japanese defenses. Countermeasures were made against the searchlights: radar countermeasures (RCM) against the radar-controlled lights, and desychronization of engines for sound-controlled searchlights. The difficulties inherent in nighttime AA defense made it possible for the B-29s to fly in relative safety at lower altitudes.

Searchlights

The searchlight defense of large cities was generally adequate, and its employment quite good, with some vital target areas using radar-directed searchlights. However, the smaller cities were woefully lacking in searchlights, averaging six to 10. The Japanese disposition of searchlights was similar to that used by the U.S. The Japanese Army used the standard 60in searchlights, especially in heavy concentrations in the Tokyo area, where they operated effectively to 33,000ft, with an estimated 25% radar controlled. The Tachi copy of the British SCL radar set was mounted in two separate units: the transmitter on a rotating searchlight controller, and the receiver antenna on a Type 96, 60in searchlight that was sited independently on a nearby high vantage point. Copies of the American SCR-268 captured at Corregidor were put into limited use, as mass production was never authorized.

The searchlights were set up in concentric circles around the area to be defended, and along the approach routes. The lights in the outer circle were designated as the "pick-up" lights, and were generally equipped with sound locator or, infrequently, radar to detect approaching bombers. These were the "flick" lights that caught the bombers in a very short search time. The manually controlled "carry" lights in the inner rings would focus on these "flicked" aircraft, and tracked them in for the AA guns or fighters, while the "flick" lights continued to search for other incoming targets. The Japanese searchlight efficiency ranged from poor to excellent, as over some areas it was well coordinated, passing lighted bombers along from battery to battery for several minutes. Japanese searchlight doctrine called for a maximum of four lights to track any one bomber. But the searchlight defense often broke down as the attack progressed and the bombers saturated the area. Often the Japanese would employ too many lights (10 to 30) on a single bomber, with the other bombers escaping without being illuminated. Because many of the Japanese cities were on large bays or the Inland Sea, the standard circular searchlight belts were difficult to create. Another searchlight disposition was to have six to 12 lights close together, and acting as one unit around a master light. Also, searchlights were stationed in outlying areas, often with stationary beams pointing straight up, as part of a fighter-searchlight team.

Once caught in a light it was difficult for a bomber to evade. The recommended procedure was to fly down a beam and out, but generally evasive action did not succeed. However, evasive action was useful in eluding enemy fighter attack and AA gun laying. Since it was difficult to escape the light beam, the apparent answer was searchlight countermeasures. The 28BS of the 314BW first tested Jet #622 paint on a mission over Tokyo. Jet #622 was a high gloss black paint that had a high specular (mirror) reflection and a very low diffuse (scattered) reflection. Jet #622 reflected the searchlight beam at a mirror angle with a minimum amount of light scattering in other directions. Although the black paint had no effect on radar controlled searchlights, the black painted bombers were difficult to track with optical fire control gun battery instruments.

AA Counter Measures

Radar countermeasures (RCM)—the dropping of rope and the use of electronic jammers—obliterated the radar screens on the enemy radarscopes for the searchlights and AA guns. The saturation of defenses by getting the maximum force over the target in the minimum time was very effective, as the searchlight defenses could only capture a limited number of bombers, and many more got through without being "flicked." Saturation also confused the radar picture, as the greater the number of bombers in a given area, the more difficult for the radar to pick up individual aircraft. The desynchronization of engines was useful against sound controlled lights, as sound locators worked on the ability of the operator to balance the sounds received by each ear. Once the VII Fighter Command arrived to escort XXIBC B-29s they would drop down to bomb or strafe searchlight positions while the bomber force was approaching the target.

8

The VII Fighter Command
Arrives for Fighter Escort

When the VIIVFC (15FG and 21FG) arrived at Iwo Jima in April 1945, it was confronted with many problems. The major difficulty was utilizing its new P-51D fighters in a new type mission; the Very Long-Range (VLR) escort and strike mission against targets on the Japanese Homeland, which were over 700mi away. Before VLR escort and strike operations could begin a navigational aircraft system had to be developed to lead the fighters to rendezvous with the bombers, or to the target. Also, an efficient ASR scheme would have to be put into place, and effective weather data would have to be made available. Navigation B-29s were employed, and the problems were resolved by installing special homing equipment that allowed the fighters to follow them.

Joint Bomber-Fighter Navigation Missions

The fighters had limited navigational equipment, and the B-29s acted as "Mother" ships to lead the fighters to and from the target. Joint bomber and fighter missions were conducted, and were of two types:

1) Fighters could fly to and from the target area with the main bomber force, in which case particular bombers had to be alerted to standby on the bomber to fighter VHF Channel "Nan" frequency. The bomb-

ers could take any calls from the Fighter Leader and relay them to the Bomber Formation Leader on the bomber-to-bomber frequency. During a joint bomber-fighter mission, if a fighter was unable to find its navigational B-29 it was to join any B-29, which was to lead that fighter back to within sight of its home base on Iwo Jima.

2) Fighters could be assigned to navigational B-29s (call sign "Dreamboat"), which were assigned expressly to convoy the fighters (call sign "Chicken") to the target area or enemy coast, where they rendezvoused with the main bomber formation. The navigational B-29s would then proceed to a predetermined rally point to rendezvous with the fighters on their return from the target to be led back to base homing on VHF Channel "Item." The radio signal was transmitted two minutes on and two minutes off, followed by identification by voice at the end of each transmission. B-29s flew 312 navigational sorties for the fighters to join the bombers for escort, or for fighter-bomber strike missions.

Collecting quick and correct weather data was a problem both for the XXIBC and VIIFC, and was somewhat remedied by B-24 and B-29 weather recon missions, and the use of a navigational B-29 that could relay weather

The VIIVFC (15FG and 21FG) arrived at Iwo Jima in April 1945. Shown are P-51s with a B-29 taxiing behind and P-61 Black Widows and Mt. Suribachi in the distance. (USAF)

Fighters could be assigned to navigational B-29s that were assigned to expressly convoy the fighters to the target area or enemy coast, where they rendezvoused with the main bomber formation. USAF)

forecasts to its charges. However, severe weather fronts could take their toll. On an escort mission to Osaka on 1 June 148 P-51s neared a heavy 23,000ft weather front two hours from Iwo. They entered the front despite the guideline never to fly on instruments except in an emergency, and 27 successfully flew through the front and on to the target, but 94 Mustangs turned around, and 27 were lost trying to penetrate the front.

Fighter Escort Missions
The first of 13 XXIBC missions with fighter escort was flown on 7 April when the 73BW attacked the Nakajima Aircraft Engine Factory in Tokyo on the war's longest fighter escort mission. The VII Fighter Command sent up about 80 P-51s with auxiliary fuel tanks from Iwo Jima, and rendezvoused with three Navigational B-29s that led the Mustangs to the rendezvous with the bombers off the Japanese coast, where the escorts flew above and three or four minutes ahead of the bombers, which were flying in a column of groups. About 125 Japanese fighters (Nicks, Tojos, Irvings, and Zekes) were alerted and were waiting over Tokyo, four or five miles north of the aiming point. The P-51s were flying in the standard finger four fighter formation, and the B-29s flew the closest formation they had ever flown, and took only six minutes to release their bombs over the target. During the sharp turn during withdrawal the Japanese interceptors were able to attack the last two bomber groups and made 450 firing runs. Many of the attacks were coordinated, executed from above, ahead and out of the sun. Some 20 air-to-air bombings were attempted, and one B-29 was rammed, and had its horizontal stabilizer torn off (it landed safely at Iwo Jima). The bomber gunners claimed an inflated 40 enemy fighters destroyed, 30 probably destroyed, and 40 damaged. The P-51s claimed 21 destroyed, six probables, and 10 damaged. Two P-51s were lost, but ASR rescued one pilot.

Fighter-Bomber Strikes
During the first months of operations Japanese fighter opposition was relatively effective, and the B-29s required the fighter escort, which destroyed 128 Japanese aircraft in the air for a loss of 35 fighters. When enemy fighter

In the four months after the VII Fighter Command began operations from Iwo it flew 14 escort operations (two were aborted due to weather), where it destroyed 128 Japanese aircraft and lost 35 fighters (27 to weather on the 1 June mission). Shown through the right sighting blister is a P-51 of the 458FS/506FG. (USAF)

opposition weakened, and the fact that B-29s flew repeated night missions that did not require fighter escort, the VIIFC fighters were released for fighter-bomber strike missions. The VIIFC had flown 11 escort missions until 29 June (it then flew only two more bomber escort missions, on 7 and 10 August). From the first fighter-bomber strike on 16 April, when 57 fighters attacked targets in the Kanoya area, the VIIFC strike operations increased in scope, as it flew 23 (six aborted due to weather) VLR fighter-bomber strike missions. The existing two fighter groups were supplemented by a third P-51D group (506FG) in late April, and a fourth P-47N group (414FG, a 20AF group attached to the VIIFC) arrived in August, but it was able to fly only three fighter-bomber strike missions before the war ended.

Summary of VIIFC Operations

From the start of operations until the end of the war the VIIFC flew 1,744 sorties in 13 escort missions (two aborts), 4,532 sorties in 38 fighter-bomber strike missions (six aborts), and 2,105 patrol and miscellaneous sorties. During the VLR campaign the VIIFC shot down 221 enemy aircraft in the air: 99 during escort missions, and 122 during the fighter-bomber strikes. The best days for the American fighters on escort were 26 aerial victories on 29 May over Yokohama, 27 on 10 June over Tokyo, and 26 during a strike mission on 11 June over Tokorozawa. Maj. Robert Moore of the 78FS and 45FS/15FG scored 11 victories and was the top ace of the VIIFC, while Maj. James Tapp of the 78FS/15FG scored 8 victories, and Maj. Harry Crim of the 531FS/21FG scored 7 victories flying from Iwo. During this time the VIIFC lost 204 P-51s and 8 P-47s to all causes (27 P-51s to weather on the 1 June mission). In combat 165 aircraft and 91 pilots were

lost, with 114 credited to enemy AA or fighters. A further 190 aircraft were damaged, 165 credited to enemy action. After a while the Japanese had no inclination to mix with the P-51s and P-47s in the air, and expertly dispersed their aircraft on the ground so that only 219 were destroyed in strafing attacks. However, as fighter-bombers the machine guns and rockets of the VIIFC destroyed 134 locomotives, 355 rail cars, 254 surface vessels, and numerous buildings and targets of opportunity.

VIIIFC VLR Fighter Escort Missions

Mission No.	Date	Fighters Sent	E/A/C Lost	D/P/D*	Target
1	4/1	108	2	21/5/7	Tokyo
2	4/12	90	4	15/6/3	Tokyo
5	4/22	104	6	9/?/?	Kanoya
7	4/30	104	1	0/1/0	Tachikawa
10	5/19	100	0	——	Tachikawa Aborted weather
14	5/29	101	3	26/9/23	Yokohama
15	6/1	148	27	1/0/0	Osaka
16	6/7	138	1	2/0/1	Osaka
19	6/10	107	0	27/7/10	Tokyo
21	6/15	123	1	——	Osaka Aborted weather
24	6/27	148	1	2/0/5	Nagoya
48	8/7	—	-	0/0/0	Toyokawa
50	8/10	2grps	0	6/1/11	Tokyo
51	8/14	2grps	1	0/0/0	Osaka

*D/P/D = Destroyed/Probable/Damaged

9

Ditching/Bailout/Rescue

Bailout

Ditching the bomber in an emergency was preferred to bailing, out as chances of being rescued were greater (for reasons that will be enumerated in the Ditching section). However, statistics tended to show the opposite, as a greater percentage of bailouts were rescued, but this was because many of that number were controlled bailouts from aircraft in trouble in the near vicinity of Iwo Jima, where immediate rescue was probable.

The airplane commander gave the order to bailout by first sounding a warning with a series of three short rings on the alarm bell when the emergency first appeared. The airplane commander gave the actual bailout order over the interphone, and with a long, sustained ring of the alarm bell. The crew had practiced repeated bailout drills on the ground, and everyone knew the procedure and their exit points, along with the destruction of designated instruments by a specific crewman. The crew in the nose compartment was to bail out through the nose wheel well when the gear was down, or through the forward bomb bay as an alternate exit. The crew in the waist was to go through the rear bomb bay, or the rear entrance door as an alternate. The tail gunner could bail out of the window at his side, or through the rear entrance door.

The most important step in a bailout was to clear the aircraft before pulling the ripcord. The crewman was to look around and try to wait at least five or 10 seconds, if altitude permitted, to pull the ripcord. Before pulling the ripcord his legs were to be straightened and feet placed together to prevent spinning and somersaulting, reducing the danger of tangling in the harness when the chute opened, and also reducing the shock of the opening chute. While looking down at the ripcord, both hands were to be used to grip the ripcord pocket attached to the harness. The left hand was to hold the harness out, and the right yanked the ripcord handle. About

two seconds after the ripcord was pulled the sharp jerk of the opening canopy was felt, and the jumper was to look up to check the canopy and shroud lines. The chute descended at about 1,000ft per minute, and had a back and forth swing. The drift was checked by looking up and then down between the legs, keeping the feet together to use them to meter the drift. The chute could not be steered, but by turning the body into the direction of the drift the jumper would land in the direction of the drift and greatly reduce his chance of injury on landing.

During a high altitude bailout it was advantageous to delay opening the chute, even though there was the anxiety of knowing if it was going to open. The free fall to a lower altitude minimized the jumper's exposure to extreme cold, lack of oxygen, excessive opening shock of the parachute, and enemy gunfire. Frostbite could occur within a matter of seconds at high altitude, and the oxygen supply in the bailout bottle could be exhausted before the jumper reached an altitude safe from anoxia. Bailing out at 30,000ft and opening the chute immediately meant over 20 minutes of floating through the cold atmosphere, whereas free falling from 30,000 to 10,000ft meant 1.5 minutes of free fall and then 5.5 minutes floating down in the chute in the comparatively less hostile skies below 10,000ft. In a free fall terminal velocity was reached within seconds, and then the jumper would travel no faster, so a free fall to a lower altitude and thicker air also lessened the jolt from the chute opening. The suggested altitude to open the parachute was 10,000ft, but a rule of thumb for the last chance of opening the chute was that at 5,000ft objects on the ground were recognizable, the horizon became larger, the ground seemed to be rushing up, and the rip cord definitely needed to be pulled. Of course, when there was cloud cover another rule of thumb came into effect: Pull the ripcord just before entering the cloud layer or under cast. During a night bailout the only suggested, reliable method was to know the bailout altitude from the navigator previous to the jump and count the seconds after bailout, knowing how long a free fall should take from bailout altitude to 10,000ft; otherwise, the rip cord was pulled after clearing the aircraft (on low altitude night missions).

Bailout over Water

When the bailout was to be over water, each crewman removed the individual life raft from its position near his station and snapped it to his parachute harness. He opened the corner of the raft pack cover, pulled out the

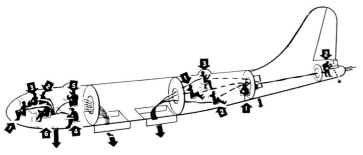
Emergency Bailout Exits

end of the lanyard, ran it under his parachute harness, and snapped it into the ring of his life vest strap. The location of the parachute packs was discussed previously. For water landings the jumper was to get ready early by throwing away anything not needed. He pulled himself back into the sling as far as possible, undid his chest strap by hooking his thumb under one of the vertical lift webs, and pushed firmly across his chest to loosen the cross webbing to undo the snap. The leg straps were freed by doubling up first one leg and then the other, unsnapping the fasteners each time. The jumper then hung onto the risers and rode the chute into the water. Before hitting the water the locking cap of the Single Point Quick Release Harness was turned 90-degrees to set the release mechanism for immediate operation. As soon as he was in the water (but not before) he would pull the safety clip and press hard on the cap to release the lock, and the harness would slide off. The Mae West was then inflated one side at a time, but never before the harness was free. If the leg straps were not released before going into the water, the life vest would hold the head above the water while the straps were unfastened or slid over the feet. If the harness or suspension lines were not freed they had to be cut free. It was important to remain clear of the parachute, and not become entangled while inflating the raft. There was a slightly different procedure for the QAC chute that had no risers on the pack or harness.

Bailout over Land

When landing the jumper was to reach up and grasp the risers with his hands, and look down at 45-degrees (not straight down), which enabled better judgment of the height above the ground. To set up for the landing his feet were to be placed together with the knees slightly bent, so that the landing would be on the balls of the feet. The jumper was instructed: "Don't be limp; don't be rigid. Just partially relax, and ride on into the ground, drifting face forward." Upon hitting the ground the procedure was to fall forward or sideways in a tumbling roll to absorb the shock. High wind landings followed the standard procedures, but once down on the ground the jumper was to roll over on his stomach and drag in the shroud lines closest to the ground, and continue hauling in the lines until the canopy was reached. The skirt of the canopy was pulled in to spill the air and collapse the chute. Tree landings were considered the easiest of all, as it was a cushioned landing. When the jumper saw that he was going into the trees he was to release the risers, cross his arms over the front of his head, and bury his face in the crook of an elbow, keeping the feet and knees together. If help was imminent it was recommended the jumper wait for help in getting down. Otherwise, the jumper was to get out of the harness and cut the lines and risers to make a rope for climbing down.

Ditching

Ditching was the "forced landing of a land-based aircraft on water." When there was choice, ditching was the preferred emergency procedure for leaving a B-29. The reasons were that the crew could remain together for mutual support, discovery, and rescue, because spotting a large raft (or rafts lashed together) was easier than spotting individuals who were scattered over a large area after bailout. However, ditching was difficult under ideal conditions, but in a damaged aircraft and/or in bad weather or sea conditions, and/or at night it was even more difficult. Ditching was perilous, in that the crew had to withstand the enormous impact of hitting the water, and then exit the sinking aircraft with the necessary survival equipment.

There were no practice ditchings, and the airplane commander and crew had to thoroughly know and coordinate the procedure through repeated dry run ditching drills.

If the bomber survived the ditching intact it could stay afloat for a considerable time. Its large fuel tanks had been at least half emptied on the inbound flight and were buoyant with air, as were the sealed pressurized crew compartments. This flotation allowed the crew time to escape with their survival gear and launch the life rafts. The B-29's fuselage structure was weak at the trailing edge of the wing, and tended to split open at that point. Also, the bomb bay doors were prone to collapse, permitting water to rush in and tear into the bomber as it skidded along the top of the water. In analyzing 45 ditchings the AAF found that the downed bombers stayed afloat between 10 to 15 minutes. By early 1945, 45% of the crews were rescued in less than five hours, 36% in 5 to 24 hours, 13% in one to three days, and 6% in three to seven days. Of 129 B-29s with 1,424 crew (just under 50% were saved) involved in ASR, 72 ditched, 24 "crashed at sea," and 33 had crew that bailed out.

The first step once an emergency arose was to initiate emergency radio procedures, as this greatly enhanced the chance of ASR finding the downed crew. Distress Procedure:

a) Radar Operator turned the IFF to the emergency position.
b) Navigator was to know the longitude and latitude, LORAN line, and nautical mileage to the nearest reference point, and the correct name of and true bearing from that reference point. The navigator then gave this information to the airplane commander and radioman.
c) Airplane commander immediately called Channel "A," and stated that he was in distress and was switching to channel "C," which was the Lifeguard and Dumbo channel, to inform them he was ditching. The airplane commander then instructed the tail gunner to throw the radio transmitter buoy out the rear escape hatch when he instructed him to do so.
d) The radio operator immediately contacted his Air-Sea Rescue Unit on 7920Kcs or 3755Kcs (CW) and gave the following coded information: "Am about to ditch, LORAN line, latitude, longitude, course, speed, and altitude." The coded message would look like this example:

00V535 V 21V537 – OPSAR – BT QUG 2300
1022N 142 31 E 320 195 8000 K
(Encoded in CSP 1270)

The radio operator waited for the Air Sea Rescue Unit to decode his message and to receive a receipt for it. While he was waiting, the radioman switched to 4475Kcs to send the previous message again to the Dumbo and Lifeguard. If he did not receive an acknowledgment from the Dumbo, Lifeguard, or ASRU he would immediately switch back to his assigned strike frequency and send an urgent signal (XXX) to his Ground Station for a bearing request. If the bomber was unable to raise any rescue unit the radio operator was to continue to repeat his position, and any information that could help in the rescue. The message was to be sent every two minutes until ditching. The rescue instructions stated:

"Keep repeating your position until you leave your key. SCREW YOUR KEY DOWN WHEN TOU LEAVE!"

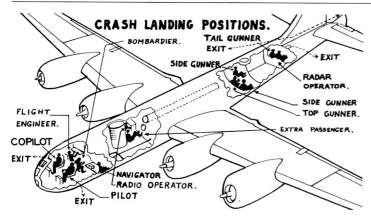

Emergency Ditching Exits

The radioman was to take the dinghy transmitter (Gibson Girl) with him when he left the aircraft.

Before ditching, the airplane commander gave the co-pilot the warning, "Prepare for ditching in XX minutes," and rang the alarm bell with several short rings. The co-pilot relayed the pilot's "ditching" message. The airplane commander then had the co-pilot relay the "Open emergency exits and throw out equipment" order to the crew (preferably above 5,000ft.). The bombardier opened the bomb bay doors and jettisoned any bombs, and the crew dumped all loose equipment out; the doors were then closed. All gunners fired off their remaining ammunition. At 2,000ft the airplane commander gave the co-pilot the order "Stations for ditching, impact in XX seconds" to be relayed to the crew. Thirty seconds before impact, the radio operator was ordered to abandon his key and take his station. The airplane commander then ordered "Brace for impact" and sent a long ring on the alarm bell

Crew ditching positions and exit procedures (each crewman acknowledged his ditching readiness over the interphone by "Navigator ditching" etc.):

Airplane commander: He opened his side window, and braced his feet on the rudder pedals with knees flexed. After ditching he checked to be sure all crew were out of the forward compartment and exited through the left window. If the plane was not on fire he would inflate his life vest while sitting on the window ledge, and then climb to the top of the fuselage and then to the left wing to secure the left life raft.

Co-pilot: He would take the first aid kit stored above the flight engineer's seat, climb out the right side window, inflate his life vest, climb on top the fuselage to the right wing, and secure the right life raft.

Flight Engineer: He was to jettison the front hatch and any other loose equipment through the forward bomb bay. His ditching position was his normal seat facing to the rear, the back of his head and shoulders braced against the back of the co-pilot's armor plate, safety belt fastened, and hands braced against the control board. After ditching he was to take the raft accessory kit from the shelf behind the airplane commander's seat and exit through the jettisoned front hatch. He inflated his life vest and climbed over the fuselage to the right wing, and assisted the bombardier and co-pilot with the life rafts.

Bombardier: Before ditching the bombardier destroyed the bombsight and bombing data, and jettisoned the disabled bombsight so that it would not crash through the front glass. He opened the bomb bays, jettisoned any bombs, and helped the crew jettison loose equipment. He retrieved the emergency signal kit from under the navigator's desk and took his ditching position sitting beside the engineer, also with his back against the co-pilot's armor plate, with a cushion behind his head, feet braced, and knees flexed. After ditching, the bombardier took the signal kit and followed the engineer through the hatch to the right wing.

Navigator: Previous to ditching gave the radioman the position, course, speed, and altitude to transmit, and gave the airplane commander the sur-

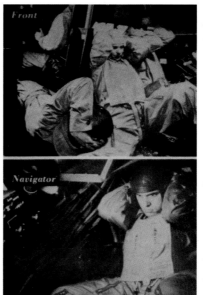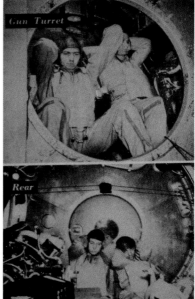

Ditching Positions (USAF)

face wind, strength, and direction. He collected essential maps, charts, and navigational equipment, put them in a waterproof pouch, and tucked them inside his clothing, along with two smoke grenades. He assisted in jettisoning loose equipment, and dropped drift flares through the release tube. For ditching he sat on the floor facing aft, and used his parachute for a cushion. He exited through the astrodome, inflated his vest, and went to the right wing.

Radio Operator: Prior to ditching he destroyed all classified material and continued to send emergency signals, and on airplane commander's orders clamped down the transmitter key. He lowered the trailing antenna to full extension, watched the height when it grounded (100 to 110ft.), and reported to the pilots. He took two smoke grenades and remained at his position with his seat belt fastened, facing aft, with his head, shoulders, and back cushioned with his parachute against the upper turret, and bracing his legs against the bulkhead. He exited through the astrodome to the right wing life raft.

Top Gunner: Crawled through the tunnel to the forward cabin, took the fire ax, and chopped out the astrodome and any projections in it. He took his position with his back and head braced, padded with his parachute, against the upper turret, and legs were braced against the pressure bulkhead with his knees flexed. He exited through the astrodome. If he did not have time to crawl through the tunnel then he was to take a position in the rear unpressurized section, and sat facing aft and braced against the rear pressure bulkhead. After ditching he was to help with throwing out (in priority) the Gibson Girl, life raft, and sustenance kits stowed in the unpressurized section. He exited through the rear escape hatch, inflated his vest, and went to the left wing.

Right Blister Gunner: Proceeded to the rear unpressurized compartment and opened and jettisoned the rear escape hatch. He took his ditching position between the radar operator and left gunner, knees flexed, feet braced, and back padded by his parachute. After ditching he was to aid in throwing out the Gibson Girl, life raft, and sustenance kits. He exited through the rear escape hatch, inflated his vest, and went across the top of the fuselage to the left wing.

Left Blister Gunner: He was to report the progress in the ditching procedure in the gunner's compartment to the co-pilot, and check that the pressure door to the bomb bay was closed. He closed the door in the armored bulkhead, and was the last to leave the rear pressurized compartment for the rear unpressurized compartment, and closed the rear pressure door behind him. Here he was to see that life raft and emergency kits were stowed in the corners of the pressure bulkhead, thus padding the Gibson Girl against impact. He took his position on the left pressure bulkhead, facing aft, back padded and pressed against the bulkhead, and legs braced. He exited through the rear escape hatch and helped with the Gibson Girl, life raft, and sustenance kits. He inflated his life vest and proceeded to the left wing.

Radar Operator: Prior to ditching he was responsible for opening the rear escape hatch and securing the raft accessory kit. He was to report the progress of the ditching procedure in the rear unpressurized compartment to the co-pilot. His ditching position was sitting in the unpressurized rear compartment against the rear pressurized bulkhead at the right, facing aft,

with hands and cushions behind his head, knees flexed, and feet braced. After ditching he took the raft kit and exited through the rear escape hatch, inflated his vest, and went to the right wing.

Tail Gunner: Prior to ditching he jettisoned the tail gunner's escape hatch and, if time allowed, the gunsight. He was to take the aeronautical kit and remain in his seat, facing aft, head and back cushioned against the back of the seat. He exited through the tail gunner's escape hatch to the left of the horizontal stabilizer, inflated his vest, and moved to the left wing.

Note that the rear pressurized compartment was evacuated in the ditching, and its occupants were positioned in the rear unpressurized compartment. This evacuation was because the pressurized doors to the bomb bays could collapse in the impact, and water would rush into the compartment.

The men designated to take the raft from its compartment were to inflate and launch it right side up. The rafts were attached to the wings by a light rope that would sever if the plane sank and started to take the raft along. If the ditching was made into the wind, the raft would swing toward the tail and boarding was easy. If there was a crosswind after ditching the plane would swing into the wind. If the raft was on the upwind side it could become wedged under the wing, and if it were on the downwind side it could be caught under the fuselage or tail. The crew had to take care that the rafts were not punctured by any jagged edges.

In a ditching it was important that the airplane commander do so before he ran out of fuel. Power and a margin of speed needed to be maintained so that the aircraft could be set down in the most advantageous sea condition available in the ditching area. The airplane commander had to be cognizant of the appearance of the sea in relation to the velocity and direction of the wind. Generally, the roughness of the sea indicated the velocity of the wind; for example, a few white crests indicated 10 to 20mph winds, many white crest meant winds of 20 to 30mph, and spray from crests indicated winds of 40 to 50mph. In ditching, the airplane commander had to fly as flat on the approach path as possible, keep the speed as low as possible, and not exceed a rate of descent of 200fps. The landing gear was to remain retracted. Flaps were to be lowered to reduce aircraft speed, and the flap angle used was to be in proportion to the amount of power available to obtain a minimum safe rate of descent with a minimum safe forward speed. A normal glide approach speed was to be used to insure control and maintain some speed after the plane flattened out so the airplane commander could choose the best area for ditching.

If the seas were calm and there was only a slight wind, the plane was to be put down on the top of a swell. With any other wind condition the

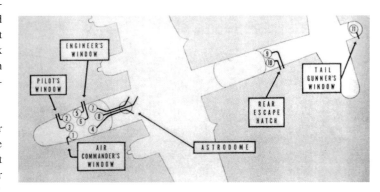

Emergency Ditching Exits (USAF)

The men designated to take the raft from its compartment were to inflate and launch it right side up. The rafts were attached to the wings by a light rope that would sever if the plane sunk and started to take the raft along with it. (USAF)

plane was to be landed upwind, near the top of a swell or incoming wave. A landing on top of a swell was always preferred, but if the landing was to be made in a strong cross wind, then it was to be abandoned in favor of an upwind landing. If the ditching had to be made across a swell, the plane was to be put down on an upslope towards the top. A downwind landing was to be avoided, as it was always dangerous. On touchdown the airplane commander tried to hold the tail down slightly so that the nose would not come down into the water and cave it in. A tail down landing would result in a violent impact and then rapid deceleration. On a clam sea the plane had a tendency to bounce, and the airplane commander had to keep the control column back hard. In average seas the tail would touch the crest of the wave first, and the airplane commander had to keep the nose up so that the forward part of the plane would hit the next wave crest at near the center of gravity.

Crash Landing

The airplane commander sounded the alarm bell and interphone announcement to prepare for a crash landing. The procedure for a crash landing had been practiced in dry runs, and was similar to that of a ditching. However, in a crash landing positions in the rear pressurized compartment were considered safe, as the deceleration was not so rapid as in a ditching, and there was not the chance of the rush of water through the pressurized doors. The airplane commander, co-pilot, navigator, flight engineer, left and right gunner, and tail gunner remained in their normal flight positions, while the bombardier, radio operator, top gunner, and radar operator took positions facing aft, with their backs braced against bulkheads padded by parachutes or cushions. The crew was to remain in the braced position and not relax until the aircraft came to a complete stop.

Rescue Plan

When a mission was scheduled, Bomber Command HQ contacted Submarine HQ (ComSubPac) at Guam, and was informed as to which submarines would be available with their positions and voice calls. This information was sent to the ASRUs (Air Sea Rescue Units) on Iwo Jima for the assignment of surface vessels and Dumbos based there. This information

was also sent to each participating Bomb Wing so that its crews could be briefed. Each Wing was to provide its own Super Dumbos, usually two for submarine cover, and the crews were rotated from combat for this special duty.

During a mission distress signals were sent to Wing HQ, which would relay it to ASR at Iwo Jima and Saipan. There also was direct communications between the downed aircraft and the rescue units at sea, but the Wing remained the center for all information about its own aircraft. It was estimated that ASR teams flew more than 2,000mi for every one of the 600 crewmen saved.

The "Buddy System"

In the "Buddy System," bombers would fly in a formation of three aircraft (a leader and two wingmen), and try to keep in visual contact (using running lights at night). A distressed aircraft would inform his formation over VHF channel "A" of his problem. The aircraft answering would become the "Buddy". If an aircraft were to abort on the way to the target the squadron leader would order the "Buddy" to accompany the distressed aircraft. If there was to be a ditching the "Buddy" was to make reports of the ditching to the Wing Air-Ground Station (Dumbo or Lifeguard). If the distressed aircraft ditched, the "Buddy" would attempt to take photos of the ditching procedure, and then turn on his emergency IFF and make calls to the Wing Air-Ground Station, Dumbo, and Lifeguard. The "Buddy" would orbit and plot his exact position, and again inform the Wing Air-Ground Station. When the "Buddy" had to leave he would drop a radio transmitter buoy near the ditched aircraft. The "Buddy" would then again orbit the ditched aircraft one last time and take photos of the scene before he left.

When the B-29s began operations from the Marianas, the Joint Chiefs of Staff designated ASR as a theater responsibility. CINCPOA assigned the Commander Forward Area (later Commander Marianas Area) to establish the Marianas Air Sea Rescue Group at Saipan, and later at Iwo Jima, and also to assume operational control of all air units involved in ASR. The Marianas Surface Patrol and Escort Group controlled all surface vessels, except lifeguard submarines, operating north of the Marianas that were under the operational control of Commander, Submarine Force, Pacific Fleet. It was obvious that previous ASR procedures would have to be greatly expanded, as there were 1,500mi of open ocean between the Marianas and Japan that were controlled by the enemy. The Bombardment Wing HQ was responsible for evaluating a distress signal and acting on it by dispatching ASR units from the various organizations. ASR units on Iwo Jima advised all rescue organizations nightly on the status of ASR searches, and the search intents for the next day.

Rescue facilities

a) Air-Sea Rescue Unit was composed of Army and Navy personnel stationed at Base and Wing headquarters, and at the Naval Air Station and Bomber Command. The ASRUs were in teletype communication with all ground stations, and with each other. All information concerning aircraft in distress was received and evaluated, and then quickly acted upon by sending the appropriate rescue organization.

b) Lifeguard Submarines were positioned across the bomber routes at the locations that the bombers were most likely to have trouble. The submarines were equipped with radar to pick up IFF distress signals; radio monitoring 4475Kc voice and CW signal, and observers on the bridge to look for aircraft, flares, rafts, etc. Submarines were usually positioned closest to the Japanese mainland, and because of this precarious location they were protected by one or two Super Dumbos.

c)   The Dumbo aircraft were the Navy's PBY and PB4Y, and the Air Force's B-17 and the B-29 Super Dumbo (B-29s specially equipped for S&R with one extra liaison officer). The Dumbos were named after the Disney flying baby elephant. The ASR procedure involved two Super Dumbos orbiting over a "lifeguard" submarine during the day, and one at night along the route of returning B-29s. They monitored the strike frequencies of the mission bombers for distress signals. They were equipped to broadcast low frequency signals on which distressed aircraft could home to reach the vicinity of the submarine. Six of these B-29s were stationed on Iwo Jima, and in May the Marianas Bomb Wings were directed to convert six more B-29s to ASR duties, with two on 24/7 call. The PBY or B-17 Dumbo search and rescue patrol aircraft flew out to 600mi, and were equipped with radar and radio. They were spaced so that any position along the route could be reached by a Dumbo in 20 to 30 minutes.

d)   The Navy positioned picket ships nearby the Marianas and Iwo Jima airfields in case of crashes shortly after takeoff, along with destroyers located along the mission routes. These vessels were equipped with powerful radar and a variety of radio equipment, and were positioned to be within four hours of rescue.

On 23 March 1945, the ASR organization was expanded by the first echelon of the AAF Fourth Emergency Rescue Squadron, which was under the control of the Marianas ASR Group. This unit had 12 OA-10s and eight B-17s carrying motorized lifeboats that could be parachuted. On the last missions of the war the ASR team consisted of 14 submarines, five surface vessels, 21 Navy patrol aircraft, and nine Super Dumbos, along with Navy surface vessels stationed off the ends of the runways during take offs. For every four men in the air there was one man waiting on the sea for rescue. Rescue personnel totaled 2,400, and were about one quarter of the personnel employed in the combat mission. ASR units rescued 596 aircrew from 83 ditched, crashed, and abandoned B-29s. The B-29 Dumbos flew 134 search sorties during this period.

Once the aircraft had ditched there were several methods of relaying the position of the life raft. The dinghy transmitter, or "Gibson Girl" (SCR-578), was a small floating transmitter that sent distress signals from the life raft. The radio transmitter buoy (AN/CRN-1) was a droppable floating transmitter that allowed any radio compass equipped with a rescue component to home in on it. The corner reflector "Emily," MX-137A-single man raft and MX-138A multi-place raft, was a foldable device for reflecting radar impulses back to the receiver of the rescue aircraft or vessel.

After the crew got into the life rafts the radioman would set up the Gibson Girl for operation. He was to limit its operation from 15 to 18 minutes and 45 to 48 minutes past GCT hour, with the crew taking turns cranking to save their energy. Included with every Gibson Girl was a yellow kite and white balloon that were used to raise the antenna of the radio, and also were effective as visual sighting devices.

Included on the raft was an assortment of visual signaling equipment. A Very Pistol with a number of colored flares was to be used only when a

searching aircraft was approaching the raft. A type AN-M8 pyrotechnic pistol in a type A-2 holder was stowed on cable guard at the co-pilot's station. A type A-8 signal container was stowed at the co-pilot's left. A pistol mount was located at about head level at the co-pilot's station. The pistol was operated by opening the breech and pulling out the unlocking lever. After inserting the signal flare the breech was relocked, and the loaded pistol was inserted into the mount, locked in a vertical position, and fired to the outside. Sea markers of florescent green dye called "Evergreen" were found to be the most easily seen color on the surface of the water. It was to be dispersed so that it left a long trail behind the drifting raft. A hand-held signaling mirror designed to be aimed at a searching aircraft or rescue vessel was provided. Aiming was difficult, but done properly on a sunny day the mirror could be a useful rescue device. At night waterproof signal lights were carried, and the Gibson Girl could also be used for signaling at night by means of its signal lamp, keyed manually when there was the possibility of nearby rescue. The "Emily" radar reflecting device (MX-137A or MX-138A) was useful both in day and at night. If the raft was not equipped with the "Emily" the crew was to raise as many metal objects as high as possible to reflect any search radar beams.

When the survivors were found their position, aircraft type, condition, number, and any markers were reported. The type of aircraft was given either by name or code:

Fighter (1-crewman)	Chicken
Dive-Bomber (2 man crew)	Hawk
Medium Bomber (3 man crew)	Eagle
Heavy Bomber (9-10 man crew)	Box Car
VHB Bomber (11-12 man crew)	Monster

The condition of the survivors was given either by name or code:

Survivor(s) in raft	Goodyear
Survivor(s) in life jacket	Yellow jacket
Survivor(s) without life jacket	Davey Jones

A typical search report was made over channel "Queen," or 4475Kc (voice), depending on the distance between the aircraft and rescue method, and was as follows:

"20 Hairy Larry 170 Monster Goodyear nine Evergreen," signifying search aircraft Hairy Larry spotted "nine survivors of a B-29 down 20mi bearing true 170-degrees from the reference point in a life raft with dye marker."

The orbiting aircraft was to remain on station with its emergency IFF ON until relieved by another aircraft, rescue vessel, or Dumbo. The orbiting aircraft was to assure itself of the identity of a submarine by radioing it to change course to the left or right. The orbiting aircraft was to zoom the position of the survivors, or lead the rescue vessel or Dumbo to them. If the orbiting aircraft had to leave before any rescue it was to drop a radio transmitter buoy or smoke bomb. Dye markers were difficult for submarines or surface vessels to see.

10

Miscellaneous

Sgt. Henry "Red" Erwin: The Only B-29 CMH Recipient

On 12 April the 313th and 314th Bomb Wings were sent to Koriyama, with airplane commander Capt. Anthony Simeral's *City of Los Angeles* as the lead bomber of the 52BS/29BG. Aboard the B-29 was Alabama native Sgt. Henry "Red" Erwin, the radio operator, who was flying his 11th mission. As the squadron lead bomber the *City of Los Angeles* was to precede in a tight formation to the IP, and Erwin was to drop flares and then a smoke bomb to mark the assembly point, about 550mi north of Iwo Jima and 175mi from the target. The phosphorous smoke marker bomb was a 20lb canister that was to be dropped through a circular drop chute near the forward bomb bay, and fused with a six second delay to allow it to fall about 300ft before exploding.

As the *City of Los Angeles* was crossing the Japanese coast, Erwin was waiting with his pyrotechnics as the first flak hit close to the B-29, throwing him to the floor. He got up and again waited near the release pipe for Simeral's signal to drop the parachute flares. The airplane commander signaled, and Erwin dropped the parachute flares through the chute, followed by the phosphorous bomb. The bomb reached the bottom of the chute and bounced briefly against the release gate at the bottom, which had been jammed by the last flare. Seconds later the bomb exploded, with a blast of white-hot flame pouring back up through the chute into Erwin's

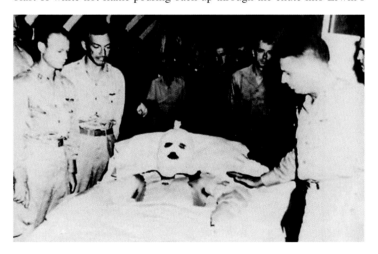

Radio operator Sgt. Henry "Red" Erwin of the 52BS/29BG aboard the *City of Los Angeles*. *City of Los Angeles* was the only B-29 Medal of Honor recipient. (USAF)

face. Phosphorous particles covered the radio operator, and the bomb, now a fireball, bounded along the compartment floor and engulfed Erwin. Erwin fell backward in horrendous pain, his nose burned off, his right ear destroyed, arms scorched, and his upper body burned. The still-burning bomb finally came to a stop at Erwin's feet and began to burn through the floor only a few feet away from the bomb bay loaded with incendiary bombs. One of the gunners thought he could smother the bomb with parachute packs, but heavy white smoke continued to pour throughout the bomber, choking everyone. Erwin reeled to his feet, nearly blind, his eyes a mass of blisters, and somehow headed toward the bomb. The heavy smoke blinded Simeral and his co-pilot, and the B-29 lurched out of control, and was diving to only 700ft, where Simeral could not safely jettison the incendiary bombs. As Simeral struggled to regain control, Erwin groped to find the burning bomb, lifted it in his hands, and slowly moved forward, away from the bomb bay, with the bomb grasped in his hands. His life vest and clothes were burned away as he felt his way around the top turret well, but was then blocked by the navigator's table. He clutched the bomb with one hand against his body to free one hand to unlatch the table. With his hands burned to the bone and entire body smoldering he followed Simeral's shouts to drop the bomb out the window. Finally, after 12 to 15 seconds of unbelievable pain and effort, Erwin reached the cockpit, found the open co-pilot's window, dropped the bomb out, and immediately collapsed. Simeral regained control of the bomber at 300 ft, climbed, and turned back to Iwo Jima after jettisoning the incendiaries. The situation seemed hopeless, but the crew sprayed the smoldering Erwin with the fire extinguisher to put out the persistent burning phosphorous particles, and the bombardier injected morphine. Erwin screamed in pain as he floated in and out of consciousness. He needed blood plasma to maintain his fluids, but no one, except Erwin, knew how to administer it. Erwin regained control of his tormented mind and body and managed to instruct the crew on how to administer the vital plasma. The morphine granted Erwin relief as he lay on the floor for the next several hours, not losing consciousness, staring at the ceiling. When the *City of Los Angeles* landed on Iwo Jima Simeral immediately braked to a stop to allow the stretcher bearers to remove Erwin to the hospital. His chances for life were considered so slim that the recommendation for the Medal of Honor was drawn up that night, and hand-carried to Guam for Gen. LeMay's immediate approval, and a display medal in Hawaii was flown specially to Guam for presentation. For the next four days Erwin's life hung in the balance as the doctors worked frantically. He recovered enough to be flown to the larger hospital at Guam, where he continued his miraculous recovery. On 18 April, still wrapped in heavy bandages, he was presented the Medal of Honor by Gen. LeMay. He was returned to the Army's burn unit at Valley Forge Hospital, PA, for extensive therapy and skin grafts, and was released in early October 1947; he took a job with the VA in Alabama, where he married and raised a family.

Surviving B-29s

Serial #	Model #	Location (B-29 *Name*)
42-24791	B-29	Beale AFB, CA (*Big Time Operator*)
42-65281	B-29	Travis AFB, CA (*Miss America '62*)
42-93967	B-29A	GA.War Veteran's Memorial, GA
44-27297	B-29	USAF Museum (*BOCKSCAR*)
44-27343	B-29	Tinker AFB, OK (*Tinker Heritage*)
44-61535	B-29A	Castle AFB, CA (*Raz'n Hell*)
44-61669	B-29A	March AFB, CA (*Flagship 500*)
44-61671	B-29A	Whiteman AFB, MO (*Great Artiste*)
44-61739	B-29A	Aberdeen, MD
44-61748	B-29A	Imperial War Museum, UK (*Hawg Wild*)
44-61975	B-29A	New England Air Museum, CT (*Jack's Hack*)
44-62022	B-29A	PuebloWeisbrod Aircraft Museum, CO (*Peachy*)
44-62070	B-29A	Commemorative Air Force, TX (*FiFi*)
44-62112	B-29A	MASDC, AZ
44-62139	B-29A	Air Force Museum, OH (*Command Decision*)
44-62214	B-29A	Elison, AFB, AK
44-62220	B-29A	Kelly AFB Heritage Museum, TX
44-69729	B-29	Museum of Flight, WA (*T Square 54*)
44-69972	B-29	U.S. Aviation Museum, CA (*Doc*)
44-69983	B-29	Atomic Energy Museum NM
44-70013	B-29	NAS Atlanta, GA (*Sweet Eloise*)
44-70016	B-29	Pima Air Museum, AZ (*Sentimental Journey*)
44-70049	B-29	Week's Air Museum, FL
44-70064	B-29	Castle AFB, CA
44-70102	B-29	Bud McGee Aviation Park, CA (*Here's Hoping*)
44-70113	B-29	Florence Air Museum, SC
44-84053	B-29B	Robins AFB, GA
44-84076	TB-29	Strategic Air Command Museum, NB (*Man o' War*)
44-84084	SB-29	Aero Trader, CA
44-86292	B-29	Smithsonian, MD (*Enola Gay*)
44-86402	B-29	Aircraft Industries Museum, KY
44-86408	B-29	Hill AFB, UT (*Hagerty's Hag*)
44-87627	B-29	8AF Museum, Barksdale AFB, LA
44-87779	B-29	Ellsworth AFB, SD (*Legals Eagle II*)
45-21639	B-29	Military Academy Museum, S. Korea
45-21748	B-29	National Atomic Museum, NM (*Duke of Albuquerque*)
45-21749	B-29	Chanute AFB, IL
45-21787	B-29	Weeks Fantasy of Flight Museum, FL (*Fertile Myrtle*)
Tupolev Tu-4		Mulino AFB, Moscow, Russia
Tupolev Tu-4		Chinese Air Force Museum, Beijing, China (2 aircraft)

Sentimental Journey, the Pima Air & Space Museum B-29

The Pima Air & Space Museum south of Tucson, AZ, received its B-29 from the Military Aircraft Storage and Disposition Center (MASDC) at Davis-Monthan, which was located directly adjacent to the Pima Museum. When the B-29s were being phased out of service they were sent to the MASCD to be scrapped, but someone there had the foresight to release several to be disbursed for display. Aircraft number 44-70016 was literally towed across the road to Pima, where it sat in the hot desert with fictitious markings for several years. Several of the original crew recognized their bomber in the early 1980s, traced its history, and began its ongoing restoration.

Records indicated that before going to Davis-Monthan the bomber had been placed in storage after WWII. In 1951 the bomber was reactivated, and was assigned to the Air Defense Command's 4713th Radar Evaluation Electronics Countermeasures (REEC) Flight, stationed at Griffis AFB, NY, where it was used to test the U.S. air defense system. The 4713 REEC Flight nicknamed its aircraft after Walt Disney's Seven Dwarfs, and 44-70016 was named *Dopey*.

Originally, 44-70016 was manufactured by Boeing's Wichita plant in March 1945. Its first crew trained at Kearney, NB, in April, and after only seven flying hours the crew flew it to Guam, arriving on 28 April. It was assigned to the 458BS of the 330BG of the 314BW(VH)/20AF, and was designated K-40. Soon the crew named their bomber after the popular song of the time, *Sentimental Journey*. The 330BG emblem, consisting of a circle around a map of North America and the designation of a specific city, was placed on the right side. Since several of the crew were from Philadelphia and that name had been taken, the name *Quaker City* was substituted. The primary crew of the *Sentimental Journey* flew 24 combat missions from the Marianas, and other crews flew eight more in her for 42 total. Its first mission was flown against the airfield and installations at Matsuyama on 4 May 1945. K-40 flew its last combat mission on 8 August 1945, but sustained battle damage, and had to land at Iwo Jima for repairs. It flew two additional "show of force" missions at the end of the war, including being part of the large B-29 formations that flew over Tokyo Bay during the Japanese surrender on the battleship *Missouri* on 2 September. Its primary crew then flew K-40 back to Mather AFB, CA, in October 1945k, and lost track of her when they returned to civilian life.

Sentimental Journey, which flew with the 458BS/330BG/314BW, is now displayed by the Pima Air & Space Museum, south of Tucson, AZ. The bomber is featured in the color photos and many black and white photos in this book. (Author/Pima)

The 330BG formed its Association in the mid-1980s, and began their fund-raising project to construct a display building for the bomber to preserve it from further deterioration in the hot desert. The building was dedicated in 1994, and K-40 appears in many of the photos contained in this book. The restoration of the bomber is continuing, and checks payable to the AAF for the K-40 Fund can be donated to the Pima Air & Space Museum, 6000 E. Valencia Road, Tucson, AZ, 85706.

Bibliography

Magazines and Pamphlets

Aeroplane, *"Development of the Superfortress,"* *11 August 1944*

Ahnstrom, D. Newell, *"Evolution of the B-29,"* *Skyways*, 1945

Air Force, *"Pacific Debut,"* *Air Force*, June 1945

All Hands, *"Pacific Cinderella,"* Bureau of Ordnance, June 1946

Boeing Magazine (*from various wartime issues*)

    "B-29: Maple Leaf Brand," Helen Call

    "Big Change"

    "Birth of the B-29," Helen Call

    "Boeing Artillery"

    "Get a Load On That Thing," Helen Call

    "Ghost Ship," Tom Potwin

    "Gun Men"

    "History's Biggest Manufacturing Job"

    "Jigsaw Picture in 40,000 Parts"

    "Minute Men of Kansas," Helen Call

    "1000 B-29s"

    "Our Destination-Tokyo"

    "Plains Plant"

    "Pressurized Cabin in the Sky"

    "Quick Change Artists"

    "Radar Had to be Streamlined," Jim Douglas

    "Sky Writing for the B-29"

    "Snooperfortresses"

    "Tokyo Diner"

    "There's a Long, Long Trailer Winding," Byron Fish

    "Wichita to Yawata," Reynolds Phillips

    "Wing Train," Thelma McMinn

    "World Wide Wings"

Boesen, Victor, *"B-29 Superfortress,"* *Skyways*, September 1944

Britton, Tom, *"Insignia of the XX Bomber Command,"* AAHS Journal, Spring 1980

Brown, John, *"RCT Armament in the Boeing B-29,"* *Air Enthusiast Quarterly* #3

Buchmann, Capt. L.P., *"B-29...Modified by Battle,"* *Air Force*, April 1945

Chinnery, Phil, *"Disposal: Boeing B-29 Superfortress, FlyPast*, January 1998

Churchill, Edward, *"What We Learned from the B-19,"* *Flying*, August 1942

Cook, G.A., *"Sighting Stations on the B-29,"* *Army Ordnance*, July-August 1946

Craig, Gary, *Norden Bombsight*, War Monthly, No.23, February 1976

Culver, Gordon, *"Superfort Samaritans,"* *Air Force*, November 1945

Davis, Maj. Luther, *"The B-29 and You,"* *Flying*, 1944

Erdmann, James, *"Monroe Leaflet Bomb,"* *Naval Institute Proceedings*.

Flight, *"B-29,"* *Flight*, August 10, 1944

Flight, *"Boeing (B-29) Superfortress,"* *July 12, 1945*

Flying, *"Building the Superfort Team,"* *Flying*, May 1945

Flying, *"B-29 Flight Engineer,"* *Flying*, July 1945

Flying, *"Radar in Air Combat,"* *Flying*, October 1945

40th Bomb Group, *The Battle of Kansas (Pt.1)*, *Memories* Issue #11, September 1986

40th Bomb Group, *The Battle of Kansas (Pt.2)*, *Memories* Issue #13, January 1987

Fuller, Curtis, *"Superfort Power Plant,"* *Flying*, July 1944

Impact, *"More on the B-29"* Impact, June 1944

Impact, *"B-29s Smack Japan"* Impact, July 1944

Impact, *"B-29s Big Bomb Bays,"* Impact, September 1944

Impact, *"29s Hit Gap Steel,"* Impact, September 1944

Impact, *"Superforts vs. Nips"* Impact, November 1944

Impact, *"Saipan: B-29 Springboard to Tokyo,"* Impact, January 1945

Impact, *"VBH Formations,"* Impact, February 1945

Impact, *"The Weather Problem in Attacking Japan,"* Impact, February 1945

Impact, *"Ditching the Superfort,"* Impact, February 1945

Impact, *"Aerial Mines Pollute Jap Waters,"* Impact, June 1945

Impact, *"B-29 Strikes,"* Impact, June 1945

Impact, *"Big Bombs for Big Bombers,"* Impact, June 1945

Impact, *"Fire Blitz,"* Impact, August 1945

Impact, *"B-29ers,"* Impact, Sept.-Oct. 1945

Impact, *"Tale of Dumbos, Super Dumbos and Subs,"* Impact, Sept.-Oct.1945

Jenstrom, Eino, *"Last Mission of Eddie Allen,"* *Air Force*, August 1980

Johnson, Robert, *"Why the Boeing B-29 Bomber, and Why the Wright R-3350 Engine?,"* AAHS Journal, Fall 1988

Karana, Max, *"B-29,"* *Flying*, August 1944

Knight, Charlotte, *"Radar Bombing,"* *Air Force*, October 1945

Krims. Milton, *"Floating Death,"* *Air Force*, September 1945

Krims. Milton, *"From Kansas to Tokyo,"* *Air Force*, June 1945

Landman, Amos, *"Seagoing Shops: Keeping the B-29s Pounding Japan,"* *Popular Science*, September 1945

Lott, Arnold, *"Japan's Nightmare-Mine Blockade,"* *Naval Institute Proceedings*, November 1958

Morse, David, *" Eye in the Sky-The B-13,"* AAHS Journal, Summer, 1981

Peacock, Lindsey, *"Boeing B-29: First of the Super Bombers,"* *Air International*, August 1989

Peck, James, *"Radar: Magic Eye that Sees the Invisible,"* *Popular Science*, January 1945

Popular Mechanics, *"Coral Nest for the Superforts,"* *Popular Mechanics*, April 1944

Putt, Col. Donald, *"Under Pressure,"* *Air Force*, October 1944

Scholin, Lt. Allan, *"Superfortress Modification,"* *Air News*, January 1945

Ringold, Herbert, *"Our Pacific Airfields,"* *Air Force*, August 1945

Ross, John, *Fire Bombing Japan,"* *Flying*, October 1945

Rust, Kenn, *Bomber Markings of the 20th Air Force*, AAHS Journal, Fall/Winter 1962.

Taylor, John W.R., *"Boeing Superfortress,"* *The Aeroplane*, March 30, 1945

Books

Anonymous, *Thrilling Story of Boeing's B-29 Superfortress*, Playmore, NY, 1944

Archer, Robert & Victor, *USAAF Aircraft Markings and Camouflage 1941-1947*, Schiffer, PA, 1997

Anderton, David, *B-29 Superfortress at War*, Scribner, NY, 1978

Bell, Dana, *Air Force Colors, Vol.3*, Squadron/Signal, TX, 1997

Berger, Carl, *B-29, The Superfortress*, Ballantine, NY, 1973

Birdsall, Steve, *Saga of the Superfortress*, Doubleday, NY, 1980

Birdsall, Steve, *B-29 Superfortress in Action*, Squadron/Signal. TX, 1978

Birdsall, Steve, *Superfortress: The Boeing B-29*, Squadron/Signal. TX, 1980

Bowers, Peter, *Boeing Aircraft Since 1916*, Aero, CA, 1966

Bowers, Peter, *Boeing B-29 Superfortress*, Warbird Tech Series #4, Specialty Press, MN, 1999

Bowman, Waldo, "*Bulldozers Come First*," McGraw-Hill, NY, 1944

Boyce, Joseph, *New Weapons for Air Warfare*, Little Brown, Boston. 1947

Bradley, F.J., *No Strategic Targets Left*, Turner, KY, 1999.

Bridgman, Leonard (editor), *Jane's All the World's Aircraft 1945/6*, Arco, NY, 1970 (reprint)

Bureau of Yards and Docks, *Building the Navy's Bases in World War II, Vol. II*, GPO, Wash. D.C., 1947

Caiden, Martin, "*A Torch to the Enemy*," Ballentine Books, NY, 1960

Campbell, John, *Boeing B-29 Superfortress*, Schiffer, PA, 1997

Chant, Christopher, *B-29 Superfortress Super Profile*, Foulis, UK, 1950

Chamberlain, Peter and Gander, Terry, *Anti-Aircraft Guns*, Arco, NY, 1975

Chilstrom, John, *Mines Away!: The Significance of USAAF Minelaying in WW-2*, Air University, Al, 1993

Coffey, Thomas, *Iron Eagle*, Crown, NY, 1986

Collison, Thomas, *The Superfortress is Born: The Story of the B-29*, Duell, Sloan & Pearce, NY, 1945

Craig, William, *Fall of Japan*, Dial, NY, 1967

Craven, W.F. & Cate, J.L., *Army Air Forces in World War II, Vol. V*, University of Chicago, IL, 1953

Craven, W.F. & Cate, J.L., *Army Air Forces in World War II, Vol. VI*, University of Chicago, IL, 1955

Craven, W.F. & Cate, J.L., *Army Air Forces in World War II, Vol. VII*, University of Chicago, IL, 1957

Davis, Larry, *Planes, Names & Dames*, Squadron/Signal, TX, 1990

Davis, Larry, *B-29 Superfortress in Action*, Squadron/Signal, TX, 1997

Dod, Karl, *The Corps of Engineers: The War Against Japan*, Office of Military History, Wash. D.C., 1966.

Dorr, Robert, *US Bombers of World War Two*, Arms & Armor, UK, 1989

DuPre, Flint, *US Air Force Biographical Dictionary*, Watts, NY, 1965

Edion, Hoito, *The Night Tokyo Burned*, St. Martins, NY, 1987

58th Bomb Group Association, 58th Bomb Wing: "Wait till the 58th Gets Here," Turner, KY, 1998

40th Bomb Group Association, *40th Bombardment Group (VH) History*, Turner, KY, 1989

Freeman, Roger, *Camouflage & Markings; USAAF 1937-1945*, Ducimus, UK, 1974

Goldstein, Donald et al, *Rain of Ruin*, Brasseys, UK, 1995

Green, William, *Famous Bombers of the Second World War, Vol.2*, Hanover, NY, 1959

Griehl, Manfred, & Dressel, Joachim, *Heinkel He-177, 277 274*, Airlife, UK, 1998

Gurney, Gene, *B-29 Story*, Fawcett, CT. 1961

Gurney, Gene, *Journey of the Giants*, Coward-McCann, NY, 1961

Hansell, Haywood, *Strategic Air War Against Japan*, Air War College, AL, 1980

Hansell, Haywood, *Air Plan hat Defeated Hitler*, Higgins, MacArthur, GA, 1972

Harding, Stephen & Long, James, *Dominator: The Story of the Consolidated B-32 Bomber*, Pictorial Histories, MT. 1983

Haugland, Vern, *AAF Against Japan*, Harper & Bros, NY, 1948

Hess, William, Johnson, Frederick, & Marshall, Chester, *Great Bombers of World War II*, MBI Publishing, WI, 1998

Holley, Irving, *Buying Aircraft: Materiel Procurement for the Army Air Forces*, U.S. Army, Wash. D.C., 1964

Hoyt, Edwin, *Inferno*, Madison, NY, 2000

Huie William B., *From Omaha to Okinawa*, Dutton, NY, 1945

Johnsen, Frederick, *The B-29 Book*, Bomber Books, WA, 1978

Johnson, Ellis & Katcher, David, *Mines Against Japan*, Naval Ordnance Laboratory, MD, 1973

Keenan, Dick (ed.), *The 20th Air Force Album*, 20AF Association, 1982

Kerr, E. Bartlett, *Flames Over Tokyo*, Fine, NY, 1991

LeMay, Curtis and Yenne, Bill, *Superfortress: The B-29 and American Airpower*, McGraw Hill, NY, 1988

Mann, Robert, *B-29 Superfortress: A Comprehensive Registry of Planes and Their Missions*, McFarland, NC, 2004.

Mansfield, Harold, *Vision: Saga of the Sky*, Duell, Sloan & Pearce, NY, 1956

Marshall, Chester, *The Global Twentieth: An Anthology of the 20th AF in World II: Vol. I*, Apollo Books, MN, 1985

Marshall, Chester, *The Global Twentieth: An Anthology of the 20th AF in World II: Vol. II*, Marshall, TN, 1987

Marshall, Chester, *The Global Twentieth: An Anthology of the 20th AF in World II: Vol. III*, Global, TN, 1988

Marshall, Chester, *The Global Twentieth: An Anthology of the 20th AF in World II: Vol. IV*, Global, TN, 1994

Marshall, Chester, *B-29 Superfortress*, Warbird History Series, Motor Books, WI, 1993

Marshall, Chester, *Sky Giants over Japan*, Apollo, MN, 1984

Maurer, Maurer, *Combat Squadrons of the Air Force World War II*, USGPO, Wash. D.C., 1969

Maurer, Maurer, *Air Force Combat Units of World War II*, USGPO, Wash D.C., 1961

McClure, Glenn, *Saipan, Then and Now*, Emerson, TX, 1972

McClure, Glenn, *Tinian, Then and Now*, Emerson, TX, 1977

McClure, Glenn, *Guam, Then and Now*, Emerson, TX, 1979

McDowell, Ernest, *Flying Scoreboards: Aircraft Mission and Kill Markings*, Squadron/Signal, TX, 1993

Morrison, Wilbur, *Point of No Return*, Time, NY, 1979

Morrison, Wilbur, *Hellbirds: The Story of the B-29 in Combat*, Duell, Sloan & Pearce, NY, 1960

Murphy, Edward, *Heroes of WWII*, Ballantine, NY, 1990

Nathans, Robert, *Fire in the Air War: Making the Fires that Beat Japan*, NFPA, Wash. D.C., 1946

19th Bomb Group Association, *19th Bomb Group*, Turner, KY, 2000

Pace, Steve, *Boeing B-29 Superfortress*, Crowood, UK, 2003

Pardini, Albert, *The Legendary Norden Bombsight*, Schiffer, PA, 1999

Pimlott, John, "*B-29 Superfortress*," Chartwell, NJ, 1980

Polmar, Norman, *Enola Gay*, Brasseys. VA, 2004

Redding, Robert & Yenne, Bill, *Boeing: Planemaker to the World*, Crown, NY, 1983

Rhodes, Richard, *The Making of the Atomic Bomb*, Simon & Schuster, NY, 1986

Rottman, Gordon, *World War II Pacific Island Guide*, Greenwood, CT, 2002

Rust, Kenn, *Twentieth Air Force Story*, Historical Aviation, CA, 1979

Rust, Kenn, *Seventh Air Force Story*, Historical Aviation, CA, 1978

St. John, Philip, *B-29 Superfortress*, Turner, KY, 1994

Shannon, Donald, *United States Air Strategy and Doctrine as Employed in the Strategic Bombing of Japan*, Air War College, Maxwell AFB, AL, 1976.

73rd Bomb Group Association, *73rd Bomb Wing: An Illustrated History*, Turner, KY, 2000

Sinclair, William, *Big Brothers, The Story of the B-29s*, Taylor, TX, 1972

Sinclair, William, *Confusion Beyond Imagination*, Whitley, ID, 1987

Stanley, Roy, *World War II Photo Intelligence*, Scribners, NY, 1981

Snyder, Earl, *General Leemay's Circus*, Exposition, NY, 1955

Stout, Wesley, *Bullets by the Billion*, Chrysler, MI, 1946

Stout, Wesley, *Great Engine and Great Planes*, Chrysler, MI, 1946

Sweeting, C.G., *Combat Flying Clothing: Army Air Forces Clothing During World War II*, Smithsonian, Wash. D.C., 1984

Sweeting, C.G., *Combat Flying Equipment: US Army Aviation Personal Equipment 1917-1945*, Smithsonian, Wash. D.C., 1989

Takaki, Koji and Sakaida, Henry, *B-29 Hunters of the JAAF*, Osprey, UK, 2001

Theismeyer, Lincoln and Burchand, John, *Combat Scientists*, Little Brown, Boston, 1947

Thomas, Gordon & Morgan-Witts, Max, *Enola Gay: Mission to Hiroshima*, Dalton Watson, UK, 1995

U.S. Navy, *Aircraft Instruments: 1945 Edition*, Navy Training Courses, USGP), Wash. D.C., 1945.

U.S. Navy, *Aircraft Materials*, Navy Training Courses, USGPO, Wash. D.C., 1953.

Vander Meulen, Jacob, *Building the B-29*, Smithsonian, Wash. D.C., 1995

Wagner, Ray, *American Combat Planes*, Hanover, NY, 1960

Werrell, Kenneth, *Blankets of Fire*, Smithsonian, Wash. D.C., 1996

White, Graham, *Allied Aircraft Piston Engines of World War II*, S.A.E., PA, 1995

Wilkinson, Paul, *Aircraft Engines of the World 1945*, Wilkinson, NY, 1945

Narratives/Interviews

Pattillo, James, Interview (transcribed) August 1998

Internet

http://b-29.org

Braugher, Joe Web Site: http://home.att.net/%7ejbaugher

Caldwell, Jack, "*Day in the Life of a Flight Engineer*," http://home.att.net/~Sallyann5/b-29 February 2001 Guest column Sallyann's B-29 Web Site

Videos

American War Eagles: B-29 Superfortress, Delta, 2001

B-29 Flight Engineer 1944, T.F. 1-3354, War Department, First Motion Picture Unit Army Air Forces, 1944

The Last Bomb, War Department, First Motion Picture Unit Army Air Forces, 1945

Biography of a Bomber, AZ Aerospace Foundation, 2001

Bomber Boys, 29th Bomb Group Association

Famous Planes: Bombers of World War II: Superfortress, Vol.2, Columbia River, 1998

Unsung Heroes: B-29 Pilots, History Channel, 1998

Warbirds of World War II: B-29 Superfortress, MM&V/Daystar, 1996

Technical and Training Manuals

B-29 and B-29A: Pilot's Flight Operating Instructions, AN 01-20EJA-1, 3 August 1945

B-29: airplane commander Training Manual for the Superfortress, AAF Manual No. 50-9, HQ AAF, Office of Flying Safety, 1 February 1945

B-29 Superfortress: Instructors Supplement to airplane commander's Training Manual, AAF Training Command, January 1945

B-29 Maintenance and Familiarization Manual, AAF, 1945

B-29 Parts Catalog, AN 01-20EJ-4, AAF, 1945

B-29 Structural Repair, AN 01 20EJ-3, AAF, 1945

Class 13-Illustrated Catalog, Clothing, Parachutes, Equipment and Supplies, AAF S-13-9, AAF Air Service Command, OH, September 30, 1943

Combat Crew Manual, XXI Bomber Command, APO 234, May 1945. (MF)

Erection and Maintenance Instructions for the Army Model B-29, TO, No. 01-20 EJ-2, 1943

Fire Warfare: Incendiaries and Flame Throwers, NDRC Technical Report, Wash. D.C., 1946

Flight thru Instruments, USN, Aviation Training Division, 1945

Gunnery in the B-29, AAF Manual No.27, July 1944

Pilot's Flight Operating Instructions for the Army Model B-29 Airplanes, AN 01-20EJ-1, U.S. Army Air Force, January 25, 1944

Pilot's Information File, 1944, War Department, AAF Form No.24, 4/1/43

Pilot's Notes, AAF Pilot School (VHB), Roswell Army Air Field, 1945

Reference Manual for Personal Equipment Officers, AAF Manual 55-0-1, HQ-AAF, Wash. D.C., 1 June 1945

Reports

AAF, *Statistical Digest*, Office of Statistical Control, December 1945.

Baker Board Report, July 1934

Brandon, Harry, "*Leaflets Announcing Incendiary Strikes*," 20AF, A-2, 4 August 1945

Combined Chiefs of Staff, *Air Plan for the Defeat of Japan*, August 1943

Driskill, Sanford, *Historical Data: "The Blitz,"* XXBC HQ, 28 June 1944

Japanese Radar Equipment, COM-ONI, Intelligence Bulletin. May 1945

Naval Analysis Division, *US Strategic Bombing Survey (Pacific War)*, GPO, Wash. D.C., Nov. 1946

Office of Statistical Control, *Army Air Force Statistical Digest*, World War II, 1945

Peterson, A., Tuck, R. & Wilkinson, D., "*Aircraft Vulnerability in World War II*," USAF Project Rand, Rand Corp. CA, 19 May 1950

Sallagar, F.M., "*Lessons From an Aerial Mining Campaign*," Rand Corp., CA, 1974

Shannin, Donald, "*US Air Strategy and Doctrine as Employed in the Strategic Bombing of Japan*," Air War College Study No. 6056, AL, 1976

Thomas, Fred, *Historical Notes: "The Blitz,"* XXBC HQ, June 1944

20 Air Force, *A Statistical Summary of Its Operations Against Japan*, June 44-August 45

20 Air Force, "*Problem of the Radar Operator, B-29 Aircraft*," 20AF HQ, 6 October 1944

US Strategic Bombing Survey (Pacific War), "*Japanese Air Power*," GPO, Wash, D.C., July 1946

US Strategic Bombing Survey, "*The Strategic Air Operation of Very Heavy Bombardment in the War Against Japan (20th Air Force) Final Report*," GPO, Wash. D.C., 1 September 1946

US Strategic Bombing Survey, Summary Report (Pacific War), GPO, Wash. D.C., July 1946

US Strategic Bombing Survey, Summary Report (Pacific War) No.53: Effects on Japan's War Economy, GPO, Wash. D.C., July 1946

XXI BC, Communications Bulletin No.1

XXIBC, "*Enemy Tactics: 25 Mission Summary*," 6 Feb.1945

XXI BC, "*Evasion of Flak*," Flak Intelligence, Air Intelligence Report, 12 April 1945

XXIBC, "*First Fighter Escort*," Air Intelligence Report, 19 April1945

XXI BC, "*Gunnery in the B-29: The Tactical Use of Equipment*, XXIBC June 1945

XXIBC, "*Japanese Air Defense*," Air Intelligence Report, 16 June 1945

XXIBC, "*Japanese Searchlight Defense*," Air Intelligence Report, 2 June1945

XXIBC, *The Jap and the 21st BOMCOM*," Air Intelligence Report, 4 May 1945

XXI BC, "*Jap Day vs. Night Tactics*," Air Intelligence Report, 12 April 1945

XXIBC, "*Jap Early Warning System*," Air Intelligence Report, 19 April 1945

XXIBC, "*Jet Black Paint*," Air Intelligence Report, 16 June 1945

XXIBC, "*Last Word in Air Sea Rescue: Airborne Lifeboats*," Air Intelligence Report, 26 April1945

XXIBC, "*Night Missions*," Air Intelligence Report, 11 May1945

XXI BC, "*Peashooter Pete Talks Tactics*," Air Intelligence Report, 5 April 1945

XXIBC, "*Psychological Warfare via B-29s*," Air Intelligence Report, 19 May 1945

XXI BC, "*655th Spots the Weather*," Air Intelligence Report, 22 March 1945

XXIBC, "*3rd Photo*," Air Intelligence Report, 19 April1945

XXIBC(HQ), *Japanese Air Force on the Defense; Its Capabilities and Intentions*, A-2 Section, 10 May 1945

XXIBC(HQ), *Flak Intelligence in the Pacific*, A-2 Section, 29 July 1945

Index

Note: Any subject listing in this index is found only in the text or captions, but not in charts or tables. The italicized page numbers indicate a photo of the subject.

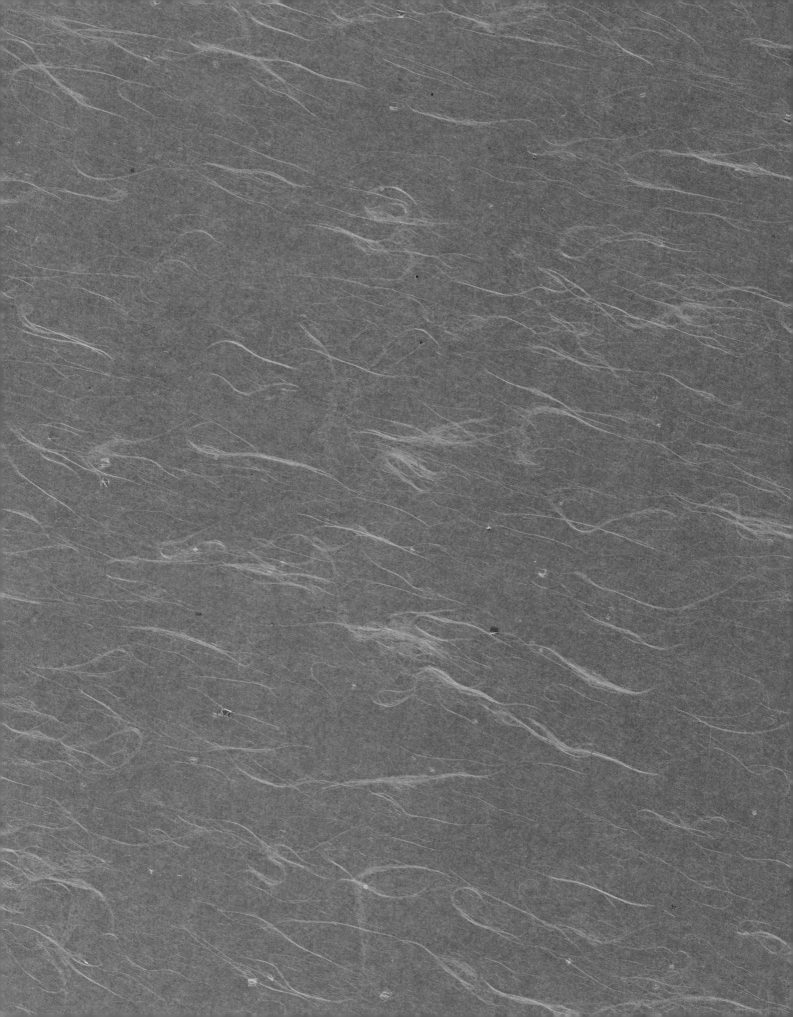